Counseling and Psychotherapy: A Behavioral Approach *by E. Lakin Phillips*

Dimensions of Personality *edited by Harvey London and John E. Exner, Jr.*

The Mental Health Industry: A Cultural Phenomenon *by Peter A. Magaro, Robert Gripp, David McDowell, and Ivan W. Miller III*

Nonverbal Communication: The State of the Art *by Robert G. Harper, Arthur N. Wiens, and Joseph D. Matarazzo*

Alcoholism and Treatment *by David J. Armor, J. Michael Polich* B. Stambul

A Biodevelopmental Approach to Clinical Child and Cognitive Control Theory *by Sebastiano Santostefano*

Handbook of Infant Development *edit.*

Understanding the Rape Victim: A Syn ..atz and Mary Ann Mazur

Childhood Pathology and Later Adjustme. rrediction *by Loretta K. Cass and Carolyn B. Thomas*

Intelligent Testing with the WISC-R *by Alan S. Kaufman*

Adaptation in Schizophrenia: The Theory of Segmental Set *by David Shakow*

Psychotherapy: An Eclectic Approach *by Sol L. Garfield*

Handbook of Minimal Brain Dysfunctions *edited by Herbert E. Rie and Ellen D. Rie*

Handbook of Behavioral Interventions: A Clinical Guide *edited by Alan Goldstein and Edna B. Foa*

Art Psychotherapy *by Harriet Wadeson*

Handbook of Adolescent Psychology *edited by Joseph Adelson*

Psychotherapy Supervision: Theory, Research and Practice *edited by Allen K. Hess*

Psychology and Psychiatry in Courts and Corrections: Controversy and Change *by Ellsworth A. Fersch, Jr.*

Restricted Environmental Stimulation: Research and Clinical Applications *by Peter Suedfeld*

Personal Construct Psychology: Psychotherapy and Personality *edited by Alvin W. Landfield and Larry M. Leitner*

Mothers, Grandmothers, and Daughters: Personality and Child Care in Three-Generation Families *by Bertram J. Cohler and Henry U. Grunebaum*

Further Explorations in Personality *edited by A.I. Rabin, Joel Aronoff, Andrew M. Barclay, and Robert A. Zucker*

Hypnosis and Relaxation: Modern Verification of an Old Equation *by William E. Edmonston, Jr.*

Handbook of Clinical Behavior Therapy *edited by Samuel M. Turner, Karen S. Calhoun, and Henry E. Adams*

Handbook of Clinical Neuropsychology *edited by Susan B. Filskov and Thomas J. Boll*

The Course of Alcoholism: Four Years After Treatment *by J. Michael Polich, David J. Armor, and Harriet B. Braiker*

Handbook of Innovative Psychotherapies *edited by Raymond J. Corsini*

The Role of the Father in Child Development (Second Edition) *edited by Michael E. Lamb*

Behavioral Medicine: Clinical Applications *by Susan S. Pinkerton, Howard Hughes, and W.W. Wenrich*

Handbook for the Practice of Pediatric Psychology *edited by June M. Tuma*

Change Through Interaction: Social Psychological Processes of Counseling and Psychotherapy *by Stanley R. Strong and Charles D. Claiborn*

Drugs and Behavior (Second Edition) *by Fred Leavitt*

Handbook of Research Methods in Clinical Psychology *edited by Philip C. Kendall and James N. Butcher*

(*continued on back*)

THE INDUCTION
OF HYPNOSIS

The Induction
of Hypnosis

WILLIAM E. EDMONSTON, JR.
Colgate University
Hamilton, New York

A WILEY-INTERSCIENCE PUBLICATION
JOHN WILEY & SONS
New York · Chichester · Brisbane · Toronto · Singapore

Library of Congress Cataloging in Publication Data:

Edmonston, William E.
  The induction of hypnosis.

  (Wiley series on personality processes)
  "A Wiley-Interscience publication."
  Bibliography: p.
  Includes indexes.
    1. Hypnotism. I. Title. II. Series.
[DNLM: 1. Hypnosis—history. 2. Hypnosis—methods.
WM 415 E24i]

BF1141.E517 1985   154.7′6   85-17882
ISBN 0-471-83112-3

Printed in the United States of America

10 9 8 7 6 5 4 3 2

To
Nellie

Series Preface

This series of books is addressed to behavioral scientists interested in the nature of human personality. Its scope should prove pertinent to personality theorists and researchers as well as to clinicians concerned with applying an understanding of personality processes to the amelioration of emotional difficulties in living. To this end, the series provides a scholarly integration of theoretical formulations, empirical data, and practical recommendations.

Six major aspects of studying and learning about human personality can be designated: personality theory, personality structure and dynamics, personality development, personality assessment, personality change, and personality adjustment. In exploring these aspects of personality, the books in the series discuss a number of distinct but related subject areas: the nature and implications of various theories of personality; personality characteristics that account for consistencies and variations in human behavior; the emergence of personality processes in children and adolescents; the use of interviewing and testing procedures to evaluate individual differences in personality; efforts to modify personality styles through psychotherapy, counseling, behavior therapy, and other methods of influence; and patterns of abnormal personality functioning that impair individual competence.

IRVING B. WEINER

University of Denver
Denver, Colorado

Preface

The idea for this book had its beginnings more than 10 years ago. Since then, the book, like its content, has had a history. In the early years little was accomplished, primarily because I was involved in writing *Hypnosis and Relaxation,* a theoretical treatise that appeared in 1981. Until that time I had developed little enthusiasm for either a history or a handbook of hypnotic induction techniques. However, through that effort, as well as further informal discussions, I became acutely aware that nowhere in the literature of hypnosis was there a single source of induction procedures ancient and modern. The available literature was primarily contemporary in orientation, with, perhaps, a single chapter reviewing techniques and theories from the distant past to the decade of the books themselves. The need was clearly there.

Thus the work began, only to be plagued by inevitable, and some not so inevitable, delays. Teaching at a small liberal arts college that prides itself on the individual attention given to its students is a full-time position. Scholarly work is accomplished on one's own time, or on sabbaticals. My sabbatical during the period of the book's development was spent in Germany as a Fulbright Scholar and a Gästprofessor, where I either handwrote the manuscript or worked on a German typewriter. Compared to its American counterpart, the latter is a curious machine, particularly when writing in the field of hypnosis. The "y" and the "z" are interchanged on the German model. Thus, when one types "hypnotized," it comes out "hzpnotiyed." Writing by hand turned out to be almost as fast and far less frustrating.

Further delay came through my own inadequacy as a linguist. Finding ready translators for the various languages (including Latin) covered in the book was not easy, even in a sleepy college town of 2500. I finally took to translating passages myself, in my laborious, dictionary guided way. But the final and most frustrating delay came when manuscript assistance expected from another quarter failed to materialize. This time, however, modern technology was at hand in the form of my trusty Kaypro-4 and the remaining third of the manuscript was completed in less than 6 months.

This, then, is the abbreviated history of a history, for that is what *The Induction of Hypnosis* is: a history of the rituals, rites, and incantations through which individuals have attempted to produce in one another the condition we now call hypnosis. However, it is not a history book alone, for it not only presents the chronological record of the past and the present but also offers the detailed verbal patterns of hypnotic induction procedures, past and present. To many, then, the book will serve as a handbook, a reference work, through which they can have dozens of induction techniques at their fingertips by a flip of the index. To others it will serve, I hope, as an interesting trek through the heritage of hypnosis, a journey that I, quite frankly, found fascinating. I guess I just never fully appreciated how ancient our modern techniques really are.

Some readers will no doubt wonder why, if *The Induction of Hypnosis* is a trek through the heritage of hypnosis, the theories of hypnosis and hypnotic phenomena through the ages are absent. Actually, they are not absent, for every induction method is, at least in part, dictated by an unspoken hypothesis of what lies at the fundamental core of what one is trying to produce. The induction procedures themselves are the theoretical history of hypnosis. Human beings behave in manners calculated to bring about the future they hope to create.

Finally, for an author of such an undertaking as this, there is always a concern that the work is as complete and as comprehensive as possible. I have no delusions that a particular reader could not fault me for failing to include this or that historic tidbit, or this or that esoteric induction technique, but what I have attempted to do is to present the major developmental trends in hypnotic induction through the centuries, fleshed out with as many of the actual methods as seemed appropriate. In that goal, I think I have succeeded. I hope the reader will agree.

WILLIAM E. EDMONSTON, Jr.

Hamilton, New York
September 1985

Acknowledgments

I wish to acknowledge the cooperation of the following publishing houses and journals: Consulting Psychologists Press, Inc., for text from the *Harvard Group Scale of Hypnotic Susceptibility,* by Ronald Shor and Emily Orne, copyright 1962 ("Reproduced by special permission of the publisher. Further reproduction is prohibited without the publisher's written permission."); E. P. Dutton, Inc., for permission to reproduce text from A. Cannon's *The Science of Hypnotism,* copyright 1936; Grune & Stratton, Inc., for permission to reproduce text from L. R. Wolberg's *Medical Hypnosis* (Vol. 1), copyright 1948, A. M. Weitzenhoffer's *General Techniques of Hypnotism,* copyright 1957, and H. B. Crasilneck and J. A. Hall's *Clinical Hypnosis: Principles and Applications,* copyright 1975; William Kaufmann, Inc., for permission to reproduce text from E. R. Hilgard and J. R. Hilgard's *Hypnosis in the Relief of Pain;* J. B. Lippincott Co., for permission to reproduce text from W. S. Kroger & W. D. Fezler's *Hypnosis and Behavior Modification: Imagery Conditioning,* copyright 1976; Plenum Press, Inc., for permission to reproduce text from D. E. Gibbons's *Applied Hypnosis and Hyperempiria,* copyright 1979; Munksgaards Publishers, Copenhagen, for permission to reproduce text from B. Ebbell's *The Papyrus Ebers: The Greatest Egyptian Medical Document,* copyright 1937; Basic Books, Inc., for permission to reproduce text from H. Spiegel and D. Spiegel's *Trance and Treatment,* copyright 1978; University Books, Inc., for permission to reproduce text from H. M. Bernheim's *Hypnosis and Suggestion in Psychotherapy,* copyright 1964; John Wiley & Sons, Inc., for permission to reproduce text from W. E. Edmonston's *Hypnosis and Relaxation,* copyright 1981; Williams & Wilkins Co., for permission to reproduce text from the 1924 and 1947 volumes of the *Journal of Nervous and Mental Disease·* the *American Journal of Clinical Hypnosis,* for permission to reproduce text from the 1959, 1964, 1979, and 1980 volumes, copyright by the American Society of Clinical Hypnosis; and the *International Journal of Clinical and Experimental Hypnosis,* for permission to reproduce text from the 1958 and 1968 volumes, copyright by the Society for Clinical and Experimental Hypnosis. Acknowledgment is also made to Stephen S. Marmer, M.D., Ph.D., for permission to reproduce text from his father's book, *Hypnosis in Anes-*

thesiology; to M. S. Laguerre, for permission to reproduce text from his book, *Voodoo Heritage,* copyright 1980; and to E. R. Hilgard et al., for permission to reproduce text from the Protocol for SHALIT, copyright 1979.

In addition to owing a great debt to all of the individuals, from pre-Christian teachers and priests to 20th century practitioners appearing in this book, I am particularly indebted to those who assisted with the less glamorous, yet infinitely more necessary, tasks of bringing the manuscript to hardcover: to the typists, Robin D. Adelstein, Sharon Geasey, Mary Hill, Shelley E. Sykes, and Lynn M. Tybursey; and to the members of the Colgate University Research Council who provided funds for the initiation of the manuscript.

W.E.E.

Contents

Illustrations

CHAPTER 1

The Ancients

The history of hypnotic induction is the history of medicine, which in turn is the history of the occult, of magical rites and rituals. Hypnosis did not begin with Mesmer, but with ancient, primitive people's attempts to understand and, more importantly, to effect change in themselves and their world (see, e.g., Ellenberger, 1970; Zilboorg, 1941).

Mesmer's induction techniques, which I will chronicle later, were not a new beginning, but the logical next step in humanity's efforts to alleviate pain and suffering. So, too, were they the logical next step in the intimately intertwined rituals of physician and priest, in the attempts of the former to extricate medical practice and the methods of handling natural disease from the latter, from the particular religious dogma of the day. Nothing has so slowed the progress of humanity's attempts to aid one's fellow beings as religious fanaticism whether in direct form from the church and its leaders or in the indirect form of those beliefs and prejudices held, often unconsciously, by the very same healers who were breaking new ground.

The direct form of prohibition by the church was most clearly seen from the 2nd to the 16th centuries, which, as Cutten (1911) outlines, saw little progress in the development of medical science. It was during this period that entire cultures were virtually exterminated in the name of various religions, with Christianity being one major offender. The great library of Alexandria, for example, was destroyed and with it vast stores of knowledge and history. The Druids, whose Irish literature was burned by St. Patrick, were themselves exterminated in 637 at the battle of Mayrath (Pokormy, 1910) in the name of enlightened Christianity. Whether their healing rituals would have added anything substantial to developing medical science we will never know, but their basic teaching—"to be pious towards the gods, to do wrong to no man, and to practice fortitude"—on the surface did not seem to warrant the destruction of an entire subculture.

Our more recent history has been hampered by the indirect forms of prohibitive attitudes residing in practitioners who could not bring themselves to consider treatment forms other than those in vogue and use at the time. To be sure, progress was slowed by the authoritative approach wherein any discovery of the student that did not agree with the prevalent dictums of the professor was immediately suspect if not discarded, but there were individual voices of courage. Zilboorg (1941) describes the case of Georget, a young

1

pupil of Pinel and Esquirol, who, on April 26, 1826, had the audacity to suggest to the *Acadamie des Sciences* that magnetism and magnetizers were not only worthy of careful and thoughtful consideration, but perhaps unworthy of the label of charlatanism and charlatans that had been ungraciously bestowed on them by his fellow Academy members. Elliotson, also a victim of such bias, not only with regard to his work in mesmerism but also in his use of the stethoscope as well, still proceeded with his investigations. Voices speaking out for a rational evaluation of new techniques and newly described phenomena were few and far between, but they did exist.

What may be slowing the negative impact of professional, religious, and lay attitudes toward progress in medical science is (a) the general educational level of the populace and (b) the logically absurd position into which those who would halt progress through rituals of supplication either to some religious idol or to some authoritative domain of influence place themselves. As the general populace becomes increasingly better educated, it is more likely to question authoritative proclamations whether from religious, political, or professional demigods, and less likely to accept rituals, those maintainers of the status quo, without results.

Attempts to constrain progress, however, often lead the prohibition to a logically absurd position easily recognized and not easily tolerated by an educated populace—professional or otherwise. For example, in 1842 the Royal Medical and Chirurgical Society received a case report of a mid-thigh amputation made during a mesmeric trance. One member claimed the patient must have been an impostor, while another suggested that the case presentation not be recorded in the minutes of the meeting! (See Bramwell, 1903, p. 10.) Moreover, in the 1970s, because of a difference in viewpoints, officers of a professional society discussed obtaining a legal injunction barring one of its members from including on his curriculum vita the fact that he had been an officer in the society!

THE HINDUS AND THE CHINESE

Although a number of authors (Bernheim, 1891/1980; Bramwell, 1903; Kroger, 1977; Ludwig, 1964; Moll, 1889/1897; Wolberg, 1948) allude to ancient Hindu practices as the beginnings of hypnotic induction procedures, none makes the case strongly or in detail. Most merely refer to the "obvious" hypnotic quality of the cataleptic and other feats of Indian fakirs and yogis without detailing their procedures or suggesting other explanations for the results (e.g., out-and-out fakery). Bernheim (1886/1964) does offer a description of an induction, but gives us no reference or source for his information:

> They accomplish this [extraordinary cataleptiform postures] by fixing the gaze on the tip of the nose for a quarter of an hour, slowing their respirations, and concentrating the attention until a bluish flame appeared at the tip of the nose. (p. 47)

In fact, although this self-induction procedure is contained in a paragraph implying that it is of ancient origin, we do not know whether or not he was describing a procedure used in India during his own time (the late 1800s).

A reference to the Chinese use of auto-techniques appears in Scholem's (1941) quote from Dennys (1904), quoted in Stoll (1904), and later abstracted by Bowers and Glasner (1958). Its emphasis is not on eye-fixation, but rather on the particular position assumed by the individual: "She sits down on a low chair and bends forward so that her head rests on her knees. Then, in a deep measured voice, she repeats three times an exorcism, whereupon a certain change appears to come over her" (Bowers & Glasner, 1958, pp. 54–55). According to Bowers and Glasner (1958) the position of the head between the knees was important in Jewish attainment of proper Kavanah for religious ecstasy.

The most compelling argument that modern hypnosis had its beginnings in the 4th to 2nd millennia before Christ is one by analogy, given the advanced stage of Hindu medicine and science. According to Muthu (1930), the Hindus had worked out "the atomic theory, the evolution theory, the theory of motion, of gravity, of sound, of light and heat potential, the presence of ether, the diurnal motion of the earth, the principle of differential calculus, the calculation of lunar periods and eclipses, the humoral theory, and the circulation of the blood, centuries before they became known in Europe" (p. 42). Little wonder that with such advancement, he also concluded that "they were early acquainted with some of the modern branches of medicine, such as hypnotism. . . . Hypnotism originated among the Hindus, who took their sick people to their temples to be cured by hypnotic suggestion, or temple-sleep, as was done in Egypt and Greece in later times" (Muthu, 1930, p. 44). In fact, Zilboorg (1941) builds a strong case that the development of the Hindu medical system *preceded* and was the basis of the Greek, Roman, and even Egyptian systems, although the opposite had been proposed a century before (Lloyd, 1847). The treatment of mental disorder, however, resided in the Hindu priesthood, so that induction rituals are more likely to be found in literary works than in descriptions of medical practice. Neither Muthu nor Zilboorg enlighten us on the actual rituals used by this "cradle of Aryan civilization" to induce the sleep cures, although Paton (1921) does indicate that in the Shang dynasty (1900 B.C.) dancing and singing were used to induce a "prophetic ecstasy" in individuals called *wu*.

However, in the various Vedas (Rig Veda, Atharva V., & Ayur V.) we do find descriptions of the rituals, some of which may form the ancient beginnings of hypnotic induction. While the Rig Veda contains a general description of medical practice, it is the Atharva Veda that describes specific disorders and their treatments. The latter covers both the primitive and the more developed medical practices of the period. It should be remembered that while the Atharva Veda contains a section on "Materia Medica" (as does the later Papyrus A. Nr. 65—Leiden) describing "materials from the vegetable kingdom, minerals, manufactured things," it primarily describes the charms system of the Ayurveda of the Vedic age. Thus, while treatment through herbs and plants was amalgamated with the charms to effect cures, the latter are considered regnant in the Atharva Veda.

The charms were mainly in the hands of the priesthood, not the physicians of the 18th through the 15th centuries B.C., because the physician was considered unclean and was viewed with fear and suspicion by the general populace. Censure was the general tone toward medicine and its practitioners in the literature of the time. For this reason apparently, the physicians made concerted efforts to relate their treatments with plant-derived drugs to the spoken charms of the Atharva Veda, the better to win the favor of the people toward themselves and their techniques. Thus, according to Karambelkar (1961), "the sage Atharvan stood for Bhesaja-medicine and was the most prominent representative of Vedic medicine" (p. 23), and "the Atharvan priest is the medical practitioner here, par excellence" (p. 115).

One thing that is most striking about Atharvan practices is the prominent role played by water in the treatment process. Despite the variety of drugs and plants used, water was most basic. Patients were sprinkled with it; they were washed with it; it was poured over them; they were immersed in it; they were made to drink it, in both its blessed and natural form. Water was even used in a crude form of instrument sterilization. But for us what is noteworthy is the historical continuity implied here. As we will observe later, water played a prominent role in Mesmer's induction techniques and was even "magnetized" and given to patients to drink as a way of inducing or continuing the magnetic condition while the patient was away from the practitioner. The use of charmed water did not begin with Mesmer, nor even with the early Christian church.

In ancient China (as well as in the China of the 1920s), the idea of a relationship between certain base metals and magical rites, particularly associated with burial rituals, began. Copper coins were placed at the corners and iron nails were strewn on the bottom of the grave to assist the movement of the deceased's spirit into a permanent resting place (Paton, 1921).

The charms or *Mantra* of the Atharva Veda used in the practice of medicine included hymns to deal with specific diseases, disease in general, to ensure long life, to accompany various water and plant cures, and to secure the growth of hair. For example (Bloomfield, 1897, p. 8):

VI, 105.   Charm Against Cough

1. As the soul with the soul's desires swiftly to a distance flies, thus do thou, O cough, fly forth along the soul's course of flight!
2. As a well-sharpened arrow swiftly to a distance flies, thus do thou, O cough, fly forth along the expanse of earth!
3. As the rays of the sun swiftly to a distance fly, thus do thou, O cough, fly forth along the flood of the sea!

In addition to the medical *Mantras* there were charms of a political nature, prayers for a successful reign of royalty, for protecting warriors in battle, for harmony and the avoidance of discord, to be successful in the home, in business, in animal husbandry, to avert evil and sin, and even to obtain a spouse, prevent miscarriage, and to obtain a male heir. The *Mantra* that most closely approximates an induction procedure, in the more modern sense, is the one designated by Bloomfield (1897, pp. 105–106) as a charm at an assignation:

IV, 5.   Charm at an Assignation

1. The bull with a thousand horns who rose out of the sea, with the aid of him, the mighty one, do we put the folks to sleep.
2. The wind blows not over the earth. No one looks on. Do thou then, befriended of Indra, put all women and dogs to sleep!
3. The women that lie upon couches and upon beds, and they that rest in litters, the women all that exhale sweet fragrance, do we put to sleep.
4. Every moving thing I have held fast. Eye and breath I have held fast. I have held fast all limbs in the deep gloom of the night.
5. Of him that sits, and him that walks, of him that stands and looks about, of these the eyes we do shut, just as these premises (are shut).
6. The mother shall sleep, the father shall sleep, the dog shall sleep, the lord of the house shall sleep! All her relations shall sleep, and these people round about shall sleep!
7. O sleep, put thou to sleep all people with the magic that induces sleep! Put the others to sleep until the sun rises; may I be awake until the dawn appears, like Indra, unharmed, uninjured!

While some may view this particular *Mantra* as more of a treatment for insomnia than as the precurser of a hypnotic induction, Satow (1923) clearly views it as a "poem which is certainly calculated to induce a hypnotic sleep, 'a magic slumber'" (p. 24).

The potential difference in interpretation comes no doubt from different translations of the same *Mantra*. Here is Satow's English translation of Grill's German translation (1889) of the same charm, and the words to which Satow was responding:

The Bull that arose thousand-horned from the tide of the sea
By him, all powerful, we submerge the people in sleep.
No breath of air moves over the land, no eye gazes out upon it.
The womenfolk are all asleep, the dogs as well, by Indra's aid.
The ladies rest on benches, or in litters sleep, or on their beds,
The fair, fragrant sex, we lull them all to sleep.
If any one so much as moves I seize upon him firmly,
holding the eye and the breath.
In this hour of deepest night I hold fast all their limbs,
Whether sitting or walking or standing and looking before him
We close his eyes as fast as this dwelling here is closed.

> *The mother sleeps, and the father, the head of the house and the dog,*
> *The whole family sleeps, and the whole little world of the household.*
> *With the drowsy spell submerge the whole people in sleep,*
> *Bewitch them, until the sun is rising; I watch until the morning light,*
> *Like Indra whole and prosperous.*
>
> (SATOW, 1923, pp. 24–25)

Phrases such as, "I seize upon him firmly, holding the eye and the breath," "with thy drowsy spell submerge the whole people," and "bewitch them," certainly give an impression different from "eye and breath I have held fast," "O sleep, put thou to sleep all people," and "put the others to sleep." However, portions of this charm appear to be a combination of laying-on-of-hands and eye-fixation techniques that gained a wider reputation with Mesmer in the 18th century and Braid in the 19th century. Curiously enough, the phrase, "I hold fast all their limbs," also seems to reflect the laying-on-of-the-entire-body, which we will note in biblical passages later on.

Even as late as the 1920s, these *Mantras,* coupled with fervent dancing, lively music, and drum beats, are used for "inducing a suggestive religious ecstasy" (Satow, 1923, pp. 26–27). According to Williams (1954), a trance was recorded in China as early as the 18th century B.C. in which music, dancing, and rhythms played a prominent role. Individuals seeking to commune with the dead entered an ecstatic (hypnotic?) state through singing and dancing: "The first evening was opened by them with bells and drums, the noise of which they altered with music of stringed instruments and bamboo pipes . . . dancing with light steps and while round and round" (p. 10).

Can we conclude then that modern hypnotic techniques had their origins centuries before the Egyptians of the 16th century B.C.? On the basis of the general climate and techniques for dealing with the unknown that prevailed at the time, it is a reasonable supposition that mesmeric and hypnotic-like inductions were used by the priests and practitioners of early Vedic medicine. Direct evidence, on the other hand, is much harder to come by, as we will see in the case of the long revered and oft-quoted *Papyrus Ebers.*

THE EGYPTIANS

Three major links between the past and the present are (a) the use of the hands in curative treatments, (b) the use of magnets or magnetized objects to induce an altered state, and (c) the induction of some form of sleep. Other lesser links include special verbal incantations, music and rhythm, and sacred liquids (e.g., specially treated water). As we will see, from the time of Mesmer until the middle 1800s the dominant form of inducing the mesmeric trance, whether to achieve a crisis or a sleep state, was passes made over the head and body with the hands. These manipulations were detailed and ritualistic, and form a major link between the present inductions of hypnosis and the rituals of the ancient past.

It was not so much the verbal rituals, the incantations, examples of which we will see shortly, that tie the curative efforts of the Hindu and the Egyptian to hypnosis, but the laying-on-of-hands as part of the total treatment regimens. (This is not to say that verbalizations did not play some part, for we know that they eventually dominated the induction procedures, but that part, historically speaking, was of lesser importance than manual manipulations.) The line of history is quite clear, from the laying-on-of-hands (with the occasional inclusion of verbal incantations) of ancient times, to the passes of the hands either in direct contact with the patient or at a distance of a few inches (without verbal utterance on the part of the practitioner), to the reintroduction of a combination of the two, and finally to the present use of predominantly verbal suggestion. In each period of the development of hypnotic inductions we will see smatterings of both physical and verbal manipulations, but the dominant transition has been from the tactile to the verbal, both often accompanied with some sort of eye-fixation technique as an attention-holding device.

The *Papyrus Ebers* is usually credited with having the first references to modern hypnotic inductions in the 12 spells or incantations contained in its 20 meters of text. However, a spell alone may not be sufficient evidence on which to conclude that our ancient forefathers were practicing hypnosis. What is more critical to historic accuracy is the use of the hands and/or the production of some altered state in the patient, often designated a trance and most often having the appearance of a relaxed, sleep-like condition.

The *Papyrus Ebers* is named for its discoverer, Georg Ebers, who found the document in a tomb in 1873 and subsequently deposited it in the University Library of Leipzig (Ebbell, 1937). Although written about 1550 B.C., the *Papyrus* contains remedies and prescriptions dating as far back as 3000 B.C. While the descriptions of some authors (e.g., Cutten, 1911; Ludwig, 1964) yield the impression that this, "the greatest Egyptian medical document," was predominantly a listing of spells and incantations, interspersed with remedies that "consisted of horrible mixtures of unsavory ingredients" (Cutten, 1911, p. 24), such is not wholly the case. Ebbell (1937) contests the views that spells and incantations were dominant—in fact, only 12 exist in the entire document—and that by their presence they provided proof that the Egyptian physicians viewed disease as a "demoniacal intrusion." Rather, he concludes: "In *Papyrus Ebers* incantations are prescribed in very few cases, chiefly against diseases where ordinary remedies failed [not so different from present medical practice] . . . , but the greater part of the affections are treated solely with naturally operating medicines" (Ebbell, 1937, p. 20).

Regarding the spells, their main purpose seemed to be to call on the aid of some diety to make the medical remedy effective, not to render some altered state in the patient, as we might expect if these incantations were related to latter-day mesmerism and present-day hypnosis. Here are the 12 spells and incantations contained in the *Papyrus Ebers* to be said with the application of specific medical treatments. (Ludwig, 1964, reported a general recital to be said *before* medical treatment.) None of these 12, or the pretreatment recital cited by Ludwig (see Ebbell, 1937, p. 29), seems to qualify as an induction of hypnosis, ancient or otherwise.

I. The beginning of a recital on applying a remedy to any limb of a man: I have come from Heliopolis with the old ones in the temple, the possessors of protection, the rulers of eternity; assuredly, I have come from Sais with the mother of the gods. They have given me their protection. I have formulae composed by the lord of the universe in order to expel afflictions (caused) by a god or goddess, by dead man or woman, etc., which are in this my head, in this my nape, in these my shoulders, in this my flesh, in these my limbs, and in order to punish the accuser, the head of them who cause decay to enter into this my flesh and feebleness (?) into these my limbs as something entering into this my flesh, into this my head, in these my shoulders, in (this) my body, in these my limbs. I belong to Re; he has said: "I will save him from his enemies, and Thoth shall be his guide, he who lets writing speak and has composed the books; he gives to the skilful, to the physicians who accompany him, skill to cure. The one whom the god loves, him he shall keep alive." It is I whom the god loves, and he shall keep me alive.—Spoken when applying remedies to any limb of a man which is ill. Really excellent, (proved) many times!

Another recital for loosening any bandage: Loosened was the loosened one by Isis, Horus was loosened by Isis from the evils done to him by his brother Seth, when he killed his father Osiris. Oh Isis, great in sorcery! Mayst thou loosen me, mayst thou deliver me from everything bad and evil and vicious, from afflictions (caused) by a god or goddess, from dead man or woman, from male or female adversary who will oppose me, like thy loosening and thy delivering with the son Horus. For I have entered into the fire and have come forth from the water, I will not fall into this day's trap. I have spoken (and now) I am young and am—Oh Re, speak over thine (Uraeus) serpent! Osiris, call over what came out of thee! Re speaks over his (Uraeus) serpent, Osiris calls over what came out of him. Lo, thou hast saved me from everything bad and evil and vicious, from afflictions (caused) by a god or goddess, from dead man or woman, etc.—Really excellent, (proved) many times!

Recital on drinking a remedy: Come remedy! Come thou who expellest (evil) things in this my stomach in these my limbs! The spell is powerful over the remedy. Repeat it backwards! Dost thou remember that Horus and Seth have been conducted to the big palace at Heliopolis, when there was negotiated of Seth's testicles with Horus, and he shall get well like one who is on earth. He does all that he may wish like these gods who are there.—Spoken when drinking a remedy. Really excellent, (proved) many times!

II. It shall be said: oh *htw*-animal! Oh *ḥtt*-animal! is repeated backwards; oh *'dn*! oh *'dnjt*! is repeated backwards.

III. Their incantation: the burdens are loosened, and the faintness departs which the worm has put into this my belly. The one whom the god has created, against him the enemy has made violations; (but) the god cures that which he has done in this my belly.

IV. Incantation for purulency: It is purulency which shall come out as *bkn*, it is purulency which shall come out as *bkn*—(the book is (here) without writing)—of my arms, as I trample Busiris and overturn Mendes. I will go up to heaven and see what is done there, (for) nothing is done in Abydos to expel afflictions (caused) by a god or goddess, by all kinds of purulency, by dead man or woman, etc., afflictions and all evil things that are in this my body, in this my flesh and in these my limbs. But if the afflictions (caused) by a god or goddess, by all kinds of purulency, by dead man or woman, etc., afflictions and all evil things that are in this my flesh, in this my body and in these my limbs, expel themselves, then I will not say (the incantation) nor repeat the recital. Spit, vomit, perish as thou arosest!—Is recited 4 times, spit on the diseased spot of the man. Really excellent, (proved) many times!

V. Thou shalt recite as a spell: I have brought this which was applied to the seat of yonder and replaces the horrible suffering. Twice.

VI. Another to expell white spots in the eyes: It is thundering in the southern sky since the evening, there is rough weather in the northern sky, as corpses fell into the water, and Re's crew were landing at their shore, because the heads fell into the water. Who shall bring them? (Who shall) find them? I shall bring them, I shall find them. I have brought your heads, I have attached (them to) your necks, I have fastened your cutoff (heads) in their place. I have brought you (i.e., Re's crew) to expel afflictions (caused) by a god, by dead man or woman etc. Is recited over gall of tortoise, (which) is pounded with honey and applied to the eyelids.

VII. Another to expel water-suffusion in the eyes (cataract): Come, malachite! Come, malachite! Come thou green one, come discharge from Horus' eye, come secretion from Atum's eye, come fluid that has come out of Osiris! Come to him and expel for him water, matter, blood, dim sight, *bjdj*, blindness, bleary eyedness, afflictions (caused) by a god, by dead man or woman, all kinds of purulency, all evil things that are in these eyes, etc. Is recited over malachite pounded with honey *nt ḥprj*, with them is pounded rush-nut, is applied to the eye. Really excellent.

VIII. Another, incantation of the fire the first time: thy son Horus is burnt in the desert. Is water there? There is no water there. There is water in my mouth and a Nile between (my) thighs; I come to extinguish the fire. Is recited over milk of (a woman) who has borne a male (child), gum and ram's hair, is applied to the burn.

IX. Another reciting: my son Horus is burnt in the desert. There is no water there, I am not there. Bring thou (woman) from the shore and liquid to extinguish the fire. Is recited over milk of (a woman) who has borne a male (child).

X. Another, incantation of fetid nose: flow out, fetid nose! Flow out, son of fetid nose (polypus?)! Flow out, thou who breakest bones, destroyest the skull, digest in the bone-marrow and makest the 7 holes in the head ill. Re's servants, praise Thoth! Behold, I have brought thy remedy against thee, thy protecting drink against thee: milk of (a woman) who has borne a male (child), and fragrant gum; it expels thee, it removes thee. Is repeated backwards. Go out to the ground, thou fetid, thou fetid one! 4 times.—Is recited over milk of (a woman) who has borne a male (child), and fragrant gum; is placed in the nose.

XI. Incantation for a breast: it is this breast which was ill for Isis in Chemmis when she gave birth to Shu and Tefnet. What she made for them was their incantation with flax (?), with t3 of fnb, with bk3t of fwt and with hair of its ibt, (things) that were brought to expel afflictions (caused) by dead man or woman, etc., are made into a twisting to the left (i.e., a left-twisted strong) and applied to afflictions (caused) by dead man or woman. Do not produce evacuation, do not produce itching, do not produce blood, beware lest bleary-eyedness arises for men.—Is recited over flax (?), over t3 of fnb, bk3t of fwt and hair of its ibt, is twisted to the left, made into 7 knots and applied thereto.

XII. Another to prevent the kite from robbing: a branch of acacia, let it stand up. The man shall say: oh, Horus, he has stolen in town and in the field; his thirst is for the birds' field; he shall be cooked and eaten. Is recited over a branch of acacia, and fk3-cakes are applied to it; that is the way to prevent the kite from robbing.

XIII. What is spoken as its effective spell: flow out, thou vessel šrtjw (the superficial venous plexus?) which šrtjw me, and which jumps (i.e., pulsates) in the midst of these limbs because thou unitest with Chons' unions. If thou examinest Chons' swelling m3' ndm nhk wj. Let me bring sacrificial gifts to Re, namely faience, in the mornings. Is recited 4 times very early in the morning.

It is also doubtful that the "laying-on-of-hands" described sparingly in the *Papyrus Ebers* has anything to do with the history of hypnotic inductions. Most of the instances of the laying-on-of-hands involved the application of ointments and salves, massage, or that carried out in the ordinary examination of a patient to determine the site of disease. For example, to expel purulency the patient was anointed with ricinus-fruits' oil and massaged for ten days, "rubbing very early in the morning" (Ebbell, 1937, p. 41). Or: "If thou examinest a man with an obstacle in his cardia, thou shalt apply thy hand to him; if thou findest that his disease consists in that his body all through (literally, his thickness) is shivering [probably refers to fever], when thy fingers are applied to him, then thou shalt say of him: it is a case of purulency which has not yet attached itself" (Ebbell, 1937, p. 49). The latter directive certainly would appear to be more a description of examination procedures than an attempt to influence either the patient or the disease. In the anatomical-physiological section (Ebbell, 1937, pp. 114–120) there is also a description of the use of hands and fingers as diagnostic devices to palpate the circulatory system in various parts of the body, again hardly a hypnotic induction-like use of the "laying-on-of-hands," unless one is willing to include physical examinations as an induction technique, which I am not.

The two instances where instructions for the laying-on-of-hands take on a curative, mesmeric–passes-like quality is in the control of pain. (It is fascinating to note in passing that the control of pain is still one of the foremost medical and dental uses made of hypnosis.) The first involves the care of a patient with "illness in his cardia, and he has pains in his arm, in his breast (mamma), and in one side of his cardia. . . . Thou shalt apply thy extended [i.e., flat] hand to him; the arm gets well and rid of pains" (Ebbell, 1937, p. 49). The second instance is in the treatment of headache: "If a man's head aches [?], then thou shalt lay thy hand on his head without his perceiving it." (Ebbell, 1937, p. 60). There follows then a description of a mixture of natron, oil, honey, and wax to be applied in bandage. Thus, if the descriptive beginnings of hypnotic inductions are outlined in the *Papyrus Ebers,* and thus early Egyptian medicine, their role was not predominant.

However, there is a papyrus, which according to its German translation (Krugsch-Pascha, 1893), does contain more direct references to early Egyptian knowledge and use of what we today call hypnosis. *Pap. A. Nr. 65* has resided in the museum of Leiden, The Netherlands since 1829.[1] Since it was dedicated to an Egyptian Gnostician and other dating data are absent, historically it is best placed somewhere around the 3rd century A.D. Whether this implies earlier Egyptian knowledge of hypnotic techniques as supposed from the *Papyrus Ebers* is not clear.

The use of the techniques to be described below was for calling forth various demons from whom knowledge could be secured through stealth. Most often this was done through the medium of a "harmless, chaste boy" through whose mouth the demons spoke, answering any questions put before them. The stealth came in the form of the "hypnotist" pretending to be one of the noted Egyptian gods (e.g., Osiris, Isis, Horus, etc.), and thus commanding the presence of the demons through the child. On occasion, the operator himself acted as medium.

What is of interest for us is the rituals used in preparing the boy to serve as medium. Apparatus for the procedure included a "purified and clean room" set aside from other rooms of the edifice (perhaps akin to the *Abaton* of the sleep temples and the *baquet* of Mesmer's chambers), a clean and new lamp filled with the "best and purist oil," and two boxes. The hypnosis of the child could be done with him or her either seated on one of the boxes facing the lamp or standing facing the lamp hung on a wooden peg on the wall.

The original Egyptian text calls for the operator "to make him [the child] close his eyes" and then later "he made him open up his eyes." It was during the intervening sleep (hypnosis) that the demons spoke. The child was "made to sleep" by repeating a long verbal incantation seven times to him.

Other parts of the total procedure described in the original papyrus are even more strikingly like later hypnotic techniques. For example: "When you perform in a room, take care that it is dark," denoting the practice, still used today, of reducing extraneous environmental stimuli. The relationship between the old and the new is even more apparent in the following: "Arrange a second box as your seat and stand the boy between your feet. Then say the motto, mentioned above, upon the boy, *while your eye fixes the mirror of his eye* [italics added]." Eye-fixation played a prominent role in all of the procedures described in this papyrus, whether it was as just described, or having the boy fixate on the lighted lamp. Except for the incantation that induced the sleep, most of the verbal rituals were not hypnosis-producing, but intended to call forth supernatural beings through which knowledge could be obtained. Like the *Papyrus Ebers,* most of the incantations seem little related to an induction procedure. However, as we will see later, a number of the more modern, prominent individuals in mesmerism and hypnosis also were caught up in attempts to use mesmerized subjects as mediums to obtain insight into the future or diagnosis and prescription in the present (e.g., Mesmer, Elliotson).

Several other similarities exist between the practices of 3rd century Egyptian and later practitioners of other rituals, including mesmerism and hypnosis. The *Leiden Papyrus* specifically designates the type of wood from which the peg, on which the lamp is hung, is fashioned—laurel. ("Hang it [the lamp] on a wall that faces East on a peg made of the wood of the laurel tree.") Specification of the wood to be used makes us wonder if the Egyptians attributed certain powers to the laurel, in a manner similar to the Druids, who used mistletoe, yew, ash, or oak for their magical wands. The choice of the particular wood usually depended on what was locally available.

Finally, what appears to be a mesmeric-like pass is described: "While saying the motto to him, pass the finger of your right hand [index finger?] over his head, up and down, and so forth." Such maneuvers, coupled with the eye-fixation described above, and the attendant apparatus and setting, would appear to indicate that the 3rd century Egyptians practiced something quite similar to hypnosis.

To ascertain the beginnings of hypnotic induction, we may have to look more to the antithesis of ancient medical practice—the religious priesthood—to find some of the historical antecedents. It is here particularly we find reference to the laying-on-of-hands. According to Bonwick (1878), for example, "We still keep up 'the-laying-on-of-hands' adopted in the mysteries" (p. 348), the initiation rites of Freemasonary in early Egypt. He also indicates that the priests and priestesses (The Egyptians incorporated women also into this most revered order of power and influence, demonstrating a degree of equality with respect to women not accorded in the

Greek and Jewish societies of ancient times.) bestowed blessings by "hold-ing up two fingers and a thumb, or three fingers, and inclining them toward the favored individuals" (p. 356). Such a gesture is quite reminiscent of those made by the Abbé Faria as he pointed at his charges while proclaim-ing, "Sleep!" No doubt the mesmerists of the early and middle 1800s would have interpreted this priestly gesture as a mesmeric pass. Lloyd (1845a), in fact, informs us that the dervishes of early Constantinople cured diseases, particularly in children, by "laying-on-of-hands." In fact, although he allows us few examples, Bonwick (1878), in his discussion of magic in ancient Egypt, quotes the author of *Art Magic:* "They [Egyptian magicians] under-stood the nature of the loadstone, the virtues of mineral and animal magne-tism . . . in fact, they were the masters of the arts now known as mesmer-ism, clairvoyance, electro-biology, etc" (Bonwick, 1878, p. 337).

The reference to "mineral and animal magnetism" is particularly impor-tant, because like the historical continuity of the use of the hands in hypnotic (mesmeric) inductions, the supposed relationship between lodestone, me-talic, mineral magnetism and the so-called animal magnetism, was based primarily on theoretically explanations dating from at least the time of Max-well (see Moll, 1889/1897). The early knowledge of and concern about the seemingly magical effects of mineral magnetism is of no less historical impor-tance than the concern with the laying-on-of-hands and other significant gestures. The continuity, which seems to appear first in ancient Egypt, although it is probably a reasonable assumption to attribute its origins even farther back (to the Hindu), appears also in the folklore of the ancient Celts (to whom iron held a special military and sociological reverence, since it was more efficient and stronger than the earlier bronze) as we will see later in this chapter. According to Homer, the Greeks too used a wand (made from gold), "which closes the eyes of mortals in sleep, and rouses them again" (Odyss. xxiv. 4; see Lloyd, 1847, p. 285). It is an easy cognitive step to the rods and wands of Mesmer's days at the *baquet.*

Amulets of various shapes, sizes, and composition also played a role in Egyptian magic and thus assume a role in the history of hypnotic induction. However, for the Egyptians, amulets appeared to have more protective than inductive powers (Bonwick, 1878). They were used to protect the bearer from evil, in particular the evil eye, which is noted as one of the ancient origins of present-day hypnosis by Moll (1889/1897). The carrying of lucky pieces (e.g., rabbits' feet, lucky coins, St. Christopher medals) even today is not forsaken for fear that abandonment of the magical ritual will lead to some disaster. The rosary plays as important a role in religion today as it did over 6000 years ago in Egypt.

The association of spoken words with induction makes its appearance more in relationship to amulets than to the laying-on-of-hands, since the recitation of certain verbal rituals spoken over the amulet increased its pro-tective powers, particularly when uttered by the right individual. The words, however, belonged to a special sect and were not to be profaned by utterance of the common person. "The words, hidden from the vulgar, had their secret influence intensified by the will of the utterer" (Bonwick, 1878, p. 341). Again, historical continuity presents itself when we recall that the "strong will" of the mesmerist of the 18th and 19th centuries was considered of great importance for the effectiveness of the passes. In present day we enjoin the hypnotist to present a façade of professional confidence and expertise to the patient, who will thereby be better able to join in the process. Also, the policy of nondisclosure of the verbal rituals to the "vulgar" is strangely reminiscent of the present-day priesthoods' attempt to limit the use of modern induction techniques and practices to the few, to protect the many, by legislative means.

Two other historical continuities need to be mentioned at this point: (a) the association of music, particular rhythms and dancing, and (b) the use of water or other liquids with inductions. Again in *Art Magic,* we find that the Egyptian magicians also "employed music to admirable effect" (Bonwick, 1878, p. 337), although its actual use, except as in the temple processions, is not explicated. Lloyd (1845a) also indicated that the dervishes of Constantinople, mentioned above, used dancing as part of their ritual. Both dancing and rhythmic musical pulsations as part of an induction procedure are clearly seen in the more recent descriptions of Haitian and other Voodoo rituals. Aaronson's rhythmically moving witches' cradle (1973) is but a present day acknowledgment of rhythmicity in hypnotic induction. So too are the rhythmic voice qualities used by present practitioners and studied by Barber (Barber & Calverley, 1964).

Specially treated (holy) water also had its place in the rituals of ancient Egypt, for the temple worshipper was sprinkled with holy water as he or she entered the temple (Brier, 1980). (In fact, those readers interested in the historical antecedents of modern religion, both in rituals and in beliefs, should consult Bonwick's *Egyptian Belief and Modern Thought.*) While we may not consider such a practice part of the direct lineage of hypnotic induction, it is; not because we use it today, but because the 18th and 19th century mesmerists made extensive use of "magnetic" water. "Magnetized" water was in the *baquet;* often mesmerism (magnetism) was achieved by having the patient drink water that had been previously magnetized. As we shall see, there was for a time a proliferation of magnetized objects (gloves, glasses, pieces of metal, etc.) used in the induction of mesmeric trances. De Puységur himself used a magnetic tree, which as we will explore, has a historical connection to the Druids' use of oak and ash for magical wands. Reflected in the folklore of ancient Ireland is the use (again by the Druids) of water and milk as liquids possessing special, magical properties. Thus the holy water, with all of its attendant supernatural attributes, of ancient Egypt has historical connections, not only with the ritual of the modern Catholic Church, but also with the induction of modern hypnosis with its acknowledged mesmeric connection (Pattie, 1967; Shor, 1979).

SLEEP TEMPLES OF EGYPT, GREECE, AND ROME

Probably the most prominently known of the ancient links to modern hypno-sis are the famed sleep temples of the Egyptians, and later the Greeks and Romans. The Egyptian temples, located along the Nile River, appeared about the 5th century B.C., and were primarily dedicated to the healing Goddess Isis (Bonwick, 1878; Cutten, 1911; Lloyd, 1845a, 1845b, 1847; Ludwig, 1964; Rogers, 1947; Zilboorg, 1941). During a nine-day incubation or sleep period, Isis was supposed to have revealed herself to the sufferer and offered both diagnosis and treatment, after "the affected was put into a magnetic sleep by the priestly magician" (Bonwick, 1878, p. 339). Temples also appeared at Memphis, where Serapis (a divinity whose healing powers were an amalgamation of Osiris—Isis' husband—and Apis, the local god) was the major religious vehicle for cure (see Cutten, 1911; Ludwig, 1964). Lloyd (1845a) informs us that this latter center (at Memphis) was where mesmerism was chiefly concentrated, although Canobus was another site where "Aeschylus assigns the cure of Io!" (p. 167).

Soon the sleep cult had spread to Greece with the construction of the Temples of Asklepios (between 186 and 320 in all—Hamilton, 1906) during the 4th century B.C., and other incubation sites as Epidauros, Kos, Trikka, Pergamos, Knidos, Crotona, and Cyrene (Hamilton, 1906; Ludwig, 1964; Rogers, 1947). Similar to their Egyptian predecessors, Grecian seekers of solace gained entrance to the *Abaton*—the sacred sleep room—only after cleansing themselves physically (by bathing) and spiritually (by making valu-able offerings to the temple; some, in fact, donated additional buildings to the temple site.) and serving a probationary period under the tutelage of the priests. According to Hamilton (1906), the *iatra* or physician's fees were "stringently exacted." Once in the *Abaton,* the patient slept. Whereas the Egyptians were visited by Isis or Serapis, the Greeks dreamed of the appear-ance of Asklepios, who cured the individual or gave treatment instructions. (Rogers, 1947, notes a similarity between the past and the present. It seems that while the incubation healings were acknowledged by many, there was a large contingent of the Greek population, particularly intellectuals, who looked upon them with disdain and ridicule, and raised the question of fraud. Mesmer's Paris experience, Elliotson's banishment from established medi-cine, as well as the experience of many modern practitioners of hypnosis have a similar ring.) So it was, somewhat later (2nd century A.D.), in the Roman Empire where Tibur Island (San Bartolomeo) and the Temple of Aesculapius (the Roman counterpart of Asklepios) became the focus of incu-bation.

Neither of the more modern summary accounts (Ludwig, 1964; Rogers, 1947) offers any detail of the procedures employed by the priests of the sleep temples. In fact, Rogers (1947) indicates that the details "remain lost secrets of the priestly cult" (p. 625), although he does opine that the relaxation preceding the incubation (εγχοιμησλδ) and that developed in the sleep itself could have laid an excellent groundwork for suggestive therapeutics. (Although Rogers does give 9 examples of the 46 cases described on the stelae at Epidauros, no procedural details are contained therein.) Hamilton (1906) merely states: "The patient . . . lies down to rest in the appointed hall, and during the night there comes to him a visitation from the god" (p. 29). However, Colquhoun (1836) did indicate that the cures were produced by the laying-on-of-hands ("the touch of the priests," p. 188). Such a technique is also mentioned by Lloyd (1845a) when he attributed the Aeschylusian cures to the "contrectation of the hand of Zeus" (p. 167). The preserved inscriptions from marble slabs from Ribur indicate that during the rule of Augustus (31 B.C.) the laying-on-of-hands was prescribed. Gaius, a blind man, was instructed to place his fingers on the alter and then to lay his hand on his eyes and thus restore his sight (Hamilton, 1906).

Bernheim (1886/1964), however, claimed that the ancient Egyptian technique was one of eye-fixation leading to hallucinations and eventual somnambulism:

> The *Mandeb* . . . use a perfectly white earthenware plate; then, with pen and ink, they draw two crossed triangles (one within the other), and fill the empty space of the geometric figure with cabalistic words. The subject chosen for this experiment then fixes his gaze at the center of the crossed triangles. After four or five minutes, he sees a black point in the middle of the plate. This black point enlarges, changes form, and is transformed into various visions which fly about in front of the subject. This hallucination frequently leads to an extraordinarily lucid somnambulism. (p. 47)

More direct references to the induction procedures used in the Greek temples of sleep have been preserved. Both Colquhoun (1836) and Lloyd (1845a) quote the same passage from Solon to indicate the use of mesmeric-like passes in the process of alieviating pain and disease:

$$\text{Πολλάκι δ'ἔξ ὀλίγης ὀδύνης μέγα γίγνεται ἀλγος}$$
$$\text{Κ'οὐκ ἄν τις λύσαιτ' ἤπια φάρμακα δ'ούς,}$$
$$\text{Τὸν δὲ κυκαῖς νούσοισι κυκώμενον ἀργαλέαις τε}$$
$$\text{Αψάμενος χειροῖν ἀιψα τίϑησ' ὑγιῆ.}$$

Quoting from Stanley's *History of Philosophy* (1666), Colquhoun (1836, p. 190) offers the following translation:

> *The smallest hurts sometimes increase and rage*
> *More than all art of physic can assuage;*
> *Sometimes the fury of the worst disease*
> *The hand, by gentle stroking, will appease.*

Lloyd (1845a, p. 159) renders the passage thus:

> Often from trifling pain great suffering arises, not to be allayed by the adminis-
> tration of soothing medicines, but touching with the hands the sufferer by
> malignant and obstinate diseases, you immediately restore him to health.

Colquhoun also informs us that Asclepiades of Bithynia recommended "frictions" until the patient reached the salutary condition of sleep.

Lloyd (1845a, p. 159) found further references to the laying-on-of-hands as
a curative manipulation (hence, we presume, the historical antecedent of the
mesmeric induction technique) in passages from Aeschulus' *Prometheus
vinctus* in which Prometheus tells Io to find solace at Canobus:

Ἐνταῦθα δή σε Ζεὺς τίθησιν ἔμφρονα
Ἐπαφῶν ἀταρβἕι χειρὶ καὶ θίγων μόνον.

*There Zeus will render you sane, stroking you with gentle hand and
simply touching you.*

and again:

Εν δ᾿ ἦν Ζεὺς ἐπαφώμενος ἠρέμα χειρὶ θεείῃ.

Zeus was represented gently stroking or soothing (Io) with divine hand.

As is often the case in researching ancient preambles to modern medical
treatment techniques, it is the poets of the time who have preserved the
culture, lay and professional. Aristophanes, in *Plutus,* describes the god
Aesculapius touching the patient to effect a cure in this remarkably detailed
narrative of the procedure:

> The blind patient, no other than the god of wealth, is bathed in the sea, then
> taken to the *temenos* of the god, where, after sundry cakes are consecrated on
> the burning altar, he is placed in bed, and his friends also prepare to pass the
> night there with him. The minister of the god extinguishes the lights, and
> enjoins them to sleep, and whatever noise was heard, to keep silence; and so
> they compose themselves. . . . The god appears, attended by two maidens,
> Inso and Panaceia, and walks round, inspecting the diseases of the patients, a
> child bringing him a pestle and mortar, and little case. . . . At length he seats
> himself by the side of the blind patient, and first touched (ἐφήψατο) his head;
> then, taking a clean handkerchief, he wiped round his eyelids, and Panaceia
> covered his head and whole face with a purple covering; the god then made a
> signal (εποππυσεν)—made the sound that the word exemplifies—and immedi-
> ately two serpents of immense size sprung from the *neos,* slid gently under the
> covering of the patient's head, and, as the narrator supposed, licked his eyes,
> and the cure was effected. (Lloyd, 1845a, pp. 163–164).

The final reference in this passage to the influence of serpents has been noted in several instances of ancient history, both with the serpents as curative agents and with males of certain sects having the power to cure snake bites with stroking:

"The Ophiogeneis of Parion in the Propontis," says Strabo, xiii., "claimed a certain relationship to serpents, and pretended to descend from a hero who was transformed into one. [A parallel mythus to that of Aesclepiadae, descendants of the serpent physician of Epidaurus.] They say that their males cure the bites of vipers, by *constantly touching* (συνεχως εφαπτομενους), like the charmers (επωδ᾽αι), first transferring to themselves the *livor* (πελιωμα), and the inflammation and pain." (Lloyd, 1845b, p. 306)

Pliny described the Ophiogeneis of Parion as "a race of men who relieved the wound of a serpent by a touch, and by laying on the hand drew the poison out of the body" (Pliny, vii, 2; cited in Lloyd, 1845b, p. 307). In addition, snake bite was treated by special water held in the mouths or used to rinse the hands of the Psylli of Africa (Lloyd, 1845b). So also did the Psyllus use their own saliva and "frictions" to aid a sufferer:

If the Psyllus found the anguish of the sound still tolerable he relieved it by his saliva, and prevented worse consequences. If he found the sufferer in extreme torment he gave him water to drink that he had held in his mouth, and in cases where the virus had gained still greater power, he lay down naked by the naked patient, and delivered him from his danger, by communicating to him, by gentle friction, and sympathetic vigour of his own body. (τοῦ χρωτός οἱ τοῦ ιδίου προσανατρίψας την ἰσχὺν την συμφυῆ.) (Lloyd, 1845b, p. 307)

This latter technique—that of using the body and body heat as a curative agent—is not at all unlike the tale of King David, which we will encounter shortly, nor of the verses of Nicander, of Colophon (Lloyd, 1845b, p. 308):

Ανδρασιν ημνναν τνμμασιν αχϑομενοις,
Ον ριζαις ερδοντες, εων δ᾽απο σνγχροα γνιων.

The Psylli cure men of venomous bites, not by the assistance of roots, but by the contact of their own bodies.

Pliny's description of the Ophiogeneis of Cyprus is quite similar to Aelian's notations on the Psylli:

Pliny xxviii. 3, mentions Ophiogeneis, of Cyprus, also a family of which Exagon, a member, ambassador at Rome, was thrown by the consuls (experimenti causa, says the Naturalist, but if at all it must be supposed by his own invitation) into a cask full of venemous serpents, who only licked him. The family had a strong odour in spring, and their sweat, as well as saliva, had a curative power. Persons were cured by being sprinkled with the water in which their hands had been washed; their very presence was beneficial. (Lloyd, 1845b, p. 307)

It is conceivable that such practices relate to the present symbolic uses of holy water as noted above, for Lloyd (1845b) also notes its use described in *Tacitus Ann.* ii 54, wherein priests out of certain families in Asia Minor "drank water of a secret fountain (*hausta fontis arcani aqua*)" (pp. 312–313), before offering prescriptions to the seekers of answers. We shall note also that magical (magnetized?) water was used for "evil" purposes as well, for example, by the Telchins, who destroyed plants and animals by "sprinkling them with magic water" (Lloyd, 1847, p. 283).

Lloyd (1845b) also notes the power of the eyes in a footnote concerning the supposed effect of staring into the eyes of either Alexander Severus or Augustus, the latter of whom took great delight in noticing that individuals avoided direct eye contact with him for fear of being dazzled, as by the sun.

Nor was the effect of music, as produced by a chorus, in the production of extraordinary effects lost on the ancients. Thus the Homeric hymn to Apollo:

προςδε, τοδε μεγα θαυμα, οου κλεος ουποτ᾽ολεισαι,
κουραι Δηλιαδες, Εκατηβελεταο θεραπναί
αιτ᾽ε επει αρ πρωτον μεν Απολλων᾽ υμνησωσιν,
αυτις δ᾽αν Λητω τε και Αρτεμιν ιοχεαιραν
μνησαμεναι, ανδρων τε παλαιων νδε͂ γυναικων,
υμνον αειδουσιν, θελγουσι δε φυλ᾽ ανθρωπων.
παντων δ᾽ανθρωπων φωναρ και κρεμβα᾽ λιαστυν
μιμεισθ᾽ ισασιν φαιη δε κεν αυτος εκαστος
φθεγγεσθ᾽.

A vast wonder, moreover, of which the fame shall never perish; the Delian virgins, ministers of the far darting god, who celebrating Apollo, Latona and Artemis, making mention of the men and women of old, sing a hymn, and charm (or sooth) the tribes of men. They can imitate the voices and accents of all men, and each would say that he himself was speaking; so their beautiful song is adapted. (Lloyd, 1845b, p. 305)

Finally, there is some indication that the lodestone, or imitations thereof, was used in heightening the psychological aura surrounding the sleep temples, if not directly in the induction procedure itself. In the Egyptian temple of Serapeion at Alexandria, a metal statue was suspended from the ceiling by a magnet, which apparently the priests used to excite superstition and wonder (Lloyd, 1847). At Trikka the magnet was used to cure afflictions of the eyes, and the mythology of Prometheus tells of a magnetic stone set in a ring probably composed of iron and gold (Lloyd, 1847).

As mentioned above, iron and its attractant, the lodestone, have played a significant role in early mythology, and, we therefore assume, in the culture of the day. This fascination with physical influence at a distance (magnetism) and its power for making the unknown comprehensible is exemplified in a passage by the Byzantine Tzetzes:

Η μαγνης 'η λιθος μεν τον σιδηρον ελκυει
ης την ολκην και την μορθην και ετερα βραχεα
και ως καθελκει προς αυτην την φυσιν του σιδηρου
προτερον προειρηκομεν· αλλα δε νυν ερουμεν,
την λιθον ταυτην την μαγνησσαν στρωμνη τινος γυναιου
λαθρω θεις 'υπο δεμνιον τη γυναικι ερωτα,
και μονη πασας ειπη σοι ταυτης τας αμαρτιας
η της στρωμνης ως προς την γην εξολιοθηση ταχει,
αν δ'εστιν αμαρτητος, αν δ'εστι των απταιστων,
εκτεινει περιβαλουσα χειρας τω σω τραχνλω,
οιδα και αλλα περισσα χηνων τε και βατραχων
οσα ποιει καθευδοντας ανδρας τε και γυναικας
τοις ερωτωσι προσλαλειν αυτων τα επταισμενα,
αρκει δε τα μαγνητιδος κ.τ.λ.

The magnet stone attracts iron; of its power of attraction and of its form, and how it draws to itself the natural quality of iron, we have already spoken. (iv. 400.) We will now mention other properties. Place this stone, the magnet, secretly beneath the coverlet of the bed of a woman, and interrogate her, and she will declare to you all her frailties, or immediately slip from the couch down upon the ground. But if she be faultless, if she be one of the untripping, she will extend her arms to throw them round your neck. I am also acquainted with other strange properties of geese and frogs, causing men and women when asleep to declare their slips to those who question them; but the instance of the magnet is sufficient. (Lloyd, 1847, p. 274)

Furthermore, we are told:

ες γαρ μιν κομισας, υπο δεμνια κατθεο λαθρη,
χειλεσιν αειδων θελξιμβροτον ατρεμας ωδην,
η δε κατακνωσσουσα και ηδεϊ περ μαλ 'εν 'υπνω,
αμφι σε χειρ' ορεγουσα ποτιπτυσσειν μενεαινει·
ει δε ε μαχλοσυνησιν ελαυνει δι' Αφροδιτη,
υψοθεν ες γαιαν τετανυσσεται εκπροπεσουσα. v. 312 sqq.

[But I tell you, to prove your wife whether she preserves her purity;] for, taking the magnetic stone, place it secretly beneath the coverlets, chanting gently with your lips a soothing song, and she, although slumbering in sweet sleep, will endeavour to embrace you with her arms; but if divine Aphrodite urges her to infidelities, she will start from the couch and fall extended on the earth. (Lloyd, 1847, p. 275)

Note in this latter passage the coming together of the use of the lodestone and music entreatment in the form of a verbal chant, perhaps, marking an early notation of the induction of an altered state by verbal means, a technique we did not fully appreciate and fully use until the 19th century. "The gentle murmer of a soothing verse is part of the magnetizing formula of Tzetzes" (Lloyd, 1847, p. 283), as was their (and the Telchins') use of "magic water" and "the evil eye."

Thus it appears reasonable to suppose that the induction techniques used in the sleep temples of Egypt, Greece, and Rome closely paralleled the methods we see later in the development of induction techniques, particularly in Mesmer's time: (a) the laying-on-of-hands, (b) the use of physical magnetism, (c) the use of specially prepared water (and/or saliva), (d) the fixing of visual attention, and (e) the use of rhythmic chants and musical forms.

BIBLICAL TIMES

According to Wolff (1951), several of God's activities, related in the Old Testament, were hypnotic in character. On the strength of the use of *tardemah,* the Hebrew word for Adam's sleep (Genesis 2:21), he claims that such events as the sleep of Saul (I Samuel 26:12) and the revelations to Job (Job 4:13, 33:15) were merely descriptions of a hypnotic trance. However, the latter (revelations to Job) appear to be merely a description of dreaming during ordinary night sleep. None of these passages enlightens us on the details of the induction procedures beyond the general statements: "And the Lord God caused a deep sleep to fall upon Adam" (Genesis 2:21), and, "because a deep sleep from the Lord was fallen upon them" (I Samuel 26:12).

Wolff (1951) does make another inference of historic interest when he suggests that the "holy water," "oil," and/or "incense" of biblical reference was in reality naphtha, whose fumes produced a hypnotic condition. Lloyd (1847) also suggested that the effect of the oracles of Trophonius "was probably due to a gaseous exhalation of the same kind as that to which . . . the *prophetic* [italics added] excitement of the Delphic priestess was due" (Lloyd, 1847, p. 273).

Ludwig (1964) reports as well that Pythia, the priestess of the Temple of Apollo at Delphi, was supposed to have fallen into an altered condition (" 'hypnotic' trance") "while inhaling fumes emanating from poppy leaves or hempen ingredients" (p. 209). Paton (1921) claims that the vapor rose through a fissure in the earth, while Björnström (1887) described the priestess seated on a tripod over the fissure inhaling not the vapor of naphtha, but those of sulphur. The ancients, too, perceived many paths to hypnosis.

The word "prophetic," in the quote from Lloyd above, is another curious connection between biblical interpretation and ancient folklore, because a number of authors (Glasner, 1955; Paton, 1921; Williams, 1954; Wolff, 1951) have suggested that this word refers to a frenzied behavior denoting mass hypnosis. Thus, when the prophets (e.g., in I Samuel 10:5–6, 10–12; 19:20–24) or the priests of Baal (e.g., in I Kings 18:26–29) were prophesying, they were, in fact, engaged in some sort of mass hypnosis.

Whether such suppositions are correct is difficult to determine and would takes us farther afield in biblical study than is warranted. What is worthy to note, it seems to me, is the general flow of continuity between ancient practices and present inductions, a continuity Hockly (1849) claimed to have found in the Old Testament book of Exodus. According to Elliotson (1848), the laying-on-of-hands as a method of cure is reported in II Kings 5:11, in which Naaman expresses disappointment at Elisha for not employing mesmerism in the cure of his leprosy: "Behold, I thought, He will surely come out to me, and stand, and call on the name of the Lord his God, and *strike his hand over the place,* and recover the leper." The italicized words were interpreted to mean "wave his hand near the place" (Elliotson, 1848, p. 257), indicating the performance of mesmeric-like passes.

Old Testament passages not only allude to the laying-on-of-hands, but also to the laying-on-of-the-entire-body (Elliotson, 1848):

> Now king David was old and stricken in years; and they covered him with clothes, but he gat no heat.

> Wherefore his servants said unto him, Let there be sought for my lord the king a young virgin: and let her stand before the king, and let her cherish him, and let her lie in thy bosom, that my lord the king may get heat.

> So they sought for a fair damsel throughout all the coasts of Israel and found Abishag, a Shunamnrite, and brought her to the king.

> And the damsel was very fair, and cherished the king, and ministered to him: but the king knew her not. (I Kings, 1:1–4)

No doubt the efficacy of this procedure lay in the body heat thus generated, rather than a transfer of any magically curative fluid, flux, or magnetism.

One element of continuity does seem to be consistent—the prominence played by the eyes in both producing special states and of the states themselves. Just as the ancients of the sleep temples may have used visionary techniques to effect cures, so too is the Old Testament replete with tales in which the eyes predominate in mystic visions. Glasner (1955) catalogs such visions as Ezekiel's eye-studded spiral wheels (1:16, 18; 10:12), Daniel's vision of eye-studded horns (7:8, 7:20), and Zechariah's seeing of a stone with seven eyes (3:9). (Could the latter be the lodestone again?) According to Wolff's interpretation (1951), God also produced eye phenomena in the form of hypnotic blindness. However, in Isaiah 29:10 we find another Genesis and I Samuel-like reference to sleep (hypnosis?), this time associated with eye closure: "For the Lord hath poured upon you the spirit of deep sleep, and hath closed your eyes." Although interesting as historical anecdotes, these passages merely describe the phenomena produced, rather than the method of production.

With the dawn of Christianity, the historical march continued, and we find in the cures of the New Testament, as wrought by both Jesus and the Apostles, the use of eye-fixation, the laying-on-of-hands, verbal suggestion, and saliva, singly or in combination. The Apostle Peter effected a cure of lameness and paralysis by an eye-fixation technique (Acts 3:2–10; 9:32–34): "And Peter, fastening his eyes upon him with John, said, Look on us" (Acts 3:4). Paul reportedly did the same in healing the cripple (Acts 14:8–10): "The same heard Paul speak: who steadfastly beholding him. . . . Said with a loud voice, Stand upright on thy feet" (Acts 14:9–10).

The laying-on-of-hands was not unknown to the Apostles. In fact, it was used on Saul (Paul) himself by Ananias: "And Ananias, . . . putting his hands on him said, Brother Saul, the Lord, even Jesus, . . . hath sent me, that thou mightest receive thy sight . . . And immediately there fell from his eyes as it had been scales: and he received sight forthwith" (Acts 9: 17–18). Later Paul used the same technique (laying-on-of-hands) to cure the father of Publius, "to whom Paul entered in, and prayed, and laid his hands on him, and healed him" (Acts 28:8).

But Paul apparently also used hypnotic techniques aggressively. In Acts 13:6–11, he produced hypnotic blindness (with a posthypnotic suggestion for the blindness to terminate in one year) through a combination of eye-fixation and the laying-on-of-hands: "Then Saul, (who is also called Paul), filled with the Holy Ghost, set his eyes on him, . . . And said . . . And now, behold, the hand of the Lord is upon thee, and thou shalt be blind, not seeing the sun for a season" (Acts 13:9–11).

Jesus, on the other hand, relied more on the laying-on-of-hands and/or verbal soothing and suggestion. His laying-on-of-hands is described in relation to the lepers by Matthew (Matthew 8:1–14), Mark (Mark 1:40–45), and Luke (Luke 5:12–14). The passage is essentially the same in all three cases: "And Jesus put forth *his* hand, and touched him, saying, I will; be thou clean" (Luke 5:13; Mark 1:41; Matthew 8:3).

Luke also tells us of Jesus' use of the laying-on-of-hands for the cure of a woman with bodily distortion: "And he laid his hands on her: and immediately she was made straight" (Luke 13:13, from Luke 13:10–17). The use of touch in Jesus' curing of the blind is also evident: "So Jesus had compassion on them, and touched their eyes: and immediately their eyes received sight" (Matthew 20:34, from 20:29–34, see also Matthew 9:27–31). (See below for additional examples.) In the case of dropsy (edema) it is difficult to ascertain whether or not the laying-on-of-hands took place: "And he took him, and healed him, and let him go" (Luke 14:4, from Luke 14:1–6). However, the use of touch is clearer in the case of fever: "And he touched her hand, and fever left her" (Mark 1:31, from 1:29–31; Matthew 8:15, from 8:14–15). The same story in Luke (4:38–39), on the other hand, omits a direct reference to physical contact.

In his cure of the women suffering from hemorrhage, a touch of Jesus' garment—initiated by the woman—was combined with soothing words. Here may be a forerunner of the later use of magnetized objects (articles of clothing, trees, and so forth) to rivet the attention of the patient (see Luke 8:43–48; Mark 5:25–34; Matthew 9:20–22). In a few cases he used direct verbal command (suggestion) alone, for example, with paralysis: "Jesus saith unto him, Rise, take up the bed, and walk" (John 5:8, from John 5:5–9); a withered hand: "Then saith he to the man, Stretch forth thine hand" (Luke 6:10, from 6:6–11; Mark 3:5, from 3:1–6; Matthew 12:13, from 12:9–14). The same tactic was used with the blind: "And Jesus said unto him, Receive thy sight" (Luke 18:42, from 18:35–43). As is the case of many practitioners today, Jesus apparently proceeded directly to treatment with little time and effort being spent in a formal induction procedure.

In two instances the Bible relates an act by Jesus that seems to be a throwback to the Ophiogeneis of Cypus and Parion and the Psylli of Africa (see above)—the use of his own spittle to effect a cure. In the case of a deaf stammerer, he combined saliva with the laying-on-of-hands: "And when he [Jesus] had spit on his eyes, and put his hands upon him, he asked him if he saw . . . [he did]" (Mark 8:23, from 8:22–26). In another case of blindness he combined his spittle with the clay of the earth to form compresses: "He spat on the ground, and made clay of the spittle, and he anointed the eyes of the blind man with the clay" (John 9:6, from 9:1–7). Again one wonders if such a use of a "magical liquid" was not another early forerunner of magnetic water.

According to Glasner (1955), the Rabbis of early Christianity were also knowledgeable in hypnotic phenomena, though many distained such practices and relegated them to the category of "sorcery." If Imber (1910) is correct, the Talmud contains a direct reference to hypnotic induction using eye-fixation in the phrase *achisath aynayim* ("holding of the eyes").

Although Christ and his immediate disciples were the first of the new religion to incorporate ancient, so-called "pagan" rituals into their own form of worship, they were by no means the last. Many of the early saints were reported to have engaged in curative methods identical to those of the past, most including the incubation, or sleep-cures, which we have noted above during the Egyptian, Greek, and Roman dominated eras. For example, we find the laying-on-of-hands attributed to St. Cosmas and St. Damian, who were put to death in 287 A.D. Most of the laying-on-of-hands occurred following the ritual of incubation, which took three forms during the early centuries of Christianity (Hamilton, 1906): (a) voluntary, where the patient came to the temple to sleep and be cured, (b) chance, where the patient chanced to fall asleep and a vision appeared to him or her, and (c) involuntary, where the patient achieved a state of readiness or receptiveness through self-suggestion, hypnosis, or miraculous intervention. The role of the priest in early Christian ritual was threefold. They cared for the infirmed (including the insane), interceded through prayer on behalf of the afflicted, and exorcised demons (Hamilton, 1906).

Basil, Bishop of Seleucia (4th century A.D.) reported that St. Thekla, whose biography he had recorded, cured him of an earache by touch when she appeared before him in a vision. But the laying-on-of-hands was not the only ritual to persist in Christian rites. The bringing forth of special fountains, a draught from which cured the sick, was also attributed to St. Thekla, and most of the churches associated with the cult of St. Michael, about whom many legends of cures exist, have a sacred fountain located nearby (Hamilton, 1906). Drinking the water from these fountains was said to bring about miraculous cures of debilitating diseases.

Apparently the curative works of St. Cyrus and St. John in the 7th century A.D. were among the most faithfully recorded. Hamilton (1906) tells us that there are numerous references to incubation prior to the curing of the individual. People slept at the church anywhere from overnight to several years before receiving the curative gestures of the saints. Mostly, the ritual involved a laying-on-of-hands. Similar to the supplicants to the earlier sleep-temples in Egypt, those in the time of Cyrus and John were required to offer money and other worldly possessions prior to the incubation period and following the restoration of their health. The prosperity and growth in the wealth of the early church was in part attributed to such offerings. There were even reported one-day cures of the rich, while the less well endowed had to wait for months or years for the balm of the sacred touch.

Throughout the first millennium Christian saints and martyrs appeared to the sick during their incubation (sleep) and by prescription, by direct touch, or by the use of specially endowed water restored health. In addition to those mentioned above, Sts. Julian, Martin, Maximinus, and Fides continued the same historical rituals, efforts which we will see continued virtually to the present in the techniques of mesmerizing and hypnotizing. According to Hamilton (1906), the practice of incubation as a prelude to additional curative manipulations persisted in the churches of Greece and Asia Minor to the time of her publication. Two points of resemblance between the temples of Asklepios and the healing churches of the late 19th century, which Hamilton notes, make it clear that some rituals have yet to cease. Both had associated with them sacred springs, fountains, or wells, which played a significant role in the cures. Also, both developed health resorts or spas in association with the religious structure. Many of these spas continue to be attractive, such as the shrine at Lourdes or such secular resorts as those at Saratoga Springs, New York, and Baniff, Canada, with their curative water source.

NOTE

1. I am indebted to Andreas Nonnenmacher and Andreas Hofferbauer for their assistance in rendering Krugsch-Pascha's German translation of the original Egyptian text into English.

CHAPTER 2

From Druidism to Perkinism

THE DRUIDS

Whether the Druids, those teachers, priests, prophets, philosophers, physicians, and soothsayers of the Celts, were, as Pokormy (1910) argues, actually pre-Celtic aboriginal medicine men discovered by the Celts in their 6th and 5th centuries B.C. invasions of Ireland, Wales, and Scotland, or the priesthood of the Celts (MacCulloch, 1911) who roamed not only Great Britain, but also Europe east to Asia Minor, the Balkans, and as far north as the present Cologne and Leipzig, they were certainly a powerful group, wielding far-ranging influence. Although their period of greatest influence appears to have been from the 3rd or 2nd century B.C. through the 5th century A.D. on the continent, Hyde (1910) claims they were first known as Hyperboreans from the 6th to the 4th centuries B.C., and it was not until the 7th century A.D. that their extensive influence was finally put at an end in Ireland and Britain. The Romans had abolished the Druidic religion in Gaul in 54 A.D. under Claudius, but did not move to accomplish the same end until 61 A.D. in Britain. However, it took Christianity incarnate in the form of St. Patrick to exterminate the Druids in Ireland in 637 A.D. at the battle of Mayrath (Pokormy, 1910). Unfortunately, along with the corporal destruction came the literary, for although many of the venacular texts from Ireland had survived the Romanization of the 1st century A.D., and the oral texts had been recorded and preserved by Christian clerics, the fires of religious fervor of the Patrickites burned brightly and with them the literature of the Irish Druids.

Second only to the Celtic kings, the Druids were consulted in virtually every decision of state, and were held in such high esteem that they had the power to stop wars (Piggott, 1968). Little wonder, then, that both real and magical abilities were attributed to them, since they were the guardians not only of religion and medicine, but also of learning in general (Reisman, 1935). Often their teachings and insights were contained not in fine "professional" literature, but in the folklore of ancient Ireland and other Celtic dominated parts of the world. The same was true of the rituals that so closely resemble the inductions whose history we are tracing.

Several allusions to hypnosis appear in the epic tale of the witch, Sin's revenge on King Muirchertach Mac Erca for killing her family. The epic relates that after long pursuit, "Sin beguiled his mind" (Stokes, 1902, p. 417), and "the king then sleeps heavily after Sin had cast the sleep-charm upon him" (p. 423). There is even mention of a magical liquid, "she cast a sleep-charm on that deceptive wine" (p. 421), and induced hallucinations, "so of the fern she made fictitious swine of enchantment" (p. 417).

Wine was not the only liquid to which the ancient Celts attributed potential magical powers; in fact, it was the least important. Far more important were milk and water, reminding us again of the uses of holy water by the Egyptians and Greeks and its later use as magnetized water by the mesmerists. Milk in the Irish myths had both curative and restorative powers. Janet, for example, dipped Tamlane in milk and hot water to restore him to his original form (Spence, updated). The Druids themselves made extensive use of water in their rituals (MacCulloch, 1911), as well as potent drinks ("drinks of oblivion"), which produced the "Druidic sleep" and are also reminiscent of the magnetized water used in the 19th century.

The Druids also made extensive use of certain woods in their rituals, particularly the oak, mountain ash, and yew, although most are more familiar with their worship of mistletoe (Constant, 1913). In Ireland divination was done with pieces of wood cut from the yew tree and used as wands (Hyde, 1910) to discover hidden items and predict the routes to be used by invaders (MacCulloch, 1911). Whether oak or ash or yew was used ritualistically seemed to depend on the vegetation of the local area, but what is important about this seeming tangent in our tour through history is that this worship in and of forests and certain sacred trees could have been a forerunner of the use of magnetic trees (e.g., by de Puységur) by the 18th century mesmerists (see also Ellenberger, 1970).

Iron, too, played a major role in Irish and Welsh Celtic folklore, as it was later to play a leading part in Mesmer's time and later in Elliotson's. The best protection one could obtain from the vagaries of the fairies, who were leading characters in the mythology, was a piece of iron. Many a folk hero, who sought the fairies in their caves, protected himself from being permanently locked in the cave by placing a piece of iron at the entrance upon entering. Thus iron was dreaded by evil and had the power to avert its nefarious intentions. Spence (undated) relates this attribution as far back as the 8th century B.C., when Bronze Age peoples encountered the iron-equipped La-Tene culture.

Averting the machinations of evil through iron was not unique to the Celts or to Celtic times, for who among us is unfamiliar with the powers of the horseshoe to bring good luck? (Few, however, are probably aware that it should have been thrown from the near hind hoof of a grey mare, found by accident, and nailed above the door with its own nails—E. Hull, "Folklore of the British Isles," cited in Spence, undated.)

The above curiosities (water, wood, iron) are of historic interest, of course, but what of the rituals and incantations used by the Druids? According to MacCulloch (1911), they seemed to be used primarily for placing the priest into a special state or trance, from which he divined information of medical, political, or military importance. Often this knowledge came in the form of a dream: "A great obnubilation was conjured up for the bard as he slept a heavy sleep, and things magic-begotten were shewn to him to enunciate," apparently in his sleep (MacCulloch, 1911, p. 249). It was not always the Druids themselves who went into the "heavy sleep" and emitted "trance utterings," but a third party over whom the priest chanted and through whom (as a medium) the future was revealed. One is reminded here of the process described in the *Leiden Papyrus* using a young, chaste boy as medium (see Chapter 1) and of the Egyptian, Greek, and Roman sleep temples in which the revelations of cures appeared in dream-like form to the supplicant.

In a number of instances the production of the revealing sleep was by verbal incantations repeated again and again until sleep ensued. Different incantations were used for different purposes; e.g., the *Cetnad,* sung through the fist, was used to discover which way a cattle thief had made his escape. Invisibility (negative hallucinations) and transformation into other life forms (positive hallucinations to the perceiver) were caused by a spell called *feth fiada,* the incantation itself being called *fāth-fīth* or *fīth-fāth* (used interchangeably and indiscriminately). This incantation was of particular value to hunters, who wished to be invisible from their quarry, and warriors, who were either made invisible to their enemies or made to appear as a fearsome beast of the forest (Carmichael, 1900, pp. 24–25).

Fāth-Fīth	Fāth-Fīth
Ni mi ort,	Will I make on thee,
Le Muire na frithe,	By Mary of the augury,
Le Bride na brot,	By Bride of the corslet,
Bho chire, bho ruta,	From sheep, from ram,
Bho mhise, bho bhoc,	From goat, from buck,
Bho shionn, 's bho mhac-tire,	From fox, from wolf,
Bho chrain, 's bho thorc,	From sow, from boar,
Bho chu, 's bho chat,	From dog, from cat,
Bho mhaghan masaich,	From hipped-bear,
Bho chu fasaich,	From wilderness-dog,
Bho scan foirir,	From watchful 'scan,'
Bho bho, bho mharc,	From cow, from horse,
Bho tharbh, bho earc,	From bull, from heifer,
Bho mhurn, bho mhac,	From daughter, from son,
Bho iantaidh an adhar,	From the birds of the air,
Bho shnagaidh na talmha,	From the creepidae of the earth,
Bho iasgaidh na mara,	From the fishes of the sea,
'S bho shiantaidh na gailbhe.	From the imps of the storm.

Although the spells had to be said while maintaining a certain posture—standing on one leg, with one arm outstretched and one eye closed—the real power of the incantations lay in the verbalizations themselves. While the idea of the importance of a particular position reflects back to the biblically described positions (though their form was different) and can be related to the emphasis of the mesmerists on the physical attitude of both patient and mesmerist, it is important to note that it is the Druids who placed major emphasis on verbal induction, only fully appreciated later in the 19th century.

Most often the incantations rhymed, so that the ability to "rime either a man or beast to death" (MacCulloch, 1911, p. 326), attributed to the Druids, may have been nothing more than production of a death-like trance state by rhyming, repetitive incantations, as was reported in the case of Captain Townsend during the 1700s (Colquhoun, 1836). The works of Snyder (1930), Silber (1968, 1971), and Snyder and Shor (1983) reflect these ancient origins.

But the rhythmic aspects of induction—if we may translate incantations thus—were not solely poetic and verbal, but musical as well. The music of the Druid charmed and caused a magical sleep in the same manner, as the Celtic tales tell of people joining in fairy dances only to fall asleep not to awaken until many years later. In fact, according to Williams (1954), music was a major pathway to the "magical sleep." The combination of music, rhythm, and dance will be seen again in the entrancing rituals of voodoo, which we will encounter later.

FIRST MILLENNIUM

The Druids were not the only people to be active in hypnotic-related rituals during the first millennium after Christ's birth. The Finns, who were, according to J. F. Campbell (see Pokormy, 1910), the true ancestors of the Druidic priesthood, described a technique for inducing sleep in others that maximized the use of music we have already encountered in the ancients. In the epic poem, *Kalewala*, Wainamoinen induces a profound sleep in the people of Pohjola by playing his harp:

> *Wainamoinen, old and truthful,*
> *Striding up to where his harp is,*
> *Seats himself as sits the harper,*
> *And begins his wondrous playing,*
> *So that all the people listen,*
> *Hearkening to his notes astounded.*
> *All the folk were joyful-minded*
> *Smiling all the women's faces,*
> *Moist the eyes of all the heroes,*
> *Kneeling all the lads to hear him.*

Drowsy thus he makes the people;
All upon the ground are lying,
All his hearers, dazed and drowsy,
All his marvelling hearers prostrate.
Old and young are wrapped in slumber
Hearing Wainamoinen's playing.
Then the cunning Wainamoinen
The immortal wizard, swiftly
Thrusts his hand into his pocket,
Seeking in the leather wallet
Haling forth the phial of slumber
Sleep he scatters on their eyelids,
Locking fast their lids and lashes,
Closing with a lock the eyelids,
Of the drowsy, wearied people,
Of the soundly slumbering heroes,
Plunging them in deepest slumber,
So they lie a long while sleeping,
All the people of Pohjola,
And the folk of all the city.

(SATOW, 1923, pp. 28–29)

Notice that not only does this champion of Kalewa induce a "trance", but he also adds eye catalepsy following the induction:

Sleep he scatters on their eyelids,
Locking fast their lids and lashes,
Closing with a lock the eyelids.

(SATOW, 1923, p. 29)

By and large, however, the first millennium did not yield a plethora of documents or descriptions relevant to the history of mesmerism and hypnosis. Greek medicine had died out between 700 and 1400; only Galen and Celsus stood out against the darkening horizon of the Middle Ages. By this time the Romans had turned their interests to the directly applicable and gloried in a strange mix of the superstitious and the practical (Riesman, 1936). However, the barbarians had not managed to destroy the Greco-Roman culture in the south (Italy and Switzerland), so the hope for the continued development of reasoned medical theory and practice remained there, and, as we will see, to the East in Arabia and the West in Ireland.

Galen, the famous and oft-echoed physician of the 2nd century, to whom physicians of the ensuing 12th and 13th centuries turned to ascertain the accuracy of their observations, exerted influence over patients by extending his thumb, as well as his first and middle fingers toward the patient (Elliotson, 1851). In addition to this Faria-like gesture, even the Roman Emperors Claudius and Vespasian (69 A.D.) carried on the early established tradition of the laying-on-of-hands to heal the people of disease (Satow, 1923). This latter emperor also touched with his foot to cure lameness, and, like Jesus before him, used his own spittle to cure blindness (Colquhoun, 1836; Ludwig, 1964). The method used by Pyrrhus, King of Epirus, is described by Marks (1947): Individuals were placed supine and Pyrrhus' great toe was passed over them, curing colic and diseases of the spleen.

This idea that the touch of powerful people (sovereigns mainly) could cure illness received a considerable thrust of credibility during the Middle Ages, when the monks of that time conceived of the idea of curing The King's Evil ("strumy, scofula [tuberculous glands], demoid cysts, sarcoma and wens") by the touch of a sovereign (hence the term The Royal Touch). Whether or not the practice of bringing the afflicted to the king actually began (as the French claim) with Clovis in 481 A.D., Riesman (1936) asserts that it was certainly used by the English King Edward the Confessor in 1043–1066. As Bernheim (1886/1964), Moll (1889/1897), Ludwig (1964), and others have outlined, this practice continued at least into the 16th century with Francis I (1515–1547), possibly the 18th century (Riesman, 1936), and even, some indicate (Moll, 1889/1897), into the 19th century with Charles X (1824–1830) in France.

Charles II of France and Phillip of Valois apparently hold the records for drawing the largest crowds to their touching ceremonies. Ludwig (1964) tells us that the latter is credited with gracing 1500 people with his touch in a single sitting, while at one session with the former, in 1684, six people lost their lives in the crush. The technique of Charles II was as follows:

> His Majesty began to touch for the Evil according to custom, thus: His Majesty sitting under his state in the banqueting house, the chirugeons cause the sick to be brought, or led, up to the throne, where they kneel; the King strokes their faces or cheeks with both hands at once, at which instance a chaplain in his formalities says, "He put his hands upon them, and he healed them." (John Evelyn's *Diary,* July 6, 1660; see Marks, 1947, pp. 135–136)

In England, although the custom lasted through Queen Anne (1714), its agreed-upon effectiveness faded by the time of the ascension of William and Mary (1689). The English added a touch of their own, in that, beginning with Henry VII (1505), each petitioner was given a "touchpiece" (a gold coin), which had the power to sustain the curative Royal Touch as long as the individual kept it in his or her possession. Thus the English use of the Royal Touch combined the laying-on-of-hands, metals, and amulets into one grand ceremony. Regardless of its accurate beginning or termination, the practice of laying-on-of-hands had enlarged during the Middle Ages to include royalty as well as the current priesthood.

Although the clergy of the Middle Ages relinquished some of their control over the treatment of the populace by including royalty, they did not by any means abdicate their ministering role. For example, *The Zoist* of 1851 contains a picture by Bernard Von Orlay (1490–c. 1560) of "St. Ewald The Fair, Healing a Possessed Woman in the Presence of Radbrad, Duke of Friesland." The Saint is seen pointing his thumb, forefinger, and middle finger at the patient, with his ring and little fingers folded back against his palm. This hand position is the usual position of directing one's influence over another seen throughout history and used in the mid-19th century for mesmerizing patients (Elliotson, 1851). St. Ewald lived in the 700s. In fact, it was through the monasteries and the cleric themselves that progress continued to be made in medicine during the Middle Ages, a period we too often perceive as void of progress and development. For example, Tours, in France, developed during the 8th century, as did the Benedictine Monastery of Fulda (in Germany). Monte Cassino was a prominent center of medical practice during the 9th century, and the medical school at Salerno dates from 529.

Just as the ancient antecedents of hypnosis resided in the East, so too were those practices akin to present-day techniques maintained in the East (India particularly) during the period 300–500 A.D. According to Das (1964), the 195 mnemonic rules of the Yoga system ascribed to Patanjali were written down during that period. Through five indirect aids (abstentions—Yama, observances—Niyama, postures—Asana, regulation of breathing—Pranayama, and withdrawal of the senses—Pratyahara) and three direct aids (fixed attention—Dharana, contemplation—Dhyana, and concentration—Samadhi) the supreme stage of Yoga, a state of pure consciousness *sans* matter, is attained. This state, called Kaivalya, is similar to hypnosis both with respect to induction and result. For example, the importance of physical position is noted in both—the Yoga usually in a "lotus-posture"; the hypnotic subject supine or at least resting comfortably in a chair. The regulation of breathing or concentration on breathing plays a role in both, and the desire of the participant to return to the state is positive in both cases.

The importance of posture was also noted by Hai Gaon, who headed a Babylonian academy (Bowers & Glasner, 1958), when he described a technique for "beholding Merkabah and the palaces of the angels on high." While whispering hymns and songs, the seeker had to "lay his head between his knees," a posture similar to that of Elijah while praying on Mt. Carmel, and to that described previously for the ancient Chinese somnambulist (see Chapter 1).

Curiously, despite the destruction of the Druidic culture by the Christianization of Ireland, it was here that the practice and development of healing techniques continued. Thus it was through the Irish missionaries that enlightenment kept its tenuous foothold in England, Germany, and the low countries (all devastated by the Hun, Goth, Vandal, and Norse). In a sense Ireland had become the cradle of both ecclesiastic and secular knowledge, which eventually took hold by the 12th century. Early in the century before (the 11th), medical literature from Arabia and the East appeared at Salerno, mainly through the efforts of Constantinus Africanus and his translations of this literature (Riesman, 1936). By the 12th century medical knowledge had begun to grow and develop outside the monasteries through the work of such individuals as Maimonides (1135–1208), and by the middle of the 12th century we find a directive that the psychoses should be treated with "soothing words and pleasing music" (Riesman, 1936, p. 37), not unlike some treatments today and perhaps a reference to hypnotic-like techniques that we have encountered in the ancient literature and will see again in the Jewish religious rituals of the 13th century.

Just as Yogi attempted to attain concentration (Samadhi), the Jewish Talmud uses the word "Kavanah" to convey the concentration that was preliminary to prayer. One method for achieving this condition, described by the Cabbalistic philosopher and mystic, Abraham Abulafia, in the 13th century, involved the concentration and mental manipulation of the Hebrew letters. As Bowers and Glasner (1958) point out, his instructions are of interest:

Cleanse thy clothes, and, if possible, let all thy garments be white, for all this is helpful in leading the heart towards the fear of God and the love of God. If it be night, kindle many lights, until all be bright. Then take ink, pen and a tablet to thy hand, and remember that thou art about to serve God in joy [and] gladness of heart. Now begin to combine a few or many letters, to permute and to combine them until thy heart be warm. Then be mindful of their movements and of what thou canst bring forth by moving them. And when thou feelest that thy heart is already warm, and when thou seest that by combinations of letters thou canst grasp new things which by human tradition or by thy self thou wouldst not be able to know, and when thou art thus prepared to receive the influx of divine power which flows into thee, then turn all thy true thought to imagine the Name and His exalted angels in thy heart as if they were human beings sitting or standing about thee. And feel thyself like any envoy whom the king and his ministers are to send on a mission, and he is waiting to hear something about his mission from their lips, be it from the king himself, be it from his servants. Having imagined this very vividly, turn thy whole mind to understand with thy thoughts the many things which will come into thy heart through the letters imagined. Ponder them as a whole and in all their detail, like on to whom a parable or a dream is being related, or who meditates on a deep problem in a scientific book, and try thus to interpret what thou shalt hear that it may as far as possible accord with thy reason. . . . And all this will have dropped from thee because of the intensity of thy thought. And know, the stronger the intellectual influx within thee, the weaker will become thy outer and thy inner parts. Thy whole body will be seized by an extremely strong trembling, so that thou wilt think that surely thou art about to die, because thy soul, overjoyed with its knowledge, will leave thy body. And be thou ready at this moment consciously to choose death, and then thou shalt know thou hast come far enough to receive the influx. And then, wishing to honour the glorious Name by serving it with the life of body and soul, veil thy face and be afraid to look at God. Then return to the matters of the body, rise and eat and drink a little, or refresh thyself with a pleasant odor, and restore thy spirit to its sheath until another time, and rejoice at thy lot and know that God loveth thee! (pp. 52–53)

Several points need to be highlighted. The cleansing instruction in the first line is reminiscent of that which preceded entrance into the Egyptian, Greek, and Roman sleep temples. The use of only white garments reminds us of the rituals of the Druids, particularly their ritual used in gathering the mistletoe, in which it was specifically prescribed that the participants be clothed in white and that the mistletoe itself be caught in a white garment as it falls from the tree, not allowing it to touch the ground. Also, there appears to be a reference to clairvoyance—"Thou canst grasp new things which by human tradition or by thy self thou wouldst not be able to know"—which was one of the benefits of trance in the ancients and continued to pervade the hypnosis literature through the time of Elliotson and beyond. (In fact, the use of clairvoyance in a third party, in the patient, or in the healer, himself or herself, to diagnose and/or prescribe treatment remains in our Western culture today in both the more fundamentalist religious practices and in some professional circles; e.g., client-centered psychotherapy.) Finally, it is interesting to note that Abulafia's instructions seem to herald the magnetic fluid of Mesmer's time; in fact, they prepared the disciple "to receive the influx of divine power," and later, "thou hast come far enough to receive the influx."

Scholem (1941) notes other similarities of Abulafia's system to that of Yoga (see above) in the attention given to breathing regulation and posture (head between the knees). He also pays attention to the rhythmic and musical qualities of verbalizing the letters in various combinations and orders, which Bowers and Glasner (1958) interpret as an additional hypnotic quality and certainly relates readily to our history of the uses of music, dancing, and rhythm in ancient hypnotic techniques.

Both clairvoyance through a medium and incantations as an induction were also noted in Mongolia about this same period (1253 A.D.). According to Stoll (1904), the Minorite monk, Wilhelm von Ruysbrock, witnessed the three-day trance of a slave girl induced by the incantations of a soothsayer of Emperor Mangua-Khan. When she awakened, she reported her dreams which were in turn used to predict the outcome of her master's illness (Satow, 1923).

According to Ludwig (1964), this same 13th century saw the use of magnetism as an explanatory concept for changes in behavior by Arnold of Villanova (1235–1312) and Roger Bacon (1214–1294), although its use for curing disease dates back to Galen (2nd century A.D.) and Dioscordies (Colquhoun, 1836). Aetius of Amida had also described the use of the magnet to relieve pain in the 6th century A.D. (The Egyptians, you will recall, used mineral magnetism for dramatic effect.)

The use of magnetism as an explanation and the concept of a vital force, spirit, or fluid linking living things leads us then to the man considered to have anticipated Mesmer (particularly in his theorizing)—Phillippus

Figure 2.1. Grave of Paracelsus. Friedhof of St. Sebastian, Salzburg, Austria.

Theophrastus, Bombast of Hohenheim (Hartmann, 1891) or Auriolus Philip Theophrastus Bombastus of Honhenheim, as Riesman (1936) gives his name. Actually his grave (see Figure 2.1), in the Friedhof of St. Sebastian (Salzburg, Austria), simply calls him "Philippus Theophrastus."

PARACELSUS AND OTHERS

No book professing to discuss the history of hypnosis can ignore the contributions of Paracelsus, although these contributions were indirect and theoretical. Paracelsus was a rebel extrodinaire. Born near Zurich in Maria–Einsiedeln in 1493, he was educated primarily by his father until he was 16. Then, after study at the University of Basal, he furthered his knowledge with such celebrated alchemists as Johann Trithemius, Abbot of St. Jacob (Würzburg), and Sigismund Rugger at Schatz (Tyrol, in present-day Austria). Whether he actually obtained a formal medical degree has not been established (Riesman, 1936). Paracelsus was widely traveled and it is through his travels—from India to the Netherlands, including an eight-year stay with the

Tartars (1513–1521)—that he gained much of the knowledge that went into his unorthodox theories, doctrines, and prescriptions. Unlike other physicians of his time, he studied much more than the works of Galen, Hippocrates, and Avicenna, whose opinions formed the dogma of most of the medical practices of the 16th century. He was open to learning from any quarter, including many hours spent with the "common" people in the taverns and other haunts of their daily life: "He collected information from the high and the low, from the learned and from the vulgar, and it was nothing unusual to see him in the company of teamsters and vagabonds on the highways and at public inns" (Hartmann, 1891, p. 6).

Consequently, the doctrines Paracelsus presented to students throughout southern Germany, northern Austria, and Switzerland were his own rather than the prevalent regurgitations of the ancients. These teachings were a mixture of common knowledge, alchemy, and academic medicine distilled through his alert and open-minded approach to illness and suffering. His emphasis on experimentation and direct experience in the training of physicians, nettled his colleagues in the profession, as did his insistence on lecturing in German rather than Latin (as was the usual academic practice) and his forceful presentation of his writings. For example, he had no fear of directly stating what he viewed as reprehensible in his fellow professionals:

> You have entirely deserted the path indicated by nature, and built up an artificial system, which is fit for nothing but to swindle the public and to prey upon the pockets of the sick. Your safety is due to the fact that your gibberish is unintelligible to the public, who fancy that it must have a meaning, and the consequence is that no one can come near you without being cheated. Your art does not consist in curing the sick, but in worming yourself into the favour of the rich, in swindling the poor, and in gaining admittance to the kitchens of the noblemen of the country. You live upon imposture, and the aid and abetment of the legal profession enables you to carry on your impostures, and to evade punishment by the law. (Hartmann, 1891, pp. 203–204)

Strong words to say the least; stronger yet, considering the time they were written. Little wonder that he was soundly condemned by the medical personnel of his time to the extent that at one point the medical faculty at Leipzig pressured the Senate of Nürnberg to withhold his right to publish his works.

Such infighting and domination has always appeared in history, whether political, social, or professional. The 1842 incident at the Royal Medical and Chirurgical Society previously noted, Elliotson's banishment from University College Hospital, and present attempts to restrict knowledge of hypnosis to the few with certain educational backgrounds all smack of the same sort of trade-unionism Paracelsus encountered. As we have discovered, and will see more of later, it was the nonprofessional, the occultist, the dabbler in magical and religious ritual, who kept knowledge alive during the hiatuses of professional progress. To the soothsayers of old and the magicians of late, we may owe a greater debt than we realize. In fact, some of the more prominent individuals in hypnosis during the present century learned many of their early techniques from stage magicians and the self-professed witches of their time.

All of this brief history of Paracelsus is not to present him as without fault. Many of his theories of medical treatment and the basis of its supposed effectiveness were patently inaccurate. He espoused occult formulae and rituals. Part of his writing dealt with alchemical formulae for making Electrum Magicum for mirrors (through which the past could be seen and heard), artificial gold, and the like. These formulae and others of his writings were generously laced with astrology. But what Paracelsus did do is captured succinctly by Riesman (1936):

> His theories regarding disease have a strongly individualistic character and show him to have been a bold, independent as well as ruthless thinker. Not that all his theories are true, actually they are for the most part far from true, but the fact that he promulgated them with such vehemence served to break the slavish obedience that had characterized medical thought for fourteen hundred years. It needed a fearless, cantankerous rebel like Paracelsus to throw off the dead hand of Galenical doctrine from the practice of medicine. (p. 344)

What of his contributions to hypnosis? As indicated above, they were primarily in establishing some of the theoretical bases of Fludd's, Maxwell's, and later Mesmer's viewpoints of the underlying principles of mesmerism. Since Paracelsus presented no practical techniques for trance induction in his writings, I will not outline his doctrines in great detail, but show where these ideas tied into later presentations. His major contribution for our purposes, then, was that he laid the groundwork, which formed the theoretical basis for the techniques used later by Mesmer and his followers.

With respect to the development of mesmerism, Paracelsus made several contributions. First, he held that the stars and all living creatures shared a common bond, which he labeled "Archaeus": "The formative power of Nature. . . . It is the principle of life; the power which contains the essence of life and character of everything" (Hartmann, 1891, p. 40). Furthermore, Paracelsus' own description of Archaeus not only introduced magnetism, but was strikingly reminiscent of the notions underlying Kerlian photography, in which there has been a recent surge of interest: "The Archaeus is of a magnetic nature. . . . The vital force is not enclosed in man, but radiates around him like a luminous sphere" (Hartmann, 1891, pp. 221–222).

While Archaeus bears a resemblence to the vital force (spiritus vitalis) of Fludd and Maxwell in the next (17th) century, Mesmer's magnetic fluid of the 1700s, forces noted by Bertrand in the 1820s and the Odic force we will encounter in the 1840s of Elliotson's time, Paracelsus coined yet another term, which he did in fact consider to be a vital force and which tied directly into his notions of magnetism and the use of magnets in the treatment of the ill: "Spiritus vitae—the vital force; a principle taken from the elements of whatever serves as a nutriment, or which may be imparted by 'magnetism'"—was the term he used. As Hartmann summarizes these views of Paracelsus: "As all things come from the same source containing the primordial substance of all things, they are all intimately related to each other and connected with each other, and are essentially and fundamentally a unity" (Hartmann, 1891, p. 65).

The remark that this unity-making vital spirit was imparted by magnetism gives us some inkling that it was Paracelsus, not Mesmer, who first described the curative powers of the magnet and the concept of "animal" magnetism. (Curiously enough, although he himself advocates Paracelsus as the discoverer here, Hartmann, 1891, notes that when the cosmology of Paracelsus and the teaching of the Eastern sages are compared they are "almost, if not wholly identical"!)

For Paracelsus, people had a magnetic power that had attractive powers, much as the lodestone is capable of attracting iron. Human magnetism attracted the vital spirit, and a "magnet" so endowed had to be made from former repositories of this vital spirit (e.g., hair, excrement, blood). Thus, as the iron magnet attracts iron objects, the vital spirit magnet attracts the vital spirit and could be used to absorb the vital spirit in a diseased part of the body and thus effect a cure. In this vein Paracelsus also seemed to anticipate Freud and others in the notion of treating a disease at its source, rather than symptomatically:

> Martial diseases are such as are caused by auras coming and expanding from a centre outwards, and at the same time holding on to their centres; in other words, such as originate from a certain place, and extend their influence without leaving the place from where they originate. In such cases the magnet should be laid upon the centre, and it will then attract the diseased aura towards the centre, and circumscribe and localize the disease, until the latter may be reabsorbed into its centre. It is useless to try to suppress the external symptoms that are caused by a disease, if we at the same time allow the disease to spread. A poisonous tree cannot be kept from growing if we simply cut off some of its branches or leaves, but if we can cause the vital essence which it draws by its roots from the earth to descend again into the roots and reenter the earth, the poisonous tree will die on its own account. By the attractive power of a magnet acting upon the diseased aura of the blood in an affected part, that aura may be made to return into the centre from which it originated, and be absorbed therein; and thereby we may destroy the herd of the virus and cure the patient, and we need not wait idly to see what Nature will do. The magnet is therefore especially useful in all inflammations, in fluxes and ulcerations, in diseases of the bowels and uterus, in internal as well as in external disease. (Hartmann, 1891, pp. 232–233)

Not only did Paracelsus anticipate Mesmer and Freud, he seems to have anticipated the compelling force of imagination on human behavior, noted later by Braid, Bernheim, and William James:

Man is that what he thinks. If he thinks fire, he is fire; if he thinks war, then will he cause war; it all depends merely on that the whole of his imagination becomes an entire sun; i.e., that he wholly imagines that which he wills. ("De Virtut. Imag.") (Hartmann, 1891, p. 172)

It is readily apparent that this controversial figure, who in his lifetime moved from place to place offering his medical knowledge for the benefit of the afflicted and upon his death willed all of his wealth and possessions to the poor, incorporated into his vast writings anticipations of much of what we call the beginnings of the theoretical base of modern hypnosis. Unfortunately for our purposes, this strange mix of alchemy, the occult, and startlingly accurate insights into some of the practices of medicine, which included detailed alchemical formulae, did not offer us anything in the way of induction techniques. Though it may seem paradoxical in a man so practical in his orientation to medicine, his was a theoretical contribution to the dawning of mesmerism and hypnosis.

Others

One of the great Jewish mystics who was living during Paracelsus' time and died about the time that Paracelsus was writing his major works (1530), related to animal magnetism and the like, Abraham ben Eliezer (of Jerusalem) was recommending a self-hypnotic technique to people facing the flames of martyrdom. His admonition was similar to Abulafia's technique reported above; in fact, he advised "them to concentrate . . . on the Great Name of God; to imagine its radiant letters between their eyes and to fix all their attention on it" (Scholem, 1941, p. 143). Thus, he urged, they would be able to endure the burning with what we would label today self-induced hypnotic analgesia.

St. Augustine also described a case of voluntary trance, though not associated with an attempt to endure the torments of burning at the stake:

St. Augustine gives a case of voluntary trance in the *De Civitate Dei* (Opera, Edit. 1569, vol. v. p. 796): "Jam illud multo incredibilius, quod plerique fratres memoriâ recentissimâ experti sunt. Presbyter fecit quidam nomine Restitutus in paroecia Calamensis ecclesiae, qui quando ei placebat (rogabatur autem ut hoc faceret ab eis qui rem mirabilem coram scire cupiebant), ad imitatas quasi lamentantis cujus libet homines voces, ita se auferebat a sensibus, et jacebat simillimus mortuo; ut non solum vellicantes atque pungentes minime sentiret, sed aliquando etiam igne ureretur admoto, sine ullo doloris sensu nisi postmodum ex vulnere; non autem obnitendo, sed non sentiendo non movere corpus, eo probabatur, quod tanquam in defuncto nullus inveniebatur anhelitus: hominum tamen voces, si clarius loquerentur, tanquam de longinquo se audisse postea referebat."

(Now there is an incredible story that very many of the brothers recently remembered: A certain priest named Restitutus in the parish of the church of

Calama, who, whenever he pleased did it [voluntary trance] (he would be asked, moreover, to do this by those who desired to witness the miraculous thing in person); by imitating the wailing of men's voices, he would so carry himself away from the senses that he would appear very similar to one who was dead; so that not only when people pinched and pricked him he felt no sensation whatever, but sometimes even when fire was applied, he would be burnt, without any sensation of pain except afterwards from the wound; besides, moreover, by the process of not feeling rather than by resisting, his body was shown not to move, because no breath was found in the man, as if he were dead: still the voices of men, if they spoke rather clearly, he would recall later as if he had heard them from afar.)[1] (Tuke, 1884, p. 374)

and again in the form of voluntary rumination:

Sunt qui et aures moveant vel singulus, vel ambas simul. Sunt qui totam caesariem capite immoto quantum capilli occupant, deponunt ad frontem, revocantque cum volunt. *Sunt qui eorum quoe voraverunt incredibiliter plurima et varia, paululum proecordiis contrectatis, tanquam de sacculo, quod placuerit, integerrimum proferunt.* Ipse sum expertus, sudare hominem solere cum vellet. Notum est, quosdam flere cum volunt, atque ubertim lachrymas fundere.

(There are those who even move their ears either singly or both at the same time. There are those who move their entire head of hair, without disturbing a single hair, down in the direction of their forehead, and whenever they wish, they recall it back to its original position. There are those who, incredibly, having consumed very many and different things, contract their stomach very little and bring forth quite whole whatever they liked, as if from a little bag. I myself have made a test of it, whenever he [they] wished for a man to get in the habit of perspiring. It is noted, when they want certain ones to cry, they [the certain ones] pour out the tears copiously.)[1] (Tuke, 1884, pp. 374–375)

During the latter part of the 16th and early 17th centuries at least two other descriptions of the personal magnetism of which Paracelsus wrote appeared in the writings of Johann Baptist van Helmont (1577–1644) and Robert Fludd (1574–1637), the latter of whom King (1837) informs us called himself Robertus a Fluctibus. Not only did Fludd write of the powerful influence of personal magnetism, but he also penned another idea often attributed to Mesmer—although Pattie (1956a) established that Mesmer's was heavily borrowed from Mead—that of the influence of heavenly bodies on human behavior. It was apparent, then, that both the concept of the unity of the universe, and thereby the ability of distant objects (e.g., stars and planets) to influence one another, and of the power of magnets, both metalic and otherwise, were strikingly influential by the turn of the 17th century.

SEVENTEENTH CENTURY

Just as Colquhoun considered Paracelsus the major 16th century predecessor of Mesmer, he assigned that role to Van Helmont in the 17th century. Actually, John Baptist van Helmont spanned both centuries, having been born in Brussels in 1579 and died in 1644. Educated as a physician, he lauded Paracelsus and made major contributions of his own (Pagel, 1972). He defended magnetism against the church and the Jesuit Father Robert, who attempted to assign the reported magnetic cures to the devil. His cause was not so much the efficacy of the treatments, but that magnetism is a natural phenomenon, having neither a criminal nor diabolical nature (Colquhoun, 1836). Like Paracelsus, Van Helmont's contributions to the soon-to-emerge mesmerism were primarily theoretical.

Robert Fludd

Robert Fludd was born in 1574 and as far as we know lived in the home of his father, Sir Thomas Fludd, in Kent until he entered St. John's College, Oxford in 1592. After his B.A. (1596) and M.A. (1598) degrees he spent six years traveling in Germany, France, Spain, and Italy. While in the latter country, he became acquainted with William Harvey, and during this six-year sojourn he adopted the views, ideas, and practices of Paracelsus and his particular brand of medicine.

So ardent was his ferver and so explicit his denunciations of Galenic medical practices (á la Paracelsus) that, although he passed his Bachelor and Doctorate of Medicine examinations in 1605, it was not until 1609 and his third reexamination that he was allowed to practice. His medical practice in London was a combination of accepted medicine (diagnosis through pulse and urine examination) and herbal and chemical treatments of Paracelsian origin. A number of his contemporaries saw him as a psychic healer, who used some unusual approaches, which brought him into conflict with some of the religious leaders of his time. In one instance, he advocated a "weapon-salve" to heal wounds. However, it was not used to anoint the wound, but rather the weapon that inflicted it!

More in keeping with his place in the history of hypnotic inductions, Fludd made use of magnetic treatments. Although William Maxwell is usually credited with early use of parts of the human body (including excreta) to form a magnetic device for treatment, a quote by this Scottish physician makes it clear that he may have borrowed the idea from Fludd:

> Among other things he (Fludd) was able to tell me of the wonders of a magnet which I had heard of but never myself tried: . . . The Fluddian magnet is nothing other than dessicated human flesh, which certainly possesses the greatest attractive power; it should be taken, if possible, from a body still warm, and from a man who had died a violent death. (Godwin, 1979, p. 9)

Figure 2.2. Robert Fludd (1574–1637) by Mattieu Merian. (Reprinted by permission of the Trustees of the National Library of Scotland.)

According to Godwin (1979), Fludd, like his idol before him, Paracelsus, left little in the way of specific treatment details, except those contained in his monumental treatise, *Medicine Catholica*. (Fludd died in London on September 8, 1637 and was buried in Bearsted Church.)

Similar theoretical contributions were also made by William Maxwell, whose collection of magnetic cures through the ages, *De Medicine Magnetica,* was written in 1679. Here he reiterated both the vital fluid notions we have encountered above and the use of magnets to move that fluid around and restore it to diseased parts of the body (Ludwig, 1964). Like Paracelsus and Fludd, Maxwell advocated the use of "magnets" made from parts of the body, including excrement, rather than magnetized iron or the lodestone. Both his and Paracelsus' ideas along these lines were the logical outcome of their (we now think, erroneous) theorizing about the nature of the universe and of humans.

We must also be aware that Paracelsus, Van Helmont, Fludd, and Maxwell were not the only individuals interested in and writing about the use of magnets with human beings during this time. Colquhoun (1836) lists Pomponatius, Rodolphus Goclenius, Athanasius Kircher, Sir Kenelm Digby, J. G. Burgrave, Sebastian Wirdig, and Joannes Bohnius, along with Van Helmont and Maxwell as the most eminent. Ludwig (1964) also adds Pietro d'Abano, Johann Trithemius, Agrippa of Netterheim, William Gilbert, and Martin Antonio Delrio. The quote Colquhoun gives from Wirdig's 1673 *Nova Medicina Spirituum* is remarkable: "Totus mundus constat et positus est in magnetismo; omnes sublunarium vicissitudines fiunt per magnetismum; vita conservatur magnetismo; interitus omnium rerum fiunt per magnetismum" (The whole world exists and is situated in magnetism; all changes come about through sublunar magnetism; life is preserved by magnetism; the perishing of all things comes about through magnetism.)[1] (Colquhoun, 1836, p. 150), and serves to indicate the prevalence of these ideas.

The groundwork for the emergence of Mesmer to prominence was clearly laid in the 200 years prior to his major work. Like any other insights of science, the seeds had been sown many years before their fruition. Even the major induction techniques of the 18th and 19th centuries had been anticipated and, in fact, extensively used in the 1600s, as were other techniques of dealing with illness that we have noted before. The use of saliva as a curative agent (see above) continued into the 17th century at least in Spain, where the *Ensalmadores* so used it (Colquhoun, 1836). Such practices and its use as a protection against the "evil eye" of a stranger who may have coveted some valuable object persisted in Northern Africa into the 19th century (Colquhoun, 1836). Clairvoyance and/or precognition as an ability or an outcome of trances also continued to prevail, so that the individuals capable thereof were looked on as prophets and prophetesses. For example, Bertrand (1823) related the case of Christian Poniatove of Bohemia who, during a malady in 1627, fell into trances and predicted events related to the church (see Sandby, 1844).

Just as we have noted that King David's (see above) salvation came from the "laying-on-of-the-entire-body," Elliotson (1848) reported the following cases handled by the same technique by the well-known 17th century physician, Sydenham:

De Methodo Medendi Morbos Per Accubitum *iunioeis*
Cap. 16.

May y[e] 19th 1662 I was called in y[e] night to M[rs] Change, whom I found very ill of a Cholera Morbus; she had many ugly Symptoms, as coldness of the Extreme parts, talking a little idly, intollerable Sickness, & felt a tingling in her Fingers & flesh outwardly. I judge it dangerous to use Dilutients especially by Clysters in a Women [*sic*] soe green (she having not lain in a Month) & y[e] Disease pressing soe hard upon my heels; Soe I ordered her to take a warm Cordial, & that a good draught of it, & her Husband to lie close to her Back naked, and her sonn of 12 years close to her Belly, & to lay on more Cloths & to warm her Leggs & Hands wth hot Clothes: She immediately fell into a moderate Breathing, & all Sympt. ceased: & after enjoyning her to keep her bed ye next day, & to eat & drink nothing save a small Quantity of Barly-broth a day for 2 days she perfectly recovered.

February 1661 I was called to Mrs Hulston, who after a very Chronical fever was fall'n into a very fatallike Diarrhea; I saw it was to noe purpose to give astringents seeing ye Disease proceeded from a decay of natural heat, therefore I took this Course, viz. I caused her Sonn a plump hot Lad of 13 years of age, & her Nurses sonn of 6 or 7 years to goe to bed to her naked, & lie ye one close to her BELLy, ye other close to her Back, w^eh they did, & as long as they continued wth her she had noe stools: but ye Boys rising at any time ye Loose-ness would immediately return. I commanded that she sould persist in ye Course till her curse should be compleat, (the Boys relieving one another by turns in ye daytime) & soe she fully recovered not only of her Looseness but allso of her Sickness in generall.

The very same course I took with one Mr Little, who had a fever a^bt 7 weeks, & at ye time Aug. 1662, soe far spent y^t his D^rs judged him a Dead-Man: he was ancient & having been much purged wth violent Medicaments, he was as weak as ever I saw any y^t recovered; I (having to noe purpose made attempts to lay his fever by inward Medicines & to raise his strength by Cordials) told his wife that nothing could preserve his life but ye putting a Boy to bed to to him: soe she procured a Link boy to lie very close to him all night, & ye next morning I found his fever allmost off, & his Eye & Countenance more lively, upon w^eh I pronounced all danger to be over, yett afterwards upon my giving him a Clyster & upon ye recess of ye Boy he began to relapse; but ye Boy being gott again & I giving noe more Clysters he perfectly recovered.

The very same way had I cured before Bp. Monk's Lady, who was an aged Woman of a very feeble & thin habit of Body, & had an Ague w^eh (tho gone) had soe weakened her y^t her Physician Dr. Ridgley looked upon her as dead; when I was sent for she had allso spitten some purulent matter & blood w^eh they shewed me in abundance upon ye Napkin. I told ye D^r y^t I apprehended y^t nothing could save her life, but a speedy transplantation of some young Spirits upon her, to w^eh he readily agreed, & a Girl of 13 years was put in close to her Coughing: But ye Girl fell sick, w^eh was attributed to her lying wth ye Lady, tho I was confident to ye Contrary, having never known any Mischief y^t way; how-ever she had first coming out upon her Petechiae, & afterwards large Ulcers upon her Breech; But Dr Ridgley & I recovered her. (Elliotson, 1848, pp. 260–261)

These illustrations, and that of King David before, are not to suggest that the process described a hypnotic or even a mesmeric induction technique. On the contrary, as suggested above, what they illustrate is the use of body heat in the treatment of disease. However, for us they illustrate much more, for they indicate that the "passes", which were to become the major form of mesmeric induction procedures, were the natural next step and a natural consequence of similar ideas prevalent in the lay and professional culture of the day and of the past. The basis of laying-on-of-hands in ancient times and the Middle Ages derived from the assumed ability of certain powerful people (priests and royalty), which itself was probably the consequence of generalization on the part of the laity. If the sovereigns of secular and ecclesiastical worlds held so much of the daily lives of the people in their hands (Even the expression anticipates the act.), why could they not, by a simple touch or passing of the hand over the person, effect wonderous changes and cures? The idea was an easy extension and specification of the general power they already wielded over the populace.

What was different about the uses of passes to affect others from the 17th century on was that it had a theoretical base, the notion of a vital spirit, a flux, a magnetic fluid that could be moved about and relocated in the person being treated. Though the passes were a logical step from what had gone before, they were also a major innovation, which we are not sure even the practitioners of the day recognized. The locus of effectiveness now lay, not solely in the operator—a powerful person whose personal power dramatically influenced others at the mere touch of a finger or a toe—but at least partially in the person being treated. It was the patient's magnetic forces that were moved and relocated, albeit by the operator's movements. Patient and practitioner had become partners in the process, though many operators then, as today, continued to attribute great power (divine and otherwise) to themselves in the process.

Valentine Greatraks

Although England produced at least three individuals who used stroking with the hand to treat various diseases—Leveret, Dr. Streper, and Valentine Greatraks (Colquhoun, 1833)—it is the latter about whom we have more information.

Valentine Greatraks was born on February 14, 1628 (d. 1680) in Affane, County Waterford, Ireland of William Greatraks and his wife, the daughter of Sir Edward Harris, Knight and Justice of the King's Bench. His early education was in his native Ireland at the Free school of Lismore, established by the Earl of Cork. Fleeing the Irish revolution of 1641, he continued his education in England until he returned to Ireland in 1646. By 1649 he was a Lieutenant in Cromwell's army in which he served until its disbandment in 1656. At that time he returned to Affane and became the Clerk of the Peace (County Cork), Registrar for Transplantation and Justice of the Peace.

"About four years since [1660; Björnström (1887) claimed it was 1662] I had an Impulse, or a strange persuasion in my own mind . . . which did very frequently suggest to me that there was bestowed on me the gift of curing the Kings-evil [scrofula]" (Greatraks, 1666, p. 22). Thus began Greatraks's work. His first case, the son of William Maher of Salterbridge, had originally been brought to his wife (She had some skill in Chirurgery.) for treatment of

Figure 2.3. Valentine Greatraks (1628–1680) of Affane, County of Waterford, Ireland. (From *The Zoist,* 1844; first published March 20, 1794 by W. Richardson, Leicester Square.)

the Kings Evil in the eyes, cheek, and throat. His wife deferred to his *Impulse,* and Greatraks applied his technique: "And thereupon I laid my hands on the places affected, and prayed to God for Jesus' sake to heal him, and then I bid the Parent two or three days afterwards to bring the Child to me again, which accordingly he did, and I saw the Eye was almost quite whole, and the Nose, which was almost as big as a Pullet's Egg was suppurated, and the throat strangely amended, and to be brief . . . within a month discharged it self quite and was perfectly healed, and so continues God be praised" (Greatraks, 1666, p. 23).

With this beginning, he spent the next three years effecting cures of the King's Evil through the combination of stroking and appealing to God to heal the disease: "And I stroked them, and desired God out of his abundant mercy to heal them" (Greatraks, 1666, p. 25). Throughout his long letter to Robert Boyle, Esq. (1666) Greatraks maintained that he was only an instrument of God's mercy and power. Nowhere did he take credit for the changes that occurred in his patients as he stroked and prayed. He felt that God had specifically chosen him for this work, although he did not know why. "He [God] always sent Patients that applyed themselves to me, and I never sought after any from the first moment" (Greatraks, 1666, p. 25). Asked if his cures might have derived simply from his own body temperature as he applied his hands to the afflicted parts, he maintained that it was a gift from God. His evidence for this assertion was simply that prior to the visitation of the Impulse he had been unable to cure his own headaches.

After three years of singular success with the King's Evil, the Impulse returned to him and instructed him to heal those afflicted with Ague (a form of malaria), a near epidemic of which had just struck. He attested to his own success with a housewife named Bateman, "on whom I laid my hands, and desired God Almighty to cure her, who in mercy heard my Prayer, and so the *Ague* run through her, and she went away immediately, perfectly cured of her *Ague*" (Greatraks, 1666, p. 25). On the Sunday after Easter (2 April 1665) Greatraks's Impulse returned yet again in the early morning. From then on, he attempted healing with whatever disease the patient presented, including dropsy, epilepsy, fevers, and chronic headaches.

As his therapeutic range grew, patients were attracted to him as nails to a magnet and he was reported to have cured thousands with his hands through "a sanative contagion in his body" (*The Zoist*, 1843, pp. 58–94). At Affane his stable, barn, and malt-house were continually overflowing with sick individuals, although he set aside only three days each week (6 a.m. to 6 p.m.) for the laying-on-of-hands. As Mesmer after him, Greatraks's notoriety gained him the close scrutiny of local authorities, in his case the Court of Lismore. Before the Court he was first asked why he practiced medicine without a license. His reply was simply because *he charged no fee* for his services and he was unaware that the law prohibited one neighbor from offering aid and assistance to another. The Court then ordered him to cease his practice of laying-on-of-hands, which he did for a short time. Two days later, in Copoqueen, where people continued to flock to him for help, he cured two individuals who were having seizures. At this point the Bishop of that Diocess ordered him to stop "laying on his hands' lest the miracles of scripture should be disparaged!" (King, 1837, p. 33). The church and organized medicine had combined to deny the populace's access to Greatraks. Throughout these confrontations with the establishments of his day, Greatraks maintained a degree of humility, not only through his insistence that the cures came from God not himself, but through his open admittance that not all of his patients were healed. In fact, his most famous failure lead to his most eminent success and spread his fame even wider than the attempts of the church to stop his practice.

In January 1666 Greatraks was called to England by Viscount Conway of Ragley Hall, Warwickshire to attend Lady Anne who suffered from severe headaches. She had been treated by Dr. Thomas Willis, Sir Kenelm Digby,

Robert Boyle, and no less a personage than Dr. William Harvey. The latter had even recommended trypanning her skull to relieve the pain (Hunter & Macalpine, 1956). For the first and only time in his treatment career (He attested.), he accepted a fee of £155, but his efforts also proved unsuccessful and Lady Anne continued to have headaches (quite possibly migraine) for 22 years until her death in 1679. What was more important about Greatraks's trip was that he stayed on at Ragley Hall for a month, curing hundreds of people who had heard of his presence and flocked to him for healing. From there he went to Worcester at the request of the Mayor and Aldermen and finally to White Hall at the behest of King Charles II himself. In April 1666 he treated a number of different maladies at St. Bartholomew's Hospital (Greatraks, 1666; Hunter & Macalpine, 1956).

His major technique of laying-on-of-hands and praying for God's help has already been described above in his own words. His technique was to apply his hand to the diseased area and rub gently downward (as in the passes of the 18th and 19th centuries), stroking the disease from the center of the body out through the periphery. In one case at York-House he reported stroking the swelling in a woman's body up through the throat and out of the mouth. However, it is in the testimonial letters accompanying his own epistle to Boyle and in the works of Stubbe (1666) and Hunter and Macalpine (1956) that we learn of some of his adjuncts to laying-on-of-hands and of the special aura that surrounded the man. Hunter and Macalpine (1956) claim that Greatraks used different techniques for different afflictions at St. Bartholomew's. For epilepsy, he laid his glove on the patient's head; for pain, he used dry hands, while for ulcers and running sores, he massaged in his own spittle. Stubbe (1666) confirmed the latter technique, which we have already discovered in ancient practices and in the work of Christ. According to Stubbe, Greatraks cured a 14-year-old boy of leprosy that he had had for 10 years: "*Mr. Greatarick* [sic] stroked him againe, and rubbed his Body all over with Spittle" (Stubbe, 1666, p. 28).

But spittle was not the only liquid treatment available to Greatraks. Two testimonial letters reported the case of Elenor Dickinson, age 45, who suffered from dropsy. In the first account it was reported that the patient "drank at the same time about 6 spoonfuls of his water, and rubbed some on her body" (Greatraks, 1666, p. 44). At first reading one might think that here was the precursor of the use of magnetized water that appeared a century later; however, the second account of this same incident clarified what actually occurred: "But not being able to come near him by reason of the throng, she snatch'd some of his urine and drank it, some of which she also put in her ears, which were so stopp'd she could not hear, and immediately she heard the noise of the people around her" (Greatraks, 1666, p. 45). Neither report indicates how she obtained this golden elixir nor that Greatraks himself was aware that he had within himself means other than his hands to cure. Stubbe, however, reported that "*Dean Rust* observed his Urine to smell like Violets, though he had eat nothing that might give it that scent"

(Stubbe, 1666, p. 11). Similar pleasant fragrances were attributed to his hands by Lord Conway and his entire body by Sir Amos Meredith (Stubbe, 1666). The reality of these attributes is unknown, but it is clear that Valentine Greatraks had established his place in the history of hypnosis and served as a major continuing link between the techniques of the first millenium and those to emerge as the beginnings of modern hypnosis in the 18th century with Mesmer.

EIGHTEENTH CENTURY

In the history of hypnosis the 18th century is usually considered to be Mesmer's century, but he was not the only individual to practice the art of hypnotic (mesmeric) induction during that time. John Joseph Gassner, the German exorcist, received great notoriety in the 1770s with his cures in Suabia, Switzerland, Tyrol, and Regensburg, Germany. It is not clear whether he was a "Swiss priest" (Ludwig, 1964) or an "ex-monk from Suabia" (Björnström, 1887), or both, but according to Colquhoun (1833) he was born in 1727 at Bratz (near Pludenz, Suabia) and was a Catholic minister at Klösterle (Bishopric of Chur). He lived for a while with the bishop of Constance, then performed a number of cures on patients with "spasmodic and epileptic complaints" while with the Archbishop of Ratisbon at Ellwangen (Colquhoun, 1833). His cures (10,000, according to Björnström, 1887) were based on exorcism in Latin to cast out the "demonds," his reasoning being that the illnesses were caused by Latin-speaking demons and the most direct route was through the common language. Essentially, his technique was first to ascertain the patient's permission to use *exorcismus probativus* (trial exorcism), then to call on the devil to produce the symptoms of which the patient complained. If the symptoms were, in fact, manifested, Gassner proceeded with the exorcism. If not, the patient was referred to a nearby physician for treatment. Thus Gassner handled maladies of the spirit only and left those of the body to the physicians of his time.

The case of Emilie, the 19-year-old daughter of a court official in Germany, illustrates his techniques. Emilie came to Gassner in the village of Ellwangen in an apparent state of remission from "convulsions." Gassner informed her that her disorder was not over, but in a latent condition, and called forth the "evil spirit" to manifest itself. The girl promptly displayed her old symptomatology, until Gassner ordered: "Cesset."

Some days later Gassner produced in Emilie a variety of convulsions and spasms through Latin commands to the "evil spirit":

> Praecipio tibi, in nomine Jesu ut minister Christi et Ecclesiae veniat agitatio brachiorum quam antecedenter habuisti! (As the servant of Christ and the Church, I command thee in the name of Jesus, let the jerking of the arm appear, as thou hadst before.)

Agitentur brachia tali paroxysmo qualem antecedenter habuisti! (Shake the arms in such a paroxysm as thou hadst before.)

Paroxysmus veniat iterum, vehementius ut ante fuit et quidem per totum corpus! (Let the paroxysm come again, more vehemently than before, and that through the whole body.) (Marks, 1947, p. 141)

In each case, Emilie's body followed the commands, producing the various paroxysms as suggested. After a thorough demonstration of his control over the "spirit," Gassner awakened the girl and pronounced her well.

So well known were Gassner's cures, that Mesmer himself is reported to have visited him in Ratisbon (Colquhoun, 1836). Ellenberger (1970), however, makes no mention of such a visit.

Mesmer

That Mesmer plagiarized much of his 1766 dissertation ("On the Influence of the Planets upon the Human Body") from Richard Mead's *De Imperio et Lunae in Corpora Humana* of 1704 is now clear (Pattie, 1956). It is also clear that his claim to originality in the use of magnets for treatment was blunted by history, and the controversy with the Jesuit Father Maximilian Hell (Ludwig, 1964; Zweig, 1932). His fame then can be attributed to two factors: (a) his ability to call attention to himself and his procedures and thus attract a group of ardent followers who would carry on his work (Ludwig, 1964); and (b) the happenstance of timing.

As I have shown in the previous pages, Mesmer came onto the medical-scientific scene when many of the theoretical and practical ideas he incorporated into his work were being discussed, used, and evaluated. Mesmer had only to highlight and publicize what had developed before to be assured of a lasting place in history. In the latter he eventually triumphed, but the course of his professional career was one defeat following another.

Born on May 23, 1734 in Iznang on the Bodensee (Lake Constance), Franz Anton Mesmer (Björnström, 1887 calls him "Friedrich Anton"; and Colquhoun—1833, 1836—refers to him as "Frederick Anthony") came to Vienna as a youth, where he pursued the study of medicine. Following his public defense of his less than original dissertation he practiced medicine and his newly labeled technique of animal magnetism until he left that city under heavy criticism by his medical contemporaries. He then traveled, during 1775 and 1776, through Bavaria and Switzerland performing magnetic cures privately and in the public hospitals of Bern and Zurich. It was during this time that he visited Gassner at Ratisbon. According to Björnström (1887), Mesmer was officially expelled from Vienna in 1777 following the Marie Paradise case. (For biographies of Mesmer, see: Ellenberger, 1970; Goldsmith, 1934; Ince, 1920.) The next year he moved to Paris.

In Paris, through the good offices of Dr. Charles d'Eslon, physician of Count Artois, he was introduced to Parisian society and developed a large and lucrative practice, primarily in his hotel at the Place Vendome where his rooms contained the now famous *baquet,* which we will describe below. His reputation, fame, showmanship, and penchant for the dramatic gained him not only attention and a constant stream of patients, but also a certain notoriety among his medical and academic contemporaries. Soon the outcry was at such a pitch that the French Academy of Medicine appointed what in contemporary terms would be called a "blue ribbon," international commission to investigate and report on Mesmer's techniques, theory, and claims. The committee's report dealt a serious blow to Mesmer and his practice, in part by attributing his results to the "power of imagination" (Franklin et al., 1784), and he left Paris professionally ostracized and isolated. Finally, after a brief stay in England, he returned to the Bodensee and lived in Konstanz from 1812–1814 (see Figure 2.4). He died across the Bodensee in Meersburg, March 15, 1815 and is buried in the city churchyard.

Mesmer seemed to view his professional contemporaries with ambivalence. While he wanted them to recognize his "discoveries," he seemed unwilling or unable to come directly to grips with their desire for a closer scrutiny of his work. For example, although in his own writings he offered to

Figure 2.4.   Mesmer's Home, 1812–1814, Konstanz, West Germany.

submit his practice to evaluation, he insisted that such evaluations be on his own terms. The investigations of the French Commission of 1784 were carried out at d'Eslon's offices because he refused admission to his own. Earlier in his career he had written letters to various academies of Europe outlining his theories and observations. All went unanswered except his contact with the Berlin Academy. However, when this one response made inquiries of him regarding his views, he refused to submit a response. It is interesting to note that of all of those learned societies to which he wrote, The Medical Faculty of Berlin alone honored his passing with a three-sided gravestone, each facet depicting a perspective of his career (see Figure 2.5).

Techniques

Mesmer's techniques paralleled his theoretical viewpoints. Initially, based on the idea of a common bond among all natural things—the vital spirit of Paracelsus, Maxwell, the ether of Newton—and Father Hell's revelations to him concerning the magnet, he proceeded to apply artificial magnets to his patients. Diseased parts of the body were stroked with magnets effecting cures, through, so the theory went, redistributing the magnetic fluid into a more efficacious alignment within the individual.

Figure 2.5.   Mesmer's Gravestone. Friedhof of Meersburg, West Germany. (Erected by the Medical Faculty of Berlin.)

However, Mesmer soon gave up the use of magnets in preference to his own personal magnetism and ability to influence the magnetic fluid of others through his own movements alone. According to Colquhoun (1836), Ennemoser attributed the development of the mesmeric pass to an observation Mesmer made while watching blood being withdrawn from a patient. It seemed to him that the magnitude of the flow of blood was dramatically influenced by his physical approach or withdrawal from the patient. Thus he concluded that the magnetic influence resided, not in the magnets he had been using, but in himself. Magnets were no longer necessary for his curative manipulations and the mesmeric pass was born.

The mesmeric pass, which, as we will see, dominated induction techniques of the 18th and 19th centuries was as follows:

First, Mesmer established *rapport* between the patient and himself by placing his hands on the patient's shoulders and staring into his or her eyes. This being done, the hands were passed over the patient (in physical contact) from head, down the arms to the fingertips. The thumb of the patient was held for a brief period before repeating the process several times. In addition to these general passes, Mesmer also applied his fingers or the palms of his hands to the afflicted regions of the body in order to manipulate the magnetic fluid. Thus the laying-on-of-hands as an influential ritual continued to pervade induction and curative techniques through the time of Mesmer.

Although the so-called mesmeric passes continued to dominate the 18th and 19th century induction techniques, it was Mesmer's use of the *baquet* and certain attendant implements that gained him considerable Parisian notoriety. The *baquet* itself (which Ellenberger, 1970, calls an "imitation of the Leyden jar") was a round oak tub about 5 feet in diameter and $1\frac{1}{2}$ feet high in which there were bottles, some with their necks pointing to the center and some to the perimeter. In addition, the tub contained water in which there was ground glass and iron filings. (The heavy use of iron, both filings and rods, also ties Mesmer's technique into the past and the previous magical properties attributed to that metal.) Bent iron rods, protruding through holes in the lid, were grasped by the patients encircling the *baquet*. Physical contact among the patients was assured by their close proximity to one another (knees touching). Second, and sometimes third and fourth, rows of patients encircled the primary group and maintained intrarow contact by each patient taking the left thumb of his or her neighbor between his or her own right thumb and forefinger. These outer circles were kept in contact with the tub (and with each other) by "magnetic" cords, which were wrapped around their waists and connected back to the tub.

The room was mirrored and darkened to a "twilight" intensity (Björnström, 1887; Colquhoun, 1836), reminiscent of the room described in the *Leiden Papyrus*. The silence that initially was broken by the strains of either a harpsichord or a harmonium (Björnström, 1887; harmonica—Colquhoun, 1836). Mesmer himself sometimes provided the music on this instrument, which depended upon glass "bells" for its tonal production. A replica is in the Corning Glass Museum, Corning, NY. Into this dramatic and electrifying (Or should I say magnetic?) atmosphere stepped Mesmer, and at times d'Eslon as his assistant (Goldsmith, 1934), attired in a violet robe made of embroidered silk. Using an iron staff (like the magic wands of before), he stroked the patients with an air of "majestic dignity" (Björnström, 1887), upon which various hysteria-like crises developed successively through the group. As each patient achieved the crisis, they were removed from the *baquet* room to a silkpadded *chambre des crises* by Mesmer's assistants until all had achieved some form of trance. What had begun as a relatively simple stroking of the individual patient had now been converted into a sort of group therapy in which the achievement of dramatic effect seemed to outweigh therapeutic concerns. The drama of the situation and Mesmer's own personal magnetism were captured in Binet and Féré's description of the scene.

> Mesmer, wearing a coat of lilac silk, walked up and down amid this agitated crowd in company with Deslon and his associates, whom he chose for their youth and comeliness. Mesmer carried a long iron wand, with which he touched the bodies of the patients, and especially the diseased parts. Often laying aside the wand, he magnetised the patients with his eyes, fixing his gaze on theirs, or applying his hands to the hypochondriac region and to the lower part of the abdomen. This application was often continued for hours, and at other times the master made use of passes. He began by placing himself *en rapport* with his subject. Seated opposite to him, foot against foot, knee against knee, Mesmer laid his fingers on the hypochrondriac region and moved them to and fro, lightly touching the ribs. Magnetisation with strong currents was substituted for these manipulations when more energetic results were to be produced. The master, raising his fingers in a pyramidal form, passed his hands all over the patient's body, beginning with the head, and going downwards over the shoulders to the feet. He then returned to the head, both back and front, to the belly and the back, and renewed the process again and again until the magnetised person was saturated with the healing fluid, and transported with pain or pleasure, both sensations being equally salutary. Young women were so much gratified by the "crisis" that they begged to be thrown into it anew; they followed Mesmer through the hall, and confessed that it was impossible not to be warmly attached to the person of the magnetiser. (Binet & Féré, 1888, pp. 10–11)

Marquis de Puységur

Probably the most famous student of Mesmer was Amand-Marie-Jacques de Chastenet, Marquis de Puységur (1751–1825). His fame, however, is not so much attributable to his association with Mesmer, as to his observations of "artificial somnambulism" during mesmerism. His concern with the potential harm of the mesmeric crises and his development of a calm, sleep-like state to replace the physical and mental torment of the crises earned him a place in the history of dynamic psychiatry (Ellenberger, 1970) and hypnosis (Edmonston, 1981), far beyond his mentor, Mesmer.

The eldest of three brothers (all students of Mesmer and descendants of one of the oldest families in France), the Marquis practiced mesmerism primarily on the family estate in Buzancy and in the public square of the village by the same name. His individual induction procedure was dominated by physical contact, as might be suspected from his training with Mesmer and the general tenor of his time.

> Consider yourself a lodestone, of which your arms, and hands especially, are the two poles; touch then, a patient, by placing one hand on the back, and the other in opposition on the stomach; figure to yourself, then, that a magnetic fluid tends to circulate from one hand to the other, in crossing the body of the patient. (King, 1837, p. 65)

De Puységur considered the head and stomach prime targets of the magnetic process:

> The experience that I have acquired confirms me in the idea, that the *head,* and the *plexus solaire,* (plexus of nerves in the stomach) are the parts of the human body, which receive most effectually, the magnetic emanations.—The eyes above all, appear to me more susceptible than any other organ. It is by a light friction on the eyes that I finish the *magnetic charge,* from whence results *somnambulism;* and it is also by a very light friction on the same organs, that I perform the *discharge*, from whence follows, awakening, and the natural state.

> The immediate touch without pressure, is that which I prefer; it often seems to me, that the magnetic action is augmented, by a light friction. (King, 1837, pp. 79–80)

Considering de Puységur's concern with prophesy and his explorations into the supposed clairvoyance of his patients, it is not surprising that he should believe the stomach to be of particular significance. From at least the times of the Pythagoreans and the Peripatetics, the soul was believed to have emitted prophesies from the stomach during the sleep of the medium, hence the rendering of, στερνομαντις, εγγαστριμαντις or εγγαστριμνθος, as "ventriloquist or belly-talker" (Lloyd, 1847).

Two additional induction techniques appear in King's (1837) translation. One is from Ducommun:

> The hand of the magnetiser, at two inches distance, gives generally a sensation of heat, scarcely ever of cold. Frequently it excites a drowsiness, or heaviness of the head, which is not unpleasant. On the stomach it often produces the effect of a weight; pulsation becomes more lively and regular; perspiration is frequently very sensible, particularly in the hands and feet; the patient gets into a state of ease, and ceases to perceive the duration of time; he may fall into a slight slumber, which the least noise may destroy. Sometimes the eyelids are contracted, he cannot raise them, although perfectly awake. (King, 1837, p. 79)

The other appears in a section titled "Extracts from Various Authors." Whether it is directly attributable to the Marquis is not clear, but we can assume that it was a, if not *the,* prevalent induction technique of the late 18th and early to middle 19th centuries:

> Suppose that you wish to magnetise [sic] a patient; sit opposite to him, take hold of his thumbs, and look steadily at him, with a permanent attention and intention, or *will* to produce the desired effect. After four or five minutes, when his thumbs have acquired the same temperature with yours, place your hands on his shoulders, let them remain there two or three minutes, then draw them very slowly along the arms, and take hold again of the thumbs; do this three or four times in succession; then, place your hands on his stomach, in such a manner that your thumbs may be in the centre, and your fingers on the sides; when you feel a communication of heat, slowly draw your hand down to his feet; then place them over his head, and slowly draw them again down to the feet, and continue in the same manner, taking care in raising your hands to his head, to turn them outwards, and extend them to both sides. The precaution never to magnetise [sic] upwards, and to separate your hands when you raised them, is recommended as essential. Touch slightly and slowly, keeping your hands a few inches from the face, and scarcely even touching the clothes; use no muscular effort; let your motions be easy and supple; your hand must not be stiff; let your fingers be a little bent, and occasionally united, for it is from the end of the fingers that the fluid flows or radiates; do not be impatient of producing effects; give yourself up entirely to feelings of sympathy, and to the wish to relieve your patient. If he feels pain in particular parts, hold your hand some time on that part; continue your operation, for about half an hour. As it is necessary that your attention should be permanent, a longer time would be fatiguing. In finishing the operation, make several long *passes,* and one across the eyes, to disseminate equally the fluid.
>
> The *relation* once well established, contact is not necessary; the action *at a distance* is often more beneficial and salutary, than that produced by immediate contact. (King, 1837, pp. 74–75)

De Puységur did not feel that movement of the hands was absolutely necessary in every case. For him, the will of the magnetizer to do good for the patient was of equal importance. In fact, even the termination of the "magnetic state" was an act of will: "When you magnetized him, your aim was to put him to sleep, and you have succeeded, solely, by the act of your will; it is also, by another act of the will, that you awaken him" (King, 1837, p. 70).

The Marquis' therapeutic works were not confined to individual treatment alone. As word of his treatments spread, he soon found himself in the position of having to offer collective treatment, what we might today characterize as group therapy. He chose as the site of these treatments the huge elm tree, which stood in the center of the Buzancy village square (see Figure 2.6). According to Goldsmith (1934), it was not just the number of people

Figure 2.6. (*a*) Amand-Marie-Jacques de Chastinet, Marquis de Puységur (1751–1825).
(*b*) The Elm Tree of Buzancy. (Reprinted by permission of Henri F. Ellenberger.)

seeking the Marquis' help that lead him to choose an outdoor setting, but
also the nature of the people involved. Since they were predominately "simple villagers and peasants," used to an outdoor life, he felt that they would
not feel comfortable receiving his treatment in a dimly lit room of the Estate
House proper. The tree, itself, was held in a certain reverence by the people,
for it was the focal point of village life, under which many important discussions of harvests and crops and local affairs were held.

His group technique was as follows: The patients sat on stone benches
beneath the tree, from which dangled ropes from its main branches and from
around its trunk. With the ropes tied to their afflicted body parts, all formed

a human chain by holding each other by the thumbs, until the Marquis commanded them to release their hold on one another. Then he touched selected individuals with an iron wand, thus rendering them capable of the clairvoyant powers of the diagnosis and treatment of others. Termination of the session was accomplished by having the patients kiss the tree, which not only awakened them from their "perfect crisis," but also rendered them spontaneously amnesic for the trance period (Ellenberger, 1970).

What we see in the group therapy above is, of course, vestiges of Mesmer's *baquet,* with all of the patients seated around and connected to a central focal object (both of wood, by the way) and interconnected among themselves to enhance the flow of magnetic fluid from person to person. The wand too is reminiscent of Mesmer's procedure around the *baquet,* but it also reminds us of the powers attributed to iron in the days of the early Druids. Nor is the central focus of a wooden object so far removed from that same period. In fact, when the actual tree used by the Marquis was finally destroyed in a storm in 1940, local farmers gathered pieces of the bark, "ascribing to them certain prophylactic or curative properties" (Ellenberger, 1970, p. 74).

Finally, in yet another ritual do we find connections with the ancient past. De Puységur, like his contemporaries, used magnetized water in the treatment of various disorders. Like the Hindu, the Greeks, Jesus, the Druids, and others before him, he attributed special curative powers to specially prepared and treated water:

> Magnetised water is one of the great means of *magnetic medicine*. A patient in crisis is the only person who can perceive the difference from ordinary water. I have no more idea of this fact, than of others I have cited, as it depends upon a sensation that I have never felt; but the reiterated experience that I have had among many patients, leaves no doubt of its reality. It is not even necessary, that the water to be magnetized, be in a glass vessel. All my patients in crisis agree in advising this water in abundance to dropsical persons, confident that it is more salutary to them, than my exterior touching. (King, 1837, pp. 77–78)

Elsewhere in King's (1837) book instructions for magnetizing water are given, although they are not directly attributed to de Puységur:

> In order to magnetize a decanter or a tumbler full of water, hold it on the palm of the left hand, and place the right hand above with the fingers closed; open and shut them by turns; move them over the surface, at a short distance, to charge the water with the fluid, in the same manner as philosophers would charge with electricity, a Leyden bottle. (p. 78).

De Puységur continued his work even after he had been sent to Strasbourg with his military regiment. Here he and a Dr. Ostertag (Goldsmith, 1934) formed two Société de l'Harmonie (named after Mesmer's Parisian society by the same name) for both the experimental study of somnambulism and the gratuitous treatment of patients. It was the latter who continued the eye-fixation induction techniques of the ancients by having patients stare at a glass ball until somnambulism overtook them.

The Chevalier de Barbarin reaffirmed the ancient ties of mesmerism, hypnosis, and medical practice to religious ideology by forming his own Animist Society of Harmony at Ostende (Belgium) in which he preached that the mesmeric cures were acts of God. In the midst of this retrograde step in the progression of understanding, he did recognize that implements such as the *baquet,* various amulets, glass balls, and the like were unnecessary in the induction of the mesmeric condition.

Bruno

In St. Dominique's account (1874) a contemporary of Mesmer and de Puysé-gur by the name of Bruno also used passes to mesmerize his patients. His passes were intended both to induce mesmerism and to diagnose the afflicted part of the patient's body:

> He established relation by means of the thumbs which he held for the space of seven or eight minutes, his will being active the while, and his attention centred on the subject. Then he resorted to passes, which he performed very slowly, along the arms, and in front of the body from head to feet, or at least as low down as the knees. He gradually drew away from the subject, continuing his passes, first at the distance of one inch, then of several inches, and only gave sufficient tension to his hands to maintain them in position.

> Bruno pretended that while passing his hand before the patient at a distance of three or four inches, the magnetizer should experience a sensation of heat or cold when on a level with the part affected; a pain in the hand, or at least a feeling that his own body is exhaling a certain vapour—i.e., fluid—which takes the direction of the part affected. (p. 23)

Bruno apparently owes his obscure place in the history of hypnosis to the fact that his works were not published until 1819 by M. Delauzanne.

Perkinism

Europe was not the only area of the world to have its run at the development of new and miraculous cures for the afflicted. In 1795 Elisha Perkins (1740–1799), a then respected medical practitioner of Plainfield, Connecticut, wrote a letter describing a new therapeutic technique. He had found that inflamed and painful areas of the body could be soothed by gently stroking those areas with a knife blade. As his experiments progressed, he discovered that lacquered metal combs worn in the hair also had a curative affect, but the most efficacious instruments were two pieces of metal, one iron, one brass, blunt at one end and pointed at the other (Holmes, 1891).

Perkins' technique was simple and direct. The metal instruments, labeled Metalic Tractors, were held, one in each hand, by the therapist and "repeatedly and gently stroked towards the heart across the affected part of the patient's body" (Carlson & Simpson, 1970). According to Perkins and his son Benjamin D. (1774–1810), also a physician, the Tractors worked on a Galvanic principle involving natural animal electricity (in contrast to Mesmer's animal magnetism).

Elisha Perkins patented his Tractors on February 19, 1796 (Carlson & Simpson, 1970) and in 1798 they were used in the Royal Hospital at Copenhagen. About this same time, armed with testimonials of the value of the Tractors from American and Danish physicians, clergy and government officials (President George Washington bought a set.), Benjamin took the instruments to England. In 1804 the Perkinean Institution was established in London and son Benjamin was pocketing a fortune (more than 10,000 pounds) from sales of the patented devices (They sold for 5 guineas—$25). Things were going so well that a physician-poet submitted a zealous defence of Perkinism entitled, satirically: "Terrible Tractoration!! A poetical Petition against Galvanizing Trumpery and the Perkinistic Institution" to the Royal College of Physicians.

Things did not, however, continue to go well when Dr. John Haygarth of Bath and others (William Falconer, Dr. Alderson) investigated the Tractors by using controlled data rather than individual testamonials. Using "tractors" made of wood—although the patients thought they were genuine Metallic Tractors—both Haygarth and Alderson achieved therapeutic success with a variety of ailments. Haygarth further found that lead, nails, pieces of bone, slate, and a tobacco pipe were equally effective! By 1811 Perkinism had died out in England and on the continent. To its credit the Connecticut Medical Society had already expelled Elisha Perkins in May 1797, primarily on the grounds of using a secret remedy that he had personally patented.

Perkins' Tractors were but a logical step from the medieval beliefs in the effects of various metals on patients. Even before Perkins, in 1771, Abbé Lenoble had used the wearing of magnetized iron to aid his patients and in 1779 Audry and de Thouret recommended such a practice to the French Royal Society of Medicine (Janet, 1925). The relationship of Perkinism to Mesmerism has been discussed in a number of articles (Carlson & Simpson, 1970; Colquhoun, 1836; Holmes, 1891). Benjamin Perkins argued that the two were quite different, mainly on the grounds of the electricity-magnetism point noted above. Most reviewers of the two techniques, however, attributed the effects of both to the imagination of the patient and its powerful effect on bodily processes. Colquhoun (1836), on the other hand, contests such as interpretation.

Thus, by the turn of the century, the induction procedures still in vogue were those directly relating to Mesmer and his techniques. The continuity from the ancients' laying-on-of-hands, eye-fixation, and the uses of specially prepared liquids (primarily water) and objects persisted. While the use of soothing verbalizations, chants, and rhythmic sounds occurred in ancient times, such techniques were not fully appreciated during the 18th century. It was for the 19th century to bring to fruition verbal induction techniques.

NOTE

1. I am indebted to John E. Rexine for his assistance in rendering the Latin text into English.

CHAPTER 3

The Early Nineteenth Century

The progress of history is continuous and unaffected by humanity's numerical notations. Our story of hypnotic induction procedures begins anew with the 19th century, not because the year 1800 yielded some dramatic changes in what had gone before but because the century mark is a convenient, arbitrary demarcation of time. Although we have seen the beginnings of the abandonment of many of the trappings of Mesmer and de Puységur's techniques, and will continue to see less and less use made of magnetized objects as "indispensable" tools of the magnetizer, the use of special objects, to which are attributed special powers, persisted well into the 19th century, and, yes, even into the present.

The practice of clairvoyance, or the use of somnambulistic individuals as diagnosticians for others' illnesses, which itself derived from the ancients' uses of dreams and dreaming individuals to foretell the future, prevailed in the 19th century. Just as we saw in the ancient sleep temples (see Chapter 1), the health care class of the 19th century placed much stock in the abilities of naive individuals to diagnose and prescribe while in the mesmeric condition. Just as de Puységur and the Societies of Harmony explored the tangent of clairvoyance through mesmerism, so too did some of the more prominent practitioners of the 19th century; for example, Bertrand and Elliotson. While such a practice is no longer relied on in the present century by health care personnel and is generally looked on with disdain, it remains an abiding interest of the public.

Eye-fixation techniques and the laying-on-of-hands both continued to be heavily used, the latter not really dropping out of general use until the 20th century. If anything, eye-fixation techniques again gained currency during the 19th century, as did the increasing use of verbal induction techniques. One of the more well known, although not fully appreciated, individuals to introduce verbal expression as the sole mesmerizing agent was the Abbé Faria.

The Abbé Faria

In the early 1800s a Portuguese priest, Jose Custodio de Faria (the Abbé Faria), came to Paris and subsisted by offering demonstrations of animal magnetism. Although discredited by a simple stage actor, his insights into the phenomena of magnetism, presented in his posthumously published book (Faria, 1819), had a profound bearing on the future directions pursued by other practitioners. Born on May 31, 1756 in Candolim, a village of Bardez, Goa, Portuguese India, the then to be Abbé Faria emigrated to Lisbon on November 23, 1771. His father, Caetano Victorino de Faria, was a descendant of a renowned Hindu family whose lineage was of the Saraswat Brahmin caste. Both of Jose Custodio's parents later entered religious orders, he becoming a priest and she a nun of the Roman Church.

From Lisbon, Faria travelled to Rome where he was an Internee in the College of "popaganda Fide" (Sharma, 1979). After his ordination was accomplished on March 12, 1780, he returned to Lisbon to pursue his calling, but soon discovered that advancement was limited and so journeyed to Paris for the first time in 1788. Sometime following the French Revolution, in which he participated, he began public demonstrations of magnetism (probably about 1802 according to Sharmin, 1979) but then left in 1811 to take a position as Professor of Philosophy at Lyceum, an academy in Marseille. The following year he accepted a similar post at the Academy of Nimes, before returning to Paris in 1813. From this point in time on he conducted public demonstrations and courses on magnetism at No. 49 Clichy Street, with the blessing and permission of the Prefect of Police. His first demonstration was given on August 11, 1813 and his last in 1816 when an actor pretended to be in a state of somnambulism, only later to announce his deception and ridicule of Abbé Faria through a caricature of him in *Magnetisomanie,* a popular farce of the time (Pattie, 1967). He died a pauper on September 20, 1819 and is buried in the cemetery of Monmarte.

Taught by de Puységur, the Abbé Faria continued to obtain a "lucid sleep" or somnambulism in his subjects. For him, the processes involved in the production of trances were the same as those involved in producing natural sleep, to the point that he thought the two—natural sleep and somnambulism—to be the same. So extensive was Faria's recognition of the sleep-magnetism relationship that he selected his subjects on the basis of their ability to fall easily into a natural sleep. This was the technique he used for selecting his 8 or 10 demonstration subjects from the 50 to 60 people who attended his daily lectures.

In a real sense the Abbé anticipated modern scales of the capacity for hypnosis, which generally begin with the subject demonstrating his or her ability to become "naturally" relaxed. Faria even attempted to change—unsuccessfully, we now know—the terminology of his time. He preferred the terms concentration and lucid sleep to animal magnetism and somnambulism, respectively. In addition, the Abbé Faria clearly recognized the impending demise of magnetic fluid explanations of mesmerism (and later hypnosis) long before the induction techniques, which took their method from the theory, had ceased to be used: "I cannot conceive how the human species could have been bizarre enough to seek the cause of this phenomenon in a *baquet,* in some external influence, in a magnetic fluid" (Faria,

1819). But the passes, the laying-on-of-hands, the use of special objects and fluids did not suddenly disappear from the practitioner's repertory of techniques.

The Abbé Faria's view of magnetism as a "lucid sleep" was reflected quite strongly in his induction techniques. He used several methods, singly or in combination. In one, the subject was instructed to sit comfortably in a chair and to close his or her eyes. After a period, during which the Abbé observed the subject to ascertain the degree of quietude attained, Faria announced "Sleep" in an emphatic, commanding tone. His technique was as follows:

> He placed the patient in an arm chair, and after telling him to shut his eyes, and collect himself, suddenly pronounced, in a strong voice and imperative tone, the word "dormez," which generally produced on the individual an impression sufficiently strong to give a slight shock, and occasion warmth, transpiration, and *sometimes* somnambulism. (Braid, 1843/1976, p. 7)

If this method was not initially successful, it was repeated several more times.

Just as his "sleep" method anticipated the extensive verbal induction procedures used today, so did the Abbé Faria's second method provide the bridge between the ancients' use of eye-fixation and Braid's technique of creating eye fatigue through the fixation method. Subjects who did not respond to the "sleep" method were instructed to stare at his hand until the eyes became fatigued (noted by increased blinking) and closed. If the individual did not show signs of fatigue or blinking, the Abbé Faria would move his hand closer to the person's face, until the eyes closed.

As a final resort, Faria used a laying-on-of-hands technique in which he touched the patient in various locations (temples, chest, knees, feet, forehead, and bridge of the nose). The palpations were apparently used to aid the patient's concentration, the better to achieve the "lucid sleep."

Joseph Philip Francis Deleuze

Another individual who was also greatly influenced by de Puységur and his work at Buzancy was J. P. F. Deleuze. Before his long, illustrious career came to a close, he had produced a two-volume *Critical History of Animal Magnetism* (1813 & 1819) and one of the first and certainly most detailed instructional manuals in the techniques of magnetism, *Practical Instructions in Animal Magnetism* (1825). It is the latter which will hold our attention.

Born in March, 1753 at Sisteron, Deleuze first sought a military career in Paris in 1772. After three years, however, he directed his energies to the natural sciences, and, in 1785, became aware of de Puységur's work at Buzancy. It was through one of his friends, M. D. d'Aix, that he received his first instruction in mesmerism (magnetism), and through which experience the world received one of the first personal accounts of being magnetized.

Subsequently, Deleuze became one of the staunchest defenders of the process and its curative powers. What lent particular credence to his defense of mesmerism was his professional stature in the field of natural science. In 1798 he became assistant naturalist of the Garden of Plants (Paris), and in 1802, the secretary of the Annals of the Museum of Natural History. In 1828 he received the appointment of librarian of the Museum of Natural History. He died in 1835.

I will dwell at length on the methods of Deleuze, because (a) they are so explicitly given in his *Practical Instruction in Animal Magnetism* (1843/1982), (b) they exemplify the techniques most in use throughout the 19th century, and (c) they demonstrate a fascinating continuity between the past and the future.

Deleuze's techniques derived directly from the theory to which he had subscribed: in essence, that a magnetic fluid was involved and had not only to pass from the magnetizer to the patient, but also had to be redistributed within the patient through the passes made by the operator. What was also noteworthy in his form of induction was the setting in which operators were instructed to use it. Deleuze advised no additional witnesses, lest they disturb the patient; a moderate temperature; and precautions to avoid interruptions during the process. In general, the only individuals he advised having present, other than the patient and the operator, were female witnesses in the case of a male operator mesmerizing a female patient. On this point he was quite explicit, lest charges of moral impropriety be brought against the operator.

His general technique was as follows:

Cause your patient to sit down in the easiest position possible, and place yourself before him, on a seat a little more elevated, so that his knees may be between yours, and your feet by the side of his. Demand of him, in the first place, that he give himself up entirely; that he think of nothing; that he not trouble himself by examining the effects which he experiences; that he banish all fear, and indulge hope; and that he be not disquieted or discouraged if the action of Magnetism produces in him temporary pains.

After you have brought yourself to a state of self-collectedness, take his thumbs between your two fingers, so that the inside of your thumbs may touch the inside of his. Remain in this situation from two to five minutes, or until you perceive there is an equal degree of heat between your thumbs and his; that being done, you will withdraw your hands, removing them to the right and left, and waving them so that the interior surface be turned outwards, and raise them to his head; then place them upon his two shoulders, leaving them there about a minute; you will then draw them along the arm to the extremity of the fingers, touching lightly. You will repeat this *pass** five or six times, always

---

* I employ here the word *pass,* which is common to all magnetizers. It signifies all the movements made by the hand in *passing* over the body. Whether by slightly touching, or at a distance.

turning your hands, and sweeping them off a little, before reascending; you will then place your hands upon the head, hold them there a moment, and bring them down before the face, at the distance of one or two inches, as far as the pit of the stomach; there you will let them remain about two minutes, passing the thumb along the pit of the stomach, and the other fingers down the sides. Then descend slowly along the body as far as the knees, or farther; and, if you can conveniently, as far as the ends of the feet. You may repeat the same processes during the greater part of the sitting. You may sometimes draw nearer to the patient, so as to place your hands behind his shoulders, descending slowly along the spine, thence to the hips, and along the thighs as far as the knees, or to the feet. After the first passes, you may dispense with putting your hands upon the head, and make the succeeding passes along the arms, beginning at the shoulder; or along the body, commencing at the stomach. (Deleuze, 1843/1982, pp. 40–42)

He also commented on the degree of energy the passes took and detailed the attitude of the hands in making contact with the patient.

In making the passes, it is unnecessary to employ any greater muscular force than what is required to lift the hand and prevent it from falling. The movements should be easy, and not too rapid. A pass from the head to the feet may take about half a minute. The fingers ought to be a little separated from each other, and slightly bent, so that the ends of the fingers be directed towards the person magnetized.

It is by the ends of the fingers, and especially by the thumbs, that the fluid escapes with the most activity. For this reason it is, we take the thumbs of the patient in the first place, and hold them whenever we are at rest. This process generally suffices to establish the communication, to strengthen which there is also one other process. It consists in placing your ten fingers against those of the patient, so that the inside of your hands are brought near to the inside of his, and the balls of your fingers touch the balls of his. The fluid seems to flow less copiously from the back of the hands than from the inside; and this is one of the reasons for turning the hands in raising them, without carrying them off too far from the body. (Deleuze, 1843/1982, pp. 44–45)

Several types of passes were described.

I think it proper to distinguish the passes that are made without touching, from those which are made with the touch, not only with the ends of the fingers, but with the extent of the hand, employing at the same time a slight pressure. I give to these last the name of *magnetic frictions*. They are often made use of to act better upon the arms, the legs, and the back, along the vertebral column.

This manner of magnetizing by longitudinal passes, directing the fluid from the head to the extremities, without fixing upon any part in preference to others, is called *magnetizing by the long pass, (magnetisér à grands courans.)* It is more or less proper in all cases, and it is requisite to employ it in the first sitting, when there is no special reason for using any other.

The fluid is thus distributed into all the organs, and it accumulates naturally in those which have need of it. Besides the passes made at a short distance, others are made, just before finishing, at the distance of two or three feet. They generally produce a calm, refreshing, and pleasurable sensation. (Deleuze, 1843/1982, p. 43)

Based on theoretical grounds, the direction of the passes was considered important, while other aspects of pass behavior was not.

You see that it is essential to magnetize always descending from the head to the extremities, and never mounting from the extremities to the head. It is on this account that we turn the hands obliquely when they are raised again from the feet to the head. The descending passes are magnetic; that is, they are accompanied with the intention of magnetizing. The ascending movements are not. Many magnetizers shake their fingers slightly after each pass. This method, which is never injurious, is in certain cases advantageous; and for this reason it is good to get the habit of doing it. (Deleuze, 1843/1982, p. 42)

The passes were also used diagnostically.

While drawing your hands slowly before your patient, at the distance of three or four inches, and holding your fingers slightly bent, you will feel, either at the ends of the fingers, or at the palm of the hand, different sensations, as they pass along before the affected organ of the patient. These sensations will be either of cold, or of prickly heat, or of slight pain, or of numbness. They will indicate to you the principal seat of the disease, and consequently the part upon which you ought to direct the action. (Deleuze, 1843/1982, p. 261)

Special consideration was given to the instances (a) when a male operator worked with a female and (b) when the patient was bed-ridden, unable to sit or stand.

In the first case, you can place yourself by the side of the person whom you wish to magnetize. First, take the thumb, and, the better to establish the communication, place one hand upon the stomach, and the other upon the back; then lower the two hands opposite to each other, one down the back, and the other at a distance down the fore part of the body, one hand descending to the feet. You may magnetize the two arms, one after the other, with one hand only.

In case the patient cannot raise himself, take your station near his bed in the most convenient manner; take his thumbs, make several passes along the arms, and, if he can support himself upright, several along the back; then, not to fatigue yourself, use only one hand, placing it upon the stomach, and making longitudinal passes, at first slightly touching through the clothes, then at a distance. You can hold one hand fixed upon the knees or upon the feet, while the other is in motion. Finish by passes along the legs, and by transversal passes before the head, the breast, and the stomach, to scatter the superabundant fluid. When the communication is established, one can magnetize very well by placing himself at the foot of the patient's bed, and in front of him; then directing, at that distance, both hands from the head to the feet, dashing them aside after each pass, so as not to conduct the fluid to himself. I have produced somnambulism by this process, without establishing the communication by touching. (Deleuze, 1843/1982, pp. 45–46)

In fact, Deleuze made great moment of the delicacy of a male operator magnetizing a female patient. Throughout *Practical Instruction in Animal Magnetism* he repeatedly remarks on this special case. His concern appears to stem from a fear that unless proper precautions were taken, the moral and ethical intent of the physician would be suspect, and worse yet, the process itself would suffer in the public eye. These concerns led to the explicit directions that the patient should be "clad in the most decent manner," and that the practitioner avoid physical contact with the patient except to hold the thumbs and "to make frictions along the feet, outside of her garments" (Deleuze, 1843/1982, p. 215). To this end he even suggested the use of a glass or steel rod as a wand to effect the magnetic induction.

Thus we see that the use of physical and at-a-distance laying-on-of-hands was not the only way in which Deleuze's detailed manual provided historical continuity with the past procedures of the ancients and his contemporaries (e.g., Mesmer). Although he did not feel that a wand was necessary, he did suggest that it was "sometimes very useful." His was not the wooden wand of the Druids and other ancients, nor the iron rod of Mesmer, but a more modern version made of steel.

It is a steel wand, in the form of a long cone, ten or twelve inches in length, about five lines in diameter at one end, and two lines at the other. It is held in such a way as to have the large end in the palm of the hand, and the straightened fingers touch it at their extremities. This is used to direct the fluid at a distance, to fix the action of the five united fingers upon any particular point. It is also used in magnetizing water; which is done by plunging it into a vase half its length, and stirring it round in the water. (Deleuze, 1843/1982, p. 89)

The mention of magnetized water again demonstrates the historical continuity of induction procedures. In Deleuze's day the use of magnetized water was still quite prevalent, to the point that several pages of his manual were spent outlining the procedures for preparing this curative agent and its applications.

To magnetize water, take the vessel which contains it, and pass the two hands alternately from the top to the bottom of the vessel. Introduce the fluid at the opening of the vessel, by presenting the fingers close to it, several times in succession. Sometimes you may breathe upon the water, or stir it round with the thumb. You may magnetize a glass of water, by holding it by the bottom in one hand, and with the other throwing the fluid upon the glass.

There is one process which I employ in preference, in order to magnetize a bottle of water, when I am certain it is not disagreeable to the person whom I magnetize. It consists in placing the bottle upon my knee, and applying my mouth to the nose. I thus throw my breath into the bottle, and, at the same time, I make passes with both hands upon all the surface. I believe this process charges strongly; but it is not necessary. It is sufficient to magnetize it by the hands.

One may magnetize a pitcher of water in two or three minutes; a glass of water in one minute. It is unnecessary to repeat here that the processes pointed out for magnetizing water, like everything else, would be absolutely useless, if they were not employed with attention, and with a determinate will. (Deleuze, 1843/1982, p. 76)

The water thus magnetized was used to produce "marvellous effects" and Deleuze took to task other magnetizers for not making more extensive use of this magnificent cure-all. It was applied both externally and internally, the latter being efficacious in the case of intestinal and stomach ailments. Magnetized water was prescribed for eight days running as a purgative, and a Dr. Roullier was reported to have used it in the same manner five or six times daily for periods exceeding a month. The water itself had to be magnetized only by the operator who was treating the patient in the usual magnetic format.

Not only could water be specially prepared for therapy use, but other food stuffs as well, particularly liquid foods such as milk (shades of the Druids and Irish mythology) and broths. Deleuze even claimed that magnetized milk was palatable to those who previously found it repugnant. Nor was magnetization limited to food materials. Other agents, such as silk and cotton materials, leaves of trees, and plates made from gold, steel, or glass were all advocated as curative implements, particularly when placed in contact with the afflicted part of the body. Deleuze reported using a magnetized handkerchief placed on the stomach of the patient to "calm spasms and nervous movements" (Deleuze, 1843/1982, p. 84), and a magnetized bandage wrapped around the head throughout the night to rid a patient of headache.

The wearing of amulets (in this case magnetized objects) to treat various internal ailments was also prescribed. The same Dr. Roullier who had his patients gulping great quantities of magnetized water also advised them to wear pieces of magnetized glass of a lenticular shape, about $1\frac{1}{2}$ inches in diameter. These amulets were suspended from a ribbon of such length as to allow the amulet to be in contact with the pit of the stomach. It was reported that these devices would adhere to the skin as long as they retained their magnetism (three to five days) after which they would have to be remagnetized in order to renew their powers. The same procedure was used with pieces of steel or leaves of trees (species unnamed). The wearing of specially treated bits of metal was not new. Abbé Lenoble used iron attached to the wrists and chest in 1771 (see Janet, 1925, p. 791), and we have already noted the importance of iron in Druidic times as related in the folk tales of Ireland (see Chapter 2). In fact, the extensive range of the uses of metals in therapy was reported as early as 1853 by Burq and is partially summarized in Janet (1925).

Deleuze also reported the use of magnetic socks to treat a patient, claiming that they "produced a warmth of the feet which could not have been obtained by any other means" (Deleuze, 1843/1982, p. 84). Such a reaction was also reported some 20 years after the publication of Deleuze's manual (1825) by a William Topham in the 1847 issue of *The Zoist*. Topham, a barrister-at-law, communicated with Elliotson that he had aided an epileptic patient by mesmerizing a kid glove and sending it to the patient through the mail. When Horner (the patient) put it on: "At first, he said that he felt a sort of warmth passing up his arm; and then, in the course of three or four minutes, he dropped asleep" (Topham, 1847, p. 129). However, the mesmerized glove apparently had some unwanted side effects, since it was further reported that later his arm and hand became rigid and painful and he had difficulty removing the glove due to the swelling in his hand.

Feelings of warmth on the part of the patients seem to have been prevalent in Deleuze's day (and beyond). Here he describes the general and most common effects of the process:

> The magnetized person perceives a heat escaping from the ends of your fingers when you pass them at a little distance before his face, although your hands appear cold to him if you touch him. He afterwards feels the heat through his clothes, in some parts, or in all parts of his body before which your hands pass. He often compares it to water, moderately warm, flowing over him, and the sensation precedes your hand. His legs become numb, especially if you do not carry your hands as low as his feet; and this numbness ceases when, towards the close, you make passes along the legs to the toes, or below them. Sometimes, instead of communicating heat, you communicate cold; sometimes, also, you produce heat upon one part of the body, and cold upon another. There is often induced a general warmth, and a perspiration more or less considerable. (Deleuze, 1843/1982, p. 59)

Concern with the eyes also enters into the observation, although Deleuze did not use eye fixation in the induction phase.

> Magnetism causes the eyes to be closed. They are shut in such a manner that the patient cannot open them, he feels a calm, a sensation of tranquil enjoyment; he grows drowsy; he sleeps. (Deleuze 1843/1982, p. 60)

He also noted effects that could disturb the operator:

> The action of Magnetism is sometimes accompanied with nervous movements, and very often a disposition to yawn; sometimes the patient experiences pains

at the stomach, and nausea, which is even followed by vomiting; at other times, he experiences colic pains.

These crises ought to give the magnetizer no disquiet. He ought to know how to calm those which are nervous, and to aid the tendencies of nature. (Deleuze, 1843/1982, p. 61)

The various effects noted in the patient could also be used as indications to the operator of how best to proceed. Deleuze outlined a number of specific patient responses and what they suggested to the operator.

If the patient feels the sensation of heat or coolness from your fingers, content yourself with magnetizing with long passes. If the action of Magnetism excites pain in any organ, concentrate the action upon that organ, in order to draw it away afterwards.

If there be manifested any heat or heaviness at the head, attract it to the knees.

If Magnetism produces a sense of suffocation, or an irritation of the lungs, make passes, beginning below the breast, and continuing to the knees.

If colics take place, and if they indicate, as they often do with women, that the circulation ought to be accelerated, avoid letting the hands stop at the breast, or even at the stomach; carry the action to the sides, and below them; make passes along the thighs, and let the hands remain some time upon the knees.

If the patient have [sic] pains at the back, make passes along the vertebral column.

If you see any nervous movements, calm them by your will, first taking the thumbs or the wrists, and afterwards making passes at the distance of several inches, or even of several feet, with the open hand.

If Magnetism seems to act too powerfully, moderate the action, and render it more soothing, by making the passes at a distance.

If the patient sleep [sic], let him sleep tranquilly while you continue to magnetize him. When you wish to rest yourself, take the thumbs of the patient, or place your hands upon his knees.

If the sitting has been long, and you are obliged to quit, rouse the patient gently, by telling him to awake, and by making passes transversely across the eyes.

If the eyes are closed fast, not attended with sleep, open them by transverse passes, but not till the termination of the sitting.

If, after being roused, the patient feels anew the desire of sleeping, you will leave him to sleep alone, taking precautions that no one shall trouble him. (Deleuze, 1843/1982, pp. 61–62)

Such detailed observations, leading to shifts in the therapeutic process were much easier made on patients being treated individually. Consequently, Deleuze did not recommend the group therapy procedures of Mesmer around the *baquet*. Instead, he presented a case for group therapy that involved a number of "therapists" all concentrating their attention on a single patient. The method was called "the chain." Before proceeding, as described below, the individual leading this form of treatment had to ascertain that (a) all who participated were in good health (except the patient), (b) all were actively interested in the patient, and (c) no one would disturb the chain once initiated. These having been established, arrange the people in a circle.

> Let them all take each other's hands, holding on by the thumbs, so that he who is on the right of the patient may touch him with the left hand, and he who is on the left may touch him with the right hand. You will form a part of this chain, and, when you wish to make passes with your hands, the two persons by the side of you will place their hands upon your shoulders or upon your knees. If you place yourself in the centre, your two neighbors will approach each other, so that the chain be not interrupted. The magnetic fluid will soon be in circulation, the patient will feel the effect strongly, and your power will be considerably augmented.

> But to have a chain good [sic], it is necessary that all who compose it should be thoughtful only of the patient, and unite constantly with you in intention; without this condition, it is more injurious than beneficial. Some persons in the chain often feel the effects of the magnetic action; they faint, or go to sleep. But that does not counteract the effects so much as a single act of inattention. (Deleuze, 1843/1982, p. 86)

Although Deleuze did not recommend the combining of groups of patients for treatment around a *baquet,* he gave a very explicit and detailed account of the preparation of the *baquet* and its general use:

> Take a wooden vessel, two feet high, larger or smaller according to the number of persons to be placed round it, having the bottom elevated an inch from the floor by the projection of the sides. Place an iron rod in the centre, to serve as the principal conductor, having a diameter of half an inch, or of one inch, descending to within two inches of the bottom, and rising above the trough two or three feet. The lower end of this iron rod should be firmly fixed in a glass foot, or in a jug, so that it may retain its vertical position. Put into the vessel bottles of magnetized water, or other magnetized substances. Cork them, and run through each cork a piece of iron wire projecting two or three inches; and arrange them in such a manner that the neck may be near the central conductor, and communicate with it by the iron wire which pierces the cork. Then place a second range of bottles above the first. If the *baquet,* or trough, is large, you can put two ranges of bottles in the same order; the neck of one being placed in the bottom of the other. This being done, you will fill the vessel with water, white sand well washed, pounded glass, and iron filings, all well magnetized. Place upon it a cover in two pieces, fitted closely together, having an opening in the middle for the central conductor. At a short distance from the circumference, at points corresponding to the spaces between the bottles, you

will pierce several holes, for the purpose of thrusting into the reservoir iron conductors, bent and movable, which are raised and lowered at pleasure, so that one may direct them against any part of the body, and pass the hands above them, to draw off the fluid. And, last, you will attach to the central conductor cords of cotton or wool, which the patients may twine around their bodies. (Deleuze, 1843/1982, pp. 81–82)

He did consider a small reservoir of magnetized water of value.

But a large bottle filled with magnetized water, furnished with an iron wire inserted into the cork and forming a curvature of from three to six inches, terminated by a knob, is a little reservoir which keeps up the magnetic action, and may be very useful. The magnetizer charges this bottle occasionally without taking out the cork. (Deleuze, 1843/1982, p. 83)

Unlike some of the early writers, Deleuze also explicated the termination processes as well as the induction. He outlined three approaches to ending a sitting. The techniques could be used singly or in combination.

When you wish to put an end to the sitting, take care to draw towards the extremity of the hands, and towards the extremity of the feet, prolonging your passes beyond these extremities, and shaking your fingers each time. Finally, make several passes transversely before the face, and also before the breast at the distance of three or four inches: these passes are made by presenting the two hands together, and briskly drawing them from each other, as if to carry off the superabundance of fluid with which the patient may be charged.

There is one more process by which it is very advantageous to terminate the sitting. It consists of placing oneself by the side of the patient, as he stands up, and, at the distance of a foot, making with both hands, one before the body and the other behind, seven or eight passes, commencing above the head, and descending to the floor, along which the hands are spread apart. This process frees the head, reestablishes the equilibrium, and imparts strength. (Deleuze, 1843/1982, pp. 42–43)

In addition, Deleuze also advised making final passes over the eyes (particularly in the case of somnambulists) as the operator announces: "Wake!"

Before briefly summarizing the techniques of Deleuze, there is one more recommendation he made. In the course of describing the precautions to be taken when a male operator is treating a female patient, he made the following statement:

It may happen that a nurse, endowed with intelligence and kindness, may perceive, with her own eyes, the efficacy of Magnetism, and feel the desire and the power of doing good. In this case, the magnetizer will excite her confidence, and get her to take his place, after giving her suitable instructions how to proceed. He will always recommend to her not to speak of it. (Deleuze, 1843/1982, p. 216)

Thus, as early as 1825, Deleuze was suggesting two things with respect to magnetism (the hypnosis of his day): (a) that lay people (nurses in his case) could, with "suitable instructions," perform treatment through magnetism and (b) that such activity must be kept semi-secret. Why the latter? The implication is that if the self-evident fact that individuals without advanced academic degrees can perform some of the treatment services then reserved for physicians and priests were to become widely appreciated that some negative consequences might accrue to the trainer, the professions, the patient, and so forth. Deleuze explains the matter more gently: "The time is not yet arrived for nurses to consider the exercise of Magnetism as one of their most important functions" (Deleuze, 1843/1982, p. 216).

Today advocacy of the training of lay individuals in the techniques and uses of hypnosis is quite open, but not without intraprofessional consequences. Byers (1975) reported training "Hypnotist Technicians" in relaxation techniques through self-hypnosis for work with alcoholics. The editor of the journal in which the article appeared was verbally chastized for allowing an article reporting such activity to be published! More recently, a major intraprofessional debate has emerged over the training of police officers in the techniques of hypnosis, particularly the work of Martin Reiser with the Los Angeles Police Department (see, for example, Reiser & Neilson, 1980). So seriously is the issue of "nonprofessional" participation in hypnotic techniques taken that the Society for Clinical and Experimental Hypnosis inserted the following statement in its code of ethics: "[It is] unethical for its members to train lay individuals in the use of hypnosis, to collaborate with laymen in the use of hypnosis, or to serve as a consultant for laymen who are utilizing hypnosis" (Society for Clinical and Experimental Hypnosis, 1979, p. 452). Thus members of this society who engage in such activity, as was suggested in 1825 by Deleuze, can be expelled from membership on ethical grounds. Whether ethical code restrictions are a prelude to restrictive legislation, legally preventing the general population from using hypnosis (Edmonston, 1980, 1982), or a genuine and humanitarian attempt to protect the masses of the population from a potentially dangerous and harmful procedure, only time and heated intraprofessional debate will clarify. However, the long departed members of the secret priesthoods of the Hindu, the Egyptians, the Druids, and the rest (as well as the medical societies of the 18th and 19th centuries) must certainly be applauding this thread of historical continuity in the application of induction techniques.

Finally, this insightful and learned gentleman (Deleuze) summarized his own technique.

1. Establish the communication by holding the thumbs, placing the hands upon the shoulders, and making passes along the arms with a light pressure, and placing the hands upon the stomach. 2. Direct the current from the head to the feet, or at least to the knees. Touching is useless. 3. Make passes, or else magnetic frictions, along the legs, to the extremity of the feet: soothe the

patient by several passes at a distance with the open hand; and, finally, throw off the superabundant fluid, by a few transversal passes. The first sittings ought to be about an hour in duration, when there is no reason to prolong or abridge them. I say the *first* sittings, because a part of the time is consumed in establishing the communication. As soon as that has been once well established the action of Magnetism is manifested at the first moment; then a sitting of half an hour, or three-quarters, provided the labor commenced is duly sustained, will be sufficient.

It is necessary to order the treatment in the most uniform and regular manner possible. The sittings must be periodical, and equal in duration. The magnetizer must be calm and self-collected; all foreign influence must be banished; all curious persons excluded, and also every other witness except the one chosen at first. (Deleuze, 1843/1982, pp. 50–51)

Billot

According to St. Dominique (1874), a practitioner named Billot began his techniques in the same manner as Deleuze, but at the second sitting began directing the magnetic fluid to the pit of the stomach. Like Deleuze, he used a steel, conical shaped wand in one hand while making passes with the other free hand. At times he placed both hands over the epigastric area, formed a fist, rubbed his thumbs over the outer surfaces of his fingers and suddenly threw open his hands toward the patient, creating "a succession of manual discharges" (St. Dominique, 1874, p. 25). Billot also magnetized trees and at times used mirrors to direct the sun's rays, along which the magnetic fluid was conducted. This latter technique may have been the forerunner of the device used by J. B. Luys (see Chapter 4).

Alexandre Jacques François Bertrand

Although de Puységur questioned the effectiveness of the mesmeric crisis and led the way from crisis to relaxation, it was Alexandre Bertrand who first challenged the basic doctrine of a magnetic fluid operating in the process of mesmerism. Bertrand's claim to this distinction came primarily through his industry if not through brilliant intellectual insights. According to Ellenberger (1970), it was General Noizet of the French army who convinced Bertrand to question the reality of magnetic fluid. However, although both sent manuscripts to the Berlin Academy on the subject about the same time, it took Noizet 35 years to publish his, but Bertrand only four.

Noizet himself was a long-time follower of the development of mesmerism. He was well acquainted with Abbé Faria and carried his ideas to Bertrand, thus being instrumental in furthering the replacement of the magnetic fluid theory with that of will and suggestion as brought to full fruition by Liébeault, Bernheim, and the Nancy School. Although proclaiming that the notion of a magnetic fluid was incorrect, his technique followed the pattern of those proclaiming its reality. His method was described by Bernheim (1891/1980):

> General Noizet also used passes. He touched the thumbs of the subject to his for some time to establish good communication between the two fluids. Next, he placed his hands on the subject's shoulders, left them there for a few minutes, and then lowered them (at a slight distance from the arms and hips) to the knees. He took the thumbs again and repeated the same maneuver several times. He would then place them on the sides so that the two thumbs joined at the pit of the stomach, or, better, he supported them on the temples and then lowered them to begin again. He continued in this way while varying the movements (always from above to below) from time to time. (p. 60)

Noizet became acquainted with Bertrand through the latter's public lectures.

Born in 1795, Bertrand offered a public course in magnetism early in his career and in 1823 published *Traité du Somnambulisme* in which he reiterated some of the older mesmeric ideas: (a) the presence of life forces unites all animal bodies in the world and (b) somnambulism is only one of the crises of animal magnetism. He outlined four types of somnambulism: (a) essential, which is seen in individuals with a particular nervous predisposition; (b) symptomatic, which occurs as a symptom of certain diseases; (c) ecstatic, such as occurs in moral or religious ecstasies; and (d) artificial, which is seen in animal magnetism. However, through a number of experiments, he arrived at the conclusion that the behavior of somnambulism was not brought about by the redistribution of a magnetic fluid, but by the will and the *suggestions* of the operator. It was with the latter idea that Bertrand established himself as the forerunner of the notions of Braid (Braid was accused of being ignorant of these ideas; see Braid, 1843/1976.), Liébeault, Bernheim, and the entire Nancy School.

Bertrand's techniques were those of his time, the mesmeric, magnetising passes. In his 1826 treatise, *Le Magnetisms Animal en France,* he noted that his patients saw the fluid emanating from his fingers when he magnetised them. He also reported effects obtained through the use of magnetised objects (handkerchiefs, gloves, pieces of money) in much the same way as others before and after him. Some of his patients even reported that the water, which he supposedly had magnetized, had a distinctive and different taste.

It was partially through an experiment he performed using a magnetized letter that he established the basic groundwork for overthrowing the magnetic fluid hypothesis. Three letters were sent to a patient, one magnetized by Bertrand, one not magnetized, and one forged in Bertrand's hand by a friend of Bertrand. All three induced a somnambulistic trance in the patient when held against his body. Suggestion of magnetism, rather than magnetism itself, seemed to be the crucial factor. Unfortunately, Bertrand died in his middle thirties (1831); otherwise, he might have established a greater data base for his new proposals.

Alphonse A. Teste

Teste was another of the forgotten but important individuals (along with Du Potet, Lafontaine, and Durand de Gros) in the history of hypnosis, hypnotic induction, and psychiatric treatment in general (Ellenberger, 1970). Born in Gray on April 16, 1814, Alphonse Teste received his doctorate in July, 1837. His books included a number of treatises on magnetism and on homeopathic medicine. His first book was on the causes, treatment, and rationale of gout. (*Dictionnaire Universal,* 1880, p. 1729)

Teste's techniques are chronicled in his *Practical Manual of Animal Magnetism.* His basic technique was that of Deleuze, which he reproduced in its entirety; however, he took issue with his predecessor on some points. He felt, for example, that the passes along the spine were unnecessary, as was the actual contact of the hands of the operator on the head and epigastrium. The latter, in fact, he felt were a distraction and added "nothing to the efficacy of the process" (Teste, 1840/1843, p. 153). He advised magnetisers against using direct touch, not only because of the questionable effectiveness of the procedure, but also "for the sake of seemliness." In this vein, then, he shared Deleuze's concern with the moral (Or was it immoral?) aura surrounding the work of a male operator with a female patient. He warned against the development of sexual and/or love relationships between the two (Ellenberger, 1970).

While he advocated Deleuze's basic technique as fundamental to beginning work with a new patient, he offered several other procedures that he reserved for subjects with whom he had worked already and who had demonstrated some facility in magnetism (somnambulism). The first was as follows:

> Most commonly, I stand up before the person I wish to magnetize, and even at a certain distance from the individual; after the few minutes of collecting one's self which should precede every experiment, I raise my hands to his forehead, and I direct my passes slowly from above, downwards, before the face, chest, and abdomen; only, each time I raise the hand, I take care to let my fingers fall so that their dorsal surface looks towards the magnetised person during my motion of ascent, and their palmar surface during the passes. This process is simple, probably too simple; so that I would not advise it to be adopted, except on persons already accustomed to magnetism, and susceptible of being readily set to sleep. (Teste, 1840/1843, p. 152)

Another technique he used was called "Magnetisation by the Head":

> You place yourself opposite the person you wish to magnetise, at first you make some long passes from above, downwards, in the direction of the arms, before the face, and along the axis of the body; after which, you extend your two hands some inches from the forehead and parietal regions, and you remain thus for some minutes. All the time the operation lasts you vary but little the position of your hands, content to carry them slowly to the right and left; then

to the occiput, so as to return them to the forehead, where you leave them for an indefinite time, that is, until the individual is asleep. Then you make passes on the knees and legs, *to attract the fluid* down, according to the expression of magnetisers. (Teste, 1840/1843, p. 154)

This procedure took approximately three minutes, and according to its author, had some potentially negative consequences: headache, "megrim," occasional "states of madness and delirium," "permanent paralysis," and "temporary catalepsies." Teste cautioned the reader lest he or she take magnetisation too lightly.

Brief descriptions of two other techniques were also contained in the *Practical Manual*. The first of these was "Magnetisation by means of the Look," which, he said, could only be used by an individual with "a sharp, penetrating look, and capable of long-continued fixedness" (Teste, 1840/1843, p. 157).

You place yourself opposite your subject; you direct him to look at you with all possible fixedness, whilst on your part you fix your eyes on him steadfastly. At first, some deep sighs will raise his chest; then his eyelids will twinkle, will become moistened with tears, will contract forcibly several times, and ultimately close. (Teste, 1840/1843, pp. 157–158)

The other procedure, called "Magnetisation by the mere Will," also depended on the patient being first trained in the "Magnetisation by the Head" technique and consisted simply in the operator "willing" the patient into a magnetized condition during conversation. This process also took only three minutes, by the account offered by M. Husson as he observed the work of Du Potet.

Teste also mentioned yet another procedure that gained currency in both Britain and India about the same time as his book was published—magnetizing through insufflation. According to his account, the breath was usually directed at the head or, occasionally, to a diseased part of the body. Apparently, this too was a technique only to be used with the previously initiated patient. As we will see below, both Elliotson in London and Esdaile in India used blowing on patients as part of the ritual of induction. Braid, curiously enough, blew on his patients' eyes *to arouse* them from the hypnotic condition. Scoresby also mentions "demesmerizing patients by breathing, or blowing softly, on the upper part of the face, over the eyes" (Scoresby, 1849, p. 38).

The length of the early sessions was to have been at least 20 minutes, longer if necessary, and carried on for eight consecutive days. The sittings were to be scheduled at the same hour of each day to facilitate the process on each successive day. Mental preparation also was important; the operator must think only of the results he wished to attain, while the patient must think of nothing. If the patient found the induction disturbing in any way, the operator was to move some distance away, retard the movement of the passes, and reduce the action of his will. Termination of the magnetized condition was by "revulsive passes on the lower extremities."

Teste also seems to have anticipated a practice used by practitioners of the present century—using a patient (somnambule in Teste's operations) to magnetize another patient. Teste actually derived the idea of using one patient with another from *Lettre d'un Médecin étranger à M. Deleuze* (Teste, 1840/1843, p. 165), and describes the procedure as a contest of will and physical power in which one patient eventually dominates the other in a positive therapeutic manner. More recently, Tart (1967) described a similar technique he called mutual hypnosis. Plapp (1976) took the idea of mutual induction a step farther in his description of a case in which the patient, a 17-year-old disturbed adolescent, hypnotized the therapist.

Teste's *Practical Manual* indicates an individual who was concerned about the welfare of his patients when they entered or were in a magnetized condition. He advised caution, a gentle attitude, and kindness toward the patient. More important, his writing reflects yet another anticipation of the practices "developed" in this century, more specifically, in the last three or four decades—the idea of making the patient, rather than the practitioner or the disorder, the focus and center of the treatment process. This orientation is evident in the following:

> When you have reason to suppose that your patient is sufficiently magnetised, wait some minutes before you address a word to him. At length speak to him, but in a subdued voice, with gentleness and kindness; and if he does not answer the question you put to him, allow some minutes to elapse before you repeat it. Then make yourself acquainted with the state of his health, as also with any thing which may annoy him, or with whatever he might wish for in order to be better. If he feel [sic] pain in any part, carry your hand to this part, make some passes there, and slight frictions, with the sincere desire of removing the pain, and you almost invariably succeed. In case he complain [sic] of heat, allow him some fresh, cool air. Ask him how long he wishes to be allowed to sleep; and in case of any experiment for purposes of demonstration, whether he consents to submit to this experiment, if it will not distress him; and when he shall have given his assent, what will be the precise moment when it is to be tried. Lastly, an obligation which charity imposes on you towards him is to interrogate him regarding his health the next day and the following days, and to take a note, if he is to be sick, of the prescriptions which he will suggest after your questions. (Teste, 1840/1843, pp. 167–168)

Furthermore, he warns against unduly fatiguing the patient and the avoidance of "the ridiculous whims of the by-standers, who are so fond of tricks and jugglery" (Teste, 1840/1843, p. 168). What is perhaps even more interesting is Teste's concern with the manner of speaking to the patient. He urges discretion, politeness, and precision in the verbal suggestions offered to the patient. He is careful to avoid the sound of a command, couching, instead, his suggestions indirectly with such phrases as "I would like you to. . . ." Most certainly, this is one of the early notations of the indirect suggestion that underplays demand or command characteristics in favor of the client-centered orientation we will see so markedly in the work of Milton Erickson.

Jules Denis de Sennevoy (Baron J. Du Potet)

According to one translator, Lee (see Du Potet, 1852/1927), the Baron Du Potet was the fourth in a succession line from Mesmer to de Puységur to Deleuze. "Neither a profound nor original thinker" (Du Potet, 1852/1927, p. 50), Du Potet carried forth the techniques of Mesmer and seemed to bask in the same sort of public notoriety, his flare for the dramatic being widespread throughout France and Britain.

Jules Denis de Sennevoy, Baron Du Potet, was born April 12, 1796 in La Chapelle (Commune of Yonne, Department of Sennevoy) and died July 1, 1881 in Paris. During his 85 years he produced at least eight books on Magnetism, the "Journal du Magnétisme" (from 1845 to 1861), and gave numerous public and private demonstrations and treatments. Erdan described him as animal magnetism's "real high priest—the fourth pontiff of the animal 'fluid'. He has something of Mesmer's nature without his ability" (Du Potet, 1852/1927, p. 47). According to this critic. Du Potet gave public seances at a restaurant, Provençal Brothers, near the Palais Royal. Other writers were less critical and considered him remarkable for his intuitive powers (Constant, 1913).

His early education history was one of avoidance of the established studies and academies. He became aware of mesmerism in 1815 and studied for five years with de Puységur, the Abbé Faria, and Deleuze. By 1820 he was working with the sick at Hotel Dieu, and in 1826 opened a school in magnetism, which was attended by many of the medical men of his time. In 1828, with the help of Elliotson, he began treating patients at the North London Hospital, and when this was disallowed by the hospital administration, continued practicing at his home, 20 Wigmore Street. He returned to France in the 1840s, where he lectured at Rheims, Bordeaux, Montpellier, and Beziers (Du Potet, 1852/1927) and produced a number of his books. At the age of 84, one year before his death, he was still attending patients, this time in Nice. He is buried in Montmartre.

Du Potet's technique clearly following that of Mesmer although his interpretations of the effectiveness of the magnetic fluid differed somewhat from the latter's. From him the passes were considered mechanical and not crucial to the effectiveness of the treatment. What was considered important was the will and intention, conveyed through the will, of the operator. When he did use passes, which he considered "the mechanical equivalent of the will" (Du Potet, 1852/1927, p. 53), they were as follows:

The Agent places four fingers of both hands on his shoulders, runs his thumbs along the inside of the shoulder-blades, letting his fingers follow loosely. The thumbs rest a moment or two under the edge of the scapula, about one inch from the end. When the Patient falls back, the Agent reverses the passes. The Patient sits with knees uncovered, right hand on knee and left hand holding a disc at which he must gaze steadily. (Du Potet, 1852/1927, p. 144).

It was the use of another disc for eye-fixation for which Du Potet became best known. He called the disc the "Magic Mirror," a totally blackened circle approximately five inches in diameter, drawn on the floor with a piece of charcoal. Constant (1913) likened Du Potet's use of the circle to the hydromancy of Cagliostro, in which the subject stared at water to achieve a condition of trance. In Du Potet's technique the subject approached the circle and stared at it until he or she began to hallucinate images within the circle and entered a condition which sounds much like the crisis of Mesmer's induction. The operator stood aside during the whole process and intervened only if the condition of the subject appeared to be out of hand. As at Mesmer's *baquet*, the subject was often removed to another room to fully recover from the experience. Du Potet described one such episode:

A man of twenty-five, full of self-confidence, and entirely sceptical about magic, approaches and observes the disc. . . . He lowers his head . . . becomes restless, looks around the black circle, never losing sight of it. He tends still further, arises himself, retreats a few steps, advances again, puckers his eyelids, becomes melancholy, and breathes loudly. He is beginning to see images in the "Mirror." His emotions, inimitable movements, sighs, tears, despair, and fury all depict the agitation in his soul. Before him are unfolded a series of events represented figuratively by the marks he notices. Sadness and joy follow one another in proportion as some part of the future passes before his eyes. Soon he becomes almost delirious with transport: he tries to seize the "Mirror," fixing a terrified look upon it, then kicks it with his feet until the dust rises. The operator rises to put an end to the scene: the subject seizes him forcibly by the head, but a few affectionate words, with magnetic passes, appease and pacify him: the disordered vital forces return to their proper place. In a neighbouring room he comes to his senses. For some time he feels a heaviness in the upper part of the head, which passes away in half an hour. He is still vague, preoccupied, and can remember nothing. (Du Potet, 1852/1927, pp. 70–71).

In his journal (*Journal du Magnétisme,* 1849–1851), Du Potet described the general trappings of his induction technique:

Magic Mirror

I trace a disc with charcoal on the floor, with magnetic intention. It must be covered over until proceedings are ready to commence. Smells and other sensations must be avoided. The operator should be prompt, alert, and ready for emergencies; he should also avoid contact with strangers. The subject should be left plenty of space. An opaque lid or cover should be at hand for placing over the Symbol (the disc in this case), if the emotions aroused are too violent. The seer will not always behold pleasant visions, and the operator must be calm and self-contained. (Du Potet, 1852/1927, p. 79)

Finally, in his description of a variation on the "magic mirror" technique, Du Potet in fact designates the condition induced in the subject as a "crisis," but one far more dangerous, in his view, than that achieved by Mesmer's patients. De Puységur's concern about the possible detrimental effects of the mesmeric crisis appears to have been realized by Du Potet in the latter's concern with the possible demise of subjects left too long in the mirror-induced condition.

Draw a circle about four or five feet wide without any pause or hesitation, yet slowly and reflectively, so as to afford time for your nervous influence to flow forth into it: therein lies the first link of your work. Then trace another and smaller circle about the size of a plate in the centre of the first with the same precautions. Take in your right hand some earth or crushed charcoal (preferably of a deep colour). Hold it for some moments and give all your being a sort of vibration which I can only compare to what one observes, without understanding it, in an animal at the moment when it is trying to get rid of superfluous electricity. Then lay the dust or charcoal in the centre of the smaller circle: pass your hand several times lineally over this surface: finger the dust so as to extend and unify it. Withdraw: and let your subject pass over the outer circle without breaking it. Tell him to gaze fixedly at the inner circle, watch him yourself, at the same time having an eye on that circle. When he shows the least sign of nervous disturbance, be ready to support him, yet leaving him freedom to move, and only assisting him thus. Listen to what he says, remember his words, interrogate him: but if he falls, as almost always happens, break both circles with your feet and hands, unless you want to see him nearly die. Five or six minutes should suffice: the operation begins and the precursory signs of the crisis appear: I can only describe what happens in this way. (Du Potet, 1852/1927, pp. 120–121)

Charles Lafontaine

Born in 1803, Charles Lafontaine belonged to an ancient and aristocratic French family. Shunning work as an administrator with his father, Lafontaine journeyed to Paris to become an actor. In the course of pursuing this occupation, he learned the skill of magnetizing and made it his life's work. He traveled throughout France giving stage performances of his "powers," curing the blind, deaf, and lame, and even assisting another actor in the perfection and presentation of a role through magnetism. (Erickson was not the first to aid a performer through hypnotic—mesmeric, magnetic—techniques.) According to De Courmelles (1819), Lafontaine's demonstrations were not confined to human subjects. In Paris, "he reduced cats, dogs, squirrels, and lions to such complete insensibility that they felt neither pricks nor blows. He could throw lizards into a sleep that would last several days" (De Courmelles, 1819; see Tinterow, 1970, p. 151).

In 1841 Lafontaine journeyed to London, lecturing there and in the provinces. On November 13, 1841 he gave a demonstration in Manchester. In the audience was a curious young surgeon by the name of James Braid.

> The first exhibition of the kind I ever had an opportunity of attending, was one of M. Lafontaine's conversazione, on the 13th November 1841. That night I saw nothing to diminish, but rather to confirm, my previous prejudices. At the next conversazione, six nights afterwards, *one* fact, the inability of a patient to *open his eyelids,* arrested my attention. I considered that to be a *real phenomenon,* and was anxious to discover the physiological cause of it. Next night, I watched this case when again operated on, with intense interest, and before the termination of the experiment, felt assured I had discovered its cause, but considered it prudent not to announce my opinion publicly, until I had an opportunity of testing its accuracy, by experiments and observations in private. (Braid, 1843/1976, p. 16)

Thus was Braid's introduction to magnetism (mesmerism). He, like a number of the better known professionals today, had been introduced to the topic through a stage performer. However, the teacher (Lafontaine) was not pleased to have so observant a pupil.

> Doctor Braid, after having attended my meetings and seeing the effects that I was producing, wanted also to make a name for himself, and to become the creator of a new system, of a new discovery. Soon he began to positively magnetize himself, while still denying magnetism and attributing always to different causes the effects that he was producing with the help of magnetism itself. (Lafontaine, 1860, p. 262; see also Tinterow, 1970, p. 398)

Lafontaine's technique owed much to that of Deleuze. It was a combination of eye-fixation and mesmeric passes from the head downward, commencing with the operator and subject facing one another, the former holding onto the thumbs of the latter. Here is a description in Lafontaine's own words:

> Before beginning the process, it is necessary to have the persons present sit down and keep quiet, because it is essential that during the process the magnetisee and mesmerizer not be distracted. One carefully observes all the sensations which could be depicted on the face of the magnetisee.

> The mesmerizer, in the beginning, will concentrate on himself and will reunite his entire will on a single idea, the one acting on the subject.

> (1) The patient and the mesmerizer will sit facing one another, the subject's knees below those of the mesmerizer, but without touching them, the mesmerizer on a higher raised seat, in order to be able to reach easily and without

fatigue the top of the subject's head; then he will touch the tips of the patient's thumbs with the tips of his own without shaking them; this thumb contact will put the brain of the mesmerizer in direct contact with the brain of the subject; the nerve fibers of this one forming an extension to the mesmerizer's nerves will serve as a conductor of the fluid, and rendering quicker and more complete the invasion of the patient's nervous system.

(2) The mesmerizer will fix his eyes on those of the subject, who will try his hardest to look at him; he will continue thus for 15–20 minutes. It is probable that during this time the subject's pupils will contract or will dilate in a manner beyond measure and that his eyelids will lower themselves to no longer rise again despite his efforts.

(3) After the closing of the eyes, the mesmerizer will continue to hold the thumbs until the moment when the eye no longer will roll under the eyelids and when swallowing no longer occurs; then he can let go of the thumb and slowly pulling away his hands in closing them, he raises them to each side of the patient until reaching the top of his head; then he lays his hands on and above the brain of the subject and he leaves them there for 10–15 seconds; then he passes them down slowly over the ears and over the length of the arms until the end of the fingertips.

(4) He will make 8–10 similar passes; each one lasting close to a minute.

(5) After having placed his hands in the same manner, he will pass them down in front of the face, the chest and all the bust, stopping from time to time at the top of the epigastrium, in presenting the point of the fingers. He will continue thus for $\frac{1}{2}$ hour or an hour.

(6) The layings on and the passes will be made some thumb's length of distance, without touching. Each time that the mesmerizer will raise his hands, they will be closed; he will make the pass slowly, from the side and not facing the subject, and this in order not to produce a coming and going in the circulation which could provoke congestion of the brain if acted on face on.

(7) The mesmerizer will also make a few passes by laying his hands above the cerebellum and by moving them down behind the ears and the shoulders to come back on the arms.

(8) From the beginning until the end of the process, he will only concern himself with what he wants to produce in order that by the concentration of his will, he provokes the emission of fluid and transmits it to the subject. (Lafontaine, 1860, pp. 62–64).

Thus we see that Lafontaine continued the traditions of eye-fixation, physical contact, and the mesmeric passes. He considered the physical contact— the holding of the thumbs—to be the most crucial part of the induction method.

By the method that we have indicated, we are demanding the preliminary contact of the thumbs, contrary to several mesmerizers who we recognize know how to do it; but we insist even more of force and of reason on this process, that the action by the contact of thumbs is more effective and more complete, that the invasion of the nervous system is more direct, more interior, since it is the nerves of the subject which serve as conductors to the vital fluid, until the nervous centers are put in exact rapport by this way with those of the mesmerizer. (Lafontaine, 1860, p. 67)

Thumb-holding was also an integral part of the attainment of general calm and well-being by the patient.

To obtain *well-being and calm* [italics added], it is necessary to take the thumbs, look into eyes of the patient, and when they are closed or when they are still open but when the pupil is dilated or strongly contracted, it is necessary to take the subject's hands into his own and to stay thus for a quarter of an hour, an hour even. (Lafontaine, 1860, p. 68)

He also provided a description of the appearance of the mesmerized subject.

The mesmerizer will recognize that magnetic sleep shows a cadaverous impassiveness from or on the face and the total lack of swallowing.

After having thus operated for a certain time, if the subject appears deep in sleep, the mesmerizer will be able to address him with several questions. (Lafontaine, 1860, p. 64)

And he offered specific instructions for achieving specific ends.

Perspiration [italics added] is obtained by holding the thumbs and by looking in the same manner, then by placing one hand on the stomach and the other on the back between the two shoulders.

The *spasms* [italics added] are produced by placing pointed fingers in front of the stomach, after having taken the thumbs and stared into the eyes.

Paralysis [italics added] and partial insensitivity are obtained by making long passes over a limb after having held the thumbs and stared, until the eyes of the subject are closed.

To produce *partial catalepsy* [italics added], it is necessary, after having held the thumbs and stared, to touch the extensor muscle of the limb, the deltoid, for example, until the moment when one will feel a light contraction which will announce that the muscle is stiffening, then make several passes over this limb, by putting a lot of action there.

Entire paralysis [italics added]—catalepsy and insensitivity are only obtained by acting stronger and longer. Sometimes, however, one sees them appear only a few minutes, but this is very rare and it is necessary that this be on subjects whose nervous system is very impressionable to magnetic action.

It is necessary in order to obtain *attraction* [italics added] to thrust with force on the head and on the shoulders, a jet of fluid by presenting the fingers, then closing them firmly and bring them together to yourself, as if they were holding strings by which your body would be directed toward the subject's and that you would draw back into yourself. Sometimes it is the epigastrium that it is necessary to attack.

One proceeds, for sleep, like it is indicated above.

To produce sleep *at distance* [italics added], one must concentrate strongly on oneself, in order that the emission of the fluid develops with violence and in a continuous manner. One can present the fingers on the side of the subject, or can cross the arms; the fluid being emitted by the entire body, is going to strike the subject on whichever side you lead it.

For the *paralysis of the senses* [italics added] it suffices to strongly charge the sense that you want to paralyze.

For the *localisation of the sensitivity* [italics added], charge strongly by passes over the limb with which you want to experiment, and when you will have produced the insensitivity, disengage a certain part of this limb by passes made briskly. You will have the sensitivity there where you wanted it.

When you have provoked sleep, if you want to obtain *somnambulism* [italics added], it will be necessary to charge the brain a little by placing the hands above it for 1–2 minutes, making several passes, then placing one hand on the stomach while the other makes passes from time to time. *Lucidity* [italics added] or clairvoyance is obtained in the same manner, by adding passes from the cerebellum to the eyes, and vice versa. *Ecstasy* [italics added] is obtained by making light passes over the organ phrenologically called religiosity. (Lafontaine, 1860, pp. 69–70)

Finally, before reporting Lafontaine's technique for de-mesmerizing the patient, it is worth noting that water also played a role—though small—in part of his procedure. When the mesmerizer found it difficult to awaken the patient, he was instructed to "regain all his calm" and "plunge his hands in fresh water" (p. 66) after which renewed passes to wake up were given.
De-mesmerization was accomplished in the following manner.

When the mesmerizer would like to wake up, he will make several passes from shoulders to feet, in order to disengage the head by dragging the fluid down; then by putting a little muscular force there he will make some long passes briskly in front of the eyes and the face, by passing them down from the side until the subject gives the sign that he is coming out of it; then he will continue the same passes in front of the chest and the entire body; then the subject should be waken up, but not yet in his normal state. The mesmerizer will make a cold insufflation on the eyes; he will touch the eyebrows from their point of origin in order to disengage the eyes entirely; finally, it will be necessary to continue the same passes, without stopping, over the entire body until the point where the subject will be completely disengaged. The mesmerizer will be able also to make several transversal passes in front of the stomach. (Lafontaine, 1860, pp. 64–65)

ENGLAND

As indicated in the preceding sections, both Du Potet and Lafontaine receive credit for carrying mesmerism (magnetism) to England, the former having a brief association with John Elliotson and the latter a brief, but as we have seen, not too cordial association with James Braid.

John Elliotson

Although we have few verbatim descriptions of the induction techniques used by him, no history of any aspect of hypnosis would be complete without the mention of John Elliotson. His tempestuous involvement with mesmerism was indicative of his general orientation toward the future. To him the future was now, and he felt little constraint of past dictums and traditions in his constant search for new, innovative techniques to apply to his suffering patients. According to various histories (Bramwell, 1903; Goldsmith, 1934; Marks, 1947; Pattie, 1967; Robinson, 1977; Tinterow, 1970), Elliotson has been credited with "the employment of quinine in heroic doses, the recognition of the value of iodide of potassium, the use of prussic acid in vomiting, iron in chorea, sulphate of copper in diarrhoea, [and] the employment of creosote" (Bramwell, 1903, p. 5). He also pointed out the influence of posture on heart sounds and was one of the first in England to make use of Laennec's stethoscope. It was not, therefore, unusual that once he became aware of mesmeric techniques that he used them as well.

Elliotson was born in 1791, received his M.D. at Edinburgh, and, after continued study abroad and at Cambridge, settled as physician to St. Thomas' Hospital until, in 1831, he became Professor of the Practice of Medicine at University College. Here his innovative nature continued to make itself felt, for the hospital associated with the medical school (then University of London) was developed (in 1834) mainly through his insistence and vision, which recognized the inefficiency of a medical school without an associated teaching hospital. It was from this same college and hospital that he resigned his appointments when in 1838 the Council of University College ordered the cessation of "the practice of mesmerism or animal magnetism in future within the Hospital" (Bramwell, 1903, p. 7).

Elliotson had begun his work with mesmerism in 1837 (Elliotson, 1843d), after observing and working with Du Potet during his brief visit to London, and for this reason Du Potet received credit for introducing Elliotson to mesmerism. Actually, Elliotson's interest was first aroused by Richard Chenevix, FRS, through his published papers in the *London Medical and*

Physical Journal in 1829, one of which was titled "On Mesmerism, Improperly Denominated Animal Magnetism" (Elliotson, 1843d). He also published in *Edinburgh Review* in 1819.

Richard Chenevix

Although an Irishman by birth, Chenevix lived in Paris and, according to Elliotson (1843d), is credited with introducing mesmerism to England in 1828. However, by his own admission he was a devout nonbeliever, in fact, even a scoffer of mesmerism. On numerous occasions, in Rotterdam in 1797, in Germany in 1803 and 1804, he refused to attend demonstrations of mesmerism. Finally, after 19 years of avoidance, he agreed to observe the technique and was so taken by the results and the magnetizer himself that he became the latter's student: "The Abbé Faria offered every means to dispel my remaining doubts, and gave me all necessary instructions to obtain total conviction from experiments of my own. I most zealously attended his labours, public and private" (Elliotson, 1843d, p. 69). Thus an Irishman living in France became the student of Abbé Faria and later brought mesmerism to England just two years before his (Chenevix) death in 1830. In the intervening year (1829) he worked in Dublin at the Hospital of Incurables.

Chenevix's technique appears to have relied heavily on the mesmeric passes of that time and described in several instances above. The hand passes were used for both mesmerizing and curing more than 160 cases. Like his predecessors and contemporaries, he also used magnetized water in the treatment process. Hand passes were always downward to mesmerize and transverse to de-mesmerize. Thus the "laying-on-of-hands" persisted as a dominant method of mesmerizing, of directing and concentrating the vital force or magnetic fluid. Neither eye-fixation nor verbal induction had gained preeminence by the 1830s, even though Faria was Chenevix's mentor.

Returning to Elliotson again, we do not find him actually practicing mesmerism until after his encounter with Du Potet in 1837. Du Potet had come to London to profit from "bringing" mesmerism to the island empire. Although he had an introduction to the Middlesex Hospital, his experiments were not well received and it was not until he became acquainted with Elliotson that he practiced more freely and with more effectiveness. Thus was Elliotson launched on the phase of his career that afforded him yet another place in history, but virtually cost him his livelihood.

Of Elliotson's actual induction techniques little is written, and we must rely for our understanding of his procedures on remarks contained in his many papers of clinical applications. In his "Cases of Cures by Mesmerism" (1843b) we find numerous references to longitudinal hand passes being made before the patient at a short distance. He speaks of a "gentle waving of the hand before his face," and "I mesmerized him by vertical passes before his face for half an hour" (Elliotson, 1843b, p. 200). The time and effort required by this technique is illustrated in the following: "I mesmerized her energetically for three quarters of an hour, . . . and . . . I mesmerized her on the first occasion for half an hour.'' Although the time alloted for the process was normally between one-half and two hours, he does note elsewhere: ''Accordingly I commenced manipulating, and to my surprise *in about two minutes,* the body became relaxed, and he sunk into a quiet and mesmeric sleep.'' (Elliotson, 1843b, p. 177).

De-mesmerism was accomplished (always by the same person who had induced the condition) by raising one or both eyelids, blowing on the exposed eyeball, blowing in the face (see Braid and Esdaile below), or by transverse passes with the ends of the fingers or thumbs. Curiously enough, Thomas Chandler, Elliotson's medical attendant and former pupil, used transverse passes with a single finger to *induce,* rather than to remove, the condition.

The Zoist

In 1843 Elliotson founded *The Zoist: A Journal of Cerebral Physiology and Mesmerism and their Applications to Human Welfare.* Thomas Wakley, then editor of the powerful and respected *The Lancet,* denied Elliotson (and others) publication of his experiments and findings regarding mesmerism and carried on a continuing and vitriolic campaign against Elliotson personally and mesmerism as a general technique. *The Zoist,* then, became mesmerism's main English language forum to which Elliotson and Esdaile (who was also denied access to the ''respected'' journals) were heavy contributors.

The Zoist presented a strange mixture of mesmerism, phrenology, cerebral organs, odylic force, and Gall's theories. In fact, Elliotson claimed that Gall practiced mesmerism, using the following technique. Gall ''placed his hand upon his [the patient's] forehead, and walking backwards and forwards several times, with his fingers over the hairy part of the front of his head, he remarked a gentle warmth, like a vapor, between his hand the upper part of his cranium; he felt a heat ascend towards his shoulders and cheeks, heat in his head, and chilliness in his loins'' (Elliotson, 1843a, p. 233). The patient indicated that his eyes were painful, his tongue inarticulate, and that he had a feeling of general weakness. Later Elliotson pointed out that Gall had instructed that ''passes must be made near particular parts, as an arm or a leg, in certain directions, with or without contact; particular parts must be pointed at; steadily looked at; touched or breathed upon'' (Elliotson, 1843a, p. 235).

W. J. Tubbs of Upwell Isle, Cambridgeshire, reported two techniques in his ''Cases of Cures of Diseases by Mesmerism.'' In the first he mesmerized the patient ''by [holding] the thumbs, and afterwards making passes from the vertex downwards.'' (Tubbs, 1844a, p. 461). He de-mesmerized the patient by blowing on him.

His second method is of interest on two counts. In the first place, he used an eye-fixation technique by pointing two fingers at the patient's eyes. In the second place, not only was an eye-fixation technique used, and elaborated on, but the induction was carried out by what would today be called a "hypno-technician"! Tubbs gave the following description of the technique used by Mrs. Jerry, his 65-year-old housekeeper: "Suspending her watch in the centre of her own chest, she took hold of the girl's two thumbs and desired her to fix her eyes on the watch" (Tubbs, 1844b, p. 127). Here, then is a combination of elements from Deleuze (holding the thumbs) and Braid (fixing vision on a bright object). With respect to using his housekeeper as a technician, Tubbs followed in the steps taken by Deleuze and anticipating the work of some contemporary practitioners.

The patient discussed above was de-mesmerized by outward pressure on the eyes with the thumb. Curiously, this same gentleman used a similar technique to *induce* mesmerism also: "I closed the lids, and pressed with each fore-finger upon the ball of the eyes" (Tubbs, 1844c, p. 265). It would almost seem as if mesmerism could be achieved by any means whatsoever so long as the method was distinguishable from what had previously been happening to the patient.

Elliotson, himself, reported using Tubbs' pointing technique in one article (Elliotson, 1844b). Later, he also advocated using the extended thumb, first and middle fingers as a means of influencing the patient. By 1846 he had combined eye-fixation and passes:

> She was placed in an easy chair, and I made very slow passes with one hand from opposite her forehead to opposite her chest, occasionally pointing my fingers without movement before her eyes instead, looking at her intently, and she looking as much as possible at me, for five and thirty minutes. (Elliotson, 1846, p. 345)

A number of the articles in *The Zoist* were concerned with identifying criminal personality variables through palpation of bumps on the skull and facial physiognomy. Thus much of which Elliotson chose (as editor) to publish turned out to be misdirected beliefs without empirical base, much the same as his contemporary detractors claimed of mesmerism. But it is in those portions of the 13 years of *The Zoist* (Publication ceased in 1856.) that we find the continuing history of the use of magnetized water, as well as magnetized objects and various metallic objects, to effect change and cure in patients.

Elliotson and the authors whose works appeared in *The Zoist* continued the ancient tradition of using specially prepared water (magnetized, mesmerized) in their techniques. Elliotson (1844a) reported the use of mesmerized water to stiffen parts of the body (which could later be relaxed through transverse passes, breathing on the patient, or touching the stiffened part). The water was mesmerized by blowing on it, the same method some used for mesmerizing patients and others used for de-mesmerizing patients. Others (e.g., DeM., 1853), however, mesmerized water by pointing their fingers at its surface.

Both S.E. DeM. (1853) and the Reverend *Jeffery Ekins* (1853, 1854) enlightened the readers on the appearance of mesmerized water. The former reported that the streams of light, which emanated from the mesmerizer's fingertips as he magnetized the water, fell to the bottom of the water, covering the entire bottom surface. After a short period, the light rose to the upper surface giving a glow to the entire volume. Then "a movement like boiling or the motion of the waves of the sea" (DeM., 1853, p. 426) took place. These same phenomena were attested to by Ekins on two occasions, except that he described the light effect as "a nebulous form like an inverted cone [that] slowly descended from the surface of the water towards the bottom of the glass" (Ekins, 1853, p. 85). He described the motion as "undulating."

In 1852 Elliotson outlined a slightly different use of water during the mesmeric process, which had been communicated to him by "a lady." Mesmerizers were instructed to keep a basin of unsoaped water handy when treating diseases, in which the hands were to be washed between passes that were in contact with the patient. The frequency of the washing was determined by the virulence of the disease being treated. The reason for so doing was because the flinging of the hands outwardly after a pass (see Deleuze above) did not eliminate all of the disease and it could thus be transferred into the basin of water where it sank to the bottom. Aside from making a basic assumption regarding the molecular weight of bacteria and viruses, this technique did recognize that contagion could be controlled through cleanliness, although this reasoning was never mentioned in the article.

Finally, *Hazard* (1849) described an elaborate mechanism for inducing mesmerism, which involved water, crystallized carbonate of lime, and brass rods, wires, and chains. The crystals were in double hexatetrahedral pyramids and covered with water. A brass wire was inserted into the crystal and another brass rod was placed at right angles to the wire above the water and below the cover of the container. Chains from the cover were attached to the hands of the patient who entered a "sleep within a few minutes." Hazard, whose name may have been more prophetic than denotational, told of a man who grabbed "my powerful electrical machine" and could not let go until Hazard *blew on it* (apparently de-mesmerizing the machine in this case).

The last author also reported using magnets suspended from a brass rod, from which hung an iron chain. The patient held the chain and became rigid and comatose. Elliotson, himself, was quite fascinated by the use of magnets and various metals in the treatment of patients. Both of these interests gained some strength from his reading in the work of Baron von Reichenbach and the latter's proposed Odic Force. In fact, as time went on, Elliotson published increasing amounts of material about von Reichenbach's work. The Baron used iron bar magnets that were $10\frac{1}{2}$ in. long, $1\frac{1}{2}$ in. broad, $2\frac{1}{4}$ in. deep, and weighed 19 lbs. The patient placed his or her hand on the magnet and was induced into a mesmeric state resembling sleep. Thus did iron (the magic metal of the Druids and other ancients) retain its preeminence as a special tool for the mesmerist.

Not only did the iron magnet produce mesmerism, but it was also perceived as glowing by those individuals who were particularly sensative to its

Odyle influence. Although the light was described as being very faint, it was reported by "sensatives" in daylight as well as at night. The north pole was blue and the south red, the "cool-and-hot" colors in present-day interpretive psychology. Curiously enough, we find that the colors blue and red are at opposite poles in present-day spiritualistic thinking in South Wales (a land not unknown to the Druids of ancient times), where individuals are considered to have "auras" of different colors (Skultans, 1974). Red is considered a bad aura, while blue, white, and purple are "good" auras. In fact, blue is thought to be a "healing color" and is especially to be desired. It would seem then that Major Buckley's clairvoyant's ability to see blue surrounding his face (see below) was not arbitrary, but, rather, another thread of historical continuity.

Reichenbach was not the only individual to report that certain of his patients perceived lights and colors emanating from the instruments of magnetism. Gregory (1909/1975) wrote of a Major Buckley that his subjects perceived a blue light around his face if they were "truely" capable of clairvoyance. The association of mesmerism with clairvoyance was quite in evidence in the middle 19th century, and *The Zoist* contained numerous references to these phenomena. What was unique about Buckley's technique was that he used passes downward from the patient's wrist to ascertain their susceptibility to mesmerism, and he made passes over *his own* face and chest to ascertain the patient's clairvoyant ability. With regard to the former, if he felt tingling and numbness while making the passes, he believed the patient to be susceptible. If the patient perceived a strong blue light in his face as he made the passes over himself, he or she was capable of clairvoyance without first being mesmerized. If, however, the light were absent or pale, the mesmeric sleep had to be first induced before clairvoyance could be achieved. Once achieved, the patient had "x-ray" vision and could see through boxes made transparent through the blue light. We will see that the ability to see through objects, whether to read materials contained therein or to diagnose illnesses, was also being reported by practitioners in America during this same period (see Chapter 4).

Returning now to special qualities attributed to various metals, Elliotson (1843d) reported that iron could relax the spasmic effects of mesmerized gold and silver. The precious metals caused patients' hands to close when stroked on the palm; iron abolished the effect.

In 1844(a) Elliotson reiterated the claim that gold (silver also) was especially good for stiffening parts of the body by making longitudinal passes with such a metal object. Two years later copper made its entry into the arena of special metals yielding special powers. Again it was through von Reichenbach's researches that we receive a description of the copper instrument—Should we call it a wand, as in ancient times?—used to produce those sensations of pleasure and warmth so often associated with the mesmeric condition. A 9 in. square copper plate was mounted on the end of a 30 ft. long copper wire and held towards the sun or the moon to transmit the appropriate rays to the patient. Once again, we see the continuation of the concept of some sort of vital force, some magnetic fluid (à la Maxwell, Fludd, Paracelsus, Mesmer, and others), which links all objects in the universe. Even in the 1840s and 1850s, the search for ways to tap into this force was still strongly in evidence.

In all fairness, however, it must be added that not all of Elliotson's editorial energies went to searching out will-of-the-wisp techniques based on mystical or religious belief systems. Just as the use of the water basin above contained a strong element of practical medical practice, so did concerns about the "powers" of various metals have practical developments. For example, the recognition of the effects of copper, although couched in terms of its having great "odic force" (even when coated with silver), may easily be interpreted as a recognition of the poisoning effects of this metal (and lead as well) when the silver plating of plates and utensils wears thin. That this recognition did not escape Elliotson is noted in an 1853 article in *The Zoist* concerning itself with the relationship between the type of mine or foundary in which one was employed (e.g., copper, iron) and the incidents of fatalities during the cholera epidemics in France in 1832 and 1849 (Burq, 1853). Workers in factories or mines using metals such as copper, brass, bronze, iron, and English and German steel had far fewer fatalities per capita than those employed in other occupations (e.g., cobblers). Burq (1853) concluded that continual contact with all of the above metals prevented the individual from contracting cholera. Copper alone was touted as a curative agent, whether rubbed on the body or taken internally through inhalation. To this end he proposed a number of metallic objects such as rings, necklaces, tools for percussion and friction, and bathtubs to be used in either the prevention or cure of the disease. By bringing this perspective to the English-speaking professional world, Elliotson maintained the historical continuity of the importance of metals in medical practice and magnetism, continuing a legacy extant in modern medicine. (John Elliotson died on July 29, 1868.)

James Esdaile

Born in Perth, Scotland on February 6, 1808, Esdaile, like Elliotson before him, graduated from Edinburgh in 1830 and immediately took up practice in the Native Hospital at Hooghly through an appointment with the East India Company. On April 4, 1845 he first used mesmerism as surgical anesthesia and launched his fame as one of the most noteworthy practitioners of the 19th century.

Although he had difficulty at first convincing the medical profession and the government to acknowledge, much less accept, his findings, he faired much better than Elliotson in England, for he was eventually granted a small hospital in which to carry on his experimental treatments. At least one reason, no doubt, was that trances (induced by passes, laying-on-of-hands, and breathing on the patient) for the purposes of curing individuals of various ills were already a part of the Indian culture. The process of *jar-phoonk* practiced by the conjurors of the time, the *jadoowalla,* derived its name from the Hindustani *jarna,* meaning to stroke, and *phoonkna,* meaning to breathe. Esdaile described his observation of a woman cured of "epilepsy and insanity" by a *jadoowalla.* Following the passes, breathing, and laying-on-of-hands, "she soon became drowsy, and appeared to sleep." On follow-up, the woman's mother reported that "this man not only put her to sleep whenever he came, but made her speak during that sleep" (Esdaile, 1852/1975, pp. 54–55).

Bagnold (1848) also reported on induction techniques practiced in India at the time of Esdaile's birth, and we have already seen (see Chapter 1) that induction techniques date far back into Indian antiquity. In Bagnold's case he described the use of eye-fixation and passes coupled with the laying-on-of-hands. It seems that in 1808 he observed a "Vergraggey" undertake to cure an ill Hindoo female. He "seated the woman on the ground with her back and head against the wall; took from his long matted hair a string of large sandal-wood beads, which *he held up before her eyes, and directed her to look at; then made passes with it from her head downwards, occasionally stopping to breathe upon or lay his hand upon her chest.* She soon became drowsy and appeared to sleep; he then retired to a little distance, and sat counting the beads, but with *his eyes attentively fixed on her,* and muttering as if in prayer" (Bagnold, 1848, pp. 250–251). A half hour later the woman was aroused by the "Vergraggey" snapping his fingers and loudly calling: "Seetartam!"

Colonel Bagnold also noted that he, too, was not immune to the effects. He reported that whenever a particular Syed sat before him, counting his beads "with a peculiar *fixed look* [he] felt a strong tendency to sleep." (Bagnold, 1848, p. 252). Later (1827), when he was at Jidda, a Turkish Durveish offered to cure him of a nervous headache. The man's method was "*to make passes over the forehead* with an iron stile" (Bagnold, 1848, p. 252). Here again we note not only the use of hand passes, but also that of a wand made from iron, as we have found continually through history. Hand passes over the afflicted area were also used for the cure of snake and scorpion bites with, the Colonel reported, miraculous success.

Bagnold was apparently well traveled, because two years later (1850) he also reported on similar mesmeric activities in Africa in 1806. There, on the small island of Goree near Cape Verd on the western coast, he observed a native magician: "seating himself on the ground, with his knees drawn up to his chin, the patient's head resting against them, he applied his fingers on each side of the neck under the ears, and in the course of a few minutes the subject was in a profound state of coma. When called upon to restore him, he did so by pressing two or three times firmly on the sternum" (Bagnold, 1850, p. 444). Clearly, this technique sounds like the application of pressure to the carotid arteries until unconsciousness is achieved.

Finally, again in India, Bagnold reported a practice that sounded much like the use of a mesmerized individual to diagnose and prescribe for others, a style of clairvoyance that ensnared de Puységur, Elliotson, and others. Called "Receiving the God into the Body," it was practiced in western India in the 1820s. The individual receiving the rite was first washed (the use of water again), then seated in a circle with others. The priest "commenced a quick but *monotonous chant,* accompanied with the sound of small brass bells, cymbals, and tom-toms" (Bagnold, 1848, p. 253, italics added). The main individual went into convulsions and his body became rigid, after which he was asked questions concerning other's health, fortune, and so forth. Here, then, in this one ritual we see the continued use being made of monotonous verbalizations (as today), rhythmic musical beats (as in both verbalizations and voodoo practices today), and water as a central cleanser and giver of powers.

In his note accompanying Colonel Bagnold's letter, Elliotson (1848) told of two instances of the use of water in the East for curative and/or trance-inducing properties. R. Monckton Milnes reported watching a sheik administering mesmerized water to epileptic children (as well as making passes over their prostrate bodies with his foot). The second report was conveyed to Elliotson by Esdaile and illustrated not only the use of water in the process but also of a wooden wand. A famous magician from Bengal showed him his technique for assuaging pain:

> He sent for a brass pot full of water, and a twig with three or four leaves upon it, about a span long, and commenced muttering his charm, at arm's length from the patient. In a short time, he dipped his middle finger into the water, and flitted it with his thumb into the eyes, and then commenced to stroke the patient's body from crown to toe with a long drawing motion of the leaves, and I saw in a moment, what I have long suspected, that if these charmers ever do good by such means, it is by a pure mesmeric process. The knuckles almost touched the body, and he said, that he would continue the process for an hour, or longer, if necessary. (Elliotson, 1848, p. 255)

Esdaile's own induction technique used the same stroking and passes that had been in vogue in the early days of mesmerism and were in use in the country of his practice. The patient was placed on a bed in a darkened room with the operator seated behind the head of the bed. Then the passes began, initially without any verbal suggestion of sleep, but later with verbal urgings to go to sleep. Initially, Esdaile had tried the European technique of having the patient seated upright:

> I placed his knees between mine, and began to pass my hands slowly over his face, at the distance of an inch, and carried them down to the pit of his stomach. This was continued for half an hour before he was spoken to. . . . [Later] I . . . breathed on his head, and carried my hands from the back of his

head over his face and down the Epigastrium, where I pressed them united.
. . . The same process was persevered in, and in about an hour he began to
gape, said he must sleep, that his senses were gone. (Esdaile, 1846/1976, pp.
43–44)

Later, however, he felt that the supine position was superior, and as his
practices became more uniform, the following became his mode of mesmerizing (carried out most often by his native assistants):

Desire the patient to lie down, and compose himself to sleep, taking care, if
you wish to operate, that he does not know your intention; this object may be
gained by saying it is only a trial; for fear and expectation are destructive to the
physical impression required. Bring the crown of the patient's head to the end
of the bed, and seat yourself so as to be able to bring your face into contact
with him, and extend your hands to the pit of the stomach, when it is wished;
make the room dark, enjoin quiet, and then shutting your patient's eyes, begin
to pass both your hands, in the shape of claws, slowly, within an inch of the
surface, from the back of the head to the pit of the stomach; dwelling for
several minutes over the eyes, nose, and mouth, and then passing down each
side of the neck, go downwards to the pit of the stomach, keeping your hands
suspended there for some time. Repeat this process steadily for a quarter of an
hour, breathing gently on the head and eyes all the time. The longitudinal
passes may then be advantageously terminated, by placing both hands gently,
but firmly, on the pit of the stomach and sides. (Esdaile, 1846/1976, pp. 145–
146)

Once again, we see, in the parenthetical remark above, the use—in Esdaile's case, the rather extensive use—of "ancillary" personnel as inducers
of the mesmerized (magnetized, hypnotized) condition, just as Deleuze had
suggested and Tubbs and others had implemented. As we indicated above,
the use of "hypno-technicians" is not new, nor, we suspect, are the intraprofessional disagreements surrounding their use.

In 1851 Esdaile returned to the place of his birth where he continued to
practice mesmerism and to attract a number of converts to the process. He
died at Sydenham on January 10, 1859.

James Braid

Yet another graduate of Edinburgh will round out our survey of Britain's
"important three" during the last century. Like Esdaile, James Braid was
also born in Scotland (about 1795 in Fifeshire). After his training in Edinburgh, he practiced in Scotland before moving to Manchester.

As we indicated above, Braid, like Elliotson, was introduced to mesmerism by a traveler from the continent, although he and Lafontaine did not
share the type of mutual admiration and rapport that Elliotson and Du Potet
had established (see above). Although Elliotson's interest in mesmerism had

been first aroused by a student of the Abbé Faria (Chenevix), it was Braid, not Elliotson, who was the English successor to Faria. His debt to Faria is to be noted in two ways: first, his extension of the Abbé's observation that the phenomenon of magnetism was due to forces and events within the subject; and second, in his introduction of a new nomenclature for the phenomenon previously known as magnetism and/or mesmerism. In fact, as Marks (1947) noted, it is Braid, with his new term of hypnosis, who brought to an end the age of mesmerism. Braid's *Neurypnology* (1843) introduced his physiological theories and the term hypnotism or nervous sleep, from the Greek *hypnos*, "to sleep." Thus he paid his debt to Faria's lead in explicitly recognizing the central importance of sleep (relaxation) to hypnosis and hypnotic phenomena, the full importance of which was not summarized explicitly until 1981 (Edmonston, 1981).

Braid's induction techniques were guided by his physiological-fatigue ideas regarding mesmerism and the one phenomenon in Lafontaine's demonstration that he felt was of singular importance—the inability of the patient to open his eyes. Lafontaine derisively described one of Braid's early methods, which he (Lafontaine) felt did not accomplish the same end as he had achieved with his demonstration subjects.

> Doctor Braid put a cork on his forehead, which he maintains with a rubber band around his head; he has the subject look at the cork, the subject is thus forced to have his eyes turned upward; all his nerves and all his muscles begin to be tired, the sight grows less clear, eyelids fall, and for an instant cannot be raised. M. Braid then tries to prove by experiences that the subjects are in a state similar to the magnetic state. (Lafontaine, 1860, p. 262)

Braid, himself, described his early techniques, first with a Mr. Walker:

> I requested Mr. Walker, a young gentleman present, to sit down, and maintain a fixed stare at the top of a wine bottle, placed so much above him as to produce a considerable strain on the eyes and eyelids, to enable him to maintain a steady view of the object. In three minutes his eyelids closed, a gush of tears ran down his cheeks, his head dropped, his face was slightly convulsed, he gave a groan, and instantly fell into profound ᵓleep. (Braid, 1843/1976, p. 17)

He then turned to Mrs. Braid: "I requested her to sit down, and gaze on the ornament of a china sugar basin, placed at the same angle to the eyes as the bottle in the former experiment. In two minutes the expression of the face was very much changed" (Braid, 1843/1976, p. 18), and she began to enter a condition similar to that of Mr. Walker's.

While the objects of fixation occasionally differed, (He used a fingertip at one point.), the basic technique was one of eye-fixation. By creating fatigue in the patient's eyes, he induced a general fatigue that eventually affected the activity of the nervous system and produced the nervous sleep (hypnosis). Later, in *Neurypnology,* he gave specific instructions:

> Take any bright object (I generally use my lancet case.) between the thumb and fore and middle fingers of the left hand; hold it from about eight to fifteen inches from the eyes, at such position above the forehead as may be necessary to produce the greatest possible strain upon the eyes and eyelids, and enable the patient to maintain a steady fixed stare at the object. The patient must be made to understand that he is to keep the eyes steadily fixed on the object, and the mind riveted on the idea of that one object. [Once the pupils have dilated] if the fore and middle fingers of the right hand, extended and a little separated, are carried from the object towards the eyes, most probably the eyelids will close involuntarily, with a vibratory motion. (Braid, 1843/1976, pp. 27–28)

According to Bramwell (1903), Braid later abandoned the prolonged gaze and simply instructed his patients to close their eyes early in the process. Once the eyes were closed, he used verbal suggestions (which he had used unwittingly before—Bramwell, 1896) both to concentrate the attention and to create the sleep and relaxation long associated with the process. His method of terminating the mesmeric state was to blow, or otherwise cause currents of cold air to strike the patient.

Braid spent much of his experimentation with mesmerism demonstrating the subjective and suggestive elements of the process. On the use of metals, magnets, and magnetized objects to induce the state he disagreed with Elliotson, and, like Haygarth before him (see Chapter 2), demonstrated that the imagination and belief systems of the patient were more important than the object used in the induction process. When he died on March 25, 1860 of cardiac arrest, Braid left a legacy of creativity and a new vocabulary through which to understand it.

Before leaving England and the first half of the 19th century, let me briefly present three other practitioners. Two of these individuals came into direct conflict with Braid and his viewpoints, and were, in his own words, "disposed of" in his 1855 treatise, *The Physiology of Fascination and the Critics Criticised:* namely, Reverend Chauncy Hare Townshend and George Sandby.

Chauncey Hare Townshend

Townshend (1798–1868), poet, friend of Charles Dickens, and collector of such items as coins, precious stones, cameos and other art works, published a number of works during the same era as Braid. His books were well thought of in their day, and reports of his work found their way into the writings of Gregory (1909/1975, p. 211ff) and Tuke (1884, p. 439ff), as well as Braid (1855/1970).

According to Sinnett (1897), Townshend, like others before him, was reluctant at first to involve himself in mesmerism. As he overcame his incredulity, he experimented more and more with the process and described a number of his experiments in the late 1830s with patients in *Facts in Mesmerism or Animal Magnetism*. Here he brought together his interests in mesmerism and in the collection of precious stones, for he describes the sensations reported by his mesmerized patients to the placing of certain stones on their foreheads. For example, diamonds brought about "agreeable" feelings; opals, a "soothing effect"; emeralds, a "slightly unpleasant sensation"; and sapphires, a "positively painful sensation." Like others working during that period, Townshend also reported on the effects of certain metals and magnets when brought near to the mesmerized individual (without their knowledge). His controversy with Braid developed from his insistence that mesmerism was induced only through the presence of another person, the mesmerizer. Braid denied that the presence of a mesmerizer was necessary and reported several instances of his patients hypnotizing themselves in his absence (Braid, 1855/1970).

Townshend's technique also differed from that of Braid, in that he continued the tradition of Deleuze, beginning first with staring into the eyes of the patient while holding their thumbs and only later, after their eyes had closed and they had entered the sleep, using the mesmeric passes. Early in his book (Townshend, 1841), he described the method of a Mr. K_____ , which was also his own.

> Mademoiselle M_____ placed herself in an arm-chair at one end of the apartment, while he occupied a seat directly facing hers. He then took each of her hands in one of his, and sat in such a manner as that the knees and feet of both should be in contact. In this position he remained for some time motionless, attentively regarding her with eyes as unwinking as the lidless orbs which Coleridge has attributed to the Genius of Destruction. We had been told previously to keep utter silence, and none of our circle—composed of some five or six persons—felt inclined to transgress the order. . . . As soon as the first symptom of drowsiness was manifested, the mesmeriser had withdrawn his hands from those of Mademoiselle M_____ and had commenced what are called the "mesmeric passes," conducting his fingers slowly downward, without contact, along the arms of the patient. (pp. 56–58)

Two things are notable here. First, we receive a glimpse of Townshend's poetic leanings in his reference to Coleridge, and second, we are informed that there needed to be a reduction of environmental stimuli to enhance the effectiveness of the process. The latter, of course, we have noted before as appearing in the later works of Esdaile (1846/1976).

The process of demagnetizing the patient could be done only by the mesmerist who originally induced the condition. It was done in a manner that Braid and Esdaile used a few years later—disturbing the air about the patient:

> Mr. K_____ again operated with his hands, but in a different set of movements, and, taking out his handkerchief, agitated the air around the patient,

who forthwith opened her eyes, and stared about the room like a person awaking from sleep. (Townshend, 1841, p. 58)

Continuing the traditions of past history, Townshend laid great emphasis on the eyes and their particular appearance. "One of the first tokens a person gives of passing into mesmeric sleepwalking is a look of stupor in the eyes, and an apparent lack of power in the eyelids to perform the usual office of nictation" (Townshend, 1841, p. 132). He maintained that the lids remained only about three-quarters closed, and in addition, differed from ordinary sleep in the following ways: "There is a compressed look about the lids, as if they were rather held down by force . . . [and] . . . the ball of the eye is in frequent and violent motion" (Townshend, 1841, p. 134). He also noted that the eye ball itself was turned upward and inward, toward the nose, giving the appearance, we suspect, of individuals participating in Spiegel's Eye-Roll Sign (Spiegel, 1972). But, Townshend did not dwell on the sense of vision alone. Rather, he claimed that all external senses were blunted in the individual in a mesmeric state.

George Sandby

George Sandby, Jun. M.A. was the vicar of Flixton, Suffolk and wrote on mesmerism during the same years as Braid. Although his book, *Mesmerism and Its Opponents* (1844), was essentially a treatise taking issue with the opponents of the phenomenon, in particular a M. M'Neilie, he later also criticised Braid and thus became one of the critics Braid criticized in 1855. Reverend Sandby asked all contenders for the role of major proponent and theorist of mesmerism of the 1840s to justify and offer proof of their particular rationale for mesmerism. Braid's suggestive theory was no exception, and thus drew the fire of the Reverend.

In his book Reverend Sandby describes briefly several people's techniques for mesmerising (e.g., Mr. Thompson, Dr. Dickson), all of which merely reconfirm that the basic method used during the 1840s was that of holding the patient's thumb and making longitudinal passes over the body from the head down. He did report one small variation in the use of hand and/or finger pressure around the eyes and forehead: "The mutual contact of the thumbs, the application of the points of the fingers near the eyes, the pressure of the hand upon the crown of the head, are the plans I have found most successful myself" (Sandby, 1844, p. 122). He, as others before and after, noted the effect of the process on the eyes of the patient and on the induction of a sleep-like condition. A female patient described the effect: "from the moment her thumb touched the thumb of the Mesmeriser, a leaden weight has settled on her eyelids, making resistance to sleep impossible" (Sandby, 1844, p. 122).

Sandby's use of the fingertips in the technique was predicated on the equation of mesmerism with "electricity," as renamed by the Americans ("electro-biology") and the Germans ("electro-physiology"), which was considered to flow most readily from a point, hence the use of the tips (points) of the fingers. We shall see more of this in the work of the New Englander, Grimes, and his electro-biology, just as we have seen the electrical connection in the Tractors of Perkins and the descriptions of the feelings associated with mesmerism by the patients.

W. Scoresby

It was in his book, *Zoistic Magnetism,* that the Artic explore and writer on maritime science, Dr. W. Scoresby, revealed the continued association of electrical references and the process and effects of mesmerism. This association was no doubt a continuation of the older ideas of a vital force or fluid interconnecting all things in the universe and one which appealed particularly to the German theorists. Considering the regions of his maritime explorations, it is also probably not a coincidence that Scoresby chose to dwell at length on the polarity aspects of the mesmeric process.

Reference to the electrical properties or sensations associated with mesmerism were evident in his description of technique:

> Passes from the head downward, quite clear of the dress, were distinctly felt, and elicited pleasurable, sometimes delightful, sensations. His fingers being pointed downward, towards any part of the body on limbs, without contact of the dress, were felt. "It was," as one said, "as if something like electrical current was coming from him to her." Upward passes always had an unpleasant effect, and changed the previously happy expression of the face into a frown. (Scoresby, 1849, p. 15)

Further references to physical magnetism appeared in his description of the usual and most efficacious form of induction:

> When, however, the subject, as was frequently the case, was placed on a sofa, or, with a curative object, on a bed, he, the operator, whilst sitting parallel and face to face, usually crossed his knees, and covered, with a view to insulation, his proximate knee with silk (which otherwise, he supposed, might act unfavorably), so as to yield the most consistent arrangements for the magnetic developments. And beyond the particulars specified, he preferred (for reasons he could not now particularize) to have the sofa in the line of the magnetic meridian, with the head of the subject toward the north.

> Thus situated, respectively, the magnetic condition was generally (first of all) developed, by merely taking the hands of the subject in his, the operator's hands, right with left, and left with right; and then steadily looking at each others eyes. After the eyes closed, and after a few minutes continuance of motionless and silent contact of the hands—he proceeded to make passes, usually with one hand at a time, whilst retaining the other hand, from the head over the face, or side of the head, downward to the extremity of the arm, or, as far as easily practicable, towards the feet—always confining the manipulations

of either hand to its proper side. In cases where the eyes could not be closed by the mere contact of hands, etc.,—passes were resorted to, partly free (two or three inches above the dress), and partly in contact with the dress of the subject, in aid of the quiescent influences. (Scoresby, 1849, pp. 60–61)

Scoresby eschewed Braid's initial technique of creating eye strain by placing an object of focus above the normal line of sight. He also described a number of variations on the above induction technique in detail, telling the reader why, in each case, they were less satisfactory than the "usual." For example, he claimed that if the operator were to be placed at one side of the patient, the "phenomena appeared to be less distinctive and the *polarity* [italics added] less sensative" (Scoresby, 1849, p. 61). If there were no contact of the hands, though the usual position with eye contact and passes be used, the process took about twice as long as usual. If the wrong hands were in contact (right to right and left to left, instead of right to left and left to right), the time required for eye closure was tripled. Coupling the wrong hands with *upward* passes was fruitless, as was hand contact without eye contact. No polarities developed if the magnetizer held both of the patient's hands in his right hand and the tips of the shoes in his left.

The polarities of magnetism were so important to Scoresby that he devoted a considerable portion of his book to their production and manipulation. "The Polarity" extended from the crown of the head to the foot, or sometimes from the shoulder to the foot, and was increased by the appropriate downward passes. The analogy to electrical phenomena was evident in Scoresby's assertion that, although the mesmerist often did not make passes fully to the feet, the feet were magnetized "inductively" as the passes were made to the upper portions of the body. He claimed that there were attractive and repellent forces (again the allusion to physical magnetism and electricity) between patient and magnetizer, such that contact between attracting parts (e.g., right hand of mesmerist with left hand of patient, and vice versa) produced pleasurable sensations in the patient, while repellent hands (e.g., right to right or left to left) produced the opposite effect. Upward passes also had a negative effect, "like rubbing upward a cat's back" (Scoresby, 1849, p. 67). The allusion to electro-motive force is completed when the author suggests (a) that the power of the mesmerist diminishes as the distance from the patient increases "in the ratio of the squares of the distance, inversely" (Scoresby, 1849, p. 71), and (b) that the attire of the patient directly influences the powers of the induction technique. Regarding the latter, Scoresby found that when his prize patient, Miss P_____ , wore silk or satin, the effects of all of his efforts were diminished, if not completely obliterated: "The *satin dress* was found to be completely *insulating,* as to external attractions and repulsions" (Scoresby, 1849, p. 74). The author did admit, however, that bringing the patient into contact with a compass, a "delicate galvanometer," and/or an "electrometer" did *not* affect any of the instruments.

The lack of reliable and measureable changes did not derail the continued references of mesmerism to physical magnetic and/or electric phenomena, as we will see in the next chapter. Nor did it affect Scoresby's (and others) de-mesmerization method. If one was mesmerized, magnetized, polarized by downward passes, then it was obvious that the process would be reversed by reversing the direction of the pass. So it was with reverse passes that he awakened his patients, although he also noted that lateral passes across the face and chest would accomplish the same end. What is particularly evident from Scoresby's treatise is confirmation of the observation that as the practitioners believed, so did they behave with respect to the induction techniques applied to patients. Braid's (and others') work to dispell the universal fluid, the magnetic and electrical "explanations" of mesmerism—hereafter called hypnosis—and to replace the pass and the stare with words of ease and comfort as induction procedures was slow to take hold, as we will see in the next chapter.

NOTE

1.   I am indebted to Ann Baumler for her assistance in rendering Lafontaine's work into English.

CHAPTER 4

The Later Nineteenth Century

A number of historians of hypnosis (Bramwell, 1903; Marks, 1947; Pattie, 1967; Shor, 1979) move from the British triumvirate of Elliotson, Esdaile, and Braid back to the continent and the contributions of Liébeault, leading to the famed disagreements between the people in Nancy and those in Paris. Others (e.g., Goldsmith, 1934) digress into Spiritualism both on the continent and in the United States. Although much of the spiritualism movement, including Andrew Jackson Davis, Phineas Quimby, and Mary Baker Eddy, certainly owes a debt to hypnotism, its forerunners and to the long, long association between religious orders and what is now called the health sciences, I will skirt much of the spiritualistic movements of the late 19th and 20th centuries in favor of the more health science related methodologies of inducing hypnosis. As we will see, we cannot completely skirt spiritualism because a number of individuals who worked originally as medical practitioners later turned to spiritualism (e.g., J. Stanley Grimes, H. G. Darling), in a reversal of the usual trend of history from devout belief to experimental investigation, suspended judgment and the willingness to doubt. However, the separation is justified, at this point, because the definition between the two groups (the religious and the applied health fields) is much clearer, both conceptually and legally, than it had been until the last century. This is not to say that counseling, including the use of hypnotic and hypnotic-like techniques, is not still conducted today by those outside "legitimate" professional health care organizations. Helping behavior between two individuals, regardless of the "credentials" held by one, will not be stifled by legislation. However, *knowledgeful* helping behavior has come of scientific (and legislative) age in this century and I intend in this book to pass on the knowledge of induction methodology gained through clinical observation and active experimentation, rather than through miraculous surprises and deep conviction alone.

In reality, Liébeault is not the next historical step from Braid et al. Mesmeric and other techniques were also flourishing in America during the 19th century (In fact, Mesmer's work was called to Washington's attention by Lafayette—Deleuze, 1843/1982, p. 344.), and it is to those practicing in the United States that we now turn our attention.

MESMERISM IN AMERICA

Although the best known early center of mesmerism in America was New Orleans, where individuals interested in the phenomenon gathered informally in the early 1830s (Tomlinson & Perret, 1975), Cincinnati, Philadelphia, New York, and Pawtucket, Rhode Island were also sites where mesmerism gained a foothold in the "new world." According to Durant (1837/1982), the first public lectures on the subject were offered by Charles Poyen in the latter part of 1836 at Pawtucket, and later at Boston, Lowell, and Nantucket. However, at least one individual had been making the study of mesmerism his standard for some 12 years prior to those historic lectures, Charles Caldwell.

Charles Caldwell

Charles Caldwell was born in North Carolina in 1772. During his medical training at the University of Pennsylvania, he labored with yellow fever victims and drew conclusions from his experiences that put him into direct confrontation with Benjamin Rush, the most renownd physician of his time. Caldwell concluded that yellow fever was (a) a domestic disorder and (b) not contagious, and he openly took on Rush and the medical establishment prior to his attaining his medical degree in 1796. Controversy continued to swirl about him when he and others advocated bringing the waters of the Schuylkill River into Philadelphia as a sanitary and preventative medicine move.

In 1812 he spoke on medical jurisprudence (a new field at that time) and spent the war as Physician General of the Pennsylvania troops. After a short period as Professor of Geology and the Philosophy of Natural History at Penn, he moved to Kentucky and spent from 1819 to 1829 attempting to establish a medical college at Transylvania College in Lexington. At the age of 77, he was terminated by Transylvania, and died four years later in 1853.

Twenty years before the publication of his book, *Facts in Mesmerism* (1842/1982), he began another advocacy that again led him into further controversy. Caldwell was among the earliest Americans to show a professional interest in phrenology, the topic that fascinated Elliotson so much and, some think, led him astray. Caldwell was no doubt influenced by Elliotson, through personal contact and the latter's writings. *Elements of Phrenology,* the first American book on the subject, was published by Caldwell in 1824. With his history of contrary opinion, it was not surprising that he took the next logical step from phrenology to mesmerism and became one of the earliest in this country to practice it.

Caldwell's small volume (1842/1982) is a compendium of the history of mesmerism, contemporary beliefs and folklore regarding it, and reports of case practices. It does not, however, explicate his induction technique(s), but merely gives general statements indicating that the patients were "thrown into" a mesmeric condition, as if the process were one of physi-

cally catapulting the patient across the room. He does, in fact, make repeated mention of the strong will of the operator, indicating strength and
effort, but not of a physical type.

Apparently, as we will see further on, many of the early Americans who
used mesmerism were devotees of Deleuze and routinely followed his instructional pattern (see Chapter 3). From such entries as the following—"So
are the 'passes' and looks employed in mesmerism" (p. 55); "I commenced
the manipulations" (p. 88); and, "The mesmerist commenced his manipulations. In a very short time their effect was visible in the extreme drowsiness
of his subject; and ere ten minutes had elapsed she was soundly asleep" (pp.
93–94)—we can conclude that the mesmeric pass, coupled with eye-fixation
had reached the frontiers of America.

Charles Poyen

As indicated above, Charles Poyen usually receives credit for bringing animal magnetism to America through his series of lectures in the New England
area. Perhaps of equal value to his lectures is his small book, *Progress of
Animal Magnetism in New England* (1837), which gives, in addition to his
own history, the history of work being done in the third decade of the 19th
century in Boston; Providence; Lowell; Nashua, NH; Taunton; New Bed-
ford; Salem; Bangor; and Nantucket. The book is dedicated to Alexander
Wright, the individual who introduced the manufacture of carpets into New
England, and practiced animal magnetism on the side.

Poyen himself was introduced to magnetism by a clairvoyant (Madame
Villetard) who was called in by Dr. Chapelain to aid in the treatment of
Poyen during his medical training in Paris in 1832. On her advice, he spent
more than a year in the French West Indies recuperating and having his
interest further roused by the planters' practice of magnetism. Fourteen
months later he settled in Lowell, MA. by way of Portland, ME. and
Haverhill, MA. There he occupied his time teaching his native language
(French) and drawing, until his interest was further stirred by the mayor, Dr.
Elisha Bartlett. He then proceeded to translate Rostan's work, but was
unable to find a publisher because "the delusion had been exploded some
fifty-three years ago by '*the great Franklin*'" (Poyen, 1837, p. 44). At the
suggestion of a would-be publisher, he gave a series of public lectures and
private instructions to create interest in the topic.

In 1836 a number of his sessions were given in his private lodgings at 176
Washington Street. As word spread, Poyen widened his geographic scope
and lectured in Boston, Bangor, Cambridge, and Providence. The latter site
drew dignitaries from Brown University (including the president—Reverend
Dr. Wayland), but it was not until 1837 that he achieved some financial
stability through his lectures, which had aroused enough interest in the topic
of magnetism for publishers for his work to venture forward. Until that time,
the majority of his work had been done at his own expense, according to his
own narrative.

A brief, 22-page book within a book follows the appendix to *Progress*. Contained therein is a chapter on the processes and specific uses of magnetism as practiced by Poyen. His method was as follows:

> If you wish to put a person into the magnetic sleep, cause him to sit as easy as possible in an easy chair, with his head reclined back, and require him to be perfectly quiet; sit down before him, place your knees beside his; then take his thumbs in such a manner that the inside of your thumbs will touch the inside of his. Concentrate your attention, and will him to sleep; after holding him thus about ten minutes, slowly raise your hands with the palms turned outward to his head, then turning the palms inward let them descend to his shoulders, and let them remain there five minutes; then let your hands descend with the fingers pointed towards the arms, at the distance of two or three inches from them to the extremities of his fingers; let your hands then ascend, sweeping them off to the right and the left, to their extent, palms outward as before; raise them as high as the head, then descend as before; thus continue from five to ten minutes, and lastly, lay the right hand upon the pit of the stomach. Remember that unless you keep your attention fixed, your will steady and unwavering, your efforts will be vain. The operation is principally intellectual; many make no use of the manipulations, and produce all the effects by the mere energy of the will, at a distance from the patient; but still the movements of the hands give some assistance in producing the magnetic current; the downward motions are magnetic, the upward are not. (Poyen, 1837, "Elements," pp. 15–16)

Although the eye-fixation is missing, the mesmeric passes are clearly there. He also makes clear the supposed power of the will of the operator in both the concentration effort of the operator and the "willing" of the patient to sleep. We see here, too, the emphasis on the stomach as a central locale for concentrating effort through touch. In an additional method, the will is paramount: "Take the patient by one hand and place the other hand on the head and exert the will" (Poyen, 1837, "Elements," p. 16).

Poyen briefly mentioned susceptibility in that he noted that some individuals are more easily magnetized than are others. Some are so susceptible that they "become somnambulists." "To awaken the patient from magnetic sleep make upward motions with your hands before his face, willing him to awaken" (Poyen, 1837, "Elements," p. 16).

The combination of passes and touchings and desire and force of will were considered the main ingredients in the applications of magnetism to specific disorders:

> For head-ache place your hand upon the part affected and exercise a constant and benevolent desire to relieve pain; and after holding it there a few minutes, pass it lightly over the head from right to left; if the pain is occasioned by the stomach, next place your hand on it and proceed as with the head. If the headache is accompanied with cold feet, after holding the hand on the head for a short time, draw the hands slowly from the head downwards, along the sides, to the knees; soon the head will be relieved and the feet become warm. If the pain has existed for years it is chronic and must have a prolonged treatment.

In rheumatism, if local, place your hand where pain is felt, hold it for fifteen or twenty minutes, then pass your hand lightly to the extremity of the feet, and thus continue for ten minutes; but if the limbs are generally affected, make passes at a short distance from them to their extremities, for an hour or more; if the disease is chronic repeat the operation daily until the relief is complete; and so of every chronic disease. (Poyen, 1837, "Elements," pp. 16–17)

Poyen readily admitted that magnetism was not effective in all diseases, but "is a valuable auxiliary of medicine, and every physician should be familiar with its principles" (Poyen, 1837, "Elements," pp. 17–18)—a position held by most of the traveling workshops and seminars in hypnosis today.

The major portion of the rest of the book is the recounting of magnetic activities in various cities through the contemporary reports in local newspapers and medical and surgical journals. Descriptions of induction procedures were very abbreviated, usually consisting of simple statements such as, "He proceeded with the manipulations." Most of the emphasis was on the non-verbal willing of the operator to effect reports, movements, or other changes in the patient. For example: "I willed him to give me his hand. Immediately, he moved his arm forward. I asked him why he did so? He answered—'If I understood you right, you wanted me to give you my hand'" (Poyen, 1837, p. 99).

Part of the chapter, which outlines the experiments Poyen conducted on a Miss Cynthia Ann Gleason, is devoted to the analogy between mineral and animal magnetism. This part reveals to us the continued concern for special properties attributed to iron, whether in the form of iron magnets or steel scissors. Both of these items were reported to have influenced the patient and caused twitchings in the limbs and fingers, which ceased when, unknown to Miss Gleason, lead or silver spoons or wooden objects were substituted for the iron object. The fascination with iron, which we recall from the Druids to Mesmer's wand, pervaded American magnetism as well during this early period of exploration.

But Poyen drew other analogies and relationships. He advocated the use of magnetized water with all sorts of ill health, even indicating that it had a basic warming effect when placed at the feet of an individual with cold feet. (Perhaps he should have tried this ploy with resistive patients.) His analogy of magnetism with electricity was couched in terms of the "shock" the patient reported when coming into contact with the magnetizer. It sounded vaguely similar to the completion of an electrical circuit: "If the hand of the magnetizer is on the head of the magnetized, and the hand of the latter touches the head of the magnetizer, that moment he experiences a shock like that of electricity" (Poyen, 1837, "Elements," p. 21).

Charles Ferson Durant

One of the most fervent devotees of the methods of Deleuze in America was Charles Durant. Born in New York City in 1805, he produced works on the classification of seaweeds and physical astronomy, as well as his 1837 book on mesmerism. His interests ran to politics, printing, lithography, and the uses of silk and silk products. He produced the first silk in America and was awarded several gold medals by the American Institute for his efforts in this field of production and manufacture.

His own interests in mesmeric phenomena were apparently aroused through the lectures of Charles Poyen, noted above. Poyen himself converted such people as Americus Potter, Thomas C. Hartshorn, and Professor Francis Wayland, President of Brown University and the individual to whom Durant dedicated his book. Much of the interest and proof of the reality of mesmerism resided in clairvoyant experiences reported by various mesmerists and their patients. Much commotion was made of certain individuals' abilities to see through objects, such as the human body, in order to diagnose and prescribe. These "super women" (most were female), with 19th century x-ray vision, were not unlike the child described in the *Leiden Papyrus,* through whom the operator could talk to the gods. Durant mentions such well-known cases in America as Mrs. Andros, Miss Brackett, Miss Parker, Miss Ebon, and Miss Ayres.

Of Durant's induction technique, it was that of Deleuze with the eye-fixation and the mesmeric passes, which I described in the preceding chapter. But other elements were becoming more prevalent by the 1840s, the concepts of imagination, operations of the mind, self-suggestion, and will. Durant even tried the latter on himself: "I tried an experiment on myself: 'I *willed*' a magnetic sleep, and it came. I tied two handkerchiefs over my eyes, and holding a book to the epigastrium, I read correctly one entire page in the REGNE ANIMAL OF CUVIER" (Durant, 1837/1982, p. 70). Not only do we see here the willing of the condition, but also the emphasis on the stomach as a sense organ. Remember that the early mesmerists often stopped their passes at the epigastrium and allowed their hand to rest there to heighten the effect of the distribution and redistribution of the magnetic fluid.

The Deleuzian induction technique was, of course, theory dependent. As long as the theory of mesmerism was that of a magnetic fluid, the fluid had to be distributed or redistributed, and the most efficient way to effect that was by passes of the hands, while holding the attention of the patient with the eyes. From his experiments, conducted in Providence and New York (18 of which were detailed in his book), Durant developed his own theory of mesmerism, which likened the magnetic fluid to that in electricity and the lodestone and passed from the eye of the magnetizer to the eye of the beheld: "In the magnetic sleep, the magnetic fluid passes from the brain and eye (North Pole) of the *magnetizer* to the eye (South Pole) and the brain of the magnetic somnambulist; the magnetic fluid is composed of globular molecules which touch each other, and form strings or magnetic cords from one brain to the other brain" (Durant, 1837/1982, p. 79). The fluid was able, so the theory went, to penetrate the pores of all substances, except one. "CERIN, an

EXPERIMENT IN ANIMAL MAGNETISM.

Figure 4.1.   CERIN deflecting the powers of the magnetizer. (From *Exposition, Or a New Theory of Animal Magnetism* by C. F. Durant, 1837).

animal fat which was discovered in a grave yard, where dead bodies had been buried many years'' (Durant, 1837/1982, p. 122) was supposedly composed of such soft globules that they ''mash together and close up all the pores'' (p. 76), disallowing passage of magnetic fluid, natural or mesmeric (see Figure 4.1). As long as the patient was not oiled with Cerin, the magnetic fluid, directed by the magnetizer's passes, will or both, penetrated the pores of the body and cleansed it of disease. Durant died in 1873.

Mesmerism and American Spiritualism

The early 1800s saw a rapid growth in spiritualism in America. Much of this growth and developing interest was directly related to mesmerism and magnetism. I do not intend to give a full account of the spiritualistic movement here, but there are certain interconnections that should be noted. For example, such individuals as J. Stanley Grimes and H. G. Darling interpreted mesmerism in terms of electrical phenomena (''electro-biology,'' Grimes called it), and despite (or because of) their medical backgrounds found the transition from mesmerism to spiritualism easy and appealing. However, it is in the nonprofessionally trained—the shoemakers, tailors, watchmakers, businessmen—that we find the major impetus for the spiritual movement in America. These individuals, too, began with the passes and eye-fixations of mesmerism.

Andrew Jackson Davis, the ''Poughkeepsie Sear,'' was born in 1826 in Poughkeepsie, NY, destined to become the major leader of the spiritual movement in America. As a boy of 16 he, along with other boys in the neighborhood, visited William Livingston, a local tailor, with the express purpose of being magnetized. Livingston had become acquainted with the skill through a series of lectures on phrenology and mesmerism by Professor Grimes.

Davis proved adept at the mesmeric sleep, through which he achieved a clairvoyant state in which he reported being able to see through his forehead, rather than his eyes. Shortly after his initiation, he became quite famous as a medical clairvoyant with Livingston as his magnetizer. In the magnetized state he dictated *Nature's Divine Revelations* and became the leader of spiritualism on this side of the Atlantic. The wonder of *Divine Revelations* and his later autobiography was that he was uneducated in the formal sense.

In his autobiography, *The Magic Staff* (1857), he outlined the technique used on him by Livingston:

> Situated in close relation to the one who intends to produce the physical sleep, the subject is compelled (in order that the state may be properly induced) to sit in an easy position—entirely quiet—with mind free alike from external intrusions and internal desires. The subject's thoughts should be calmly concentrated; to accelerate the accomplishment of the end. At length he will become wholly passive, while the operator is active. Care should be taken to exclude all unfavorable circumstances that might render the operation either tedious or unsuccessful. (Davis, 1857, p. 204)

Here we have outlined essentially the same juxtaposition of operator and subject as described by Deleuze and used by most of that era. As we have noted throughout this history, the instruction to reduce external and internal distractions continues. Davis then describes his own sensations while being mesmerised:

> I felt the operator's chilly hand pass and repass my brow, the chamber of thought. The living blood which had flowed undisturbed through my youthful form during its brief existence seemed well-nigh arrested. The ten thousand avenues of sensation were illuminated with the livid flames of electric fire. Anon, all was intensely dark within. Dreadful and strange feelings passed over my body and through my brain. My emotions were painful. (pp. 204–206)

From here on he describes his internal ruminations about the sensations and feelings he was experiencing in eloquent and mystical phrases. Much of his description revolved around the fear that he was dying as he entered the mesmeric condition. Such a concern, as well as an indication of deep somnambulism and amnesia, was expressed in his description of trance termination:

> I awoke to physical consciousness, mentally revolving in a circuitous form. The darkness continued (with my ascending movement) to increase and expand, till I gained the margin that bounded the ocean of the dreaded oblivion, whose restless waves conveyed me to the longed-for state of thought and wakefulness. My senses, the windows of the soul, were again opened; light

broke in upon my dimmed vision; sound vibrated throught the labyrinths of my ear; sensation flashed over my whole frame; and I moved, shouted, and opened my eyes. But how joyfully surprised! I was in precisely the same position as when I first seated myself for the experiment. . . . I could remember nothing, except my mental sufferings; and somehow, in my bewilderment, I did not feel quite certain that I had not died. I could not realize that I had, in reality, returned from the dark "valley of the shadow of death." (Davis, 1857, p. 209)

Davis's early experiences were clearly of a mesmeric nature, but his eventual calling appeared to be elsewhere as a leader of spiritualism. It has also been suggested that the work of Mary Baker Eddy and Christian Science use the same basic principles as hypnosis and mesmerism (Watkins, 1964). Certainly, the historical connections are clear. Phineas Parkhurst Quimby (1802–1866), a watchmaker who had on occasion assisted surgeons by magnetizing their patients, treated Mary Baker Eddy for hysterical paralysis in 1861. While following her rehabilitation under the care of Quimby, she launched her faith cure today known as Christian Science.

New Orleans and Cincinnati

It was probably the combination of a French heritage and an active proponent of mesmerism that New Orleans is given credit as the main center of magnetism in America. Informal meetings of interested individuals began about the same time Poyen was lecturing in New England, but it was not until April 1845 that the *Règlement de la Société du Magnétisme de la Nouvelle-Orléans* published its constitution. Through its president, M. Joseph Barthet, and his correspondence with Baron Du Potet and the *Journal du Magnétisme,* which Du Potet edited, the activities of the New Orleans group became widely known.

The scanty information uncovered by Tomlinson and Perret (1975) indicated that Barthet lived in New Orleans in the 1840s and 1850s and died in France in 1863. He was apparently an indefatigable correspondent, since the *Journal du Magnétisme* contains innumerable letters from him from the middle of the 1840s through the 1850s. Magnetic therapy was offered by the Society and its members without opposition from the two medical societies, the French-speaking *Société Médicale de la Nouvelle Orléans* and the English-speaking *Physico-Medical Society*. Their methods were of two kinds: (a) the usual passes prevalent in that period; and (b) the use of clairvoyants, individuals who diagnosed and prescribed while in the mesmeric condition. Nicolas (1852) did outline some of the passes in more detail:

Pass 1. The position pass. If the subject is not confined to his bed, you must, in order to magnetize, seat him comfortably and place yourself in front of him, making sure that the subject has his back turned to the magnetic pole indicated by the magnetic needle.

Pass 2. The rapport pass. It is performed in the following way: You take the thumbs of the subject, one in the right hand and the other in the left hand, in order to establish perfect equilibrium of temperature.

Pass 3. The fascination pass. Look intently at the subject and concentrate on the power you have to magnetize.

Pass 4. The occlusion pass. It is performed by touching lightly the closed eyelids of the subject. In this way his eyelids become heavy and are soon motionless.

Pass 5. The longitudinal pass. This pass is accomplished by placing your open hands on the crown of the shoulders of the subject and then running them down the length of his arms, barely grazing him, except for his hands, which you should touch lightly. These passes must be repeated 10 to 12 times.

Pass 6. The temporal pass. It is performed by placing the palm of both hands, shaped to form a concave surface, on the temples of the subject. During this pass, which should last at least a minute, the magnetizer should concentrate exclusively on the goal to be accomplished.

Pass 7. The frontal or cervical pass. This is accomplished as follows: With the palm of the left hand you hold the forehead of the subject, making sure your fingers are turned toward the occiput. Place the fingers of your right hand, bunched together, on the epigastrium in order to follow the movements of respiration and circulation. You should press lightly on the epigastrium for at least a minute.

Pass 8. The occipital or polarizing pass. Leave the left hand on the forehead in the position described for the preceding pass. Place the inner surface of the fingers of the other hand at the base of the cervical.

Pass 9. The pectoral pass. It is accomplished by placing the palm of the hands on the front of the shoulders in such a way that their eminence is resting on the axillary plexus. Gently rock the upper part of the subject's torso several times.

Pass 10. The projection pass or continuous stream pass. This is performed by casting onto the sensorium and the crown of the skull the magnetic fluid gathered in the air with both hands, being careful each time to move the fingers. (p. 22)

These passes, like those most used during this period, were predicated on the concept of a magnetic fluid within and without the patient, which had to be directed and redirected by the hypnotist. In reality, only passes five through ten seem to be manipulations. The first four appear preliminary to the remaining six, although the final six could be used either singly or in various combinations. The gentle rocking motion mentioned in passes eight and nine are again reminiscent of Aaronson's witch's cradle (1973).

Nicolas (1852) also acknowledged that these ten passes were not the only methods of magnetizing: "To produce a sleeping state, some magnetizers simply move one hand or both to a spot close to the forehead, from the epigastric region; others utilize the simple method of touching; others tell the patient to close his eyes, to turn his thoughts inward, and, after a few seconds of quiet immobility, order the patient to fall asleep, using a firm tone of voice" (p. 23). Verbal inductions were making their entrance into America.

Nor did Nicolas (1852) leave the reader without a way to end the magnetized condition:

> To awaken the subject you must proceed in an inverse fashion. Four passes are necessary to achieve this result.
>
> Pass 1. The "disocclusion" pass. This is performed by touching the subject's eyelids with your thumbs, moving from the inside to the outside.
>
> Pass 2. The transversal. This is done by putting your palms in front of the eyes of the subject and then bruskly [sic] separating them with a movement from the inside to the outside.
>
> Pass 3. The drawing off. This is done by placing the bunched fingers of the right hand on the epigastrium and withdrawing them several times, making sure to move them outwards, away from the subject.
>
> Pass 4. Disengagement. This is performed by placing the palms on the head, then on the chest of the subject, making sure that you shake them while you sweep away the electric fluid. This pass must be repeated until the subject is fully awake.[1] (pp. 22–23)

The New Orleans Society lasted through the 1850s, but shortly thereafter ceased to function regularly. Tomlinson and Perret (1975) opine that it was the combination of the coming Civil War, the death of their dynamic and active President, and insufficient economic support.

Though the mesmeric activities in New Orleans may have been better known, the formalization of the Phreno-Magnetic Society of Cincinnati actually preceded that of the New Orleans group. Organized on June 14, 1842, the Cincinnati group produced its first journal issue, *The Journal of the Phreno-Magnetic Society of Cincinnati,*[2] in August of that same year. This one, and perhaps only, issue of their journal (Webster, 1976) was explicit in its reporting of the various experiments that occurred at the Society's first Monday of the month meetings, except for the method of inducing the magnetic sleep of the subjects.

From what is available, we can deduce that both eye-fixation and passes were used. For example: "The operator . . . proceeded to mesmerize the subject by the influence of his eye and will and succeeded in three and one half minutes" (Webster, 1976, p. 279). It is interesting to note that the inductions in Cincinnati were much shorter in length than those occurring in New Orleans, Philadelphia, and anywhere else for that matter, 3 to 5 min. having been the usual. Elsewhere, passes as a mode of induction are indicated by, " 'Mr. Vallentine was now awakened by the reverse passes' "

(Webster, 1976, p. 280). We must assume that the passes were made in the same manner as was the general practice of the day (see, for example, Deleuze above), but evidence indicates that bar magnets were also used for special effects and for the magnetization of parts of the body: " 'His arm was then magnetized with the [bar] magnet; . . . the arm was then relieved by the reversed passes made with the magnet' " (Webster, 1976, p. 281).

The Phreno-Magnetic Society of Cincinnati, however, was short-lived and may not have lasted beyond the year of its formation in 1842. Meanwhile, the center of attention shifted geographically back to the East coast and to the phenomena known as electro-biology.

Electro-Biology

Three of the main proponents of magnetism as electro-biology were Grimes, Mr. Lewis, and Stone. Born in 1807 (d. 1903), Dr. J. Stanley Grimes taught medical jurisprudence at the Castleton Medical College, some years after Caldwell had introduced the topic at the University of Pennsylvania. He also taught at the first women's college in the United States, Willard Institute. Like so many of the other individuals who contributed to the history of mesmerism and hypnosis, his interests were varied and far ranging. According to Tinterow (1970), he was an early proponent of evolutionary theory in America, an adherent of phrenology, and one of the first to recognize the value of suggestion in understanding mesmerism—prior to and independent of Braid's later notions of monoideism. Although initially a staunch opponent of superstition and the occult, he later drifted into spiritualism himself. One of his most interesting proposals was that the seat of consciousness lay in the lower brain stem, the medulla. Today, of course, we denote the central core of the medulla (and pons and midbrain) as the RAS, which is associated with levels of cortical arousal and excitation.

In 1848 Grimes independently developed techniques and discovered phenomena similar to those reported by Braid. He called the influence he had on patients *electro-biology*. More important, however, was his introduction of verbal suggestion to the process of inducing mesmerism and hypnosis (Durand, 1860/1970). While he probably used eye-fixation and passes, as did others of this period, he found verbal suggestion to be an advantage in producing the condition. Here, then, we have one early indication of a movement away from physical passes on the part of the operator to "passes" of a verbal nature.

Grimes's message of "electro-biology" was carried to the continent by Mr. Lewis (This may have been Dr. Winslow Lewis cited in Poyen's book, 1837.), Mr. Stone, and Dr. Darling. The 1851 *Zoist* (Vol. 9, No. 23, March, p. 107) mentions Dr. Warren, Dr. Darling, Mr. Lewis, and Mr. Stone from America demonstrating their induction technique for electro-biology (see below). The latter gentleman, Stone, is credited by Durand (1860/1970) with publishing one of the early books on the topic in London in 1852. However,

Darling had already revised and edited the work of John Bovee Dods, a minister of the American Universalist Church (1795–1872), which included both his (Dods's) and Grimes's notions on "electrical psychology." Dods (1850) actually gave 12 lectures before the U.S. Congress on the topic!

Lewis's technique was outlined by Gregory (1909/1975) after first noting several fundamentals of the mesmeric situation: "A passive and willing state of mind in the patient, . . . intense concentration on the part of the operator . . . (and) perfect silence" were essential (Gregory, 1909/1975, p. 2). Just as in present-day techniques, the willingness of the subject, the undivided attention of the operator, and a nondistracting setting were perceived as necessary for the methodology proper to be applied.

Intensity of gaze was what set Lewis's technique apart from his contemporaries'. Lewis's total method was direct eye-fixation of the patient: "Mr. Lewis produces the same state (the mesmeric state) by gazing for five minutes only, with extreme earnestness and concentration, at the subject, while the latter gazes either at him, or at an object in the same direction" (Gregory, 1909/1975, p. 68).

H. G. Darling is credited by several sources (Durand, 1860; Moll, 1897) with having brought electro-biology to England in 1850. People familiar with Braid's writings and methods recognized it immediately as basically the same process and phenomena. Darling, however, combined the Braidian technique of fixing the eye with the older use of passes with the hands, and with verbal suggestions that *allow* the patient to enter the desired condition. This latter innovation was brought to fruition by Milton Erickson and others, as we will see later.

The center piece of Darling's induction technique was a small disc of zinc with a copper center, which was held in the palm of the left hand of the patient and fixated for 10 or 15 minutes. The fixation disc served historical continuity in several manners, although it is probable that few of the practitioners of that day recognized the fact. The choice of particular metals may well have been influenced by the notion of electro-biology and the conductance properties that zinc and copper possessed. It was also during this period (1850s) that *The Zoist* published a number of articles on the suspected curative powers of certain metals, with copper and iron (ancient history again) being the most often mentioned, although even "English steel" received mention in an 1852 article (*The Zoist,* Vol. 10, No. 29, October 1852). These articles, which it is not necessary to detail here, were a mixture of magical belief, as in the case of much of Baron Reichenbach's Odic Force speculations, and of more firmly based hypotheses that the particular mine or foundry in which a worker might be employed (copper, iron, etc.) might be related to the types of diseases contracted (see Chapter 3). The history of attributing special powers to certain metals was continued unconsciously by Darling's technique, although the older mainstay, iron, was losing out to metals that conducted galvanic currents, electricity, and/or "odic forces" more efficiently, such as copper and zinc.

It is important to keep in mind that Darling, himself, did not attribute special properties of an electric or galvanic sort to the metals contained in the disc. He felt that the coin "simply assists in enabling the subject to concentrate his thoughts, and thus to bring himself into a state of abstraction favourable to the further operations" (Gregory, 1909/1975, pp. 67–68). Some of the "further operations" Darling obtained from his subjects were catalepsies (inability to open the eyes, to open the jaw, to separate the hands when placed together palm to palm, to remove the hands from the forehead when placed there by Dr. Darling); anesthesias and somatosensory halluci-nations, both positive and negative; post-hypnotic suggestions and amne-sias; positive and negative hallucinations; and the assuming of various per-sonalities. Most of these phenomena were accomplished through verbal suggestion followed by the general allowance suggestion of "Now you can."

Like Braid before him (see Braid, 1843/1976, pp. 27–28), Darling found the effects of staring at the disc to be fatigue, eye-closure, drowsiness, and finally, entrance into a mesmeric (hypnotic) condition, with its attendant amnesia. "The first is a twitching of the eyelids, which begin to droop, while, even when the eyelids remain open, there is in many cases, a veil, as it were, drawn before the eyes, concealing the operator's face and other objects. Now also comes on a drowsiness, and, after a time, consciousness is sud-denly lost, and on awaking the patient has no idea whatever how long it is since he fell asleep, nor what has occurred during his sleep" (Gregory, 1909/ 1975, p. 3).

Once the patient has stared at the hypno-disc, Dr. Darling, "ascertains . . . which of them have been affected, by desiring them, singly, to close the eyes, when he touches the forehead with his finger, makes a few passes over the eyes, or rather presses the eyelids down with a rapid sideward motion, and then tells them that they cannot open their eyes." If they can open their eyes, "He generally takes hold of one hand, and desires them to gaze at him intently for a moment, he also gazing at them [as per Mr. Lewis], . . . and stated " 'Now you can' " (Gregory, 1909/1975, pp. 65–66).

Thus, Darling and the others who took electro-biology eastward across the Atlantic combined the induction techniques of the past, present, and future in their uses of special metals, eye-fixation, passes, verbal commands and suggestions, and the beginnings of nondirective, you-are-allowed-to sug-gestions exemplified by "Now you can."

Joseph Pierre Durand (Durand de Gros—J. P. Philips)

Writing under the pseudonym of Philips, J. P. Durand (Durand de Gros) was a French physician who resided in America until his return to France in 1853, and, according to Ellenberger (1970), read a paper at the Fourth Inter-national Congress of Psychology in 1900. During his stay in America he became interested in Grimes's electro-biology and attempted to transplant those views with little success back to his native France (Durand, 1855). He is far better remembered for his theory of polypsychism—the division of the human into anatomical sections, each with its own psychic ego, all under the control of a generalized Chief Ego—which, along with "dipsychism" (Ellenberger, 1970), formed the early bases of Janet's dissociation and Hilgard's divided consciousness views of hypnosis.

According to St. Dominique (1874), Durand initially used a silver coin as the focal point for an eye-fixation induction. Later he adopted the "hypnotic disc," which was constructed in a manner similar to that reported used by Dr. Darling above. "The size of a two-franc piece," it was constructed of zinc, convex in shape "and traversed in the center by a piece of copper wire, three or four lines in diameter" (St. Dominique, 1874, p. 68). The red (copper) on gray (zinc) held the attention of the patient's eye and produced the magnetic sleep. "After causing the subject to be seated, the disc is placed in his hand, which rests flat on his knees, and he is told to keep his eyes constantly fixed on it. This constitutes the whole process" (St. Dominique, 1874, p. 68; see also Tinterow, 1970, p. 390).

Here we have an induction technique consisting only of the subject's concentrated staring until the mesmeric condition set in. Durand did not use verbal suggestion of eye strain or fatigue as we now do with the prevalent eye-fixation inductions. The supposed effects of the metal on the body are evident in Durand's theory of what was occurring during the prolonged staring of the patient. Sensations of tingling were produced in the palm of the hand, traveled up the nerves of the arm to the head, and produced a "strange feeling" and tranquility there. Metals and their effects on the body still held a fascination for the mesmerizers of the 1840s and 1850s—even in America.

Samuel Underhill

Dr. Darling et al. and the gentlemen from New Orleans, Cincinnati, Rhode Island, and Pennsylvania were not the only individuals engaged in mesmeric activities during the middle and later 19th century in America. Indications are that there were a number of practitioners plying the trade throughout the States. Rather than chronicle all who traveled, lectured, and magnetized, I have chosen one, Samuel Underhill, as representative of the general Deleuzian method in vogue and the historical continuity of the practice of using magnetized water in his operations.

Dr. Underhill's book (1868/1902) was a series of lectures in which he reported various treatments he had administered in and around the Ohio area in the early 1840s. In Lecture 6, he relates his method:

> Well, to begin, your patient ought to sit comfortably. If an adult, a little lower than the magnetizer—with no one but the magnetizer to look him in the face. He should have the magnetizer sitting immediately before him, not leaning back too much, as this would put him too far from the magnetizer. His head should not fall back, as this would soon be uncomfortable, and his eyes should

fix calmly on those of the magnetizer . . . Now, let the magnetizer, sitting before the patient near as he well can, with the patient's feet between his own, take his thumbs by placing the ball of his thumb to the ball of the patient's, bringing the fore-finger across the nail of the thumb, that he may not strain the thumb back too far for comfort, and throwing his fingers as far over into the hand of the patient as may be, he has as good a contact and position as can be selected. (Underhill, 1868/1902, pp. 92–93)

At this point the magnetizer concentrated his will and effort and proceeded with passes that were intended to establish better rapport with the patient and produce the "magnetic sleep."

Now, collecting your thoughts and fixing your eyes and mind on the patient, exert firmly the intention to magnetize. . . . After holding the thumbs a few minutes, draw your hands away, and turning the backs of your hands towards the patient, you will move them apart the width of the patient's body, and a little more, and thus you will carry them up to the shoulders of the patient. Placing the fingers here a few moments, you will pass them lightly down the arms a few times—and always carrying them up in the same position as at first. You will next place them a moment on the head, the thumbs placed on the forehead just above the nose. Then you will pass them over the face, and then placing the thumbs on the pit of the stomach, and the fingers around the sides, you will keep them there two minutes. Then pass them down to the knees. (Underhill, 1868/1902, pp. 93–94)

According to Underhill, the first symptom of the state is that the thumbs and hands become cold and moist, a condition that should continue throughout the mesmerizing. If the hands became warm in the process, he advocated walking the patient briskly about the room and reinitiating the whole process. He also pointed out that the operator may speak to the patients in a normal, if not loud, voice without fear of arousing them from the magnetic condition. Most of his contemporaries maintained quiet during the process, lest the patient be distracted. Underhill did agree, however, that ambient disturbances be kept to a minimum during the initial phases of the induction.

Like the generally used techniques of his time, Underhill's method was like that of Deleuze and was intended to move the magnetic fluid from the magnetizer to the patient. But Underhill used another kind of magnetic fluid quite freely with his patients—magnetized water: "To magnetize water, you will take a tumblerful [sic] and fix your eyes upon it, hold your hand over it with the fingers extended, slowly moving them round over it for one minute" (Underhill, 1868/1902, p. 113). While it took one minute to magnetize a glass of water, it took five to prepare a bottle. The water was recognizable by his patients from ordinary, unmagnetized water, having either a sweetened or a carbonated taste. The water was used as a medicine or drunk regularly by the continuing patient to facilitate each successive mesmerization. Thus, while others in America kept alive such historically ancient techniques as the use of special metals, passes, and eye-fixation, Underhill, and no doubt many others, furthered the cause of magical fluids as adjuncts to and direct treatments for their patients' ills. (See Chapter 3 for the British uses of magnetized water.)

J. W. Cadwell

Just as Underhill represented the more itinerant professional individuals engaged in magnetism or mesmerism, I have selected "Professor" J. W. Cadwell as representative of the group of lay individuals traveling in the United States during the latter part of the 19th century giving stage performances and teaching techniques to all who could afford the $15 fee.

Cadwell roamed the eastern United States during the 1860s, 1870s, and 1880s, giving lectures (more than 250) as far south as Baltimore and as far west as Columbus, Ohio. He concentrated his efforts, however, in New England, primarily in Lowell, MA. and Providence, RI. Although most of his performances were given to large audiences, he occasionally mesmerised a person on the spot to instruct him or her in the phenomenon with which they were unfamiliar. For example, he told of a shopkeeper, in whose store he wanted to place a handbill advertising his lecture in Richmond, VT. When the shopkeeper queried, "What is psychology?", Cadwell had him place his hands, palm down on the counter and forcefully stroked the man's hands, drawing his fingers off of the end of the man's. While he was making these "passes", Cadwell talked incessantly (distracting verbalization), until after three or four passes, the man found he could not raise his hands from the counter.

His induction technique, on or off stage, was what we would call today a "rapid induction procedure," starting first with eye contact (not necessarily prolonged fixation) and then quickly offering the subject a suggestion of either physical immobility (Eyes will not open; hands are stuck together; cannot say name.) or cognitive inability (Cannot remember own name.). For example, at a Lowell, MA. lecture, a declared nonbeliever in mesmerism volunteered: "I looked at her steadily for half a minute, and until I had her undivided attention, and then in an earnest voice I said to her that she had forgotten her own name" (Cadwell, 1882, pp. 33–34). She in fact had.

In many ways Cadwell's stage techniques closely paralleled, or were identical to, methods used by both the ancients and the 20th century practitioners. He insisted on no interfering remarks or noises from the onlookers (reduced ambient stimulation). He established rapport with the intended subjects through small talk and then, when he had determined that they were highly susceptible to his influence, quickly proceeded with attempts to control some physical activity, as above. He was careful to use only volunteers with whom he determined he had an excellent chance of succeeding. "Street corner loafers" and inebriated individuals were quickly eliminated from the initial volunteers or made to sit with their backs to the audience with their eyes closed during the entire performance. Those who made good eye contact with him and responded positively to his first challenge (eye catalepsy) were used for demonstration. Those who could open their eyes were sent back to their places in the audience, and he quickly challenged the remaining subjects with catalepsies and amnesias. "Almost invariably I find that people with very full temples are generally easy subjects, while those with very hollow temples are very hard to control. Soft, light-haired people are very much easier to mesmerize than those with black coarse hair. *The eyes of good subjects will roll upward as the eyes are closing* [italics added]; if they do not, it is an indication that they are not easy subjects" (Cadwell, 1882, p. 46). In this quote, we see what appears to be the direct precurser of Felkin's (1890) sign of the hypnotic condition and Spiegel's Eye-Roll Sign of hypnotic susceptibility almost a century before Spiegel's work (Spiegel, 1972).

Although Cadwell began by having his subjects close their eyes for three or four minutes and challenging them to open them, he felt that the most critical factor in the induction was verbalization: "From the moment you commence your first effort, talk—keep talking—talk on—a steady round of talk. Talk is cheap, but it is more important than all other things combined. Whether you touch your volunteer or not, talk to him constantly" (Cadwell, 1882, p. 49). What he seems to be describing here is a "distraction technique," which was more fully developed in the 20th century. He did not care so much what was said, as the manner in which the verbalizations were presented: "Let every articulation of the voice indicate that you intend and expect to succeed; otherwise you had better not begin" (Cadwell, 1882, p. 60). Nothing succeeds like the suggestion of success.

What is so interesting about Cadwell's techniques is that they are the same techniques prevalent in today's stage performances and in the demonstrations given at professional meetings and workshops. Those who remember Erickson's demonstrations will recognize the selection of demonstration subjects through a quick analysis of their capacity for attentiveness; the ignoring of some volunteers while concentrating on others; the stream of conversation, often distracting the subject from other, more physical manipulations and suggestions occurring at the same time; the rapid, and sudden suggestion of a catalepsy, a hallucination. We have already noted that Spiegel's eye-roll susceptibility measure was there as well in Cadwell's little book, which the author published himself and "pronounced the most wonderful and interesting book ever written."

HYPNOSIS COMES OF AGE

Ambroise Auguste Liébeault

Born September 16, 1823, A. A. Liébeault first became aware of animal magnetism two years before he completed his medical degree in 1850. Generally presented as a quiet country doctor who plied hypnosis with the

French peasants in Pont-Saint-Vincent, near Nancy, he was influenced by Braid's writings and the induction method of Abbé Faria. Whether he was, in fact, the kindly, fatherly country doctor who charged patients if they required medication and treated them gratus if they required hypnosis, or a rather sloppy diagnostician, who ignored instances of his patients' noncompliance with his suggestions (See Pattie's description of Delboeuf's account of Liébeault.) has never been settled.

Bramwell was struck by the air of gentleness and calm that pervaded the overflowing waiting rooms at Nancy. (Liébeault settled there in 1864 and was seeing 50 to 60 patients a morning.) He was also impressed with the observation that almost all of the patients were easily hypnotized. Bramwell gave two descriptions of Liébeault's techniques. The first exemplified the "gentle doctor" image: "Two little girls, about six or seven years of age, no doubt brought in the first instance by friends, walked in and sat down on a sofa behind the doctor. He [Liébeault], stopping for a moment in his work made a pass in the direction of one of them, and said: 'Sleep, my little kitten,' repeated the same for the other, and in an instant they were both asleep. He rapidly gave them their dose of suggestion and then evidently forgot all about them" (Bramwell, 1903, p. 32). Delboeuf's (1889) description also implied a very casual approach; stating that Liébeault placed his hand on the patient's forehead and offhandedly remarked, "You are going to sleep" and manually closed the patient's eyes. Bramwell's (1903) second description implies that it was somewhat more elaborate than that:

> The patient was first placed in an arm-chair, then told to think of nothing and to look steadily at the operator. This fixation of the gaze was not maintained long enough to produce any fatigue of the eyes, and appeared to be simply an artifice for arresting the attention. If the eyes did not close spontaneously, Liébeault requested the patient to shut them, and then proceeded to make the following suggestions, or others resembling them:—'Your eyelids are getting heavy, your limbs feel numb, you are becoming more and more drowsy,' etc. This was continued for a minute or two; then Liébeault placed his hand upon the patient's body, and suggested the sensation of local warmth. (pp. 41–42)

Liébeault's own description of his technique reflects Bramwell's description:

> While the subject keeps his eyes on those of the operator, his senses are isolated from external and internal impressions. You direct him to simply imagine sleep and healing. You announce the initial phenomena of sleep to him—heaviness of the body, the desire to sleep, heaviness of the eyelids, and insensibility. When you perceive that the eyelids are fluttering and become heavy, when the eye takes on a surprised look, when the pupil oscillates or dilates, you say, "Sleep." And if the eyelids don't close, you repeat the same series of affirmations several times. Then your thumbs are placed on each lowered eyelid while you continue the suggestion. If, at the end of a minute, nothing has happened, you put it off until the next day. (Bernheim, 1891/1980, p. 64)

AMBROISE LIÉBEAULT (1823–1904)   HIPPOLYTE BERNHEIM (1840–1919)

Figure 4.2.   Ambroise Liébeault (1823–1904) and Hippolyte Bernheim (1840–1919). (Reprinted by permission of Henri F. Ellenberger.)

Here we see verbal suggestion, rather than physical eye fatigue, being used as the main vehicle of the induction of the sleep-like condition, which from here on in time was to be known as hypnosis. It was, in fact, Bramwell, after visiting Liébeault for two weeks in 1889, who credited him with the "development of modern hypnotism" (Bramwell, 1903, p. 32). However, Liébeault was not without his connections to the past. Forel (1906) reports that he used laying-on-of-hands with children, particularly those under the age of three. Also, he did use eye-fixation and passes with adults, although they were, apparently, more of a casual wave of the hand than a deliberate, mesmeric-like gesture. More important for historical continuity, Liébeault was reported by Delboeuf (1889; see Pattie, 1967) to have kept a bottle of magnetized water on hand for the treatment of infants (see also Forel, 1906). Specially prepared fluids remained a part of the process, even into the last quarter of the 19th century.

Following a celebration in his honor on May 25, 1891, Liébeault discontinued active practice, although he continued to contribute to the literature until his death on February 17, 1904 (see Hilger, 1912).

Hippolyte Marie Bernheim

Were it not for Bernheim, Liébeault would not have been as well known as he was in his day and as he is today. In 1882, the latter successfully treated a former patient of Bernheim's for sciatica. Since Bernheim had worked with the same patient without success for six months, he visited Liébeault's clinic to learn his technique. From this beginning, their continuing association formed the Nancy School (along with Beaunis and Liégois), which held views regarding hypnosis that differed greatly from those espoused by Charcot at the Salpêtrière.

Born in Mulhouse, Alsace-Lorraine in 1840, Bernheim received his medical training at Strasbourg before moving to Nancy and his clinical practice. Bernheim placed heavy emphasis on the suggestive element in hypnosis, the notion which formed the basis of his (and Liébeault's) disagreement with Charcot, who perceived the phenomenon as manifestations of pathology. Another basis of his suggestive argument was the data base he and Liébeault amassed in the process of successfully hypnotizing 85 percent of more than 10,000 patients they treated.

Bernheim's induction procedures were similar to Liébeault's described above. He first obtained their attention through some type of eye-fixation, then made gestures and other passes over the patient and completed the induction with verbal suggestions to sleep. Here, in his own words, is his technique:

> I begin by saying to the patient that I believe benefit is to be derived from the use of suggestive therapeutics; that it is possible to cure or to relieve him by hypnotism; that there is nothing either hurtful or strange about it; that it is an *ordinary sleep* or torpor which can be induced in everyone, and that this quiet, beneficial condition restores the equilibrium of the nervous system, etc. If necessary, I hypnotize one or two subjects in his presence, in order to show him that there is nothing painful in this condition and that it is not accompanied with any unusual sensation. When I have thus banished from his mind the idea of magnetism and the somewhat mysterious fear that attaches to that unknown condition, above all when he has seen patients cured or benefited by the means in question, he is no longer suspicious, but gives himself up, then I say, "Look at me and think of nothing but sleep. Your eyelids begin to feel heavy, your eyes tired. They begin to wink, they are getting moist, you cannot see distinctly. They are closed." Some patients close their eyes and are asleep immediately. With others, I have to repeat, lay more stress on what I say, and even make gestures. It makes little difference what sort of gesture is made. I hold two fingers of my right hand before the patient's eyes and ask him to look at them, or pass both hands several times before his eyes, or persuade him to fix his eyes upon mine, endeavoring, at the same time, to concentrate his attention upon the idea of sleep. I say, "Your lids are closing, you cannot open them again. Your arms feel heavy, so do your legs. You cannot feel anything. Your hands are motionless. You see nothing, you are going to sleep." And I add in a commanding tone, "Sleep." This word often turns the balance. The eyes close and the patient sleeps or is at least influenced.

> I use the word sleep, in order to obtain as far as possible over the patients, a suggestive influence which shall bring about sleep or a state closely approaching it; for sleep properly, so called, does not always occur. If the patients have

no inclination to sleep and show no drowsiness, I take care to say that sleep is not essential; that the hypnotic influence, whence comes the benefit, may exist without sleep; that many patients are hypnotized although they do not sleep.

If the patient does not shut his eyes or keep them shut, I do not require them to be fixed on mine, or on my fingers, for any length of time, for it sometimes happens that they remain wide open indefinitely, and instead of the idea of sleep being conceived, only a rigid fixation of the eyes results. In this case, closure of the eyes by the operator succeeds better. After keeping them fixed one or two minutes, I push the eye-lids down, or, stretch them slowly over the eyes, gradually closing them more and more and so imitating the process of natural sleep. Finally I keep them closed, repeating the suggestion, "Your lids are stuck together; you cannot open them. The need of sleep becomes greater and greater, you can no longer resist." I lower my voice gradually, repeating the command, "Sleep," and it is very seldom that more than three minutes pass before sleep or some degree of hypnotic influence is obtained. (Bernheim, 1884/1964, p. 2)

Thus Bernheim's technique was quite modern. He began by gaining rapport with the patient and allaying the patient's anxieties. Having clarified any misconceptions the patient may have had, he proceeded with what we would today call an eye-fixation technique, coupled with verbal suggestion for sleep, tiredness, and heaviness.

However, children, some adults, and individuals highly resistive to the techniques required special consideration:

As soon as they are able to pay attention and understand, children are as a rule very quickly and very easily hypnotized. It often suffices to close their eyes, to hold them shut a few moments, to tell them to sleep, and then to state that they are asleep.

Some adults go to sleep just as readily by simple closure of the eyes. I often proceed immediately without making use of passes or fixation, by shutting the eye-lids, gently holding them closed, asking the patient to keep them together, and suggesting at the same time, the phenomena of sleep. Some of them fall rapidly into a more or less deep sleep.

Others offer more resistance. I sometimes succeed by keeping the eyes closed for some time, commanding silence and quiet, talking continuously, and repeating the same formulas; "You feel a sort of drowsiness, a torpor; your arms and legs are motionless. Your eyelids are warm. Your nervous system is quiet; you have no will. Your eyes remain closed. Sleep is coming, etc." After keeping up this auditory suggestion for several minutes, I remove my fingers. The eyes remain closed. I raise the patient's arms; they remain uplifted. We have induced cataleptic sleep.

Others are more rebellious, preoccupied, unable to give themselves up: they analyze their own feelings, are anxious, and say they cannot sleep. I command them to be calm. I speak only of drowsiness, of sleepiness. "That is sufficient," I say, "to gain a result. The suggestion alone may be beneficial even without sleep. Keep perfectly quiet and do not worry." (Bernheim, 1884/1964, pp. 2–3)

Beaunis, a contemporary of Bernheim's at the Nancy School, also leaned heavily on eye-fixation without much emphasis on the verbal suggestion to sleep:

The method most frequently used, and which we might call "classical," is fixed gazing. I say to the patient: "Look at me very steadily," and at the end of a little time his eyelids close and he sleeps. After the subject has been hypnotised several times any method will reinduce the condition. (Bramwell, 1903, p. 42)

Bernheim also cited another contemporary, Brémaud, to illustrate his thesis that the important element in induction (and de-induction) is the suggestion relayed to the patient through whatever the hypnotist may do. Brémaud, using a technique of Donato (a Belgian stage hypnotist), operated as follows:

He asks the subject to lay the palms of his hands upon his own, stretched out horizontally, and to press downward with all his might. The subject's whole attention and all his physical force is absorbed in this manoeuvre. All his innervation, so to speak, is concentrated in this muscular effort, and so the distraction of his thoughts is prevented. "The magnetizer" says Brémaud, according to Donato, "looks at him sharply, quickly, and closely, directing him by gesture (and by word, if need be) to look at him as fixedly as he is able. Then the operator recedes or walks around the patient, keeping his eyes fixed upon him and attracting his gaze, while the subject follows him as if fascinated, with his eyes wide open, and unable to take them from the operator's face. If once carried away by the first experiment, the simple fixation of the gaze suffices to make the subject follow." (Bernheim, 1884/1964, p. 16)

Even in de-hypnosis, Bernheim found support for his suggestion thesis. Donato described awakening a subject by merely blowing on his face, while others, amateurs who had induced the hypnosis in the first place, could not arouse the subject despite all their efforts (blowing, slapping, and shaking). To Bernheim the explanation was simple: The frantic efforts of the untrained suggested to the subject that awakening was difficult and the subject followed that suggestion, refusing to be aroused. When, however, a person of known authority appeared, the subject awakened at a single puff of air.

Bernheim's own method of terminating hypnosis was verbal, coupled with physical touching only when the patient was slow to open his or her eyes. Initially, he merely stated: "It is all over. Wake up!" If they were slow to open their eyes, he said, "Your eyes are opening. You are awake!" If they still did not respond, he would choose some arbitrary spot on the head and tell the audience (so that the patient would hear it), "It is sufficient for me to touch this point to cause the eyes to open immediately." (Bernheim, 1884/1964, pp. 17–18). He then touched the spot and the patient awakened.

Thus Bernheim made it clear in both of his books (Bernheim, 1884, 1891) that he considered the passes and eye-fixation mere ploys for gaining and maintaining attention. Later (1891), he wrote that the success of gestures, touching, and so forth was dependent on their association with the suggestions of sleep and hypnosis, which were most effectively carried out verbally. In many respects he considered the single word "sleep" to be the most effective way of obtaining hypnosis: "Experience teaches that the simplest and best method for impressing the subject is by words" (Bernheim, 1891/1980, p. 65).

Thus Bernheim (who died in 1919) carried on the legacy of the Abbé Faria and Liébeault, his teacher and friend. Not only had hypnosis come of age, but the use of verbal suggestion and instructions became the major hypnotic induction vehicles.

Jean-Martin Charcot

Charcot, however, was not yet ready to give up the older procedures totally. He was, after all, the other giant of this era of hypnosis, having established his own territory, practice, and theory. For an individual so completely intolerant of the views of others, who, according to Pattie (1967), never hypnotized anyone, and who worked with a limited number of hysterical women, Jean-Martin Charcot holds an unusually revered position in the history of hypnosis as the individual who refocused interest in hypnosis and achieved its recognition by the scientific community (Chertok, 1967). No doubt part of this fame was the halo effect generated from his earlier successes in pulmonary and kidney diseases and the scleroses and ataxias (Ellenberger, 1965). The rest derived from the well-documented controversy between his Paris School and that at Nancy in the late 1800s, and the importance of his concern with scientific rigor, which was not fully appreciated until this century (Shor, 1972). Although the "suggestion" viewpoint of the Nancy School has been dubbed the "winner" of the controversy (Pattie, 1967), it is curious that it is the painting by A. Brouillet of Charcot demonstrating a case of "grand hystérie" that is remembered by the students of the history of hypnosis and psychiatry.

Charcot was born in 1825 (d. 1893) in Paris where his father was a carriage maker. Early in his medical career—when he was a resident—he was briefly assigned to the Salpêtrière, to which he returned in 1862 to build a cadré of devotees and to become the "prince de la Science" and the "Napoleon of Neuroses" (Ellenberger, 1965). His first interest in hypnosis was probably stirred by Charles Richet in 1878, leading eventually to his methodologically flawed work in the field and the Paris-Nancy controversy. While much has been written about the latter and Charcot's three stages of hypnosis, little has appeared about his (or rather his assistants') induction techniques.

According to Forel (1906), Charcot believed in the direct influence of magnets and metals as well as direct stimulation of portions of the head. Björnström (1887) tells us that Charcot (Here is probably meant, Charcot's assistants.) used a modification of Braid's visual fixation technique "by placing pieces of glass close to the bridge of the nose, by which procedure the convergency of the eyes is increased and sleep comes more rapidly" (Björnström, 1887, p. 16). Björnström also seems to confirm Forel's report of the use of magnets, but claims that Charcot used auditory and/or tactile stimulation as well. "A blow on a gong or a pressure on some 'hypnogenic or hysterogenic' zone [See Pitres's zones in Chapter 5.]—such as an ovary, the top of the head, and so forth—or the approach of a magnet will act on hysterical women" (Björnström, 1887, p. 16).

The varied methods used at the Salpêtrière were, it seems, less intended to induce a general hypnotic condition as to produce the three stages outlined by Charcot—lethargy, catalepsy, and somnambulism. Lethargy was achieved by eye-fixation and the closing of the eyes; catalepsy was obtained by converting lethargy through the opening of the eyes; and somnambulism by converting catalepsy through stroking the forehead (see Forel, 1906; Marks, 1947.) Bernheim described the sequence slightly differently in 1884: "the production of catalepsy with anaesthesia by fixation upon a bright light, . . . the sudden disappearance of the light, replacing the catalepsy by a sleep with relaxation, or lethargy, . . . [and] finally the friction of the head, transforming this lethargic state into somnambulism" (Bernheim, 1884/1964, p. 120). In 1891, he described the now accepted sequence of events—lethargy, catalepsy, and somnambulism—however, Björnström's (1887) account is like that of Bernheim's 1884 presentation. The first stage is catalepsy, induced either slowly through Braid's eye-fixation method or rapidly by the introduction of a sudden, alerting stimulus such as an unexpected flash of light or noise. The lethargic stage was produced by eye-fixation and pressure applied to the eyes through the closed lids. Somnambulism, so Björnström reported, was either produced by eye-fixation and manipulations, or secondarily from the other two stages by pressure on and stroking of the head.

Whatever is the correct sequence of events, it is clear that those working under Charcot were given to using a number of different inductions, singly or in combination. These inductions were more reminiscent of the past and less predictive of future trends in induction methodology than those used by Liébeault, Bernheim, and the rest of Nancy. If, then, the Nancy School was the "winner" in the war of theories, it was also the "winner" in furthering the induction methodologies from the past (e.g., Abbé Faria), which were to dominate the forthcoming 20th century.

Countess C. de St. Dominique

Although hypnosis was coming of age through the efforts of Liébeault, Bernheim, Charcot, and others, the maturation was not without backward strides. The past continually made its impact felt.

In 1874 a book was published in London by a Countess C. de St. Dominique which reflected the continuing interest in magnetized water and other objects: "Water is magnetized by directing the tips of the fingers towards the surface of the liquid, by holding in the hand the vessel containing it, by warm insufflation over it, and lastly by discharges of fluid from the hand" (St. Dominique, 1874, p. 73). The Countess noted one prerequisite for the water's effectiveness; the patient had to be "under the influence of magnetism," unlike previous uses of specially treated water where the water itself induced the condition.

Any object can, according to this treatise, be magnetized and thereafter induce the magnetic condition in individuals with whom it is brought into contact. The method was simple: "Magnetized objects are prepared by keeping them in the hand for the space of fifteen minutes, with the firm will of impregnating them with the agent destined to act on the subject" (St. Dominique, 1874, p. 72). The author warns against too casually using magnetized objects, for they were capable of influencing individuals who were unaware of their power, a power that could not be rendered impotent without "a regular course of demagnetization." Sheets of magnetized paper were reported to retain their influence ever after being burned! A similar, indestructability with regard to marble was attributed to Du Potet by Poyen (1837):

> A large marble pestle, after being magnetized, was wholly immersed in muriatic acid, in which it was kept until the acid had reduced the mass to about one half of its original size, it was then drawn out, well cleansed, and presented to the somnambulist, who fell asleep as soon as he had touched the whole mass of marble. ("Elements," p. 21)

The Countess's technique was given in detail:

> Place your chair at a few inches from the subject's knees, and sit with your legs sufficiently open to enclose those of the subject, without, however, touching them, keeping the body and head erect. Ask the subject to keep his eyes constantly fixed on yours, to place his hands on his knees, to keep his thoughts centered on you and to strictly avoid their being diverted.
>
> Then take both his hands in yours, his left in your right and his right in your left, your thumbs resting in the hollow of his palms, which they fill, and allow them to rest on the knees of the subject. The object of this first operation is to establish the magnetic relation by the multiplied effects of contact.
>
> Meanwhile, the operator's eyes are performing their part; he keeps them steadfastly fixed on those of the subject, without allowing himself to be disturbed by his looks, his laughter, his tears, or the slight nervous twitchings which might agitate him.
>
> At the end of two or three minutes employed in establishing magnetic relation, gently withdraw your right hand, hold it extended as if conferring a benediction, and bring it before the eyes of the subject, your middle finger pointing to

the centre of the nose, which it must approach within a few lines only. After the space of a moment, this operation should be repeated with the left hand, both hands acting respectively on the eyes. Maintain this position for ten minutes without lifting your eyes from those of the subject—whether the latter be closed or shut is immaterial. It being admitted in principle that the fluid escapes from every part of the operator's body, but principally from its most pointed extremities, the fingers are naturally looked upon as the best conductors: the magnetizer is made aware of this by a certain heat, a kind of tingling which he feels in these parts; and the subject, by something of a similar sensation, which he in turn experiences at their approach. On the other hand, the close proximity of the fingers to the eyes will cause him to squint slightly, which is sufficient to produce the magnetic sleep. After a few minutes his eyes become closed, and this is a first result. (St. Dominique, 1874, pp. 54–56)

In addition, she pointed out certain exceptional methods, which were used occasionally:

The operation, which consists in holding the hand extended before the eye of the subject, is unquestionably the most important act of magnetization, that which more than any other ensures the "engagement" of the brain.

Practice will point out the variations or additions which may be introduced in the above process. When the subject is thought to become sensitive, or that he is favourably disposed, the effect is hastened by imparting, and almost imperceptibly, a tremulous movement to the hands for the purpose of discharging a greater abundance of fluid. When the moment for completing the sleep is supposed to be arrived at, the tip of one of the middle fingers should be applied to the root of the subject's nose. On persons whose phrenological organ of veneration is particularly developed, the application of the hand on the anterior fontanel has sometimes produced a good effect, which in others has been obtained by pretending to surround the temples, the eyes, or the cerebellum with the palms of the hands. Some operators perform magnetic passes before the face, from the eyes to the chin, while others strongly press the thumb and first finger on the eyes with the firm determination to produce sleep. (St. Dominique, 1874, p. 56)

The technique, then, is a combination of eye-fixation, passes, and phrenological pressures.

St. Dominique also noted a phenomenon that long interested those concerned with clairvoyance in the 18th and 19th centuries, and continues to be described today (Erickson, 1952)—namely, somnambulism. She noted that this is a rare occurrence, and, while it can occur independently of the magnetic condition, usually is produced only after many magnetic sessions. She detailed the methods of four individuals—Loisson, Lafontaine, Cahagnet, and Millet—for producing somnambulism, warning, however, that these methods—dramatically like those used for ordinary magnetism—are effective only on individuals who are already somnambulists. Here are the techniques:

M. Loisson recommends holding the hands for a certain time over the head of the subject, directing warm insufflations over the two thumbs brought together under the nostrils and between the eyes; then, leaving one hand in that position, the other should be placed above the epigastric region, and finally, insufflations should be made on the two thumbs placed over the pit of the stomach, while the fingers encircle the ribs.

According to M. Lafontaine, when sleep is already established, the hands should be placed for a minute or two over the head of the subject, and his brain be charged; after which one hand should be placed over the chest for the space of half an hour, with occasional passes.

M. Cahagnet is in favour of placing the hand over the exterior fontanel, allowing it to rest there for ten minutes, bringing it gently down in front of the forehead to the root of the nose, simply presenting the tips of the fingers before those organs, enveloping the head in fluid, using both hands for the purpose; depositing a portion of the fluid on the temples and eyelids, acting with particular energy on the latter, with the firm will that they shall close.

M. Millet selects a sensitive subject, and places himself before him as if for the purpose of magnetizing him. He requests him to divest his mind of all care and trouble, and seeks to inspire him with confidence, since a sense of fear or repulsion will raise insurmountable obstacles. Bending his hand to the shape of an arch, he presents his fingers opposite the root of the nose, and performs passes over the face down to the chin, by a simple twist of the wrist, the arm remaining stationary. (St. Dominique, 1874, p. 160)

Interestingly, St. Dominique also made a distinction between magnetism and the "hypnosis of Dr. Braid." She viewed the latter as "a process of magnetization" with the advantage that it could be used for group inductions (provided there were enough Darling discs to go around), but the major detraction that it "is violent in its action, and tires the subject much more than does ordinary magnetization" (St. Dominique, 1874, p. 70). She preferred the tried and true animal magnetism.

However, despite the Countess's preference, Braid had renamed the process, and hypnosis was maturing, born of and certainly not discontinuous with the older forms of magnetism and mesmerism.

Contemporaries to Controversy

Because the controversy between the Paris and Nancy Schools regarding the basis of hypnosis has so overshadowed our thinking of the history of hypnosis, we often forget that a number of other practitioners and investigators were active during the same period and throughout the last two or three decades of the 1800s. Here I will highlight only a few of those individuals.

Charles Richet

Richet (1850–1935) was a man with varied and far-ranging interests. A noted physiologist of his time and 1913 Nobel laureate, his personality was described by Dessoir (see Ellenberger, 1970) as "a strange mixture of scientific rigor and poetic indulgence." He introduced automatic writing in psychopathology, pointed out to his contemporaries that de Puységur had already written about their "discoveries" a century before, and founded the *Sociéte de Psychologie Physiologique* with Charcot. His "poetic indulgent" side came to fruition with the publication of a novel, *Sister Marthe,* about the development of multiple personality in the context of the treatment of nervous systems through hypnosis. He authored the book under the pseudonym of Charles Epheyre.

While Liébeault was working outside of Nancy, Richet was advocating hypnosis—he called it "somnambulisme provoqué"—in Paris. His induction technique was based primarily on that of Mesmer, the holding of the thumbs and passes over the head and upper body. Eye-fixation was considered helpful, but not necessary. Bramwell (1903) provided an English translation of Richet's 1884 description:

> I place my patient in an arm-chair in front of me, in each of my hands I take one of his thumbs, and squeeze them somewhat strongly and with fairly uniform pressure. After continuing this for three or four minutes, I generally find that nervous patients experience a sensation of heaviness in the arms, elbows and wrists. I then make passes with outstretched hands; these consist of uniform movements from above downwards in front of the eyes, as if I desired to close them. At first I thought it necessary to make the patient look fixedly at some object, but it now appears to me that this was a useless complication. Steady gazing has perhaps some influence, but it is not indispensable. (Bramwell, 1903, p. 43)

Jules Bernard Luys

Richet and Charcot were not the only individuals engaged in hypnotic use and investigation in Paris in the 1880s. Although Luys (1828–1895) recognized that sounds (tuning fork vibrations, the tick of a watch, verbal commands) could produce the artifical sleep called hypnosis, he concentrated on eye-fixation methods and received some attention by bringing mechanical methodology to eye-fixation as an induction technique. Using a rotating mirror, such as was in use for attracting meadow larks, he induced hypnosis by having his patients stare at the device. Hart (1896/1982) described the device as "a framework of small mirrors, rotated by a clockwork movement, before which the subjects for experiment are placed, and as they gaze at it they fall into various attidues [sic] of slumber, fascination, catalepsy, hysteric hallucination, or whatever else one may please to call it" (Hart, 1896/1982, p. 87). (See Figure 4.3.) So attractive was the device, at least to larks and hypnotists, if not their patients, that a number of modifications appeared. One was described by Bramwell (1903): "After seating the patient in a comfortable chair, I arranged a small moveable mirror above his eyes, and placed a lamp in such a way as to throw a bright light upon it. The patients

Figure 4.3.   Group of eight people under the influence of a rotating mirror apparatus (after Luys). (From *Hypnotism, Mesmerism and the New Witchcraft* by Ernest Hart, 1896).

were told to look fixedly at the mirror as long as they could keep their eyes open. In some instances the eyes closed rapidly and hypnosis quickly appeared'' (Bramwell, 1903, p. 48). One is easily reminded of the lighted candle in the *Leiden Papyrus,* and Braid's lancet case as foci for creating eye fatigue and thus hypnosis.

Probably one of the most generally negative views of hypnosis, and of J. B. Luys in particular, came from the pen of the London surgeon, Ernest Hart (1835–1898). A fair portion of Hart's book (1898/1982) discussed his 1892–1893 visit to Luys's wards at the Hôpital de la Charité, which he described as surpassing those effects and performances ''to which we have all been more or less accustomed at the theatres of magic and the conjurers' halls on the boulevards of Paris or in Piccadilly'' (Hart, 1896/1982, p. 71). Through observation and controlled repetitions of experiments he had observed, he concluded ''that Hypnotism, when it is not a pernicious fraud, is a mere futility which should have no place in the life of those who have work to do in the world,'' and ''that for curative purposes hypnotism is very rarely useful, generally entirely useless, and often injurious'' (Hart, 1896/1982, preface to second edition & p. 68).

Despite his generally negative opinion, he recognized what has become one basic tenet of present-day hypnotic inductions, the central role and focus played by the subject or patient in the process: ''To produce these effects there is no cleverness wanted on the part of the hypnotiser, there is no special power in this matter resident in him; anyone can hypnotise and everyone can hypnotise if he is patient enough, and either scientifically intelligent or ignorantly fanatic. The marvel and the mystery is in the individual operated upon" (Hart, 1896/1982, p. 66). The central importance of this viewpoint will become clearer at the end of this chapter and in my exposition of the 20th century techniques.

Frederik Björnström

Not all of the activity on the continent in the latter part of the 19th century was occurring in France. Frederik Björnström (1833–1889), Professor of Psychiatry at the Stockholm Hospital, published his book (1887) to summarize what was known at the time and convey his own views regarding hypnosis. He was one of the earlier writers to discuss the relationship between hypnosis and law, a topic that still consumes considerable debate.

Rather than present a verbatim account of his own preferred method, Björnström reviewed a number of techniques, most of which have been chronicled above. He does mention G. Gessman of Vienna who combined the holding of the thumbs with strokings and concern with the stomach as a "sense organ." Gessmann said:

> I sit down opposite her, make her close her eyes, take her hands in mine so that the four thumbs are pressed against each other, tell her to be quiet, and to yield unresistingly to the first inclination to sleep. When she has fallen asleep—generally within ten or twenty minutes—I increase the sleep by some strokings over her head and chest, and try to induce her to talk; this I easily achieve by placing one hand on her head and taking one of her hands in my other hand, while I—speaking towards the pit of her stomach—ask: "Do you hear me?" (Björnström, 1887, p. 16; See also Gessmann, Chapter 5)

Björnström felt that hypnosis could be produced through a number of widely differing techniques. Vision could be irritated by bright lights, audition by either sudden sounds (gongs or drums) or monotonous sounds like a ticking clock, or the rhythms of songs or chants. By his account, Binet and Féré exhausted the sense of olfaction with musk, thus inducing hypnosis. The tactile sense approach appeared to be a throwback to the phrenology prevalent in the days of Elliotson. In general, the tactile method called for direct pressure on the visual or auditory senses, by pressing on the eyes or the external auditory meatus. The relation to phrenology appears in the notion that certain areas of the body were considered "hypnogenic zones," particularly sensative to hypnotic influence through touch and stroking (see Pitres, Chapter 5). These areas were the top of the head, the forehead, the base of the thumb, joints, and the area of the ovaries.

One set of instructions that Björnström did provide was usually absent in many of the writings of this period: de-hypnotization. The process of de-hypnotizing the patient appears to have been "common" knowledge, so that many writers did not include instructions for what some may have considered to be the more important part of the total process. Again, Björnström points to the multiplicity of effective methods, but does outline a series of maneuvers to pursue if the patient does not awaken on the first attempt:

The simplest and most common method is to blow on the eyes or forehead. This may be done with a pair of bellows instead of with the mouth; or a few drops of water may be dashed on the face. If this proves unsuccessful, the eyelids are raised and the blowing is made a little stronger straight into the eyes. If then awakening does not follow, pressure may be made (in hysterical women) on the ovarian region or on other hypnogenic zones. For by pressure on the same spot, many hysterical persons can be hypnotized when awake, and wakened when asleep. The same means seems to have opposite effects, depending on the state of the persons. Blowing on only one half of the head, while the other half is separated by a screen, wakens only one half of the body. The subject is wakened psychically by the simple cry "Awake!" addressed to him. (Björnström, 1887, p. 19)

In a real sense, the techniques used to arouse the patient were strikingly like those used to induce hypnosis in the first place. The blowing and the water splashed in the face could as well serve as a sudden, unexpected stimulus—the type used at the Salpêtrière to induce catalepsy. Björnström points out the apparent paradox that the same stimulus (e.g., pressure on the ovarian region) will render opposite effects depending on the particular condition of the subject at the time of the stimulus presentation. He may have been inadvertently anticipating the present-day concern for the role of the patient/subject in the effectiveness of any induction or de-induction technique. He may also have inadvertently anticipated the present-day concern with brain hemisphere function, as it relates to hypnosis and hypnotic functioning, for he discusses the production of aphasia by "frictions" on the left side of the head.

August Forel

While Björnström worked in Sweden, Forel (1848–1931) promoted hypnosis in Zurich. His book, first published in Stuttgart in 1889, went through 12 editions. His major contribution to keeping interest in hypnosis alive was his use of the procedure therapeutically in the Cantonal Insane Asylum (Burghölzli) where he was the Director.

Although Forel did not outline his own induction technique in detail—stating, rather, that he recommended the method of Liébeault and Wetterstrand (of Stockholm)—he did comment on a number of points that are today considered basic to the therapeutic applications of hypnosis. He warned, for example, against using a mechanical, automatic approach to the hypnotic situation on the part of the hypnotist. The operator must be constantly alert, innovative, and flexible in her or his approach to the patient. (Erickson's "utilization technique" [1959] may owe a debt to Forel and Bernheim on this point.) He should avoid arousing anxiety and/or negative "autosuggestions" regarding the process. Forel advocated Oskar Vogt's general approach. Vogt did not give direct commanding suggestions to the patient, but, rather, "hinted" at what he intended the patient to do or perceive. His verbal delivery was in a quiet, gentle tone of voice, so that the

AUGUSTE FOREL (1848–1931)

Figure 4.4. Auguste Forel (1848–1931). (Reprinted by permission of Henri F. Ellenberger.)

"freedom of will" of the patient would not be disturbed. (Again, the nondirective or indirective approaches of today owe a debt.) In Forel's words: "The old rule remains the same: kind, consistent, and firm" (Forel, 1906, p. 213).

Forel did give one specific, which appears to be his own, in his chapter, "Hints to the Practitioner." He suggested that the chair to be used for the patient either have no arms at all or be upholstered. The chair should be placed against a wall to be used later in the process when arm catalepsy is suggested. Other than this directive, Forel either outlined or reproduced the induction procedures of others (e.g., Bernheim). One of these techniques is of interest, because it foreshadowed the present-day approaches wherein the operator is careful, on initial contact with the patient, to avoid any statements that are easily refuted or not true. For example, if the patient is wearing a blue sweater, the hypnotist might comment, "You are wearing a blue sweater today." This statement is irrefutable and the patient immediately begins to accept the concept that what the operator says is true. Thus verbal conditioning begins from the outset, and further, more complicated suggestions are more readily accepted by the patient. Forcing an event to occur, while coupling its occurrence with the verbal suggestion for that event, is evident in Grossmann's technique:

First of all, I suggest suggestibility to every patient. I find it best to deal with the sceptic with the following little experiment: I say to him that I am going to press on his conjunctiva with my finger, although he will scarcely believe it, without producing any reflex closure of the lids—that is, without his blinking. The experiment nearly always succeeds, for, as I have pointed out in a previous work, the conjunctiva of almost every person becomes anaesthetic by fixing at the same time the attention on this sort of suggestion. The fact that the suggestion has succeeded frequently increases the suggestibility to such an extent that the command to sleep, simply following at once on this, suffices to cause hypnosis to appear forthwith. In other cases I get the patient to sit on a chair, without leaning back, or, still better, to rest on a sofa in a half-sitting, half-lying position, and to fix me intently with his eyes for a few seconds. I then suggest to him that [he] feels a sensation of warmth traversing his limbs, and especially that his arms, which are resting on his knees, are becoming as heavy as lead. Having said this, I raise them a little, catching hold of them by the wrists, and cause them to fall suddenly by a slight push of my hands. They fall back on the knees apparently as heavy as lead, and the patient actually feels a marked tiredness in his arms; this I have had confirmed by nearly everyone. If I do not observe the somewhat dazed expression, or trances of it, which may only last for a few seconds, I then use the principal trick. I ask the patient to close his eyes, or I close them myself quickly; then I seize his wrists, the forearms being flexed upwards, and suggest that he is becoming so tired that he can no longer keep up, but must sink back. I gradually press him backwards myself by imperceptible pushes, until his head is resting on the back of the chair, and, provided that it is still necessary, give the command to sleep. (Forel, 1906, pp. 210–211)

Thus, while Forel did not present a unique induction procedure of his own, he did summarize a number of approaches that clearly foreshadowed the basic techniques used in present-day hypnotic induction procedures.

Otto Georg Wetterstrand

Like Forel, Wetterstrand, working in Sweden, was practically oriented. However, if Forel's book reflected the march from special metal objects, magnetized water, mesmeric passes, and so forth to verbal suggestion in the context of a client-centered atmosphere, Wetterstrand's approach could be interpreted as mainly a step backwards, or at least a running in place.

Wetterstrand's Stockholm clinic was certainly a sought-after place. Forel visited there in 1890 and Bramwell in 1894. The atmosphere in the clinic was primarily one of silence. The conduction of sound was contained through heavy carpeting in the two rooms that Forel described. Apparently, Wetterstrand's patient population had expanded by 1894, for Bramwell describes the clinic as consisting of three rooms. Nonetheless, silence and darkness were described by both visitors. There was a steady flow of patients from 9 a.m. to 1 p.m. each day. Patients were first screened for suitability and were conducted into the treatment rooms. Hypnosis took place in front of others waiting for treatment, so that new patients observed returning patients being rapidly placed in the hypnotic condition. This "group" approach seemed to increase the susceptibility of those waiting for their turn, in much the same manner that Erickson, during large audience demonstrations, would hypnotize one individual on stage while the rest observed, and became more susceptible themselves. Unlike Erickson, who gave suggestions loud enough for all to hear, Wetterstrand whispered his suggestions individually to the patients. If he wanted to give the same suggestion to more than one patient, he raised his voice appropriately. Wetterstrand's clinic must have had somewhat the atmosphere of Mesmer's *baquet,* with a number of patients in varying degrees of hypnosis as he (Wetterstrand) moved among them inducing the hypnotic condition and offering therapeutic suggestions.

Curiously, one does not obtain the impression of a throwback to induction techniques and procedures of a time gone by in Wetterstrand's own writing. In his book (1893/1902) he describes his induction technique without a hint of the grand showmanship implied in the writings of Forel and Bramwell:

> But how are we to proceed to produce hypnosis easily and quickly? If we adhere to the explanation first given by Liébeault, that sleep is the result of a psychic act, the answer is not difficult. We tell the patient that sleep will most probably cure his disease, and that he will enjoy a quiet, refreshing slumber, which all can get under the same circumstances and without any disagreeable after-effect. We ask him to sit down and to concentrate all his thoughts upon sleep. Then, while fixing our eyes upon him, we suggest a heaviness in the lids and the limbs and an increasing impossibility to move. Continuing to speak about sleep and its symptoms which soon are to make their appearance, we finally say that they are already there. (In the case of most people, sleep has come in less time than is needed to write these lines; others, who prove less susceptible, resist longer.) He is then told that the sleep, or even the lightest slumber, is beneficial, and if that state be not obtainable, we make him witness the result upon one or two, who previously have proved good subjects, and we often gain thereby our purpose. Sometimes we succeed in hypnotizing a person who two or three times before had resisted our efforts. (p. 4)

Here, then, is a simple use of verbal suggestion to induce hypnosis, based on his adherence to the Nancy School's theoretical position. However, Bramwell (1903) indicates that Wetterstrand's overall method was clearly related to those of a few decades prior to his period.

> In addition to making verbal suggestions, Wetterstrand employed passes more largely than is usually done by members of the Nancy school; these were made over the eyes, face, and arms, and always with contact. Sometimes he would touch the forehead with one hand, while with the other he pressed heavily over the region of the heart. Before commencing the passes, he generally requested the patient to look at his eyes, but this was never continued long. The patients rested quietly for about an hour, while Wetterstrand passed from one to the other whispering suggestions audible only to the person addressed. (pp. 42–43)

Wetterstrand was also given to converting natural sleep into hypnosis through the following method:

> One hand is laid carefully and lightly on the sleeper's forehead, the body is gently stroked with the other, and, in a subdued voice, the patient is told to go

on sleeping. When questioned he replies, and *rapport* is established. (Bramwell, 1903, p. 47)

Wetterstrand's book (1893/1902), which is basically a resumé of his clinical practice, including 128 detailed case histories of cures of virtually every malady from hysteria to poliomyelitis, epilepsy, stuttering, chorea, and heart disease, also indicated his use of chloroform as an adjunct to his usual hypnotic induction. In resistive cases he added "a few drops of chloroform" to his suggestive patter and was able to turn the patient thenceforth into an excellent hypnotic subject. This is a combination about which we read little today.

F. van Eeden and van Renterghem

Both van Eeden and van Renterghem operated a private clinic in Amsterdam during the last decade of the 19th century, and, like Wetterstrand, were mainly interested in the therapeutic applications of hypnosis. Van Eeden, in a presentation to the Second International Congress of Experimental Psychology in London in 1892, decried the use of the word hypnosis because it had become associated with performers and stage hypnotists and therefore detracted from the actual value of suggestive therapeutics. This position regarding stage hypnotists was not so different from the concerns of present-day "professional" users of hypnosis.

Bramwell (1903) stopped at Amsterdam to visit with van Eeden and van Renterghem in 1893 on his tour of the clinics of Europe. His description of their technique indicated that it was essentially that of Wetterstrand, "quiet, prolonged resting in a darkened room, combined with softly whispered suggestions" (Bramwell, 1903, p. 43). Thus these well-known practitioners of Amsterdam, as Wetterstrand in Sweden, used techniques that harkened all the way back to the sleep temples of the ancients, *sans* the appearance of a diety to make therapeutic suggestions.

Albert Moll

Long before Albert Moll (b. May 4, 1862) wrote his now classic, *The Study of Hypnosis* in 1889, he was well known for his work on sexuality and psychopathology. His efforts concentrated on the libido, which he viewed as "stages of evolution of the sexual instinct" (Ellenberger, 1970, p. 704). Thus his efforts in this area led from Dessoir to Freud to Jung.

Moll's *Study of Hypnosis* presented one of the most comprehensive summaries of the history of the phenomenon, in addition to his own theoretical views (see Edmonston, 1981), and descriptions of various experiments made by him. It is in the context of the latter that we glean some pictures of the induction techniques used by Moll (1889/1897):

I request him [a young man of twenty] to seat himself on a chair, and give him a button to hold, telling him to look at it fixedly. After three minutes his eyelids fall; he tries in vain to open his eyes, which are fast closed; his hand, which until now has grasped the button, drops upon his knee. (p. 31)

Here we have a technique reminiscent of Dr. Darling's zinc and copper disc. The boy was aroused by blowing on his eyes.

With a 53-year-old woman, Moll (1889/1897) used downward mesmeric passes and awakened her with passes in the opposite direction, but with the palms outward (backs of the hands toward the patient):

> When she has seated herself on a chair I place myself before her; I raise my hands, and move them downwards, with the palms towards her, from the top of the head to about the pit of the stomach. I hold my hands so that they may not touch her, at a distance of from two to four centimetres. As soon as my hands come to the lowest part of the stroke I carry them in a wide sweep with outspread arms up over the subject's head. I then repeat exactly the same movements; that is, passes from above downwards, close to the body, and continue this for about ten minutes. At the end of this time the subject is sitting with closed eyes, breathing deeply and peacefully. (p. 32)

He then offered the patient a series of physical challenges, such as eye and limb catalepsies to which she complied.

The third experiment, with a boy of 16, found the patient imitating Moll's (1889/1897) every move following this induction:

> I request him to look me straight in the eyes. After he has done this for some time I take him by the hand and draw him along with me. Then I let go, but our eyes remain fixed on each other's. (p. 33)

In this case, the hypnosis was terminated by Moll's ceasing to stare at the patient.

Finally, a verbal induction procedure was described, with a 41-year-old male patient:

> [He] seats himself on a chair. I tell him that he must try to sleep. "Think of nothing but that you are to go to sleep." After some seconds I continue: "Now your eyelids are beginning to close; your eyes are growing more and more fatigued; the lids quiver more and more. You feel tired all over; your arms go to sleep; your legs grow tired; a feeling of heaviness and the desire for sleep take possession of your whole body. Your eyes close; your head feels duller; your thoughts grow more and more confused. Now you can no longer resist; now your eyelids are closed. Sleep!" (Moll, 1889/1897, pp. 33–34)

Moll then described a series of instructions for visual hallucinations and comments that hypnosis has, in this case, been induced through the image of sleep. The patient is aroused by saying to him, "Wake up!"

With these four experiments Moll illustrated that there were (and are) multiple induction paths to hypnosis, and further, that different individuals respond to different techniques differently. Thus, later on in his book, he suggested that, while one method may not work with a particular patient, another might, so that the hypnotist should be well armed with a number of different induction techniques. Moll reviewed a variety of techniques, which he classified as the mental (directing the subject's imagination, as seen in the techniques of Faria, Braid, Bernheim, etc.) and the physical (stimulating the senses, as in techniques used by Braid early on, Du Potet, Luys, Charcot, etc.). These methods have been described above, so there is no reason to repeat them here. However, Moll did make one comment that is of interest. Noting that others have proposed that "monotonous singing and uniform whirling movements" produce hypnosis in Northern Africa and the East (The dervishes were most often cited.), he offered a contrary opinion: "I have, however, myself, often watched the howling and dancing dervishes at Cairo and Constantinople, without being able to detect any indication of autohypnosis" (Moll, 1889/1897, p. 43).

Sigmund Freud

Freud, like a number of present-day practitioners, was introduced to hypnosis by observing a stage hypnotist, Hansen, who traveled in Germany and Austria. Freud studied under Charcot and visited Bernheim and Liébeault. He was much impressed with the latters' use of hypnosis in front of new patients, so that they would be more easily hypnotized when their turn came. Freud's disappointment with hypnosis and his subsequent abandonment of it as a treatment method is well known (see, for example, Ellenberger, 1970; Marks, 1947; Pattie, 1967), and is occasionally characterized by lecturers as a failure of Freud as a hypnotizer; it is clear from his own writing (Freud, 1891) that his induction techniques were those of his era, those which others (Wetterstrand, van Eeden & van Renterghem, Forel, Bernheim, & Liébeault) had found quite successful for their purposes. Apparently he used the eye-fixation method of Braid and the verbal suggestions of sleep, either individually or in combination. Why he was "unsuccessful" was probably more a case of his own expectations of "deep hypnosis" and the fact that so small a percentage of patients were able to achieve the levels of hypnosis he desired for his explorations into the nervous disorders. Consequently, Freud contributed little to our history of the development of induction procedures.

J. Milne Bramwell

Bramwell was one of the two most often mentioned individuals practicing hypnosis in the last decade of the century in England (the other was C. Lloyd Tuckey). He was a physician in private practice who came later to hypnosis, about 1889, but rapidly expanded his knowledge and skills through a number of visits to clinics throughout the continent. His book, *Hypnotism* (1903), briefly summarized the techniques used in the clinics, as well as other methods with which he had become familiar through travel, lectures, and informal meetings. His own technique was modified over the years, beginning at first with a combination of Braid's eye-fixation on a Luys-like light-reflecting mirror, and mesmeric passes:

> After seating the patient in a comfortable chair, I arranged a small moveable mirror above his eyes, and placed a lamp in such a way as to throw a bright light upon it. The patients were told to look fixedly at the mirror as long as they could keep their eyes open. In some instances the eyes closed rapidly and hypnosis quickly appeared; in others, even after half an hour's gazing, there was no apparent result. When this was the case, I requested them to shut their eyes, and made passes without contact over the face and upper part of the body, at the same time adding a few suggestions. (Bramwell, 1903, p. 48)

At other times he took a page from Wetterstrand, passing from patient to patient in the clinic room offering a verbal induction:

> I passed rapidly from one to the other, saying to each in turn: "Look at my eyes! Your eyelids are getting heavy, you cannot keep them open, they are closing now, they are fast!" As the eyelids closed, which they almost invariably did at once, I made an energetic pass in the direction of the patient's face and said: "Sleep!" (Bramwell, 1903, p. 49)

These two approaches were used on his own patients, individuals with whom he was already familiar.

As he began seeing people who were strangers to him, he found that the notion that observing others already in hypnosis was facilitating to one's own hypnotizability, was not correct. His new patients found the group atmosphere disturbing. Consequently, he reverted to the use of a darkened room and the Luys's mirror. However, even that had its difficulties.

> Each patient was then taken singly, and fixed gazing at a mirror in a darkened room again resorted to. In addition, I frequently made them look at my eyes while I made verbal suggestions. I also procured one of Luys' revolving mirrors, but found it worse than useless. The instrument was driven by clockwork, but could not be stopped until it ran down, and there was no method of regulating its speed. It made a loud and disagreeable noise, which from time to time became more marked and irregular, and irresistibly suggested an infernal machine on the point of exploding! (Bramwell, 1903, p. 49)

Necessity drove him to reconstruct the mirror arrangement to eliminate the disturbing elements, even to the point of his modification producing a uniform and soothing sound.

As the years went on, Bramwell developed his own method, which he described, and then cautioned the reader that "no stereotyped method is employed." Thus, like Moll, he stressed flexibility in the approach to different individuals or to the same individual at different times. He began with an approach that is strongly stressed today—that of establishing rapport with the patient by allaying any anxiety or misconceptions she or he may have concerning hypnosis.

> I then say: "Presently I shall ask you to look at my eyes for a few seconds, when probably your eyelids will become heavy and you will feel impelled to close them. Should this not happen, I shall ask you to shut them, and to keep them closed until I tell you to open them. I shall then make certain passes and suggestions, but I do not wish you to pay much attention to what I am saying or doing, and above all you are not to attempt to analyse your sensations. Your best plan will be to create some monotonous drowsy mental picture and to fix your attention upon that. You must not expect to go to sleep. A certain number of hypnotised persons pass into a condition more or less closely resembling sleep; few do so at the first sitting, however, and you must only expect to feel drowsy and heavy." After these explanations, and having darkened the room and instructed any spectators to remain quiet, I place my patient in a comfortable chair and request him to look at my eyes, at the same time bringing my face slightly above and about ten inches from his. The patient's eyes sometimes close almost immediately. Should they not do so, I continue to look steadily at him and make suggestions. These are twofold; the patient's attention is directed to the sensations he probably is experiencing, and others, which I wish him to feel, are suggested. Thus: "Your eyes are heavy, the lids are beginning to quiver, the eyes are filling with water. You begin to feel drowsy, your limbs are becoming heavy, you are finding it more and more difficult to keep your eyes open, etc." (Bramwell, 1903, pp. 50–51)

This procedure contains many of the elements we use in present-day inductions. In addition to the pre-induction rapport-gaining period, he is asking the patient to just let the process take place and not try to analyze it closely ("I do not wish you to pay much attention to what I am saying or doing."). He also suggests monotony, heaviness, and the idea of sleep. The introductory instructions of the *Harvard Group Scale of Hypnotic Susceptibility* include a number of these, particularly the idea of "just letting it [hypnosis] happen." Clinicians the world over will readily recognize the efficacy of calling the patient's attention to "sensations he probably is experiencing," clearly a verbal conditioning ploy. Finally, Bramwell drew on practices of the ancients and his contemporaries in his use of a darkened room, or, more generally, a reduction of ambient stimulation.

As his clinical skills developed, he combined what he had first seen and applied as two distinct elements, the induction of hypnosis and curative suggestions. But he occasionally used additional aids in the induction procedure, primarily narcotic drugs and chloroform, in order to overcome initial resistance to the induction. He was unsuccessful in transforming natural sleep to hypnosis in the manner of Wetterstrand, but he was successful at hypnosis-at-a-distance. A report that first appeared in *The Lancet* in 1890 and was subsequently retold many times in the literature tells of Bramwell giving a hand-written note to a dental surgeon—a Mr. Turner—to be shown to one of the surgeon's patients. The patient, with whom Bramwell had previously worked, read the note and immediately entered a condition of hypnosis sufficient for dental surgery. The note read: "Go to sleep by order of Dr. Bramwell, and obey Mr. Turner's commands" (a correspondent, 1890).

Like Moll, Bramwell outlined two classifications of maneuvers for terminating hypnosis, physical and psychical (mental). The former included blowing on or rubbing the patient's eyes or splashing cold water into the patient's face. He also noted that forcibly opening the eyes would terminate hypnosis. Psychical methods were mainly attributed to the Nancy school and consisted of verbally suggesting that the patient wake up. Sometimes the signal took the form of counting, but what was essential, Bramwell relates, was that the patient understand the meaning of the stimulus, physical or psychical.

Others

The reader may wonder why I have not mentioned all of the many hundreds of individuals who were working during the last part of the 19th century, many of whom were quite well known either in the practice of hypnosis or in other areas of scientific endeavor. Most added little to the various techniques being used at the time and illustrated above. Binet and Féré (1888) offered a concise summary of the techniques at the time of their writing, but did not outline a method that could be considered uniquely their own. Heidenhain and Weinhold are mentioned in a number of texts as advocating monotonous auditory stimulation (the ticking of a watch) as an induction technique. The former is also credited with hemi-hypnosis by stroking one side of the patient's head (Binet & Féré, 1888; Björnström, 1887). Pitres' zones hypnogènes have already been mentioned.

Krafft-Ebing, who introduced us to hypnotic age regression (1889) and was better known for his studies of sexuality and its relationship to psychopathology, combined eye-fixation, with passes and verbal suggestions, as was the vogue of this period in the history of hypnotic induction procedures. He "would look steadily at the patient, even hold his hands or make movements like passes from the vertex down over the eyes, while he verbally and in a rather monotonous but pleasant voice impressed him with what he expected to be the result in regard to either physical or mental sensations" (Petersen, 1897, p. 127).

August Voisin received some attention at the 1889 International Congress on Hypnotism when he reported reasonable success (10%) at hypnotizing severely psychotic patients in Paris. Whether his method constituted an innovative technique or the mere application of immobilization and fatigue the reader can judge from Bramwell's (1903) description:

> The patient, either held by assistants or placed in a strait-jacket, had his eyes kept open, and was compelled to look at the light of a magnesian lamp or at Voisin's fingers. If necessary, the process was continued for three hours;

suggestions meanwhile being made. The patients, who at first usually struggled, raved and spat in the operator's face, eventually became exhausted and, in successful cases, passed into a condition of deep sleep. (p. 43)

Methods for inducing hypnosis have appeared in diverse publications, not just the medical and psychological literature. The British Society for Psychical Research published a report on mesmerism (hypnosis) in the first volume of their proceedings (Committee on Mesmerism, 1882). Early in the report the committee presented Braid's eye-fixation method using a coin held 15 inches in front of the subject so that the eyes turned inward and upward. Later they described the method used by "Mr. G. A. Smith of Dulwich, S.E.," which, while it generally follows the mesmeric pass format, adds a stroke that I did not find mentioned elsewhere.

> The subject is placed in a chair, with his hands in his lap, and he is told to direct his attention exclusively to a coin or other bright disc of metal, which is placed in his hands. Mr. Smith, meanwhile, draws his hands, at intervals, slowly downwards across the subject's head and face, always in the same direction. His hands, generally, do not touch the surface of the skin, nor even approach very near to it. After a time varying from two to twenty minutes has been thus occupied, Mr. Smith raises the subject's head, closes the eyes, and presses his thumb on the forehead between the eyes. . . . *Mr. Smith then strokes the muscles at the corner of the mouth* [italics added]; and, after a short interval, both eyes and mouth being closed, he is told to open them. If the subject is a good one, he fails to do this, and it is very strange to watch the contortion of his features, and his evident vexation, whilst he endeavours to thwart the mysterious influence which has sealed his lips and eyes. (Committee on Mesmerism, 1882, p. 221)

Both this approach and Braid's were advocated for boys between the ages of 12 and 20.

Finally, *Christian A. Herter*'s induction technique (which appeared in *Popular Science Monthly,* 1888) was, again, not that different from what was transpiring at that time. However, it (like Bernheim's method) includes elements and subtleties that the 20th century practitioners use to advantage. He begins by allaying the patient's anxieties through *rapport* and allowing them to observe others in hypnosis. The technique proper consisted of verbal suggestion and challenges—not being able to open the eyes or awaken. But it is Herter's admonishment to the operator that he or she turn every action (or inaction) of the subject to the advantage of the process, to heighten the hypnotic process, that constitutes a clear link to what is taught to 20th century practitioners. The process of inducing hypnosis during the latter part of the 19th century developed from a dependency on mesmeric-like passes and the uses of various specially prepared objects (magnets, metals, water, etc.) to verbal suggestion and its ability to reorganize the imagination of the patient or subject. The realization of the effectiveness of the subtleties of verbal communication in the hypnotic situation, which paralleled the development of suggestion, imagination, and cognition as theoretical constructs of hypnosis, is clearly stated in Herter's induction method and its rationale.

This [inducing the hypnosis or artificial sleep] is very simple, and it is always well to assure the subject that you do not intend to make use of any supernatural means, and that there is no magnetism of any kind about your procedure. Where persons are very skeptical of your ability to put them to sleep, it is a good plan to hypnotize a few patients in their presence, as an evidence of what you are able to do. Having thus obtained the subject's confidence, the physician asks him to look him intently in the eye, and to think of nothing but of going to sleep. The subject should be seated in a comfortable position, preferably with his back to the light. The recumbent position is not usually necessary. While the patient's eyes are still fixed, as just described, upon the operator's eyes, the latter says, in a monotonous but distinct tone: "Your eyelids are getting heavy, very heavy. Your eyes are red and moist. You are getting sleepy, very sleepy, very sleepy. Now you are nearly asleep. Your eyelids are shut; you can not open them, because you are asleep, fast asleep. Try as hard as you will, you can not open them. You can not wake up," etc. While these words are being uttered, the lids begin to drop and the eyes really look sleepy, and, if the subject is a good one, the pupils can generally be seen to dilate and contract alternately.

If two fingers of one hand slightly separated be held before the patient's eyes, he rolls his eyes down, following the fingers as they are moved down until the eyelids actually close. When the eyes close the subject is almost asleep, and a few judicious words affirming that he is asleep complete the hypnotizing.

In order to obtain good results it is necessary to watch the subject very carefully. Every sign of submission to the hypnotic influence should be immediately turned to account. Thus, if the eyes are seen to close suddenly, the subject should be at once told that he is asleep and can not wake up. If, instead, the operator adheres to a rigid formula, he may affirm the presence of sleep too soon, and the subject loses confidence, and the trial fails. *The great secret of success is to watch closely, and suit the words to the symptoms of sleep as they develop*. The importance and the difficulty of doing this well can only be appreciated after trial.

The *rationale* of this mode of hypnotizing is very simple. It consists essentially in an imitation of the processes of ordinary sleep by means of verbal suggestion. The attention is fixed by making the subject look into the physician's eyes, which thus answer the same purpose as Braid's glass knob. The heaviness of the eyelids, the dryness and subsequent moistness of the conjunctiva, and the gradual approach of somnolence, are natural episodes which usher in ordinary sleep. These we actually bring into existence by acting on the imagination through speech. It is a case of verbal suggestion in the waking state. The skill of the hypnotizer consists in making the subject believe he is going to sleep; that is all. It is not necessary that he should possess any peculiarities of temperament and voice, as has been supposed. Strokes and passes are useless, except in so far as they heighten suggestion. In short, everything lies in the subject and not in the hypnotizer. (Herter, 1888, pp. 760–761)

NOTES

1. I am indebted to Ross Ferlito for his assistance in rendering the French text into English.
2. Gravitz (1983a) also notes two other journals being published in America during the same period: the *St. Louis Magnet,* 1845; and the *Magnet,* published in New York between 1842 and 1844.

CHAPTER 5

The Turn of the Century

The latter portion of the 19th century was one of the great periods of scientific and intellectual curiosity and development. Hypnosis was no less touched by the fervor of activity that took place during the 1890s. In fact, the growth spurt of interest in things hypnotic began in the 1840s. Felkin (1890) reported the publication of some 476 books and papers on the subject between that period and 1890. The English began the trend with the writings of such luminaries as Braid, Esdaile, and Elliotson but were soon outdistanced by the volume of publications appearing on the continent. Most of the English language papers and books appeared between 1843 and 1853, while those published in Belgium, Holland, Greece, Poland, the Scandinavian countries, Russia, France, and Germany proliferated in the last half decade of the 1880s. By far the most prodigious output came from Germany and Austria where some 118 books and papers were issued between 1886 and 1888.

This trend for the British to be overwhelmed in the arena of productivity troubled several of the better known English and Scottish practitioners. Felkin, for example, noted that "information published in the English language can hardly be considered as either original or more than a drop in the bucket" (Felkin, 1890, pp. 4–5). Tuckey (1889/1900) revealed his concern when he noted in the 4th edition (1900) of his 1889 book that, of the 141 items published on hypnosis in 1889, only 7 came from English sources and 16 from the United States. A drought had occurred in the country from which the Victorian Era derived its name, but Tuckey saw an English renaissance in the making with the works of Felkin, Kingsbury, Vincent, and others.

Charles Lloyd Tuckey and Others

C. Lloyd Tuckey was one of the most influential physician-practitioners of hypnosis in Britain during this period. (The other was J. Milne Bramwell— see Chapter 4.) A visiting physician to Margaret Street Infirmary, he held membership in a number of professional hypnosis societies of the time on the continent and abroad; for example, Fondateur de la Société D'Hypnologie and the American Society for the Study of Inebriety. His name appeared constantly in issues of *The Lancet* of the period (Thomas Wakley, of Elliotson's day, no longer held the fate of publications on hypnosis in his hand), and on Oct. 8, 1889 announced the formation of the Hypnotic Society.

Tuckey held hypnosis to be "merely a psychical preparation or vehicle for suggestion." Thus hypnotic treatment was a two-step procedure: first the induction, then the treatment. "This condition being induced, it remains for the treatment to be applied" (Tuckey, 1889/1900, p. 151). His method of induction was essentially that of Liébeault. The patient, with whom a confident rapport had been established, was seated comfortably, told to "think of nothing at all," and concentrated their vision on the fingertips of the operator, held slightly above the normal plane of vision (much like Braid during the 1840s). Then it was suggested to the patient: "Your sight is growing dim and indistinct; your eyelids are becoming heavy; a numbness is creeping over your limbs; my voice seems muffled to you; you are getting more sleepy; you cannot keep your eyes open" (Tuckey, 1892, p. 43). If this method failed, Tuckey modified his procedure by using a bright metal disc or coin as a fixation point and rubbing the forehead of the patient. Unlike Moll and Bramwell, he was unwilling to make more than three or four attempts at hypnosis with a particular patient before declaring him or her unhypnotizable.

Tuckey did note one other method of induction, which sounds like a page out of hypnosis in the early part of this 19th century in America—pseudo-paralysis. Used with patients with whom he had previous contact it simply involved announcing to the patient "You cannot move that arm (or leg)." This simple directive was sufficient to induced a profound condition of hypnosis. Max Dessoir (according to Tuckey) used a variation that utilized repetitive motion as an induction ploy. He (Dessoir) is reported to have once told a postal worker to make the motions of stamping letters and then announced: "Now, you cannot stop doing that!" (Tuckey, 1889/1900, p. 138). Thus the hypnotic condition was induced through suggestions for motor activity or inactivity.

Finally, Tuckey did not take well to the "fascination" technique: "looking fixedly and pertinaciously into the subject's eyes at the distance of a few inches, and at the same time holding the hands. In a few minutes all expression goes out of the face, and the subject sees nothing but the operator's eyes, which shine with intense brilliance, and to which he is attracted as *a needle to a magnet* [italics added]" (Tuckey, 1889/1900, p. 163). Although he recognized that in some instances such a technique might be justified—as with Voisin's work with the insane—he generally felt that the patient's personality was unduely subjugated and suppressed in the process. Tuckey and his colleagues were moving more toward the client-centered approaches of the 20th century.

Tuckey's therapeutic manipulations were similar to those of Poyen, described in Chapter 4—placing the hands on the afflicted part of the body and applying either friction or the warmth of the touch. Terminating the hypnotic condition was done with a simply verbal command to awaken, or, if this failed initially, reinforcing the directive with a fanning of the patient or blowing gently on the patient's eyes (similar to the technique of Braid).

R. W. Felkin

R. W. Felkin was the Scottish contingent of Great Britain's movement to recapture preeminence in hypnotic publication. His book, *Hypnotism or Psycho-Therapeutics* (1890), originally appeared as a series of papers in the *Edinburgh Medical Journal*. His fields of expertise were diseases of the tropics and climatology, on which he lectured at the Edinburgh School of Medicine. He was also adept at languages for it was he who translated Hilger's *Hypnotismus und Suggestion* in 1912.

Felkin's book (1890) is a detailed compendium of the literature of his time, covering not only the most prevalent induction techniques, but also the physiology of hypnosis, theories of hypnosis (particularly the sleep theory of Preyer of Jena and the biochemical notions of Lauder Brunton), and such "modern" concerns as the physical and physiological condition of the eye during hypnosis and the difficulty of ascertaining the presence or absence of the hypnotic condition in a particular subject or patient. Regarding the latter, a detailed explication would take us too far afield for this book, but Felkin noted the following observations for ascertaining the success of a hypnotic induction: (a) the condition of the eyes—a "convulsive rotation upwards of the eyes" (see Eye-Roll Sign, Chapter 8); (b) the mask-like appearance of the face; (c) the general lethargy and retarded reaction time to suggestions for movement; and (d) changes in the retina under ophthalmoscopic examination (For more modern data along this line, see Strosberg & Vics, 1962.).

Felkin's summary of induction techniques adds little to what has already been presented earlier. He noted two classes of induction methods: physical suggestions and physical impressions. The former, of course, was the Nancy School technique described above by Tuckey. The latter took many forms, all of which depended on fixating one or more of the senses: the visual by staring at a particular object; the auditory by attending to monotonous, repetitive sounds such as the ticking of a clock or the beating of a drum; the tactical by pressure on the eyeballs or a gentle stroking of the skin. Physical passes remained an oft-noted technique, although the ideas of literal animal magnetism had for some time been losing favor. Phrenological pressure points, 1–4 cm in diameter and appearing on both sides of the body, were said to create instantaneous hypnosis, according to A. Pitres and de la Tourette.

One final method noted by Felkin deserves passing note because we have seen it before with Bramwell (see above) and will see it again with modern telephone hypnosis later on. The technique is that of hypnosis-at-a-distance. Bourneville and Regnard claimed to be able to hypnotize patients by merely holding their hand over the patient's head. Such a procedure was attributed to "imagination" when Bourneville instructed a patient to fall asleep at precisely 3 p.m. in her home, which she did.

George C. Kingsbury

George C. Kingsbury was another of the practicing physicians of Britain to produce a book summarizing hypnotic activities of the period. His induction technique, like most of his English contemporaries, was that of Liébeault, modified with stroking the patient's face, arms, and/or chest, while verbally suggesting sleep. He, too, mentions the famous hypnosis by correspondence of Bramwell, and also reports that Dr. deJong of the Hague used his appointment cards in a similar manner. In fact, any object may be used as a signal at a distance, a method capitalized on by George Estabrooks while teaching students better study habits through hypnosis in the 1960s. Estabrooks gave the students a 3″ × 5″ file card with a cue word printed on it, which the student used any time he wished to enter hypnosis.

Kingsbury also took note of a technique that was meeting with some success among the medical community: the use of chemical intervention to set the stage for hypnotic induction. Some claimed hypnotic induction per se by this means. Wiffs of chloroform and morphia were the most prevalent substances used, although Heidenhain was reported to use nitrite of amyl. Kingsbury felt that such techniques were unnecessary and unwise.

Like others of the 19th century, Kingsbury reported the upward roll of the eyes as a final sign of the presence of hypnosis. He also explicated a number of aids to hypnosis that have appeared in the literature for eons: the cooperation of the patient, a quiet environment free from sensory distractions, and a minimum of observers. In addition, he placed the induction of hypnosis into favorable time and seasonal frameworks. The morning was said to be the best time to induce hypnosis and the summer season more efficacious than winter. The latter notion was attributed to Ringier.

One thing that Kingsbury's book made clear was that the reliance and fascination with physical magnetism in the realm of hypnosis was not yet at an end. In fact, this will become even clearer when we explore some of the writings of Gessmann below. Although he reports negative results (as did Voisin, Forel, Bernheim, and Tuckey), there was still the concern that one could produce hypnotic effects with bar magnets. The folklore of the attraction of the North magnetic pole and the repulsion of the South still persisted also. Luys had continued to report such effects, and it was still believed in some circles that subjects perceived a yellow light from the North pole of magnets and blue from the South—the opposite relationship from that reported by Reichenbach in his "sensatives."

Finally, Kingsbury noted what by that time had become the standard method of de-hypnotization. The patient was merely given a verbal signal to awaken; that failing, fanning or blowing on the patient was added. If both methods failed to arouse the patient, Kingsbury suggested that a time period be suggested, after which the patient would awaken.

Ralph Harry Vincent

R. H. Vincent also adhered to the same techniques for terminating the hypnotic condition as Kingsbury, except that he added sprinkling with water when ordinary verbal instructions to awaken failed. Allowing the patient to "sleep it off" was the final ploy, as above. He did note that Pitres of Bordeaux not only suggested hypnotic sensative zones for induction, but also *zones hypno-fénatrices,* the stimulation of which had an awakening effect.

Nor were Vincent's inductions much different from those of Tuckey and Kingsbury. They involved the same fixation of vision accompanied with the following: "The eyelids are quivering; the eyes are tired: the sleep is coming" (Vincent, 1893/1897, pp. 79–80). He, too, concentrated on changes in the eyes with induction, but also offered one symptom "nearly always present—a peculiar, deep, catching inspiration" (Vincent, 1893/1897, p. 80). Nothing else was new with respect to his own inductions; he also favored the morning hours for inducing the hypnotic condition.

What Vincent's book did provide for the English-speaking professional was a brief summary of induction techniques used on the continent. Professor *Oskar Berger* of Breslau claimed that the mere warmth of his hands was sufficient to induce hypnosis, even when the hands were held at some distance from the patient. Professor *J. Purkinge,* also of Breslau (and Prague), preferred stroking the forehead, as did his compatriot in Tübingen, *H. Spitta. Jean de Tarchanoff* thought that these gentle stimulations of the skin produced an electricity that was the effective agent. In fact, the notions of induction through electrical instruments and "galvanising currents" were quite prevalent on the continent. Professor *Adolph Weinhold* of Chemnitz used an electric battery and Professor *Albert Eulenburg* galvanised the head to create a lethargic condition. Breslau seemed to be a center for experimentation with different induction procedures, for here also a Professor *Hirt* used electrical means. What should arrest our attention regarding electrical or galvanic means for inducing hypnosis is its continued use into the 20th century, in fact, into at least the 1970s. As we will see in Chapter 6, Ferenc András Vögyesi of Budapest advocated the use of an instrument he called the "Faraday-Hand" until his death in the late 1970s. Neither the idea nor the application originated in the present (20th) century.

Both the use of physical "passes" and fascination (a steady, penetrating gaze by the operator into the patient's eyes) continued as induction techniques. Mason (1901) reported cases induced by both means to the Neurological Section of the New York Academy of Medicine on October 12, 1888. He hypnotized one young lady by having her stare at his coat button while he held her thumbs. In fact, so effective was the technique that pinching and slapping the patient failed to arouse her. Only nontouching passes were effective. Jeaffreson (1892) reported the same technique during ophthalmic examinations. The past lingers on, and on, and on.

The laying-on-of-hands technique persisted, but by this time, had been refined primarily to the head region and more particularly the eyes. Vincent noted the Paris physician *Ch. Laseque's* technique of applying moderate pressure on the eyeballs themselves to induce hypnosis. Practitioners today still gain and maintain rapport with the patient through the tactile sense, often by holding or gently rubbing the head and/or eye region. Another persistent induction and explanatory device was our old friend magnetism.

The use of magnets in hypnosis and other curative manipulations continued into the 20th century, despite the insistence by Tuckey, Kingsbury, Vincent, and other professionals that, at best, it was the suggestions, stated or implied, with the magnets that were the effective component. Vincent claimed that Parisians Ballet, Binet, Féré, Landowzy, and Proust, as well as Benedikt of Vienna, all subscribed to the power of the magnet in hypnotizing. This attraction to magnets and their uses in hypnosis was noticeable on the continent, particularly in Germany.

Germany

As indicated above, the most prolific geographic area during this last decade of the 19th century was Germany. In addition to mention of Albert Moll in the last chapter, I have already noted the induction techniques of less well-known figures such as Weinhold in Chemnitz, Spitta in Tübingen, Preyer in Jena, and the Breslau group of Berger, Purkinge, and Hirt.

One of the best known professional residents of this latter city was *Rudolf Heidenhain,* Professor of Physiology at the University of Breslau. Heidenhain told of his initial and subsequent dealings with hypnosis in a lecture to the Silesian Society for Home Culture on January 19, 1880. What prompted his increased interest in the phenomena of hypnosis was the public performances of a mesmerist, Herr Hansen, in Breslau. Here is Heidenhain's description of Hansen's method:

> Mr. Hansen makes the subjects of his experiments stare fixedly at a faceted and glittering piece of glass. After this preliminary proceeding, he makes a few "passes" over the face, avoiding actual contact; he then lightly closes the eyes and mouth, at the same time gently stroking the cheeks. . . . After a few more passes over the forehead, [the subjects] fall into a sleep-like condition (Heidenhain, 1906, p. 4)

Furthermore, "Mr. Hansen, when carrying out his stroking manipulations, evidently works with great muscular effort. He flexes and extends his hands with great force; consequently, his hands become very moist and warm" (Heidenhain, 1906, p. 35). The difference between the condition of the skin of the operator and that of the subject maximized the stimulating effect, so thought Heidenhain. Heidenhain himself tried a number of different techniques prevalent during that period: eye-fixation, monotonous sounds such as ticking watches or clicking the fingernails, and gentle, rhythmic skin stimulation. He found that different individuals responded differently to different techniques: a Dr. Kröner only by cutaneous stimulation, a Mr. Poper only by staring at Heidenhain.

However, Heidenhain's main contribution to hypnosis was not in developing unique induction methods, but in his attempts to explain the process physiologically. He viewed the induction procedures as a means of increasing sensory irritability to enhance central nervous system inhibition. Comparing human hypnotic behavior with animal behavior following CNS lesions, he eliminated the corpora quadrigemina (superior and inferior colliculi) as being directly affected and opted for a general inhibition of the cortex, specifically the "ganglion-cells".

It followed logically from such theorizing that the termination of hypnosis would be best effected by some sudden, arousing stimulation. Thus Heidenhain also subscribed to the use of "sudden blowing on the face, a knock on the hand, a cry in the ear . . . [and] . . . touching the face with cold fingers" (Heidenhain, 1906, p. 37) as appropriate de-hypnotizing maneuvers. Thus Heidenhain, along with W. Preyer, Professor of Biology at Jena and Berlin, attempted to put hypnosis and its induction on a more solid, biological basis.

While others, like *Hans Schmidkunz* at the University of Munich, were producing works not dissimilar from the array of summary books I have mentioned above, *G. Gessmann* (1887) was investigating the relationship between magnetism and hypnosis in Vienna, following Hansen's 1880 demonstrations.

Following a brief summary of data on hypnotic susceptibility, Gessmann offered a detailed description of a measurement device developed by the Parisian physician, *Ochorowicz*. The device consisted of a hollow steel cylinder about 5 cm long and 4 cm in diameter, weighing 170 grams. In reality it was a flat bar magnet bent into a tubular shape into which the subject placed his or her finger. According to its inventor (Ochorowicz), approximately 30% of people perceived a peculiar sensation while so doing, indicating that they were easily hypnotized. Such a prediction worked equally well with sick and healthy individuals. Although Gessmann replicated this percentage, he also reported that some individuals who did not perceive the sensations were easily hypnotizable and some others who did turned out to be refractory. However, he welcomed the invention of such a device as a first step in exploring either "Stahl- oder Elektromagneten."

Gessmann's (1887) own susceptibility measuring technique followed clearly from his investigations into physical magnetism:

> I attend to a person from the audience, as a rule a woman, who, through her pale look, nervous sensativeness, alluring eyes, etc., appears to be qualified for the experiment. A strong electrical development takes place in my body, so to speak, so that I am not in a position to try to electify too robustly a built individual. In order to prove this, I grasp two fingers of each hand of this person in my right hand, wait a second and then ask if they notice a particular sensation. The person, from whom always issues an affirmative reply and indeed describes the sensation of pins and needles in his arms and upper body (and later a feeling of the arms going to sleep), is qualified for the attempt. So I say: "Please listen carefully to what I say to you. Hold my finger tight . . . tighter . . . still tighter . . . so . . . and now you can no longer let go of my hand." This is always the case. Through a stroke of my left hand over the

subject's forearm—with a direct touch—I keep the spasm of the hand muscle in this position, reinforce it, and now it is impossible to let go.

To reverse this condition, I blow upon the spasmotically constrained hands and say, "Now you are again free, please let go," and thereby relax the spasm.

This kind of experiment serves me as a preliminary probe into the suitability for hypnosis. Those individuals who succeed in the above described research are always good mediums [subjects] and need only a little effort to enter hypnosis.[1] (pp. 105–106)

Gessmann's induction technique was also based on his interest in physical magnetism, for it mainly involved contact between the operator and the subject, with little in the way of verbal suggestions. It also contained an element that we have not seen since some time back in our history—the notion of communicating with the patient through his or her stomach:

I place myself in relation to the person who will be induced into the artifical nervous sleep, close the eyes, take his hands in mine—so that the four thumbs become pressed against one another—and ask the subject to keep quiet and yield unresistingly to the inclination to enter sleep.

As a rule the person falls asleep in between two to ten minutes. I deepen the sleep with a few passes over his head and chest and seek to speak to the sleeper by laying one hand on his head, taking hold of his hands with the other and speaking against the pit of his stomach. I first ask: "Do you hear me?" I must repeat the question five or six times before an answer is forthcoming. At first this is faint, scarcely audible, yet with repeated questions, spoken as loud commands, the speech of the sleeper becomes clearly perceived.[2] (Gessmann, 1887, p. 106)

His method of terminating the hypnosis was by commanding, "Wake up!"

France

The French were no less active during the final years of the 19th century than were their colleagues to the North and West. *H. Durville*, for example, was clearly on the same wavelength as Gessmann. The first volume of his small, two volume work, originally published in 1895, presented his theory of physiological or human magnetism, which was based on the movement of atoms rather than on the older notions of the transmission of a magnetic fluid. The body was said to be polarized in a manner similar to that of a magnet; the right side of the body, positive, and the left, negative. The dividing line was a longitudinal axis from the top of the head to the anal-genital area. The polarity was said to be reversed in left-handed individuals. So pervasive was the magnetic force that Durville claimed to have found it in parts of dead animals and humans and even in inorganic bodies. Here was clearly a throw-back to the days of Fludd and Maxwell and all of the ancient notions of a vital spirit uniting everything in the universe. Little wonder he was the founder and general secretary of the Magnetic Society of France.

Durville's methods followed directly from his theoretical notions. Obviously, since "the magnetic force radiates around us," it was the job of the operator to manipulate this atomic movement in order to aid the patient. Manipulation was accomplished through passes, impositions, applications, stroking, rubbing, and breathing. The passes were not that different from what has been described several times before. In the longitudinal pass the hands were held at a distance of 3 or 4 in. from the body, starting at the head and sweeping down the body with the palms flat and the fingers slightly spread. Usually this was done with the operator standing in front of the seated patient. When the hands reached the level of the patient's knees, they were formed into fists and raised close to the operator's body until they were high enough for another long downward pass. Dehypnotization occurred with transverse passes, in which the operator crossed his arms in front of the seated patient and then uncrossed them laterally until he had the appearance of a crucifixion standing before the patient.

Imposition involved the presentation of either the palm of the hand or the finger at a distance of 2 to 8 inches from an afflicted body part and holding this "pointing position" for periods of 1 to 5 minutes. Such a procedure was often combined with movement, either rotary or perforating. The latter was a rotary movement that imitated a corkscrew, as if the therapist was attempting to bore a hole into the ailing organ. Application was imposition with physical contact being made with the patient, a simple laying-on-of-hands. This procedure was used in conjunction with stroking and rubbing, the former being a light touching and the latter being strong or weak frictions either in a longitudinal or a rotary pattern. None of Durville's methods were new; nor were they old, if one considers modern massage as a curative procedure. Only the theorizing behind the action is different.

Finally, it should be mentioned that Durville also advocated the use of a variety of objects, which, he thought, were endowed with the capacity to retain magnetic charge. Liquids were his favorite, with cotton and wool stuffs and metals close behind. He particularly mentioned silk in this regard. Nor did he forget the gaze as a powerful way to influence his patients, and lastly, the breath, emanating as it does from one of the principle sources of the magnetic force in the body, the lungs. So powerful did he consider this latter essence that he claimed to have been able, through "hot insufflation," to return life to the dying. "The lips slightly parted, leaving the mouth half open, are placed upon the skin, or better still, upon some light piece of clothing covered with a clean towel or handkerchief; and in pressing, so that the breath does not escape, and as if it could penetrate the skin and the subcutaneous tissues, you force it energetically by a prolonged expiration" (Durville, 1900, p. 96). Old traditions and ideas die slowly and the progress of understanding is a series of advances and retreats. Our only hope is that each advance surpasses the previous retreat.

Major centers of activity were Paris and Bordeaux, although, as we will see, practitioners were not restricted to those two locales. One of the better known of the Bordeaux group was *Travaux Azam,* Professor of the Medical Faculty at Bordeaux. Although his book on hypnosis and alterations of the personality was well received when it appeared (1887) and was often quoted thereafter, his contribution to procedures for the induction of hypnosis was minimal. When queried regarding his preferred induction technique, he responded: "The procedure of Braid" (Crocq, 1896, p. 257). Even the well-known director of the *Revue de l'Hypnotisme, Edgar Bérillon* used either fixation on a bright, shiny object or on the eyes of the operator, coupled with the following verbalization:

Look fixedly in my eyes. Your eyelids are going to get tired. They are becoming very heavy. You feel the need to close them. You are becoming lethargic. The lethargy of mind is spreading to your arms and legs. You feel a sensation of calm, of rest, of well-being. You are going to feel sleepy. The need to sleep arrives. You are going to sleep as if you were in your bed. Sleep! (Bérillon, 1891, pp. 20–21)

Occasionally he would manually close the eyelids.

The technique of *Fontan* and *Ségard* (1887) was quite similar:

Cause the eyes of the client to be fixed on yours (with your glasses off, if you wear them), . . . and speak with firmness, in an uninterrupted fashion, determinedly monotonous, your voice becoming softer little by little:

"You are going to sleep; dream only of going to sleep; the sleep that you are going to obtain is very natural, very simple to accomplish; it is not fatiguing, but, to the contrary, is entirely beneficial. Sleep (return often, intentionally to words which contain the idea of sleep)—It is good—The state that occurs. You are no longer distinguishing my features—Your gaze is becoming confused, your ideas also are confused—Your eyelids are fluttering—They are heavy, heavy—It is as if you had weights on them which, in spite of you, cause them to close. You are putting yourself to sleep, it is perfect—See how my voice seems to come to you from afar." In order to augment this illusion, lower your tone imperceptibly. It helps also to speak to the assistant.—"Look there, he is going to sleep—There, he sleeps—not a sound." (p. 67)

These authors also offered advice if the induction procedure did not work as well as the operator expected:

Sometimes the patient protests and maintains that he is not going to sleep at all. He is helped, by his own manner of speaking, to make sure if he speaks the truth or if he deludes himself. "Does the spasm of the eyelids become more pronounced? Is his voice less and less strong, like that of an individual overcome by sleep?" . . . Complete hypnosis will not delay. (Fontan & Ségard, 1887, pp. 67–68)

Even for the case of the apparently refractory patient, procedures for success were provided:

> If, without hesitation, without trouble, he moves his eyelids; if he replies to you in an assured tone, do not be discouraged. . . . Insist that the act of sleeping will neither prevent him from hearing you nor speaking to you; [there is] a material bond, a mode of communication holding him and you together. [Continue in this manner], according to your individual dispositions and appreciation [of the situation], for some seconds to five or ten minutes; [then] suddenly, and with a decisive intonation, say to the patient, "Close your eyes, sleep" and, by surprise, lower his upper lids with two fingers, maintaining their closure with a little compression on the eyelids. Say to your assistant that, in a few seconds the subject will sleep. Under your fingers you will feel a palpable quivering; the movements of swallowing will become more frequent and fuller; respiration will become regular; finally, often after a deep sigh, the patient will definitely yield to the influence of the hypnotist. (Fontan & Ségard, 1887, p. 68)

Here we find much of what we find in modern, client-oriented, Ericksonian-type inductions. Following the eye-fixation, there is the monotonous commentary on the condition of the eyelids and other behaviors observed by the hypnotist, spoken in a soft, lulling tone of voice. Lowering the vocal volume to give reality to the suggestion that the voice of the operator is "coming from afar" is a modern classic ploy to reinforce the "truth" of the operator's utterances. So, too, are the double-bind ploys of having the patients specifically attend to their own behaviors in order to assess the accuracy of their own resistance and the double-bind procedure of informing the patient that even his or her behaviors, which seem to verify resistance to the procedures (opening the eyes, speaking to the operator), are what is expected in the hypnotic "sleep." In fact, Fontan and Ségard's procedure could easily have been published as a standard induction technique in 1987 as in 1887.

One French investigator, *Albert de Rochas d'Aiglun,* was quite concerned with the lack of attention being given to deep states of hypnosis, and blamed it, in part, on the unwillingness of investigators to couple their research with the "practice of magnetism." Thus they:

> have restricted themselves to producing hypnosis by feeble means, like a sudden noise, a pressure on the ocular globes or vertex, [in short] by procedures which end abruptly as soon as the first result is produced: such as, for example, the fixation of gaze, which ceases to act as soon as the subjects have closed their eyes. [On the other hand] the magnetizers act in another fashion. By using passes they prolong their action on the subject for a quarter of an hour, a half an hour, and sometimes longer. (de Rochas, 1892, p. 6)

His point was that the induction of hypnosis should be a more prolonged procedure if the practitioner desires deeper conditions of hypnosis than those achieved through the prevalent methods.

Claverie (1889) appeared to verify this concern with briefer induction procedures when he summarized the hypnotic techniques of his fellow Frenchmen:

> One puts another to sleep by fixing his attention and his gaze on a brilliant object, by looking at him fixedly in the eyes, by producing a sudden noise close to him, by a pressure of the hand on the parts of the body recognized as hypnogenic [Here he refers to Pitres' work.]; [and] finally by suggestion, by a single verbal command and sometimes, that which is most wonderful yet, by an order given from a distance, without possible communication between the operator and the subject. (p. 20)

Four years before the turn of the century *Jean Crocq,* from the faculty at Nancy, produced a book in which he reported the responses of the authors of that period to a series of questions regarding the nature of hypnosis and hypnotic phenomena. To the question, "What procedure of hypnosis and waking up do you prefer?", he received the following responses:

Sanchez Herrero (of Madrid): "The fixation of the gaze of the subject in mine, or in my hypnotic device, and suggestion." [His device is described by Milechnin as follows: The "hypnotizing apparatus" consisted of a metal stem, about a metre long, with twenty component parts articulated in four different directions, and ending in a compass with dull points, holding two magnificent diamonds. This portable apparatus could be fastened to the subject's bed and adjusted in such a manner that the diamonds would be four centimetres from the subject's eyes. [Milechnin, 1965b, p. 28.]

Marot (of Paris): "Electisme. Visual fixation, pressure on the eyeballs, breath in order to wake up, everything accompanied by suggestions: you sleep, etc. . . . wake up."

A. Voisin (of Paris): "I use several hypnotic procedures: application of the hand on the brow and the eyelids, fixation of the eyes, fixation of the eyes on a brilliant point, on a rotating mirror. I prefer the waking up by suggestion."

Beaunis (of Paris): "At bottom, the procedure is of little importance. I use most especially visual fixation for hypnosis and blowing with a verbal command for awakening."

Pitres (of Bordeaux): "That of Braid." [Curious that he did not report using his own theoretical, hypno-inducing sensative body points.]

G. Ballet (of Paris): "Visual fixation in order to fall asleep; breath on the face for waking up."

Varinard (of Paris): "Following the subject or following his actual state." [?]

Ochorowicz (of Varsovie): "Application of the hand on the head for hypnosis, a light massage and suggestion for waking up."

Joire (of Lille): "Visual fixation accompanied by passes made with the hands. For waking up, breathe on the eyes."

Dumontpallier (of Paris): "Verbal suggestion."

Brémaut (of Brest): "The sleep by persuasion; the spoken methods of force have grave consequences. Waking up by a command to wake up or a light breathing on the eyeball. This last method seems to me very often to be a suggestion."

De Jong (of the Hague): "The procedure of verbal suggestion."

Le Menant des Chesnais (of Ville-d'Ayray): "I believe Bernheim's method for putting patients to sleep and waking them up is the best. That is what I use. But at the moment of waking up, I never forget, following the recommendations of Luys, to tell the patient that I am going to wake him *completely*. I believe, with Luys, that the use of this word is very important and I repeat it several times. On the other hand, in order to prevent my patient from being put to sleep by a layman [or novice], I forestall this by suggesting during sleep that henceforth he will only be able to be put to sleep by a doctor and that he will resist all other individuals who seek to put him to sleep, resisting more energetically the more the other insists." [Here we have two points that have become the foundation of modern hypnotic procedures: (a) telling the patient to become "fully awake and fully alert" at the termination of hypnosis, and (b) "protecting" the patient from untoward effects at the hands of less rigorously trained individuals.]

David (of Narbonne): "The procedure of Liébeault is the most practical."

Lajoie (of Nashua, New Hampshire): "By spoken suggestion."

Henrik Petersen (of Boston): "The will, the stare, and the spoken word." [The succinctness of an American response.]

Burot (of Rochefort): "Verbal suggestion with the application of the hand on the forehead."[3] (Crocq, 1896, pp. 256–258, Italics added)

THE TWENTIETH CENTURY BEGINS

Although the opening of the 20th century brought us such innovations as waffle-wrapped ice-cream and ice-ladened tea at the St. Louis World's Fair, little new emerged in the induction of hypnosis. True, the Second International Congress of Experimental and Therapeutic Hypnotism was held in Paris in 1900, attended by some of the same well-known people as were active at the first one in 1889 (e.g., Richet, Azam, Voisin, Vogt, Brown-Sequard), but the trends from mechanical to verbal inductions remained the same. The masters of the late 19th century remained the much-quoted idols of the 20th—Luys, Björnström, Forel, Wetterstrand, Moll, Bramwell, and Tuckey.

Even the controversies within and without the professional ranks continued, little changed, into the dawning of the new century. Within the medical ranks, controversy regarding the public display of hypnotic techniques, whether by "lay people" or by trained physicians, raged. Norman Kerr, in

England, now lifted the cudgel against his fellow physicians, particularly those on the continent. So enthusiastic were his denunciations of hypnosis that at times he bordered on a near full return to the past of espousing hypnosis as a satanic procedure. For example, for Kerr pain deserved not to be alleviated through hypnosis except when it threatened the life or sanity of the patient. This approach echoes the 1842 response of the Royal Medical and Chirurgical Society of London to Dr. Ward's report of a mid-thigh amputation under hypnosis (see Chapter 3).

Furthermore, Kerr felt that the repeated consequences of hypnosis might "lead to deterioration of brain and nerve function, a physical decadence, and a moral perversion" (Kingsbury, 1891/1967, p. 100). What is curious about Dr. Kerr's strident rebuke of his colleagues's use of hypnosis was not only his return to the past, but also his anticipation of the future. Although it was true that Belgium had prohibited the public display of hypnosis in 1891 and that by 1895 both Hungary and Austria had prohibited its use by everyone except physicians (Argentina did both in May, 1891—prohibited public display and restricted its use to physicians—W. C. K., 1891), his attack against his colleagues's public presentations struck a pose similar to the controversy over the teaching of hypnosis in brief seminars that split the Society for Clinical and Experimental Hypnosis and led to the formation of the American Society of Clinical Hypnosis six decades later.

While Kerr was railing against hypnosis and its application, G. H. Savage was of a different mind. In his Harveian Oration at the Royal College of Physicians of London on October 18, 1909, he took up where Tuckey had left off: "The investigation of hypnotism is a thing that should not be ignored in England. When other nations are carefully investigating the physiology [Heidenhain and Preyer, for example, in Germany] and the therapeutic value of this potent influence, it is certainly rather a pity that England should be in the background." (Savage, 1909, p. 41) Such a call to arms certainly had its effect, for as the early years of the 1900s passed, an increasing number of English language publications were produced.

However, for the first decade or decade and a half of the new century, continental publications continued to dominate the field. In 1900, for example, *Jean Filiatre* brought out his practical course in hypnosis entitled, *Hypnotisme et Magnétisme*. In the text Filiatre presented four methods used either singly or in combination to induce hypnosis: (a) *le Regard* (eye fascination or fixation), (b) *la Parole* (verbal suggestion), (c) *les Passes* (gestures and movements of the hands), and (d) *la Pensée* (concentration on an idea or thought). None of these manipulations are particularly new to the reader by this time, simply reflecting a continuity with the past. Filiatre advocated eye-fixation on the base of the nose of the hypnotist, thus indicating that the prevalent eye-fixation for the French was the "fascination" or staring eye-to-eye between hypnotist and patient. He noted that this technique was the ordinary method used by professional hypnotists.

Verbal suggestion was considered the basis of personal influence and should be offered in a persuasive and gentle voice, with assurance and conviction. La Pensée differed from la Parole by the fact that the latter involved having the patient concentrate totally and explicitly on a single idea. Such a procedure he felt was the basis of autohypnosis. It was, however, the use of passes that seemed to fascinate Filiatre the most, for he conceptualized them in the context of literal magnetism. He assigned them a special place in the production of hypnosis: "through the passes the hypnotist is able to produce a special state in the subject which is neither produced through verbal suggestion, eye fixation on a brillant point, nor expectant attention" (Filiatre, 1909, pp. 103–104).

Despite this fascination, Filiatre concentrated on constructing a "hypnotic sphere," which he called "The Fournier Hypnotic Sphere," named for the M. Fournier, the manufacturer. After a brief review of other mechanical methods of inducing hypnosis, which included Mesmer's *baquet,* Ochorowicz's hypnoscope (see above in the discussion of Gessmann's work), Luys's revolving mirrors, other bright objects such as magnesium or limelight lamps, gongs, drums, tuning forks, and whistles, he described his own *Boule hypnotique Fournier*. From the advertisement in his book, the instrument has the appearance of a small mace of about 8 to 12 in. in length. The basic core is a cylinder about 1 in. in diameter. At one end is a small sphere, perhaps $1\frac{1}{2}$ in. in diameter, while three-quarters up the cylinder from this sphere is an enlarged spherical area about 3 in. in diameter. Above that remains another inch of the core cylinder, on which there is a metal cap, shaped somewhat like a crown. By turning this cap at the top of the instrument, one could allow vapors of chloroform or ether to be emitted, as per the "infallible method of Dr. Liébengen." The Fournier Sphere had two particular advantages, according to its creator: (a) patients who were otherwise refractory to hypnosis became hypnotizable and (b) it was a major labor-saving device for the hypnotist. In fact, a major selling point (It cost 5 Francs and could be bought by mail order) was the latter; in that, the hypnotist no longer had to look forward to the extreme fatigue caused by the eye-fixation and verbal suggestion methods.

In addition to its potential as a chloroform emitter, The Fournier Sphere was used primarily as an eye-fixation device. The small sphere at the bottom of the instrument was used for prolonged fixation without the blinking of the eyelids. The large sphere, three-quarters of the way up the device was used when the patient was in a sitting position, and the very tip of the top, crown-shaped cap was used as a Braidian fixation point, since it was constructed of a highly shiny metal. To convince the reader of the value of his instrument, Filiatre presented testimonials from his French colleagues, Drs. Liébengen and Charpentier, and from as far away as America—a Dr. B. Harwley of New York. In addition to this interest in devices mechanical, Filiatre was also one of the earliest to remark on hypnosis by telephone (see Weitzenhoffer, 1972, and Gravitz, 1983).

What is particularly noticeable about Filiatre's and other's work is the continuing interest in the "magnetic passes" and various mechanical devices for the induction of hypnosis this late in our history. The passes particularly, including the simple laying-on-of-hands and tactile rubbing of the patient, and a number of the instruments were rooted in ideas of magnetism and, later on, electricity. There was still, in the first decade of the present century, the prevalent idea that hypnosis involved the passage, or redirection, of some force from the hypnotist to the patient. While verbal suggestions were gaining ground as the preferred method of induction, the search for some quick, magical technique continued well into the present, as we will see.

The notion of a force, a power exerted by the hypnotist, was apparent in another Frenchman's writings, *Louis Moutin.* To determine the susceptibility of a particular subject, Moutin (1887) placed one hand between the subject's shoulder blades, pressed moderately, and asked for a report of the sensations felt. If, after 3 or 4 min., the subject reported "heat" (or cold or electric charge or cramping) and then reported "unbearable heat" when Moutin quivered his fingers, the subject was hypnotizable. It was in the next maneuver that we see the continued reliance on notions magnetic. Moutin next gradually withdrew his hand and the patient (reportedly) began to follow Moutin by walking backwards wherever the unseen hand led. To Moutin, the operator acted as a magnet and the subject as a piece of metal.

By 1907, Moutin had modified his technique somewhat to an eye-fixation, physical pass method:

> We take the hands of the subject and apply our thumbs against his. We look into the person's eyes and have them do the same, remaining thus for 10 to 15 minutes, watching the physiological effects. . . . The time allows for eye-closure but not sleep.
>
> We then release the hands of the subject and stand up facing the subject in order to make our movements freely. Raise the hands and place them some centimeters above his head. Leave them there for 20 seconds and descend laterally to the height of the ears. The fingers are toward the cerebellum, where we stop them for several seconds.
>
> Make passes for five to six minutes, then apply the hands, one on the forehead and other on the cerebellum. Leave them there for five or six minutes. In order to place our hands we place ourselves at the right or left of the subject. Then, sit again opposite the subject, raise one hand to the root of the nose and bring it down slowly to the top of his chest. Raise it again and continue the passes until absolute insensibility and immobility are achieved.[4] (Moutin, 1907, pp. 44–45)

One of the most read of the European writers of this first decade was *Paul Dubois,* a practicing physician in Bern, Switzerland. His book, *The Treatment of Nervous Disorders* (1904/1909), had, by 1909, been translated into two German editions and six English editions and had appeared in its third

French edition. The book, which was originally delivered as a series of lectures to the Faculty of Medicine of the University of Bern, is a compilation of twenty years' experience in the treatment of nervous disorders. Dubois was not taken in by the continuing magnetic movement, for he noted that even Mesmer's successor, Deslon, recognized the central point played by the imagination in inductions: "In spite of these clear statements of Deslon they [modern hypnotizers] could not see it; the magnetizers continued their passes, and the public waxed enthusiastic over this mysterious agent" (Dubois, 1904/1909, p. 214).

Since the book was focused on the study of nervous disorders, Dubois did not dwell on particular induction methods. It is clear that he was of the Nancy School, for he concluded that Bernheim was the only individual to reach a logical conclusion about hypnosis. He did provide us with a method used at the time by a traveling "suggestor" by the name of *M. Krause.* By 1904 Krause had been on the circuit offering séances in the towns of Germany and Switzerland. His method was to tell a member of his audience to put her head back, open her mouth, and close her eyes. Then he states: "You cannot open your eyes!" When the subject opened her eyes, she was sent back to her chair. The same occurred with the second subject, until the audience began to doubt the effectiveness of the operator. However, when the third subject opened his eyes, Krause stated: "Yes, you succeeded in opening your eyes very well, but did you not have some trouble? It wasn't quite as easy as in the normal state?" (Dubois, 1904/1909, p. 118). From that point on, the rest of the subjects conformed easily to his suggestions, and his performance was a success through verbal suggestion. Although Dubois obviously disdained such public displays, he recognized the method as supporting verbal suggestion, often very cleverly offered, as fundamental to the emerging techniques of induction. The reader should notice too the relationship between Krause's verbal conditioning of the subject through suggested doubt and the indirect methods used by Erickson (see Chapter 6).

One remark in Dubois's work, which has little to do with hypnotic induction, but perhaps did portend the gathering storm of World War I and the eventual curtailment of investigations into hypnosis on the continent was his chiding his German colleagues for not fully recognizing the import of Briquet's 1859 work on hysteria. He thought the Germans would naturally "take these didactic descriptions seriously." When they did not, he taunted Germany, "a country of profound and sometimes obscure philosophies," for leaving it to the French to lead the way in the study of the psychological problems underlying nervous disease (Dubois, 1904/1909, p. 15).

However, the opening of the century revealed a continuing presence of German scholars in the study of hypnosis. *L. Loewenfeld* of Munich, for example, produced a monumental work (1901) several years before Dubois delivered his lectures. Loewenfeld's book was probably the most comprehensive of the time, offering, among other things, chapters on the history of hypnosis, hypnotizability, theories of hypnosis, the treatment of pathologies with hypnosis, the relationship between hypnosis and sleep, and group hypnosis. His chapter on the techniques of hypnotic induction concentrates on the last decade of the 1800s, including the various techniques that I have outlined thus far; for example, various eye-fixation methods, including Luys's mirrors; Preyer's use of a continuous gaze at a candlelight elevated above the normal visual plane (shades of Braid and the *Leiden Papyrus*); Hansen's technique and the procedure of having the patient stare at the fingers of the hypnotist. He also provided the reader with an extensive explication of the use of passes or strokes, which he pointed out was born of Mesmer's theory not his method.

Bernheim's methods (see Chapter 4) were given prominence and appear to have formed the bases of Loewenfeld's (1901) own procedure, which combined eye-fixation with verbal suggestion for fatigue and sleep:

> I bring two fingers of my right hand before the eyes of the patient and allow him to fixate upon them. Or I stroke repeatedly with both hands over his eyes from above downward. Or I ask him to gaze into my eyes steadily, in the course of which I seek, at the same time, to regulate all of his thought toward the introduction of sleep. I do it thus, with approximately the following words: "Close your eyelids; you cannot open them anymore; you notice a heaviness in your arms and legs; you hear nothing more; your hands are immobilized; you can see no more; the sleep comes over you." Then I add with a commanding tone, "Sleep!"[5] (pp. 109–110)

The two fundamentals, Loewenfeld felt, were (a) the fixation and (b) monotonous stimulation, which worked to accomplish the three phases of the procedure. "The first phase is to cause weariness and drowsiness, essential for the entry into hypnosis; the second phase has the aim of achieving the hypnotic sleep; and the third deepens the sleep"[6] (Loewenfeld, 1901, p. 114).

Loewenfeld also mentions, almost in passing, various physical magnetic and electric methods, as well as the use of drugs (chloroform, morphine, bromides, paraldehyde, etc.) to facilitate the participation of otherwise refractory patients. We should notice that as newer hypnotics and sedatives were developed they were added to the previously meager list of chemical supplements to the standard induction techniques.

One method the author covered, which has not been presented as yet, was Die Fractionirte Methode of *Oskar Vogt* (b. April 6, 1870; d. July 31, 1959).

> The principle encountered in this procedure is that one puts patients to sleep, not in a single period, as in the usual methods, but through awakenings, one after another, from very short, intermittent hypnotizations. This procedure has the great advantage that through questions of the patient during the wakeful periods, which obtain information on the effectiveness of the suggestions, one can reorient and remold the psychological conditions of the previous hypnosis

period. The obtained information on the effectiveness of the suggestion will then become the point of departure for subsequent suggestions. One is thus able to adjust the suggestions to the individuality of the person and to the exact degree of susceptibility encountered in later hypnosis periods. You can return to and strengthen suggestions in such a way as to dominate the formation of hypnosis more and more and use one's influence, in particular, in successive deepenings.[7] (Loewenfeld, 1901, p. 116)

This step-by-step approach of Vogt was based in his psychophysiological conceptualization of hypnosis, which he, like Pavlov, considered to be on a continuum between full wakefulness and deep sleep. His concept of hypnosis as "artificial sleep" preceded Pavlov's similar interpretation. His "fractioned method" was the forerunner of Schultz's autogenic training (see Chapter 6), with the exception that Vogt's technique was therapist directed, while Schultz's was patient implemented. Luthe (1969) gave this account of a single phase in Vogt's technique:

Patient comfortably relaxed, looks at the therapist's eyes with slightly upward position of the eyes, therapist's hand on forehead, local warmth from therapist's hand used for promoting spreading feelings of warmth and eye closure, sequence of "artificial sleep" with rapport; termination after 2 or 3 minutes: "Now I count to 3 and you are fully awake and comfortable, 1, 2, 3, awake and comfortable." (Luthe, 1969, p. 57)

Another German who had made the acquaintance of Oskar Vogt and adhered to his fractionation method was *W. Hilger,* a practicing physician in Magdeburg. Often this "intermittent treatment," as Vogt referred to it, was used by Hilger and others to ascertain the clarity of communication between physician and patient. Shortly after the induction, the patient was instructed to open his or her eyes and report on the progress of the treatment, discomforts that may have arisen, and/or the general ability to comply with the suggestions offered. Such a procedure for enhancing communication is a basic part of much that is taught today in our more client-centered approaches.

While others advocated the use of natural sleep as an entry into hypnosis, Hilger used hypnosis as a cure for insomnia. Using either a "memory-picture" or a corner of the ceiling of the room as a visual attention holding stimulus, Hilger told the patient to concentrate on the act of breathing:

It is quite sufficient to breathe in a quiet rhythm, and to repeat to one's self by syllable, "I may now rest, I do not need to work now, I do not need to make any plans now"; then say, "I may now sleep, I am sleepy, I will now sleep, I sleep now." (Hilger, 1912, p. 60)

Hilger's own method was, like so many of his time, grounded in the technique of Liébeault:

We let the patient lie on a comfortable couch, as far as possible in the position he usually adopts when going to sleep, in a quiet, slightly darkened room; then give some simple explanation of the action of hypnotism, so that the patient may be calm and not expecting any wonderful happenings, rather that simple rest or possibly sleep is to set in.

We sit down, say, to the left side of the patient near the head of the couch, lay the right hand on the patient's forehead, and request him to quietly look at the doctor's eyes (in doing this the patient's eyes are rather turned upwards), or we may direct his eyes to a fixed point on the ceiling of the room or on a wall of the room, to fix the gaze there. We then give the suggestion that the eyes are becoming tired and closing, the breathing quiet and regular (taking on the type as in sleep), that the thoughts are quieter and more indifferent, that the rest is becoming deeper, and so forth. (Hilger, 1912, p. 62)

Meanwhile to the south, *Joseph Lapponi,* chief physician for Popes Leo XIII and Pius X, was publishing his *Hypnotism and Spiritism.* In it he took note of a fact that not many of his professional colleagues were openly willing to admit and placed himself at variance with others who felt that hypnotists had to have some special qualities in order to be successful: "Any person [can] induce hypnosis in a susceptible subject" (Lapponi, 1907, p. 60). He noted also that various methods operated equally well, particularly when applied in a quiet, calm environment, devoid of distractions and dimly lit.

We can only assume that Lapponi's method was eclectic because his brief discussion about induction merely reiterated the five groups of inductions outlined by Chambard: psychic, sensory, mechanical, physical, and narcotic. Psychic means included concentrating on lively, imaginative images, or the opposite of abstaining from thought and imagination, much as the Bonzes of Japan and the Brahmins of India. Lapponi also included the sudden appearance a stimuli (a "shock") and the belief, which the subject may have, that the hypnotist has a particular power. Regarding the latter, he mentioned such individuals as Loewenthal, Reuss, Berson, Carpignon, Teste, and Guidi who were reported to have induced hypnosis by giving their patients cards, letters, flowers, or specially prepared "bread-pills," which the patients thought endowed with the power to induce the condition. We have already encountered this method with Bramwell and Estabrooks, mentioned above.

Sensory means included both rapid and sudden sensory stimulation and slow, monotonous fatiguing of the different sensory organs. In addition to the usual visual (staring at brilliant objects), auditory (a blast of a trumpet, the explosion of a petard), and tactile (rubbing) methods, Lapponi also mentions the elevation or depression of external, room temperature. The latter procedure has seldom been reported in the literature, no doubt because of the elaborate preparations it would have entailed. Mechanical methods did not involve mechanical devices as the name might imply, but, rather, mechanical manipulation of the body or parts thereof. Rapid and violent turning of the subject's head was one example and either compression and massage of the eyeballs or convergence of the optic axes through staring at one's own nose were others.

It was the physical methods that better fit the usual interpretation of mechanical means. Here magnets or electricity were used, in particular the "electric bath." Although the latter is not described, the reader can allow her or his imagination to fill in the gaps in the following comment: "By means of electric baths hypnosis may be induced either when the subject is being charged with electricity, or after the charge has been made, when sparks are drawn from him" (Lapponi, 1907, p. 66). Finally, narcotic means involved those drugs mentioned a number of times above and intoxicating substances like alcohol. "During the period of delirium resulting from the use of these various narcotic substances the hypnotic state is very often induced" (Lapponi, 1907, p. 66).

England

The British, heeding Tuckey and Savage's call to arms, produced a number of books and articles on hypnosis during this same period (1900–1920). *Edwin Ash,* the anesthetist at St. Mary's Hospital, Paddington, published two articles in *The Lancet* (1906) outlining his work with a number of patients. Initially, he used a "hypnoscope" constructed of a 6–8 in. diameter piece of ebony into which was inserted a 1 in. diameter bright metal disc. "The method used at first was fixed gazing at the small polished disc set in the centre of a larger disc of ebony. But it was soon found that by diverting the subject's attention to one hand which I slowly moved from the height of about 18 inches from the forehead down to the level of his eyes and then rapidly past them, hypnosis was as readily produced in susceptible people" (Ash, 1906, p. 217). Despite the opposition of individuals like Dr. Kerr (see above), Ash, like many others, gave public demonstrations, one of his being to the Psycho-Therapeutic Society at Bloomsbury Mansions on November 5, 1906.

To the North, *Hugh Crichton Miller,* an Edinburgh physician, constructed his induction technique on a remark by Tuckey and thus became known as the innovator, in England, of "collective hypnosis." Tuckey had noted that it was sometimes easier to hypnotize a new patient by having them observe the induction of one or two other, usually more practiced, patients. Wetterstrand, van Renterghem, van Eeden, and Bérillon had used group techniques for sometime, as, of course, had Mesmer himself. Miller (1912) presented four advantages to hypnotizing three or more patients at once in a large, dark, quiet room:

> 1. The suggestive power of imitation. The very sound of a neighbor breathing slowly and deeply, obviously asleep, is worth hours of suggestion from the most persevering physician.

2.   The self-conscious patient, who ordinarily is one of the most difficult to influence, is relieved for most of the time of the feeling that he is the centre of the physician's interest.

3.   If there are six patients present it is obvious that for every three minutes the physician is making suggestions to a given patient that patient has fifteen minutes' rest, during which those suggestions can "soak" in.

4.   The saving of time to the physician is immense, for in an hour he can treat efficiently some half-dozen patients, who taken individually would have occupied about three hours of his time, and been less efficiently treated even then. (Miller, 1912, p. 133)

As others of his day, Miller was a strong proponent of monotony in the form of suggestions for sleep and what he called "mind drill," or the attention to quieting, restful mental images. Some of the attention-holding devices used by his patients were as follows: "a familiar walk, the parade at Margate, the sign of infinity, Tschaikowsky's 'Symphonie Pathétique', the bunkers of St. Andrew's golf course, [and] garden planning" (Miller, 1912, p. 132), although Miller, himself, preferred rhythmic breathing as "the most simple and fundamental form of mind drill" (Miller, 1912, p. 143).

A number of the British practitioners made considerable use of the laying-on-of-hands in their induction procedures. *J. F. Woods,* for example, placed one hand on the patient's epigastrium and gently stroked the forehead with the other. "Let him relax his muscles to the full, and let no sound be heard but the rhythmic movement of your hand as you stroke the upper part of the face, or, possibly, the arms" (Miller, 1912, p. 126). Woods felt that silence was much more effective than "the continual drone of the voice." Miller (1912) also reported on another physician, *Adkin,* whose physical contact procedure was more dramatic than that used by many of his colleagues. The operator stood to the seated patient's right and grasped the temples with the thumb and first three fingers of the right hand. The hypnotist's left hand grasped the back of the subject's neck, shutting off the flow of blood to the head! The patient was told to close his or her eyes and think of nothing but sleep, while the operator rolled the head from left to right until the subject was "asleep." While the head was being rolled, the practitioner said: "You are so tired and sleepy that you cannot hear any sound but my voice; if any one calls you, you will not answer, you cannot hear them; when I count ten you will be sound asleep" (Miller, 1912, p. 126). After the count of 10, the patients were told they were sound asleep. Meanwhile the rotation of the head was slowly diminished, along with the pressure on the back of the neck. Finally, the left hand was placed over the patient's heart, pressing as he or she exhales and releasing the pressure as he or she inhales.

Although the tendencies to adhere to methods and theories of the past persisted in the continued use of "magnetic" and electric implements and the use of hands-on procedures, a strong element of the future was making progress, in the form of more concern for the client and more attention to explaining the process to the client prior to its application. One of the earlier practitioners to present such client concern was *Bernard Hollander*. Although he did not emphasize the directing of his own energies toward having patients well informed, the point was there in his statement of technique:

> The patient lying down on a couch or seated in a lounging chair, in which he has a comfortable rest for his head, the first step is to induce in the patient a mental state of calm and relaxation; a mental state which causes the patient to become receptive to the impressions that we wish to make upon his or her mind. The best plan is to have the patient seat himself in a comfortable position, and *then talk to him a little to remove his fears and in order to induce a placid, easy frame of mind, which will react upon the physical condition* [italics added]. He is asked to resign himself, not think of anything, not to distract his mind by thinking of the effects he will experience, to banish every fear, and not be uneasy or discouraged if he fall not asleep at once. He is then told to concentrate his attention upon sleep, to try to go to sleep; and, to assist him in this effort by preventing his taking in distracting ideas through his eyes as they wander around the room and see the pictures, books and furniture, we may get him to fix his gaze upon some bright and shining object. Thus, fixity of attention, passivity and concentration are produced. He is instructed not to try to keep his eyes open, and not to close them voluntarily, but merely to let the lids go as they will. The physician may now keep quiet for a time, or else by a monotonous talk he may encourage the patient in his effort to go to sleep. (Hollander, 1910, p. 48)

What we note here is not only the concern that the fears of the patient be allayed, but also the implication that a cognitive dissociation should take place. Is this technique a forerunner of neodissociationism or the continuation of Janet's original dissociation ideas? We may never know, but we will see the cognitive dissociation view made more explicit in the work of Wingfield below.

Though Hollander may have been a bridge for the dissociation approach, he parted ways with many of his contemporaries and practitioners of the present when he noted that "no suggestion should be made, unless the patient is really in a perfectly passive state, or has actually gone to sleep" (Hollander, 1910, p. 49). For him, treatment was a two-step affair, curative suggestions following the first step, induction.

A. Betts Taplin, Liverpool President of the Psycho-Medical Society of Great Britain, was another of the British practitioners who were now explicating what many practitioners, at least since the time of Liébeault, had been doing. Taplin began his procedures—following a thorough physical examination—by explaining the theory of treatment and generally gaining the patient's trust and confidence. Due deference was paid to a quiet, calming environment, to the extreme point that even the wallpaper should be of a soothing color. Treatment per se often did not begin until the second session, wherein he started with a laying-on-of-hands by placing his left hand on the seated patient's forehead. This beginning point was crucial for Taplin, for the hand and its application must be precisely executed. Here is his brief treatise on hands and their effects: "The decided slap of the large, cold, heavy hand will almost startle him [the patient]; the tremulous, nervous hand will worry him; the clammy, perspiring hand will annoy him; the hard, knobby, bony hand will irritate him; whilst the soft, normally warm hand, applied with gentle pressure, will soothe and calm him" (Taplin, 1918, pp. 57–58).

Following the application of this warm, soothing hand, a bright object was presented on which the patient fixed his gaze while the following words were spoken by the physician in an equally soothing voice: "You are feeling tired, sleepy and comfortable—your eyes are growing more heavy and misty, you are going to sleep. [The thumb and forefinger of the left hand applied gentle pressure to the outside of the eyeballs and the verbal instructions continued.] You are feeling comfortable, warm, drowsy, heavy in your eyelids, your legs, arms, and all over" (Taplin, 1918, pp. 58–59). The hand was then moved back to the forehead and the right hand applied to the epigastrium intermittently.

Taplin was also not averse to using the physical passes of old, and would sometimes use a method he characterized as "suggestion, pure and simple." In this procedure he merely told the patient to close his or her eyes and allow his or her thoughts to "drift into some restful, dreamy channel," while he maintained gentle pressure on the eyeballs. He then said, "Now all your muscles are relaxed, you are feeling comfortable all over, a comfortable tired feeling, your eyes are growing heavy, you are beginning to feel sleepy all over, sleep, sleep, sleep" (Taplin, 1918, p. 61). These last verbalizations were accompanied with monotonous passes from the crown of the head down the body. Therapy usually took about 15 or 20 min., after which the patient was awakened ("wide awake, clear and very well") by counting to either 5 or 10, depending on the perceived depth of the hypnosis.

Several things about Taplin's work should strike us. First, although there is certainly the lingering of the past as noted above, there are clear elements of the progressing 20th century. Simply counting was used to terminate hypnosis, a move away from the older Braidian methods of blowing on the patient or startling him or her with other sensory stimuli suddenly presented. The attention paid to the patient and his or her understanding of the treatment procedure *before* it was applied was another ambience to the induction techniques which we will see gain increasing currency as we progress through the present century. (In fact, it is a professional shame that informing patients about their pending treatment, hypnotic or otherwise, is not more universally applied than it is even today.) But despite the more modern moves of a client-centered approach and a counting de-induction technique, one ancient facet of hypnosis had not changed—and, in fact, still has not changed—by Taplin's time: the conceptualization of hypnosis as a condition of relaxation, calm, peace, both cognitively and physically. Taplin incorporated both forms of relaxation into his induction when he told the patient to "let your thoughts wander away from the present into any restful channel" (Taplin, 1918, p. 58) and admonished him to relax the muscles and feel drowsy. The relaxation-hypnosis equation is powerful and pervasive.

However, Taplin was not the only individual writing in the first two decades of the 20th century to advocate a strong client-centered position. *Hugh Edward Wingfield,* another past president of the Psycho-Medical Society of Great Britain like Taplin, and a consulting physician at the Royal Hants County Hospital, was also an adherent to the procedure of spending time with the patient making sure he or she understood the principles underlying hypnosis before beginning the induction. Curiously enough, not only did Wingfield present the client-centered approach, but also what, in modern times, has become known as "divided consciousness" or "neodissociation" (see Hilgard, 1977). During his initial contact, he told the patient that whenever we concentrate our attention on something with sufficient intensity, "our consciousness always tends to split in two. . . . Unaware actions . . . are governed by a part of consciousness split off from the rest, and the split-off part possesses so little power of criticism that it accepts suggestions quite readily" (Wingfield, 1920, p. 50). Here, then, is a statement quite similar in theory to the ideas of neodissociation and in practice to the instructions given experimental subjects when queried regarding the "hidden-observer" phenomenon.

Having conveyed these dissociative concepts to the patient, Wingfield proceeded by having the patient lie down and relax his or her muscles. He then produced a cut-glass crystal for eye-fixation and told the patient, "Whilst you are looking at it, I want you to blink as much as ever you like; let your eyes get as heavy as ever they can, and let yourself become as drowsy as possible, and do not rouse at all" (Wingfield, 1920, p. 51). This was followed by continued eye-fixation and rubbing the forehead, then: "Your eyes are getting heavier now; you are becoming drowsy, they are half closed" (Wingfield, 1920, p. 52). At times stroking of the patient's arms was used, as well as concentration on a monotonous metronome beat. At no time did Wingfield attempt this method, for which he claimed 92% effectiveness on the first trial, for more than 3 min., usually only 2. No doubt he could have doubled his patient load in the same time period if he had adopted Miller's earlier group induction procedure, but most of the practitioners of the day continued with individual therapy techniques.

How, then, should we summarize this period of the first two decades of the 20th century? We have seen the continuation of the old and glimmers of the new. Although the more mechanical, magnetically based methods were losing their impact to the verbally based methods, the laying-on-of-hands retained its place in the armamentarium of practicing hypnotists. Certainly, increasing attention was being focused on the personal needs and anxieties of the patients. Through it all, however, one interpretation of hypnosis was, and is, glaringly regnant—the relaxation, sleep basis of almost all induction techniques. Perhaps Hollander and Wingfield best summarized the conditions prevalent in hypnotic inductions of the period when they reproduced the characteristic of inductions according to Sidis (Hollander, 1910, p. 55; Sidis, 1898, p. 87; Wingfield, 1920, p. 40):

1. Fixation of the attention.
2. Monotonous environment, to produce monotony of impressions and intellectual drowsiness.
3. Limitation of voluntary movements by relaxation of the muscles.
4. Limitation of the field of consciousness.
5. Inhibition of ideas by making the mind a blank.

Thus, through this period (1900–1920), the productivity balance was beginning to shift to the English language as exemplified by the above items and a host of lesser known, and, for our purposes, lesser value, works; for example, Reinhardt, 1914; Hutchison, 1919. The latter example does, however, deserve special mention because it was one of the earliest works on hypnosis published by a female physician. In 1912 *Alice M. Hutchison's* book was unique in this regard, as well as in its quality.

America

In America, publication on hypnosis had not begun to approach the fevered pitch that was to begin after World War II. True, individuals like Morton Prince, William McDougall (Although English by birth, he spent his last years at Duke University.), and William James explored the phenomena of hypnosis; Prince, its therapeutic possibilities; McDougall, its physiological properties; and James, its place in history and the philosophy of psychology. In 1908 McDougall, in his article on the state of the brain (inhibition) during hypnosis, took passing note of the prevalent methods of the time. Apparently they were much the same on this side of the Atlantic, including eye-fixation, monotonous verbal or mechanical stimulation, and various passes. As we will see in Chapter 6, Erickson was beginning his interest in hypnosis at Wisconsin in the late teens and early twenties. According to Shor (1979), he offered a graduate seminar in 1923, at the request of another investigator whose work began during the first two decades of this century, Clark L. Hull.

One rather curious publication appeared in 1903 from the Chicago area. It was a book published by it authors, Mr. & Mrs. *Herbert L. Flint*, entitled *Practical Instruction in Hypnotism and Suggestion*. In it, Mr. Flint outlined methods for achieving many of the same hypnotic phenomena we encounter in other books of the past and present, but his sequence of presentation was what brought my attention to his book. Unlike anyone I had encountered before or afterwards, Flint presented instructions for ending the hypnotic condition *first* (following the usual preliminary discussion of defining the condition and reviewing its "scientific history"). Thus the novice operator is given the procedure for awakening *before* he or she is given the methods of induction. A unique approach, but quite logical. The technique itself was simple enough; he instructed his pupils to say "All right, wide awake!" to the subject. Should that not have the desired effect immediately, he admonished the operator to continue to exude confidence (lest the subject become concerned) and to give the subject a count of 1 to 10 to awaken. If this also failed to awaken the subject, he resorted to upward passes such as I described in previous chapters. Finally, Flint felt it advantageous for the operator to smile at the subject on awakening as a positive suggestion of the pleasantness of the condition. Flint felt that "too little attention is paid to this part of the work [the awakening process] by most writers on this subject" (Flint, 1903, p. 154). Therefore, he included awakening instructions with each "test" he taught in the book, tests such as visual (butterfly) and tactile (flea, molasses) hallucinations, catatonic suggestions, and anesthesias.

He taught three basic methods of induction, all using the fundamental factors of the laying-on-of-hands and eye-fixation. In all three the subject was seated comfortably in a chair with his or her hands on the knees and feet flat on the floor. In the first, the hypnotist interlocked the thumbs of his two hands, curved the fingers inward, and made passes from the subject's forehead down the shoulders to the arms and hands, pressing briefly on the latter before beginning the next pass. The thumbs disengaged as the pass progressed from head to shoulders, but were reintertwined on the upward sweep. While the passes were being made, verbal suggestions for sleep were simultaneously issued.

The second method used a different pass pattern. The thumb of the right hand was on the top center of the forehead with the fingers on the subject's left temple. The operator's left thumb was on the subject's right temple, with the fingers at the base of the back of the skull. Both hands were slowly drawn forward and outward until they were about a foot away from the face. The pass was repeated 30 to 40 times. While making these motions, the operator fixated the subject's eyes and said: "Your eyelids are getting heavy; they are feeling tired. You will find you want to close them. You are getting sleepy, sleepy" (Flint, 1903, p. 87). Finally, the third method involved gross bodily movement on the part of the operator. Again standing in front of the seated subject, the hypnotist looked intently into the eyes of the subject (and vice versa), while grasping the subject's right hand in his own right hand and placing his left hand so that the thumb rested between the eyebrows and the first two fingers were spread at the top of the forehead. Now the operator began to move toward and away from the subject, coming as close as 6 in. from his or her eyes and as far away as 3 ft., for about 5 min. Again, verbal suggestions for fatigue and sleep were continuously offered. The final test for the effectiveness of the procedures was to challenge the subject to open his or her eyes which had been "made fast." Often this challenge was issued concomitant with increased pressure from the operator's fingers on the subject's forehead.

Flint disavowed any such induction as an instantaneous method, offering his total financial worth and half of his profits from the next 5 years if someone could teach him how. Instead, he concentrated on the attributes and general health care of the hypnotist. The voice, for example, was to be positive, pleasing, and earnest; the eyes penetrating and steady. He even went so far as to prescribe a diet for the hypnotist consisting of more vegetables, less meat, and general moderation in the quantity consumed. In short, Flint's book was an interesting compilation of practical advice, but not one likely to catch the eye of his professional contemporaries.

Probably the most well-known American publishing in hypnosis and many related fields at the turn of the century was *Boris Sidis* (b. Oct. 12, 1867; d. Oct. 24, 1923), to whom both Hollander and Wingfield deferred. A friend and student of William James, he began his researches into suggestibility at the Harvard Psychological Laboratories and completed much of his early work at the Pathological Institute of the New York State Hospitals. He was one of the original editorial board members of the *Journal of Abnormal Psychology,* started in 1906 by Morton Prince, and published a variety of articles there ranging from clinical case studies of psychopathology to speculations on the causes of social upheaval. His books also displayed his varied interests (e.g., *The Psychology of Laughter,* 1913), but centered primarily on normal and abnormal psychology and the treatment of nervous or mental disorders. Since he held both the Ph.D. and the M.D., he opened his own psychiatric institute in 1914 in Portsmouth, New Hampshire, the Sidis Psychotherapeutic Institute, later renamed Dr. Sidis's Maplewood Farms, in 1922.

Sidis's concern was not directly with hypnosis, but with suggestibility and how it operated in the human organism. Consequently, when he did hypnotize, he used "the method of Nancy." But Sidis's major contribution was the notation of the "hypnoidal" state, a condition somewhere on a continuum between waking and hypnosis. The condition was of considerable value in working with cases of psychopathology for history, diagnostic, and treatment purposes. In addition, much of his experimentation with the hypnoidal condition was in the realm of the amnesias and multiple personalities. The method for achieving this condition, which Sidis called "hypnoidization," but which Goldwyn (1929) later contended should be called "hypnoidalization" to avoid confusion with the induction of the hypnoid state—a semi-hypnotic or hysterical abnormal condition—was simply enough:

> The patient is asked to close his eyes and keep as quiet as possible, without, however, making any special effort to put himself in such a state. He is then asked to attend to some stimulus, such as reading or singing. When the reading is over, the patient, with his eyes still shut, is asked to repeat it, and tell what

comes into his mind during the reading, during the repetition, or after it. Sometimes, as when the song-stimulus is used, the patient is simply asked to tell the nature of ideas and images that entered into his mind at that time or soon after. (Sidis, 1898, p. 224)

Later, he modified his technique to include more obviously monotonous stimulation:

The patient is told to close his eyes and keep very quiet. He is then asked to attend to some monotonous stimulus, such as the beats of a metronome, or listen to a continuous note produced by a tuning-fork, or to smell some pleasant odor, or simply to submit himself to a gentle massage in which touch and pressure are of uniform intensity. This should be carried out in a room where it is dark and quiet. Fatigue, physical and mental, especially emotional, is a favorite condition. A predisposition to sleep is helpful. It is, therefore, best to make first attempt—late at night, when the patient is both tired and sleepy. In most cases darkness, quietness, repose, fixation on a bright point and listening to the monotonous buzzing of an inductorium are conditions favorable to the induction of the hypnoidal state, and even at the very first attempt. (Sidis, 1907, p. 73)

A year later, *J. E. Donley* (1908) described his own variation on Sidis's theme.

The patient is first placed at ease by a few minutes' conversation, during which he is instructed regarding what is about to be done. He is then requested to lie upon a couch, the head of which has been placed close to a faradic wall plate. With his eyes closed he is directed to listen to the monotonous vibration of the ribbon rheotome, and to concentrate attention either upon nothing at all or upon the particular idea or group of ideas or images suggested to him by the physician. (Donley, 1908, p. 149)

Ten years later *Goldwyn* (1929) reported essentially the same procedure, which he had renamed "hypnoidalization." It, too, placed the patient in a comfortable position in a dimly lit room, with tight clothing loosened, and had him or her concentrate on some monotonous stimulation until the hypnoidal state was achieved. Goldwyn, however, made great moment of distinguishing between the hypnoidal and the hypnotic conditions. The latter, he stated, was an abnormal condition in which the subconscious became regnant by the diminished function of the conscious mind. In the hypnoidal state, however, both the conscious and the subconscious were diminished in activity. Whether such a distinction was warranted, it was a considered viewpoint during the Sidis, Prince, et al. period. What should strike the reader, on the other hand, is the similarity or virtual identity of the "hypnoidalization" technique with hypnotic induction techniques of that period and today. Particularly with the passing of the notion of hypnosis as an abnormal phenomenon, we can subsume Sidis's method under the general heading of a hypnotic induction method. All the characteristics were there—concern for the patient's welfare and comfort, an environment of reduced stimulation, eye and/or mental-fixation, and suggestions (verbal or otherwise) for fatigue and general lethargy.

This same general format was adhered to by *F. H. Gerrish,* (1909) who also spent a considerable amount of prehypnosis time explaining matters to the patient. He told his prospective subject (a) that all people are suggestible, (b) that he will accept suggestion more easily during hypnosis, (c) that no harm will come to him, (d) that hypnosis does not involve the surrender of will, (e) that there will be no unpleasantness, (f) that he must not consciously try to resist the suggestions, and (g) that the use of the word "sleep" is a convenience and not a statement of the condition. Rather, he told his patients that hypnosis was a transitional condition between sleep and waking. This latter point sounds much like Sidis's idea of a hypnoidal state and belies the distinction made by Goldwyn (1929). (It also mimics the modern Russian view—see Edmonston, 1981.) Not everyone at that time was convinced of the "abnormality" of the hypnotic condition. In fact, to further the sleep-hypnosis analogy, Gerrish instructed his patients to concentrate on sleep as he placed his hand on their foreheads: "Try to sleep, think of nothing but sleep, keep your thoughts fixed upon going to sleep. Your lids are heavy, they are drooping, you are going to sleep. Every moment you are getting more drowsy; you feel the sleep stealing over you. The lids are closing; you are almost asleep. Now the eyes have closed; you have gone to sleep" (Gerrish, 1909, p. 103). He applied this technique to cases of drug addiction, phobias, obsessions, and seasickness.

Another American whose works also appeared at this time was a physician practicing in New York City, *John Duncan Quackenbos*. Quackenbos trained at the College of Physicians and Surgeons and taught at Columbia University for the period 1871–1894, until he resigned his chair to devote full time to the application of "suggestive therapeutics to the eradication of criminal traits, hereditary and acquired" (Quackenbos, 1907, p. 6). His experience with more than 7000 cases (a number of them young boys in Manhattan) led to the publication of his philosophy of suggestive therapeutics in 1907. His previous book, *Hypnotism in Mental and Moral Culture,* had already been translated into Japanese and Armenian.

The general characteristics of Quackenbos's induction techniques were not different from what we have already encountered, involving, first the fixation of the gaze on some bright object; second, the establishment of the patient's confidence in the therapist; and third, the delivery of monotonous suggestions for sleep. He, like Taplin and Wingfield noted above, spent fully an hour or two prior to induction explaining each step of the induction and the proposed suggestive therapy. "It is useless to begin by insulting his [the patient's] intellect" (Quackenbos, 1907, p. 33). Despite the lack of substantive innovation in his procedure, I have reproduced it here to illustrate the detail to which the author was willing to go to ensure the patient's understanding and confidence. It is essentially the same method he had published in his earlier (1900) *Hypnotism in Mental and Moral Culture*.

After the patient was comfortably reclining on a lounge, he began.

I wish you to look at this diamond (or select any convenient object in the line of vision) in a dreamy, listless manner, with a blank expressionless stare, thinking of nothing, not concentrating your mind or focussing your eye upon it, but relaxing the ocular muscles so that it has a confused outline. Abstain from that effort with the eyes that you are accustomed to make in order to see a near object distinctly. Rather look through the stone and past it, as you look at a dead tree standing between you and a distant view contemplating. The reason for affecting this vacant look is thoroughly scientific. Darwin has shown, in a treatise on the emotions, that every mental state has a corresponding physical expression, and that if you assume one you are likely to experience the other. Anger, for instance, expresses itself physically in violent language, clenching the fists, slamming a door, etc. And a man may make himself angry by doing these things. So he can put himself into a devotional frame of mind by assuming the attitude of prayer, and you may help to bring on the congenial state of musing or wool-gathering by simulating the languid look which is natural to this state. This is the reason why I ask you to look at the jewel, which has no power in itself to induce abstraction. The power is in you. What often happened when you are reading a newspaper of a warm afternoon in that

> *"Season atween June and May*
> *Half prankt with spring, with summer half imbrown'd,*
> *A listless climate made when sooth to say*
> *No living wight could work, ne cared even for play,"*

(THOMSON'S "CASTLE OF INDOLENCE")

will now take place. You remember, as you read on, the type begins to swim beneath your eyes, the effort to concentrate your mind fails, all activity is irksome, the sense of passiveness deepens, the muscles relax, the paper drops from your hand, and you are launched into a world of airy visions. So now you are to be wooed out of this consciousness, and to pass into a light slumber in which you can be made to see the truth and adjust yourself thereto.

Make no effort, for there is nothing you can do to encourage the approach of the favorable mind state. Do not wonder what is going to happen, for nothing is going to happen. Do not be apprehensive, or suspicious, or distrustful. Do not desire that anything shall take place, nor watch to see what may occur—nor seek to analyze what is going on in your mind. You are as negative, indolent, and indifferent as you can be without trying to be. Your idle unconcern is justified only by confidence, and this you have in me, in yourself, and in the outcome of the treatment. You have confidence in me, first, as a man of science who is qualified by education and experience to perform this service for you, and who is going to do it wisely and conservatively for your good; and, secondly, you have confidence in me as a friend to whom you have laid bare your heart, who is in sympathy with you, who is sincerely desirous of helping you, and who is going to help you by showing you how to help yourself—a friend is the one who makes you do what you can, not the person who does for you and so destroys your independence. And then you have faith in yourself. You are sure that you can be helped, that you are adequate to the accomplishment of your purpose when appropriately inspired, that you cannot be deceived or influenced against your better judgment, even if my intent were malevolent. No harm can possibly come to you when lost in this sleep. So with confidence in me, in yourself, in the occasion, the instrumentality, and the outcome of the treatment, you are about to abandon yourself without mental reservation, reluctance, or misgiving, to a pleasant current that drifts you along with it toward the sphere of sleep—for that is all that it is, the same sleep you enjoy every night, only that you have voluntarily selected me to go with you into this sleep as a companion and friend, to apprise you of your own powers, and to point out to you the way of escape from your trouble through the spontaneous operation of these powers.

You are to expect the familiar signs of the approach of sleep, and they are all associated with the failure of the senses and the stand-still of the brain—heavy eyelids, reluctant ears, muscles and skin indifferent to stimuli of temperature, humidity, penetrability, etc. Already that delightful sensation of drowsiness "weighs your eyelids down and steeps your senses in forgetfulness," and you yield to the impulse as the curtains are dropped between you and the outside world of color and light. And your ear seeks to share in this rest of the senses. As darkness is the sleep of the eye, so is silence that of the ear; and your ear secures silence by deadening itself to sound impressions. The sounds of my voice lost interest for you, and force and incisiveness, and seem to be receding into a mysterious remoteness whither you are disinclined to follow them, leaving you in a state of delightful relaxation. A grateful sense of surrender to some pleasing influence which you cannot resist, and would not if you could, descends upon you and enwraps your whole body in its beneficent embrace, and you are physically happy. Refreshing sleep has come to you. (Quackenbos, 1907, pp. 33–36)

Should this more client-concerned approach not attain the desired effects, Quackenbos shifted to a more direct, authoritative technique reminiscent of the middle 1800s. Placing the patient in a straight-backed chair, he took hold of both of the patient's hands and stared him or her, eyeball to eyeball, into "a state of suggestive sleep." The procedure took about 15 min., but was reported to be extremely fatiguing to the operator, "who looks into the subject's soul from eyes 'as unwinking as the lidless orbs of the Genius of Destruction' " (Quackenbos, 1907, p. 37). Such high drama was rewarded by an "expression of surrender" and deep inspirations as the patient entered the hypnotic condition.

Although it is clear that Quackenbos was given to dramatic presentation and the fundamentals of his technique were not particularly innovative, his writings illustrate the progression toward the future we saw in the British practitioners. The increasing concern for the patient's welfare and willingness to make the patient a partner in his or her own treatment, in addition to the growing attitude that much of the therapeutic work is actually accomplished by the patient rather than the practitioner probably laid the foundation for much of what was to come. No doubt these growing attitudes played a part in the development of what I have called the New Nancy School of Coué in the roaring 1920s.

BETWEEN THE GREAT WARS

The New Nancy School

In 1920 Charles Baudouin, Professor at the Jean Jacques Rousseau Institute and the University of Geneva, dedicated his book, *Suggestion and Autosuggestion,* to the founder of the New Nancy School of hypnosis, Émile Coué. Born on February 26, 1857 in Troyes, Aube, France, the son of an Eastern Railroad Company worker, Coué studied chemistry at the École de Pharmacy in Paris and opened his own drug store in 1882 in Troyes. During 1885 and 1886, he observed Liébault and was much impressed with his methods, so much so that, after a number of years of studying hypnosis both on the continent and in the United States, he moved to 186 Rue Jeanne D'Arc in Nancy and opened a free clinic where he was purported to have treated between 15,000 and 40,000 patients annually.

In 1921 Coué was visited by a Dr. Monier-Williams of London, who was so impressed with the auto-suggestive techniques of the New Nancy School that he opened a free clinic in London himself. As Coué's fame spread, a series of "Coué Institutes" were opened. The mother institute was the Société Lorraine de Psychologie, operated by Coué and his wife from their home in Nancy. Here, for 5 francs, one could become an active Member, or for 10 francs, a Social Member. In London, a Miss Richardson started the Coué Institute for the Practice of Conscious Auto-Suggestion, and in 1922 an institute opened in Paris under a former student, Mademoiselle Anne Villneuve. Coué's trip to America, also in the early 1920s, yielded preparations for a National Coué Institute in New York City. By 1922 the Coué League of America had been formed, with Archibald Stark Van Orden (Ramsey, New Jersey) as its secretary and main proponent.

What was Coué's method that had so captured two continents and had lead Baudouin to refer to him as a "steadfast worker and pioneer"? The basic mechanic of the method was simple indeed, and is captured in the following passage from one of his books:

> All that is necessary is to place oneself in a condition of mental passiveness, silence the voice of conscious analysis, and then deposit in the ever-awake subconscious the idea or suggestion which one desires to be realized.

> Every night, when you have comfortably settled yourself in bed and are on the point of dropping off to sleep, murmur in a low but clear voice, just loud

enough to be heard by yourself, this little formula: "Every day, in every way, I am getting better and better." Recite the phrase like a litany, twenty times or more. (Coué, 1923, p. 26)

To enhance the ritual, Coué instructed his patients to tie 20 knots in a piece of string and count off the repetitions as one might say the rosary.

Although one of his other books (Coué, 1922) offers the phrase as "Day by day, in every way, I am getting better and better" to be said both in the morning on arising *and* in the evening on retiring, the phrase embodies the principles underlying the New Nancy School. Coué believed strongly in the powers of autosuggestion; thus cure came not from the practitioner, but from the patient himself or herself. Furthermore, the most significant effects of autosuggestion occur in the subconscious or unconscious, under certain principles or laws.

Coué (1922, p. 38) offered two principles governing his method:

1. It is impossible to think of two things at the same time.
2. Every thought that completely fills our mind becomes true for us and has a tendency to transform itself into action.

The heavy reliance on the patient's unconscious, the belief in the power of the unconscious, through autosuggestion, to effect cures through the transformation of thought into action, and the notion of what Baudouin called the Law of Reverse Effort (Baudouin, 1920, p. 121) bear a striking resemblance to the principles taught in the 1950s and 1960s by Milton Erickson and his colleagues in the Seminars on Hypnosis, discussed below. With knowledge of Coué's method and the underlying principles, it is easy to see the historical continuity between that method and the emphasis placed on client-centered responsibility for treatment outcome and the importance of the unconscious by modern hypnotherapeutic techniques. Thus many of the Ericksonian techniques being so highly idolized nowadays are little more than the modern restatement of Coué's New Nancy School method, which, in turn, was the 20th century development of the methods of Liébault.

Even the "laws of suggestion" proposed by Baudouin (1922) appear quite similar to those in vogue today:

1. *Law of Concentrated Attention.* An idea that becomes a suggestion is one on which spontaneous attention is concentrated.
2. *Law of Auxiliary Emotion.* An idea that is wrapped in emotion is more likely to become a suggestion.
3. *Law of Reverse Effort.* Conscious efforts to counteract a suggestion only serve to intensify its action. (Here we see stated the principle behind such Ericksonian-like utterances as: "The more you try to resist entering hypnosis, the more relaxed you become.")

4. *Law of Subconscious Teleology*. The unconscious finds a way to realize suggested ends.

As with many modern techniques, Baudouin considered the first and third principles the most important. But even more important was the groundwork Baudouin and Coué considered primary in the realization of suggestion, whether auto or hetero-relaxation. This was the condition through which "the desired suggestion will come into being with the minimum of effort" (Baudouin, 1922, p. 151). Relaxation was considered the royal pathway to the subconscious and thus the realization, in action, of the autosuggestions necessary for their patient's well-being. Relaxation has had a long symbiosis with hypnosis and suggestive therapeutics (Edmonston, 1981).

Returning now to Coué and his method, we should note that he did not rely solely on his patients' repetitive utterance of the litany of "Every day, in every way, etc." In his treatise, "How to Teach People to Make Autosuggestions: Advice and Instructions to his Pupils and Disciples" (Coué, 1922, pp. 38–52), he offered specific suggestions on technique. He emphasized a positive approach, praising, never reproaching patients. The confidence of the practitioner was critical and was to be conveyed through bearing, the firm, commanding, warm tone of voice, and general unflappability in the face of a cold, unsympathetic patient. With these ideas in mind, the pupil was then directed to go through a series of four experiments with the patient to establish a suggestive pattern. First, the patient was instructed to stand straight and stiff and to allow the practitioner to pull him or her backwards as if he or she were anchored at one spot on the floor. Second, the patient was instructed to think: "I am falling backward . . . I am falling backward, . . . etc.," while the practitioner held his right fist on the back of the patient's neck and the left hand on the patient's forehead. Then the practitioner gently removed his right fist and applied a slight, almost imperceptible pressure on the forehead, as the patient continued to think: "I am falling backwards." (The technique of assisting movement during demonstrations of hypnotic suggestion was used often by Erickson, see Chapter 6.)

The third experiment advised by Coué involved the patient facing the practitioner in a standing position, with the latter fixing his gaze on the base of the former's nose while placing his hands on the patient's temples. The patient was then told to think: "I am falling forward" until, with gentle pressure from the practitioner, the action occurred. The final experiment also involved the fixed gaze of the practitioner on the base of the patient's nose, but this time the patient was told to clasp his or her hands together and think: "I cannot get my hands apart. I cannot do it."

In these relatively simple suggestive tasks, we see the development of the patient's suggestibility through the use of a positive approach and imperceptible prodding by the practitioner in the context of suggested motor responses (or inhibition thereof). Naturally, we are clearly reminded of the sway test now attributed to Hull (1933), the various quick tests of hypnotizability, and parts of the longer, modern scales of susceptibility that are discussed in Chapter 8.

Once the suggestive rapport was established between the patient and the Coué method practitioner, Coué offered the following:

Sit down and close your eyes:

I will not try to put you to sleep; it is not necessary.

I request you to close your eyes simply for the purpose that your attention may not be distracted by the things you see around you:

Now impress upon your mind that every word I say is going to fix itself in your brain and be firmly imprinted, engraved, embedded there:

My words will always stay there fixed, imprinted, embedded, and without your will or knowledge, in fact wholly unconsciously on your part, you yourself and your entire organism are going to obey:

I tell you, first of all, that every day, three times a day, at morning, noon and evening, at the usual meal hours, you will be hungry, that is to say: you will feel the pleasing sensation that makes you think: "Oh! I am ready to eat with great satisfaction":

You will indeed eat with great pleasure and enjoy your food, of course without over-eating; you will be careful to chew your food thoroughly so as to transform it into a sort of soft paste which you will then swallow:

Your food will be properly digested and you will not feel the slightest discomfort, inconvenience, or pain—neither in the stomach nor in the intestines:

You will assimilate your food well and your organism will profit by it in making blood, muscle, strength, energy—in a word: LIFE.

Having digested properly, the function of excretion will be perfectly normal:

Every morning, on rising, you will feel a desire for an evacuation; without ever requiring medicine or artificial means of any kind, you will obtain entirely normal and satisfactory bowel movements.

Furthermore, every night, from the moment you wish to sleep to the time at which you desire to awake in the morning you will sleep a profound, calm, wholesome, unbroken sleep, during which you will have no nightmares; upon waking you will feel well, cheerful, and ready for active work.

If at times you have been sad and depressed; if you have been brooding and worrying, this will cease from now on, and instead of being sad, depressed and worried, you will feel cheerful, very cheerful, even gay; you may have no cause for your gaiety, just as you may have had no reason for your depression. Moreover I say that even if you have had any real reason for being sad or depressed, you are NOT going to be so.

If it happens, sometimes, that you have fits of impatience and ill temper, you will never have them again. On the contrary you will always be patient; always master of yourself; and the things which worried, irritated and annoyed you will henceforth leave you absolutely indifferent and perfectly calm.

If you are at times attacked, pursued, haunted by bad and unwholesome ideas, by apprehensions, fears, aversions, temptations, or grudges against others, all will gradually fade away and be lost as in a passing cloud and will finally disappear completely; as a dream vanishes on awakening, so will all your vain imaginations vanish.

I say that all your organs are performing their functions properly:

The heart beats normally, the circulation of the blood is as it should be:

The lungs are in fine condition:

The stomach, the intestines, the liver, the bladder, the kidneys and the biliary duct are all functioning properly:

If at this moment one of them should not be acting normally, this abnormality will be less day by day and very soon it will have vanished completely and the organ will be in perfect working order.

Further, if there should be any lesions in any of these organs they will improve day by day and soon be entirely healed. (In this connection I will say that it is not necessary to know which organ is afflicted in order to heal it. Under the influence of the autosuggestion "Every day, in every way, I am getting better and better," the Unconscious exercises its influence on the particular, diseased organ.)

I must also add, and it is of extreme importance, that if up to the present, you have lacked confidence in yourself, I tell you that distrust in yourself will gradually disappear and give place to self-confidence, based on your knowledge of that force of incalculable power which is in you.

This self-confidence is absolutely necessary for you and every other human being to have. Without it you will never get anywhere; with it, you may accomplish whatever you want to (within the laws of nature, of course).

You are now going to have confidence in yourself and this confidence enables you to believe that you can reach each goal you set for yourself (if it is a natural one):

And that you will do well all that, in the course of duty, you have to do.

So then, when you wish to do something that is natural, or when you have a duty to perform, always think that it is an easy thing to do. The words: "It is difficult, impossible, I cannot, it is beyond me, I cannot help myself" . . . must disappear from your vocabulary. Think: "IT IS EASY. . . . I CAN." Believing a matter to be easy, it becomes so for you, although it may seem difficult to others. You will do it quickly and well, without fatigue, because you do it without effort. (Coué, 1922, pp. 45–47)

Here again, as we have seen before and will see further on the induction used is a potpourri of therapeutic suggestions and instructions to be in a receptive condition. Notice the generalized aspect of the suggestion patter. Coué believed in making his suggestions as general as possible, leaving the specific work to the subconscious.

Once these suggestions were made—"in a monotonous, soothing voice"—de-induction was accomplished by saying:

> In short, I mean that from every point of view, physical and mental, you are going to enjoy excellent health, better health than you have been able to enjoy hitherto.
>
> I am now going to count three, and when I say "three" you will open your eyes and come out of the passive state in which you are now.
>
> You will come out of it very quietly, without feeling in the least drowsy or tired.
>
> On the contrary you will feel strong, vigorous, alert, active, full of life.
>
> Moreover you will be cheerful, fit and well in every respect: "ONE . . . TWO . . . THREE." (Coué, 1922, p. 48)

Finally, it should be noted that Coué eschewed the role of curer, of healer. This was the role of the patient; his role was merely that of facilitator, teaching the patient how best to use his or her own inner powers of the subconscious. Nor did he, like practitioners of other faith healing, minimize the role of the physician: "Let me add most emphatically that I do not advise you to dispense with a doctor's services. Obviously there are many cases in which his advice and medicine and care are absolutely indispensable. . . . I want both patients and doctors to understand that auto-suggestion is a most formidable weapon against disease" (Coué, 1923, p. 45).

Thus autosuggestion was one of the three cornerstones of Coué's New Nancy School; it was autosuggestion, not heterosuggestion, that was paramount in hypnosis. The other two were the domain of the subconscious, in which autosuggestion manifests its effectiveness, and the law of reverse effect. Apparently because of the nature of the times, Coué attempted to "physicalize" the latter with such statements as: "In the conflict between the will and the imagination, the force of the imagination is *in direct ratio to the square of the will*" (Baudouin, 1920, p. 125). Be that as it may, the New Nancy School had a long and lasting effect on the general approaches used in treatment through hypnosis.

One reason for its continued popularity through the 1920s and 1930s was Coué's main advocate, *Charles Baudouin,* mentioned above. Baudouin added little to the induction procedures used at the time; his role was to perpetuate Coué's methods, in much the same way Bernheim had done for Liébault. Probably his major contribution was the recognition of the importance of the subject's subconscious attitudes and ideas in education, that the successful teacher is the one who can communicate with his or her pupils' unconscious, rather than their conscious frame of reference.

The Roar Before the Fall

The post-war (WWI) years saw many changes in Western society, but few in hypnotic induction procedures. The Germans, despite the desperate times caused by the outcome of the war, continued to contribute to our attempts to understand hypnotic phenomena (e.g., Birnbaum, 1927; Bruhn, 1926; Kronfeld, 1925; Sanders, 1921; Schilder, 1921/1956). *Hans-Theodor Sanders* presented two methods of induction, the eye-fixation method and the suggestion method. Essentially, they were the same as I have outlined above. His termination method was also as described before, a counting method: "I will now count to three. At 'three' you will awaken" (Sanders, 1921, p. 18). Whereas Sanders merely described his induction methods, *Arthur Kronfeld* (1925) offered specific verbalizations to accompany his techniques. In one case he gave the subject these instructions: "I will transfer you into a sleep-like condition, and while in this condition my influence on your nerves and mental activity will become extraordinary. To that end, you will need to go along inwardly and with great sympathy with all that I say. Relax your limbs, then look at my eyes with great concentration"[8] (Kronfeld, 1925, p. 213).

The previous words were spoken with a moderately forceful voice, standing in front of the patient. Brief pauses were interjected between each suggestion. Then, while the subject fixated on the base of his (the operator's) nose, he continued:

> Your limbs are completely relaxed. You look at me unswervingly. More and more you feel the influence of my look. Your breathing gets quiet and regular. Under the influence of my eyes you become more quiet and passive. All of your own mental functions fade more and more, as a tiredness overcomes your eyes and nerves, you feel well, weak and tired. Your limbs are heavy and motionless. It becomes increasingly difficult to hold your eyes open; the eyelids flutter; the eyeballs burn; the environment sinks more and more; the eyes close. [The eyes were closed manually, if they did not close themselves. Then he continued.] Always it becomes dimmer. You are wholly cut off from the environment, wholly passive and under my influence. You are in a sleep-like condition. You hear only what I say; you hear nothing else. You think only what I want [you to]; you think of nothing else. You sleep deeply and quietly. The eyes remain tightly closed. Your limbs are under my influence.[9] (Kronfeld, 1925, p. 214)

In yet another method, the patient lay down on a couch and listened to the hypnotist say:

> "Close your eyes. Think to yourself that you are very tired and will go to sleep gently and quietly. You exclude all inner restlessness and all of your own thoughts. Relax all your limbs; allow no trace of your own activity. You breath quietly and deeply. I will now make my influence over your nerves effective by making light strokes [passes] over your body." Then one begins to execute, in slow movements at intervals of 5 to 10 seconds, light, rhythmic passes with the

fingertips of both hands from the forehead of the subject downward over his chest and abdomen to the femur. At each three to five passes one utters the following: "You observe how you slowly become calm and quiet. Your breathing is quiet and rhythmic. With each stroke [pass] you feel the growth of my influence. The environment sinks more and more. You are overcome with deeper rest and passivity. You feel very well and adjusted. You sink still deeper into a sleep-like condition. My influence over you grows further still. Your limbs are wholly without volition. You hear only what I say to you. You think only what I want [you to]. Your body comes under my influence still more; you cannot open your eyes anymore.[10] (Kronfeld, 1925, pp. 214–215)

Christian Bruhn's book (1926) was a compendium of what was occurring in Germany in the early part of the 1920s with regard to hypnosis. In it, he discusses 15 different German "scholars in hypnosis" and offers an appendix of brief testimonials by 50 other professors and physicians on experiments conducted by Schrenkt. But of the methods of induction, little new is presented since he mentions only Hansen's method of eye-fixation and Mann's use of music played first on a music box and then on an harmonium ("The music is haunting" [p. 31].). The same paucity of innovation is true of *Karl Birnbaum's* 1927 book on the psychological healing methods and *Gustav Heyer's* chapter on hypnosis.

One of the better known German works on hypnosis during this period was *The Nature of Hypnosis* by *Paul Schilder,* the second edition of which appeared in 1922. In it he reviewed a considerable amount of the literature relating to hypnotic phenomena, including various physiological effects (e.g., on striated muscles, the circulatory system, the skin, the endocrine system, etc.). His induction method, however, was not any different from his colleagues'. Following some reassuring comments, he stood behind the patient, rubbed the latter's forehead, and offered suggestions of fatigue, sleep, and relaxation. In addition, Schilder also claimed to be able to induce hypnosis from sleep by softly speaking to the patient while asleep, as well as through narcotics. He eschewed the use of both chloroform and scopolamine, which he considered dangerous. The latter drug was apparently used by Kausch, who administered as much as 0.0015 gram (plus 0.01 gram of morphine) when the recommended maximum dose was only 0.0005 gram. Schilder reported that N. Kaufmann used veronal or a derivative (e.g., medinal) but that it had to be administered two hours before the intended hypnosis procedure. The usual dose was 0.5–1.0 gram, but on occasion was elevated to 1.5 grams. Schilder, himself, seems to have preferred paraldehyde, which he considered a safe drug for hypnotic purposes when administered in doses of 4 to 12 grams. The University of Vienna Clinic, under H. Hoff, concurred despite the side effect that the patient might enter a state of deep sleep, making the rapport necessary for hypnosis impossible.

Unlike some of his contemporaries or his colleagues of the past, Schilder felt that the termination of hypnosis should be slow, not sudden or rapid.

Thus the patient was informed that he or she would awaken slowly and when awake feel alert and rested, without any untoward effects. Both his induction and his deinduction were as modern as today, the basic elements having taken seed in the late 1800s and flowered in the early 1900s.

In France *Georges de Dubor* summarized a number of the older methods (Bernheim, Richet, Moutin) before presenting his own three-step procedure. As with others, he started by placing the patient at ease with informative conversation and then fixated his own eyes on the bridge of the patient's nose, while the patient stared at his. Taking the patient's thumbs in his hands, he then proceeded to suggest sleep and relaxation. This method failing, he manually closed the patient's eyes and continued with the verbal suggestions. If this, too, did not achieve results, he opted for physical passes and sometimes for gently rocking the patient's head to and fro—a sort of slow motion edition of the rapid and violent head turning Lapponi described (see above). Dubor also made it clear that there was still a lingering belief in hypnogenic zones of the body, zones on which pressure produced instantaneous hypnosis, Mr. Flint notwithstanding. The phalanges of the hand, the base of the nails, the bend of the elbow, and the extremity of the nose were all said to be such locations, although Dubor did recognize that in some patients they were totally absent.

Nor were the reported influences of magnetism entirely dormant in the 1920s. It is to Dubor again that we are indebted for the reminder that old beliefs die slowly, for he reviewed the works of Moutin, Van Velsen, and M. Boirac, all of whom had a strong affinity for the power of magnetism. The latter, *M. Boirac,* claimed as late as 1907 that he was able to make the skin of a patient move by merely waving his hand above it. Even more dramatic, he claimed to be able to make the feet of a sleeping subject rise and fall from the bed with upward or downward movements of his hands at least 3 yards from the subject! No less dramatic, perhaps, but more directly understandable and possibly quite a bit more dangerous was the method described by a Dr. Steiner in Java (also mentioned by Dubor). In it, the operator uses his or her thumbs to compress the carotid arteries until the subject droops and falls into a deep sleep. The *one* drawback, Dr. Steiner reported, was, alas, the subject only remains in the sleep condition for a short period (hopefully).

For Dubor awakening was a well-trod path. First, the subjects were informed that they were about to be awakened and then the eyelids were lifted while the operator blew directly on the eyeballs. That failing, upward passes were instituted, and, when all else failed, the subject was brusquely ordered to awaken and his or her hands and feet were struck sharply—quite a contrast to Schilder, above.

In 1923 the English translation of *Louis Satow's* book *Hypnotism and Suggestion* appeared. It is an excellent source book for the ancient history of hypnosis and hypnotic inductions. For example, it is well indexed, something most books of this period were not. However, like its contemporaries, it is devoid of references, so it is extremely difficult to trace original source material. Of his own technique, Satow showed us little new. His method was basic. First, the patient was instructed to look fixedly into his eyes and think of nothing but sleep. Then he enjoined: "Your eyelids are growing heavy . . . very heavy. . . . Your eyes are growing rather dim. . . . You can't see distinctly any longer. . . . Your eyelids are heavier . . . heavier still . . . heavier and heavier. You can scarcely keep them open any longer. . . . You are closing your eyes." [After the eyes close, he said] "Now you are asleep" (Satow, 1923, p. 67). It was a simple, direct eye-fixation technique, but not new or different from contemporary practices.

The English of this period also brought us few innovations in induction. *William Brown* (1922)—a reader at Oxford and lecturer at Bethlem Royal Hospital—for example, merely reiterated the old Braidian eye-fixation technique, coupled with rubbing the patient's forehead. *Henry Yellowless* (1923)—Medical Superintendent at the York Retreat—called attention to the three factors essential for hypnosis: bodily relaxation, mental concentration, and suggestion, and re-presented Braid's technique. Knowles (1926), in his System of Personal Influence and Healing, mentioned three induction methods also: suggestion, passes, and use of the "Radio-Hypnotic Crystal." Unfortunately, he did not elaborate on the latter, but the name implied that the patient was "tuned in" on hypnosis, much as one would the old crystal radios.

American writings were beginning to have their impact. Although the verbalizations used by *William Wesley Cook,* Professor of Physiological Medicine at the National University of Chicago, were not new—involving the usual fatigue invoking words while the patient fixated an object—his mechanical eye-fixation device was a bit unique in the use of modern technology that conveyed the ancient "power" of the eye. It consisted of a black, polished hard disk of rubber into which was fixed an artificial eye. A small metallic rod was fixed on the back of the device, by which the patient held the instrument at arm's length above the level of his or her head. Cook also concerned himself with the general environment in which the hypnosis occurred—not a new concern, but one that had temporarily receded from the literature. He described the usual quiet room, free from distractive decorations and outfitted with heavy carpet. But, in addition, he was one of the first to note that the room should be distant from vehicular traffic on the streets outside—the automobile had arrived! He, like others, warned against disturbing wallpaper, but he also analyzed the use of colors in the room. Red and yellow were to be avoided (as was direct sunlight—a cloudy day was optimal), light blue preferred, and pale green acceptable. Temperature should be between 68 and 78 degrees Farenheit; thus hot summer days and cold winter ones were to be avoided. Nor did Cook forget the olfactory sense; certain odors were to be avoided—tobacco, garlic, onions, for example—while others were preferred—heliotrope, lilacs, and tuberoses. Simple, monotonous music was considered enhancing, an idea not unlike Mesmer's *baquet* preludes on the harmonium.

Theorists like *Morton Prince* were hard at work trying to uncover the essence of hypnosis (He called it "a state of dissociation and synthesis."—1923, p. 239)—but it was *Wesley Raymond Wells* who called attention to a type of hypnosis, and thus a different kind of induction technique, that had been noted on and off since the time of de Puységur—waking hypnosis. This particular view of hypnosis and its inductive consequences will be presented later in Chapter 6, but it should be noted here that this innovative induction consisted of avoiding verbal suggestions for relaxation and sleep and manipulating the subject's attention by direct suggestion. A number of authors before and after Wells's work (1923) would have called this simply direct suggestion or nonhypnotic suggestion, and it is, in fact, difficult to assess what differences if any exist, for Wells was particularly circumspect in the description of his technique. At any rate, the theoretical implications of "waking hypnosis" or the "alert trance," as it is presently called, have been discussed in Edmonston (1981) and the induction of such a condition will be discussed later.

Probably the most important work to be done during the 1920s was the development of Progressive Relaxation by *Edmund Jacobson*. Begun in 1908 at Harvard University, carried on at Cornell University, and brought to fruition at the University of Chicago, progressive relaxation was (and is) a training program in negative muscular action leading eventually to complete relaxation of both the musculature and mental activity. Jacobson's work started with an interesting series of studies on the startle response to sudden, unexpected sounds. In these investigations it was noted that the normal startle (He called it in 1925 the "involuntary start.") response was much more exaggerated when individuals were tense than when they were relaxed. Thus investigations into the accomplishment of relaxation were begun, culminating in the publication of the technique in 1924. A later book (1929) on the method saw new editions appearing into the 1960s, so pervasive was the interest in the technique. In fact, the fifth edition of his book, *You Must Relax,* appeared in 1977.

The technique of Progressive Relaxation bears a striking resemblance to hypnosis, as we will see. It begins with the patient lying down on a comfortable couch in a quiet atmosphere. Practice sessions take from $\frac{1}{2}$ to 1 hour and can be conducted individually or in groups up to eight. First, the patient is taught to recognize muscular contraction through either movement or simple contractions. Then he or she progressively relaxes muscle groups, beginning with large groups. The order that Jacobson recommended is as follows:

Left biceps, l. triceps, l. hand flexors, l. hand extensors, right biceps, r. triceps, r. hand flexors, r. hand extensors, l. calf, l. foot extensors, l. leg flexors, l. leg extensors, l. thigh flexors, l. thigh extensors, abdomen, respiratory muscles, erectores spinae, l. pectoral group (forward extension of arms), l. interscapular group (backward movement of shoulder), r. pectoral group, l. interscapular group, elevators of shoulders, shrugging, bending head to right, to

left, forward, back, holding it up stiffly, wrinkling the brow, frowning, closing
eyelids tightly, with lightly closed lids turning eyes to look toward right, left,
up, down, straight forward. . . . Smiling, rounding lips to say "O"; protruding
tongue, retracting tongue, closing jaw tightly, counting one to ten, swallowing,
complete the list. (Jacobson, 1924, p. 571)

The physician who teaches the patient does so with a minimum of verbal
interaction (like a nonverbal induction), teaching by allowing the patient to
experience rather than be told how. What verbalizations take place are
labeled "instructions," not "suggestions." Emphasis is on relaxation being
the opposite, the negative of contraction, and that the patient should do the
negative of contraction to achieve relaxation. Relaxation should involve *no
effort,* since it is the opposite of doing something, and doing implies effort.
Jacobson also made a distinction between tenseness and strain, believing
that no one could really control the relaxation process until able to discrimi-
nate these two feelings. Often this distinction must be made clear to the
patient by passive movement of a body part by the physician. For example,
extending the arm forward and inward creates sensations both in the scapu-
lar and the pectoral regions. The latter are often overlooked by the patient,
but through passive movement can be brought to his or her attention and
labeled "tension," while the former is labeled "strain."
     The final stages of the Progressive Relaxation, the eyes and speech mech-
anisms, are crucial for the relaxation of mental functioning. At no time are
the patients instructed to stop thinking or to make their mind a blank. Instead, such mental peace and relaxation is accomplished by prolonged practice at relaxing the eyes and the face and speech apparatus. Eye relaxation
starts with wrinkling the forehead and then letting it flatten out for ten
minutes or more, then the eyelids, and then the eyes themselves. To help the
patient feel tenseness in the eyes, he or she is instructed to look right and left
and note the sensations. All of this is done with the eyelids shut. Now, with
the eyes open, the practitioner stands at the foot of the couch with his or her
index fingers held 3 ft. apart on a horizontal plane. The patient looks back
and forth at the fingertips, noting the tensions of movement. Progressively,
the practitioner moves the fingers closer and closer together until the patient
is staring at a single fingertip and noting the tension of staring. Although not
accompanied with verbal suggestions, such a maneuver is not uncommon in
hypnotic induction techniques proper. Such commonalities accentuate the
possibility of a close relationship between the process of relaxation and that
of hypnosis, as I have alluded to above and stated elsewhere (Edmonston,
1981).
     That the process is similar—but not identical—to hypnotic induction,
particularly nonverbal, arm levitation types, is clear from both method and
outcome. However, it is also clear that Jacobson's proposed methods of
objectively measuring the degree of relaxation achieved mirror a number of
observations and measures applied to estimates of hypnosis and hypnotic

depth. Here are the external signs of progressive relaxation the physician observes. I have italicized those that appear most similar to hypnotic measurement observations.

> (1) Palpation of the muscle group; (2) *passive movement of the part;* (3) *observation of the regularity and force of respiration* [italics added]; (4) visual observation of the flaccidity of the muscle-group or region; (5) *the absence of movement or contraction, including speech and winking of the closed eyes* [italics added]; (6) the presence of a sudden involuntary start or jerk, often generalized, which often marks the onset of advanced relaxation in an individual who has been previously hypertense; (7) *increasingly slow responses to interruption, or the failure to respond;* (8) *the sleepy-eyed appearance of the individual who arises after successful relaxation;* (9) *when the individual learns to relax the eyes while open, their vacuous appearance, with the facila musculature so relaxed that it is expressionless, is characteristic* [italics added]; (10) graphic records of respiration, pulse, eye-movements, or of the tone of internal organs may be employed. (Jacobson, 1924, pp. 574–575)

Thus Jacobson gave to the literature a detailed process that is strikingly similar to hypnosis in both its induction and the observations used to ascertain its occurrence.

The Depressing Thirties

The world-wide economic depression appears to have had no less effect on the study of hypnosis than it did on general productivity. The 1930s formed a major hiatus in publications about hypnosis. True, Erickson was doing his early work at this time, but his real impact did not occur for another two to four decades. Hull and his students were hard at work through the 1920s and 1930s, and his classic work summarizing many of the studies appeared in 1933. However, little of the latter's work pertained directly to the development of hypnotic induction techniques. Rather, it was more concerned with quantifying the phenomenon through experimental investigations (see Edmonston, 1967). Thus a considerable amount of groundwork was being laid during this period for the explosion of hypnosis literature following the second World War.

There was one continuing trend, which we noted in the 1920s when discussing Schilder's work—the use of narcotics to aid hypnotic induction. *P. Brotteaux* (1936) reported a number of investigations on the combined use of scopolamine and chloralose. His "scopochloralose" treatment was applied 2 to 4 hours prior to the presentation of verbal therapeutic suggestions. However, even this narcohypnosis could not be considered entirely new, although it did involve a newer combination of drugs.

Although Baraduc reported using a cylinder phonograph in the treatment of 10 patients in 1902, and Hull perhaps used recordings in the 1920s (see

Gravitz, 1983a), it was not until the 1930s that gramophone disk recordings were capitalized upon. In 1930 *George H. Estabrooks* produced a 12 in. Victrola record of a standardized induction technique. Estabrooks (b. Dec. 16, 1895; d. Dec. 30, 1973), a Canadian who spent most of his teaching career at Colgate University, recorded $4\frac{1}{4}$ min. of sleep induction (as per Bernheim and the old Nancy School) with further instructions on one side of the record for the inability to use the right arm and to open the eyes. These instructions were followed by a 5 sec. pause before resuming with brief wake-up instructions. The second side contained the same induction, followed by a challenge to bend the right arm and then verbalizations to transfer rapport from the record to a live operator in the room with the subject. This latter maneuver could only be accomplished if the subject had given prior written permission for such transfer. Finally, as on the first side, there was a 5 sec. pause followed by the wake-up instructions.

Although Estabrooks reported his record as "simply an effort to produce a standardized laboratory technique for experimental purposes" (Estabrooks, 1930, p. 116), it was the first time that a standardized, repeatable induction had been available for the general professional public. (Jenness used Estabrooks's phonograph inductions in his laboratory at the University of Nebraska in 1933.) Not only did his record provide a standardized procedure, but it also allowed for awaking the subject, and, if desired, a method for transferring an already hypnotized subject to another operator (the first being the record), again in a standardized format. The use of sound recordings (now mainly on electromagnetic tape) has now become commonplace, and many professional societies (e.g., American Society of Clinical Hypnosis, Society for Clinical and Experimental Hypnosis) provide tapes of inductions and treatment patters for the practicing professional. There are, in fact, also video tapes available, so that the viewer may not only hear the verbalizations and the particular inflections with which they are delivered but also see the physical interaction between operator and patient. Again, the professional societies are the most reliable source for these training aids.

Meanwhile, in the 1930s, some reports of technique were still appearing. *H. H. Hart,* for example, reporting on the work in various psychiatric clinics, indicated that his technique involved "a dark room, freedom from noise, physical relaxation of the patient on a couch, the monotonous repetitions of suggestions of sleep" (Hart, 1931, p. 601). Nothing really startlingly new here. *Ludwig Mayer,* in Germany, presented a number of case studies in which he used the patient's conception of hypnosis to form the base of the particular induction instructions used (Mayer, 1934). Here, then, we have an anticipation of Erickson's utilization techniques, which we will explore in Chapter 6. In a somewhat similar vein, *William Sargant* and *Russell Fraser* in England were suggesting that a darkened room, verbal suggestion, and elaborate rituals were unnecessary for the induction of hypnosis. Instead, they suggested hyperventilation, particularly with hysterical patients, as a route to the hypnotic condition.

> *Without telling the patient he is to be hypnotized* [italics added], he is asked to
> lie on a couch and to concentrate on breathing as deeply as possible, either in
> rhythm with the movements of the clinician's hand, or at some other com-
> mand. This rhythm should be regular, and as rapid as is consistent with the
> patient's ability to take respirations of a maximum depth. . . . When some
> degree of gaseous alkalosis has been produced by two to four minutes of
> hyperventilation, the patient begins to feel dizzy and confused, and in hysteri-
> cal subjects there is increased suggestibility. This can be rapidly gauged by the
> readiness with which the eyes follow a quickly moving finger, by a more
> automatic quality of the respiratory rhythm, and by increased willingness of
> response to requests to breathe deeply. A few other commands should now
> be given to test the degree of suggestibility present, and the patient is usually
> found to be in a state of light hypnosis. (Sargant & Fraser, 1938, p. 778)

Unlike the general trend of the 20th century toward better communication
between patient and physician, Sargant and Fraser appear to be proposing
the opposite, in that there is a deliberate attempt not to inform the patient of
what is to transpire. Yet there is a utilization quality to the technique; they
used what the patient brought to the situation—his or her breathing mechanism and the natural tendency for the body to go toward alkalosis with
hyperventilation.

Alexander Cannon (Medical Director of the Isle of Man Clinic), on the
other hand, was most explicit that the patient should be fully informed
regarding what was to occur and what was expected of him or her. Touted by
the dust cover of his book, *The Science of Hypnotism* (1936), as being "one
of the few men to be admitted into the secrets of the Orient," Cannon wrote
a number of books on the occult and mysticism. In his hypnosis book he
presented two basic induction methods as uniquely his own. The first, he
called the Occidental Method, in which, after giving some preliminary information to his reclining subject, he said, "I am going to press my fingers on
the whites of your eyes, and although you will scarcely believe it, your eyes
will not close, but will remain wide open; they won't blink. You see your
eyes have already lost their power of feeling (and are anaesthetic)" (Cannon,
1936, p. 49). This was certainly different from the usual pressure on the
closed eyelids we had encountered in the early part of this century! According to the author, the method was nearly always successful.

If, however, success was not forthcoming, Cannon shifted to an eye-
fixation method, using first his own eyes then a bright colored light from his
"hypnoscope" as a focal point. His "hypnoscope" made use of different
colored filters through which light was shown. It was battery operated,
looking somewhat like a large (approximately 8 inches in diameter) projection disk set on top of a flashlight handle, which contained the batteries. A
lens in the center of the disk focused the light beam, the color of which was
chosen to match the individual patient. In cases where the room was well lit,
he used a tuning fork and had the subject fixate the space between the
vibrating tongs. While the subject fixated the chosen object, Cannon said:

Look steadily at this [object], but do not strain your eyes; you will soon see two lights and a glow or halo will form around them: think of nothing, and let your mind go blank. Your sight is growing dim and indistinct; your eyes will soon feel heavy, very heavy, and your eyelids will tend to close. Keep your eyes open as long as you can, and so try to resist this feeling of tiredness. (Pause.) Numbness is creeping over your limbs, your arms and legs. (Pause.) My voice seems muffled to you; it is becoming more muffled to you. (Pause.) You are getting more sleepy; you cannot keep your eyes open. You now breathe slowly and deeply, slowly and deeply, slowly and deeply, slowly and deeply. Now as I pass my hand [on the patient's forehead] over your eyes, your eyes will close; your arms and legs, especially your arms, are becoming warmer and warmer, and more heavy [This instruction is similar to Schultz's autogenic exercise.] They are becoming heavier and more and more numb. Relax more; let yourself go! (Cannon, 1936, pp. 50–51)

These induction instructions were followed by a series of challenges, primarily catalepsies, and whatever therapeutic suggestions as may be necessary. His method of terminating the condition was by counting from one to seven, the latter being "the perfect number" of ancient mysticism.

Cannon's second method was also an eye-fixation method, taking a page from the work of William Cook (see above). He used an artificial eye as the fixation point, but instead of having it embedded in a disk of black rubber, it was laid on a piece of black cloth held in the patient's left hand. Both of the patient's hands supported this fixation device while resting in his or her lap. The artificial eye was of medium size with a blue iris made to look as if the pupil were slightly dilated. (The author even supplied the manufacturer's address—the daughter of a Dr. O. Millauro, 43 Tavistock Square, London—and the price—two guineas.) Staring at the eye was accompanied by suggestions for changes in vision and increasing fatigue for a period of 2 minutes. If the patient was not hypnotized by then, Cannon moved his hand over the patient's eyes and down to the artificial eye. If the room were dark, a green or blue light was projected onto the eye and a purple ray from the hypnoscope was projected onto the forehead between the eyebrows. The use of purple was based on his belief in the effects of certain colors on the "mind-power" of individuals. Purple was purported to heal.

Cannon used a number of other methods as well. One was suggestion without hypnosis, which involved issuing authoritative instructions without the preliminaries of an induction. Another was "Erskine's Method," in which the operator fixated the left eye of the patient, while commanding, "Look at me!" Following a 10 count, the patient was challenged to open his or her eyes or to arise from the chair. The inability to meet either challenge signaled the onset of hypnosis. Alex Erskine, however, did not mention such a procedure in his book (1932). He, instead, reported merely having the patient sit comfortably in a chair while he (Erskine) counted aloud. With each successive number, the patient opened and closed his eyes until sleep ensued.

One of the other methods Cannon used sounded much like Völgyesi's Faraday-hand technique, in that the patient was charged (literally) with a static electricity machine between points on the solar plexus and the nape of the neck, the lower spine and the forehead, and the nape of the neck and the lower spine for 10 min. each, and then placed in physical contact with a hypnotized somnambulist. All of this was to exorcise a "possessing entity." The method originated with a *Dr. Carl Wickland* in the United States.

Borrowing another page from his American colleagues, Cannon produced a number of gramophone records intended for the treatment of a variety of diseases. One particularly caught my attention, because it seemed to combine the new technology with the older Coué method. It was called "Dr. Cannon's 'Rejuvenation Record' " and began with music extolling the wonders of a new day and the rejuvenating powers of the sunshine and happiness. The record continued with suggested feelings of youth and health and contained the following Coué-like expression: "Every day in every way, I feel younger and younger" (Cannon, 1936, p. 114). Old ideas and new technology mark the history of induction procedures.

Autogenic Training

One method, which first made its appearance in the 1930s, was a new idea that used old technology—the ability of the patient to concentrate on his or her own bodily functions. In 1932 the German psychiatrist *J. H. Schultz* first published a book on a series of exercises that the patient undertook himself or herself in order to improve general functioning and/or to correct some aspect of functioning. The technique developed from his and Oskar Vogt's work around the turn of the century. Since the 1930s, eight editions of his book have appeared, and his student and collaborator *Wolfgang Luthe* has edited a six-volume set of *Autogenic Therapy,* which includes reviews of the method, its applications, and research literature. The process was little known this side of the Atlantic until the late 1950s and early 1960s, when Luthe brought the process to Canada at the University of Montreal. He has subsequently introduced the method to the Far East at Kyushu University.

The method is essentially similar to autohypnotic techniques, but involves seven well-defined, standard exercises, taking two to three months of practice for initial mastery and six months or more for full appreciation. The Standard Exercises are performed twice daily for brief periods, much like the regimen advocated in Transcendental Meditation. The patient is usually in a supine position (although sitting postures are described) with the eyes closed and repeats the exercise verbalizations to himself or herself, after instruction by the practitioner. The series takes the patient from simple muscle relaxation to eventual control of all the major regions of the body. The verbal formulae for each exercise are deliberately simple, positive declarative statements, avoiding such formulations as "My right arm is not cold any more," or, "I want my right arm to be warm." "Passive," rather than "active" concentration is the mental activity necessary for success at the exercises. Here are the Standard Exercises.

1. *Heaviness:* "My right (left) arm is relaxed." This formula is often coupled with "I am at peace." Initially, the formula is repeated for only 30 to 60 seconds. Similar statements are added as practice continues to include the other arm and both legs: "My right arm is heavy. . . . My left arm is heavy. . . . Both arms are heavy. . . . My right leg is heavy. . . . My left leg is heavy. . . . Both legs are heavy" (Schultz & Luthe, 1969, p. 34).

2. *Warmth:* Following reiteration of the First Standard Exercise, the patient repeats, "My right (left) arm is warm." Again, the exercise progresses through both arms and both legs.

3. *Cardiac Regulation:* "Heartbeat calm and regular." (Carried out for 90 to 180 seconds and thought with the right hand on the chest over the heart, and following the instructions for the second exercise.)

4. *Respiration:* "It breathes me." (Practiced for about 100 seconds in combination with the first three exercises.)

5. *Abdominal Warmth:* "My solar plexus is warm." (Practiced for about 100 seconds in combination with the first four exercises.)

6. *Cooling of the Forehead:* "My forehead is cool," or, "My forehead is slightly cool." (Practiced for 2 to 4 minutes in combination with the first five exercises.)

The general termination procedure for the exercises involves a rigid, step-by-step sequence of behavior: "(a) flexing the arms vigorously, (b) breathing deeply, and (c) opening the eyes" (Schultz & Luthe, 1969, p. 45). Each exercise is to be mastered before attempting the next and a thorough mastery of the first four was considered a must before progressing to the last two. Each exercise is practiced for approximately two weeks before attempting the next. Once mastered, however, the patient can turn on the entire sequence in a matter of 20 or 30 seconds by repeating to himself or herself the following general formula patter:

My arms and legs are heavy [repeated several times]. . . . (I am at peace). . . . Heartbeat calm and regular. . . . It breathes me. . . . My solar plexus is warm. . . . My forehead is cool. (Schultz & Luthe, 1969, p. 142)

As the patient becomes increasingly skilled at applying the Standard Exercises, he or she begins to extend the practice periods to an hour or more. Now the patient is ready for the seven Meditative Exercises, in which spontaneous colors, specific colors, concrete and abstract objects, and other people are visualized. The more advanced Meditative Exercises include experiencing selected feeling states and obtaining "answers from the unconscious." Since it is through the Standard Exercises that the Meditative Exercises are achieved, much like therapeutic suggestions are enhanced through the hypnotic induction, I will not detail the Meditative Exercises here.

Schultz's method, particularly the Standard Exercises, appears to constitute a self-hypnosis technique, the only new one of its kind during this part of the 20th century.

The Fiery Forties

Both the war years and those immediately following were lean for publications on or containing techniques of hypnotic induction. Except for Schultz (1953), who was continuing his work from the 1920s, publication on the continent virtually ceased.

One trend was continuing to make its appearance—autohypnosis. While the past, both distant and recent, had produced an emphasis on heterohypnosis (hypnosis induced in one person by another), more practitioners were using and developing techniques for teaching the patient to hypnotize himself or herself (e.g., Duckworth, 1922; Hunt, 1923; Leavitt, 1910; Winbigler, 1923). Perhaps this movement was due in part to the waning emphasis on hypnosis being some sort of power one person wields over another and in part to the more client-centered concerns of many health care specialists. It may also be partially attributed to the realization that through such procedures, a single practitioner could serve more patients more effectively.

In 1941 *Andrew Salter* produced a brief article outlining three methods of autohypnosis. The first he called "autohypnosis by post-hypnotic suggestion." He began with a discussion of hypnosis, indicating to the patient that post-hypnotic suggestion is effective and that he (the operator) will give the patient post-hypnotic suggestions making it possible for him (the patient) to effect subsequent hypnosis by himself. Part of this pre-induction discussion centered on assuring the patient that he or she will have no trouble awakening from hypnosis should the need arise. Salter then induced hypnosis through which he offered a simple posthypnotic signal, which the patient could use to recreate the trance at a later time (e.g., the patient was instructed to tell herself or himself "fast asleep" five times in order to become hypnotized).

In the second method, Salter provided the patient with a set of general written instructions, which he or she was to memorize. After Salter assured the patient that no one hypnotizes anyone else, but rather merely shows them paths to follow in his or her own hypnotization, the patient repeated the memorized passages to herself or himself either aloud or mentally. Although the written instructions needed to be appropriately developed for each patient, they were similar to the following:

I feel very comfortable. My arms are so relaxed. My feet feel very relaxed and heavy. I feel so very comfortable and relaxed. My whole body feels comfortable and relaxed. I just want to sleep. I feel so comfortable.

My eyes are getting heavy, so very heavy. They're closing bit by bit, they feel so heavy and relaxed. I feel them closing more and more. I want to sleep, and I want my eyes to close.

Now I am fast asleep, in the deepest possible hypnotic sleep. I am in a deep sleep, as deep as the deepest hypnotic sleep I have ever been in. I have complete autohypnotic control of myself. I can give myself autohypnotic suggestions and awaken whenever I wish. I can talk to the person who gave me these autohypnotic instructions, yet I will still remain fast asleep. I will follow such instructions as he gives me, yet I shall still have autohypnotic control. (Salter, 1941, p. 429)

Note that this method clearly places the control and responsibility in the control of the patient, in that he or she can accept or reject suggestions from the practitioner. It is doubtful that all practitioners would feel comfortable with such an arrangement, but it did reveal the increasing trend for patients to be accepted as partners in their own treatment, rather than cases to whom treatment is applied.

The third method is not that much different from the first, except that the patient is drilled through heterosuggestion in the format of autosuggestion. Specific, suggested behaviors are used. First, falling forward is taught, then the Chevreul pendulum, then heaviness for separate limbs, and finally the entire body. Once taught, the subject can turn the condition on and off like "an electric light."

It was not until after the war that publications outlining variations on the older induction techniques began to appear again, although some work was proceeding during the war. Watkins's book on hypnotherapy with the war neuroses (1949) certainly demonstrated that, but it was not until the late 1940s that the publication rate began its upward spiral toward the explosion of literature in the 1970s and into this decade.

Jerome M. Schneck (1947), *J. H. Conn* (1949), and *Morris H. Adler* and *Lazarus Secunda* (1947) all reflected another trend that was appearing in the 20th century—the induction of hypnosis without using any reference to hypnosis in the induction verbalization. It was Schneck's viewpoint that mention of the word hypnosis merely "stirred up resistance, apprehension and fear" on the part of the patient. Therefore, he used only suggestions of relaxation, drowsiness, and sleep and reported that the condition achieved produced the same phenomenon as ordinarily induced hypnosis.

Adler and Secunda's method (1947) had the same intent as Schneck's— the avoidance of the word, hypnosis. Patients were taught how to relax and concentrate. They sat in a comfortable chair, with their head inclined forward and their hands hanging limply over the arms of the chair. In this position, they were instructed to fixate their gaze on the thumb and forefinger of the right hand. The verbalizations that accompanied the concentration and relaxation were as follows:

> I am going to ask you to close your eyes soon, but continue to concentrate on your thumb and forefinger. As you concentrate I shall count, and as I count you will become more and more relaxed. As you do so you will feel your thumb and forefinger draw closer and closer together. When they touch you will then know you are in a deep state of relaxation [not "hypnosis," but relaxation].
>
> [While counting in rhythm with the patient's breathing], continue to concentrate on your thumb and forefinger. As I count you will feel your thumb and forefinger draw closer and closer together, as you become more and more relaxed. When they touch you will know you are in a deep state of relaxation. [When they touch, say], Now you know you are in a deep state of relaxation. (Adler & Secunda, 1947, pp. 191–192)

To involve other muscle groups, to give the patient a sense of accomplishment, and to further the relaxation process, further instruction was offered:

> As I count further you go into a deeper state of relaxation. As you do so, your left hand gradually, and without effort on your part, moves from the arm rest and comes to rest on the chair beside you. . . . Now you know you are in a deeper state of relaxation. . . . Without further counting you will continue to relax more and more, as you do so, your hand will rise without effort, and touch your face. However, your hand will not and must not touch your face until you are in the deepest state of relaxation. Then, the touching of your face will be a signal that you are in a profound state of relaxation. (Adler & Secunda, 1947, p. 192)

Of course, what we have here is the use of a standard induction procedure—hand levitation—as a deepening technique. Also note that it is the patient who is basically self-administering the points of reinforcement for relaxation. Each step of the way, the patient is receiving personal feedback regarding his or her progress, another way of involving patients in the treatment process and providing them with the feeling of active participation. Also note that Adler and Secunda's process capitalizes on the symbiosis of relaxation and hypnosis (see Edmonston, 1981).

De-induction for Adler and Secunda was a standard one to five count with instructions that at the count of five the patient would be wide awake. As we have seen before, they also emphasized a gradual awakening during the count.

Samuel Kahn, a former clinical professor of neurology and psychiatry at both Georgetown and George Washington Universities and the chief psychiatrist for the Army induction boards of New Jersey and Delaware, outlined three basic techniques for inducing hypnosis: (a) Father Authority, sternly telling the subject to fall asleep, (b) Mother Influence, using a soothing, caressing voice, and (c) Eye-Fixation, called "nervous fatigue." His Freudian leanings appear in the names he chose for the first two. The Father Authority procedure consisted simply of commanding the subject to go to sleep, a method that some attributed to Freud and which may have contributed to his disenchantment with hypnotic techniques. The Eye-Fixation method was the usual, as was the Mother Influence, in which the often heard verbalizations were spoken in a monotonous and soothing tone of voice:

> Relax and sleep, sleep, sleep, nice refreshing, relaxing sleep. Think of nothing except what I tell you. Hear my voice, hear my voice, hear my voice only. Pay attention to what I say. Relax and listen to me. Do as I tell you. Do as I tell you. You will soon fall asleep, sleep, deep sleep, fast asleep. Sleep, sleep, you may close your eyes when you want to. Then remain relaxed and sleep. Fast asleep, sleep, deep, sleep, sleep! Your eyelids are quivering. You are so tired. You want to sleep. Sleep, fast asleep. You are falling fast asleep. (Kahn, 1947, p. 48)

Nothing particularly new or startling here, except perhaps the Freudian-like nomenclature. However, Kahn did advise that children respond more readily to direct, rather than indirect suggestion and that women, being "more emotional, insecure and masochistic than men," were more susceptible to suggestion and flattery. From the perspective of the 1980s, there is little need to comment on the latter view, other than to place it in its proper historical perspective (with the Victorian era). Notions of techniques to be used with children, on the other hand, are fairly rare in the writings just following World War II. No doubt most patients were adults, but it is somewhat surprising to see the heritage of Abbé Faria's gentleness with children to be partially reversed by a call for direct (i.e., authoritarian) approach.

Alexander Cannon, whose book I discussed above, offered a less direct, but more devious method for ensuring patient compliance with the hypnotist's suggestion. In fact, he himself called these "hypnotic secrets" a "trick method" (1949). Essentially, he challenged the patient to make movements, which, by their particular posture, were physiologically impossible to make. For example, he placed the patient in a comfortable chair with his head resting on the back, hands on the chair arms, and feet far forward and then challenged him to arise. Even more startling is his instruction to the patient to lean against a wall with his left shoulder, hip and foot against it and his head inclined toward the wall. In this position, the patient is told that he cannot raise his right foot, which indeed he cannot. Attempting such a maneuver oneself is quite convincing. Such "gimmicks" were used to convince the patient of his or her susceptibility, but having made his point, Cannon went on to produce unconsciousness by pressing on the inferior jugular veins "for one minute or so." Then he quickly gave hypnotic suggestions intended to transform this physiologically produced unconsciousness into an ordinary trance condition. Should the patient awaken before all of the suggestions had been uttered, he applied pressure with his thumbs to the patient's "carotid arteries, vagus nerves and carotid body . . . until he is 'off' again" (Cannon, 1949, p. 19). Considering what he had written in 1936 about his concern for keeping the patient well informed, these tactics seem out of character and somewhat less than client-centered.

During this same period of history, *Margaret Brenman* and *Merton M. Gill* (who were both at the Menninger Foundation) were publishing a number of items regarding hypnotherapy, with a decided psychoanalytic orientation. In their survey of the literature in hypnotherapy (1947), they reproduced several standard methods of induction, such as the "sleeping method" as presented by Bernheim and others (e.g., Kraines, 1941), Sidis's hypnoidization and Wells's "waking hypnosis." Their own technique (Brenman & Gill, 1946) stressed a flexible approach relying on no single procedure. This, they said, will yield a much higher percentage of success than more rigid adherence to set verbalizations.

They also presented a section on drug hypnosis, which we have seen occasionally running throughout this history. Particularly with the war, the use of drugs appears to have been given a new impetus, as indicated by *J. Stephen Horsley*'s book (1943), that by *Grinker and Spiegel* (1943), and some of Kubie's work (1943). The barbiturates (sodium amytal and pentothal) were, and probably are, the most often used and were recommended, particularly in cases of resistance to the usual verbal techniques. Stungo (1941) had also reported using evipan sodium in a 10% solution. He felt that the narcotic and the hypnotic conditions were indistinguishable, although Brenman and Gill contest this on the grounds of inadequate measuring devices for both states. It was often reported that after the first narcohypnotic session the patient became more susceptible to standard inductions regardless of the narcotic administered. The reasons for this observation are not clear, nor is it a universally held viewpoint.

Lewis R. Wolberg. In 1948 Lewis R. Wolberg produced what was destined to be the premier text on the applications of hypnosis in psychiatry. His two volume work, which has gone through innumerable reprintings, covers medical hypnosis from induction to application. Wolberg outlined applications to most psychiatric illnesses through case presentations and discussions of the literature in behavioral therapies and psychoanalytic therapies.

A student of Erickson, Wolberg was very concerned that the presentation of hypnosis to the lay public through magazines and other media was stunting the development of the full therapeutic values of hypnosis. He felt that both the public *and the medical profession* needed protective laws to eliminate "quacks, charlatans and showmen" from "the public platform." In fact, the whole of his last chapter in Volume 2—"The Future of Hypnosis"—was devoted to a call for legislative action by the federal government. As of this writing, however, no such steps have been taken, although some of the separate states do restrict the use of hypnosis under practice of medicine laws. Of course, as we have seen, a number of the countries on the continent had enacted such legislation in the last century.

Wolberg's first volume is of the most interest to us here, for it contains verbatim accounts of techniques that still pervade our induction methods today—hand levitation, eye-fixation, and relaxation. As we have seen developing during the 20th century, he paid close attention to the needs and concerns of the patient. Most of the initial session with a particular patient was spent encouraging motivation and dispelling misconceptions regarding hypnosis, such as the fear that being hypnotized is a sign of a weak mind, hypnosis is injurious, the fear of never awakening from hypnosis, and the concern that hypnosis will not be effective. These concerns having been allayed, Wolberg proceeded to test the susceptibility of the patient with such measures as the hand clasp test (your hands are glued and you cannot get them apart) and the postural sway test (you are falling forward, or backwards). The testing of susceptibility to suggestion prior to the introduction of hypnosis proper is one step that most practitioners today have eliminated, feeling that it is easier, and less time-consuming, to proceed with an induction and discover the patient's hypnotic ability in the course of the treatment.

Wolberg considered the hand-levitation technique (see also Chapter 6), which he learned from Erickson, the "best of all induction procedures" because of the direct participation by the patient in the induction process. However, he cautioned that it is also the most difficult method because of the length of time the operator must expend. Here is a transcript of the technique as used with a patient having anxiety neurosis.

> I want you to sit comfortably in your chair and relax. As you sit there bring both hands palms down on your thighs—just like that. Keep watching your hands, and you will notice that you are able to observe them closely.

> What you will do is sit in the chair and relax. Then you will notice that certain things happen in the course of relaxing. They always have happened while relaxing, but you have not noticed them so closely before. I am going to point them out to you. I'd like to have you concentrate on all sensations and feelings in your hands no matter what they may be. Perhaps you may feel the heaviness of your hand as it lies on your thigh or you may feel pressure. Perhaps you will feel the texture of your trousers as they press against the palm of your hand; or the warmth of your hand on your thigh. Perhaps you may feel tingling. No matter what sensations there are, I want you to observe them. Keep watching your hand, and you will notice how quiet it is, how it remains in one position. There is motion there, but it is not yet noticeable. I want you to keep watching your hand and wondering when the motion that is there will show itself.

> It will be interesting to see which one of the fingers will move first. It may be the middle finger or the forefinger, or the ring finger or the little finger or the thumb. One of the fingers is going to jerk or move. You don't know exactly when or in which hand. Keep watching and you will begin to notice a slight movement, possibly in the right hand. There, the thumb jerks and moves, just like that.

As the movement begins you will notice an interesting thing. Very slowly the spaces between the fingers will widen, the fingers will slowly move apart, and you'll notice that the spaces will get wider and wider and wider. They'll move apart slowly: the fingers will seem to be spreading apart, wider and wider and wider. The fingers are spreading, wider and wider and wider apart just like that.

As the fingers spread apart, you will notice that the fingers will soon want to arch up from the thigh, as if they want to lift higher and higher. (The patient's index finger starts moving upward slightly.) Notice how the index finger lifts. As it does the other fingers want to follow—up, up, slowly rising. (The other fingers start lifting.)

As the fingers lift you'll become aware of lightness in the hand, a feeling of lightness so much so that the fingers will arch up, and the whole hand will slowly lift and rise as if it feels like a feather, as if a balloon is lifting it up in the air, lifting, lifting, –up –up –up, pulling up higher and higher and higher, the hand becoming very light. (The hand starts rising.) As you watch your hand rise, you'll notice that the arm comes up, up, up in the air a little higher –and higher –and higher –and higher, up –up –up. (The arm has lifted about five inches above the thigh and the patient is gazing at it fixedly.)

Keep watching the hand and arm as it rises straight up, and as it does you will soon become aware of how drowsy and tired your eyes become. As your arm continues to rise, you will get tired and relaxed and sleepy, very sleepy. Your eyes will get heavy and your lids may want to close. And as your arm rises higher and higher, you will want to feel more relaxed and sleepy, and you will want to enjoy the peaceful, relaxed feeling of letting your eyes close and of being sleepy.

Your arm lifts –up –up—and you are getting very drowsy; your lids get very heavy, your breathing gets slow and regular. Breathe deeply—in and out. (The patient holds his arm stretched out directly in front of him, his eyes are blinking and his breathing is deep and regular.) As you keep watching your hand and arm and feeling more and more drowsy and relaxed, you will notice that the direction of the hand will change. The arm will bend and the hand will move closer and closer to your face –up –up –up—and as it rises you will slowly but steadily go into a deep, deep, sleep in which you relax deeply and to your satisfaction. The arm will continue to rise up –up –lifting, lifting –up in the air until it touches your face, and you will get sleepier and sleepier, but you must not go to sleep until your hand touches your face. When your hand touches your face, you will be asleep, deeply asleep.

Your hand is now changing its direction. It moves up –up –up toward your face. Your eyelids are getting heavy. You are getting sleepier, and sleepier, and sleepier. (The patient's hand is approaching his face, his eyelids are blinking more rapidly.) Your eyes get heavy, very heavy, and the hand moves straight up towards your face. You get very tired and drowsy. Your eyes are closing, are closing. When your hand touches your face you'll be asleep, deeply asleep. You'll feel very drowsy. You feel drowsier and drowsier and drowsier, very sleepy, very tired. Your eyes are like lead, and your hand moves up, up, up, right towards your face, and when it reaches your face, you will be asleep. (Patient's hand touches his face and his eyes close.) Go to sleep, go to sleep, just asleep. And as you sleep you feel very tired and relaxed. I want you to concentrate on relaxation, a state of tensionless relaxation. Think of nothing else, but sleep, deep sleep. (Wolberg, 1948, pp. 117–120)

Wolberg considered the old, tried and true method of eye-fixation a simpler, but not as effective, procedure. The object he chose for fixation did not matter, although he preferred a metal object that could reflect light. It was placed about 10 to 12 in. from the patient's eyes and above the normal line of vision, as we have encountered many times before. The accompanying verbalization went something like the following:

I am holding an object above your eyes, look at it steadily. You may pick out a spot of light on it, if you desire, and focus on that intently. At the same time relax and do not resist suggestions. Keep concentrating on the idea of sleep and do not permit any other thoughts to enter your mind. Just focus your eyes on the object. You may possibly notice that your eyes may want to travel in one direction or in another direction, but they will always return to a spot on the object. Keep your eyes fixated on this object, keep looking at it as long as you want; and as you keep looking at it, I want you to relax yourself and make your mind passive. Stop resisting; relax.

As you relax you will begin to notice that your arms get heavy, your legs get heavy, your eyes get tired, you get heavier all over. A sense of drowsiness is creeping over your entire body. Keep looking at the object and blink as much as you like. Let your eyes get as tired and drowsy as possible.

You are getting drowsy now. Soon your eyes will tire and water. Wink if you wish. Your lids will get so heavy they will start shutting. Relax and get sleepier. Your eyes are watering. Your lids keep closing. Your eyes get tired, watery and they burn. They become fatigued. Your eyelids are heavy, and get heavier and heavier. Your eyes are very tired. Soon they will close.

Keep thinking about sleep, how it would feel to be asleep. You notice that you are getting sleepier and sleepier. Keep staring at the object as hard as you can and as long as you can, and you notice that your eyelids are getting heavier and heavier. Your eyes burn, feel tired and a sense of sleepiness creeps over you. You are getttng sleepier and sleepier and sleepier. You are getting very, very sleepy, and your eyelids get heavier and heavier, and they will close and you will go into a quiet restful sleep.

Now your arms and legs are heavy like lead. A warm feeling spreads over your body, a drowsy feeling as if you are floating on a cloud. Let yourself relax and sleep, go to sleep. It is pleasant to relax. Let yourself get sleepy. Sink into a deep, deep sleep. You are relaxed and comfortable. Breathe deeply, very deeply and slowly, just like that. With each breath your sleep gets deeper and deeper. Your eyes have practically closed. You are almost asleep, deeply asleep. Go to sleep, relax and sleep, just sleep, sleep, sleep. (Wolberg, 1948, pp. 121–122)

Should the patient's eyes not close, a counting method was introduced:

> You notice that your eyelids become heavy, and I am going to count from one to ten. As I do, your eyelids will get heavier and heavier, and when I reach the count of ten your eyelids will close, and you will keep them closed until I tell you to open them up. One—they are getting very heavy. They are getting heavier and heavier and heavier. Two—your eyelids are getting very heavy. You feel sleepy all over. You get sleepier and sleepier. You feel sleepy all over. You get sleepier and sleepier. Your eyes are getting very, very tired. They burn, they smart and they water, and as I approach the count of ten, your lids get so heavy that you cannot keep them open. Three—they are getting heavier and heavier. Four—you go into a deeper and deeper and more quiet state of relaxation. You become sleepier and sleepier all over. Five—you're getting sleepier and sleepier and sleepier. Six—you notice that your eyelids have become very heavy. It is very, very difficult to keep them open. They are beginning to close. They are closing, closing, closing. Seven—they are getting very, very heavy. Eight—they are getting so heavy that when I reach the count of ten they will close, and you will go into a very restful sleep. Nine—they are getting very heavy. They begin to close. They are getting heavier and heavier. Ten—they close, and you keep them closed until I tell you to open them up. (Wolberg, 1948, pp. 122–123)

Despite Wolberg's strong aversion to the performances of stage hypnotists, he took note of the therapeutic value of their favored technique—eye gaze, or having the patient fixate on the eyes of the operator. (This is another trend we have seen develop during this century. Professional individuals increasingly eschew this technique and relegate it to performers, magicians, and other "lay" persons. Not too long ago, such a procedure was considered quite appropriate and efficacious for health care personnel. Again, I interpret this shift to be related to the increasing client-centered approaches that have begun to pervade health care, at least in this country, in the last 50 years.) The value, as Wolberg saw it, was in the establishment of an authoritative relationship with the patient, which was considered of particular value with the addictions and psychopathic personalities. Even so, it was not an easy method to master, and he suggested that the hypnotist should practice staring, unblinkingly, at near objects (12 in.) several time periods per day until he or she can stare for extended periods without blinking or shifting the eyes. Once having locked onto the patient's eyes, the operator says:

> Look steadily into my eyes. As you do your eyes will get heavy. Your arms are getting heavy, very heavy. Your legs are getting heavy, heavy, heavy. Your body is getting heavy. You are getting heavy all over. You are getting sleepy, sleepy, sleepy. Your eyes are heavy and tired. Don't close them until you can't keep them open any longer. Your eyelids are heavy like lead. You are going into a deep, deep sleep. (Wolberg, 1948, p. 126)

The final procedure Wolberg outlines is sleep (relaxation) instructions coupled with visualization on the part of the patient. The visualization is not dictated to the patient, but rather chosen by the patient. Thus an active involvement is assured and the patient is given the impression that he or she, in the main, is contributing to the therapy process. Here are the words Wolberg used with a patient who chose a mountain scene for visualization.

I should like to have you lie down on the couch and relax yourself all over. I should like to have you become aware of any tensions that exist in your muscles. First concentrate on your forehead, loosen up your forehead. Loosen up the muscles in your face, straighten out your neck, loosen that up too. Now the shoulders. Loosen up your body; stretch out your arms and legs.

Let yourself get lazy all over, from your head right down to your feet. Now fold your hands on your chest and as I talk to you try to visualize things exactly as I talk about them. First become aware of the pressure of the pillow against your head. Concentrate on the back of the head and become aware of how the pillow presses against it. Now the pressure of the pillow against your shoulders; the pressure of the couch against your back. Now shift your attention to your thighs and think of how the couch supports your whole body. It is as if your body sinks into the couch and is supported by it completely. Now I want you to visualize yourself in a comfortable place, the most comfortable place you know, a place where you would like to stretch out, forget your worries and your cares, so you can sleep. Perhaps it will be at the seashore or in the mountains or some other place if you prefer. (The patient here prefers to think of the mountains.)

As you lie there I want you to start breathing deeply and slowly. As you do, relax yourself even more. Make your body limp so that when I raise your arm it will come down limp of its own accord. (The arm is raised, and it falls down unsupported when released.) I want you to relax the rest of your body the same way, from your forehead to your toes. Stretch out and breathe deeply. Good, like that.

Now as you lie there, relaxed, breathing deeply, imagine you are on a mountain top on a sunny day. Everything is peaceful and serene. You are lying in the shade in tall soft grass. You watch the deep blue sky overhead. Perhaps you see one or two billowy clouds floating lazily by. Everything is peaceful and serene like your mind must be now. All around you are tall fir, spruce, and pine trees. The scent of pine penetrates your nostrils and makes you feel fresh and relaxed. And in the distance there are lakes, the surface as smooth as glass. Watch the lakes and your mind will become peaceful and quiet like the surface of the water. Your body is relaxed. Your mind is relaxed. Relax and sleep, deeper and deeper. Sleep more deeply, go to sleep.

As you start getting sleepy, your arm, your right arm will get light like a feather. It will get lighter and lighter and then it will lift –up –up –up. The sleepier you get, the lighter your arm will feel and the higher it will lift until it touches your face. As you relax, your hand and arm lift and rise higher and higher, and when your hand touches your face, you will be asleep, deeply asleep. Your arm is rising slowly now, just like a feather——up –up –up— higher and higher and higher. It is getting closer to your face, you will be asleep, deeply asleep. Now your hand has touched your face and you are asleep. (Wolberg, 1948, pp. 124–125)

Wolberg also presented another technique of which we have seen little so far in our review, the quick induction signal. In many cases the patient will need to enter hypnosis on a number of occasions during treatment. It is not efficient to have to proceed through an entire induction technique on each occasion, particularly when initial techniques can take up to ½ hour or more. Consequently, it is advantageous for the operator to establish a signal with the patient that will allow the latter to enter hypnosis almost instantaneously and thus preserve the majority of the appointment time for therapeutic suggestions. Wolberg merely said to the patient before the termination of a standard-induced hypnosis: "You are deeply asleep at the present time. Now listen to me carefully. From now on it will not be necessary to go through the process of hypnotizing you each time you come here. When I give you a certain signal like . . . [tapping the desk, hand on the shoulder, or any other clearly defined stimulation which is not likely to occur in ordinary social intercourse] . . . you will very easily and immediately enter into a state of sleep as deep as the one you are in now" (Wolberg, 1948, p. 159).

In addition to the above, Wolberg makes mention of both mechanical devices and drugs used to augment induction. Regarding the former, he attributes their use to the apprehension of the physician, rather than the patient, allowing that the use of such devices allays the anxieties of the operator so that hypnosis may proceed. Primary among such instruments is a metronome or some other method for presenting a rhythmic auditory stimulus. Those that couple a small light flashing in time with the sound are considered more effective. The same effect can be achieved by attaching a piece of metal foil to the tip of the metronome arm and reflecting light from it. Another device, which Wolberg himself found effective, was the visual spiral illusion. A black and white spiral painted on a disc is attached to a rheostatically controlled motor (such as an electric fan motor). The subject fixates this "moving" spiral while the operator instructs: "Keep your eyes fastened on the wheel. As you watch it, you will notice that it vibrates. The white circles become more prominent, then the black. Then it seems to recede in the distance and you feel as if you are drawn into it. Your breathing becomes deep and regular. You get drowsy, very drowsy. Soon you will be asleep" (Wolberg, 1948, p. 143).

Wolberg viewed hypnotic drugs as a temporary means for aiding the resistant subject in achieving hypnosis. Although he had tried nitrous oxide and oxygen inhalation, he found no advantage over such drugs as sodium amytal and paraldehyde. Six to nine grains of the former were administered intravenously one-half hour prior to hypnosis. One to two drams (3.89–7.77

grams; Schilder, see above, proposed 4–12 grams.) of the latter were administered 10 min. prior to hypnosis.

Wolberg also instructed in the processes of self- and group-hypnosis, the former in the form of a case study (see Wolberg, 1948, Vol. 1, pp. 170–180) and the latter by presenting an exact verbal transcript. Self-hypnosis was a process of teaching the patient, step by step, to self-induce hypnosis and to test oneself for various phenomena (e.g., catalepsies). Group hypnosis was used to increase suggestibility in new patients (much as Wetterstrand had in the last century) and as a therapeutic vehicle itself. To enhance the probabilities of compliance with the induction, Wolberg began by informing the group that most symptoms were the result of an inability to relax. He then proceeded as follows:

I should like to demonstrate to you how easy it is to relax. I should like to have you bring down your arms and your hands, resting them on your thighs. Place your feet firmly on the floor. Settle back in your chair; start loosening the muscles in your body, close your eyes; breathe in deeply and regularly and relax.

Relax your body and your mind. Relax yourself all over. Begin by relaxing the muscles of your forehead. Loosen up the muscles of your forehead. Then take the wrinkles out of your face. Shrug your shoulders. Notice how tense your back is. Shrug your shoulders and loosen your back. Let your arms feel as if they weigh a ton. Let them fall and rest on your thighs so that you have no inclination to move them. Then shift your attention to your legs. Let your legs feel heavy.

As you sit there breathing deeply, you will feel your arms growing heavy and your legs growing heavy. Your eyes will feel tired, and your eyelids will be as heavy as lead. Your body is getting heavier and heavier. Your eyes are getting tired, very tired. They are closed and you have no desire to open them. You are going to fall asleep, deeply asleep. As you relax, it is impossible for you to help sleeping. It is impossible for you to open your eyes. They are glued together firmly. They are heavier and heavier, and they continue to stay stuck together as you feel yourself sinking into a deeper and deeper sleep. Keep breathing in deeply and go to sleep, deeply asleep. You will find now that your eyes are so firmly glued together that it is impossible to open them. The harder you try to open them, the heavier they feel. Try and you'll see that the harder you try to open them, the heavier they feel. (Wolberg, 1948, pp. 181–182)

For those who did not meet the challenge, he pressed his fingers on the closed eyelids and told them to "continue to sleep." This procedure was followed by a suggestion for a quick induction signal for subsequent sessions, and he then used these subjects as models for those who were still having difficulty responding to the induction procedure.

What Wolberg has done is to present a lasting document of induction and hypnotherapy that supplies the bridge from the 1940s to what I arbitrarily call the modern period of hypnotic induction in the next chapter. His work remains a standard text and, as we will see in Chapter 6, a standard reference work to which we can relate many of the induction techniques still in vogue today.

NOTES

1. Author's translation.
2. Author's translation.
3. I am indebted to Nellie K. Edmonston for her assistance in rendering the French text into English.
4. I am indebted to Nellie K. Edmonston for her assistance in rendering the French text into English.
5. Author's translation.
6. Author's translation.
7. Author's translation.
8. Author's translation.
9. Author's translation.
10. Author's translation.

CHAPTER 6

The Modern Period

The last 20 to 35 years of the present century have witnessed an increasing interest in and publication about hypnosis and hypnotherapeutic applications. Though much of the work reported during this period actually began in the 1920s and 1930s (e.g., Erickson's investigations), much of it was not brought to full fruition until the 1950s, 1960s, and 1970s.

Major innovations in induction procedures, as we will see, have not occurred. Instead, what we will encounter are primarily variations on historical themes. Eye-fixation coupled with verbal suggestions for rest and relaxation remain the most often used techniques. Visual and other stimuli for holding the patient's attention differ slightly from the past, with modern technological advances, but attention riveting is the first step in most inductions. Ideomotor techniques, particularly hand levitation, are also heavily used, as is progressive relaxation through verbal suggestion alone. Monotony and rhythm continue to dominate hypnotic inductions.

However, most practitioners and investigators no longer heed the call from the past of magnetism; now such approaches are couched in terms of electicity (see, for example, Völgyesi, below). Thus, by and large, "mesmeric" passes are a thing of the past. Not so, however, for the ancient ritual of the laying-on-of-hands. Many practitioners, but virtually no experimental investigators, retain the need to couple their soothing verbal suggestions with direct physical contact with their patients, usually placing their hands on the forehead or shoulder of the patient. Mechanical devices no longer abound in induction techniques, although a few remain and are still being developed. Emphasis also seems to have shifted from the "power" of one individual over another to a more cooperative approach to therapeutic applications of hypnosis, wherein the patient is a full and willing partner in his or her own treatment. No doubt a part of this emphasis shift can be attributed to the overall "client-centered" approaches to psychotherapy that received a major push to the forefront through the works of Carl Rogers, Abraham Maslow, and the writings of the existentialists both here and abroad. Often the client-centered approach is coupled with Freudian-like views of the unconscious, so that induction techniques are directed to communicating with the patient's unconscious in order that the patient, through his or her own unconscious processes, can diagnose and treat. Such procedures can be seen to have their historic roots in the use of hypnotized third parties as clairvoyants to diagnose and treat; modern approaches have merely developed the seer and the patient into one frame. The past is not a category to be dispensed with, but a process evolving through time.

Early in this arbitrarily defined modern period, *Frederik F. Wagner* proposed a variation on the standard hand-levitation technique of hypnotic induction. Noting that initiation of hand movement was not difficult, but that completion of the movement upwards to the face (as is demanded in most procedures) was, he proposed a folding hands alternative. In it, the patient sits in an upright position with both hands resting on his or her thighs, the fingers together. Suggestions are then offered for both hands to become light and rise slightly off the thighs with the fingers spread and flexed. When this is accomplished, further suggestion directs the palms of the patient's hand to face inward toward one another and become increasingly attracted to one another. As the hands move together, additional suggestions for drowsiness, heaviness, and deep breathing are initiated and reinforced by the intertwining of the fingers and the clenching of the two hands together. As the hands clench together with increasing force, the condition of relaxation deepens, until, when the hypnosis is fully achieved, the hands are allowed to unclench and rest comfortably again on the thighs. Here, then, is a simple variation on the more physically demanding hand-levitation techniques, which attends more to the patient's apparent needs for comfort and reduced exertion. Not a new method, per se, but a modern update.

The early part of the 1950s also saw a continuing, perhaps growing, interest in narcotic hypnosis. Again, *J. Stephen Horsley* is its advocate. From his early work in the 1930s on, he strongly urged more use of the barbiturates as an entry ploy into hypnosis. However, he continually recognized that the basic difference between simple narcosis and narcotic hypnosis was the presence and active participation, through the offering of suggestions, of the operator in the latter. The major advantage of drug induced hypnosis, he tells us, is speed, the rapidity with which deep hypnotic conditions can be achieved, and therefore the time efficiency of the treatment procedure.

T. O. Burgess (1956) summarized the use of chemicals for hypnotic induction, and pinpointed such techniques for the "resistant or refractory patient." He indicated that oral administration of 3 grains of sodium amytal $\frac{1}{2}$ hour before induction or 1–2 drams of paraldehyde 5–10 min. before induction are effective aids. If one chose an intravenous route, a 2.5% solution of Nembutal at the rate of 1 cc per minute will produce a light condition of unconsciousness in which suggestions are effective. Respiratory rhythm needs to be carefully monitored.

Burgess also reported on various gaseous techniques. With nitrous oxide, the suggestions for hypnosis (eye-fixation, relaxation method) are initiated as soon as the mask is removed following "deep, even respiration." Carbon dioxide is also recommended, although Burgess admitted to finding no literature on its usage. He suggested using it as some obstetricians do—three to five breaths of 30% CO_2, 70% O_2. If the first application does not render the patient amenable to a standard hypnotic induction, he suggested several CO_2 comas about 15 min. apart—a chemical variation on Vogt's fractionation technique.

I. Rothman (1957) advocated using Vogt's technique in conjunction with $1\frac{1}{2}$–15 grains of amobarbital sodium administered intravenously. Thus, once the patient is drowsy, he or she is verbally directed into and out of hypnosis a number of times in a short time span. He also suggested that the meprobamates should facilitate hypnosis, because of their tranquilizing effect, although he noted that no literature on their use in this way existed. Like Burgess, Rothman reviewed the various inhalation methods, adding both ether and trichlorethylene to the list we have seen before. Again the latter has not been tested, and the former has application restrictions making it at times difficult to use—premedication preparations (empty stomach, atropine administration) and the consequent excitement on the part of the patient. Dehypnotization could be aided, Rothman wrote, by administering amphetamine ($\frac{1}{2}$–2 cc), d-desoxyephedrine hydrochloride (1–3 cc), caffine and sodium benzoate ($7\frac{1}{2}$ grains) or pentamethylene tetrazol ($1\frac{1}{2}$ to 3 grains). In Sweden, Sigvard Lingh and Anne-Lie Form (1969) reported that Valium did not enhance hypnotic susceptibility, despite its general calming effect.

Since there was growing professional acceptance of hypnosis as a valid treatment modality, more practitioners turned their attention to developing methods for bringing the procedures to those patients who, for one reason or another, were refractory or at least resistance to this treatment avenue. *John G. Watkins* reported in S. J. Van Pelt's *British Journal of Medical Hypnotism* a technique for overcoming a subject's direct, active opposition to hypnotic induction. He challenged a 21-year-old nurse to resist his attempts to induce hypnosis and offered her a cash reward if she were successful. She closed her eyes, plugged her ears, and talked and shouted continuously, while he attempted trance induction. Near her ear, he made the following statements:

> My voice will gradually reach you, and you will hear it in spite of your shouting. You will begin to feel very uncomfortable. There will be a pain in your head which will grow and grow. It becomes stronger, much stronger. After a while it will be come excruciating. It will be unbearable, and everything in you will cry out for relief. But the only way out of this intense pain will be to enter a deep sleep, etc. (Watkins, 1951, p. 29)

After 3 min. of listening to these repeated suggestions, the subject stopped some of her shouting, saying, "My God but it hurts." At 6 minutes she threw the cash reward—which he had allowed her to hold—back at him and said, "Here, take it;" and entered a deep hypnotic condition. Once she had accepted the initial suggestion of pain, the only escape he offered her was to give up her resistance and enter hypnosis.

Rather than place patients in such double-bind situations, *Milton V. Kline* developed a technique for shaping the imagination. Refractory subjects were first asked to imagine, "in their mind's eye," a house, a tree, a person, and an animal. This was practiced with their eyes open, until they were able to have the appropriate images. Then he told them, "Close your eyes and in your mind's eye visualize yourself as you are here; sitting in the chair (or lying on the couch) *except the image of yourself has his (her) eyes open"* (Kline, 1953, p. 228). From here on, all of the therapist's suggestions were ostensibly directed at the image of the subject for which the subject reported responses. Thus a standard eye-fixation induction was applied to the image. Finally, however, Kline stated to the subject, "Now you are feeling just like the image, going deeper and deeper asleep." The entire process, claimed the author, took an average of 10 min. for 15 previously refractory subjects.

Another method for handling uncooperative subjects or patients was advised by *Berthold Stokvis* of the Neatherlands. His method, like many others calculated to overcome resistances, involved using some naturally occurring phenomenon, usually physical or physiological, and convincing the patient that its occurrence is due to hypnosis. Having accomplished that, most follow-up suggestions are readily effective. Stokvis applied a method of color contrast at the Leyden Psychiatric Clinic. The patient was given a grey cardboard sheet 14 cm × 23 cm on which were located two strips of paper, one light yellow, the other blue, 3.2 cm × 8 cm in length. The colored strips were placed parallel to one another so that a 5 cm strip of the grey background appeared between them. The patient is told to concentrate visually on the grey strip between the two colored strips and note that soon additional colors will appear (as is naturally the case, due to the color contrast phenomenon). However, and here is where the manipulative maneuver enters, the patient is told: "When you have seen the color phenomena appear, that will be the proof that the hypnotic state is going to set in. In fact the appearance of the colors is the first sign of the effect of the hypnotic influence; it is a kind of fatigue phenomenon of the eyes" (Stokvis, 1952, p. 380). The operator then continues a soft and monotonous verbal patter describing the various changes occurring in the visual field of the grey cardboard, coupling these remarks with suggestions of increasing fatigue and relaxation: "As you observe the color phenomena, you will find that your eyelids are getting heavier and heavier . . . still heavier all the time . . . you will feel that you are getting more and more tired . . . tired and weary . . . and you will soon get so tired that you would just love to shut your eyes [etc.]" (Stokvis, 1952, p. 381). It is certainly not uncommon, in fact encouraged, for practitioners to use any and all naturally occurring phenomena, spontaneous or consciously manipulated, to aid induction. Erickson's utilization techniques are probably the psychological pinnacle of such techniques (see below).

As we saw in Chapter 5, the role of colors per se was of some interest to individuals using hypnosis. Cannon, you will recall, projected different colors onto the patient's forehead with his hypnoscope, while projecting others into the patient's eyes. Different colors were purported to have different effects, purple being most often used, because of its "healing" powers. (It is curious to note in this context that the most noted hypnotic healer of this century, Milton H. Erickson, was reported only to be able to perceive the color purple, and that most of his clothing and surrounding environmental trappings were decorated in shades of purple.) *Jean Bordeaux* (1950) reported studying the effects of different colored environments on patients for more than 30 years and developed a hypnoscope of his own. It consisted of a collapsible metal shaft on a heavy base (for stability) to which were attached four radial arms that could be fixed in any position on the circumference of the circle produced by the arm length. Thus all four could be in different positions, overlapping completely or overlapping partially. At the end of each arm was a 15 in. different colored transluscent plastic disc (one red, one green, one blue, and one yellow). A 25 watt bulb was mounted on the back of the upright post so that it could shine through one or any combination of the discs, creating a focal point of any color in the visual spectrum. Ten years of experimentation with different colors as eye-fixation points failed to yield "any constantly recurring reactions upon which to postulate what might be termed a principle or rule" (Bordeaux, 1950, p. 14). However, Bordeaux concluded that lavenders and soft purples were far more effective as soothing, subduing stimuli than were blues or other colors. In addition to this interpretation, he reported that chiropractors were using spectacles with one blue and one yellow lens to induce a hypnotic-like state in 15–30 min. The spectacles were, by the way, worn by the patient, not the chiropractor. Wilkie (1975) also attended to colors during induction. He used a visualized blackboard for his technique and asked the patients what color chalk they preferred for drawing on the board. "I relate the colour to the following interpretation: WHITE, desire to communicate; RED, anger and aggression; GREEN, envy and jealousy; BLUE, coldness and frigidity; YELLOW, fear and cowardice" (Wilkie, 1975, p. 126). The bases of these interpretations are not given, nor is the reason for the omission of purple.

Returning to Stokvis and refractory patients for a moment, he also advocated an "imitation-method" of induction (1960), in which the practitioner breathed in and out aloud and deliberately yawned and gaped, creating an imitation situation. Hypnosis was induced through the patient naturally imitating these actions.

The refractory patient was also of concern for *Bernard C. Gindes,* who took some pages from the stage hypnotists in developing a variety of induction techniques. It was clear to Gindes that the stage hypnotist was under far greater time pressure to produce effects than the physician. The stage hypnotist had to capture the confidence of the audience rapidly and present the situation so rapidly that a person had little or no time to analyze and think about the situation. "The attack must be rapid to be *effective*" (Gindes, 1951, p. 152). Gindes believes that in a number of inductions one must misdirect the subject's belief systems to capture his or her imagination and thus manipulate his or her expectations. To that end, he presented several induction techniques to be used with refractory (or other) patients.

The first was a variation on the Chevreul pendulum phenomenon. Two crossed lines of equal length are drawn on a surface and a small object is tied to the patient's forefinger. The patient leans on the elbow of the arm to which the object is tied so that the object swings just above the crossed lines. He or she is instructed to keep the object over the cross and to fixate the cross. However, as he or she does so, the hypnotist gives suggestions for weariness, fatigue, blurring vision, and so forth. Because of the awkward position of the arm and the fixation of the eyes, both do, in fact, become fatigued, so that the operator's words describe physical reality, but are perceived as describing a hypnotic reality in which the patient was initially hesitant to participate. This method, Gindes says, is of particular value with children.

Social influence is another technique used by the stage hypnotist, which Gindes feels can be helpful with resistant patients. Seat the patient between two others so that their line of vision is perpendicular to his. Tell him that you will count and that on the count of one he is to turn his head to the left (or right) and look into the eyes of the person next to him. Then on the next count he is to turn his head and look into the eyes of the other person, and so forth, all the while adding suggestions for entering hypnosis. Soon the patient will notice that one or both of the others are looking different (read, hypnotized), and will begin to wonder if he, too, is looking like they are. "If they are going into hypnosis, I must be too." The power of social influence and imitation soon effect the induction.

Group influence coupled with a physical phenomenon was the basis of yet another method for handling resistant patients. In this case, Gindes had a group of patients face a wall, pressing their outstretched hands as hard as they could against the wall. Repeated suggestions were given for increased pressure, until finally he suggested that they could not withdraw their hands. The fact that they could not is sufficient to convince them of the effectiveness of hypnotic suggestion.

As suggested above, the manipulation of physical phenomena is a favorite ploy for increasing the possibility of success with a particular induction procedure. Gindes stands behind the patient, who is also standing, and makes contact passes of his hand from the nape of the patient's neck down to the small of the back. (Passes are not yet a thing of the past.) Each pass is forcefully applied so that the patient is moved forward and forced to offer counter-resistance to remain erect. Thus each time the operator's hand is removed to place it again on the nape of the neck, the patient naturally sways slightly backwards. The passes are continued until the patient literally falls backwards into the therapist's arms, at which time the usual verbal suggestions of relaxation and sleep are introduced to solidify the condition.

Finally, Gindes uses another physical method, which, nonetheless, relies on verbal suggestion to convince the refractory patient (or any others for that matter) that the physical maneuvers are effecting hypnosis. In a manner much as we saw in many of the techniques at the turn of the century, Gindes places his left thumb and forefinger on the bridge of the patient's nose and the fingers of his right hand on the patient's inion. Pressure from the two hands is equally applied. He then informs the patient that he is pressing on "certain nerves" that will facilitate hypnosis. "I am now pressing on certain nerves; when I release my fingers, you will fall back and be in a deep, sound sleep. Do not be afraid of falling; my arm is directly behind you and I will catch you. Now breathe very deeply; think only of sleep, think of nothing else, but concentrate all your attention on sleep" (Gindes, 1951, pp. 152–153). Then he imperceptibly reduces the pressure exerted by the right hand, *but not the left*. The result, of course, is that the patient is being physically pushed backwards, although, if the maneuver is properly executed, he or she is unaware of the physical manipulation. Soon the patient falls backwards and is further verbally encouraged to enter a deeper and deeper condition of hypnosis.

Thus what we basically see in these methods of handling refractory patients is the convincing of the patient that natural physical events are the result of the hypnotist's manipulations and that they (the patients) can in fact enter hypnosis. As is also evident, a number of these maneuvers involve swaying phenomena and, except for the physical contact made by the therapist, are not that much different from generally used sway tests for hypnotic responsiveness. *Frank A. Pattie,* whose illustrious career in hypnosis has spanned at least half a century and included teaching positions at The Rice Institute and the University of Kentucky and an unparalleled knowledge of Mesmer and his activities, also reported an induction method using sway techniques that can more rightly be labeled "an invasion of personal space technique," although he himself categorized it as a "waking suggestion" technique.

With the subject standing in front of him, Pattie has the individual look into his eyes and clasp his or her hands and hold them in front of his or her nose. Then the subject is told that he or she will sway in response to Pattie's suggestions. However, while suggesting swaying backwards and forward, Pattie himself sways toward and away from the subject with his own palms facing the subject at shoulder level. Concomitant with the forward invasion of the subject's personal space, the subject moves backwards, and, as Pattie recedes, moves forward to regain proper balance. (Pattie assisted me in the selection of subjects for an investigation by using the response to these sway suggestions as a measure of responsivity to later hypnotic induction. As the swaying occurs, Pattie further suggests that the subject will have to take a step backwards to maintain his or her balance. Then he challenges the subject with the suggestion that he or she cannot take the necessary step backwards and stations someone behind him or her to prevent a complete fall. At this point, Pattie reports he is able to demonstrate all of the usual hypnotic phenomena, including positive and negative hallucinations and amnesia.

Some subjects attempt to disrupt the rapport he has established by ceasing to meet his eyes. He merely instructs them: "I will be able to control your actions even when you are not looking into my eyes" (Pattie, 1956b, p. 2/8). Pattie cautions the reader that this authoritative, dominating method is inappropriate for therapeutic purposes and is better applied in the experimental investigative laboratories of academe. However, that these approaches are still in use even today shows that the permissive attitudes of the 20th century have not yet completely taken over hypnotic inductions. In fact, Pattie's occasional demonstrations of authoritative techniques at the Seminars in Hypnosis was in stark contrast to, but no less manipulative than, those of the other participants, even Milton Erickson.

MILTON H. ERICKSON

Milton H. Erickson was the best known practitioner of medical hypnosis during the middle of the 20th century. His more than 150 publications and his active professional life, both in the practice of psychiatry and his leadership in various professional organizations, attest to his efforts to bring the therapeutic uses of hypnosis out of the last vestiges of occultism and magical ritual. Erickson was born in Aurum, Nevada on December 5, 1901 and died in Phoenix, Arizona on March 25, 1980, just nine months prior to the First International Congress on Ericksonian Approaches to Hypnosis and Psychotherapy, developed in his honor. According to Haley (1967), Erickson had the unusual early experience of journeying east in a covered wagon, when his family moved to a farm in Wisconsin.

Erickson was precocious in his interest in and activity in hypnosis. He began hypnotizing individuals while still a freshman at the University of Wisconsin and it is reported (Haley, 1967) that by his junior year he had hypnotized hundreds of people and was giving demonstrations to the faculty and staff of the psychology department, the medical school, and Mendota State Hospital. His graduate education was at the University of Wisconsin and the Colorado General Hospital, where he achieved the M.A. and M.D. degrees in 1928. After two years of additional training at Colorado Psychopathic Hospital and a short period as a psychiatrist at Rhode Island State Hospital, he moved to the Worcester State Hospital, becoming Chief Psychiatrist on the Research Service until moving back west to Michigan in 1934. There he directed research and training at the Wayne County General Hospital and Infirmary; from 1940 to 1948 he rose from assistant to associate professor of psychiatry at Wayne State University College of Medicine and simultaneously held a full professorship in that same university's graduate school. Before repairing to Phoenix, Arizona in 1948, Erickson also held a visiting professorship of clinical psychology at Michigan State University.

Although Erickson was a fellow in both the American Psychiatric Association and the American Psychological Association, as well as the American

Psychopathological Association and the American Association for the Advancement of Science, his most notable professional achievements were the founding of the American Society of Clinical Hypnosis (ASCH) in 1957 and the *American Journal of Clinical Hypnosis* in 1958. The founding of the American Society and the journal grew out of internal disagreements within the Society for Clinical and Experimental Hypnosis, of which Erickson was an active and forceful member. His (and others') disagreements with other people in the latter society developed in part from a controversy regarding the efficacy and ethics of teaching the techniques of hypnosis in two- or three-day seminars offered around the country at various hotel sites. Controversy escalated to rupture and ASCH was born. Meanwhile Erickson (along with Edward E. Aston, Seymour Hershman, William S. Kroger, and Irving I. Secter) continued to offer "Seminars in Hypnosis" all over the United States, until the founding (again by Erickson) of the American Society of Clinical Hypnosis—Education and Research Foundation, which Erickson directed for a number of years.

Techniques

"Trance induction is not a standardized process that can be applied in the same way to everyone. There is no method or technique that always works with everyone or even with the same person on different occasions" (Erickson & Rossi, 1979, p. 3). Thus, in his last year, Erickson summarized 50 years of applications of hypnotherapeutic techniques that were at once indirect, subtle, versatile, flexible, and highly effective. Although earlier on, he viewed induction as that which preceded therapeutic intervention: "[There] is the need to recognize that trance induction is one thing, and trance utilization is another (even as surgical preparation and anesthesia are one thing, and the surgery is another)" (Erickson, 1952, p. 83); his naturalistic and utilization techniques made it clear that the blending of hypnotic induction and the introduction of therapeutic suggestions was so homogenized that neither therapist nor patient recognized precisely when one left off and the other began. For the patient, even the demarcations between wakefulness and hypnosis were blurred. Thus the imperatives of the suggestions offered to the patient were so subtle as to take effect virtually without the patient's awareness. For example:

> *You really can't conceive of what a trance is*—no, I can't, what is it?—*yes, what is it?*—a psychological state, I suppose—*A psychological state you suppose, what else?*—I don't know—*You really don't know?*—no, I don't—*you don't, you wonder, you think*—think what—*yes, what do you think, feel, sense?*—(pause)—I don't know—*but you can wonder*—do you go to sleep?—no, tired, relaxed, sleepy—*really tired*—so very tired and relaxed, what else?*—I'm puzzled—*puzzles you, you wonder, you think, you feel, what do you feel?*—my eyes—*yes, your eyes, how?*—they seem blurred—*blurred, closing*—(pause)—they are closing—*closing, breathing deeper*—(pause)—

tired and relaxed what else?—(pause)—*sleep, tired, relaxed, sleep, breathing deeper*—(pause)—*what else?*—I feel funny—*funny, so comfortable, really learning*—(pause)—*learning, yes, learning more and more*—(pause)—*eyes closed, breathing deeply, relaxed, comfortable, so very comfortable, what else?*—(pause)—I don't know—*you really don't know, but really learning to go deeper and deeper*—(pause)—too tired to talk, just sleep—*maybe a word or two*—I don't know (spoken laboriously)—*breathing deeper and you really don't know, just going deeper, sleeping soundly, more and more soundly, not caring, just learning, continuing ever deeper and deeper and learning more and more with your unconscious mind.* [Erickson's words are in italics.] (Erickson, 1959, pp. 6–7)

Indirect Techniques

Not only were Erickson's verbal techniques of induction indirect and lethargically dramatic, but also his nonverbal manipulations as well. His 1976 book with the Rossis (Erickson et al., 1976) describes a combined verbal and nonverbal technique he used on a certain Dr. S. Erickson: He shook hands with her as he told her to begin counting backwards from 20 to 1. However, he did not immediately release her hand, as one normally does in a handshake greeting. Rather, he continued to hold her hand, applying very subtle and delicate pressures on different parts of her hand with his fingers. By the time he finally did release the patient's hand, she was confused and unsure of exactly when he did stop having physical contact with her. As a consequence of this timeless release of her hand, it remained in midair in a cataleptic pose. In addition, while he was greeting her, his gaze focused not on her face but on the wall behind her head. As with the hand manipulation, the intent of having his eyes appear to look through her was to jar her hold on reality and create puzzlement and confusion. Confusion thus established, Erickson asked the patient if she thought she were awake, compounding further her "imperfect touch with reality." Confusion is the key word here, for in his commentary on this particular induction he noted: "In all my techniques, almost all, there is a confusion" (Erickson et al., 1976, p. 85). Erickson felt that through his indirect manipulation of the patient's reality contact he so confused the lines between reality and unreality, between wakefulness and trance, between the conscious and the unconscious that he could communicate more directly with the individual's unconscious processes and be in a more commanding position through which to help the patient.

The subtleties of Erickson's tactile manipulations were made clear to me when I was invited to be a demonstration subject for ideomotor behavior at a workshop for advanced hypnotherapeutic techniques. Erickson held my right forearm in a horizontal position such that Erickson's thumb and small finger were on the undersurface and his index, middle, and ring fingers on the oversurface. Thus holding the arm, Erickson proceeded to offer a brief didactic lecture to the audience on ideomotor behavior. As he did so, my arm began slowly to rock forward and backwards around the fulcrum of Erickson's hand, until by the end of the lecture the arm was rocking a full 3 or 4 in. from the horizontal and *was no longer supported by Erickson's hand.* What Erickson had done was to provide virtually imperceptible cues for the movement by applying alternating pressure with his thumb and ring fingers and his index and small fingers. In addition, he eventually released the arm from the control of his hand in such small incremental steps that I was not aware of when the release occurred. Erickson's perceptive and tactile manipulative skills would have put Sir Arthur Conan Doyle's fictional detective to shame.

In addition to the subtle creation of a confusion during induction, the other key descriptor of his methods was "naturalistic." Erickson took whatever the patient brought to him, naturally, and used those behaviors to effect a trance. It was far more effective, he felt, to use the individual's own internal processes for induction and therapeutic intervention than some contrived, ritualistic verbal incantation intended to be all powerful for all people. It was better to use the imagery of the patient, than to provide the imagery for him or her through reality objects. Far better to have patients imagine a crystal ball, than to dangle one before them on the end of a watch chain. Initially, patients are inherently more interested in their own natural processes, thoughts, images than in anything the hypnotist could provide from his or her own reality set.

Erickson often used the patient's own symptomatology as a vehicle for induction. Rather than having the individual focus *away* from the distressing symptom, be it an injured body part or a compulsive act, he more often than not had the patient over-focus on the distress, while he (Erickson) cleverly manipulated the situation to the end of a hypnotherapeutic trance. A fine example of his utilization techniques was given in his 1959 paper by the same name (Erickson, 1959). The paper contains 16 case examples, several of which were of incidents involving his own children. One example was that of a patient of 30 to 35 years who was "unhypnotizable" because of extreme restlessness and a compulsion to pace around the room. Unlike the psychiatrists who had previously attempted to work with the young man, Erickson did not view the pacing as an obstacle, but rather asked the patient, "Are you willing to cooperate with me *by continuing to pace the floor, even as you are doing now?*" (Erickson, 1959, p. 5). For the next 45 minutes Erickson verbally guided the patient's pacing, to the right, to the left, toward and away from the chair in which Erickson eventually intended the patient to sit. Initially, his verbal instructions were given in the same tempo as the patient's pacing, but gradually he slowed down the tempo so that the pacing became slower and more lethargic. In addition, Erickson gradually introduced references to the chair and the idea of sitting in it. "Now turn to the right away from the chair in which you can sit; turn left toward the chair in which you can sit." (Erickson, 1959, p. 6). Chair references were then escalated to, "the chair which you will soon approach as if to seat yourself comfortably" (Erickson, 1959, p. 6), until finally direct instructions were given to sit in the chair and enter a profound trance condition. Even the last instruction was not without its client-centered aura, for Erickson told the patient to enter a profound trance *as he related his own history*. Again he gave the patient something to do that was inherently interesting to him—his own history—as the context in which the hypnotic condition was achieved. In Erickson's words: "It meets both the patient's presenting needs and it employs as the significant part of the induction procedure the very behavior that dominates the patient" (Erickson, 1959, p. 6).

Patients are interested in themselves, not in the practitioner's ideas, imagery, and hypnotic paraphernalia. Erickson's use of imagery, which was extensive, relied on this observation. The patient's own imagery was far more captivating than that of the hypnotist. And imagery was not confined to the visual sense; all senses were liable for use in an induction method. For example, Erickson reports using auditory imagery of a metronome instead of the presence of the real object, as Luys had done in the 1700s. The advantage of personalized imagery rather than either hypnotist imagery or the mechanical device itself is illustrated in the following subject report: "When I listen to the imaginary metronome, it speeds up or slows down, gets louder or fainter, as I start to go into a trance, and I just drift along. With the real metronome, it remains distractingly constant, and it keeps pulling me back to reality instead of letting me drift along into a trance" (Erickson, 1961, p. 72).

The subtle, indirect, client-centered approaches of Erickson do not imply that he had no standard approach to patients. As one peruses his published works on inductions, it is clear that he had some consistent, fairly standard methods which he used. What made him so unique among hypnotherapists was his facility to perceive the subtleties of the situation and to turn what in other's mouths was merely a standardized incantation into a dynamic, patient-oriented induction technique. His "standard" starting points were not so much different from what has been in use throughout most of the 20th century.

Confusion Technique

Although Erickson did start from standard procedures, as presented below, he was clear in his perception that the attention getting and attention holding devices were not the "desiderata of hypnosis." Insufficient attention was directed, he felt, to what the subject was experiencing. Nonetheless, as early as the 1940s (Erickson, c. 1940s), he spoke of three standard approaches to the induction of hypnosis: visualization, hand-levitation, and confusion techniques. Since Erickson used individualized visualization techniques in which he allowed the patient any visual imagery she or he desired and then proceeded to mold that patient-centered imagery into an induction method, I will concentrate on his confusion and ideomotor patterns of induction.

As he developed the *confusion technique,* Erickson recognized that what needed to occur was the combination of a perfectly comprehensible situation to which the patient could readily respond and an irrelevancy, a *non sequitur,* to which the patient could not respond with sufficient rapidity without extensive "mental reorganization." Thus the patient is caught in a state of bewilderment and enters the hypnotic condition. Originally the *confusion technique* centered on the confusion of past, present, and future, for it was intended to facilitate hypnotic age regression. Only later did it become apparent that the method could be used as a general procedure. Here is an outline of the original technique (Erickson, 1964a, pp. 185–187):

1. Mention of some commonplace item of everyday living such as eating.
2. Relating that item as an actual fact of possibility for the subject for the current day or *present.*
3. Mention its absolute probability in the *future,* specifying some one particular day of the week, preferably the current day.
4. Comment on its probable occurrence (the eating) on that same day in the *past* week.
5. Comment on the identity of the day preceding the named day of the past week, emphasizing that such a day is a part of the *present* week even as it will occur in the *future* week.
6. Add that today's day had occurred last *week,* even *last month,* and that learning the names of the days of the week had constituted a *childhood problem.* (Thus the period of regression desired is subtly introduced.)
7. Mention that just as in the past a certain month would follow the *present month* even as the *present month* had been preceded by the *previous month* during which a meal had been eaten on some named weekday. And that weekday had been preceded by another weekday just as the previous week had a day of an earlier ordinal position. (For sake of clarity to the reader, let us assume that the current day is the second Friday of June 1963, that *next* Friday eating will occur even as it did *this* Friday, and as it undoubtedly did *last* Friday, which was preceded by a Thursday just as it was earlier in the *present month* and would be in the *future weeks.* Days, weeks, months, past, present and future all intermingled.)

   Then one proceeds with mention that last month (May) had a Thursday, in fact, several Thursdays, each preceded by a Wednesday while the month of April preceded May, another *childhood task* of learning the months of the year. (Thus, from Friday June 14, 1963, by a simple valid statement, an underlying implication of time is employed to arouse thoughts of *childhood,* or any chosen past time, without seemingly direct suggestion to that effect.)

8. This intermittent and varied reference to the present, future, and past is continued with increasing emphasis upon the past with an implication of the actual past as belonging to the present and then to the future. Again to clarify for the reader, one might say "Not only did you (Reader, please bear in mind that it is the second Friday of June 1963) eat breakfast on Wednesday of last week but before that, you ate dinner on Tuesday in May, and *June was then in the future,* but before May was April and

before that was March and *in February you probably had the same thing for lunch* and you didn't even think of having it *next* April, but of course on January 1st, New Years Day, you *never even thought of the 14th of June 1963,* (an implication of possible amnesia developing) it was *so far in the future,* but you certainly could think of Christmas, December 1962, and wasn't that a nice present you got—one that you didn't even dream of on Thanksgiving Day in November and what a Thanksgiving dinner, *so good* (A present tense description of a series of ideas with an emotionally charged validation of the actual past as the present and then the future), but Labor Day came in September of '62 but before that was July 4, but on January 1st of 1962 you really *couldn't think of July 4th* because it was (this use of "was" implies a present tense) just the beginning of 1962. And then, of course, there was your birthday in 1961 and maybe on that birthday you *looked forward* to your birthday in 1962 *but that was in the future and who could guess a year ahead about the future?* But the really wonderful birthday was your *graduation year birthday. Twenty-one and a graduate at last!"* (An item of fact you have carefully learned and to which you lead and finally state in terms of present reality and utter and pleasing emphasis. Or one could continue as above to the 17th birthday or the 10th or whatever year might be desired.)

9. Thus there has been a rapid and easy mention of realities of today gradually slipping into the future with the past becoming the present and thereby placing the mentioned realities, actually of the past, increasingly from the implied present into the more and more seemingly remote future.

10. Significant dates which are in themselves indisputable are selected and, as the backward progress in time orientation continues to the selected time, some actual positive strongly tinged emotional event is mentioned.

11. Throughout, tenses are watched carefully and one speaks freely, as in the illustration given of the 21st birthday. It *is* the year of 1956, hence one speaks joyously of the instructorship that *will begin in September* which is yet to come. (Reorientation in time by implication and emotionally validated by vivifying the emotions of the past.)

12. Throughout the entire time, each statement is made impressively, with adequate and appropriate inflections, but before the subject in his attentiveness has any opportunity to take issue with or to dispute mentally what has just been said, a new utterance has just been offered to claim his thought and which arouses more effort toward further new understandings, with only a frustration of effort to respond resulting.

13. Finally, a clear-cut definitive, easily grasped and understood statement is uttered and the striving subject seizes upon it as a Rock of Gibraltar in the running flow of suggestions that has kept him helplessly following along. (Graduation day and birthday—emotionally potent and coincidental and a valid fact.)

14. Reinforcement of the patient's re-orientation in the past by a "specific orientation" to a "general" orientation such as a vague general reference to his "father's job," and by wondering, "Let's see, did it rain the last week?" and followed by mention of the instructorship. (Two general

vague possible ideas followed by the validity of the instructorship all to fixate the regression to the past as the present.)

15. Following up with the specific statement, "Now that it is all over, (the graduation) what shall we do now?" and let the subject lead the way, but carefully interposing objections to some impossible remark such as "Let's go down to Lake Mendota and have a swim." (This is "impossible" since a bathing suit becomes an immediate reality.) Instead, one agrees that it would be nice to go to Lake Mendota, there to watch the waves, the birds and the canoes, thereby leading to hallucinatory activity and, as this develops, hallucinatory swimming may then follow.

Temporal confusion was also the basis of the verbal patter presented in the Seminars on Hypnosis mentioned above. This particular patter was credited to Seymour Hershman, an obstetrician-gynecologist practicing in the Chicago area, and was called an "indirect induction technique." It is the patter that hundreds, perhaps thousands of physicians, dentists, and clinical psychologists first learned as a confusion technique in the 1950s.

The methods of going into any hypnotic trance vary with each individual. The common concept is that one needs to be unconscious or asleep. This is not true. Actually, in a deep trance, you should be able to hear, to see, to feel and experience anything that may belong in the situation. For example, it might be extremely necessary for you in a deep trance to hear the traffic noises. It might be very necessary for you, as an individual, to hear the traffic noises because you do not know how your unconscious mind works or what it needs. The baby who gets tired and wants to sleep can very easily teach you a great deal. It hunts up its favorite doll and discards it. It finds its favorite toy and discards it. It gets big sister's reader, examines it and discards it. And then, seemingly discouragedly, picks up an old block, and takes it to bed and falls asleep immediately. And yet, your assumption would be that it would be the favorite doll or the favorite toy, and not just a block picked up at random. Actually, it was not a block picked up at random. It was hunted for, because in that particular state, the child wanted something special. It doesn't make sense to the adult. But it makes a tremendous amount of sense to that child, although the child cannot recognize or understand it. And so, any subject going into a trance, going very deeply into hypnosis may hang on to what seems to be full conscious contact with his surroundings. But, of course, that full conscious contact with the surroundings serves a purpose for the unconscious. Perhaps this is the only way that the unconscious knows of distracting the conscious mind so that it can do its own thinking, its own feeling, its own organizing.

In the matter of going into a trance state, there is a need for you to recognize that it is the experience of the unconscious that is the important thing. Now the question may come to your mind: when am I going to hypnotize you? The answer to that question is that the time is not at all important. You are here and I am here. The time really should be picked by your unconscious mind. For all you know, you may already be in a light trance. What difference does it make whether you think you are wide awake. Perhaps it is a very useful thing for you

to think that you are wide awake. Perhaps you may think that you are beginning to go into a trance. Perhaps that is useful. But let's rely upon what your
unconscious mind is actually doing. Now every patient with a problem has the
feeling that the problem should be helped in this or that way. Actually, the help
should be given in a way that the patient's unconscious can best use it. It may
be very interesting for you as you sit here to recall that the time is now just past
4:30, and as you sit and think about the time, it is interesting to remember that
today is (date). Yesterday, (date) also at 4:30, you may have been sitting
around the house, or going for a ride, or having cocktails at your relatives, or
thinking about what you were going to do at 5:30, or maybe at 6:30, or maybe
at 7:30. And yesterday being (date), you know too, that the day before, on
(date) you also were doing something at 4:30 which may have been interesting.
Or maybe at 4:30 on Friday or Thursday or Wednesday of the week before, or
some Wednesday in November, you may have been thinking at 4:30 in the
afternoon of what might be interesting to do at that time. And as those thoughts
occurred, you were reminded of the fact that last June on a Saturday afternoon, you were doing something that seemed interesting. And thinking about
last June in the afternoon, brings back the fact that yesterday afternoon you
were also engaged in some activity. And what was it you were thinking yesterday? And what was it you were thinking last June 1956, and what was on your
mind in June of 1953 and 1952, because also in June on a Saturday afternoon,
some thoughts were going through your mind. You were engaged in some
activity, whether you were interested or whether you were not very interested,
and you were thinking of something else to do, it reminded you that in 1952, in
1951 and in 1950—many years and days—there were Saturdays at 4:30 and at
5:30 and at 3:30 and at 2:30 in the afternoon—times when you had just arose or
were just going to sleep, when you were rested and when you were tired. Nice
summer days and spring days and fall days back in 1949 and 1948, you had
many very pleasant days in June. Sometimes it was on a Saturday. Sometimes
on a Sunday. And then there were Mondays and Tuesdays. And in 1952 and in
1953 and in 1951, you had some very pleasant Saturday afternoons. And all
the time as you think of these things and the wonderful things that you were
doing and the things that were not so interesting, wondering what you would
like to do that evening, whether it should be done in June or in July or in
August, whether the year should be 1954 or 1953 or even 1952. And you were
reminded some evenings of the fact that you wanted dinner and what did you
have for dinner on Saturday in 1953, and what did you have for dinner on
Saturday in 1952, and what did you have for dinner on Friday and on Thursday
and on Wednesday and on Tuesday. And all these things are returning to you
and you think about them, and as you do, you notice a drowsiness and a
sensation of relaxation that creeps over your body, and you remember that it
was very pleasant that June Saturday in 1951, at 4:30, and you wondered what
you might be doing at 6:30 that evening. What you might be wanting to eat that
Saturday in June 1951, or was it 1952. The June and July and August nights on
Saturdays, and you relax and revel in the fact that you had some pleasant
experiences. Some of those times, you were sleepy as you may be becoming
now, and you allowed that sleepiness, when it overtook you, to allow you to
relax completely and let your eyes close if you desired and really relax and to
sleep deeper and sounder. You were very comfortable on those afternoons

when you lay down to sleep. You were very comfortable and you enjoyed relaxing and allowing your head to relax and your eyes and allowing yourself to sleep deeper and sounder and think about a day in July or June or in August or in September, in 1954, or in 1953, or even in 1952. You might even think about what might happen in 1958, next year, in December two weeks before Christmas or three weeks before Christmas, or even a month before Christmas about Thanksgiving time, or even in November, or October, and of the very pleasant things that might happen to you at that time. And the nights when you might be very relaxed, very restful, very sleepy, and you just might want to sleep soundly and deeply, remembering that in 1957, you were sleeping very soundly, very deeply, very comfortably, very relaxed, and as you speculate on those things, the thought comes to you that it is (date), and even now, you feel sleepy, relaxed, restful, and drowsy. And you allow the sensation to grow stronger and stronger because it is a nice pleasant sensation. And it grows stronger and stronger as you think about the fact that it is very relaxing and very restful, and as the relaxing, restful, sleepy sensation creeps over you and grows stronger and stronger, it allows you to really relax and to rest and to sleep comfortably and to think about many pleasant things.

As you awaken in the next few minutes feeling very refreshed and relaxed, you will undoubtedly realize that you have been completely relaxed, completely hypnotized—a very comfortable, relaxing sensation—knowing that the next time will be much more simple, and much more easily accomplished. You will find that by merely thinking of the fact that you are back again now to (date), that you can easily allow your eyes to open and awaken feeling very relaxed and very comfortable. (Erickson, et al., undated, pp. 24–25)

These rather simple verbalizations are easily mastered, but by so mastering are liable to become inflexible, rigid, hypnotist-centered, rather than client-centered. It took someone like Erickson to develop, *on the spur of the moment,* a confusion patter that fit the individual patient in the individual situation. Here, for example, is an individualized general confusion patter he used with a patient who had entered therapy with a bitter, hostile, and resentful attitude toward the medical profession for its inability to relieve him of continuing episodes of pain.

You *know and I know* and the doctors you *know know* that there is *one answer* that you *know* that you don't want to *know* and that I *know* but don't want to *know,* that your family *knows* but doesn't want to *know, no* matter how much you want to say *no,* you *know* that the *no* is really a *yes,* and you wish it could be a good *yes* and so do you *know* that what you and your family *know* is *yes,* yet you wish that *yes* could be *no* and you *know* that all the doctors *know* that what they *know* is *yes,* yet they still wish it were *no.* And just as you wish there were *no pain,* you *know* that there is *but what* you *don't know* is *no pain* is something *you can know.* And no matter what you *knew no pain* would be better than what you *know* and of course *what you want to know* is *no pain* and that is *what* you are *going to know, no pain.* [All of this is said slowly but with utter intensity and with seemingly total disregard of any interruption of cries of pain or admonitions of "Shut up".] Esther [John, Dick, Harry, or Evangeline, some family member or friend] *knows* pain and *knows no pain* and so do you wish to *know no pain* but *comfort* and you *do know comfort* and *no pain* and as *comfort increases* you *know* that *you cannot* say *no to ease and comfort* but *you can* say *no pain* and *know no pain* but *you can* say *no pain* and *know no pain* but *know comfort and ease* and it is *so good* to *know comfort and ease and relaxation* and to *know it now and later* and *still longer and longer as more and more relaxation* occurs and to *know it now and later* and *still longer and longer as more and more relaxation and wonderment and surprise come to your mind as you begin to know a freedom and a comfort you have so greatly desired and as you feel it grow and grow you know, really know,* that *today, tonight, tomorrow, all next week and next month,* and at Esther's [John's] 16th birthday, and what a time that was, and those *wonderful feelings* that you had then seem almost as clear *as if they were today* and the *memory of every good thing* is a glorious thing. (Erickson, 1964a, pp. 202–203)

These verbalizations, and improvisations thereon, may take from 5 minutes to an hour to rivet the patient's attention, but through the subtle introduction of different ideas in the patter (feelings of ease and comfort, happiness) many patients develop immobility and even catalepsies as they attempt to understand this confused array of contradictions and plays on words. Finally, Erickson introduces negative ideas, in the form of negative words, to convey to the patient the hypnotist's confidence in the patient's ability to handle the negative positively.

And now *you have forgotten* something, just as *we all forget* many things, *good* and *bad,* especially the *bad* because the *good* are *good to remember* and *you can remember comfort and ease and relaxation and restful sleep* and *now you know that you need no pain* and *it is good to know no pain* and *good to remember, always to remember,* that in *many places, here, there, everywhere* you have been at *ease* and *comfortable* and *now* that you *know* this, you *know* that *no pain is needed* but *that you do need to know all there is to know about ease and comfort and relaxation and numbness and dissociation and the redirection of thought and mental energies and to know and know fully all that will give you freedom to know your family and all that they are doing and to enjoy unimpeded the pleasures of being with them with all the comfort and pleasure that is possible for as long as possible* and *this is what you are going to do.* (Erickson, 1964a, p. 203)

Ideomotor Techniques

From at least the early 1920s on Erickson was fascinated with ideomotor behavior such as automatic writing and hand levitation. He saw clearly the possibilities these seemingly involuntary, uncontrolled movements had for trance induction. The latter, hand levitation, became one of his mainstays for the initial induction of hypnosis, because the hand and arm movements provided a physical, tangible event that could be used to communicate with the patient's unconscious and also convinced many resistant patients of the reality of hypnotic phenomena.

The intricate intertwining of hand levitation and communication with the patient at the unconscious level was illustrated in one example from his 1959 article on utilization techniques.

Then, with utter simplicity, the subject is told to sit quietly, to rest his hands palm down on his thighs, and to listen carefully to a question that will be asked. This question, it is explained, is possible of answer only by his unconscious mind, not by his conscious mind. He can, it is added, offer a conscious reply, but such a reply will only be a conscious statement and not an actual reply to the question. As for the question itself, it can be one of several that could be asked, and it is of no particular significance to the personality. Its only purpose is to give the unconscious mind an opportunity to manifest itself in the answer given. The further explanation is offered that the answer will be an ideomotor response of one or the other hand upward, that of the left signifying an answer of "no," that of the right a "yes," to the question asked the unconscious mind.

The question is then presented: "Does your unconscious mind think that you can go into a trance?" Further elaboration is offered again, "Consciously you cannot know what your unconscious mind thinks or knows. But your unconscious mind can let your conscious mind discover what it thinks or understands by the simple process of causing a levitation of either the right or the left hand. Thus your unconscious mind can communicate in a visibly recognizable way with your conscious mind. Now just watch your hands and see what the answer is. Neither you nor I know what your unconscious mind thinks, but as you see one or the other of your hands lifting, you will know."

If there is much delay, additional suggestions can be given: "One of your hands is lifting. Try to notice the slightest movement, try to feel and to see it, and enjoy the sensation of its lifting and be pleased to learn what your unconscious thinks."

Regardless of which hand levitates, a trance state supervenes simultaneously, frequently of the somnambulistic type. Usually it is advisable to utilize, rather than to test, the trance immediately, since the subject tends to arouse promptly. This is usually best done by remarking simply and casually, "It is very pleasing to discover your unconscious can communicate with your conscious mind in this way, and there are many other things that your unconscious can learn to do. For example, now that it has learned that it can develop a trance state and to do it remarkably well, it can learn various trance phenomena. For instance, you might be interested in _____," and the needs of the situation can then be met. (Erickson, 1959, p. 8)

Although the technique is one of hand levitation, the essence was one of communicating with the patient's unconscious and capitalizing on the patient's inherent interest in her or his own processes. Erickson interpreted the situation as follows: "It is necessary for the subject to go into a trance in order to discover the answer to the question" (Erickson, 1959, p. 9). With ideomotor behavior also, Erickson did not ignore the client-centered orientation.

So powerful is the patient's individuation of the induction process that hand levitation may at times occur without the hypnotist being aware of it. Erickson (1961) reported a case in which he offered repeated suggestions for right-hand levitation without apparent effect. Only when he noticed that the patient's eyes were starting into space at shoulder level (rather than looking at her hand on her lap) did he issue the directive to move her left hand to the same height as the right. She promptly moved her left hand to the level of her shoulder, indicating that kinesthetically and visually (to her) her right hand had risen to shoulder level, when in fact it had remained in her lap.

Erickson did not provide a set patter for hand levitation to be used with all patients. However, through the teachings of the Seminars on Hypnosis, a patter was provided for the use of newcomers to the field until they themselves were comfortable enough with the hypnotic situation to be able to attend to and better use what the patient brought to the encounter. The following was also attributed to Seymour Hershman.

Hand Levitation Induction Technique

Perhaps you'd like to just sit comfortably in the chair and let your hands rest lightly on your thighs. You may watch your hands, stare into space or even close your eyes. The important point is to begin to notice the feelings and sensations in your hands and in your fingers. Notice if you will that you can really feel a great many sensations. You can feel the texture of the cloth, the warmth of your thighs, perhaps a little tingling sensation in your fingers or in the palms of your hands. As you notice these sensations, you may begin to feel other sensations, perhaps a drowsy feeling, a relaxation of your entire body, and other things. You may be interested in noticing the beginning of a feeling in one of your fingers of motion. It may be in your left little finger, your right index finger, your left middle finger. And begin to feel that sensation becoming stronger and stronger—and just wonder and speculate as to whether that finger will move to the left or to the right or up or down.—There, you probably noticed the slight movement of that finger—good: Now begin to feel it moving still more and notice the lightness of that finger. That's right. It's now beginning to lift—now feel the lightness of the finger next to it, now the next one, and feel the entire hand now lifting, lifting, LIFTING, LIFTING, HIGHER AND HIGHER AND HIGHER. And as that hand lifts higher and higher, notice that the feeling of comfort and relaxation continues to spread and increase. You can continue to feel more and more relaxed—and as that hand is lifting—lifting—LIFTING—LIFTING—you might consider the possibility of allowing one of the fingers to touch some part of your face. It would be of value to you perhaps not to let that contact be made until you are really ready to allow yourself to go into a very deep trance. That's right: Now it's getting closer—closer—CLOSER—almost ready to touch now and when it does, you can really go into a very deep Hypnotic trance and learn to utilize Hypnosis to accomplish a great many things that will be of value to you.—Very good.— Now you may allow your hand to remain in contact with your face or it may slowly drop into your lap while you go still more deeply relaxed (asleep) etc., etc. (Erickson et al., undated, p. 23)

Aston of the same Seminars on Hypnosis group (Erickson et al., undated) combined a levitation movement with a personalized visual imagery technique. He called it the "sleep game" for children.

Ask patient if he can remember the details of a movie or television program he has seen. Almost always the answer will be in the affirmative. If it is, say, "Now close your eyes and don't open them until I ask you to. When it seems that you have the picture in your mind's eye, hold it there, but you are to let me know by raising your right arm." Wait for 15 or 30 seconds for the patient to raise arm. If he doesn't, urge him to concentrate more—"Keep trying; you'll get the picture and when you do your right arm will raise of its own accord, without any effort by you. It's beginning to raise from your lap now. You don't have to help. It will raise by itself—there it goes! Up and Up and Up!", etc. After arm raises even a little, "Keep the picture there and you will find that you'll hear nothing but my voice until I tell you otherwise. As you keep looking at the picture you are going into a deep, pleasant sleep. Stay asleep, but let your arm go back to your lap—and all the while you still see the picture." Now lift the arm up again and for a moment hold it out straight from his shoulder and say, "Now your elbow will bend and your hand will come nearer and nearer your face until it actually touches your face. As it touches your face you will relax still more and you will go much deeper, much deeper asleep, but always seeing the picture in your mind. Here it comes! Your arm is bending and coming nearer and nearer your face. Nearer and Nearer!" At the instant the hand touches say, "deep, deep-asleep!" several times. Put patient's hand back in his lap and continue to deepen as patient holds picture in his mind. (Erickson et al., undated, p. 20)

One other ideomotor induction technique came out of the Seminars on Hypnosis group, which combined an initial eye-fixation with ideomotor movement of the fingers. Developed by Irving I. Secter, a dentist who used hypnosis in both his private practice and his teaching at Roosevelt University in Chicago, it is called the "Coin Technique."

Coin Technique

All you have to do is follow my instructions exactly as I give them to you. I place this coin in the palm of your hand. Close your fingers gently over the coin; only just tight enough so that when we turn the hand over, the coin will not fall. Now stretch your arm straight out in front of you. Stick your thumb out to the side. Keep your eyes fixed on the thumb nail. Do not remove your eyes from the thumb nail until I ask you to do so.

While your eyes are occupied with your thumb, pay all your mental attention to the coin, the relation of the fingers to the coin and to one another. Now here is the way this works. I will soon start counting from one up. As you pay attention to the fingers and the coin, you will soon begin to feel your fingers relaxing. With each count, they will relax and open just a little. Soon the fingers will be stretched out far enough so that the coin will fall. The falling of the coin will be a signal for TWO THINGS TO HAPPEN simultaneously. Your eyes close and your whole body slumps or melts into the chair AS IF you were going DEEP, DEEP ASLEEP.

Sometimes the eyes get so tired from staring at the thumb that they close even before the coin drops. That is okay. Once the eyes close, keep them closed. Then you can pay ALL your attention to the coin and the moving of the fingers. When the coin drops just relax quickly and deeply.

(You may repeat the instructions at this point. The additional time will create greater fatigue in the eye muscles and encourage earlier eye closure, a desirable event.)

Let us now begin with the count. ONE. Eyes closing, fingers opening. Soon, the fingers will start to relax and open, the eyes to get heavy and close. With each count, just a little more. TWO. Fingers opening, eyes closing. Pay attention to the movement of each finger separately. Soon your eyes will be so tired and your eyelids so heavy that it will be more comfortable to keep them closed. It takes tensions to keep them open. That is the opposite of what you want. Don't work at keeping them open. THREE. That's fine. Fingers continue to open. Notice the finger tips leaving the palm of your hand. First one and then another. FOUR. When the coin falls, just relax all over. FIVE. You are doing fine. With each count, a little more movement. SIX. The coin is about to leave your fingers. It's gone. DEEP, DEEP, RELAXED. Just as if you were DEEP ASLEEP. Continue to breathe slowly and deeply as you do in the night time sleep. You have done very well. Everytime you do this, you do it better. (Erickson et al., undated, p. 26)

Resistant Patient Technique

Perhaps the most worrisome patient for the hypnotist is the resistant individual, one who either for unknown reasons cannot participate in the hypnotic process, or consciously and deliberately resists any obvious attempts on the part of the hypnotist to assist entrance into the hypnotic condition. It was with these patients that Erickson was proported to be the master. Here again the basis of his method was confusion, but a confusion based on levels of communication rather than conscious temporal or spatial irrelevancies. As is clear from what has gone before, Erickson was a firm believer in the importance of unconscious processes in hypnosis. He believed that to be successful the hypnotist must incorporate the patient's unconscious in the process through subtle, indirect instructions that placed the patient in double and triple binds. It was with the resistant patient that Erickson's communications with the unconscious were particularly effective in by-passing the consciously expressed desire of the patient to thwart the hypnotist's efforts.

The transcript of Erickson's dealings with a particularly hostile and uncooperative patient shows clearly his use of "direct, indirect and permissive suggestions intended to channel his reactions into receptive and responsive behavior'' (Erickson, 1964c, p. 9), hidden in the context of apparently casual remarks. After forcefully telling the patient to sit down and shut up, and that he (Erickson) would proceed at his own pace, the following instructions were given:

> You have come for therapy, you have requested hypnosis, and the history you have given of your problem leads me to believe strongly that hypnosis will help you. However, you state most convincingly that you are a resistant hypnotic subject, that others have failed despite prolonged efforts to induce a trance, that various techniques have been of no avail and that reputable men have discredited hypnosis for you as a therapeutic aid in itself. You have frankly expressed your conviction that I cannot induce a trance in you, and with equal frankness you have stated that you are convinced that you will resist all attempts at hypnosis and that this resistance will be despite your earnest desire and effort to cooperate. (To resist hypnosis, one recognizes its existence since there can be no resistance to the nonexistent and its existence implies its possibility. Thus the question becomes not one of the reality or value of hypnosis, but simply a question of his resistance to it. Thereby the ground is laid for the use of hypnosis but with his attention directed to his understanding of resistance to it. Hence, hypnotic induction is rendered a possibility by any induction technique not recognizable to him.)

> *Since you have come for therapy* and you state that you are a fault-finding uncooperative patient, let me explain some things *before we begin.* So that *I can have your attention,* just sit with your feet flat on the floor with your hands on your thighs, *just don't let your hands touch each other in any way.* (This is the first intimation that more is being communicated than the ear hears.)

> Now so that *you will sit still* while I talk, just look at that paperweight, just an ordinary handy thing. By looking at it, you will hold your eyes still and that will hold your head still and that will hold your ears still and *it's your ears I'm talking to.* (This is the first intimation of dissociation.) No, don't look at me, just at the paperweight because I want your ears still and you move them when you turn to look at me. (Most patients tend at first to shift their glance, so eye-fixation is effected by a request not to move the ears, and rarely does it become necessary to repeat this simple request more than three times.) Now when you came into this room you brought into it *both of your minds,* that is, the front of your mind and the back of your mind. (''Conscious mind'' and ''unconscious mind'' can be used, depending upon the educational level, and thus a second intimation is given of dissociation.) Now, I really don't care if you listen to me with your conscious mind, because *it doesn't understand your problem* anyway or you wouldn't be here, so *I just want to talk to your unconscious mind* because it's here and close enough to hear me so you can let your conscious mind listen to the street noises or the planes overhead or the typing in the next room. Or you can think about any thoughts that come into your conscious mind, systematic thoughts, random thoughts because *all I want to do is to talk to your unconscious mind and it will listen to me* because it is within hearing distance even if *your conscious mind does get bored* (boredom leads to disinterest, distraction, even sleep). If your eyes get tired it will be all right to close them but be sure to keep a good alert, (a disarming word so far as any assumed

threat of hypnosis is concerned) *a really good mental or visual image alertly* in your mind (an unrecognizable instruction to develop possible ideosensory visual phenomena while the word "alertly" reassures against hypnosis). *Just be comfortable while I am talking to your unconscious mind since I don't care what your conscious mind does.* (This is an unrecognizable dismissal of his conscious attention following immediately upon a suggestion of comfort and communication with only his unconscious mind.)

Now before *therapy can be done,* I want to be sure that you realize that *your problems just aren't really understood by you* but that *you can learn to understand them with your unconscious mind.* (This is an indirect assertion that therapy can be achieved and how it can be done with more emphasis upon dissociation.)

Something everybody knows is that people can communicate verbally ("talk by words" if warranted by low educational or intelligence level) or by sign language. The commonest sign language, of course, is when you *nod your head yes or no.* Anybody can do that. One can signal "come" with the forefinger, or wave "bye-bye" with the hand. The finger signal in a way means "yes, come here," and waving the hand means really "no, don't stay." In other words one can use the head, the finger or the hand to mean either yes or no. We all do it. *So can you.* Sometimes when we listen to a person we may be *nodding or shaking the head not knowing it* in either agreement or disagreement. *It would be just as easy to do it with the finger or the hand.* Now I would like to ask your unconscious mind a question that can be answered with a simple yes or no. It's a question that *only your unconscious mind can answer.* Neither your conscious mind nor my conscious mind, nor, for that matter, even my unconscious mind knows the answer. *Only your unconscious mind knows* which *answer can be communicated,* and it *will have to think either a yes or a no answer. It could be by a nod or a shake of the head, a lifting of the index finger,* let us say, the right index finger for the yes answer, the left index for a no since that is usually the case for the right-handed person and vice versa for the left-handed person. *Or the right hand could lift or the left hand could lift. But only your unconscious mind knows* what the answer will be when I ask for that yes or no answer. And not even your unconscious mind will know, when the question is asked, whether *it will answer with a head movement, or a finger movement,* and *your unconscious mind will have to think through that question* and *to decide, after it has formulated its own answer, just how it will answer.* (All of this explanation is essentially a series of suggestions so worded that responsive ideomotor behavior is made contingent upon an inevitable occurrence, namely, that the subject *"will have to think"* and *"to decide"* without there being an actual request for ideomotor responses. The implication only is there, and implications are difficult to resist.)

Hence, *in this difficult situation in which we find ourselves* (this establishes a "relatedness" to the patient) we will both have to sit back and *wait and wait* (participatory behavior) *for your unconscious mind to think the question through, to formulate its answer, then to decide,* whether by head, finger or hand, *to let the answer happen.* (This is a second statement of suggestions and instructions in the guise of an explanation. Seemingly, the subject has been asked to do nothing, but actually he is directly told to be passive and to permit an ideomotor response to occur at an unconscious level of awareness signifying an answer that he has been told carefully to "let happen" as another and definitive contingent result of mental processes. In all of this procedure, there have been implied or indirect suggestions given that the conscious mind will be unaware of unconscious mental activity, in essence, that he will develop an anamnestic trance state.)

In other words, I will ask a question to which *only your unconscious mind can give the answer,* and concerning which your conscious mind can only guess if it does at all; maybe correctly, maybe wrongly, or maybe have only some kind of an opinion, but, if so, only an opinion, *not an answer.''* (This a lessening of importance of his conscious thinking not recognizable to him, and a further implication of a trance state.)

Before I ask that question, I would like to suggest two possibilities. (1) Your conscious mind might want to know the answer. (2) Your unconscious mind *might not* want you to know the answer. My feeling, and I think you will agree, is that you came here for therapy for reasons *out of the reach of your conscious mind.* Therefore, I think that we should approach this matter of the question I am going to put to your unconscious mind for *its own answer* in such a way that *your own deep unconscious wishes to withhold the answer or to share the answer with your conscious mind are adequately protected and respected.* This, to me, is a fair and equitable way of dealing with one's self and one's problems. (This is what he knows he wants from others, but has not quite recognized that he wants fair and equitable treatment for himself.)

Now, to meet your needs, I am going to ask that yes or no question and *be prepared to be pleased to let your unconscious mind answer,* (this is an unrecognized authoritative suggestion with a foregone conclusion permissively stated) and in doing so, either *to share* the answer with your conscious mind or *to withhold it, whatever your unconscious mind thinks to be the better course.* The essential thing, of course, *is the answer, not the sharing nor the withholding.* This is because any withholding will actually be only for the immediate present, *since the therapeutic gains you will make* (also an unrecognized authoritative statement given in the guise of an explanation) will eventually disclose the answer to you *at the time your unconscious mind regards as most suitable and helpful to you.* Thus, *you can look forward to knowing the answer* sooner or later, and *your conscious desires, as well as your unconscious desires, are the seeking of therapy and the meeting of your needs in the right way at the right time.* (This is a definitive suggestion given as an explanation and a most emphatic positive suggestion.)

Now how shall this question be answered? By speech? Hardly! You would have to verbalize and also to hear. Thus, there could be no *fair dealing* (socially and personally potent demanding words) with your unconscious mind if it wished, for your welfare, to withhold the answer from your conscious mind. How then? Quite simply, by a muscular movement *which you may or may not notice,* one that can be done at either a noticeable voluntary level or *one that is done involuntarily and without being noticed,* just as you can nod your head or shake it without noticing it when you agree or disagree with a speaker, or frown when you think you are just trying to call something to mind.

What shall that muscle movement be? I think it would be better to mention several possibilities (simply "think" or "mention," apparently not demanding, ordering or suggesting), but before doing so, let me describe the difference between a conscious mind muscle response and that of the unconscious mind. (Muscle response is mentioned while his attention is being fixated; a maneuver to maintain that attention for the future introduction of related but delaying material. The reader will note the previous use of this psychological gambit of mentioning a topic and then entering into a preliminary explanation.) The conscious mind response cannot be withheld from you. You know it at once. You accept it and you believe it, perhaps reluctantly. There is no delay to it. It springs to your mind at once and you promptly make the response.

An unconscious mind response is different, because *you do not know what it is to be. You have to wait for it to happen* and consciously you cannot know whether it will be "yes" or "no." (How can a muscle movement be a "yes" or a "no?" The patient has to listen intently for some reasonable explanation.) *"It does not need to be in accord with the conscious answer* that can be present simultaneously in accord with your conscious mind's thinking. *You will have to wait,* and perhaps wait and wait, *to let it happen. And it will happen in its own time and at its own speed.* (This is an authoritative command but sounds like an explanation, and it provides time for behavior other than conscious, in itself a compelling force . . .).

Now what shall the movement be? Most people nod or shake their head for a "yes" or a "no," and the question I am going to ask is that kind of a question, one requiring either a simple "yes" or a simple "no." Other people like to signal by an upward movement of the index fingers, one meaning "yes," the other "no." I usually, as do most people (the phrases "I usually" and "most people" indicate that *naturally it is to be expected of both of us that behavior common to most people will occur*) like to use the right index finger for "yes" and the left for "no," but it is often the other way around for left-handed people. (Let there be no hint of arbitrary demands, since the patient is resistant and this suggestion is one of freedom of response even though an illusory freedom.) Then again some people have expressive hands, and can easily, voluntarily or involuntarily, move their right hand up to signify "yes" or the left to signify "no." ("Expressive hands" is only an implied compliment, but most appealing to any narcissism. Indeed, it is not at all uncommon for a person to beckon with a finger or to admonish with a finger or a hand.)

I do not know if your unconscious mind wants your conscious mind to look at some object, or to pay attention to your head or fingers or hands. Perhaps you might like to watch your hands, and if your eyes blur as you watch them fixedly while you wait to see which one will move when I ask my simple question, such blurring is comprehensible. It only means that your hands are close to you and that you are looking at them intently. (Even if the patient's eyes are closed this paragraph can be used unconcernedly . . .).

Now (at long last, and the patient's eagerness is at a high point) we come to the question! I do not need to know what is to be your choice of the movements to be made. You have your head on your neck and your fingers are on your hands and you can let your hands rest comfortably on your thighs or on the arms of the chair. *The important thing is to be comfortable while awaiting your uncon-*

scious answer. (In some way comfort and the unconscious answer become unrecognizedly contingent upon each other, and the patient naturally wants comfort. Equally naturally he has some degree of curiosity about his "unconscious answer." Also, another delaying preliminary explanation is being given.) Now you are in a position for any one or all of the possible movements (an unrecognized authoritative suggestion). As for the question I am to ask, that, too, is not really important. What is important is *what your unconscious mind thinks and what it does think neither you nor I consciously know. But your unconscious does know since it does do its thinking but not always in accord with your conscious thoughts.*

Since you have asked me to induce a trance, I could ask a question related to your request, but I would rather ask a simpler one (a possible threat of hypnosis removed). Hence, *let us* (we are working together) ask a question so general that it can be answered by any one of the various muscle ways described. Now here is the question to which I want you to listen carefully, and then to wait patiently to see or perhaps not to see, what your unconscious answer is. (After so much apparently plausible delay, the patient's attention is now most fixed; he is, so to speak, "all ears" in his desire to know the question and such desire has to have an unrecognized basis of acceptance of the idea that his unconscious mind will answer). My question is, (said slowly, intently, gravely) Does your unconscious mind *think* it will raise your hand or your finger or move your head? (Three possibilities, hence the conscious mind cannot know.) Just wait patiently, wonderingly, and let the answer happen. (He is inescapably bound by that word "think." In other words, his resistances have been by-passed by making responses contingent upon his thought processes in response to seemingly nonhypnotic discussion of various items and his false belief that he cannot be hypnotized is nullified by a pleasing unconscious awareness that he can cooperate.) (Erickson, 1964c, pp. 10–15)

OTHER APPROACHES

Erickson, of course, was not the only practitioner working in the middle 20th century, although his productivity and the thousands of references to his work might lead the casual reader to think so. Clearly, he was a dominant figure, but not the only figure.

The remaining 1950s saw the continued growth in adherents to the client-centered doctrine, as well as the continued use of technology for purposes of inductions and the teaching of techniques. *J. M. Schneck* (1953), for example, followed in Estabrooks's path and produced several audio-recordings of his own induction methods, which he duely reported in the *British Journal of Medical Hypnotism*. In addition, the British child psychiatrist, *Gordon Ambrose,* was modifying, slightly, relaxation techniques for use with children. He proposed three rules for hypnotizing children, the latter of which indicated how little the standard techniques had to be modified to accommodate them: (a) gain their confidence, (b) inform them concerning what will happen, and (c) apply any technique (Ambrose, 1952).

A little later (1956), Ambrose teamed with a British obstetrician and gyne-cologist, *George Newbold,* to produce one of several "handbooks" on hyp-nosis to appear in this century. The book covered the application of hypnosis to a number of medical specialty areas and included a copy of the Hypnotism Act of 1952, which prohibited the exhibition of hypnosis for public entertain-ment purposes in Great Britain. Pursuant to our interest, Ambrose and New-bold also reviewed medical hypnosis induction techniques in vogue at that time, cautioning practitioners not to restrict themselves to any one method alone. They also urged the importance of the way in which suggestions and questions assessing the success of those suggestions were phrased, as did Gindes (1951) before them. Never, they implied, query the patient about a particular effect in a manner that implies that the effect might not have occurred. This is a standard rule for the teaching of hypnotic techniques. If, for example, you have suggested a visual image to the patient and want to know if he or she is, in fact, perceiving the image, ask him or her to clarify some aspect of the image rather than ask: "Do you see it?" To ascertain the presence of a suggested pastural scene for the patient, one might ask: "What is the color of the leaves on the trees?" Or: "How many trees are there in the scene?" Both of these questions imply that you have no doubt that he or she is responding to your suggestion. All you wish to know is some detail of the image.

Aside from these now basic principles for induction, Ambrose and New-bold covered standard eye-fixation, sway ("falling"), and "confusional" techniques. Terminating hypnosis was through a simple counting routine preceded by suggestions for feelings of well-being and the removal of any unusual suggestions that might have been given in the course of the hypnotic session.

Another practitioner of the time, Baltimore-based psychiatrist *Harold Rosen,* took issue with the usual brief trance termination techniques applied throughout history. Writing primarily in a simple, declarative style, Rosen interpreted the use of simple commands for termination as based on the "arrant nonsense" that the patient plays a passive role in the hypnotic process. His psychodynamic orientation led him to suggest that at least some difficulties in dehypnosis were "a problem involving symptom-precipi-tation by the nondynamic mishandling of hypnotically induced behavior" (Rosen, 1953, p. 225). Thus, he noted that a number of his colleagues, faced with a difficult de-induction, allow the patient to "sleep it off," while others reuse another induction or a hypnotic phenomenon (e.g., dreaming) to aid the patient's termination of the hypnotic condition. Some even advocate subconvulsive metrazol. Rosen, himself, handled difficult terminations by treating the behavior as a symptom in a total therapeutic picture (Rosen, 1954). Erickson, he noted, often used the unwillingness to terminate the trance as a means for its termination, in much the same way that he used resistances to overcome resistances (see utilization techniques above).

Although eschewing the authoritative approach to induction, Rosen did admit to using "the exceedingly authoritative short-cut" of challenging the patient to open his or her eyes while they are closed and rolled upward and inward—generally a physical impossibility. His preferred method was the simple eye-fixation technique of Wolberg, although he also adhered to essentially a utilization technique in which every movement, every symptom, every response of the patient is used in the induction (see Erickson above).

By the late 1950s and early 1960s, another mechanical, actually electronic, devise was making its appearance as an induction device. Television, unlike the devices I have described thus far, was not used directly in hypnotic inductions, although it certainly had that potential as an eye-fixating apparatus, but indirectly. The mental visual image of a television set was, and is, used extensively as a means for holding the patient's attention, while suggestions of relaxation and rest were presented. With children, particularly, was this method of attention-getting found applicable. The technique consisted of having the child close her or his eyes and imagine a TV screen and proceed to watch her or his favorite program—thus the specifics of the verbalizations accompanying the method were always slightly different, but definitely up-to-date. *Milton J. Marmer* (1959), Clinical Professor at the UCLA School of Medicine, in his little noted book detailed what he called a "television imagination game" induction method for use with children. "Lassie" was a popular show at that time, so, after the child had raised her or his hand to indicate that the imagined TV was operating and indicated that "Lassie" was the show of choice, he said:

> Lassie is walking up the hill with Jeff. It is a quiet, peaceful day and Lassie is feeling very good, but she is getting a little tired and sleepy. Now Lassie is lying down in a very comfortable position and she has closed her eyes. She likes the calm, peaceful feeling it gives her. Notice how tired Lassie is, how very drowsy she is. She is beginning to feel sleepy. She is so drowsy that she is falling asleep. Lassie is going to take a nice long nap and she is going to remain asleep until she is awakened. Lassie is breathing deeper and deeper and getting deeper and faster asleep. (pp. 93–94)

As the child watches Lassie go into a pleasant, deep sleep, the child imitates Lassie. Thus this is an indirect technique strikingly similar to that described earlier by Kline (1953) in which the patient watches a visual image of himself or herself being hypnotized.

In addition to standard techniques such as hand levitation, coin technique, and confusional procedures, Marmer offers specific verbalizations for gaining rapport with the surgical patient (or with any other patient anxious about impending treatment) and a 21-step relaxation induction. First, he notes a labeling that has become almost a standard practice with many practitioners. Instead of presenting the upcoming hypnotic induction as hypnosis, he prefers to use the phrase "an exercise in relaxation," because of the many negative connotations surrounding the former term. The substitution of "relaxation" for "hypnosis" may be more appropriate than one might think (Edmonston, 1981) and certainly has the advantage of reducing initial, misguided fears and anxieties.

The gaining of the confidence of the patient initially is not new, but the presentation of a specific verbal patter is rare.

> You may be a little upset about the anticipated surgery [or any other treatment] and consequently may have become a little bit tense. Most people are that way and I find this reaction a very usual one. I understand how you feel. I assure you this can be easily remedied and reversed. I'm going to help you relax, by teaching you a method of relaxation. It will enable you to relax completely and will make you feel calm and very comfortable. All you have to do is just listen to what I tell you. If it seems reasonable and sounds meaningful to you, you will be interested in following my suggestions. You will be awake throughout this exercise and will have the privilege of refusing to carry out any or all my suggestions. Be assured that I will offer only beneficial suggestions to you that will help you relax completely, and make you feel calm and comfortable. . . .
>
> Try to give me your full and complete attention. I am asking you to remain receptive but passive, so that my words may have an impression upon you. Try to use your imagination. Do not analyze your sensations and let my words absorb your entire attention. (Marmer, 1959, p. 37)

This introduction is followed by the induction techniques. Here is his relaxation technique.

> Make yourself comfortable. Assume the position which is most comfortable for you in bed.
>
> 1.   Gently close your eyes. It will be so much more comfortable for you. It will make you feel more restful and serene. It will calm you down and bring you greater peace.
>
> 2.   Most tension is muscular. If you relax all the muscles of your body, you will find that you can rest more comfortably and completely.
>
> 3.   Let us start by relaxing the legs. Let go your entire legs from the toes to the hips. Start by relaxing the toes.
>
> 4.   Relax each of your toes. It may seem strange to you at first, but you soon will find it very easy. You will be able to do it, because you want to.
>
> 5.   Now relax the rest of your feet and your heels. It feels so good. Doesn't it? It feels as though you have just taken off a very tight pair of shoes.
>
> 6.   That is fine. Now, relax your lower legs, relax all the muscles in the calves of your legs. Relax your thighs. Relax all the muscles from the knees to the hips.
>
> 7.   You have done well.
>
> 8.   You have relaxed your legs completely. All the tension has left your lower extremities and now you will be able to do the same with your upper extremity. Start relaxing your arms from the finger tips to the shoulders. As you relax each finger and then each hand, you will feel the comfort of warmth in your hands and you will continue by relaxing your arms.

9.   That is fine. Just fine. Now relax the muscles of your abdomen and your diaphragm, so that you will breathe slowly and deeply—slowly and deeply—in and out, in and out, so that you will feel the air all the way down to the pit of your stomach.

10.   Now you are breathing very deeply—very deeply, breathing in and out, in and out, so that with each breath you will feel more deeply and more completely relaxed. You will feel very good. Very, very good.

11.   As you continue breathing deeply and regularly, try to relax the muscles of your neck. The neck muscles are usually so tense, they almost feel as though they were tied into knots. You do want to relax your neck muscles. This will release all the strain and tension and will give you great relief and comfort.

12.   Now relax all the muscles of your face. Remove the furrows from your brow and relax all your face muscles so that, now, you will be relaxed all over your entire body. You may part your lips if you wish, and if you feel like swallowing, just go ahead and swallow. It will make you feel so much better.

13.   You have done everything wonderfully well and have succeeded in relaxing your entire body completely. You are now comfortably relaxed all over and feeling wonderful. You will be able to relax this way whenever you want to.

14.   Now, I would like you to remain relaxed and to enjoy this wonderful state of relaxation for a little while, after which I will give you some suggestions that will help you to sleep better, to be calm and peaceful, relaxed and comfortable and to help you in recovering your health more quickly. (Marmer, 1959, pp. 38–40)

The remaining six steps of this induction concerned themselves with suggestions about recovery and presurgery preparations the next morning.

Marmer also noted that an authoritative technique was appropriate in some cases. He did not specify which cases were appropriate, merely saying that with practice the practitioner would intuitively know when to use such an approach. He simply faced the patient and said, "Look at me. Look into my eyes. Keep looking into my eyes. I am going to count to five and your eyes will close and you will feel very relaxed. 1–2–3–4–5. Your eyes will close. They are closing tighter and tighter and you feel relaxed, very relaxed" (Marmer, 1959, p. 46).

André M. Weitzenhoffer

In 1957, André M. Weitzenhoffer produced the most comprehensive text of modern hypnotic techniques then available. This work was the second part of an originally projected trilogy on hypnosis, its foundations, techniques, and applications. The first part, the foundations, was published in 1953 and has long served as a comprehensive review of the research literature until that period. The techniques volume, actually begun in 1948, was developed to be used as a text for both introductory and advanced courses in hypnosis.

In fact, in his preface, Weitzenhoffer indicates which chapters should be used for introductory and which for advanced students.

Weitzenhoffer (b. Jan. 16, 1921) received his Ph.D. from the University of Michigan in 1956. He spent several years in the Stanford, California area in 1957 as a fellow at the Center for Advanced Study in the Behavioral Sciences, and from 1957–1961 as an assistant professor at Stanford University. It was during 1957 that he completed his techniques book. Within the field, Weitzenhoffer has always been known as a careful investigator whose works exemplify an attention to detail that has made his publications (books, tests, and journal articles) outstanding examples of comprehensive literature coverage. In addition, he is the senior author of all of the original Stanford Scales of Hypnotic Susceptibility and the Stanford Profile Scales of Hypnotic Susceptibility, the best documented and most used scales of this nature in the world today. The mark Weitzenhoffer has left on the literature of hypnosis is outstanding; he has done as much, if not more, for the understanding of hypnosis and hypnotic phenomena than other, better known individuals at work in this modern period. He is now retired from his last position with the Veterans Administration in Oklahoma City and Professor of Psychiatry and Behavioral Science at the University of Oklahoma Medical Center.

Several of the techniques appearing in Weitzenhoffer's book deserve reprinting here. The first is an eye-fixation, relaxation method that illustrates three stages, in sequence, of induction: description of the effects subject will experience, giving the suggestions in the present tense to reinforce the idea that they are actually happening, and emphatic, direct presentation of the suggestions.

> I want you to look upward at a spot on the ceiling and to fixate your eyes on it. Any spot will do. You may imagine one that you can look at comfortably. Do not worry if your eyes stray away or you blink. That is all right. If you do, just bring your eyes right back to the spot and keep looking at it as steadily as you can. Don't be tense. Just relax and listen closely to my voice, to what I say. I want you to relax. . . . Think of relaxing. Feel your body relaxing. . . . As you do so you will find that your body becomes relaxed. . . . You will relax more and more. As you keep looking at the spot above your head and listen to my voice you will find that your entire body becomes relaxed. Your feet are becoming relaxed, your legs are becoming relaxed, your arms and your hands are becoming relaxed, your entire body is becoming relaxed, and now you will find that you are also becoming drowsy. You are going to get more drowsy. Just listen to my voice. . . . it makes you feel drowsy, sleepy. . . . You feel a heaviness coming over your body. Your body is getting heavy, very h-e-a-v-y. Your hands are getting h-e-a-v-y. Your arms are becoming h-e-a-v-y. Your arms and your hands are heavy. Your feet are getting h-e-a-v-y. Your legs are getting h-e-a-v-y. Your entire body is becoming h-e-a-v-y, v-e-r-y h-e-a-v-y. You are d-r-o-w-s-y . . . s-l-e-e-p-y. A feeling of pleasant drowsy warmth is coming over you. Soon you are going to sleep . . . deeply . . . soundly. . . . A pleasant warmth is coming all over your body, just like when you fall

asleep. . . . Your eyes are getting heavy. You are becoming sleepy. Your eyes are getting heavier and h-e-a-v-i-e-r, s-o heavy and you are feeling s-o s-l-e-e-p-y. . . . Think of sleep, of nothing but sleep.

You are going to go to sleep very soon. . . . My voice makes you sleepy . . . makes you want to sleep. . . . Your eyes are heavy, they are closing. You cannot keep your eyes open. They are closing. In a moment you find it impossible to keep your eyes open and they blink. . . . They will blink more and more and shortly they will close because they are getting heavier and heavier and you find it harder and harder to keep them open. (It is best to coordinate this suggestion with actual blinking of the subject's eyes. Some subjects are able to keep a very steady unblinking stare and the above suggestions will often lead to their blinking. If they do not, it is best not to insist on this since it is actually not essential.) You are now v-e-r-y s-l-e-e-p-y. . . . Your eyes are s-o h-e-a-v-y you cannot keep them open. They are closing, closing more and more, more and more. . . . (If you find that the subject is not showing any indication of closing his eyes at this point, tell him in a firm tone of voice:) All right, now close your eyes and keep listening closely to what I say. (Then go on with:) Your eyes are now closed and you are going deep asleep. . . . (Very often a subject who has responded poorly to eye-closure suggestions may nevertheless develop some degree of hypnosis after closing his eyes to the command. Also, some individuals pass into a relatively deep hypnosis quite early in the process but maintain their eyes open and for some reason do not respond well to suggestions of eye closure. In any case, continued with:). . . . They are now closed and you are going into a deep sleep. . . . a d-e-e-p-e-r and d-e-e-p-e-r sleep . . . a sounder and sounder sleep. . . . You will pay attention to nothing but the sound of my voice. You will not awaken until I tell you to. Nothing will bother you. Any time in the future I suggest sleep or say the word "sleep" to you, you will immediately pass into a deep sleep. You are now going to sleep deeply . . . v-e-r-y d-e-e-p-l-y. (These last few suggestions are important and should be given to the subject soon after his eyes close. They should be reiterated a number of times subsequently. They will give you a much better control over the subject than you would have otherwise.) (Weitzenhoffer, 1957, pp. 206–207)

Until this point, I have not examined deepening techniques, since such procedures usually follow the induction procedures and may be more a part of treatment suggestions than the induction per se. In addition, there is a general view now that the depth of hypnosis is not related to hypnotherapeutic effectiveness, that some patients can respond to intense therapeutic intervention in what would otherwise be evaluated as light stages of hypnosis. On the other hand, some practitioners advocate deepening the condition before proceeding with treatment. Deepening the trance condition was, for Weitzenhoffer, a three-stage affair. First, continuing suggestions to assist the subject or patient to become increasingly more relaxed were offered. Second—actually concomitant with the first—periods of silence were interspersed among the continuing suggestions for greater and greater relaxation. The number and length of these silences had to be intuitively developed by the practitioner, for, as Weitzenhoffer rightly pointed out, nothing teaches like practice, practice, practice. Third, the subject is given a series of challenges in order of graded difficulty to perform as he or she becomes increasingly hypnotized. This third stage is used primarily to ascertain the degree of hypnosis achieved and is well reflected in the series of challenges that comprise Weitzenhoffer's Stanford Scales and the group Harvard Scale developed therefrom (see Chapter 8).

Sleep . . . deeply . . . profoundly . . . sleep. Your eyes are heavy . . . v-e-r-y h-e-a-v-y. . . . They are stuck tight, so completely stuck that you cannot open them however hard you may try. YOU CANNOT OPEN YOUR EYES NOW. TRY! YOU CANNOT OPEN THEM . . . try hard. . . . All right, now stop trying. You are going deeper asleep . . . much deeper. Lift your arm up. (As you say this take hold of his hand and gently guide his hand and arm straight out to the side at shoulder height or up above his head.) "Extend it straight. Make a fist . . . a tight fist . . . TIGHTER! Your arm is stiffening, your entire arm is becoming STIFF! RIGID! LIKE A BAR OF IRON! YOU CANNOT BEND YOUR ARM YOU CANNOT MOVE IT. Try. YOU CAN'T . . . try hard. . . . All right now, you can move it." (With some subjects you may have to give more countersuggestions than this.) "Slowly lower it to your lap. As you do so you sink into a very deep sleep . . . d-e-e-p-e-r and d-e-e-p-e-r." (If the subject lowers his arm slowly enough you can add "When your hand touches your lap you will be in a very D-E-E-P sleep. . . . You are going deeply asleep . . . d-e-e-p-l-y asleep." In any case, as the subject's hand comes to rest on his lap, continue with:) You are now d-e-e-p asleep. S-l-e-e-p! D-e-e-p, d-e-e-p asleep! . . . Your body is now very relaxed. You have no desire to move. You only want to s-l-e-e-p . . . d-e-e-p-l-y . . . s-o-u-n-d-l-y. . . . You want to do whatever I tell you to do. You can hear me quite well. You will be able to answer my questions and do everything I tell you to do, but you will remain deep asleep. Even if I tell you to open your eyes you will not wake up until I tell you to. Each and every time in the future I tell you to sleep you will immediately go into a deep sleep. As soon as I say "sleep" or mention the word "sleep" your eyes will get very heavy, you will get very sleepy, your eyes will close, and you will go soundly asleep. . . . This will happen each and every time I tell you to go to sleep . . . that I say the word "sleep." (If you wish you can substitute here some other signal, or preferably add it to the above instruction. More about this later.) But now sleep . . . d-e-e-p-l-y, s-o-u-n-d-l-y. . . . I am going to stop talking to you for a few moments, but you will continue to go deeper asleep and will not let anything disturb you. . . . You hear only the sound of my voice. When I speak again to you, you will not be startled. . . . Now sleep . . . d-e-e-p-l-y . . . profoundly. (Stop talking now for 5 to 10 minutes, then in a very low voice, even a whisper, resume your suggestions, gradually but fairly rapidly increasing the volume of your voice.) You are now deep asleep. You can hear everything quite well but you will pay attention only to the sound of my voice. (Remember you said earlier that the subject would hear nothing but the sound of your voice. With a very suggestible subject this may have the effect of making him deaf to other sounds, so you must be careful to remove this effect if present.)

You are deep asleep, but you can go even deeper asleep than you are now. You want very much to be in the deepest sleep possible because it is a very pleasant experience, because it will be very beneficial to you. (You should beware in giving any suggestion of pleasantness in connection with suggestions since this can have disturbing consequences with some subjects. This is particularly true with psychotics and psychoneurotics. It is important to consider this when using hypnosis in psychotherapy, especially if a positive transference has begun or is ready to begin.) You are going to sleep much more deeply and all the suggestions I shall give you will be very effective. (It is possible that saying this may associate response to suggestions and deep sleep together. If the subject should then decide that he is not deeply hypnotized, it might tend to interfere with his response to suggestions. In view of this you may prefer not to associate the two.) I shall now count to five, (Any other number is suitable—although I find five a good figure.) and as I do so you will begin to sink into a much deeper sleep and at the count of five you will be very, very sound asleep. So sound asleep that when I tell you to wake up later on (It is preferable to say "when I tell you to wake up" rather than "when you wake up" because the former reaffirms the contingency of waking upon the hypnotist's command, whereas the latter does not and can be interpreted by the subject as giving him some control over the matter of waking.) you will have no memory of anything that was said or done while you were asleep. It will be just as if no time had passed and you had not slept." (Again it must be emphasized that there are circumstances in which these last statements are contradicted. This is true, for instance, with therapy cases who have a tendency to be disoriented anyway.) Now I shall start counting. One . . . You are going to go deeply, much more d-e-e-p-l-y asleep. Two . . . you are going d-e-e-p-e-r and d-e-e-p-e-r asleep. With each count you sink deeper asleep. With each word I say, with every breath that you take you go more deeply asleep. Three . . . S-l-e-e-p, d-e-e-p-l-y, s-o-u-n-d-l-y, s-l-e-e-p. My voice makes you want to sleep. (This associates sleep with a stimulus which is continuously present.) always d-e-e-p-e-r and d-e-e-p-e-r. You can feel yourself s-i-n-k-i-n-g into a very, v-e-r-y deep sleep . . . sinking . . . s-i-n-k-i-n-g into a d-e-e-p-e-r and s-o-u-n-d-e-r sleep in which you hear nothing but my voice which sounds as if it were coming from far, far away. (Starting with "three" begin to soften and lower your voice so that by the time you say the last "far away" you are speaking quite softly—but loud enough for the subject to hear you clearly.) Four . . . You continue to go deeper asleep as I count, as I talk to you. All the suggestions I shall give you in the future will be very effective. You will do everything I tell you to do. You have no fear of hypnosis because it can only be beneficial for you. . . . You know that it cannot harm you. You are very responsive to my suggestions and you will continue to become increasingly more responsive. Even as I talk to you, you go deeper and deeper asleep. . . . Any time that I tell you to see, hear, smell or feel something you will see, hear, smell or feel it as a reality. You will experience it fully, realistically. You will have very real experiences. Every time in the future that I tell you to do something when you are hypnotized and only then. (This provision is asked to eliminate the possibility of the subject posthypnotically becoming completely dominated by the hypnotist. This is a matter of ethics as well as a safeguard for both subject and hypnotist.) You will carry it out without question. . . . I will always be able to remove and change any suggestion that I give you now, have given you or shall give you. (This is an extremely important point, and this suggestion should always be given quite early and reiterated on a number of occasions. If you do not use the particular phase of deepening under discussion, you should make a point of giving this suggestion earlier. Now allow a few moments of silence.) . . . Continue to sleep. At the next count you will be deeply, soundly asleep. (Again allow a few moments of silence.) Five . . . Deep, d-e-e-p asleep! You are now very deeply and soundly asleep. You will not awaken until I tell you to or unless something should happen to me or endanger your life. Otherwise you will remain deep asleep and will do everything I tell you. Anytime in the future that I say or suggest sleep (include mention of signal if you have given one) you will instantly, immediately go into a deep sleep, even deeper than the one you are in now. When I wake you up later you will have no recollection of anything but having slept. (Weitzenhoffer, 1957, pp. 215–218)

Two facets should be noted about these deepening instructions. First, they contain elements similar to those appearing in the deepening procedures following eye-closure in the standard induction of the Stanford Scales. Second, they involve counting techniques. A step-by-step counted progression has become a basic induction procedure during this century, although it has never been clear whether the operator is merely counting time or counting some gradated steps of increasing or decreasing hypnosis. (It is also not clear whether the operator is counting for his or her or the patient's need.) Presumably, both are the case. Although counting constitutes a part of most inductions, Weitzenhoffer presented a unique counting method that served to regulate two behaviors (eye-opening and closing) in an alternating fashion, thus achieving hypnotic induction.

I am going to count and I want you to follow me closely. When I say "one" you will close your eyes and keep them closed until I say "two." When I say "two" you will open your eyes. Then when I say "three" you will close them again and keep them closed until I say "four." Do you understand? (If the subject seems to show some confusion you can demonstrate for him what you want. Some hypnotists make it a standard practice to demonstrate these instructions while giving them.) You will keep on opening and closing your eyes as I count until they get very tired. You will find it increasingly difficult to open your eyes. They will get heavier and heavier. You will find yourself becoming more and more drowsy and sleepy. After a while your eyes will have become so-o-o heavy and you will be so-o-o sleepy that your eyes will close and remain closed and you will go into a deep, sound sleep. You will have no desire to open your eyes, you will only want to sleep, to sleep deeply and soundly. (Weitzenhoffer, 1957, p. 289)

He cautions that the operator should pay close attention to the subject during this process to assess the degree of compliance. Combining suggestions of fatigue and relaxation with the counting increases the effectiveness of the method, but hypnosis can be achieved through the counted movements alone.

Quick methods of induction are always welcomed by the busy practitioner or the experimental investigator attempting to gather data on as many individuals as possible in a brief period. The first is not unlike some of the techniques I have presented before and involves an authoritative, dominating demeanor by the hypnotist.

> With your subject standing in front of you place your hands on his shoulders, bring your face close to his, about 8 or 9 inches away and fixate the bridge of his nose. As you do so say: "Look at my eyes and think of sleep. You are going to go to sleep, quickly, soundly. . . . You are going to go into a deep, sound sleep. Keep looking at my eyes. As you do so you feel a heaviness coming over your body. . . . You are growing heavy. . . . Your legs are heavy, very heavy. Your arms are heavy, very heavy. Your arms and your hands are very heavy, like lead. Your entire body is heavy . . . s-o heavy . . . s-o heavy. Your eyelids are getting heavy. . . . You are getting drowsy . . . sleepy. . . . You are tired. . . . Your body is so heavy. . . . You want to sleep. Your eyes are so heavy you can't keep them open. They are closing . . . closing . . . closing. . . . You cannot keep them open. . . . You're going to sleep. . . . Your eyes are closed. Sleep! DEEP ASLEEP!" (Weitzenhoffer, 1957, p. 229)

A second quick induction method is used following preliminary suggestibility testing of the subject with either a sway test, a hand-clasp test, or an eye-catalepsy test. In the first of these tests, the degree of response to suggestions of swaying (while the subject stands with the eyes closed) is noted. In the second, the subject is told that he or she cannot disengage the intertwined, interlaced fingers of both hands; and in the third, they are told that their eyes are "glued shut" and will not open. Ordinarily, the third test immediately precedes the induction instructions.

> All right, stop trying to open your eyes, you are now going to go to sleep. SLEEP! . . . DEEP ASLEEP! (Following eye-catalepsy suggestions your hand will be above the subject's forehead. Now, moving your hand downward in front of his face, form a V with the index and middle fingers and gently press the subject's closed eyes for a brief moment. Then place both hands on the subject's shoulders. All of this should take only a moment and produce no obvious break in the suggestions. In many cases the subject will now be in a relatively deep state of hypnosis, but it is best to carry the induction a little further before testing for depth. You may regard the remainder of this procedure as part of the induction proper or as part of the deepening phase; in any case we give it here because it makes use of a different approach. With your hands lightly grasping the subject's shoulders, very gently move his body in a slight, slow rotary swing with his feet as pivot. At the same time give further suggestions.) You are now sinking into a deep . . . d-e-e-p sleep. You will not wake up until I tell you to. . . . Waves of sleep are coming over you. . . .

You are going deeper and deeper asleep. . . . There is a heaviness in your body. . . . Your arms and hands are heavy, v-e-r-y heavy. . . . Your feet and legs are s-o heavy. . . . Your entire body is getting so h-e-a-v-y. You feel yourself sinking into a d-e-e-p, sound sleep. Sleep . . . deeply . . . soundly. . . . S-l-e-e-p. (At this point take hold of his forearm, raise it horizontally to his side saying at the same time:) Now raise your arm. . . . Make a tight fist. (Proceed to give the arm rigidity suggestions for deepening the hypnosis as was done in the first method. After the challenge, have the subject lower his arm slowly, guiding it if necessary and suggest that the trance is deepening. As soon as his arm is by his side, continue as follows:) You are now deep asleep and you are going to go into an even deeper sleep. . . . Take deep breaths. . . . That's right, breathe deeply and slowly. . . . With each breath that you take you sink (This word sometimes causes anxiety.) into a deeper and sounder sleep . . . a d-e-e-p, d-e-e-p, sound sleep. . . . Continue to breathe deeply. . . . Sleep. . . . You have but one desire . . . one thought . . . to sleep deeply. . . . Breathe deeply . . . sleep deeply. . . . More and more deeply. . . . Each and every time in the future that I tell you to sleep, suggest sleep, or say the word "sleep" you will instantly go into a deep, sound sleep, deeper and sounder than you are now. You will not wake up until I tell you to unless something happens to me or your life is endangered. You will remain deep asleep. Nothing will bother you. Listen only to the sound of my voice. (Weitzenhoffer, 1957, pp. 230–231)

A third rapid induction method involves not cataleptic eyelids, but cataleptic hands. Unlike the hand-clasp test above, the subject merely holds the palms of his or her hands together and is instructed as follows:

In a few moments your hands are going to become tightly stuck together, stuck so tightly that if you tried to take them apart you would not be able to do so. But you will not try. Now your hands are beginning to stick together they are stiffening, getting stiffer and stiffer, tighter and tighter. They are sticking together, sticking tight . . . tighter . . . still tighter. . . . THEY ARE STUCK TIGHT! Now your eyes are becoming heavy, heavier and heavier, very heavy. In a few moments when I tell you, you will be able to take your hands apart, but your eyes will be so completely stuck closed that you will not be able to open them. Now your eyes are sticking fast. They are tightly stuck. You can take your hands apart, but your eyes are completely stuck and you cannot open them. The more you try the harder it is. You can't open your eyes. (Usually by now the subject will have tried, but if he does not, challenge him.) You CAN'T. . . . Stop trying. DEEP ASLEEP! DEEP, DEEP ASLEEP! (As you say this apply gentle pressure with your fingers upon his eyes.) Just relax, you are going to go deeply asleep. You are sinking, sinking into a very deep sleep." (Weitzenhoffer, 1957, p. 302)

As with the second rapid induction procedure above, Weitzenhoffer used the physical ploy of eye-catalepsy in mass or group hypnosis. After some introductory remarks to the audience or group, the following verbal instructions were given:

I would like to ask you now to participate in an interesting experiment. Please place both of your feet flat on the floor. If you have any rings on your fingers it would be best for you to remove them and place them in your pocket or handbag. Now clasp your hands together like this (demonstrate) and keep them this way in your lap. Breathe deeply, just like I do (demonstrate). Keep breathing deeply and just listen to my voice. As you keep breathing deeply, imagine that every muscle in your body is relaxing, think of your entire body relaxing. As you do this your arms and hands are relaxing, your legs are relaxing, your entire body is becoming relaxed, very relaxed, and you keep breathing deeply, regularly. Now close your eyes. With your eyes closed keep breathing deeply and relaxing. Your arms and hands are beginning to feel heavy, your legs are growing heavy, your entire body is growing heavy, heavier and heavier, and you feel yourself becoming pleasantly drowsy, sleepy. . . . Just listen to my voice. Think of nothing but what I tell you. As you keep relaxing more and more and getting drowsier and sleepier you will find that your hands are becoming stuck together. In a little while they will be so tightly stuck that you will not be able to take them apart until I tell you that you can. But right now you just listen to my voice. Your hands are heavy, very heavy. Your arms are heavy, very heavy. Your legs and your feet are very heavy. Your entire body is very heavy, so-o heavy . . . and you are so drowsy, so-o sleepy. Just let yourself go to sleep. You feel yourself drifting away into a pleasant, restful sleep. You can hear everything I say and you will keep listening to me. Nothing will bother you. You will pay attention to nothing but my voice. You are comfortable and going into a deep sleep. And now as I speak to you, you will find that your hands are stuck together, that they are so completely stuck together that you cannot pull them apart. The more you will try the more completely stuck they will get. You will remain asleep, your eyes closed and as I count your hands will get still more tightly stuck together. One . . . they are sticking even more. Two . . . they are stuck tight. Three . . . tighter. Four . . . still tighter. Five. . . . They're stuck tight, you can't take them apart; *they're stuck fast and you can't take them apart.* Try. You CAN'T! You CAN'T. . . . Now stop trying, and just relax. You can now take your hands apart, but now your eyes are sticking, sticking more and more. *They are stuck fast and now you can't open your eyes, no matter how hard you try.* YOU CANNOT OPEN YOUR EYES, THEY ARE STUCK TIGHTLY CLOSED. . . . All right, now stop trying and relax. You are going deep asleep, deep asleep. You are sinking into a deep sound sleep. Deeper and deeper. (Weitzenhoffer, 1957, pp. 307–308)

Then, in a manner similar to the stage hypnotist, he told the group to hold their right arms above their heads, make a tight fist with the right hand, and keep the arm there until instructed otherwise. This challenge gives the group operator an idea of who is the most responsive and to whom further individual instructions should be given.

A variation of the above group technique involved counting. The audience is instructed to clasp their hands together, look at the operator's eyes, breathe deeply and rhythmically, and pay attention to the counted instructions.

One—As I count you will find yourself relaxing and soon you will fall asleep.

Two—You will find this a pleasant and interesting experience.

Three—As you relax more and more, a feeling of heaviness comes over you.

Four—You feel yourself getting pleasantly drowsy. Soon you will sleep.

Five—As you become increasingly sleepy and relaxed your hands are becoming stuck together.

Six—Your hands are sticking fast together.

Seven—Tight.

Eight—Tighter.

Nine—Your hands are stuck. You cannot take them apart. Try!

Ten—Stop trying and as you do so you go deeply asleep.

Eleven—If your eyes are not closed, close them.

Twelve—You go deeper and deeper asleep.

Thirteen—You are soundly asleep.

Fourteen—I may waken some of you later, but if I do, you will go right back to sleep as soon as I tell you to do so.

Fifteen—Sleep deeply . . . soundly. You will not awaken until I tell you. Stay as you are until I speak to you again. (Weitzenhoffer, 1957, p. 309)

One of the most notable things about these induction methods, which appear in Weitzenhoffer's book (1957), is that he emphasizes the testing of the depth of hypnosis achieved through a series of challenges. This "standardization" of the degree of hypnosis clearly marks his work throughout his career, and also marks him as an experimental investigator primarily. Although it is through much of his effort that we can better describe the degrees or levels of hypnosis that subjects experience, this same demand for rigorous standardization of procedures sets him apart from many of the practitioners of today, who often care more for end results than standardized approaches. However, it is the constant interplay of the search for end results and the demand for replicable procedures that has brought us to the level of understanding we have today.

THE SIXTIES

During the 1960s a number of books containing hypnotic induction techniques appeared (e.g., Elman, 1964; Erickson, Hershman & Secter, 1961; Hartland, 1966, 1971; Kroger, 1963—second edition, 1977; Meares, 1960; Teitelbaum, 1965). Most contained reiterations of the variety of techniques that I have outlined already. The Erickson, Hershman, Secter book (1961), for example, contained a number of printed transcripts of seminars given to physicians, dentists, and clinical psychologists throughout the country. The techniques contained therein have already been presented. The same is true of the Teitelbaum (1965) and the Hartland (1971) books.

Hartland's book is probably the best handbook of hypnotic inductions and hypnotherapeutic suggestions from Great Britain in this period. The author, *John Hartland,* was a president of the British Society of Medical and Dental Hypnosis, and life president of the Midlands Branch of that organization. In the Midlands he was affectionately known as "Dad," the members of that branch of the British Society being called "Dad's Army." His book presents the standard techniques verbatim, as well as many of his personalized verbalizations for clinical practice with a variety of general medical, psychosomatic, and psychiatric disorders. His approach was not an induction method, but a hypnotherapeutic procedure he labeled an "ego-strengthening technique." It bears a striking resemblence to the Coué technique of "Everyday in everyway, you are getting better and better." In its delivery, the ego-strengthening technique does resemble an induction procedure because special attention is paid to such "factors as rhythm, repetition, the interpolation of appropriate pauses, and the stressing of certain important words and phrases" (Hartland, 1971, p. 198). Here, then, according to Hartland, is a program of continuing hypnotherapeutic suggestions that makes use of the same voice characteristics and delivery as the formal induction, but allows the general practitioner to treat virtually any disorder, following any number of induction procedures.

Dave Elman's book (1964) also presents much of its material through transcripts of interactions the author had with a variety of subjects and students. He did present a quick induction, which he titled "the handshake technique" in which he tells a prospective subject that he will shake his or her hand three times. On the first shake, their eyes will get tired; on the second they will wish to close them; and on the third the eyelids will be closed. He then shakes the hand three times, counting each shake and accompanying each count with suggestions for the above behavior. This technique, which he states was developed in his early years of working with hypnosis, is, however, only a beginning and should be considered just that, a quick initial step in the process of hypnotization.

Meares's Dynamic Technique

Ainslie Meares, a psychiatrist in private practice in Australia and former president of the International Society for Clinical and Experimental Hypnosis, was born in 1910 and educated in Australia, receiving his M.D. degree in 1958. His prolific output includes 14 books and more than 60 articles on psychiatry. His book, *A System of Medical Hynosis* (1960), is based on work accomplished during the preceding two decades (see, for example, Meares,

1954a, b) and includes, along with a survey of the standard induction techniques, an extensive review of the applications of hypnosis and suggestive therapy in psychiatry and general medicine. His own orientation is psychodynamic and is clearly reflected in his comment: "Hypnosis involves the abandonment of ego control" (Meares, 1958, p. 28).

His own individual approach to the induction of hypnosis was deeply colored by his orientation, and was therefore labeled a dynamic technique. If ego control is lost, then it followed that the patient would make certain defensive maneuvers to protect against such loss. The essence of his approach was to incorporate these defensive ploys into the induction, so that no matter whether the patient cooperated or resisted, hypnosis would be accomplished. The reader will naturally notice the similarity in the basis of approach to the general client-centered views and to Erickson's utilization techniques, which were developed during the same time span. Meares felt that the older, standard induction procedures failed because they either attempted to overwhelm the ego defenses (e.g., the eye-fixation authorative approach) or to reduce them through monotony and/or step-by-step counting.

Since there is no specific verbal patter to accompany his technique, Meares explicated his method by example. If a relaxation induction is attempted and the patient responds, not by becoming immobile, but by restlessness, the therapist concentrates on the restlessness and verbally directs its movement throughout the body. The approach is switched from one of relaxation to one of movement, possibly even worked into an arm-levitation technique. If the patient then responds by not moving the arm, but by slumping and sleep, a sleep technique is put into play. Some patients, he tells us, will defend their ego by simulating the behavior suggested in the induction. This, too, is handled by allowing the patient his or her defense and proceeding as if he or she were not simulating. As subsequent sessions increase, the patients can progressively allow themselves to respond appropriately, rather than defensively, to the induction. "The patient should be merely helped and guided by the therapist, so that ego control is abandoned voluntarily" (Meares, 1958, p. 26). Thus, "the technique aims to turn the patient's defenses against him and use them in the hypnotic induction" (Meares, 1958, p. 24).

Kroger's Double-Bind and Feedback Techniques

William S. Kroger (b. April 14, 1906), a physician in California, received his M.D. degree from the Northwestern University School of Medicine in 1930. He is the author of several books on hypnosis and related topics and an early member of the Seminars on Hypnosis. In his *Clinical and Experimental Hypnosis* (1963/1977), he outlined the many induction techniques presented above, including the increasingly popular visualization variation of having the patient imagine a TV screen, the scene on which is used for a progressive relaxation induction. One unique technique appearing in this volume is called the "blood pressure method," but could well have been included under mechanical techniques. An ordinary blood pressure cuff is attached to the patient's arm and inflated. Then, as the air is released from the cuff, making a soft hissing noise, the operator suggests that the patient is becoming progressively more and more relaxed as he or she hears the escaping air, until by the time the air hissing stops he or she will be in a deep state of hypnosis.

For a period Kroger was involved in the ever-present search for an instrument that would induce hypnosis. In 1959 he and Sidney Schneider announced the Brain Wave Synchronizer (BWS) together with some rather impressive normative data. Developed between 1948 and 1957, the apparatus was essentially a photo-stimulator, the rate of which could be adjusted to match frequencies in the range of the electroencephalograph (0–50 Hz). The patient was placed before the BWS and told to "concentrate on the center of the instrument. When your eyes become tired and heavy, as they will, just let them close and feel yourself going deeper and deeper into a relaxed state" (Kroger & Schneider, 1959, p. 96). No further instructions were given. The patient could be either seated or reclining and the distance from the apparatus was not considered critical.

During a 1-year period, the machine was tested on 2500 patients, individually, and in groups ranging from 15 to 110 in number. Although no criteria of the degree of hypnosis achieved was presented, the authors reported that 80% of the subjects reached some level of hypnosis and that 50% became deeply hypnotized within the first 5 min. of watching the BWS. Such findings were extremely encouraging because of both the savings in time afforded by the instrument and the implications for understanding the brain mechanisms concomitant with hypnosis. For a while, in the late 1950s and early 1960s, a rash of such machines made their appearance in physicians' and dentists' offices across the United States. Some where photic stimulators, some audio, some combinations. A number of dentists used stereo-audio–generators, which the patient controlled through a series of rheostats allowing any mix of white noise or music.

The honeymoon of the BWS was short lived, however. In 1964 Hammer and Arkins did a well-controlled study of its effectiveness using compulsive response to a complicated "posthypnotic" suggestion. They tested the effectiveness of the BWS alone and with 15 min. of a relaxation hypnotic induction, and with two different frequency settings (11 and 30 flashes per second). The response to all combinations of the above were measured and it was shown that the BWS was "incapable of bringing about a trance state without the aid of verbal suggestion" (Hammer & Arkins, 1964, p. 86). It did appear that the use of alpha rhythm visual stimulation was more effective (with verbal suggestion) than the beta range (30Hz), but the efficacy of yet another mechanical device had been laid to rest.

However, the use of more modern technology in a visual image induction process continued and is represented by the "escalator technic," also in Kroger's book (1977). In this case, the patient visualizes standing at the top of a down escalator and as he or she visualizes moving down with the stairs suggestions are issued for progressive relaxation. Kroger actually presents this method for use in deepening an already existing condition; however, it can as easily be used as an initial approach. One of the deepening uses he makes of the escalator method is combining it with an autohypnosis technique. The autohypnosis method used is a simple counting to oneself and interspersing self-suggestions of progressive relaxation, heaviness, numbness, and fatigue with the numbers. Then, to deepen the condition, the patient is instructed to produce a visual image of an escalator and proceed as above.

Kroger and his present co-author, Fezler, stress the importance of conveying to the patient the notion that to learn to control complex symptom patterns during hypnosis the patient must first gain control over simple patterns. Thus Kroger and Fezler assist the patient to "build a 'control' system" by moving from the simple to the complex in a progressive fashion. First, however, they allay the patient's fears with the following information:

> Hypnosis is a process whereby, because you relax better, you hear better. And whenever your hear better, whatever I say to you or whatever you say to yourself will "sink in" better. If it sinks in better, you will respond better. This allows greater awareness. Since you are more aware, you naturally cannot be asleep. You go into a superalert state whenever you desire and you come out of it whenever you wish. You are always in control. You will remember everything you said during the induction procedure. There is never a time when you cannot get up off the couch, walk around the room or do whatever you wish. You can do anything during hypnosis that you can do out of it, but you can do it more effectively under hypnosis because your concentration is greater and there is less distraction. This means you can talk, dance, or take an examination while in hypnosis! (Kroger & Fezler, 1976, p. 29)

Kroger and Fezler's "Double-Bind" hypnotic induction technique is as follows:

> First you will look at a spot directly above your forehead. Pick a spot on the ceiling just above your hairline. Keep staring at it. As you keep staring at it the first sensation that you will learn how to control is that of *heaviness*. Your lids are getting *very, very heavy*. Getting *heavier* and *heavier*. Your eyes are beginning to blink. (If the patient's eyes blink or the individual swallows one can say "see you just blinked" or swallowed, as the case may be. These act as reinforcers to suggest that the patient is doing fine.) Your eyes are blinking and you just swallowed, that's a good sign that you are going deeper and deeper relaxed. And now at the count of 3 if you *really* wish to gain mastery and control over your symptom (one can mention whatever the symptom may be) you will gently control the closing of your lids. At this point you will notice that you want to close your lids because they are getting very, very tired. Promptly, precisely and exactly at the count of 3 you will close your lids, not because you have to but because you really want to. Don't close your lids too rapidly, but

close them gently at the count of 3. Your eyes are closing, lids are closing *tighter* and *tighter* together. And I really want you to feel that *tightness,* good, this is still another sensation that you are gaining control over.

Now let your eyeballs roll up into the back of your head. (At this point the operator can place his thumb and forefinger gently over the forehead just above the eyes.) Now let the eyeballs roll back down into their normal position. And as they return to their normal position you will notice that your lids are *stuck* even *tighter* and *tighter* together. (Here the operator can lightly place his thumb and forefinger over each eyelid to reinforce the suggestion.)

Now I'd like to have you imagine that your entire body from your head to your toes is becoming very, very relaxed. However, your body will not relax just because you tell it to do so. Rather, it will only relax if you pair this suggestion with the memory which once produced the desired response. Perhaps it would be nice if you would imagine yourself taking a soothing warm bath. You are relaxing *deeper* and *deeper.* And the more vividly that you can see *all* the familiar sights of your own bathroom, the deeper relaxed you will go. And the more vividly that you can see yourself in your own bathtub, the deeper relaxed you will go. And the more vividly that you feel the imaginary warm water up to your armpits, the deeper relaxed you will go. You are doing fine, just fine. Your breathing is getting slower, deeper, more regular, slower, deeper and more regular. (It is at this point the patient needs reinforcement because he is wondering how he is doing.)

Now if you *really* wish to go deeper, and gain more mastery over yourself so that *you* can control the removal of your symptoms you will first learn how to raise your arm in a controlled fashion. Listen very carefully for the following instructions. Carry these out to the best of your ability. The better you control the raising of your arm the better you will be able to control your symptom. (This heightens motivation.) You may raise either your right arm or your left arm, whichever arm you choose. But raise it in the following fashion (the patient thinks he has been given a choice, but actually this double-bind remark gives him no choice but to raise one arm or the other). Here are the instructions for the raising of your arm. Listen carefully for the instructions. Raise either your right arm or your left arm about 2 or 3 inches at a time and then pause 30 or 40 seconds. During this pause perhaps you might be willing to suggest that as your arm lifts higher and higher, with each cogwheel-like movement it will get lighter and lighter—another sensation that you are controlling. And the lighter your arm gets as it rises, the deeper relaxed you will go. You will raise your arm at the count of 3, not because you have to but because you really want to! Now do not raise it too rapidly (another double bind) 1,2,3, slowly the arm is lifting, lifting, lifting, lifting, and as it lifts higher and higher with each movement notice how your arm is getting lighter and lighter. And as the arm gets lighter and lighter notice how your state of relaxation is getting deeper and deeper. You are doing fine.

Your breathing is getting slower, deeper, more regular. (At this point the arm is allowed to slowly rise to a 75-degree angle. The patient does not realize the operator is one up and the subject in reality is one down. Since the former is setting the rules of the game, the patient does not know what to expect.

However, since he has begun to notice certain feeling states occurring, he attributes these to the suggestions of the operator. Little does he realize that *he* is producing them.)

As your arm is now approaching a straight, vertical, perpendicular position you will notice that you can develop still another sensation, that of *stiffness*. Your arm is now lifting higher and higher to where your fingers, hand, forearm, and arm are all stretched straight toward the ceiling. Paradoxically, you will notice that the *stiffer* your arm gets from the fingers to the hand, to the wrist, to the elbow to the shoulder, the *deeper relaxed* you will go. Your arm is now stiff, very rigid, like a bar of steel from the fingertips down to the elbow to the shoulder. (At this point no challenges are issued such as "you can't bend your arm," rather it is suggested that the stiffer the arm gets the deeper relaxed the patient will be and the better he will be able to control the symptom. Here the operator can gently stroke the outstretched arm from the fingers to the shoulder. Utilizing the ideosensory response with an ideomotor response produces a synergistic effect. The stroking must be performed very lightly, because it is precisely at this point that the arm develops catalepsy.) Notice the stiffness of your outstretched arm. You are doing fine.

Now, if you wish to control other sensations and gain still more mastery over your symptom, listen very carefully to the following suggestions. At the count of 3 you will slowly, ever so slowly, about an inch or two at a time allow your arm to fall to your side and with each 2 inches or so that it falls, your arm will become as limp as a wet noodle. It will become limper and limper as it slowly drops to your side. Is it not surprising how many sensations that you are gaining control over? Also, is it not remarkable how many sensations are built into the body? Now don't let the arm drop too rapidly (another double-bind remark). Allow it to drop very, very *slowly*. And with each motion that your arm moves downward, perhaps, you might be willing to suggest to yourself that when your arm returns to your side or touches any part of your body, that will be a cue or signal for every *muscle* and every *fiber* in your body to develop complete relaxation. (Notice how we are working within the framework of the patient's own personality in a permissive manner even though the technic is authoritative in nature). Now as your arm is about to reach your side or touch the chair (or couch) perhaps you could allow that to be a cue for every muscle in your body to relax completely. (The arm now falls limply to the side. At this point it is wise to use a positive reinforcing maneuver such as lifting the arm gently between the forefinger and thumb at the patient's wrist and letting the arm slip from between the operator's fingers. If the patient is male, one can insert the middle finger under the sleeve and lift the arm up about 6 or 8 inches and allow it to slip away so that it drops with a thud.)

Now you are in a very deep state of relaxation and I am going to give you several suggestions for terminating it. One route you will be able to control. The other route will be one that I can use, provided and if it is with your permission. Any time that I touch you on your right shoulder with your permission you will promptly close your eyes, let your eyeballs roll up into the back of your head (the operator can lightly touch the lids and the forehead above the eyes with his thumb and forefinger). You will let your eyeballs roll up into the back of your head to prevent yourself from falling asleep. As you know, for many individuals lid closure can trigger the onset of sleep. We want to trigger the onset of super-alertness! Next you will let the eyeballs roll back down into their normal position and you will quickly drop into a deep state of relaxation.

A touch on the left shoulder will be the signal for you to open your eyes, feeling wonderful, refreshed, relaxed. Notice that at no time did I use the words sleep, trance, or unconsciousness. (This is emphasized again and again as many patients will state, "Doctor, I know I wasn't hypnotized, I heard everything you said." This makes it clear to the patient that hypnosis is not a sleep state.) Now you can put yourself into this deep, meditative, self-reflective, contemplative state by yourself. (A touch on the left shoulder is the one which enables the patient to open his eyes. A touch on the right is the cue to enter into hypnosis.) In many thousands of inductions using the above technics we have never had a patient fail to open his eyes. (Kroger & Fezler, 1976, pp. 30–32)

Once again, toward the end of the above induction, we note the mix of suggestions beyond simple induction with the induction proper.

Kroger and Fezler are also aware that it is of value to both the patient and the practitioner for the former to be able to engage in the hypnotic process without the presence of the latter. Not only does the ability to self-hypnotize build confidence in the patient of his or her own abilities to cope with difficulties, but it is also a time-saving device in an overall treatment program. Here is their "Feedback" technique for autohypnosis:

It has been stated that one picture is worth a thousand words. For instance, if you say, "I will be confident," the words must be implemented by a picture of yourself as the confident person you want to be. If you keep fortifying this image with appropriate suggestions, eventually these mental impressions will give rise to the confident feelings that you seek.

I know that this technic seems simple, but if you keep implanting positive images into your mind, they will become a part of your personality. Do not expect immediate results when you begin to use autohypnosis and don't ask "what's wrong?" All you have to do to attain autohypnosis is to use what we call sensory or visual-imagery conditioning. This is an old technic that has been the basis for many different types of prayer.

Anyone can learn and practice autohypnosis, but to achieve the best results you must carefully consider what you wish to accomplish. Through self-exploration you can establish reasonable goals for improvement. Don't think that you have to be "out of this world" to be in autohypnosis. This idea has been produced by novels, comic strips and motion pictures. Actually, you will only be in a very deep state of relaxation and concentration. You may develop a feeling of detachment or you may experience a very pleasant sinking feeling, or you may get a feeling of peace and serenity. At times you may not even feel a definite change; it may just seem as if you had your eyes closed and heard everything at all times. However, if you aim for a deeply relaxed state, you will reach it.

After you are satisfied that you have achieved autohypnosis you may give yourself further suggestions to deepen it if you wish. Also, remember that it is not too important to reach a deep state on your initial attempts. Just realize that you are trying to establish a conditioned response which will cause you to react instantly to any cue that you wish to use. Through frequent repetition, the cue will bring on the autohypnosis.

During every attempt to achieve autohypnosis, visualize yourself going *deeper* and *deeper*. At first you may experience some difficulty, but as you stick to it you will be able to picture yourself deeply *relaxed*. Always use the visual imagery techniques whether or not you think you are under hypnosis. The images will become clear as you constantly repeat the appropriate suggestions. As you continue to work with yourself, you will develop confidence in giving yourself suggestions. To be effective, they cannot be given in a hesitant manner but with enthusiasm and anticipation. If you follow these instructions, you will see results of your suggestions and efforts.

When you practice this on your own at home, begin by selecting a quiet place and arrange to spend an uninterrupted 10 minutes three times a day practicing there. Seat yourself in a comfortable chair with your hands resting in your lap and your feet on the floor, or recline in the position in which you are now, fix your eyes on a spot on the ceiling above eye level.

Then begin counting to yourself slowly from 1 to 10. Direct your attention to your eyelids and, between numbers, tell yourself repeatedly that your eyelids are getting *very, very heavy,* and that your eyes are getting *very, very tired.* Again and again say: "My lids are getting *heavier* and *heavier*. I feel my lids getting so *heavy,* and the *heavier* they get, the *deeper relaxed* I will become, and the better able I will be to follow all suggestions I give myself. My lids are getting *very heavy*. It will feel so good to close my eyes."

By the time you count to 2, think of enough suggestions like the ones just mentioned so that you actually feel the heaviness of your eyelids. When you are sure that your lids are indeed heavy, count to 3 and let your eyes roll up into the back of your head for a few seconds. Then say, "My lids are now locked so tight that I doubt very much that I can open them. My lids shut tighter and tighter and tighter, and as my lids lock tight, I begin to feel a nice, calm, soothing, relaxed feeling beginning in my toes, moving into my legs and into my thighs as I keep counting. It's the same feeling that I have in my jaws when my dentist injects Novocaine into them; the same feeling that I have when I fall asleep on my arm; the same feeling that I have when I sit too long in one position; the identical feeling that I would have in my legs if I sat cross-legged on them for very long. A numb, wooden feeling starting in my toes is beginning to move up, up, up from my toes into my legs."

Next, count 4 and say, "By the time I have counted to 5, my legs from my toes to my thighs will be just as heavy as lead. I can feel my legs relaxing from my toes to my thighs. I can feel them getting *heavier* and *heavier* and *heavier . . .* 5. They are so *heavy* now that I don't think I can move them." Then double back for repetition. "My eyelids are locked *tight,* so *tight* that I don't believe I can open them. My legs from my toes to my thighs are completely *relaxed.*"

Each time you retrace these autosuggestions, you stamp in the learned response pattern.

You continue in this way, "By the time I have counted to 6 and 7, my fingers, hands and arms will be very, very *heavy*. I am beginning to feel that same numbness moving up from my fingers to my shoulders. A *heavy,* detached feeling is moving up from my fingers to my hand, to my wrist, past my elbows, up to my arm, to my shoulder. Both my arms, from my hands to my shoulders, are getting very numb—a heavy woodlike numbness. When I have counted to 7, my arms will be just as *heavy* and relaxed as my eyelids, as numb as my legs are now, as if I have been sleeping on them."

Don't worry if you forget the exact words. The exact words are far less important than the effect that you are trying to achieve: a feeling of numbness all the way from the fingertips to the wrist, to the elbow, to the shoulder, to the neck. In practice, this may be a bit more difficult to accomplish in the first few sessions at home, but the feeling will come faster in subsequent attempts. It is most important that you never become discouraged and that you not tire yourself by spending more than 30 minutes a day in practice.

When you finally reach the point where, by the count of 7, your limbs are sufficiently relaxed, you repeat again all the suggestions you have given yourself, adding: "My legs are so *heavy* that I don't believe I can move them. My eyes are locked so tight that I doubt that I can open them. My arms are so *heavy* that I cannot lift them, and, by the time I have counted from 7 to 8, my trunk will be *relaxed*."

Now go back to the lids, legs, and arms. Then say, "By the time I count from 8 to 9, my chest will have relaxed, too. With every breath I take, I can just feel myself going *deeper* and *deeper* into a *relaxed* state. My back and abdomen are getting very, very *numb*. I can feel the muscles in my chest *relaxing* . . . 8. My entire body, from my neck down, is *relaxed* . . . 9. I am completely *relaxed*. I can't open my eyes. I can't move my legs. I can't move my arms. I feel my whole body *relaxed,* thoroughly and deeply. It is so refreshing to remain in this deep, quiet state."

"I will now relax my neck and head, so that, at the count of 10, I will be completely relaxed from my head to my toes. I can feel that with every breath I take I am becoming calmer and *deeper relaxed* . . . *deeper* and *deeper relaxed* . . . into a calm, soothing, *refreshing* state. Everything is just getting more and more *relaxed*. I feel as if I am floating away . . . falling *deeper* and *deeper* . . . not asleep, but just thoroughly relaxed . . . 10. I am completely relaxed. My eyes and limbs are as heavy as lead. My entire body feels numb, heavy, woodenlike, as I go *deeper* and *deeper*."

By picturing yourself deeply *relaxed* in your mind's eye, you will go *deeper*. If you can imagine yourself in your own bed comfortably *relaxed,* this can be a stimulus for *deepening* the relaxation. If you think of this again and again, you set in motion a response that ultimately will allow you to achieve a *profound* state of relaxation. As you become more proficient with autohypnosis, your practice sessions become shorter until finally the mere blinking and closing of the eyes will trigger hypnosis. Rapidity with which autohypnosis can be induced increases with practice.

It is well to remember that you can deepen the autohypnosis by your own efforts and that the depth depends largely on how well you follow the principles that you are learning. It also is most important to have the proper frame of mind if you wish to achieve effective autohypnosis. If you approach it with a "prove-it-to-me" attitude, nothing will happen. To attain ultimate success, self-confidence and persistence are necessary! (Kroger & Fezler, 1976, pp. 35–37)

Other Methods

It was inevitable with the increasing literature on Skinnerian-type behavior modification programs that such a stepwise "shaping" of hypnotic behavior would occur. In 1959 *G. R. Pascal* and *H. C. Salzberg* presented such a systematic approach. There was really nothing new in what they asked of or suggested to the subject. What was innovative was the well-planned reinforcement for incremental behaviors that increasingly approached the ultimate end behavior. Each step toward a fully hypnotized condition was suggested and reinforced before moving on to the next. Thus the subject's behavior was shaped step-by-step to hypnosis through vocal reinforcement by the operator for successfully carrying out each suggested behavior.

Initially, time is spent with the subject allaying any anxieties or fears and informing the subject that hypnosis is a set of behaviors best learned by remaining relaxed and attending to the instructions. The following sequence of incremental behaviors is then presented and reinforced.

1. *Kohnstamm Phenomenon.* The subject presses his or her arm against a wall, then steps away from the wall and relaxes the arm. The arm rises out from the side of the body in an ideomotor fashion.

2. *Body Sway.* Suggestions for falling backwards are given.

3. *Breathing Coordinated Relaxation.* The subject now lies on a couch and is instructed in the process of relaxation by feeling tension when the breath is held and relaxation when it is expelled.

4. *Total Relaxation.* Suggestions for muscle relaxation and generally effortless bodily function are given.

5. *Arm Levitation.* Following suggestions for left arm analgesia and lightness, suggestions for arm levitation are given. The arm is stopped in mid-air and tested for analgesia.

6. *Continued Arm Levitation.* Suggestions for continued movement of the arm to the face are coupled with suggestions for progressively deeper and deeper relaxation and sleep.

7. *Active Trance Behavior.* The subject is now instructed to sit up, open the eyes while remaining in the trance, and perform several tasks (draw a grammar school picture and write a number).

8. *Amnesia*. Posthypnotic amnesia is suggested for the act of drawing and writing, with the cue phrase for the recall of the number being: "What's the number?"

9. *Posthypnotic Suggestion*. The subject is told that when the operator lights a cigarette, after trance termination, he or she will remove his or her shoe to remove pebbles from inside. Amnesia for this suggestion was also invoked. This procedure is conveyed with the subject lying on the couch again.

10. *Termination*. Hypnosis is terminated by a simple 1–10 counting routine, after which the two posthypnotic suggestions are tested.

According to the authors, 52% of their subjects were able to achieve a "somnambulistic trance" as indicated by responses to the posthypnotic item, while 62% responded to the posthypnotic amnesia. These data were replicated by Giles (1962), who also found a high percentage of subjects (55.2%) able to achieve "deep hypnosis." Thus what we have here is not a new technique, as I indicated at the outset of this discussion, but a more efficient format of presenting various hypnotic suggestions to achieve enhanced response to both induction and subsequent suggestions. No doubt additional use of the general principles of behavior shaping will continue to appear in the literature, as soon as practitioners become personally convinced of its efficacy.

A number of the older methods continued to be reported during the sixth decade. *Dietrich Langen,* the late professor of the University of Tübingen (b. Nov. 16, 1913; d. Mar. 20, 1980), combined the older autogenic training with the still older Eastern visual fixation to achieve hypnosis. He called the technique "Graduated Active Hypnosis." The first two steps of the method were the first two exercises from Schultz's training method—self-suggested heaviness and warmth. These are practiced daily for 1 to 2 min. each. At first the patient concentrates on the thought, "My right arm is heavy," then moves successively to, "Both arms are heavy; both arms and legs are heavy; the whole body is heavy; [and finally] peace—heaviness" (Langen, 1965/ 1966, p. 30). The same progressive approach is used with the warmth exercise. Preceding each of the following with "peace—heaviness," the patient concentrates on: "Right arm quite warm; both arms are warm; both arms and legs are warm" (Langen, 1965/1966, p. 30). When these exercises have been mastered, the patient is able to accomplish both the relaxation and warmth within 1 min. by thinking, "Peace—heaviness—warmth."

At this point Langen leaves Schultz's method and introduces an eye-fixation exercise based on Eastern meditative practices. The patient is instructed to fixate his or her vision on the operator's fingertips held about 20 cm. in front of and above the horizontal visual plane. With or without verbal suggestions, patients enter hypnosis, signaled by tiredness that becomes progressively deeper and deeper. Although standard measures can be applied, Langen preferred not and, in fact, avoided telling the patient anything that might color expectations. Thus Graduated Active Hypnosis is achieved primarily through autosuggestion, after which therapeutic suggestions can be introduced. To terminate the condition, the patient merely reverses the original instructions and concentrates on, "Arms strong—breathe deeply—eyes open," as in the autogenic training method of arousal.

Meanwhile, *Anatol Milechnin* of Uruguay was writing of producing hypnosis through a "natural procedure." In a series of articles (Milechnin, 1964a,b; Milechnin, 1965a,b,c; Solovey & Milechnin, 1957) he presented the concept that an understanding and accepting attitude was basic to "positive" hypnosis, while the authoritarian attitudes of most of the older inductions lead to "negative" hypnosis. He likened the natural procedure to a caring, soothing, mothering attitude, as one might encounter when a mother sings softly and lullingly to a baby. Thus the approach is a "mother hypnosis," which is induced by a concerted effort to avoid any mention of the word hypnosis in the induction. Instead, the technique is to present the condition to adults as a state of relaxation, nothing more. Induction, therefore, is accomplished with continuing, soothing verbalizations enjoining the patient to relax and "loosen up" the musculature so that no tension remains. He also intersperses long (5 min.) periods of silence on the part of the operator among the soothing, mothering verbalizations: "Go on relaxing . . . you are comfortable . . . your muscles are all relaxed . . . relax further . . . and enjoy this condition . . . in a few minutes I will speak to you again" (Milechnin, 1964b, p. 12).

Milechnin felt that the process of creating "positive" hypnosis was one of stimulating "stabilizing emotions," and he noted four factors involved: (a) the need on the part of the patient for "stimulating stabilizing emotions," (b) adequate rapport between patient and practitioner, (c) the application of soft tactile stimuli, and (d) vocal stimuli. With children, his methods used a soft, low voice and gentle stroking of the back or hands, with a minimum of the former. In fact, he appears to prefer a nonverbal induction modeled on that used by *Brother Vitricio* of Brazil in producing "Lethargia" in the 1950s. Brother Vitricio placed one hand on the patient's sternum and the other on the patient's sixth or seventh thoracic vertebrae and gently compressed the thorax in rhythm with the patient's breathing. At the same time the patient is gently swayed backward and forward through alternating pressures from the two hands. Slowly the hand on the back is moved up the spinal column to about the third or fourth cervical vertebrae until the patient's head droops forward, indicating the onset of "lethargia." Milechnin, who notes that quite similar procedures are used by religious cults such as the Macumbas to induce similar conditions (see also the section on Voodoo in this chapter), uses the same method, but sways his patients sidewards instead of backward and forward. As the swaying continues, the patient's head soon droops flaccidly, indicating the onset of hypnosis (Milechnin, 1964a).

Milechnin's preference for nonverbal techniques appears to stem from his conviction that the meaning of the words used in induction procedures has far less value than the attitudes and emotionality conveyed by whatever process is employed in induction. He cites, for example, the work by Sears and Talcott (1958) in which they hypnotized 30% of their subjects with verbal patters spoken in languages foreign to them. Comprehension of the meaning of the words used in verbal induction methods may be unnecessary for some subjects.

Like others, Milechnin recognized the problems of the resistant or refractory patient. His solution was always individualized, constructed to fit the particular patient and the particular situation. In some instances, he was quite comfortable with "well-meaning deceit," as in the technique used by Casullo Devoto (see Milechnin, 1965b), with fearful children in the dental office; in others, he saw the value of an authoritarian approach. Devoto informed the young patient that he had some special water (see Chapters 1 and 2), which removed the sensation of pain wherever it was applied. He then sprayed some ethyl chloride on the child's hand and pricked it with a needle to prove the veracity of his statement. From there on, a lulling, relaxing induction is carried out, including having the child wash his or her mouth out with water, which makes the gums and teeth "analgesic."

Milechnin also concerned himself with the attributes of the general environment in which hypnosis was to occur. He, like many before him, advocated a quiet environment, clean, decorated in soft colors, and devoid of metallic furniture and instruments and distributing sounds, lights, and odors. He considered 15°C to be optimal and after lunch to be preferred. Like Taplin before him (see Chapter 5), he felt that the operator's hands should be warm, not cold, and should convey comfort and tranquility to the patient. In fact, one of his methods for terminating the hypnosis was by placing a cold object on the patient's forehead.

Milechnin felt that the optimal method for inducing "the positive hypnotic emotional state" was through relaxation, particularly the relaxation of the voluntary musculature. Stabilizing emotions are accompanied by muscular relaxation; therefore, the achievement of muscular relaxation would lead directly to a stabilizing emotional effect. The verbal patter to accomplish this effect is as follows:

Be comfortable . . . as comfortable as you can . . . choose the most comfortable position . . . the position in which you feel better. . . .

Loosen the muscles of your neck . . . relax . . . loosen the muscles of your face . . . of your forehead . . . let all the muscles of your face relax . . . be nicely relaxed. . . . Relax the muscles of your arms, and let them repose . . . comfortably relaxed . . . the muscles of your legs . . . let all your body relax. . . .

And while the body is resting comfortably . . . soft . . . loosened-up . . . let your mind also rest tranquilly . . . relax all your body and enjoy this state . . . this relaxed state . . . comfortable . . . and very pleasant. . . .

You can relax still more . . . and enter a deeper repose . . . rest more and more deeply. (Milechnin, 1964b, p. 11)

What is interesting about Milechnin's approach is not the verbalizations used—they are standard fare—but the emphasis on relaxation not hypnosis. Because of the many negative connotations that have accrued to the word hypnosis during the centuries of its use, many practitioners avoid the term and label their process relaxation instead. Evans (1967) tested the efficiency of using such an approach with approximately 300 subjects during a 5-year period. His studies asked the question: "Is it possible, in an experimental setting, to induce deep hypnosis without S's awareness or knowledge that the experimental procedure involves hypnosis?" (Evans, 1967, p. 73). Evans informed the subjects that he was investigating the "effects of relaxation on behavior" and that his or her main task was to relax completely. Then an eye-fixation, relaxation induction procedure was administered while the subject lay on a couch staring at a spot on the wall trying to make his or her mind go blank. Many of the instructions were tied to the breathing rate and rhythm of the subject, and such visual images as a pendulum swinging in time to the inhalations and exhalations. Deepening the relaxation was accomplished by counting slowly from 1 to 21 or 31.

After 30 min. of such instructions, Evans administered usual hypnosis challenges such as arm rigidities, visual and auditory hallucinations, illusions, amnesias, anesthesias, and age-regression to assess the success of his technique. Two important findings were evident: (a) a rating scale measure of the depth of "hypnosis" achieved echoed the usual distribution of depth found in groups of subjects who have received a traditional hypnotic induction; and (b) "At least half of the Ss, even under some pressure, did not seem to recognize that an attempt had been made to induce hypnosis" (Evans, 1967, p. 79). Thus relaxation instructions, without mention of hypnosis, elicited the same responses, in the same distribution format, as hypnotic induction instructions; and were not recognized as inducing hypnosis.

Evans's experimental work gives practitioners yet another way (He called it an "indirect induction.") of inducing hypnosis without the impediments of negative connotations regarding hypnosis, and adds to the data base implying that relaxation is the basis of hypnosis (see Edmonston, 1981).

Julio Dittborn, from the University of Chile, offered a different approach (1968), although he related it to Evans's method in that neither required informing the subject that the intent of the procedure was hypnosis. Although presented as an excellent technique for the selection of hypnotic subjects, the author vascillates between referring to the method as a selection procedure and an induction procedure. His data show that all of the subjects who perform the task adequately are excellent subjects by more standard measurement means. However, it is clear that the method is inductive also.

The subject is seated in a chair, given a piece of paper and a pencil, and instructed:

Now we are going to use a method of inducing sleep . . . now you are going to just write down in lines across a page the word SLEEP again and again—right where you are, sitting in the chair. As you write the word SLEEP over and over again, you will feel yourself getting sleepier and sleepier . . . more and more sleepy. Just let this feeling come over you . . . don't resist it . . . but don't try to bring it about either. Just let it happen. After you enter sleep, I may speak to you. This will not wake you up. You will remain sleepy even when hearing my questions and answering them. (Ask S to repeat the instructions to be sure he understands them.) Let's start now. (Dittborn, 1968, p. 54)

Subjects who respond well to this procedure do so before completing a single page, and, if Dittborn's examples are representative, do not complete more than about 10 lines.

Following the deterioration of writing (linearity is lost, the writing becomes faint and distorted), 2 min. of suggestions for relaxation and sleep are given. If the procedure is being used to select hypnotic subjects, a number of challenges are then issued, visual images, hallucinations, and so forth; otherwise, one could proceed to therapeutic or experimental endeavors. Termination of this sleep–relaxation–hypnosis condition is accomplished by the operator informing the subject that he will count backwards from five to one to arouse him or her. The operator then waits for 2 min. before beginning the count, a touch that we have seldom seen in most de-induction procedures.

Still the search for more physiologic and/or electromechanical methods continues. Our European colleagues appear a bit more interested in such pursuits, however, as exemplified by Baykushev's discussion of the hyperventilation technique (1969). Baykushev, from the I. P. Pavlov Medical Institute in Plovdiv, Bulgaria, instructs his reclining patients to breathe deeply at the rate of 15 or 16 Hz. As the patient hyperventilates at this rate, suggestions predicting the various physiological changes the patient is experiencing are given, thus giving the patient the impression that these responses are due to the hypnosis, which he has been informed is being induced. As the feelings of giddiness, tingling, and tetany appear, the operator offers suggestions that lead to a hypnotic condition. Using eye-closure and hypnotonia or a waxy flexibility of the extremities as criteria, he reports that only 2 of 56 neurotic patients failed to respond positively to this type of induction procedure.

The Eastern Europeans have shown the most interest in mechanical, particularly electrical, means of inducing hypnosis, and their interest continues in what Hall (1973) has called electrosleep and Barabasz (1976) called cerebral electrotherapy (CET). The process was first used by Livenstsev at the First Moscow Medical Institute in 1949, and was again reported at two International Symposia held in Graz, Austria in 1966 and 1969. The primary purpose of the procedure is direct treatment of anxieties, insomnias, and depression, but it has been reported to be successful in assisting hypnotic induction.

Electrodes are applied to the supraorbital foramina and either the occiput or mastoid process, and a mild pulsating current is passed between them

(0.1–0.25 MA, 10–40 V). The pulses are of 0.25–1 msec duration at a frequency of 10–100 Hz. The voltage is individually selected by adjustment until the patient reports a "tingling" at the electrode positions (generally between 12 and 20 V). With the patient lying down, the "tingling" treatment is administered for 1 to 3 hr. daily (5 or 6 times per week) for up to 50 treatments.

According to Hall (1973), there are "virtually no contraindications" to the treatment, unlike with the earlier Japanese models (see below). When used as a adjunct to hypnosis, the procedure is combined with the usual, relaxation suggestive induction verbalizations. Barabasz (1976) found the procedure, when coupled with hypnosis per se, to be a "powerful variable" in the treatment of insomnia in depressed patients. Devices for electrosleep, or as Hall labeled it, electrohypnosis, are produced by Medexport (Moscow); Ectron Ltd., Letchworth (UK); F. Lewis & Co., Island House, Llanbadoc, Usk, Monmouthshire (UK); Tri-tonics, P.O. Box 638, Euless, Texas 76039; and Lafayette Instruments in Pennsylvania.

Meanwhile, another eastern European was investigating an electrical device for facilitating hypnotic induction. According to A. Spencer Paterson, *Ferenc Andras Völgyesi,* of Budapest, was one of the pioneers in the objective study of hypnotic phenomena. He was, until the time of his death in 1978, one of a handful of active scientists who had studied with Pavlov. Needless to say, he was greatly influenced by the latter in both his work and his theorizing and concentrated most of his efforts on nervous-system–hypnosis explanations of the phenomena. Perhaps even more prominent in his works was the perceived connection between "animal hypnosis" and similar behavior in the human. Here Völgyesi was heavily influenced by the work of W. Preyer (1841–1897), then Professor of Biology at Jena and Berlin, who in turn based much of his work in animal hypnosis on previous studies of Johann Nepomuk Zermak (1828–1873) at Leipzig. The beginnings of these works Völgyesi attributed to Father Kircher's 17th century magnetizing of a common fowl. Völgyesi's extraordinary work with crustacea, snakes, frogs, owls, buzzards, peacocks, magpies, storks, chickens, crocodiles, lions, and chimpanzees is detailed, both verbally and pictorially, in *Hypnosis in Man and Animals,* and formed much of the basis for his work with human patients.

Born February 21, 1895 in Budapest, Völgyesi first became interested in hypnosis as a schoolboy in 1909 when he witnessed a performance at a showbooth. After attending innumerable such demonstrations, he tried it himself and was so successful that it was three days before anyone could awaken his first (female) subject, and only then by a Dr. S. Sebok, a "magnetizer" from the Budapest Voluntary Rescue Society. As a medical student in 1911, he formed the Freiwillige Ujpest Rakospaloter Rettunggesellschaft for the study of hypnotic phenomena from both a laboratory and a clinical perspective. A hiatus in his hypnotic work occurred during the war years (1912–1914), but shortly thereafter (1918) he opened private practice in Budapest and continued his inquiries into hypnosis. From 1917 (the year of his medical degree) through 1963, he treated 62,000 patients with hypnosis (3800 of which were reported in his 1920 book, *Hypnose,* using hypno-therapeutic suggestions on 800,000 occasions!) According to Dr. Völgyesi, the records of all of these individual incidences have been carefully preserved.

For 33 years (1917–1950), Völgyesi remained convinced that verbal suggestion alone was sufficient to induce hypnosis. However, the more he considered the mechanical induction devices such as Luys's revolving mirrors, Joire's compass-like instrument, Ochorowitz's and Gessmann's hypnoscope, Stokvis's color contrasting cards, and Wetterstrand's Braidian-like use of a silver spoon to reflect a candle's light into the eyes of the patient (much like the priest described in the *Leiden Papyrus*), the more he questioned the power of words alone to hold the attention of Pavlov's first and second signal system analyzers (Edmonston, 1967, 1981). Thus he developed the "Faraday-Hand," which, along with the laying-on-of-hands on the patient's forehead, eyes, and face, he used for decades in his practice.

The "Faraday-Hand" is a device consisting of two electrodes through which an electrical current is passed to the patient. Although Paul Ranschburg (also of Budapest) placed the electrodes on the temples of the patient, Völgyesi preferred to have the patient hold one electrode in the left hand while he held the other in his left. The circuit was completed when he placed his right hand on the patient's forehead, neck, and/or eyes, producing a "stimulating effect" (see Figure 6.1). The power supply for the device was a standard wall plug (we must assume the standard 220 V European supply). Power was fed through a Wagner-Hammer rheostat so that the strength of the current could be regulated so that it was not uncomfortable or injurious "to the doctor." "The strength of the current is about 1 to 1.5, sometimes 2 to 2.2 milliamps, of 40 to 50/65 volts and 20 to 30 cycles" (Völgyesi, 1966, p. 154). Often the application of the current alone was sufficient for hypnotherapeutic treatment, although Vögyesi recognized that the light on the apparatus and the hum of the rheostat contributed to the effect.

At times he applied the electrode he held directly to various muscles and nerves in the head and neck region, creating specific and intense sensations and involuntary motor movements (see Figure 6.1). But in general he used a mild current, which, he stated, induces passivity (akin in his thinking, I suspect, to the passivity noted in "animal hypnosis"). Once the passivity had been achieved, Völgyesi turned to verbal suggestions. Often they were intermixed, as is the prevalent situation today. Here, for example, is a segment of the latter:

> As your head drops forward, you close your eyes . . . you feel pleasant numbness, your limbs are relaxed, the excitement is over . . . you breath deeply, regularly, you do not mind what I do to you . . . you will be as you were before you were ill . . . you feel absolutely fine . . . free in every part of your being . . . you can only be influenced for good, you feel a kindly warmth, your heart beats peacefully . . . the pain has gone . . . your organism follows

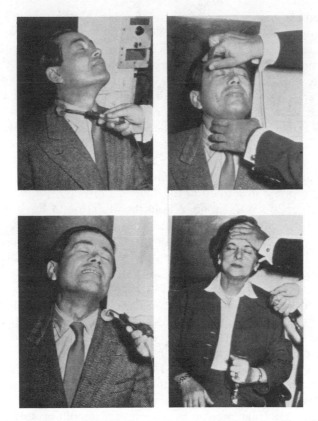

Figure 6.1. Völgyesi's Faraday-Hand, showing various methods of application. (From Völgyesi, *Hypnosis of Men and Animals*. Copyright 1966, Williams & Wilkins Co., Baltimore. Reprinted by permission.)

> my instructions exactly . . . you are your own master in every respect . . . you are now a new person . . . cheerful . . . on the brink of recovery . . . your willpower is increased, etc. (Völgyesi, 1938/1966, p. 156)

At times he merely states: "Your eyes are closed, you breathe deeply" and went on to curative suggestions. Meanwhile, there was a heavy emphasis on the hands-on effect, as in the following:

> We sometimes support the patient's forehead with our left palm and gently stroke the nape of the neck with our right. Then almost imperceptibly we draw the head forwards between our two hands. As we hold the forehead in our left hand, we gently press the eyelids together with our fourth and fifth fingers. [See Figure 6.2.] Your limbs are relaxing . . . you breathe deeper and deeper . . . excitement is gone, the heart beats regularly, you are already feeling peaceful . . . you are wholly in command of yourself . . . you are repeating continuously: I get better daily, I cannot be upset. When there is the least

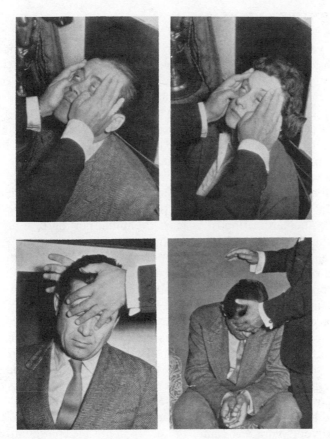

Figure 6.2. Völgyesi's laying-on-of-hands technique. (From Völgyesi, *Hypnosis of Men and Animals*. Copyright 1966, Williams & Wilkins Co., Baltimore. Reprinted by permission.)

provocation, you close your eyes quickly and repeat: "I feel fine, what others can do, I can do better. I am my own master, in charge of my intentions, in charge of what I do, I am afraid of nothing and nobody!" (Völgyesi, 1938/1966, p. 156)

Thus Völgyesi stood virtually alone in these middle decades of this century with regard to "animal hypnosis" and the Faraday-Hand. Whether his use of an electricity delivery system to induce passivity, and hence hypnosis, is a throw-back to the magical rituals of the distant past or an advancement based on animal models and Pavlovian theory is perhaps less important than the awareness of the reader of the potential dangers to the patient of such devices, unless carefully constructed and monitored. Völgyesi's only comment on this point was: "The method, even after years of application, has proved to be without danger to the doctor" (Völgyesi, 1938/1966, p. 154). No doubt his patients were reassured by this observation.

THE SEVENTIES AND BEYOND

The last 15 years, as with the main part of the 20th century, has been devoid of quantum leaps forward in the development of hypnotic induction procedures. Mostly, what has been produced has been refinements of the old, standard techniques or a particular practitioner's "pet" method, often only their own preferred visual image or verbal instructions for eye-fixation or hand levitation. The main trend of the 20th century has been the development of rigorously standardized verbal patters of induction to be used in laboratory investigations of hypnosis and hypnotic phenomena. As we will see near the end of this chapter, there are verbal patters for eye-fixation-closure inductions, which are now generally agreed on and used by most experimental investigators and some practitioners. What this trend has allowed is the standardization of at least the initial portion of a process that previously has been noted for the individuality of its application, rather than an agreed-on format. With the development of videotape equipment, even the method of delivery can be standardized, so that *no* variation occurs in the induction. Ulett, Akpinar, and Itil (1971, 1972) have reported using a videotaped induction and suggestions in a laboratory setting. The results (distribution of depth of hypnosis) compared favorably with more individualized approaches. Clinically, usage has developed with the videotaping of various practitioner's teaching sessions (e.g., Erickson) and are available through the major hypnosis societies. Audiotapes (cassettes usually) have been in use for sometime and also are available through professional societies and numerous commercial houses. Their effectiveness in laboratory settings had been favorably evaluated as early as 1963 (Barber & Calverley, 1963; Hoskovec, Svorad, & Lanc, 1963). No doubt the continuation of these developments will serve us well in the long run, particularly in attempts to understand both the process and the phenomena of hypnosis.

In the meantime, individualized, practically oriented inductions still dominate. In fact, in the clinical applications of hypnosis, inductions expressly suited and fitted to the individual patient are preferred by most practitioners. Laboratory rigor is found too confining, too inflexible for day-to-day medical, dental, and psychological practice. Consequently, practical handbooks emphasize inductions not only suited to the individual patient, but also to the individual illness or therapeutic procedure as well. Thus the American Society of Clinical Hypnosis has produced *A Handbook of Therapeutic Suggestions* (1973) in which verbal patters are reproduced for therapeutic situations such as anxiety, drug abuse, habit patterns, migraine, obstetrics, pain, study habits, surgery, warts, hemorrhage, gagging, and so on.

Harry Arons, of the "Association to Advance Ethical Hypnosis," has written and/or edited a number of how-to books, offering a variety of individual induction techniques. In one, *Prize-Winning Methods of Hypnosis,* there is a negative evaluation of another of the electro-mechanical induction devices that were marketed during the late 1960s and early 1970s. This machine, of Japanese manufacture, produced electrical pulses that were directed to the patient's eyeballs and base of the skull through electrodes strapped in place. Patients subjected themselves to these electrical jolts while listening to a tape recorded, relaxation induction verbalization. The relaxation instructions seemed to be the more effective partner in the induction, but more important, the correspondent (Leo P. Gendreau) reported unpleasant after effects lasting up to five days after experience with the machine. Gendreau thought this particular machine, with its eye-pulsing jolts of electricity, "a very dangerous tool." This is certainly a different evaluation from those offered by Hall (1973) and Barabasz (1976) above. Although the machines themselves are probably not effective in hypnotic induction and in some cases are dangerous to the patient or the practitioner, or both, the development of such machinery allows the practitioner an addition tool with which to convince the resistant patient that hypnosis is occurring. Nielson (Arons, 1969), for example, has patients hold electrodes, which are unattached to any real electrical source, to enhance the effectiveness of a standard relaxation induction verbal patter.

Two other techniques appearing in Arons's book (1969) should be noted because one harkens back to a method we observed in the last chapter, and the other highlights a continuing search. The first, attributed to Maurice E. Bryant, involves placing the patient's head in an awkward angle to the rear with the operator's hand on top such that his forefinger is visible above the patient's forehead. The operator then instructs the patient to focus on his fingertip and begins to rotate the patient's head in an uncomfortable circle. This procedure is continued while the operator offers verbal suggestions of fatigue, relaxation, and deep sleep. Here then is a method quite similar to Adkin's which I described in Chapter 5.

The other method, which calls our attention to the continuing search for more rapid induction procedures, is by William J. Bryan, and is called the "Oriental Pressure-Point Method." The patient is placed on a couch or bed in a sitting position and told that this method of induction takes only two-fifths of a second. Then placing one hand on the patient's forehead and the other on the back of his or her head, the operator suddenly pushes the patient to a supine position while loudly announcing, "SLEEP!" Dr. Bryan reports that what makes this technique effective is, in part, three fabrications he presents to the patient in order to raise his or her expectation levels. First, there is nothing "oriental" about the method. Second, the time the method takes is rapid, but not necessarily as rapid as "two-fifths of a second" would imply; and third, no real "pressure points" are used. Use of the patient's expectations and beliefs regarding hypnosis are a favorite approach by many practitioners today and certainly the desire for induction procedures that use a minimum of both the patient and the practitioner's time are still highly prized.

The interest in rapid inductions has been traced back to the stage hypnotists of the 1940s by *George Matheson* and *John F. Grehan* in their recent

(1979) presentation of their own rapid induction. (However, we should not forget that the *Abbé Faria* induced hypnosis with a single word, "Dormez," more than a century and a half ago.) *A. A. Moss* did offer a rapid induction method in 1955, in which he initially practices the subject in obtaining absolute passiveness in his hand and arm for 3–5 min. This is done by the operator raising and dropping the arm until all movement is unassisted by the patient. Then he has the patient breathe in and out five or six times, relax his or her feet, legs, and body, breathe in and out three or four times again, and become deeply relaxed.

Matheson and Grehan's technique is probably even more rapid acting. It is based on Hartland's modification of an arm catalepsy method often used by Erickson in demonstrations. The therapist picks up the patient's hand and arm at the wrist, holding it in a horizontal position, but slowly releasing contact until the patient holds the arm in this cataleptic pose. If catalepsy does not occur, the operator suggests feelings of heaviness instead, and lets the patient's arm fall back to his or her lap. Here are the verbal instructions that accompany the "Surprise Cataleptic Technique":

Before we proceed I would like to make two important points.

First, the important thing here is what you do, not what I do.

Secondly, please don't try to make anything happen. Just let things happen.

All I am going to do is to pick up your arm like this. That's fine. Now, just let your eyes close, take a nice long comfortable deep breath in all the way. And as you breathe out quietly, let the rest of your body begin to relax all over.

I would like you to let your eyes remain closed until I ask you to open them. Now the first thing you will notice here is that your arm has remained up in that position, and I think you will agree that it is sort of floating there, without any real conscious effort on your part.

As you realize this, you can be aware now that you have very easily slipped into a trance state, and you can drift even deeper. (Matheson & Grehan, 1979, pp. 298–299)

The therapist then proceeds with any other appropriate suggestions.

More recently, *J. Hariman* (1980) reported essentially the same technique, and *Graham R. Wicks* (1982) reported a slight modification thereof. In the latter, the patient is asked if he or she wishes to enter hypnosis, then his or her hand and arm are fully extended above his or her head as the therapist says, "Close your eyes, take a deep breath and hold it" (Wicks, 1982, p. 118). Then, after telling the patient to "let the breath out slowly and let the rest of your body relax deeply," the following rapid induction instructions are uttered: "In a moment or two I will bring your arm gently down to the resting position, and as it comes down you can feel yourself going more and more deeply relaxed, but you will not go very deep until your arm comes to rest" (Wicks, 1982, p. 118). The process takes 10–20 sec. *Joseph Barber's* rapid dental analgesia technique (1977) takes 10 min., but includes more than a rapid induction.

The search for rapid inductions is based, of course, on the concept of time efficiency. But there are other ways to save time during hypnotic inductions. One is by using group techniques where one practitioner can serve more than one patient in the same time period. The actual methods used, however, are no different from those used in individual hypnosis—eye-fixation progressive relaxation, arm levitation, or combinations thereof. Any will do, but Serlin (1970) does advise using techniques wherein the group of patients can begin by closing their eyes. In this way some privacy is achieved, even in the group.

Self-hypnosis is another way of saving time, but mainly that of the practitioner. As we have seen before, patients can be taught to self-induce hypnosis. Usually this approach is initiated during an interpersonal session in which the practitioner teaches the patient one, or several, methods of self-hypnosis. Again, the actual techniques used do not differ from those in the usual one-on-one sessions. This was made clear in a book by Freda Morris (1974) in which she suggested eye-fixation of a candle (shades of the *Leiden Papyrus*) as the initial self-hypnosis induction procedure. (Earlier, Morris—1970—had presented the interesting hypnotherapeutic maneuver of mutual hypnosis, wherein the patient induces hypnosis in the therapist and instructs the therapist that she or he will be effective in hypnotizing the patient. Again, standard induction methods were used.)

Another hypnotic induction procedure, which has gained currency during the modern period, is a time- or at least transportation-saving method that uses a mechanical device, the telephone. Filiatre (1909) made passing reference to the use of this device (see Chapter 5), and Gravitz (1983b) notes that, according to Moll, Jules Liegeois used the telephone in hypnosis before the turn of the century. J. O. Crone also described treatment by telephone shortly after the turn of the century (1903). However, it has only been more recently that the literature on this mechanical method has grown (Cooperman & Schafer, 1983; Owens, 1970; Stanton, 1978; Weitzenhoffer, 1972a). Owens (1970), for example, describes a telephone technique he used on 16 reported cases. With the patient seated by the phone and the instrument held in his or her nonpreferred hand, the operator tells the patient to inhale and exhale six times, increasing feelings of relaxation with each cycle. By the end of the six breaths, hypnosis had been achieved. Deepening was accomplished by having the patient imagine himself or herself on the top floor of a building, descending from level to level until the deepening process was complete. Each level was announced by the patient over the phone as "A," "B," and so forth. Telephone de-induction is through suggesting arm levitation of the preferred hand and arm until the index finger contacts the chin and the patient awakens. Weitzenhoffer's telephone technique (1972a) is more rapid because he establishes a quick induction signal with the patient in a regular office visit. He combined the word "sleep" with the patient's first name in a sentence or a phrase as a rapid induction. For telephone use, he added suggestions that would allow the patient to assume a comfortable position before becoming fully involved in hypnosis. He also added the suggestion that if he (Weitzenhoffer) ceased speaking to the patient for more than 5 min., the trance would be terminated. Thus, Weitzenhoffer, even in the use of a "mechanical" device—the telephone—concerned himself with the patient's general welfare, should anything happen to the therapist in the course of the procedure. As I have pointed out before, this client-centered attitude is one of the major marks of hypnotic inductions of the latter part of the 20th century.

All of the practitioners associated with the early Seminars on Hypnosis (e.g., Irving I. Secter, Seymour Hershman, Edward E. Aston) advocated the client-centered orientation, as do a number of clinicians today. *Melvin A. Gravitz* (b. December 8, 1927), a practicing clinical psychologist, for example, calls his unpublished induction technique:

A naturalistic approach in that it assumes that the patient/subject knows best how to achieve the desired behavior. It is an eclectic approach based on the construct that the subject knows best how to go about the process. My role is to facilitate by building an expectancy set and, in a sense, pointing the way. I do this by investing an initial visit with the subject in which we develop rapport, answer questions (to clarify misconceptions), and tell the subject what hypnosis is and what it is not. My purpose is to tell the subject how to behave with trance. (Gravitz, 1983c)

Following these preliminaries, he proceeds with basic, standard induction methodologies, modified slightly to fit the individual needs of his patient.

Shirley Sanders, a clinical psychologist in private practice (Ph.D., 1967, from the University of Kentucky under Frank A. Pattie's tutelage), is another individual who leaves the "work" of hypnotic induction to the patient. Most often she offers the client a comfortable image and lets him or her talk himself or herself into the hypnotic condition, often monitored with thermal biofeedback. Recently (Sanders, 1983), she described a technique of induction, which capitalized on the children's game of making faces. She calls the procedure ideo-kinesthetic, and it was developed on a patient who had the self-destructive habit of biting the interior of her mouth.

The technique consists of the client first taking deep inhalations, and then blowing out the cheeks and lowering the mandible as the air is expired. The deep breathing increases relaxation (the central focus of this and most hypnotic techniques), both initially and as a trance deepening maneuver, while the blowing out of the cheeks and the lowering of the jaw offers a kinesthetic association to relaxation and, in the case of this patient, to previous childhood memories of face games. The cheek and jaw movement also relaxes those portions of the anatomy, thereby preventing them easy access for biting. The essence of the technique is captured in the following excerpt:

Th: . . . . Just close your eyes and take long, slow, deep breaths. That's fine. . . . Tell me what is happening.

Pa: I am just relaxing, breathing in and out.

Th: Fine. Now, take deep breaths, and begin by blowing out the cheeks and dropping the lower jaw. Do you notice any difference?

Pa: Yes.

Th: What do you notice?

Pa: It's freer . . . more flexible.

Th: Yes—Now take a deep breath.

Pa: . . . Even before I blew out, I felt something relax. I hadn't felt it this way before. The tension really just went out.

Th: Very good. . . . Then when you dropped your jaw, did you feel anything?

Pa: Yes.

Th: What did you feel?

Pa: It's looser and easier.

Th: Yes, It's looser and easier and even freer, more flexible, and more under your control. . . . Just allow that free, flexible feeling to become more natural, let it begin to move down your neck into your shoulders, more natural, more normal, more flexible, more free. Yes. Let it move all the way down your arms to your fingertips, to your back, and your body, . . . free, flexible, easy.

Pa: (patient stretches, breathes deeply.)

Th: Just blow out your cheeks.

Pa: Yes. That's more comfortable.

Th: Yes, and it seems easier to smile, (This was in response to a smile). . . . Now, just explore just how free your jaws and cheeks and mouth are now. Describe whatever you feel.

Pa: It feels loose and free and flexible.

Th: Yes, it does, and it makes your entire face more comfortable, more relaxed, and it feels good.

Pa: It does, it does feel good.

Th: I bet this exercise reminds you of an earlier time, a time when you were little, when you were a kid and played games like blowing out your cheeks and making faces.

Pa: Yes, I did play face games when I was little.

Th: It brings up those earlier times and places and you enjoy it, because play is fun and it is something you can do to have fun, . . . not for any other reason, but just to enjoy it . . . (pt. smiles) . . . and you're even discovering things about your tongue and your teeth. All kinds of discoveries, that maybe you kind of blocked out, and this gives you more control, because you're relaxing. It's a free kind of control, not an over-control. That's what makes it comfortable. . . . Just enjoy it. It's perfectly normal and natural for this kind of muscle exploration, a rediscovery of the wonders of the body, of the face, the tongue. It's really wonderful. (Sanders, 1983, pp. 2–3)

Jonathan Venn has recently (1984) offered an induction technique that concentrates the patient's attention by having him or her direct his or her attention to a sequence of body parts forming a spiral progression from inward outward. It is called the "spiral technique" and is based on the Hindu theory of *chakras*. The number of body locations on which the patient concentrates can vary, but usually starts with the heart and winds outward from there. For example, from heart to throat to left shoulder to left hip to right hip to right shoulder to left elbow to left knee to right knee to right elbow, and so on, to hands, feet, and head. The practitioner names the parts to be focused on and indicates that the patient is to notice the way the part feels right now. Through the focusing process, then, the patient enters a condition of relaxation in which therapeutic suggestions can be accepted. The whole process, depending on the number of body parts chosen, takes 2–30 min. In a similar manner, self-relaxation can be taught.

Harold B. Crasilneck and James A. Hall

Harold B. Crasilneck (b. April 4, 1921) and James A. Hall (b. February 13, 1934) have been collaborating and publishing together since the late 1950s. Both are practicing clinicians: Crasilneck, a clinical psychologist who received his Ph.D. from the University of Houston in 1954; and Hall, a psychiatrist who received his M.D. from the University of Texas Southwestern Medical School in 1961. Their initial publication efforts, concentrating on physiological measurements of hypnosis, have blended into more clinically oriented articles on the use of hypnosis with smoking problems, pain, obesity, and other maladies.

The general approach, noted by Gravitz, has been the hallmark of Crasilneck and Hall's clinical practices as well. These authors, who use the "monotonous repetition of suggestions for relaxation and rest" as their induction technique, spend time explaining the various parameters and stages of hypnosis to the patient. Initial *rapport* is thus considered crucial to the success of the induction. Once the induction proper is begun every effort is made to make "the transition from waking to the trance state . . . as gentle as possible" (Crasilneck & Hall, 1975). It is considered vitally important that the therapist, through his or her demeanor, voice inflection and tone, choice of words, and enunciation, convey trust and calm to the patient. Clear and accurate presentation of both the induction and the therapeutic suggestions makes for an easy, clear, and accurate response on the part of the patient.

Crasilneck and Hall (1975) regularly use eight different induction methods, chosen at any given time to match the individual patient and situation.

Hand Levitation

At the start of hand levitation the patient is asked to sit comfortably with his hands resting in a cupped position on his thighs. We consciously suggest that he spread apart the fingers of his dominant hand. He is then told,

"Take a deep breath and start staring at one of the knuckles on your hand. . . . Just listen to my voice. . . . Try and pay no attention to other sounds and noises. . . . If you have extraneous thoughts, don't worry about it, but try to focus your thinking on what I am saying and on your hand that is cupped. . . . Notice how relaxed your breathing has become. . . . Good . . . and now begin to notice some facts about your hand. . . . It's becoming more sensitive. . . . Pay attention, for example, . . . to the texture of the material of your clothing, to the heat in your hand. . . . You can feel these things occurring and as you do, nod your head gently yes . . . good . . . and now in a moment one of the fingers will move slightly. . . . I don't know which finger, but it will move slightly. . . . Good . . . now your hand will begin to feel rather light, feathery and floaty. . . . The wrist feels like a string is around it, attached perhaps to some balloons gently pulling your arm up . . . light . . . feathery . . . floaty . . . coming up . . . up toward your forehead . . . good. Coming up and when your hand touches your forehead, you will be well relaxed, at ease and in a good state of hypnosis. . . . Now as your hand touches your forehead, . . . your eyes will close . . . your eyes are closed . . . your hand will return to your lap with normal sensation returning to your hand and you are now extremely relaxed and so drowsy, at ease, relaxed, so *very* relaxed . . . throughout your body . . . relaxed and at ease."

Eye Fixation

Ask the patient to sit comfortably in a chair or if hospitalized to be as comfortable as possible in the bed and then begin your eye fixation.

"Put your right hand on your abdomen and let your left hand and arm rest comfortably to the side. . . . Uncross your legs so that you won't put prolonged pressure on them. . . . Now, if you will, please look at this coin that I am holding . . . keep your face looking forward, but I am going to hold this coin slightly above the level of your eyes so that you will strain slightly to look at the object . . . now fixate your vision on the coin, . . . good . . . your breathing is deep and relaxed. . . . You notice that as you continue staring at the coin your eyes become tired and they are beginning to blink . . . yes . . . the lids are blinking. . . . Your eyes are tearing . . . watering from staring at the object and they want to close and they are now closing, closing, closed. . . . Let them remain so very heavy, relaxed, and at ease . . . breathing easily . . . free from tension, tightness, stress and strain, having now entered a good level of hypnosis and responding to my suggestions extremely well . . . relaxed and at ease . . . free from tension, tightness, stress and strain."

The therapist should take care not to hold the coin in such a strained position that his own arm becomes fatigued during the induction.

Theater Technique

This technique is especially good in the induction of patients with psychological problems, for it allows the patient to project his own conflicts and turmoil into the technique.

The patient sits comfortably in a chair with his feet on an ottoman, or if hospitalized, he is lying comfortably in bed. His dominant hand is placed on the abdomen and the other rests comfortably at the side next to his body. What follows is a typical session using the theater technique for hypnosis.

"I want you to close your eyes and begin to concentrate on the fact that you can relax your entire body . . . the muscles, the nervous system . . . just relaxed . . . your breathing . . . so relaxed . . . your entire body free from other thoughts for the moment . . . just listening to me. . . . I want you to concentrate on your right hand . . . concentrate on the breathing of your abdomen . . . the texture of the material in your clothing. . . . Your hand is becoming more sensitive to touch and sensation. . . . As you are doing this, nod your head, yes. . . . Good . . . a deeper and a sounder state . . . you are doing fine . . . normal sensation returns to your hand. . . . Now I give you the suggestion that your right leg begins to feel quite heavy . . . like it is in sand . . . so heavy that you cannot lift your leg. . . . Now normal sensation returns to the leg. . . . Now you are aware of a slight irritation on the top of your right hand, like a fly walking across the hand . . . as you are aware of this, brush it away. . . . Good . . . now a much deeper and relaxed and more profound state. . . . Now listen very carefully to what I describe. . . . You are entering a theatre and you walk down to the first row of seats and sit down . . . front row center. . . . As you are doing this, nod your head, yes . . . good. . . . Now you envision a bright red curtain on the stage . . . fine. . . . Now you are aware of white spotlights on the red curtain . . . very good. . . . Now the curtain gently begins to rise and you can see [whatever the therapist wants to suggest]."

Should the patient be phobic of being alone, we have suggested that they are accompanied to the theater by the therapist.

Television Approach

We have generally used the television approach with children. The child is asked to rest comfortably in the chair and/or bed. We then usually proceed in the following manner:

"We are going to play a game if you like, and this is going to help you get well . . . but you have to cooperate and help me so that I can help you. . . . Now close your eyes and begin to see what is apparently a television set like you have at home. . . . See it? . . . Good . . . just relaxed and at ease . . . breathing easily . . . just relaxing all over . . . listening to every word I say. . . . Now the television set comes on and you can see one of your favorite programs coming on and as you do, nod your head, yes. . . . Good. . . . Now just let the television scene fade out and you are going to become very relaxed and able to do what I tell you . . . just relaxed and at ease."

Coin Technique

The patient sits upright in a chair for the coin method. He is asked to extend his dominant arm forward at a level even with his shoulder. The palm is up, and a coin, usually a quarter or fifty-cent piece, is placed on the ulnar edge of the patient's hand. He is told,

"Breathe in a relaxing fashion concentrating your thoughts on the coin, but listening to my voice. . . . Now I am going to start counting, and as I count, your hand will begin turning. . . . Do you understand? . . . Good . . . and the coin will fall off. . . . When the coin falls off . . . your eyes will close and you will be relaxed . . . extremely relaxed and drowsy and at ease . . . capable of entering a very deep level of trance . . . the arm will be dramatically relaxed . . . it feels like a heavy weight, then this feeling will spread throughout your body . . . heavy . . . relaxed and at ease. . . . Do you understand? . . . Good . . . now do exactly as I have instructed you to do. . . . Now the coin falls and you are in a state of hypnosis."

Non Verbal Technique

There are times when a patient cannot talk to the therapist because of illness or because he is no longer conscious. In such instances the patient can either squeeze the therapist's hand with prearranged signals for yes and no or use ideomotor finger signals, such as lifting and lowering an index finger. Even blinking of the patient's eyelids may be used for prearranged signals for yes or no.

Chiasson's Method

Chiasson, an obstetrician, has developed a popular method of induction that relies on linking normal physiological responses with suggestions for hypnotic induction (Syllabus, Am Soc Clin Hypn, 1973, p. 14). The patient is instructed to place his hand in front of his face, palm facing away from him, with the fingers held together. A distance of about a foot from the face is recommended. This position places a natural strain on the fingers, which spontaneously tend to spread apart. This natural response is linked with the suggestion that "as your fingers spread, you will fall into a hypnotic state." Suggestions are also usually given that the entire hand will approach the face and that when the hand touches the face, the subject will enter a deep state of hypnotic trance. Should there be any difficulty in the induction, it is helpful to add the suggestion that "each time that you breathe out, your hand will approach your face a little bit more." This last suggestion utilizes the normal tendency of the hand, when held in this position, to move toward the chest during expiration. We have found Chiasson's method particularly useful with persons who resist a relaxation approach.

Relaxation Technique

The patient sits comfortably in a chair with his feet on an ottoman and his legs uncrossed. If hospitalized, he lies comfortably in bed. These positions are most conducive for the relaxation technique. After the patient assumes a relaxed position, we start our session.

"Now just concentrate your thoughts on my voice and let your body relax as deeply as you can. . . . Take a series of breaths as deep as you like. . . . Good. . . . Your eyes, especially your eyelids, will begin to feel very very heavy, drowsy and somewhat sleepy . . . yes, they begin to blink . . . and as they do they are becoming very, very heavy. . . . It's hard to keep them open. . . . Your eyes are watering . . . blinking rapidly . . . tired. . . . Let them close . . . so heavy you can hardly keep them open and they are now closed. . . . The feeling that you can attain in your body is of complete and total muscular relaxation . . . you are just relaxing into a deep and relaxed state. . . . You are just listening to my voice . . . and you are drifting into a very, very pleasant state of mind and body . . . free from all tension, tightness, stress, and strain . . . listening to my voice guiding you into a complete and total state of relaxation . . . your mind . . . your body . . . the muscular system . . . the nervous system . . . limp relaxed muscles . . . your respirations are the epitome of relaxation. . . . Now your entire body will become completely and totally relaxed . . . your head, your face, neck, shoulders, back, chest, arms, hands, abdomen, buttocks, pelvis, thighs, legs, and feet . . . just completely relaxed . . . completely, totally relaxed . . . your mind and body . . . free from tension, tightness, stress, and strain." (Crasilneck & Hall, 1975, pp. 55–59)

The authors caution that none of these induction verbal patterns can be used verbatim with all patients. They will, of necessity, need to be tailored to the idiosyncrasies of the patient and/or the disorder to be treated. Children form a special group of patients, which I feel needs particular attention to initial *rapport* and a gentle progression from nonhypnosis to hypnosis and vice versa. Here is an example that contains both an induction and therapeutic suggestions regarding asthma.

"Look at a spot on the ceiling. As you continue looking at this spot, you will begin to relax as much as possible. You will notice that your eyelids begin to feel heavy . . . yes . . . starting to flutter . . . and so just let them close and relax just as much as you can. Let your arms and hands hang limp at your side . . . your body is so relaxed . . . your legs and feet at ease."

If the patient is younger than 13 years of age, we usually hold the child's hand to establish the best rapport and sense of security possible. Children are then told the following:

"How cooperative you can be indicates that you are in a state of hypnosis. If you can cooperate with your mind, you can also relax every muscle in your body, but especially the muscles that control the breathing in your chest . . . and you can become much more relaxed and as you feel yourself relaxing still more, squeeze my hand, yes. . . . Good . . . just relax as much as you can. Now I want you to imagine that you are looking at your television set at home . . . can you see it? Good, now you are going to see the set come on and a movie of cowboys riding on horses. As you see this, nod your head.

. . . Good. . . . You will notice that the horses are running very fast and they are breathing hard and fast . . . like your breathing . . . can you see this? Can you feel this? . . . Good . . . but now the horses are beginning to run more slowly. . . . Breathing is becoming slower and easier and your breathing is slowing down. [The therapist should talk in tempo to the patient's breathing rhythm.] . . . That's it. . . . The horses are slowing down . . . slower now . . . walking . . . breathing almost normal. . . . The wheezing is much less . . . so relaxed. . . . The television scenes fade out. . . . Just let yourself be as comfortable as possible . . . all over . . . secure, relaxed and at ease. I take your hand again. Now I give you the suggestion that you will smell a nice odor. . . . You can smell this nice odor. . . . You can smell this nice odor and when you do . . . squeeze my hand. . . . Good. . . . Now a very deep and sound state of relaxation . . . and breath deeply and slowly, deeply and slowly . . . enjoying the nice odor and you see that your rapid and hard breathing is slowing down . . . your wheezing is less . . . relaxed, so relaxed and at ease . . . free from tension. . . . Your lungs and chest muscles are so relaxed. Smelling the nice odor and now you see your breathing is deep and relaxed, taking deep relaxed breaths . . . so relaxed and at ease. Now the odor is gone. I release your hand. Anytime you need to relax yourself you can do so . . . by closing your eyes and giving yourself these same suggestions just as I have or anytime you are ready to work with me. . . . If I take out my fountain pen and tap it on my desk five times, you can enter this same depth of trance. Do you understand? . . . Good. . . . Remember that you can enter this deep state and your asthma will become controlled. As I slowly count from ten to one, backward, you will be fully awake and your breathing will be normal and the asthma will be gone." (Crasilneck & Hall, 1975, pp. 123–124)

At times the authors combine parts of several techniques with children. In the following they combine part of the coin technique and the television method to capitalize on the ability of most children to engage in visual imagery.

Please look at this coin I am holding in my fingers slightly above your eyelids . . . just keep looking at the coin, and you will notice that very soon your eyes will begin to feel tired and they will start to blink and want to close, and as you feel them getting heavy, just let them close . . . heavy eyelids . . . closing, closing, and closed . . . good . . . so relaxed and at ease. Now, notice your one hand that is resting on your stomach. It comes up and down with every breath you take . . . can you feel this happening? . . . Good . . . up and down, and a deeper sleep . . . a much deeper sleep. Now you won't pay any attention to your hand . . . but think about your leg . . . the right one. It begins to feel just sort of heavy like it feels like concrete . . . heavy . . . so heavy. . . . You can't raise it . . . try . . . try again . . . but it won't move . . . good. . . . Now, normal feeling returns to your leg and a much deeper and sounder and relaxed state. . . . So relaxed . . . so drowsy . . . your right arm and fingers. As I count to three, slowly . . . your right arm and fingers will become so straight and strong and hard. You won't be able to budge or bend your arm or fingers . . . . 1 . . . 2 . . . 3, good. It feels like a steel bridge . . . your arm so strong and rigid . . . try to bend it . . . you can't. . . . Regular feeling now returns to your arm and hand . . . good . . . and still a deeper state of relaxation . . . so sleepy. . . .

Do you have a television at home? If you do, nod your head . . . yes . . . good. . . . You will now see the set come on and a funny picture is on the screen . . . a cowboy clown . . . you see it . . . he is doing something real funny . . . you're smiling. . . . O.K. . . . the television picture fades out and you are so drowsy and relaxed . . . lying there like a rag doll . . . so relaxed and at ease. . . . Every muscle in your body is very relaxed as you watch the T.V. screen in your imagination . . . completely and totally relaxed . . . so comfortable . . . so completely at ease . . . simply watching this funny picture . . . and now as this picture fades out, you will go into a deeper, a sounder state . . . so comfortable and so secure . . . free from tension and tightness and stress and strain. . . . You are now going to hear some very beautiful music, your favorite kind of music . . . and as you hear your favorite music you will think of other pleasant thoughts . . . things you like to do . . . things you really like . . . and as this is occurring you will nod your head slightly "yes" [the child responds]. . . . You are tremendously relaxed, as much as you have ever been relaxed. . . . You are secure. . . . You have a really strong desire to overcome your problem . . . your unconscious mind is strong and powerful . . . and is going to work hard for you and get you well. . . . I now give you the suggestion that . . . [here the specific therapeutic suggestions are included]. (Crasilneck & Hall, 1975, p. 179)

As with most practicing clinicians, Crasilneck and Hall will often combine or meld the induction technique with therapeutic suggestions, so that both the patient and the reader of published descriptions may be hard pressed to discern where one left off and the other began. Crasilneck, for instance, has indicated that he often uses two suggestive methods following hypnotic induction to enhance the patient's realization that they can in fact gain some control over undesirable symptomatology or behavior. He has used hypnotic arm catalepsy and glove anesthesia with more than 2000 patients for this purpose and reports that one year follow-up shows 87% permanent symptom control. Following hypnotic induction, this dialogue is presented:

You are relaxed—deeply relaxed—in a deep state of hypnosis. The most powerful source of control in your body and your psyche, is now in your unconscious mind allowing you to follow these hypnotic suggestions. You will extend your right arm and make a fist—good—now as I count to three that arm will turn into a steel-like state. So tight, so rigid—that it's like a board which has been soaked in water for days—like a cement block—very hard—immovable. Now feel that arm and the strength you have in that arm, with your other hand. Good. You can feel the strength—that super-human strength in the muscular rigidity. Nod your head as you perceive it. Good. Now your right arm returns to normal—I remove the hypnotic suggestion. Normal sensation returns to your arm. Good.

Now the finger that I touch will begin to lose feeling—its called hypnoanesthe-
sia—as I touch this finger with this blunt nail file you will be aware that you are
losing feeling in that finger. As you are aware of this please nod your head—
good. Now open your eyes and observe that I am thumping this finger—watch
as I stimulate it with the nail file. If you feel nothing nod your head. Good.
Close your eyes. Now then, normal sensation returns as I gently pass the file
over the finger. When normal sensation has returned nod your head. Good.
Now open your eyes. Now that the finger has returned to normal, again, I will
stimulate the finger but with much less intensity. When you feel it nod your
head. Good. (Crasilneck, 1984)

Essentially, he is saying to the patient: "If you can achieve that strength in
your hand and if you can block pain in your hand then you will have the same
strength to discontinue . . . [a given symptom or behavior pattern]."

Crasilneck and Hall accomplish dehypnotization in the same manner as
most present day clinicians, by counting backwards from a certain number
(10, 20, etc.), while giving suggestions for increasing alertness and awakening. Upon reaching the number 1, the patient is told to open his or her eyes
and be fully awake and alert, or variations thereon.

Other Approaches

As I indicated in Chapter 5, *Wesley Raymond Wells* (1923) recalled our
attention to a type of hypnosis that appeared to be the equivalent of what
others labeled direct suggestion or nonhypnotic suggestion. (Neither the
technique nor the condition were new in the 1920s, as I have made clear
elsewhere—Edmonston, 1981). The induction of this "waking hypnosis," as
Wells called it, eschewed any mention of relaxation or sleep, manipulating
the behavior of the subject by direct suggestion. However, despite the fact
that the condition and its induction appear to be the anithesis of what has
traditionally been understood to be hypnosis through the centuries, it does
form an area of curiosity and investigation that has attracted a number of
individuals working in hypnosis. Wells (1923) did not make explicit his
method of induction, merely offering the reader a contrast to traditional
sleep inductions. He stated only that his technique did not mention sleep,
nor were there any indications of sleep in the subject. He thought Wingfield's
(1920) or Coué's methods (1922) to be most closely allied to his own.

More recently, Ludwig and Lyle (1964) published a study comparing
"hyperalert trance" with traditional hypnosis with a group of "post-addict"
patients. Their "alert induction" involved having the subjects rapidly pace
the floor; spin around, sweeping the room with their eyes; do knee-bends;
rotate their heads (while seated); and tense various muscle groups. During
these activities, suggestions were presented intended to create muscular
rigidity and immobility in the muscles used in the activity. In addition, the
subject was "continually bombarded with statements telling him he was

'keyed up', 'on edge,' 'nervous'" (Ludwig & Lyle, 1964, p. 72). The authors report that a comparison on standard hypnotic challenges showed similar response patterns in the "hyperalert trance" to those in traditional hypnosis. The lack of a counterbalanced methodology in their study delays confirmation of this interpretation. This is particularly true when considering data from other studies that show that instructions to be alert produced significantly different response patterns from those produced by traditional inductions (e.g., Bartlett, Faw, & Libert, 1967; Davis & Kantor, 1935; Gibbons, 1974, 1975, 1976; Ham & Edmonston, 1971).

Don E. Gibbons, in fact, has coined a new term, "hyperempiric induction," to describe his induction of an alert condition. The term implies that the hyperempiric induction enhances experience through suggestions, not of lethargy and relaxation, but of increased alertness and "mind expansion." The examples of hyperempiric inductions that appear in his book (1979) involve visual imagery, coupled with suggestions of increasing awareness of the senses and general alertness. In "On The Beach At Night," the subject is guided through a quiet beautiful ocean scene, noting various visual, auditory, and other sensory aspects. As the subject watches the beautiful scene, the image of a boat with an old man at the oars approaches from the mist, the voyager enters the boat, and is transported to a distant silvery island. (It is interesting that Gibbons should chose an image of a boatman helping the subject "cross over," since such imagery is replete with connotations of death, not exalted, hyperalert life.) As the traveler imagines himself or herself reaching the island and leaping ashore, the operator says:

> All the vast resources within you have been freed for their fullest possible functioning. And while you remain within this state of hyperempiria, the quality of all your experiences will be infinitely keener; and you will be able to discern new and greater levels of reality and of meaning which will enable you to discover new dimensions of experience, greater and more profound than those you have encountered previously. (Gibbons, 1979, p. 33)

Similar encouragements end "The Awakening Lotus Bud," "The Cathedral," and the "Riding Through a Rainbow" inductions.

Investigators at *Ernest R. Hilgard's* laboratories at Stanford University have also investigated "alert trance" phenomena (e.g., Bányai & Hilgard, 1976; Liebert, Rubin, & Hilgard, 1965). Their method of inducing "alert hypnosis" was by modifying a standard eye-fixation induction technique by eliminating all references to relaxation and/or sleep and substituting in their place concepts of activity and alertness. Bányai and Hilgard (1976) even placed their "active-alert induction" subjects on a Monark bicycle ergometer and had them pedal continuously during the induction. Whether such procedures actually constitute hypnosis, as traditionally understood, has been seriously questioned both in the experimental (Ham & Edmonston, 1971) and in the theoretical literature (Edmonston, 1981); however, investigations continue both here and abroad (see, for example, works by *S. Kratochvil* in Czechoslovakia).

Continuations of, as well as elaborations and variations on, the shaping techniques reported earlier by Pascal and Salzberg (1959) are still in evidence. They are called by different names—skill learning, modeling, task motivation, goal-directed guided imagery, and so forth. All involve instructional sets, as do hypnotic inductions, intended to elicit certain behaviors in the subject/patient. Probably the major difference between these newer instructional sets and the older induction methods is that their effectiveness is tested by the measurement of a standard set of behaviors, through the tests I will describe in Chapter 8. The argument appears to be that if these different instructional sets elicit the same behaviors, to the same degree, as traditional inductions, we will have produced tools to aid us in better understanding hypnosis by showing it is a matter of social learning, or behavior shaping or goal-directed guided imagination or expectation, or a relaxation response.

The latter appears most likely to the present author because of the historical, clinical, physiological, and experimental similarities between the two phenomena. In the context of this book it is particularly noteworthy that the induction of the trophotropic response *Herbert Benson* coined "the Relaxation Response" is similar if not identical to that used in the induction of hypnosis.

Benson (Benson et al., 1974) outlines four basic elements in the production of the relaxation response: (a) a mental device, (b) a passive attitude, (c) decreased muscle tonus, and (d) a quiet environment.

The *mental device*—Benson calls it "an object to dwell upon" in his popular book version—is some sort of a constant stimulus, something on which the subject concentrates to the relative exclusion of all else: "a sound, word, or phrase . . . or fixed gazing at an object" (Benson, 1975, p. 38). How like Braid's later monoideism is the concentration on a single compelling idea as a device through which to enter hypnosis. Or compare Braid's lancet case on which his patients concentrated their visual attention until fatigue and hypnosis overtook them. Consider also Chevreul's pendulum, or staring into the operator's eyes as devices for arresting the attention of the subject. Virtually all of the present-day induction techniques begin with some method for arresting the subject's attention—eye fixation; hand levitation in which the hand and forearm are watched carefully and attended to by the subject as, dumb-struck, he or she watches the limb rise in the air with no apparent effort; television, movie, or other visual imagery techniques; and even "the relaxation technique" in which the subject's attention is progressively drawn to various muscle groups to monitor his or her degree of tension or relaxation. Even the words of the operator can serve as a "mental device" to aid the subject in the task of excluding the external, the logical, the sensory input.

A *passive attitude* aids the concentration on the "mental device" just as hypnotic operators enjoin their subjects to "let the cares of the day fade into the background.'' Should the individual become distracted during the process, he or she is directed to bring the attention back to the technique (the mental device). In the Stanford scales (see Chapter 8) we find: "Just relax. Don't be tense. Keep your eyes on the target. Look at it as steadily as you can. *Should your eyes wander away from it that will be all right . . . just bring your eyes back to it* [italics added]" (Weitzenhoffer & Hilgard, 1959, Form A, p. 14). The similarity is clear; in the passive attitude, concentration on the mental device is maximized.

The passive attitude has another feature that is quite similar to hypnosis: The meditator is to be a participant, not an observer. He or she is not to be concerned with performance, is not to wonder how well the technique is working, but is merely to let the technique take effect. It is similar to the individual trying to go to sleep. As long as the person *tries*, he does not sleep, but once he becomes passive, not actively observing himself for signs of sleep, slumber ensues. In hypnosis it is the same. What do we tell our subjects? "Your curiosity will be satisfied [regarding what the experience will be like] before we are through, but you can best get the answers you want *by just letting yourself be a part of what goes on and by not trying to watch the process in detail* [italics added]. . . . Hypnosis is largely a question of your willingness to be receptive and responsive to ideas, and *to allow these ideas to act upon you without interference* [italics added] (Weitzenhoffer & Hilgard, 1959, Form A, p. 8).

Or further: "Your eyes will be so tired, will feel so heavy, that you will be unable to keep them open any longer and they will close perhaps quite involuntary. *When this happens, just let it take place* [italics added]" (Weitzenhoffer & Hilgard 1959, Form A, p. 14).

Like the foregoing, *decreased muscle tonus* is also encouraged during hypnosis. The subject is placed in a comfortable position, either seated or supine, often told to loosen tight clothing, and remove contact lenses in preparation for the induction procedures. While there are some operators who claim to induce hypnotic trances while the subject is standing, such a procedure is the rare exception. Even while standing, the subject inclines the head and droops the shoulders as the hypnosis takes effect.

Esdaile and others made a *quiet* (if not darkened) *environment* equally a part of the induction of hypnosis. Such an environment is used to TM training because, perforce, it reduces environmental distraction and what tendencies the subject may have to waver from the mental device. In addition, the eyes are often closed during the TM session. Again, the similarities to the practice of hypnosis are striking. If the eyes are not closed at the outset (as they are in the usual relaxation induction technique), they soon close early in the process.

Practitioners need only consider for a moment the nature of the environment they prefer and attempt to create for their patients during hypnosis to be convinced that a *quiet environment* is not a setting unique to TM practice and the elicitation of Benson's relaxation response.

The four elements used to elicit the relaxation response are basic to the induction of hypnosis. Practitioners of hypnosis have been using them for centuries.

Standardized Inductions

As I have pointed out several times in this chapter, the rate of development of new induction techniques in recent years has diminished. Instead, individuals working in the field have been more content to use standardized procedures. This has been particularly true because of the increasing number of experimental investigators, who are more concerned with consistent methodology than with ultimate effect. The majority of these nonpractitioner investigators (e.g., Kenneth Bowers, Patricia Bowers, Frederick Evans, John Kihlstrom, Joseph Reyher, Michel Sabourin), as well as practitioners (e.g., Kenneth Graham), rely on standardized induction procedures such as contained in the Stanford Scale, the Harvard Group, and SHALIT Scale (see Chapter 8). Since the eye closure inductions vary little from one another, I reproduce only one here. The following is from the Harvard Group Scale of Hypnotic Susceptibility (Shor & Orne, 1962). The Harvard was chosen for illustration because its eye closure instructions are quite similar to the eye closure instructions on each of the Stanford Scales.

This standardized induction technique has two parts, one the basic induction, and the other a set of verbalizations used to deepen the subject's state of relaxation after the eyes have closed. This induction (or slight variations thereof), applied almost universally by experimental investigators, follows induction patterns that I have traced from the most ancient of times, through the *Leiden Papyrus* and Braid, to modern times. The patient's eyes, through staring at a fixed point, concentrate the attention while suggestions are offered for increasing relaxation, heaviness of body parts, and, of course, the closing of the eyelids. Eyelid closure, just as exploited by Hull in his time-to-enter-trance studies, is considered the overt sign that the subject has entered a hypnotic condition.

Eye Closure

Now I want you to seat yourself comfortably and rest your hands in your lap. That's right. Rest your hands in your lap. Now look at your hands and find a spot on either hand and just focus on it. It dosen't matter what spot you choose; just select some spot to focus on. I shall refer to the spot which you have chosen as the target. That's right . . . hands relaxed . . . look directly at the target. I am about to give you some instructions that will help you to relax and gradually to enter a state of hypnosis. Just relax and make yourself comfortable. I want you to look steadily at the target and while keeping your eyes upon it to listen to what I say. Your ability to be hypnotized depends partly on your willingness to cooperate and partly on your ability to concentrate upon the target and upon my words. You have already shown yourself to be cooperative by coming here today, and with your further cooperation I can help you to become hypnotized. You can be hypnotized only if you are willing. I assume that you are willing and that you are doing your best to cooperate by concentrating on the target and listening to my words, letting happen whatever you feel is going to take place. Just let it happen. If you pay close attention to what I tell you, and think of the things I tell you to think about, you can easily experience what it is like to be hypnotized. There is nothing fearful or mysterious about hypnosis. It is a perfectly normal consequence of certain psychological principles. It is merely a state of strong interest in some particular thing. In a sense you are hypnotized whenever you see a good show and forget you are part of the audience, but instead feel you are part of the story. Many people report that becoming hypnotized feels at first like falling asleep, but with the difference that somehow or other they keep hearing my voice as a sort of background to whatever other experience they may have. In some ways hypnosis is like sleepwalking; however, hypnosis is also an individual experience and is not just alike for everyone. In a sense the hypnotized person is like a sleepwalker, for he can carry out various and complex activities while remaining hypnotized. All I ask of you is that you keep up your attention and interest and continue to cooperate as you have been cooperating. Nothing will be done that will cause you embarrassment. Most people find this a very interesting experience. (Time: 3′35″)

Just relax. Don't be tense. Keep your eyes on the target. Look at it as steadily as you can. Should your eyes wander away from it, that will be all right . . . just bring your eyes back to it. After a while you may find that the target gets blurry, or perhaps moves about, or again, changes color. That is all right. Should you get sleepy, that will be fine, too. Whatever happens, let it happen and keep staring at the target for a while. There will come a time, however, when your eyes will be so tired, will feel so heavy, that you will be unable to keep them open any longer and they will close, perhaps quite involuntarily. When this happens, just let it take place. (Time: 1′10″)

As I continue to talk, you will find that you will become more and more drowsy, but not all people respond at the same rate to what I have to say. Some people's eyes will close before others. When the time comes that your eyes have closed, just let them remain closed. You may find that I shall still give suggestions for your eyes to close. These suggestions will not bother you. They will be for other people. Giving these suggestions to other people will not disturb you but will simply allow you to relax more and more.

You will find that you can relax completely but at the same time sit up comfortably in your chair with little effort. You will be able to shift your position to make yourself comfortable as needed without it disturbing you. Now just allow yourself to relax completely. Relax every muscle of your body. Relax the muscles of your legs. . . . Relax the muscles of your feet. . . . Relax the muscles of your arms. . . . Relax the muscles of your hands . . . of your fingers. . . . Relax the muscles of your neck, of your chest. . . . Relax all the muscles of your body. . . . Let yourself be limp, limp, limp. Relax more and more, more and more. Relax completely. Relax completely. Relax completely. (Time: 2′15″)

As you relax more and more, a feeling of heaviness perhaps comes over your body. A feeling of heaviness is coming into your legs and your arms . . . into your feet and your hands . . . into your whole body. Your legs feel heavy and limp, heavy and limp. . . . Your arms are heavy, heavy. . . . Your whole body feels heavy, heavier and heavier. Like lead. Your eyelids feel especially heavy. Heavy and tired. You are beginning to feel drowsy, drowsy and sleepy. Your breathing is becoming slow and regular, slow and regular. You are getting drowsy and sleepy, more and more drowsy and sleepy while your eyelids become heavier and heavier, more and more tired and heavy. (Time: 1'25")

Your eyes are tired from staring. The heaviness in your eyelids is increasing. Soon you will not be able to keep your eyes open. Soon your eyes will close of themselves. Your eyelids will be too heavy to keep open. Your eyes are tired from staring. Your eyes are becoming wet from straining. You are becoming increasingly drowsy and sleepy. The strain in your eyes is getting greater and greater, greater and greater. It would be so nice to close your eyes, to relax completely, and just listen sleepily to my voice talking to you. You would like to close your eyes and relax completely, relax completely. You will soon reach your limit. The strain will be so great, your eyes will be so tired, your lids will become so heavy, your eyes will close of themselves, close of themselves. (Time: 1'20")

Your eyelids are getting heavy, very heavy. You are relaxed, very relaxed. There is a pleasant feeling of warmth and heaviness all through your body. You are tired and drowsy. Tired and sleepy. Sleepy. Sleepy. Sleepy. Listen only to my voice. Pay attention to nothing else but my voice. Your eyes are getting blurred. You are having difficulty seeing. Your eyes are strained. The strain is getting greater and greater, greater and greater. (Time: 50")

Your lids are heavy. Heavy as lead. Getting heavier and heavier, heavier and heavier. They are pushing down, down, down. Your eyelids seem weighted, weighted with lead, heavy as lead. . . . Your eyes are blinking, blinking, blinking . . . closing . . . closing. . . . (Time: 35")

Your eyes may have closed by now, and if they have not, they *would* soon close of themselves. But there is no need to strain them more. Even if your eyes have not closed fully as yet, you have concentrated well upon the target, and have become relaxed and drowsy. At this time you may just let your eyes close. That's it, eyes completely closed. Close your eyes now. (Time: 35")

You are now comfortably relaxed, but you are going to relax even more, much more. Your eyes are now closed. You will keep your eyes closed until I tell you otherwise, or I tell you to awaken. . . . You feel drowsy and sleepy. Just keep listening to my voice. Pay close attention to it. Keep your thoughts on what I am saying—just listen. You are going to get much more drowsy and sleepy. Soon you will be deep asleep but you will continue to hear me. You will not awaken until I tell you to do so. I shall now begin to count. At each count you will feel yourself going down, down, into a deep, comfortable, a deep restful sleep. A sleep in which you will be able to do all sorts of things I ask you to do. One—you are going to go deeply asleep. . . . Two-down, down into a deep, sound sleep. . . . Three—four—more and more, more and more asleep. . . . Five—six—seven—you are sinking, sinking into a deep, deep sleep. Nothing will disturb you. Pay attention only to my voice and only to such things as I may call to your attention. I would like you to keep on paying attention to my voice and the things I tell you. . . . Eight—nine—ten— eleven—twelve—deeper and deeper, always deeper asleep—thirteen—four- teen—fifteen—although deep asleep you can clearly hear me. You will always hear me no matter how deeply asleep you feel yourself to be. . . . Sixteen— seventeen—eighteen—deep asleep, fast asleep. Nothing will disturb you. You are going to experience many things that I will tell you to experience. . . . Nineteen, twenty. *Deep asleep!* You will not awaken until I tell you to do so. You will wish to sleep and will have the experiences I shall presently describe. (Time: 3'40") (Shor & Orne, 1962, pp. 5–7)

In addition to eye-closure techniques, the second most often used stan- dardization inductions are those involving suggestions for arm levitation, such as is contained in SHALIT (see Chapter 8).

Now, please just close your eyes and keep them closed until I tell you to open them. Continue to pay attention to your hand and to what I say to you. Now, as you continue paying attention to your hand you will soon feel a tendency for the hand to rise. Let me position your hand. (HYPNOTIST: LIFT HAND SLIGHTLY AND FLATTEN IT ON TABLE.) That's it. . . . You may find your fingers arching a little as the palm of your hand leaves the table. Your hand feels light, and the feeling of lightness grows as your hand rises, with your elbow supporting your arm. Your hand is beginning to move with no effort . . . it is starting to rise. The hand is feeling very light, like a feather, ready to float up and away.

Your hand is rising, lifting, lifting up in the air. . . . That's right, perhaps slowly at first, but it is lifting up . . . up . . . and I am going to count to twenty and that will help your hand to rise. . . . *One,* your hand is lifting up . . . more and more up. Soon your elbow will lift from the table, if it has not already lifted up. *Two,* rising even more. . . . *Three,* still higher . . . lifting, lifting, lifting.

Four . . . still higher . . . lifting, lifting, lifting . . . and as your hand begins to rise or continues to rise, you feel yourself becoming more and more hypno- tized. *Five* . . . you may wonder whether your hand will eventually reach up in the air, high above your head, as high as your arm will reach. You don't know and I don't know. There is no hurry; just let it move at its own pace. *Six, seven* . . . moving, moving, lifting, lifting.

Eight . . . You will be interested in noticing how the movements take place in order, how the hand begins to rise, then the elbow lifts up, and eventually the arm reaches up and the hand is high above your head, as though the hand were being pulled up. *Nine.* . . . Your hand continues to float up, as you find yourself thinking only of drifting more and more into hypnosis, leaving all cares behind . . . it feels so good. . . .

Ten . . . lifting, lifting . . . your hand feels as light as a feather, floating up, reaching slowly for the ceiling. . . . That's it. . . . *Eleven, Twelve.* . . . Up,

up . . . and when your hand is lifted up you'll feel yourself deeply hypnotized
. . . it feels so good just to let things take place by themselves in this pleasant
state. . . . *Thirteen, fourteen.* . . . There's no hurry . . . your hand moves at
its own pace, steadily reaching up, lifting, lifting. . . . *Fifteen, sixteen.* . . .
Your whole body feels so relaxed.

You become more and more comfortably relaxed and hypnotized as your hand
rises . . . rises . . . lifts . . . lifts. . . . *Seventeen, eighteen.* . . . Everything is going well as your hand lifts up, rises up, reaches up. . . . *Nineteen.*
. . . You drift more and more into a comfortable state of hypnosis as you feel
your hand continuing to float up . . . it feels so light . . . it lifts itself . . . it
doesn't need anything to pull it up. . . . Up, higher and higher . . . all by
itself . . . more and more up in the air. . . . *Twenty.* . . . That's it; it has
gone far enough. (Hilgard et al., 1979, pp. 1–3)

Since SHALIT is primarily meant as a device for measuring hypnotic
responsiveness, and I am presenting it here as a basic example of an arm
levitation induction technique, I have omitted the instructions for measuring
how far the arm being observed has risen above the table top. In the
SHALIT proper, measurements are taken following each paragraph above.

THE DRUIDS REVISITED

Before we become too complacent and self-satisfied with the progress that
has been made throughout the centuries in induction procedures, let us look
at several, current induction activities. In Chapter 2, we explored the use of
poetry and rhyming by the Druids to "rime either a man or beast to death"
(MacCulloch, 1911, p. 326). I noted then that in 1930 Snyder, a Haverford
College Professor of English, had produced a book of *Hypnotic Poetry*. In
1983, he and *Ronald E. Shor* updated portions of the book and again listed
the poems having "trance-inductive potency." They are: R. Browning's
Love Among the Ruins; Burn's *Auld Lang Syne, John Anderson,* and *My Jo;*
Byron's *The Isles of Greece;* Coleridge's *Kubla Khan* and parts of the *Rime
of the Ancient Mariner;* passages of Fitzgerald's *The Rubáiyát of Omar
Khayyám;* Gray's *Elegy Written in a Country Churchyard;* Keats's *La Belle
Dame sans Merci* and most of *The Eve of St. Agnes;* Kipling's *The Long
Trail;* passages from Longfellow's *Evangeline;* Masefield's *Sea-Fever;* Poe's
Annabel Lee and *To One in Paradise;* Seeger's *I Have a Rendezvous with
Death;* Shelley's *The Indian Serenade* and *My Soul is an Enchanted Boat;*
Tennyson's *Break, Break, Break, Crossing the Bar* and *The Song;* and Whit-
man's *O Captain! My Captain.*

What is intriguing about Snyder and Shor's presentation (1983) is their
analysis of the poetic techniques used to produce this clinically observed
hypnotic inducing effect. First, there is the absence of alerting features and
abrupt shifts in the poem, so that the listener—the poems are to be read

aloud to another person or groups of people—can be listlessly uncritical as the words sweep over them. Second, these poems capture the attention of the listener through a regular and soothing rhythm and rhyme that is repetitiously presented, often through a repeated refrain. (Here we see the fixation of attention, as in eye-fixation techniques, and the repetitive monotony so often advocated in formal hypnotic inductions.) The soothing aspect comes from both repetition and the "vowel-liquid effect" of the poet's choice of words. Finally, trance-inductive poems weave their effect through vague, often difficult to understand passages. (Here perhaps is a similarity to the confusion techniques I have outlined above, and to the vagueness of much of the Druids' rhyming methods.) Even the authors' description of the general environment for the reading of trance-inductive poems sounds similar to the suggested atmosphere for hypnotic inductions. "The audience should be quietly relaxed, comfortable, in sympathetic rapport with the reader who is preferably an authority-figure, and there should be minimal outside distracting noises" (Snyder & Shor, 1983, p. 6). The reader should remember, as the authors remark, that much of what is proposed regarding the effects of poetry derives from "clinical" observation and has not been subjected to more rigorous investigation. Since their list of trance-inductive poems is shadowed by a list of similar, but not trance-inducing poems, controlled experimentation is clearly possible.

Another writer, *Samuel Silber,* a physician in the New York City area, has centered much of his work in hypnosis on what he has called the Poetic Hypnogram. Silber first introduced the hypnogram in 1971 and recently (1980) published three induction and two specialty hypnograms. He claims that hypnotic poetry, with its rhymes and rhythms, rearouses the memories of security and safety of fetal days and induces a condition useful in the treatment of a variety of disorders. Here are three induction hypnograms, and one that was used to deepen the hypnotic condition.

I. Progressive Relaxation from the Head Downward with
Ego-Augmenting Adjuncts

*Rest and relax in most peaceful repose
That begins in your head and spreads down to your toes;
From your neck muscles down through your arms, legs and back,
You'll feel soothed smooth and soft like a feather-filled sack.
The sound of my voice will maintain your attention
And rout all anxiety and apprehension.
Your lids will get heavy and close when they please
To put mind and body completely at ease.
You'll shut out the world as your eyes gently close.
And you'll shed aches and pains doubts and worries and woes.
As your confidence grows you'll get blessed relief,
With increased self-esteem, from depression and grief
Continuous calm relaxation is spreading,*

The goal is in-sight now to which you are heading.
You're thankful because you've been offered the chance
To help play your part in attaining this trance.
You're proud of your warm willful co-operation
That helps you achieve blissful true relaxation
As love's sweet low lullabyes can't leave you tense,
So slumber now softly soothes your every sense.
Rewards on awaking await your new learning,
New vigor and hope with all old strengths returning.
Henceforth you will know you're safe, sound and secure
With your mind keen and clear self-reliant and sure.
With the power and precision you always admire.
Your considered decision will gain your desire.
With zest zeal and enterprise in all you do.
Your efforts will make dreams and plans all come true.
Your disordered rhythms of life will now start
Producing a normal beat like a good heart.
You'll do what you choose, what you will, what you must.
And plant in your self what you have in me—Trust
One part of your brain becomes hyper-alert,
While the other's asleep, but on call not inert
Each breath makes your sleep become deeper and deeper
Producing a partly alert en-tranced sleeper.
With every breath now you'll sleep deeper and deeper
And deeper and deeper etc.

II. The Eyelid Flutter Technique—or Modified Eye Fixation with Upward Eye Roll and Flutter

As one prays raise your gaze firmly up to the skies
And try seeing your forehead with uptilted eyes,
Roll them upward and inward till you feel the strain
As if you would view the inside of your brain
As in wide open window shades move down to cover them
Let your eyes stare way up while your lids slide down over them.
Let them flutter and flicker and flicker and flutter
In flurries far faster than words that I utter,
They'll flutter and flicker, first slower than quicker
Now halting then hastier, speedier, slicker—
Let your eyes wink and blink almost fast as you think
As your inner world grows watch your outer world shrink.
You'll succeed as you heed my safe lead as your guide
To get a true view of what lies stored inside.
Now your fluttering lids help prepare you for dozing
Your eyes muscles tighten, your eyes can't help closing.
Then with tensions released your tired eyes shut down tight
To rest and relax as in sound sleep at night—
Dreamy deep soothing sleep that lets the soul expand.
And helps you to do what you've wanted and planned,

Soon your legs and your arms and your body will be
Like an orbiting astronaut's weightless and free.
Each part of your body responds on its own
With a free willing eagerness it's never known.
Revealing a wealth of great hidden resources
That overcomes all with immense inner forces.
Now your warm trust in me I'll implant in you too
And we'll tap vast potentials when I give the cue
And deep well-springs of power will now strengthen you.

III. Relaxation Through Imagery with Supportive Encouragement

Fall sound asleep in slumber deep
Relaxed to rest in a snug nest
Of silvery dreams webbed of moonbeams
And starry night's peaceful delights.
Your tired eyes close in sweet repose
Relieving strain, banishing pain.
While your tense back's muscles relax
Lassitude flows from head to toes,
Languor anoints tendons and joints.
Legs, arms and knees; you float at ease
In calm care-free tranquility,
'll tensions gone like night at dawn.
As you forsake the world awake
You'll only heed sound word or deed
That you and I feel can apply
To the designed goal in your mind
We'll both select, use or reject
Whate'er you need help you succeed.
Geared to attain your cherished gain.
Now you can view the inner you
Bringing to light your source of might.
Past failures teach grasp to match reach,
And help you strive till you arrive,
Firing your soul to gain each goal.
So mobilize and energize
Your Power Within that makes you win.
With strength immense thru confidence.
You'll dominate and control Fate;
With sacred spark, dispel the dark.
Put fears to rout dispel self-doubt
And sense of shame and sin and blame;
Conquer self-spite and see how bright
The world can be with your will now free.

IV. Imagery with Lilting Rhythm and Seductive Sound—Excellent for Deepening

As your eyes gently close you'll find open to you
A vast realm reserved only for inner view,

So retreat into reverie, restful serene,—
Away from disturbance by the waking scene;
Sail safely with me on your subconscious stream.
Drift drowsily into the realm of the dream—
Concentrate on my words place all else out of bounds,
So you'll heed what you need, not irrelevant sounds.
Lapse languidly into a light placid mood,
Let arms and legs loosely loll in lassitude,
Let your muscles relax as your mind follows me,
Unburden your body and soul and be free.
We'll resolve vexing problems dredged out of the deep
While tender thoughts gently enfold you in sleep.
Peace and power pervade your soul like healing balm
Bringing strength and tranquility with peaceful calm.
When you wake all your yearning and longing and hoping
Will bring you new strength for more capable coping.
So completely relax while you breathe calm and deep
And with every breath now you'll fall deeper asleep.

(SILBER, 1980, pp. 213–215)

The modern use of poetry in hypnosis is not the only thread of continuity between us today and the Druids of ancient times. The Druids used music as well in their rituals, and just as music was the major pathway to the Druidic "magical sleep," so too is the combination of music, rhythm, and dance fundamental to initiation, continuance, and termination of possession (often characterized by a "trance like" condition) by a *loa* (diety) in the modern Haitian practice of Vodun (Voodoo).

Voodoo, the major religion of masses of Haitians, is a blend of African beliefs, brought to this side of the Atlantic by imported slaves, and French Catholicism. While it pervades the general life-style of a large number of people who have been reared since early childhood in the Vodun beliefs and rituals, it is the group rituals of possession that both Bowers (1961) and Ravenscroft (1965) relate to hypnosis and hypnotic techniques. Both authors, reporting on personal observations made in Haiti, perceived close resemblances between the conditions of the possessed and the hypnotized. Initially, the subjects of possession resemble classical hysteria (Metraux, 1972), stumbling and falling about in an uncontrolled manner, often displaying spasmodic convulsions. Their expression may be vacant or anguished and is accompanied with profuse sweating and mild tremors. Although occasionally preceded by a sleep period, it is the hysterical-like crisis that announces the beginning of possession. The group atmosphere in which these rituals take place, the role of the *hungan* (priest), and the behavior of the possessed all remind us of the behavior of Mesmer's patients at the *baquet*. In addition, both Bowers (1961) and Ravenscroft (1965) interpret the facts that possessed individuals were exonerated of any responsibility for their behavior and have amnesia for all that transpired during possession as indicative of further similarity to the hypnotic condition. Even the concern regarding whether the trances of possession are genuine or simulated (Metraux, 1972, p. 129) parallels some of the modern concerns for the genuineness or role enactment in hypnosis and the use of simulator models in hypnotic research.

However, it is in the rituals of possession that we see a clearer historical link between modern Haitian Voodoo and hypnosis of both the past and present. While possessions are reported to occur virtually anywhere and anytime, spontaneously in the individual (in the market place, on a bus, at home), in the presence of family members during a family ritual, or during a large gathering expressly for the purpose of enhancing possession; it is the rituals of the latter that most resemble some aspects of hypnotic inductions, old and new. Three parts of the ritual show a striking resemblance to activities we have encountered in our earlier review of hypnotic rituals. First, in the middle of the area used for the Voodoo ritual is a center post around which the majority of the action takes place, in much the same manner that Mesmer's *baquet* and de Puységur's Elm of Buzancy served as the focus of their trance-inducing rituals. Second, the *hungan* draws a *vèvè* (ritual drawing) specific to the particular *loa* he wishes to call forth on the ground in front of the center post. Bowers (1961) described a heart being fashioned with flour, which was probably the vèvè of *Loa* Ezili Fréda Daomé (see Laguerre, 1980, p. 196). The reader will recall that Du Potet (1852) drew his "magic mirror" on the floor in charcoal and had his patients stare at it until a crisis ensued (see Chapter 3). Third, the *hungan* often uses ritualistic movements that closely resemble those of the hypnotic induction techniques of the 18th and 19th centuries. Whether to overcome resistance to possession or just to facilitate possession in the absence of resistance, the *hungan* stares at the individual, makes ritualistic passes over his or her face, and gently wipes sweat on them. Either staring at or having the subject stare at an object remains a central focus of many of our modern hypnotic inductions, and certainly the passes of the *hungan* appear to mimic the mesmeric passes of the last century. The use of a magical fluid—in this case, perspiration—most clearly resembles the use of "magnetic water" described in the last few centuries, and actually goes as far back in time as the period of Jesus (see Chapter 1). In fact, Ackerknecht (1948) tells us that the shamans of Siberia and the Ga people of West Africa also continue to use spittle as a magical means of transmitting power and curing illness. Thus, in the use of a central focusing object, the drawing of symbols on the floor of the ritual chamber and in the gestures toward and the touching of the possessed do we see apparent similarities between the Haitian Voodoo ritual and hypnotic induction.

However, the true central focal point of the Haitian ritual is the songs, with their rhythmic, dance-invoking cadence played out by the ever-present drums. Although Mesmer played music to his patients at the *baquet* on his harmonium, it was not the syncopated, rhythmic beat of the *Rada* or *Petro* or *Assoto* drum. His was melodic and soothing; theirs, rhythmic, demanding movement and dancing. Voodoo has often been called the "dancing religion" because drum rhythms and dances are used to call forth the *loa*, to invite him or her to take possession of one of the revelers. The songs have an educational and a liturgical function in the ritual, and serve as a means of communication between the *loa* and the possessed human. Initially songs of invitation are chanted, which invite the *loa*, whose *vèvè* has been drawn, to come and join the congregation. For example:

> *Gran boa ilé o, Gran boa ilé sousou pandian man*
> *mpa korivé*
> *Gran boa solid o, gran boa ilé ilé o*
> *Atibon solid o, gran boa ilé ilé o*
> *Atibon ilé sousou pandian man ilé ilé o*
> *Atibon ilé sousou pandian man mpa korivé.*

> *Gran Boa the islander,*
> *Is a powerful spirit.*
> *Atibon is a powerful spirit.*
> *Atibon, the islander, is about to appear.*

> (LAGUERRE, 1980, p. 163)

Once the particular spirit has appeared, welcoming songs follow.

> *Agaou Konblé sé loa nan onfò a*
> *Mdi émi é*
> *Agaou sé loa nan onfoa*
> *Mrélé agaou konblé agaou létan agaou dlo agaou*
> *boa agaou tònè*
> *Mdi agaou konblé sé loa nan onfò a*
> *Mdi ié émié sil rivé*
> *Sé loam nan onfòa ochè nago.*

> *Agaou Konblé, you are the spirit protector of my temple.*
> *I welcome you.*
> *Agaou, you are the spirit protector of my temple.*
> *My name is Agaou Konblé, Agaou Létan, Agaou Bois, Agaou Tone.*
> *Agaou, you are the spirit protector of my temple.*
> *I welcome you.*
> *You are here, the spirit protector of my temple.*

> (LAGUERRE, 1980, p. 168)

And having been welcomed, the spirit is enjoined to help with distress and illness, as in:

Latibonit o voié rélé moin
Io dim solé malad
Solé malad li kouché
Lèm té rivé moin join solé couché
Sé diléré sa poum antéré solé
Sa fèm la pèn o poum antéré solé
Sé régrétan poum antéré solé
Solé malad li kouché.

On the Artibonite river, I was,
And someone called me and told me
That Solé was sick and in bed.
When I came to Solé's place
I found him in bed.
It will be difficult and painful for me
If I have to bury Solé.
He is in bed.

(LAGUERRE, 1980, p. 172)

Finally, the spirit is bid ado through various songs of farewell and the ritual is essentially at an end.

A number of the variety of songs used, only briefly illustrated above, are reminiscent of the entreaties offered in the *Papyrus Ebers* in which there are appeals to a diety to make effective the treatment process applied. It is doubtful that a direct lineage between the Haitian songs and present-day hypnotic induction techniques can be ascertained, but certainly the rhythmic chanting of the rituals, with their requests for spiritual intervention, appear related to many of the ancient precursors of modern methods (e.g., the Druidic chants). The one aspect of the songs that both Bowers (1961) and Ravenscroft (1965) felt was directly related to modern hypnotic techniques was the use of the drums to produce a rhythmic, syncopated beat, which acted to entrance the possessed. It is true that the first disequilibrium stages of possession are often heralded by the dancers "falling to the drums," synchronizing their movements to the beat produced by the drummer. In fact, it is often not clear whether it is the drummer or the *hungan* who is in control of the ritual, for it is the drummer, with his subtle changes of rhythm, that moves the entire Voodoo ritual this way or that (Bowers, 1961). The recognition of the power of the drum and its message is embodied in the fact that anytime a government attempts to suppress "paganism," its initial proclamations outlaw the use of the drum (Metraux, 1972).

Is there, then, a direct link between the present-day rituals of Haitian Voodoo and modern hypnotic techniques? Some (Bowers, 1961; Ravenscroft, 1965) certainly think so. Many, however, may be more comfortable with recognizing the historical parallels, but leaving the equation of fundamental principles to be delineated by more rigorous investigation than is presently available. It has yet to be clearly demonstrated that the rhythmic thumps of the drums are the inorganic counterparts of the pulsating delivery of a verbal induction procedure, but that speculation is worthy of notation and possible further investigation.

To end a history of the induction of hypnosis with a description of Voodoo practices may leave the reader's faith in progress and her or his belief in the serious intent of the author a bit shaken. Is this all we have to show for 50 centuries of application and investigation? No, it is not. Have we arrived only to see ourselves depart? I hardly think so. Let us agree that progress is slow; progress is tedious. However, the reality of progress lies in the refinement of our methods, the sharpening of our instruments. And it is in the latter, the development of our measuring devices, chronicled in the following chapters, that the evidence of our progress from the past to the future is most apparent.

CHAPTER 7

Early Categories of Hypnosis and the Concept of Depth of Hypnosis

The concepts of stages of hypnosis, depth of hypnosis, and the capacity for hypnosis (susceptibility) are historically and conceptually intertwined. Although the ancients seemed to pay little attention to developing schemes to describe different stages of the induced conditions they observed, they did note that changes occurred in the individual operated on following whatever ritual "induction" they used. The major component of these changes, as witnessed by the Hindu, the Egyptians, the Druids, and so on, appeared to be a relaxation-sleep factor. Individuals subjected to the inductions became more relaxed in appearance and behavior and, finally, assumed the countenance of sleep, hence the sleep temples of Egypt, Greece, and Rome. Beyond the general notation that ancient hypnosis changed a person from an alert, awake, active condition to one of lethargy, relaxation, sleep, we have little evidence that ancient peoples differentiated as many stages in the process as did their ancestors of the 18th and 19th centuries.

During the 1700s and 1800s, each of the major theorists developed his own descriptive categories of the various behaviors observed during the induction and period of the trance. Even Mesmer, who was concerned with the curative powers of the crisis, recognized that there was at least one additional stage of the mesmeric condition—the coma. He described his magnetism in two stages: the crisis, which resembled hysterical convulsions, and the coma or apparent unconsciousness and insensitivity to external stimuli. Mesmer saw little value to the latter, but even with his expectations pointed toward the crisis, he observed the coma or sleep-like phase.

De Puységur, like his teacher, described two basic stages of the magnetism: first, one of relaxation and apparent sleep, followed, second, by a phase in which the subject could fulfill suggestions motorically and engage in verbal intercourse with the operator or whomever the operator might designate. The latter phase was of particular interest to de Puységur because during it he could affect the behavior of his subjects and assist them with their ills. King's (1837) translation of de Puységur's *Essay of Instruction on Animal Magnetism* indicates that the Marquis did, in fact, note varying degrees of mesmerism.

Sometimes, we procure from a patient, only a simple sigh; in another, the effect of magnetism is to cause him to shut his eyes, without the power of opening them himself; then he understands every thing, but is not completely in the magnetic state. This state of half crisis is very common. (p. 68)

De Puységur did not consider the "half crisis" as satisfactory as complete somnambulism, for "he [the magnetiser] can learn nothing from his patient" (King, 1837, p. 69). De Puységur was fascinated by somnambulism, or "deep hypnosis," because it was believed that through this condition clairvoyance could be achieved. It was through the somnambulist that physicians could obtain diagnoses and treatments for other patients. The somnambulist was reported to be able to transcend the ordinary senses of sight and hearing and perceive through physical objects that ordinarily block the wave-forms of sensory transmission.

Fascination with supernatural powers has always been with the human race, as we have seen in our review of the induction procedures of the ancients, and the uses to which they were put. Remember, for example, the youth described in the *Leiden Papyrus* through whom the priest could directly contact the gods. Nor did the somnambulist and her or his special powers escape the notice of such latter day hypnotists as Elliotson, who, like de Puységur, had part of his attention drawn down the clairvoyance-somnambulism pathway. The latter, for example, found somnambulistic, sense-transcending abilities in his most celebrated case, Victor Race. "There is no need of my speaking to him; I simply think in his presence, he hears me, and he answers me" (St. Dominique, 1874, p. 150).

St. Dominique (1874) distinguished two types of somnambulism, natural and artificial. The distinction hinged on whether the condition was induced by an operator (artificial) or occurred spontaneously (natural), such as in sleep-walking. In either case the individual in the condition was reported to demonstrate extraordinary powers of intuition and insight bordering on the miraculous. However, the major identifying characteristic of the condition of somnambulism was amnesia for all that took place during the period of hypnosis. *Hypnotic coma* is the phrase Braid (1855) used to describe this rare condition. Hypnotic coma denoted

That still *deeper* stage of the sleep in which the patient seems to be quite unconscious at the time of all external impressions, and devoid of voluntary power, and in whom no idea of what had been said or done by others during the said state of *hypnotic coma* can be remembered by the patient on awaking, or at *any* stage of *subsequent* hypnotic operations. (Braid, 1855/1970, pp. 370–371)

As we will see later on, amnesias (usually suggested) are still considered indicative of the most advanced (deepest) stages of hypnosis. Scales developed to assess either the depth of hypnosis or an individual's capacity for (susceptibility to) hypnosis all reserve performance of amnesic tasks for the deepest stages of the condition. Curiously, the Davis and Husband (1931) hypnotic susceptibility scale attributes complete amnesia only to a medium trance state, although theirs is the only modern scale to retain the older term, somnambulism. More modern scales of the last three decades all pose an amnesia task for the subject as one of the more difficult challenges, met only by those who have achieved the most profound stages of the hypnosis. In fact, it is becoming increasingly clear that cognitive (and sensory altering) tasks are among the most difficult for subjects to perform following a hypnotic induction. I will detail these scales later.

Before looking at some of the representative stages of hypnosis schemes of the 19th and 20th centuries, we should consider what is meant by "depth of hypnosis," for all of the schemes and measures of either hypnotic depth or capacity imply a continuum of depth. Not only is a depth continuum implied by scaling procedures, but it is also made quite explicit in the verbalizations that accompany the modern induction techniques. Key words in these verbalizations are "down" and "deep." Patients or subjects are told that they are going "down into a deep state of relaxation or sleep." Techniques such as the escalator method have the subject visualize moving "down" the escalator as he or she goes into a "deep" state of hypnosis. Seldom, if ever, does an operator use the up escalator as an induction technique, but rather reserves upward movement for coming "out of the trance." The one exception to this "down–in," "up–out" vertical direction of the depth continuum is the arm-levitation technique, in which one enters hypnosis (this phrase could be construed as a horizontal movement) as the arm rises. However, often subsequent arm movement downward is used to "deepen" the trance. Clearly hypnosis is conceived as an up–down, vertical continuum, wherein more hypnosis is down and less hypnosis is up.

But what is the nature of this vertical continuum? Its nature is simply a wakefulness–sleep continuum. Ever since the fluidic theory lost credence and induction techniques moved from physical passes intended to redistribute magnetic fluid in the subject to verbal suggestions intended to convey a particular cognitive set, the wakefulness–sleep continuum has been explicit in virtually all the procedures of induction. Measurements of hypnotic capacity also reflect the transition from wakefulness to sleep in their initial instructions to the subjects, enjoining the relaxation and/or sleep as a means of being able to meet more of the challenges that are used to measure either the depth of trance achieved or the capacity for trance at some subsequent time. Each of the schemes for categorizing the stages of hypnosis reviewed below imply, if they do not make quite explicit, the importance of a wakefulness–sleep continuum in conceptualizing what occurs in hypnosis.

Stages of Hypnosis

Many of the early 19th century practitioners of hypnosis did not concern themselves with differentiating among varying degrees of the condition. Rather, they contented themselves with producing the magnetized state (of-

TABLE 7.1.   Kluge's Stages of Hypnosis (1811)

1. Waking: Senses and musculature fully active.
2. Half-sleep: Eyes feel heavy and close; patient still hears. (Incomplete crisis)
3. Magnetic sleep: Deep, refreshing slumber; amnesia on awaking.
4. Simple somnambulism: Talking and acting in response to operator.
5. Clairvoyance: Increased interior consciousness.
6. Ecstasy: Far-seeing in time and space; insight into past, present, and future events.
7. Trance: (No behaviors given)

Source: Adapted from Björnström, 1887, p. 20.

ten referred to as somnambulism) and effecting cures or other behavioral changes in their patients. At most, they might have noted that certain "symptoms" appeared after induction. The symptoms of the patient's inability to open the eyes on their closure and being in a state of sleep or slumber were most often mentioned. Others were sensory insensitivity (particularly to anyone other than the operator) and the loss of memory for events occurring during the hypnosis, as one experiences on awaking from a night's sleep. All of these observations, although not drawn into a graduated scheme pay deference to the underlying continuum of wakefulness–sleep made explicit in the more formalized categories of others. Without taking note of the different stages of hypnosis, there was little reason to develop methods of assessing an individual patient's capacity for responding to the induction techniques. As I will note further on, the modern-day susceptibility scales ultimately evolved from the recognition of individual differences in responsiveness to induction techniques, which had made clear that hypnosis (magnetism, mesmerism) was not a unitary condition, but occurred in a matter of degrees, each degree denoted by different behaviors.

Kluge in Berlin in 1811 noted seven degrees of hypnosis (see Table 7.1). This early classification, certainly more elaborate than that of Mesmer or de Puységur, placed somnambulism and memory loss in the middle of the progressive process, not at the end. It was another 80 years before schemes such as Liébeault's (see below) proclaimed these categories to be the most profound condition achievable in hypnosis. Probably one of the main reasons for Kluge considering "Clairvoyance, Ecstasy and Trance" to be the "deepest" end of the continuum is the concern in the early and middle 1800s with being able to use the somnambulant patient as a diagnostic and prescriptive tool. As I mentioned in the chapters on induction techniques of this period, many individuals of professional renown were caught up in spiritualistic–clairvoyant–prediction-of-the-future phenomena. No wonder that some of the early categorizations of the stages or degrees of hypnosis should reflect this orientation. The same progression toward clairvoyance as the most extreme degree of hypnosis appears in the early classifications of Eschenmayer in 1816 and Lausanne in 1818. (See Tables 7.2 and 7.3.)

TABLE 7.2. Eschenmayer's Stages of Hypnosis (1816)

1. Magnetic perception: Senses move to the pit of the stomach, fingertips, or toes; increased internal instinct; insight into condition of others.
2. Magnetic clairvoyance
3. Magnetic sympathy (with magnetizer)
4. Magnetic divination

Source: Adapted from Björnström, 1887, p. 20.

Bertrand (1823) proposed a blending of the notions of somnambulism with those of clairvoyance and supernatural powers by outlining four types of somnambulism: (a) essential, which is seen in individuals with a particular nervous predisposition; (b) symptomatic, which occurs as a symptom of certain diseases; (c) ecstatic, such as occurs in moral or religious ecstasies; and (d) artificial, which is seen in animal magnetism. The mixture of somnambulism and clairvoyance was still evident into the third decade of the century in both America and the British Isles. The great spiritualist movement leader in the United States, Andrew Jackson Davis (1857), outlined four states of the condition that lead to his wonderous clairvoyant powers.

No. 1.   The Ordinary State. Separate Personal Spheres. Represents the operator and subject beginning the magnetic process.

No. 2.   The Psychological State. Partial Blending of Spheres. Favorable to sympathetic and transitional phenomena.

No. 3.   The Somnambulic State. Complete Blending of Spheres. Brings out excursional, examining, and medical clairvoyance.

No. 4.   The Superior Condition. Mental Spheres Separated. Lead to independent clairvoyance and intentional wisdom.

TABLE 7.3. Lausanne's Stages of Hypnosis (1818)

Half-Crises
1. Sensation of heat or cold.
2. Heaviness in head and limbs; eyes closed.
3. Hears but cannot answer.
4. Light slumber: dreams remembered.
5. Deep sleep.
6. Sweet and light sleep: following by feeling of delight.
7. Apparent sleep: no movement; hears and answers.
8. Dim perception of disease; sympathy or antipathy toward others.

Real Crises
9. Clairvoyance of self: self-prescription, cure.
10. Incomplete clairvoyance: of others.
11. Complete clairvoyance: of others; remedies and cures ordered.
12. Far-seeing predictions.

Source: Adapted from Björnström, 1887, pp. 20–21.

The spheres referred to a diagrammatic representation of the four states that showed the magnetizer seated in front of the subject, each surrounded by an ellipse depicting their sphere of influence and communication. In the Ordinary State two separate, non-overlapping ellipses symbolized the separateness of the personal spheres. In the Somnambulic State, one large ellipse enclosed both the magnetizer and the subject. Clairvoyance occurred in both the third and fourth state, depending on what sort of predictions were called for, medical in the third and transcendent "vision" in the fourth.

Both the blend of somnambulism with clairvoyant powers and a final, transcendent, "universal lucidity" degree of hypnosis were also evident in Britain about the same time that Davis was active in America. Colquhoun (1836) gave the following classification of the degrees of magnetism (hypnosis);

The *first* degree presents no very remarkable phenomena. The intellect and the senses still retain their usual powers and susceptibilities. For this reason, this first degree has been denominated the degree of *waking*.

In the *second* degree, most of the senses still remain in a state of activity. That of vision only is impaired; the eye withdrawing itself gradually from the power of the will. This second degree, in which the sensibility is partially disturbed, is, by some magnetizers, called the *half-sleep,* or the *imperfect crisis*.

In the *third* degree, the whole of the organs, through the medium of which our correspondence with the external world is carried on (the senses), refuse to perform their respective functions, and the patient is placed in that unconscious state of existence which is called the *magnetic sleep.*

In the *fourth* degree, the patient awakes, as it were, within himself, and his consciousness returns. He is in a state which can neither be properly called sleeping nor waking, but which appears to be something between the two. When in this state, he is again placed in a very peculiar relation towards the external world. . . . This fourth degree has been distinguished in the writings of the animal magnetists by the name of the *perfect crisis,* or *simple somnambulism.*

In the *fifth* degree, the patient is placed in what is called the state of self-intuition. When in this situation, he is said to obtain a clear knowledge of his own internal mental and bodily state;—is enabled to calculate, with accuracy, the phenomena of disease which will naturally and inevitably occur, and to determine what are their most appropriate and effectual remedies. He is also said to possess the same faculty of internal inspection with regard to other persons who have been placed in magnetic connexion (*en rapport*) with him. . . . From this fifth degree, all the subsequent magnetic states are comprehended under the denomination of *lucidity,* or *lucid vision* (Fr. *Clairvoyance;* Germ. *Hellsehen*).

In the *sixth* degree, the *lucid vision* which the patient possessed in the former degree, becomes wonderfully increased, and extends to all objects, near and at a distance, in space and in time: hence it has been called the degree of *univer-*

sal lucidity. This exalted state of the faculties, as may easily be supposed, is comparatively of very rare occurrence. (Colquhoun, 1836, pp. 280–282)

Two things are particularly noteworthy about Colquhoun's classification. First, it clearly progresses from a waking condition through various depths of sleep to increasing degrees of clairvoyant powers. Second, Colquhoun made is clear that he was writing of a continuum of stages, "No patient . . . can reach the higher degrees of magnetism, without having previously passed through the lower" (Colquhoun, 1836, p. 282). Although he did allow that some individuals could attain the later stages of the condition with such rapidity that the observer might not be able to perceive the transitions, his resolve that these stages were progressive was firm.

Colquhoun (1836) also recognized that there were both inter-individual and intra-individual differences in responsivity. "It is a very great mistake of the ignorant to suppose that the higher states of magnetism can be produced in all individuals, and at all times [in the same individual]" (Colquhoun, 1836, p. 282). In fact, he chided his French colleagues for attempting to attain somnambulism in all of their patients. Today, the recognition of the rarity of somnambules is universal. Individual differences form the bases for our present-day scaling techniques of the capacity for hypnosis.

Braid too described various stages of hypnosis. Although in *Neurypnology* (1843/1976) he outlined two stages, the "prodigiously exalted" stage, followed by "a state of depression, far greater than the torpor of natural sleep" (p. 29), Bramwell (1903) attributes a number of stages to him. According to Bramwell, Braid divided the many stages into three major categories: (a) slight hypnosis; (b) deep hypnosis; and (c) hypnotic coma. Braid, like Pavlov later, viewed hypnosis as a continuum of stages, each running into the other. During Braid's deep hypnosis occurred the two stages he noted in *Neurypnology:* the alert and then the deep, or sleep-like, phase. He warned that he did not consider it appropriate to attempt the hypnotic coma during the first session with a patient; it should be used only after the patient had had experience with the earlier stages. The hypnotic coma was similar to what others have labeled somnambulism. However, it is both in Braid's notation of the lethargic stage following the alert and in Bramwell's description of Braid's "slight hypnosis" that we see the continuing recognition of a wakefulness–sleep continuum is describing the stages of hypnosis.

During the period of the middle 1800s, there were no new and dramatically different schemes for classifying the stages of hypnosis. Björnström (1887) did make one passing comment worthy of note. He indicated that in 1852 Ennemoser distinguished between "physical" and "psychical" phenomena during hypnosis. This may have been one of the earliest explicit attempts to categorize the progression from physical feats (catalepsies) to amnesias (cognitive, psychical) noted in the stage schema above. Later, in the 1880s, Max Dessoir divided hypnotic behaviors into those involving the voluntary musculature and those involving the special senses. Although omitting the cognitive, this later classification did recognize that, as hypnosis progresses, sensory distortions occur or are possible. More recently, Rachman (1968) has extended the muscular-cognitive dichotomy to general relaxation and effective desensitization therapy. In a manner similar to the older hypnotic view that the therapeutic effectiveness of hypnosis depended on the patient being deeply hypnotized, somnambulistic, memory impaired, Rachman suggests that it is not so much the muscular relaxation, but the cognitive "feeling of calmness" that is crucial for effective therapy. Regardless, the same general continuum of wakefulness–sleep or lessened physical and/or mental activity pervaded the 19th century classification systems.

Liébeault continued in the same vein. Like Faria before him, he was concerned with the "lucid sleep," so concerned in fact that his descriptive terms for the stages of hypnosis were couched in sleep and sleep-related terms. Essentially, there were six stages of hypnosis, as seen in Table 7.4. Each of the first four stages was accompanied by behavioral signs through which the operator could gauge the stage of hypnosis. For example, during drowsiness there was said to be heaviness of the head and difficulty opening the eyes. As the individual progressed through the second drowsiness stage and the light sleep phases, such behaviors, as catalepsy and, finally, the inability to focus attention on other than the hypnotist appeared. Even the conceptual differences between the Nancy and Paris schools did not obviate the recognition of the persistent continuum of wakefulness–relaxation in the classification of the stages of hypnosis.

Both of Liébeault's somnambulistic stages (light and deep) were marked by total amnesia upon "waking", but in the latter the degree of hallucinatory potential was broader and the submission to the hypnotist more profound. Basically, this phase is just a continuation of the progression of relaxation–sleep that, from his observations of patients, Liébeault felt to be linear.

Liébeault's later co-worker, Bernheim, also developed an essentially linear scale of the stages of hypnosis, consisting of nine steps, which Hilgard et al. (1961) have collated into two major stages—one in which memory is retained, and one in which it is not. As in the previous scales, Bernheim's first degree consists of drowsiness coupled with various bodily sensations—

TABLE 7.4.   Liébeault's Stages of Hypnosis (1889)

1. Drowsiness
2. Drowsiness (catalepsies possible)
3. Light sleep
4. Deep sleep
5. Light somnambulism
6. Deep somnambulism

Source: From Edmonston, 1981, p. 57.

TABLE 7.5. Depth of Hypnosis According to Bernheim (1891)

Memory Retained on Waking

1st degree. Torpor, drowsiness, or various suggested sensations such as warmth, numbness.
2nd degree. Inability to open the eyes if challenged to do so.
3rd degree. Catalepsy suggested by the hypnotist and bound up with the passive condition of the subject, but may be counteracted by the subject.
4th degree. Catalepsy and rotary automatism that cannot be counteracted by the subject.
5th degree. Involuntary contractures and analgesia as suggested by the hypnotist.
6th degree. Automatic obedience; subject behaves like an automaton.

Amnesia on Waking

7th degree. Amnesia on waking. No hallucinations.
8th degree. Able to experience hallucinations during sleep.
9th degree. Able to experience hallucinations during sleep and posthypnotically.

Source: From Hilgard et al., 1961. Copyright 1961 by the American Psychological Association. Reprinted by permission.

warmth, numbness. As the subject moves progressively through the degrees, a linear progression of what we have come to accept as hypnotic behaviors ensues, ending with posthypnotic hallucinations. (See Table 7.5 for an outline of Bernheim's degrees of hypnosis.) Hilgard et al.'s (1961) organization of Bernheim's nine degrees serves to highlight the fact that during the latter two decades of the 19th century the observations persisted that the ultimated stages of hypnosis entailed major cognitive changes, particularly amnesias. Thus, although we do not find reference to somnambulism per se in Bernheim's classification, we do find the cognitive behavioral changes, which not too many decades before were considered characteristic of the somnambule, clairvoyant or not.

The final representative of the Nancy School in the 19th century, Forel, did keep the term somnambulism in his three-stage description of hypnosis: (a) drowsiness, in which suggestions are not uniformly effective; (b) hypotaxy, in which catalepsies appear; and (c) somnambulism, in which amnesia for events during hypnosis is featured. However, Forel was not the only individual of that era to rely on a three category classification system. Wetterstrand (1897) informs us that Fontan and Ségard, Van Eeden, Van Renterghem, and Moll all relied on three stages of hypnosis, which he (Wetterstrand) related to Liébeault's stages. Their first stage was Liébeault's first and second; their second, his third and fourth; and their third, his fifth and sixth. Lloyd Tuckey also offered a three category classification, like that of Forel: (a) light sleep, (b) profound sleep, and (c) somnambulism (Vincent, 1893/1897).

Despite the conceptual differences between the schools of thought at Nancy and Paris, the recognition that hypnosis was a progressive process moving from wakefulness to somnambulism was evident in both schools' classification systems. However, Charcot's three stages of hypnosis were not necessarily linear, as was implied in Liébeault's and Berheim's classification systems. Charcot (1882) wrote that the stages (cataleptic, lethargic, and artificial somnambulism), as well as "secondary forms" and "mixed states," could occur "suddenly, originally, and separately" or could be produced in succession by appropriate manipulations by the operator. In the latter case, the classifications were considered to be phases of the same process.

The Cataleptic State, which was produced by sudden auditory or visual stimulation, prolonged eye-fixation, or opening the eyes of an individual already in the Lethargic State, was described as follows:

> The subject . . . is motionless and, as it were, fascinated. The eyes are open, the gaze is fixed, the eyelids do not quiver, the tears soon gather and flow down the cheeks. Often there is anaesthesia of the conjunctiva, and even of the cornea. The limbs and all parts of the body may retain the position in which they are placed for a considerable period, even when the attitude is one which it is difficult to maintain. The limbs appear to be extremely light when raised or displaced, and there is no *flexibilitas cerea,* nor yet what is termed the stiffness of a lay figure. The tendon reflex disappears. Neuro-muscular hyperexcitability is absent. (Binet & Féré, 1888, p. 156)

Sensitivity to pain is lost; however, the operator can produce hallucinations and movement through suggestion. In other words, the patient can be active in this otherwise immobile condition.

The Lethargic State, which is produced either by eye-fixation or by closing the eyes of an individual already in the Cataleptic State, was described as follows:

> At the moment when he falls into the lethargic state, the subject often emits a peculiar sound from the larynx, and at the same time a little foam gathers on the lips. He then becomes flaccid, as if plunged in deep sleep; there is complete insensibility to pain in the skin, and in the mucous membrane in proximity with it. . . . The limbs are relaxed, flaccid, and pendent, and when raised they fall back again as soon as they are left to themselves. The pupils are, on the other hand, contracted, the eyes are closed or half-closed, and an almost incessant quivering of the eyelids may usually be observed. There is an exaggeration of the tendon reflex; neuro-muscular hyperexcitability is always present, although it varies in intensity. (Binet & Féré, 1888, p. 157)

The flaccidity may be either generalized or partial; however, the muscles can be made to contract by mechanical pressure on the appropriate tendons—with the exception of the face region.

The State of Artificial Somnambulism was produced either directly by eye-fixation or secondarily to lethargy or catalepsy by pressure applied directly to the head. This state also could be converted into either of the other two, into Lethargy by applying pressure to the cornea of the eyes through the eyelids, or into Catalepsy by raising the eyelids and admitting light.

Somnambulism was difficult to distinguish from the other states, particularly Catalepsy:

> The eyes are closed or half-closed; the eyelids generally quiver; when left to himself the subject seems to be asleep, but even in this case the limbs are not in such a pronounced state of relaxation as when we have to do with lethargy. . . . Excitement of the nerves or of the muscles themselves, and percussion of the tendons, do not produce contracture. On the other hand, various methods, among others, passing the hand lightly and repeatedly over the surface of a limb (mesmeric passes), or, again, breathing gently on the skin, cause the limb to become rigid, but in a way which differs from the contracture due to muscular hyperexcitability, since it cannot, like the latter, be relaxed by mechanical excitement of the antagonist muscles; it also differs from cataleptic immobility in the resistance encountered in the region of the joints, when the attempt is made to give a change of attitude to the stiffened limb. To distinguish this state from cataleptic immobility, strictly so called, it is proposed to distinguish the rigidity peculiar to the somnambulist state by the name of *catalepsoid rigidity;* it might also be called *pseudo-cataleptic.* (Binet & Féré, 1888, pp. 158–159)

Bramwell (1903) also reported a somnambulistic stage (see Table 7.6). He added this stage to Max Dessoir's two-part classification of (a) slight hypnosis, in which only the voluntary musculature could be affected, and (b) deep hypnosis, in which the special senses were affected. Bramwell, as others, used amnesia as the behavioral sign of somnambulism and noted that this stage was the one in which the subjects were "alert" in the sense that they could fulfill suggestions of movement and other overt behavior.

Alertness as a stage of hypnosis has persisted from the time of Mesmer to the present. Mesmer, you will recall, observed a crisis followed by a coma, the former being considered a more alert condition than the latter. De Puységur also perceived both a sleep phase and an alert phase; the latter he divided into two types. First, there was a type of alertness or arousal of the nervous system brought about by the particular form of induction used with the patient—reminiscent of the crisis, hysteria-like behavior of Mesmer's patients. Second, there was an alertness that occurred within the mesmeric trance itself, which allowed the patient to fulfill suggestions that would be difficult, if not impossible, to perform in the general lethargy of mesmerism per se. Braid spoke of an alert condition during Deep Hypnosis, during which subjects carried out complex motoric movements. Binet and Féré also made note of a period during hypnosis when the patient was alert—usually

TABLE 7.6.   Bramwell's Stages of Hypnosis

1. Slight hypnosis: Changes in voluntary muscles inducible.
2. Deep hypnosis: Slight hypnosis phenomena, plus changes in special senses.
3. Somnambulism: Large variety of reactions; amnesia on waking.

Source: Adapted from Bramwell, 1903, p. 155.

preceding the deepest, somnambulistic phase. Tamburini and Seppelli (1882) described two conditions of hypnosis through plethysmographic measures, a lethargic and a cataleptic condition.

Moll (1889/1897), for example, described active and passive types of hypnosis, although from his description he seemed to be dealing more with what occurs during the hypnotic condition (de Puységur's second type) than what happens on induction. Subjects in passive hypnosis could not be sufficiently aroused to respond to various suggestions of the hypnotist, while subjects in active hypnosis were able to follow postinduction instructions and respond to questions. To Moll, it was the presence or absence of muscular relaxation that denoted the type of hypnosis obtained. "The passive form has a great external likeness to natural sleep, while the active might be taken for a normal state on superficial observation" (Moll, 1889/1897, p. 78). (We know now, of course, on detailed observation that hypnotized subjects cannot satisfactorily simulate wakefulness [Reyher, 1973].) What gives us the clue that Moll's active hypnosis is de Puységur's second type (alertness—wherein the subject becomes relatively aroused to fulfill some suggestion) is his notation that: "Hypnosis often shows itself as passive at the beginning" (Moll, 1889/1897, p. 78).

The discussion of alertness on the part of hypnotized subjects has continued into the 20th century. However, it has taken on a slightly different character from in the past, in that the literature seems to be oriented not so much toward alertness to action occurring within hypnosis as toward a separate condition called "alert trance." A fuller discussion of the latter designation can be found in Hilgard (1977) and Edmonston (1981) (see also Chapter 6). In the main, however, present-day practitioners have relied on a rather simple classification system using three or four categories: light (hypnogogic), medium (moderate), and deep (somnambulistic), defined by the patients' ability to meet a progression of verbally delivered challenges starting, more often than not, with eye-catalepsies and ending with complex hallucinatory patterns and amnesias.

Whether we recognize alertness in the context of an otherwise relaxed, sleep-like condition for the purpose of effective response to suggestions or as a separate condition, the very term itself implies a wakefulness–sleep continuum through which patients pass as they enter the condition known as hypnosis. Probably the most elaborate schematic presentation of this continuum came from Russia, beginning with Pavlov's work on the conditioned response. Sleep and its precursor, inhibition—both at the cortical, cellular level and at the general behavioral level—were viewed as difficulties in the sequence of observed events leading to conditioned salivary and leg flexion responses in dogs. Pavlov and his co-workers noted that if the US (the reinforcing agent) was delayed by as much as 30 seconds in the process of elaborating conditioned responses (CRs), the dogs tended to fall into a passive state, only to become alert again in the moments just preceding the onset of the US. He attributed this tendency of the animal to slip into a profoundly passive state in the midst of a situation that ordinarily would call for alert action to *internal inhibition,* which formed the cornerstone of his notions of the wakefulness–sleep continuum.

Any monotonous, repetitive stimulation, unaccompanied by other external stimulation, eventually leads to inhibition and sleep. Thus the continual presentation of a CS to a dog without the subsequent presentation of the US leads not only to the eventual extinction of the conditioned response but also to drowsiness and sleep. This phenomenon was noted regardless of the noxiousness of the CS. Whether the CS was a potent electric shock or a gentle stroking of the dog's skin, the inhibitory response was elicited to its repetitious presentation.

In this manner, then, we may understand why most hypnotic induction techniques involve repetitive stimulation—passes and strokes in the last century and words in the present. Just as Pavlov's dogs habituated to the repetitious stimulation and their central nervous systems entered an inhibitory phase, so too do human subjects enter hypnosis through repetitious external stimulation. Monotony, relaxation, inhibition, and hypnosis were considered to be the same process by Pavlov.

While wakefulness and profound or total sleep are the endpoints of the continuum, a plethora of intermediate stages have been noted by most 19th and 20th century observers. Pavlov noted three major progressive phases through which the dogs went as they reacted to the experimental situation. His dogs were trained to make two responses, one secretory (salivation) and the other motoric (food intake). In wakefulness both responses were evident. However, if the animal were allowed to stand in the experimental harness a short while before the experiments began, the first phase became apparent by the disappearance of the secretory response, but not the motoric (Pavlov, 1928). If the beginning of the experiment was delayed still further, a second phase was attained in which the response pattern was reversed; that is, the secretory response was present, but the motoric absent. Finally, a prolonged delay resulted in both responses being eliminated in the third phase—sleep. Even more striking was the fact that if the animal were gradually awakened, the exact *reverse* response–appearance sequence occurs. First, the secretory response returned without the motoric, then the motoric was apparent without the secretory, and finally, both were elicited.

These three phases noted by Pavlov in his experimental animals closely resemble the three categories of sleep outlined by Platonov (1955/1959): "broken-up, partial and total sleep." "Broken-up" sleep most closely resembles wakefulness and is akin to the first phase outlined above. Thus CRs that were last elaborated (secretory, in the case of Pavlov's work) are temporarily lost, while the motoric are retained. In partial sleep (the second phase) there is increasing inhibition but there continues to be commerce with the external world, reminding us of Kluge's "half-sleep" state and the first few stages of Liébeault and Bernheim. Finally, at the stage of total sleep (phase three), the animal loses both responses and may hang limply in the harness.

Pavlov made several other observations of his animals. As inhibition increased, he noted other changes in the dogs' responses to a variety of stimuli. First, there occurred a phase in which both weak and strong stimuli were capable of eliciting a response. This phase of partial sleep he called the *equalization phase,* because stimuli of different strengths were equipotential. As inhibition continued, a *paradoxical phase* was entered, when the magnitude of the effect and the strength of the stimulus enter an inverse relationship. Now weak stimuli are more potent than strong stimuli, and paradoxically, a weak stimulus elicits the response that cannot be aroused by a strong one. Finally, just preceding complete cortical inhibition (total sleep), an *ultraparadoxical phase* is attained in which formerly excitatory stimuli act as inhibitors and inhibitory stimuli elicit excitation.

But what has all of this work on dogs and conditioned responses to do with hypnosis and ways in which practitioners categorize the behavioral changes noted in their patients? It was through his observations on his animals that Pavlov drew certain conclusions (later elaborated by Katlov, 1941/1959, and Platonov, 1955/1959) regarding the wakefulness–sleep continuum, a continuum that practitioners noted in their hypnotic patients. As we will see, the primacy of words (relatively weak stimuli compared with the concrete events they represent) in 20th century induction and suggestive procedures echoes both the equalization and paradoxical phases noted above.

The following table (Table 7.7) may help clarify the relationship between Pavlovian dogs and hypnotized humans because it summarized Pavlov's theory with respect to sleep, wakefulness, inhibition, and excitation. Here we see the progressive states of the organism from full wakefulness to total sleep, with the concomitant degrees of inhibition noted. One further clarification needs to be made with respect to Table 7.7. In what we may perceive as a confusion of language, the term "hypnotic sleep" was used for animal (nonhuman) hypnosis, while "suggested sleep" was reserved for what we understand as human hypnosis. I will not discuss Pavlov's notions on animal hypnosis, since my main thrust here is to present his wakefulness–sleep continuum as it relates to hypnosis in humans. A more detailed summary of this phase of partial sleep can be found in Edmonston (1981).

The degree of differentiation of partial sleep, and particularly the subdivision designated "suggested sleep," gives some clue to the importance this stage held for Pavlov. It was here that many of his observations on dogs were elaborated into an understanding and classification of hypnosis in humans. As seen in Table 7.7, suggested sleep (hypnosis) is the most elaborate and complex of the various stages of sleep. Although still working from his data on dogs, Pavlov noted an aspect of inhibition that pertains even more dramatically to the human animal than to the dog—the second-signal system, the verbal processes. In human beings, responses are progressively lost in the process of "hypnotization" in accord with the progression noted above, but both phylogeny and ontogeny play greater roles in people than in

TABLE 7.7. Schematic Presentation of Pavlov's Theory

State of Organism	Phase	Degree of Inhibition
Wakefulness		Minimal $(E \to \infty; I \to 0)$
"Broken-up" sleep		↓
Partial sleep		
Natural partial sleep		
Hypnotic sleep		
(1st-signal system)—CR sleep		
Suggested sleep		
(2nd-signal system)		
First stage		
First degree		
Second degree		Decreasing cortical excitation
Third degree		Increasing cortical inhibition
Second stage		
First degree		
Second degree		
Third degree	Equalization	
Third stage		
First degree		
Second degree		
Third degree	Paradoxical	
	Ultraparadoxical	↓
Total sleep	Complete inhibition	$(E \to 0; I \to \infty)$ Maximum

Source: Reprinted with permission of the publisher from *Handbook of Clinical & Experimental Hypnosis* by J. E. Gordon (Ed.). Copyright © 1967 by Macmillan Publishing Company.)

the dog. It is speech that is first inhibited in humans (phylogeny), and it is inhibited in accord with ontogeny. "The more complex and ontogenetically later conditioned bonds of the speech-motor analyzer are inhibited first as the subject lapses into a state of suggested sleep and are disinhibited last as the subject awakens from this state" (Platonov, 1955/1959, p. 75).

Speech provides the most obvious, the most natural conditioned stimuli in people's repertory of responsivity. And it was through speech primarily that the monotonous stimuli necessary for the induction of hypnosis were achieved.

> The method of inducing hypnosis in man involves conditions entirely analogous to those which produce it in our dogs. The classical method consisted in the performance of so-called "passes"—weak, monotonously repeated tactile and visual stimuli, just as in our experiments upon animals. At present the more usual method consists in the repetition of some form of words, describing sleep, articulated in a flat and monotonous tone of voice. (Pavlov, 1927, p. 404)

Here, then, we see Pavlov directly relating his theoretical viewpoint to the historical progression of hypnotic induction techniques I have related in the previous six chapters.

Pavlov attributed this heavy involvement of speech in hypnosis to his notation of a second-signal system, which refers to the verbal or inferential capacities of human beings, the ability to engage in abstract thought. This latter function "is achieved because the image of objects and actions expressed in words and ideas replaces their concrete effect on the organism" (Platonov, 1955/1959, p. 16). The concrete effect is the function of the first-signal system. So that to the extent that animals (and humans) engage in concrete imagery, and that imagery has an effect (elicits a response of some sort, motoric or visceral) in the organism, we are dealing with what Pavlov called the first-signal system. The dog and the person may both salivate to a morsel of food, but only the person will salivate to the word food. Although both the outward signs and the basic format of the internal inhibition in hypnosis were viewed as similar to Pavlov, it was the concept of rapport zones that further differentiated animal and human hypnosis. "The *rapport zone* produced in the sleeper by verbal suggestions is a more or less confined centre of concentrated excitation isolated from the remaining regions of the cortex" (Platonov, 1955/1959, p. 43). This then is the manner of hypnotic induction, internal inhibition produced through circumscribed excitation zones established by monotonous verbal patter.

As early as 1851, Wood made the same distinction:

> I think one great difference between natural sleep and that produced in magnetism is this—in the former, *all* nervous centres are tired out, and *all* repose; in the latter, those of sensations and volition are chiefly affected—and they being lulled to rest, the others retain their wonted activity. (Wood, 1851, p. 433)

But the rapport zones serve more of a function than merely making induction possible. It is through these zones that the hypnotist maintains the capability of eliciting further hypnotic phenomena by additional verbal suggestions. Kubie and Margolin (1944) echoed this same point, although they extended it into a psychoanalytic interpretation of the dissolution of the boundaries of the ego:

> It is characteristic of the onset of the hypnotic state that the subject appears to lapse into "sleep" while maintaining at least one sensori-motor contact with the outside world, and further that by the gradual elimination of other sensori-motor relationships the hypnotist becomes for a time the sole representative of or bridge to the outer world. . . . According to this description, the onset of the hypnotic state can be defined as a condition of partial sleep, in which one or two open channels of sensori-motor communication are maintained between the subject and the outside world. (p. 612)

If the process of hypnosis was conceived of as a process of increasing inhibition, interspersed with zones of rapport, then the subsequent elicitation of hypnotic phenomena was a process of disinhibition. As suggestions calling for some sort of alert action were offered, other areas of the cortex became uninhibited to fulfill the task required. Thus the Russians also were making the distinction between the general process of hypnosis—inhibition, sleep—and subsequent periods of partial alertness within the general condition. For them hypnosis was at least a two-step process, first relaxation and inhibition, then disinhibition to take suggested action. We have already encountered such notations in the works of de Puységur, Braid, Moll, and others.

With this admittedly brief and superficial background of Pavlov's work and theorizing, let us concentrate on the subdivisions of suggested sleep in Table 7.7. This portion of the table incorporates the work of Katkov (1941/1959). Nine degrees of hypnotic depth are presented, with their corresponding indices, which allow the practitioner to fractionate hypnotic depth behaviorally. Since Katkov's scheme is presented in detail in Platonov (1955/1959, pp. 425–428), the following is a brief summary, showing the progression of hypnotic depth.

First Stage, First Degree.   This degree has been called the prehypnoidal state, in which the patient reports pleasant sensations of restfulness. All sensibility is retained, and the patient can be easily awakened. Although the eyes are generally closed, they need not be.

First Stage, Second Degree.   There is now an inhibition of the "kinesthetic system" and a growing feeling of heaviness. The eyes are closed, and although the patient still retains usual sensitivity to his or her environment and can easily awaken, the latency of motor reactions lengthens.

First Stage, Third Degree.   The patient now exhibits a pronounced increase in verbal, as well as motor response, latency. Although the patient reports that he could have terminated the hypnosis or resisted the hypnotist's suggestion if he wanted to, "he just did not feel like it."

Second Stage, First Degree.   Inhibition of the second-signal system is more pronounced, and there now appear the symptoms of catalepsy. The patient is now very "sleepy," motor latencies are prolonged, the breathing is regular, and interest in environmental sounds is lost.

Second Stage, Second Degree.   By this time spontaneous analgesias are noted, but suggested illusions are not yet available.

Second Stage, Third Degree.   As increasing inhibition of the second-signal system continues, some suggested illusions begin to be effective, provided the patient's eyes remain closed. In particular, negative olfactory illusions can be elicited. The patient reports that his own thoughts have receded to the background and only the verbal suggestions of the hypnotist retain importance.

Third Stage, First Degree.   By this point, the patient is operating mainly on the first-signal system (excluding the rapport zone). Consequently, motor latencies to suggestions are shorter than in previous degrees. Illusions, with the eyes closed, are now easily evoked in all spheres except visual and auditory. Auditory illusions can be elicited with difficulty, yet there is no spontaneous amnesia.

Third Stage, Second Degree. With the exception of the rapport zone, the patient's spontaneous use of his second-signal system is obliterated, and positive hallucinations in all senses can be effected. However, the patient's eyes are still closed during hallucinations; opening them destroys the illusion and often initiates awakening. Partial spontaneous amnesias appear.

Third Stage, Third Degree. Only the rapport zone of the second-signal system remains, awaiting the suggestions of the hypnotist. It is during this degree of suggested sleep that all of the phenomena usually associated with "deep trance" are manifested—positive and negative hallucinations, total spontaneous amnesias, age regression, and so forth. For Katkov, and for the Pavlovian scheme, this degree is what others have labeled somnambulism, the plenary trance, or simply deep hypnosis (Erickson, 1967).

During the third degree of the second stage of suggested sleep, the human patients (as did Pavlov's dogs) attain an equalization phase of responsiveness, in which either the word or the actual stimulus calls forth the illusion. Thus the "weak" stimulus (the word) attains equalization with the "strong" (the actual event).

The paradoxical phase, in which weaker stimuli—words, in the case of the human—achieve regnancy over stronger, is highly significant for the understanding of many deep-trance phenomena. This phase appears in the third degree of the third stage of suggested sleep, in which hallucinatory, amnesic, and regressive behaviors are elicited. Thus, in the human, the capability of words to call forth negative hallucinations in the face of impinging environmental stimuli to the contrary may be viewed as an example of a universal phenomenon across species. The only basic difference between Pavlov's dogs and humans in the paradoxical phase is that the latter are responding to second-signal stimuli (words) and the former to first-signal stimuli. The same is noted even more so in the ultra-paradoxical phase.

While it is readily apparent from more recent data on hypnotic depth scaling and the development of quantitative susceptibility scales (see the next chapter) that the progression of behavioral changes in hypnosis is not as orderly as in Table 7.7 and the categories of hypnosis proposed by others of the last and this century, Katkov's sleep hierarchy serves as a prime example of the detail that the classifications of hypnotic behaviors had reached by the 1940s. Other examples will be encountered in the various hypnotic depth scales of the other decades of the 20th century, scales that were the forerunners of the array of measurement techniques intended to assess the capacity for hypnosis and predict an individual's future performance during hypnosis.

CHAPTER 8

Measuring the Capacity for Hypnosis

Categorizations of different stages of hypnosis and the development of depth scales, formats for measuring what particular stage a patient had achieved, had preceded attempts to assess the potential capacity for hypnosis. It was one thing to be able to state after the fact what stage of trance the subject had achieved; it was quite another to be able to predict the future and gauge beforehand what stage a particular individual might achieve. Certainly for the practitioner who felt the need to have his or her patients in a particular stage of hypnosis before offering therapeutic suggestions, knowing beforehand how well the patient would respond was of value. Naturally, then, a scale that could successfully predict the future was desirable both for clinical practice and for studying the variables underlying the observation that some individuals respond more profoundly to hypnotic inductions and suggestions than do others.

Although the modern quantitative measurement of the capacity for hypnosis began in the 1930s, the recognition of individual differences in ability was noted a century before. Poyen (1837) took note in his American lectures that some individuals responded more easily to the manipulations of the magnetizer than did others. What the nature of these differences were was not revealed, but Caldwell (1842) a few years later was more explicit.

> Women are mesmerisable more easily, and in a larger proportion than men; and delicate, sensitive and weakly women more easily than robust and less sensitive ones.
>
> Men can be mesmerized as certainly and as deeply as women; though not I say in so large a proportion.
>
> Persons, when in perfect health, are as certainly, and, I believe, as easily mesmerised, as when they are sick. . . . I have known mesmeric sleep to be retarded, and rendered less perfect, if not actually prevented, by indisposition. (p. 115)

Caldwell's last point is of particular historic interest because at the time there was some controversy regarding the effects of malady on the capacity for hypnosis. According to the most prevalent belief, ill people were thought to be the most susceptible, an idea that extended through the time of Charcot and the notions of hypnosis as a form of hysteria. Moll, Liébeault,

Forel, and Tuckey, among others, agreed with Caldwell's view. They considered the unhealthy, the mentally unsound, and individuals of low intellectual ability to be incapable of hypnosis, although, as we noted in Chapter 4, Voisin claimed some success hypnotizing a severely disturbed population. More recently, quantitative data also (see, for example, Gill & Brenman, 1959; Hilgard, 1965) bear out Caldwell's contention, since neuroses and psychoses do not enhance the capacity and probably slightly reduce it.

Another one of Caldwell's points also had a rather modern ring. He suggested that "a very large majority of mankind have been found mesmerisable" and he found "doubtful" and "improbable" that "some persons are insusceptible of the mesmeric influence." Many practitioners today consider all individuals to have a capacity for hypnosis, to some degree or another, and even those who appear to be insusceptible can benefit from therapeutic suggestion. Bernheim, of course, was an early proponent of the idea that even if the patient failed to respond to the induction technique they could still obtain therapeutic benefit by following his suggestions. Binet and Féré (1888), on the other hand, felt that suggestion needed a fertile field to be productive. "In order that the suggestion should succeed, the subject must be either spontaneously or artificially in a morbid state of receptivity" (Binet & Féré, 1888, p. 176).

Caldwell was one of the earlier individuals to quantify his opinions by indicating that 14 out of 15 individuals were mesmerisable. This ratio (93%) is surprising like the figures of later 19th century practitioners summarized in Table 8.1 below, wherein only 9% were reported to be refractory or nonsusceptible. Even compatible figures that reflect the data of the middle 20th century (See Hilgard, 1965) are not far from Caldwell's 1842 estimate, showing a refractory group of 20% in a predominantly college, rather than patient, population.

Braid also quantified his observations on the individual differences in the capacity for hypnosis. In *Neurypnology* (1843/1976), he reported hypnotizing 64 of 76 strangers (84%) during various lectures. These figures, which are comparable to the susceptible-refractory figures for the 20th century, included 32 children, all of whom proved susceptible. This is somewhat surprising because later in that same section of the book he indicates that he considered children, along with "those of weak intellect, or of restless and excitable minds" (Braid, 1843/1976, p. 25), to be more difficult patients.

Deleuze appeared to agree with Braid's perception of restlessness and excitability, but not with his conclusion regarding children.

In general, magnetism acts in a more sensible and efficacious manner upon persons who have led a simple and frugal life, and who have not been agitated by passions, than upon those with whom the course of nature has been troubled, either by habits of luxury or by remedies. . . . Magnetism, therefore, cures much more promptly, and much better, persons who reside in the country, and children, than those who have lived in the world, who have taken much medicine, and whose nerves are irritated. (Deleuze, 1843/1982, pp. 24-25)

The efficacy of hypnosis for those living simple, uncomplicated lives reminds us of de Puységur's notable success with the peasants of Buzancy and makes some logical sense with respect to children, who, despite where they might reside, have simply not lived long enough to have experienced the stresses and irritations of adult life. The hypnotizability of children has been the topic of more extensive study during this century, as we will see below.

Deleuze's concern with children was not restricted to their hypnotizability. Like others of the early and middle 1800s, Deleuze concerned himself with detecting who did and who did not have the capacity *to hypnotize*. Children over age seven were reported to be good operators. They learn by imitation, are not distracted during the process, and carry it off effortlessly. However, he warned that they should not be permitted to engage in the practice "because it would injure their growth and weaken them" (Deleuze, 1843/1982, p. 25). The ability to hypnotize was perceived as a natural given, a strength of will and power, which when used reduced the strength of the operator. How different it is today. Although there is some recognition that some individuals are more effective hypnotists (e.g., Erickson), the emphasis of the professional societies is on training, not native capacity or ability. If one is intellectual enough and perseveres long enough to obtain a doctoral degree, then, with "proper" training from an "appropriate" source anyone can hypnotize. Not so in the middle 19th century.

Through the 1840s there was little concern with predicting the capacity for hypnosis in prospective patients. The emphasis, as outlined in the last chapter, was on the various categories of hypnosis obtained through the induction procedure. Practitioners attempted hypnosis with all patients and noted the degree of their success. Strange how history folds back on itself, for even today many practitioners initially proceed with induction rather than present the time-consuming susceptibility scale challenges to their patients. Although manuals for various seminars training professionals in hypnosis mention quick tests of susceptibility (hand clasp, clock visualization, sway test), only Spiegel's Eye-Roll Sign has been accompanied with recent data (Spiegel, 1972). Even this quick test is not wholly accepted (see below).

One of the earlier notations of a brief hypnotizability test was that of Gregory's description (1909) of Major Buckley's work in the 1850s. "Major Buckley first ascertains whether his subjects are susceptible, by making with his hands passes above and below their hands, from the wrists downwards. If certain sensations, such as tingling, numbness, etc., are strongly felt, he knows that he will be able to produce the mesmeric sleep" (Gregory, 1909, p. 160). Notice that the operator was not a visual observer of behaviors that might have indicated a capacity for hypnosis, but a tactile sensor of electric-like sensations. Buckley, you will recall (see Chapter 3), was also the individual who selected his clairvoyant, "deeply" susceptible subjects on the basis of their ability to perceive a blue light around his face as he made mesmeric passes over his own countenance. Today we observe and measure visually the behaviors of prospective subjects to verbal challenges, rather than sense the "vibs".

As indicated in the last chapter, the later decades of the 19th century saw an increasing interest in categorizing various levels of depth of hypnosis. With this interest grew also the interest in prediction. In Chapter 5, I described an instrument, called the *hypnoscope,* designed by the Parisian physician Ochorowicz. It consisted of an iron ring magnet into which the prospective patient inserted his or her finger. If the patient reported "certain sensations in the skin and twitchings of the muscles," hypnotizability was most probable; if not, they were probably not susceptible. Little evidence was ever produced for the accuracy of the device.

Moll, as suggested above, rejected the prevalent notions of the last two decades of the 19th century that neurasthenia, pallor, hysteria and general weakness of the will, or general feebleness were predictive of success at being hypnotized; quite the contrary. It was, he felt, the healthy, even the muscularly robust, who demonstrated the best capacity for hypnosis. In fact, he relied on two factors that appeared to anticipate in part the work of Hilgard 70 years later (1965): the best subjects were those who can (a) maintain a passive state; and (b) fix or narrow their attention. He also commented on the age factor, indicating that, in his experience, children under three were not hypnotizable and those between three and eight, only with difficulty. Sex was of little value as a predictor, women being no more or less hypnotizable than men.

As the 19th century entered its last decade, the movement for increasing quantification of the parameters of hypnotizability gathered energy. Practitioners and investigators alike (They were often one and the same in those days.) wanted to know what percentages of patients/subjects were susceptible to hypnotic induction and in what degree. Clinicians such as Van Eeden, Van Renterghem, Liébeault, Bernheim, Berillon, and others were keeping records of the percentages of their successes. In 1892 von Schrenck-Notzing (see Bramwell, 1903) reported the First International Statistics of Susceptibility to Hypnosis in which he pooled the observations of 15 investigator–practitioners in different countries on more than 8000 cases. What he found was that only 6% were held to be refractory to the induction procedures. His figures and those of others gathering data around the turn of the century appear in Table 8.1.

In addition to the data in Table 8.1, Bernheim reported 75% success with 5000 patients between 1882 and 1886, and 80% with 10,000 some years later. Berillon also reported an 80% success rate with 250 children. By 1893 Wetterstrand's patient population had grown from 3209 to 6500, with a decrease in the refractory percentage. Forel's success rate exceeded 95% with 1000 patients in 1898. Loewenfeld (1901) reported the following success rates: Bottey, 30%; Binswanger, 50%; Morselli, 70%; Peronnet, 75%; Lloyd-Tuckey

TABLE 8.1. Distribution of Susceptibility to Hypnosis: Nineteenth Century Studies

Investigator	Date	Cases (N)	Distribution of Susceptibility (In Percent)					Total Susceptible
			Refractory: Nonsusceptible	Drowsy– Light	Hypotaxy Moderate	Somnambulistic– Deep		
Peronnet	ante-1900	467	25	10	20	45		75
Forel	ante-1898	275	17	23	37	23		83
Lloyd-Tuckey	ante-1900	220	14	49	28	9		86
Bramwell	ante-1900	200	11	24	26	39		89
Von Schrenck-Notzing	ante-1900	240	12	17	42	29		88
Mosing	1889–1893	594	12	42	17	29		88
Hilger	ante-1900	351	6	20	42	32		94
Von Schrenck-Notzing (pooling of 15 reports)	1892	8,705	6	29	50	15		94
Liébeault	1884–1889	2,654	5	22	62	11		95
V. Eeden & v. Renterghem	1887–1893	1,089	5	43	41	11		95
v. Renterghem	ante-1900	414	4	52	33	11		96
Wetterstrand	1890	3,209	3	36	48	13		97
Velander	ante-1900	1,000	2	32	54	12		98
Vogt	ante-1900	116	0	2	13	85		100
Total cases		19,534						
Range of percentages			0–25	2–52	13–62	9–85		75–100
			9	29	36	26		91

Source: From Hilgard, Weitzenhoffer, Landes & Moore, 1961. Copyright 1961 by the American Psychological Association. Reprinted by permission.

& Delboeuf, 80%; Forel, 83%; Bernheim, 90%; Liébeault, 92%; v. Schrenck-Notzing, 94%; Wetterstrand & Ringier, 95%; Van Renterghem, 97%; Velander, 98%; and Vogt, 100%.

Bramwell found a curious relationship between hypnotizability and his familiarity with the patient. In 100 patients from his own practice (27 males, 73 females; ages 4–76; Mean, 23.42) he found none "refractory," 12 achieved "slight hypnosis," 40 "deep hypnosis," and 48 "somnambulism." (From 500 of his own patients, he also reported only 2 failures.) In 100 patients not from his own practice (42 males, 59 females; ages 9–70; Mean, 34) he reported 22 refractory, 36 slight hypnosis, 13 deep hypnosis, and 29 somnambulism. Bramwell (1903) concluded that the differences were primarily due to the severity of the disorders in each of the two groups. In the former, 24 were either healthy or suffered only minor afflictions, while only 14 fell into those categories in the latter. He reiterated the stand of Moll, Bernheim, and others that severity of disorder was inversely related to the capacity for hypnosis.

Although we generally calculate the "beginnings" of quantitative scales of susceptibility from about 1930, it is clear that the golden age of Victoria produced some of the early attempts to scale the capacity for hypnosis in relation to the eventual depth of hypnosis achieved. Bramwell (1903) gave us a sampling of these attempts in his discussion of this point. In addition to the data for von Schrenck-Notzing's pooled observations and those of Van Eeden and Van Renterghem in Table 8.1, Bramwell recorded the distribution of susceptibility-depth for 755 of Liébeault's patients (see Table 8.2). These figures are comparable to those in Table 8.1. Interestingly enough, the somnambulistic category for the highest level of responsibility (somnambulistic-deep) in the 19th century is about 10–15% higher than that reported for 20th century scales (see Hilgard, 1965). The most probable reason for the difference is that most of the data for the 19th century came from clinical and

TABLE 8.2.   Distribution of 755 Cases of Liébeault by Sex and Depth of Hypnosis Achieved

	Men	Women	Total	Proportion (in percent) Men	Proportion (in percent) Women
Somnambulism	54	91	145	18·8	19·4
Very profound sleep	21	34	55	7·3	7·2
Profound sleep	108	163	271	37·6	34·8
Light sleep	52	99	151	18·1	21·1
Somnolence	21	50	71	7·3	10·6
Uninfluenced	31	31	62	10·8	6·6
Total	287	468	755		

Source: From Bramwell, 1903, p. 60.

private practice and those for the 20th century come from college populations of volunteer and coerced–volunteer subjects.

Children formed a special group when it came to the capacity for hypnosis.
Beaunis, recasting Liébeault's data to reflect more readily the age factor,
showed that there was indeed a decline in the percentage of individuals
capable of somnambulism with increasing age and a concomitant increase in
the refractory percentage. Maximum hypnotizability appeared to be up until
the age of 14, with 26.5% of children age 1–7 and 55.3% of those age 8–14
being characterized as somnambules. These percentages dropped to 11% by
old age. Between ages 14 and 63, the percentage of failures ranged between 4%
and 14%, the latter appearing in the age group 56 and up (Felkin, 1890). The
findings with respect to children have been replicated in more recent times
with more modern scaling techniques (Barber & Calverley, 1963; London,
1965), which showed that ages 9–14 are the prime susceptibility ages in more
than 900 children. Wetterstrand reported working with children as young as
$2\frac{1}{2}$, and Berillon had an 80% success rate with 250 children of all ages.

By the beginning of the 20th century, the following conclusions had been
drawn about the capacity for hypnosis: (a) Children, up to age 14 were more
responsive than adults; (b) Except for the higher capacity found in children,
age was of no major consequence; (c) Neither nationality nor social class
influenced susceptibility, although these points were contested by some.
(Felkin, 1890, for example, thought French, Spaniards and Italians were
easier to hypnotize than the English, Germans, Dutch, or Swedes, while
others concluded that the higher classes were more responsive to induction,
in contrast to 18th century thinking.); (d) General health and intellectual
level were positively related to susceptibility, as was the ability to narrow
and focus one's attention; and, finally, (e) The personality characteristics of
the operator were important to the success of the venture. On the latter point,
Bramwell, Moll, Forel, and others concluded that mechanical knowledge
and application of technique was insufficient for the practitioner to be successful. The operator had to "be enthusiastic, patient, confident, and fertile
resource in varying his methods" (Bramwell, 1903, p. 70). Today's clinician–investigator could well take a lesson from that quote, for while the
mechanical application of a single induction technique will obtain some measure of success with some patient/subject populations, the individual armed
with a host of techniques and the agility and flexibility to apply them as suits
the patient's needs will serve his or her patients best.

Thus, as we have seen throughout this book, the past foretells the future.
The modern, quantitative scales for measuring the capacity for hypnosis
began, if not centuries ago, at least many decades before the present century
opened. Now let us explore the "modern" scales of susceptibility.

Modern Susceptibility–Depth Scales

As indicated above, the modern, quantitative measurement of the capacity
for hypnosis began in the late 1920s and early 1930s. The movement was

almost entirely an American affair. Initially, scales originally intended to tell the practitioner the stage of hypnosis achieved by her or his patient was converted for predictive use. In general, the early scales were the same and involved, first, putting the subject through an induction procedure—usually a relaxation eye-closure technique—and then offering a series of challenges that the subject may or may not meet. Once the progression of difficulty of the challenges was established, a numerical value was given to various stages (depths) of hypnosis. As we will see, the last development was to quantify the stability of the assumed linearity among the various challenges, to include the induction itself as a challenge, and to produce a predictive score. These scores were then used to give the practitioner some idea of what hypnotic phenomena could or could not be expected in subsequent therapeutic sessions.

But herein lies a conceptual difficulty, which has of late erupted into an intramural dispute between the two individuals responsible for the development of the most widely used "susceptibility" scales today, the Stanford Scales and their various subsequent offshoots. Including an induction technique—eye-fixation and eye-closure in most cases—as one of the scored challenges converts what is intended to be a scale to predict future behavior under conditions of hypnosis into a measure of the depth of hypnosis obtained by the induction procedure. Weitzenhoffer (1980a), the principle author of the Stanford Scales has recognized this fact, along with several other flaws in the development of the scales, and drawn the fire of Hilgard (1981a) and others (e.g., Bowers, 1981a,b). However, Weitzenhoffer is correct in highlighting the misnomer of all scales purporting to measure the capacity for hypnosis that precede the challenges with an induction technique. The only scales that measure the capacity for hypnosis without the confound of an induction are the Barber Suggestibility Scale (Barber & Calverley, 1963b) and the Creative Imagination Scale (Barber & Wilson, 1977, 1978/79; Wilson, 1976), but we will examine them later in this chapter. With this recognition in mind, let us turn to the development of scaling techniques.

White Scale

In 1924 Morgan and Travis (see Morgan, 1924) noted that individuals who were more readily hypnotized were (a) better able to lose themselves in daydreaming and reverie and (b) responsive to weaker than normal stimuli while in such reverie. Acting on the latter supposition, Morgan developed a test to predict hypnotizability. Subjects were placed in a dark room and told to lose themselves in reverie while staring at an illuminated crystal ball. Meanwhile, a tone was presented to the subject through earphones, and he or she was to press a telegraph key upon perceiving the tone. The subject was not to attend to the tone, but only to respond when aware of it. Tested before, during, and after reverie, subjects who were found to respond to a weaker stimulus during reverie were those who were more readily hypnotized. In other words, those subjects whose threshold for auditory stimulation was decreased during reverie were more susceptible than those in whom the threshold remained the same or was increased. Here, then, was an early, true scale measuring the capacity for hypnosis without the introduction of an induction technique prior to the measurement.

M. M. White's scale (1930), however, was otherwise. The scale involved a series of challenges (rather than just one, as with Morgan) to which the subject's behavior was noted and assigned a number. The challenges were as follows:

1.   Stiff fingers. "Your fingers are getting stiff. You cannot move them. You will try but they will not move."

2.   Counting. "You will count to four, but you will leave out three because you cannot say three. You will try to say three but cannot. Count now."

3.   Alphabet. "You will say the alphabet as far as f, but you will leave out d because you cannot say d. You will try to say d but you cannot say d. Now begin."

4.   Petting cat. "You will open your eyes and not wake up. See the gray cat in your lap. Pet it. After the cat is removed you will brush the fur from your lap."

5.   Singing. "You will close your eyes now and go deeper to sleep. In a few minutes you will hear a woman over at the Fine Arts Building singing 'America' . . . . I hear her now, do you?"

6.   Pencil. "Open your right hand and turn the palm upward. Now when I count three, you will not be able to feel a single thing in your hand. One—two—three." (Whereupon a pencil was placed in the subject's hand and he was asked whether anything was in his hand or not.)

7.   Writing name. "You will open your eyes now and not wake up. You will take this pencil (operator indicated) and write your name on this piece of paper (operator indicated). You will leave out all the vowels in your name because you cannot write a single vowel."

8.   Addition. "You will now add these columns of figures (operator indicated) as rapidly and accurately as you can. Here is a pencil." The subject was allowed to add one minute; then he was given a second series of columns of figures. The order in which the two series of columns were given was alternated from subject to subject. There were six columns of figures in each series. Each column consisted of six four place numbers. During the addition of the second series, an assistant read aloud from a case history of a neurotic.

9.   Placing book. "When I count three you will be awake. After you wake up you will see a book on the table in front of you. When you see me put my hand in my pocket you will place this book on the chair beside you." (White, 1930, pp. 294–295)

As is readily apparent from challenge nine, the scale was measuring depth of hypnosis achieved, not potential for hypnosis at some future time. The challenges were preceded by an unspecified induction of "eye-fixation and verbal suggestion." Those subjects showing "no sign of hypnosis" (again unspecified) were considered nonhypnotizable. The scores derived from the challenges (either by measuring the time required for the subject to respond, or authoritative opinion of which tasks were more difficult) were compared to other variables the author considered to be possible predictors of hypnotizability: subject's height, weight, grades in psychology courses, intelligence (Otis), extroversion–introversion score (Neyman-Kohlstedt), and score on a sway test. The postural sway test, first used by Moutin in 1890 (Weitenzenhoffer, 1972b) and later popularized by Hull (1933), highly correlated to scores on White's scale, as did extroversion scores. Although White (1930) did not produce a true susceptibility scale, he did move history along the quantitative path by scaling his challenges and assigning numbers to the subject's responsiveness, an important step forward from the classification systems of the latter part of the 19th century.

Davis and Husband Scale

Shortly after White's publication followed the Davis and Husband (1931) and the Barry, MacKinnon, and Murray (1931) scales. The former, presented in Table 8.3, is clearly a series of graduated challenges given to the subjects and scaled from 0 to 30. It also began with an eye-fixation induction technique fashioned after Braid's method, progressed through four major categories of trance (hypnoidal, light, medium, and somnambulistic), and ended with negative visual hallucinations, although the authors noted that somnambulism could not really be considered to have been achieved unless total amnesia was present. Amnesia as the mark of "deep" hypnosis, somnambulism, some say "real" hypnosis (Braid called it hypnotic coma.), has persisted well into the present century.

These authors also attempted to relate the scores achieved on their scale with other variables in the hope of finding additional concomitants of hypnosis. The correlations were, as is consistent throughout the literature, disappointing. Although intelligence for both men and women did significantly correlate with the Davis and Husband scores (.37 and .31, respectively), maladjustment, prejudice, and affectivity did not. Introversion, contrary to White's earlier finding, did show a trend toward relating to hypnotic depth in women. What we see here, then, is the growing interest in relating hypnotizability to other traits of the individuals concerned, in a quantitative format. What investigators were attempting to do, whether they realized it or not, was to bring hypnosis into the realm of the normal and remove it from the general public's perception of an abnormal behavior. If hypnosis could be placed on a continuum with other usual, acceptable human behaviors as Pavlov and other Russians, for example, were doing, and could be shown to relate to other less "abnormal" behaviors, then a general acceptance by both the public at large and the professional community might be achieved. As this was achieved, investigators and practitioners could expend more time studying this form of human behavior and less time defending themselves from cries of charlatanism, occultism, and so forth.

TABLE 8.3.   Davis and Husband's Hypnotic Susceptibility Scoring System

Debt [sic]	Score	Objective Symptoms
Insusceptible	0	
Hypnoidal	1	
	2	Relaxation
	3	Fluttering of lids
	4	Closing of eyes
	5	Complete physical relaxation
Light trance	6	Catalepsy of eyes
	7	Limb catalepsies
	10	Rigid catalepsy
	11	Anaesthesia (glove)
Medium trance	13	Partial amnesia
	15	Post-hypnotic anaesthesia
	17	Personality changes
	18	Simple post-hypnotic suggestions
	20	Kinaesthetic delusions; complete amnesia
Somnambulistic trance	21	Ability to open eyes without affecting trance
	23	Bizarre post-hypnotic suggestions
	25	Complete somnambulism
	26	Positive visual hallucinations, post-hypnotic
	27	Positive auditory hallucinations, post-hypnotic
	28	Systematized post-hypnotic amnesias
	29	Negative auditory hallucinations
	30	Negative visual hallucinations; hyperaesthesias

Source: From Davis and Husband, 1931. Copyright 1931 by the American Psychological Association. Reprinted by permission.

Probably because of its apparent linear simplicity, the Davis and Husband scale was used more than any others until the advent of the Stanford individual scales and the Harvard group scale (see below). Two aspects of the Davis and Husband scale have persisted to the present: the use of an eye-fixation induction procedure and the notation of progressive relaxation as initiating the trance and becoming increasingly profound as the trance progresses. Even Hull (1933), who did not develop a depth-susceptibility scale per se, used the time necessary for the eyes to close with continued suggestions of eye fatigue, drowsiness, and lid fluttering as an indicator of hypnotizability.

Barry, MacKinnon, and Murray Scale

In the same year that Davis and Husband presented their scale, Barry, MacKinnon, and Murray (1931) published their study of hypnotizability as a personality trait. As White and Davis and Husband before them, they began with an induction technique and then proceeded to measure, in their own words, "the degree of hypnosis." Curiously, their technique was a combination of eye-fixation, verbal instructions for relaxation and sleep, and mesmeric passes and strokings. Somehow the latter seemed out of place by the third decade of the 20th century, even if it was intended to soothe rather than to redistribute magnetic fluid. Here is their description:

> To obtain suggestibility the subject was directed to lie on a couch with head slightly elevated and eyes focused upon the head of a pin stuck in the opposite wall. The usual procedure for inducing relaxation, drowsiness and sleep (i.e., statements in a subdued, monotonous voice accompanied by pressure on the forehead and stroking) was employed for about five or six minutes before specific suggestions to measure the degree of hypnosis were given. (Barry et al., 1931, p. 9)

Their Hypnotic Index had possible scores of 0–5 (see Table 8.4.) and consisted of a series of five suggestions plus a score for the degree of presence (or absence) of amnesia. The suggestions were challenges not to be able to (a) open the eyes, (b) raise the arm, (c) bend the arm, (d) separate the fingers, and (e) speak their name.

Friedlander and Sarbin Scale

In 1938 Friedlander and Sarbin, attempting to explore further the confusing literature on personality traits and hypnotizability, developed their own scale of hypnotic depth (see Table 8.5). In reality, they combined pieces from other scaling attempts. As with all of the scales before, and most after, theirs was not a hypnotizability, susceptibility scale, but a depth of hypnosis scale, for the challenges on which the measurement was partially based were preceded by an eye-fixation, relaxation induction technique. The five chal-

---

TABLE 8.4. Barry, Mackinnon, and Murray Hypnotic Susceptibility Scoring System

Negative Suggestions

0	No suggestion carried out. No tendency at all for them to be carried out.
1	No suggestion carried out but clear evidence of difficulty in surmounting them.
1.5	One suggestion carried out.
2	Two or three suggestions carried out.
3	All suggestions carried out.

Amnesia

0	No loss of memory and no difficulty of recall.
0.5	Difficulty, but final memory.
1	Partial loss of memory.
2	Complete or almost complete loss of memory.

Source: From Friedlander and Sarbin, 1938. Copyright 1938 by the American Psychological Association. Reprinted by permission.

TABLE 8.5. Friedlander-Sarbin Scale of Hypnotic Depth

	Score Value
Final lid closure (Hull)	
1. Eyes close in Period I	5
2. Eyes close in Period II	4
3. Eyes close in Period III	3
4. Eyes close in Period IV	2
5. Eyes close in Period V	1
6. Eyes do not close	0
Negative suggestions test (Barry et al.)	
(Total the time required to resist "failed" items. Give one point for each multiple of ten seconds.)	
1. All five suggestions passed	5
2. Four suggestions passed	4
3. Three suggestions passed	3
4. Two suggestions passed	2
5. One suggestion passed	1
6. None passed	0
Test of Hallucination (Davis and Husband)	
1. Distinct hallucination, no prodding needed	5
2. Faint hallucination, prodding needed	3
3. No hallucination	0
Amnesia (Barry et al.)	
1. No items recalled	5
2. One item recalled	4
3. Two items recalled	3
4. Three items recalled	2
5. Four or five items recalled	1
6. More than five items recalled	0

Source: From Friedlander and Sarbin, 1938. Copyright 1938 by the American Psychological Association. Reprinted by permission.

lenges were those of Barry, MacKinnon, and Murray (1931)—inability to open eyes, raise arm, bend arm, separate fingers, and say name. Measurement of the time required for the eyes to close was based on Hull's (1933) use of time-to-respond as a measure of the effectiveness of a particular suggestion, the hallucination task on Davis and Husband (1931), and the amnesia score on the number of challenges remembered after the subject awakens (similar to Barry et al., 1931).

Using a small light source as the "target" for the individual being measured to fixate, Friedlander and Sarbin (1938) presented the following verbal instructions, which are a combination of instructions intended to put the subject at ease and to induce hypnosis.

I.   Keep your eyes on that little light and listen carefully to what I say. Your ability to be hypnotized depends entirely on your willingness to cooperate. It has nothing to do with your intelligence. As for your will power—if you want, you can remain awake all the time and pay no attention to me. In that case you might make me look silly, but you are only wasting time. On the other hand, if you pay close attention to what I say, and follow what I tell you, you can easily learn to fall into an hypnotic sleep. In that case you will be helping this experiment and not wasting any time. Hypnosis is nothing fearful or mysterious. It is merely a state of strong interest in some particular thing. In a sense you are hypnotized whenever you see a good show and forget you are part of the audience, but, instead, feel you are part of the story. Your cooperation, your interest, is what I ask of you. Your ability to be hypnotized is a measure of your willingness to cooperate. Nothing will be done that will in any way cause you the least embarrassment.

II.   Now, relax and make yourself entirely comfortable. Keep your eyes on that little light. Keep staring at it all the time. Keep staring as hard as you can, as long as you can.

III.   Relax completely. Relax every muscle in your body. Relax the muscles in your legs. Relax the muscles in your arms. Make yourself perfectly comfortable. Let yourself be limp, limp, limp. Relax more and more, more and more. Relax completely. Relax completely.

IV.   Your legs feel heavy and limp, heavy and limp. Your arms are heavy, heavy, heavy as lead. Your whole body feels heavy, heavier, and heavier. You feel tired and sleepy, tired and sleepy. You feel drowsy, drowsy and sleepy, heavy and drowsy, drowsy and sleepy. Your breathing is slow and regular, slow and regular.

V.   Your eyes are tired from staring. Your eyes are wet from straining. The strain in your eyes is getting greater and greater, greater and greater. You would like to close your eyes and relax completely, relax completely. (But keep your eyes open just a little longer. Try to keep your eyes open just a little longer, just a little longer.)[1] You will soon reach your limit. The strain will be so great, your eyes will be so tired, your lids will become so heavy, your eyes will close of themselves, close of themselves.

VI.   And then you will be completely relaxed, completely relaxed. Warm and comfortable, warm and comfortable. Tired and drowsy. Tired and sleepy. Sleepy. Sleepy. Sleepy. You are paying attention to nothing but the sound of my voice, listening to nothing but the sound of my voice. You hear nothing but the sound of my voice.

VII.   Your eyes are blurred. You can hardly see, hardly see. Your eyes are wet and uncomfortable. Your eyes are strained. The strain is getting greater and greater, greater and greater. Your lids are heavy. Heavy as lead. Getting heavier and heavier, heavier and heavier. They're pushing down, down, down. Your lids seem weighted, weighted with lead, heavy as lead. Your eyes are blinking, blinking, closing, closing.

[1] Omitted on second reading.

VIII.   You feel drowsy and sleepy, drowsy and sleepy. I shall now begin counting. At each count you will feel yourself going down, down, down, into a deep comfortable, a deep restful sleep. Listen carefully. One—down, down, down. Two—three—four—more and more, more and more. Five—six—seven—eight—you are sinking, sinking. Nine—ten—eleven—twelve—deeper, and deeper, deeper and deeper. Thirteen—fourteen—fifteen—sixteen. (If eyes closed): You are falling fast asleep. (If open): Your eyes are closing, closing. Seventeen—eighteen—nineteen—twenty. (If closed): You are sound asleep, fast asleep. (If open): begin at II and repeat. (pp. 458-459)

These induction instructions took about 8 minutes and were repeated, omitting Paragraph I, if the subject failed to close his or her eyes by the end of the first read-through. If the subject's eyes closed during the first reading, the paragraph during which the response took place was noted and Paragraph VIII was read. If the subject's eyes were still open after the second reading, he or she was instructed directly to close the eyes. Thus the induction never took much more than fourteen minutes.

After the induction, the following verbatim instructions were read:

1.   Your eyes are tightly shut, tightly shut. Your lids are glued together, glued together, tightly shut. No matter how hard you try, you cannot open your eyes, you cannot open your eyes. Try to open your eyes. Try hard as you can. (Ten second pause.) Now relax completely, relax completely.

2.   Your left arm is heavy. Heavy as lead. Your arm is heavy as lead. You cannot raise your left arm. You cannot raise your arm. Try hard as you can, hard as you can. You cannot raise your arm. Try hard as you can, hard as you can. (Pause ten seconds.) Now relax completely.

3.   Extend your right arm. Straight out. Straight out. Your arm is rigid. Rigid and stiff. Stiff as a board. No matter how hard you try, you cannot bend your right arm. Try to bend your arm. Try hard as you can, hard as you can. (Pause ten seconds.) Now relax completely, relax completely.

4.   Put your fingers together. Interlock your fingers. Your fingers are interlocked, tightly interlocked. You cannot separate your fingers. Try hard as you can, hard as you can. (Pause ten seconds.) Now relax completely, relax completely.

5.   You cannot say your name. No matter how hard you try you cannot say your name. Try to say your name. Try as hard as you can. (Pause ten seconds.)

6.   Now relax completely. I am going to wake you up. When you awake, you will remember nothing of what has happened, nothing of what has happened. I shall count to ten. At eight you will open your eyes. At ten you will be wide awake and feeling cheerful. But you will remember nothing of what has happened. After you awake, you will hear someone calling your name. Ready now, one, two, etc.

7.   (When the subject awakens, wait ten seconds. If no response, ask: "Do you hear anything?" If reply is "Yes," ask, "What?" If "No," ask, "Did you hear your name being called?"). (Friedlander & Sarbin, 1938, p. 459)

Performance was scored according to Table 8.5, and the degree of hypnosis achieved assigned a numerical value.

Several things are important about the scale developed by Friedlander and Sarbin. First, the investigators measured the reliability of their scale, and found test–retest correlations of .79 and .82. The scale was stable over time with the same subjects. Second, they found that the sex of the subject made little difference; one in four or five females being "good" subjects, and one in five or six males. Third, and more important, the Friedlander and Sarbin Scale is the direct precursor to the most elaborately developed and researched scales in the history of the measurement of hypnotic depth—the Stanford Scales of Hypnotic Susceptibility, Forms A and B; which, in turn, are the ancestors of the Stanford Scale, Form C; the Harvard group version of the Stanford scales, and various more recent offspring.

All of these scales will be examined below; however, there are two other scaling efforts that should be mentioned first.

LeCron–Bordeaux Scale

LeCron and Bordeaux (1949) recognized that the Davis and Husband (1931) and Friedlander and Sarbin (1938) scales tapped only a limited number of behaviors from the wide range that could be suggested during hypnosis. They therefore developed a lengthy scale that consisted of 50 different symptoms to be observed and scored two points each if present. The behaviors were divided into six stages of hypnotic depth (Insusceptible, Hypnoidal, Light Trance, Medium Trance, Deep Trance, and Plenary Trance), and ranged from simple relaxation and fluttering of the eyelids, through catalepsies, feelings of detachment, sensory illusions, amnesia, age-regression, and negative and positive hallucinations to the termination of spontaneous activity (plenary condition). Like the Eysenck and Furneaux Scale below, LeCron and Bordeaux's scoring system never enjoyed the popularity achieved by the Davis and Husband and Friedlander and Sarbin Scales. The reasons for this are unknown, because it was certainly more elaborate than either of its predecessors.

Eysenck–Furneaux Scale

In 1945 Eysenck and Furneaux published an investigation of "primary and secondary suggestibility" in which they presented their own scale to measure these two aspects of behavior related, it was firmly believed by them, to hypnosis. Throughout most of the history of hypnotic inductions, it was believed that verbal and/or motoric manipulations created in the patients/subjects a condition of hypersuggestibility, a condition in which they would comply more readily with suggested behaviors than prior to an induction. Hull (1933) concluded that hypersuggestibility was one of the cardinal symptoms of hypnosis, and a number of investigators since have attempted to clarify the relationship between the degree of response to suggestions following an induction technique and that which we see in everyday life when one person complies with an indirect "command" from another.

Eysenck and Fureaux (1945) divided suggestibility into two types: primary, suggestions for ideomotor behaviors such as body sway, the Chevreul pendulum effect; and secondary, indirections such as hallucinations, illusions. Nine tasks were presented to their original 60 patient-subjects, three measuring primary suggestibility (body sway—$2\frac{1}{2}$ min. of verbal suggestions for falling forward, press and release—verbal suggestions that the subjects grip on a rubber ball was getting stronger or weaker, Chevreul pendulum) and six measuring secondary suggestibility (picture report—suggested memory for items not in a picture viewed for 30 sec., ink blot test—suggestions of responses to be seen, odor suggestion, two weight comparison tests, heat illusion). In addition, hypnosis was induced by an eye-fixation, verbal suggestion induction. Eighteen behaviors both during and after the induction were scored for the subject's compliance and a hypnosis score derived for comparison purposes with the test of primary and secondary suggestibility. Three post-hypnotic suggestions were also scored (increased body sway after hypnosis, changes in line-length estimates, pick up and shake a box present in the room).

The Eysenck–Fureaux Scale was, like those preceding and those discussed below, a depth scale, a measurement of compliance with suggestions contained in their induction and offered after the induction. The items scored were eyes tired, eyelids heavy, eyes closing, complete relaxation, incapable of activity, feels "miles away," feels pleasant warmth, arm falls irresistibly, cannot raise arm, glove anesthesia, both arms stiff and rigid, cannot raise arm when eyes are open, illusion of bell ringing, complete catalepsy, cannot hear buzzer, illusion of leg movement, illusion of light bulb lighting up, and spontaneous amnesia. Comparisons between scores achieved on these items and those tapping the two forms of suggestibility made the authors conclude that primary and secondary suggestibility were two unrelated traits and that only the former (primary) related to hypnotizability. In fact, the test most highly correlated with the hypnosis scores was the relatively simple body sway test.

Except for this one published item, the Eysenck–Fureaux Scale received little use and less notoriety, although the authors did replicate their work on two groups of 70 and 100 other patients. What was unusual about their scaling effort was that it was done on a patient population (at the Mill Hill Emergency Hospital for Nervous Disorders). One major change to occur between the early and the modern (1930s on) attempts to measure hypnotic depth and later susceptibility was in the nature of the populations on which the scales were developed. Prior to the 1930s patient populations were exclusively used, and quite logically so, since the concern of the practitioner was the effectiveness of a treatment modality (hypnosis) with ill individuals. As the experimental investigators entered the picture and the emphasis of many of the authors became an analysis of the variables underlying and related to hypnosis, rather than the prediction of treatment effectiveness with patients, more homogeneous test populations were sought. These were found in the captive audiences (We now call them "subject pools.") of America's colleges and universities. It may not be an exaggeration to say that we now have almost as much data on the college sophomore as we have on the laboratory rat.

Consequently, with the exception of Eysenck and Fureaux's work, all of the other modern scales discussed thus far were developed on college populations. The distribution of "susceptibility" appears in Table 8.6. The average percentages in each of the four, somewhat arbitrary, categories of susceptibility-depth are not extremely different from those for patient populations of the 19th century, which appeared in Table 8.1. If anything, Table 8.6 is somewhat skewed toward the "refractory" and "light" categories compared with Table 8.1, but that might be expected by the composition of the two sample populations. Although it has long been noted that illness works against hypnotic capability, patient populations usually come to the hypnotic situation with a different order and kind of motivation, which could account for the generally higher percentages in the upper categories of Table 8.1. With the exception of appearing to find a few more refractory individuals, the modern scales categorize individuals in about the same distribution as the depth category systems of the last century.

Stanford Hypnotic Susceptibility Scales

Until the late 1950s, the Friedlander–Sarbin Scale was the most used susceptibility-depth scale by experimental investigators. Since the Stanford scales were modeled on the Friedlander and Sarbin Scale, with some modification by Weitzenhoffer (1956), it is not surprising that they closely parallel the original's verbalizations, particularly in the induction procedure, which is eye-fixation with verbal instructions to relax. Compare, for example, the third portion of the Stanford Scale, Form A induction, with Paragraph III of the Friedlander–Sarbin Scale above.

> Relax completely. Relax every muscle of your body. Relax the muscles of your legs. . . . Relax the muscles of your feet. . . . Relax the muscles of your arms. . . . Relax the muscles of your hands. . . . of your fingers. . . . Relax the muscles of your neck, of your chest. . . . Relax all the muscles of your body. . . . Let yourself be limp, limp, limp. Relax more and more, more and more. Relax completely. Relax completely. (Weitzenhoffer & Hilgard, 1959, p. 14)

The original Stanford Scales were published in 1959 (Weitzenhoffer & Hilgard, 1959) and consist of two forms, A and B (SHSS:A, SHSS:B). An outgrowth of studies on individual differences in responsiveness to hypnotic induction procedures, their purpose was to provide a scale, or set of scales, which could be used in different settings with different populations, yet offering comparable data. With slight variations, Forms A and B are identical. Both are individually administered, begin with a postural sway test followed by an eye-closure, relaxation task that is a slightly expanded version of Paragraphs I through VIII of the Friedlander–Sarbin Scale and is basically

TABLE 8.6. Distribution of Hypnotic Susceptibility–Depth Scales 1930–1980 in Adult, Nonpatient Populations

Scale Used	Date	Cases (N)	Distribution of Susceptibility (Depth), (In Percent)				
			Refractory; Nonsusceptible	Drowsy; Light	Hypotaxy; Moderate	Somnambulistic; Deep	Total Susceptible
Davis & Husband	1931	55	9	47	15	29	91
Barry, MacKinnon & Murray	1931	73	16	37[a]	29[b]	18	84
Barry, MacKinnon & Murray	1938[c]	57	25	31[a]	14	30	75
Friedlander & Sarbin	1938	57	33	50[a]	12	5	67
Friedlander & Sarbin[d]	1956	200	23	59	15	3	77
Friedlander & Sarbin[d,e]	1958	74	3	51	30	16	97
Stanford Hypnotic Susceptibility Scale: Forms A & B	1958–9	124	13 (Scores 0–1)	32 (Scores 2–4)	31 (Scores 5–7)	24 (Scores 8–12)	87
Stanford Hypnotic Susceptibility Scale: Form C	1962	203	11 (0–1)	35 (2–4)	30 (5–7)	24 (8–12)	89

	Year	N					
Stanford Hypnotic Susceptibility Scale: Forms A & B, Revised	1965	533	10 (0–1)	32 (2–4)	28 (5–7)	30 (8–12)	90
Barber Suggestibility Scale (Objective Scores with Hypnotic Induction)	1978/9	186	8 (Scores 0–1.5)	13 (Scores 2–4)	31 (Scores 4.5–6.5)	48 (Scores 7–8)	92
SHALIT (Stanford Hypnotic Arm Levitation Induction Test)	1979	25	7[f]	21	47	25	93
Total Cases		1587					
Range of Percentages			3–33	13–59	12–47	3–48	67–97
Mean of Percentages			14.36	37.09	25.64	22.91	85.64

[a] Combined Friedlander & Sarbin's categories III & IV.
[b] Adjusted Friedlander & Sarbin's original data.
[c] Data from Friedlander & Sarbin (1938).
[d] Modified by Weitzenhoffer (1956).
[e] Hilgard, Weitzenhoffer & Gough (1958).
[f] Estimate based on 25% of the "lower percentage."

337

the most prevalent hypnotic induction technique in use today. More often than not, investigators wishing to test subjects under hypnotic conditions will use the eye-closure patter from the Stanford Scales as the induction procedure. Consequently, these scales, as noted above, are measures of responsiveness achieved following an induction procedure. That in Forms A and B the response to the induction procedure is scored as part of the quantitative scale does not eliminate the fact that an induction has taken place and the scales tell us how well a subject is doing, as well as how well he or she might do in the future following another hypnotic induction.

The items to be scored in the Stanford Scales appear in Table 8.7. The comparability of Forms A and B is evident. Form B is virtually a mirror image of A. Test manuals provide a verbal patter to be presented to the subjects verbatim.[1] Following the instructions for each task, the subject's response is observed and scored + or −, according to the criterion noted. Possible scores range from 0 to 12, inclusively. Since the scales were intended more for laboratory investigation than for clinical practice (although the authors do note there is no reason why they should not be used by the practitioner), statistical and factorial analyses of all of the Stanford Scales have been extensive. Reliabilities are quite high (Forms A and B, .83; Form C, .85; and the Stanford Profile Scales, .69 to .85), showing that no matter how we name these scales (susceptibility, depth) they are measuring a stable variable, a stable trait.

In 1962 *Form C of the Stanford Scales* (SHSS:C) was published (Weitzenhoffer & Hilgard, 1962). This new form was needed to expand the variety of hypnotic experiences tapped by scaling and to offer a scale in which the items were of graded difficulty (Hilgard, 1965). Both of these goals are indicated in Table 8.7, but the major scoring change in Form C from Forms A and B is the omission of a score for response to the eye closure instructions, which in this new form are designated as an induction procedure. The elimination of this item in the scoring does two things: (a) It allows the investigator to insert whatever induction method he or she may wish; and (b) It makes the score derived from the scale more purely a hypnotic depth score, since the score for response to induction is not confounded with responses to post-induction suggested tasks. Form C is also individually administered.

In the same year as the publication of the original SHSS:C (1962), a group administered and scored adaptation of the SHSS:A appeared. The *Harvard Group Scale of Hypnotic Susceptibility, Form A* (HGSHS:A) (Shor & Orne, 1962) can be administered directly or by tape-recording to groups of almost any size. It consists of 12 scored challenges, which with two exceptions (see Table 8.7) are identical to those appearing on the SHSS:A. Scoring is done by the subjects themselves through filling out a standardized questionnaire. Possible scores range from 0 to 12. Scores from the HGSHS:A were found to be compatible with those obtained from the individually administered scales. Total scale reliability was .83 (Shor & Orne, 1963).

TABLE 8.7. Items of the Stanford Hypnotic Susceptibility Scales, Forms A, B, and C; and the Harvard Group Scale of Hypnotic Susceptibility, Form A (HGSHS:A)

Item	Form A	Item Order	Form B	Item Order	Form C	Item Order	HGSHS:A	Item Order
Postural Sway	Backward	1	Backward	1				
Head Falling							Forward	1
Eye Closure (Induction)	Form A	2	Form B	2	Form B		Form A	2
Hand Lowering	Left	3	Right	3	Right	1	Left	3
Arm Immobilization	Right	4	Left	4	Left	8	Right	4
Finger Lock	In Front of Chest	5	Overhead	5			In Front of Chest	5
Arm Rigidity	Left	6	Right	6	Right	5	Left	6
Moving Hands	Together	7	Apart	7	Apart	2	Together	7
Verbal Inhibition	Name	8	Home Town	8				
Communication Inhibition							Shaking Head NO	8
Hallucination	Fly	9	Mosquito	9	Mosquito	3	Fly	9
Eye Catalepsy	Eyes Closed	10	Eyes Closed	10			Eyes Closed	10
Posthypnotic Suggestion	Change Chairs	11	Rise; Stretch	11			Touching Left Ankle	11
Posthypnotic Amnesia	<4 items	12	<4 items	12	<4 items	12	<4 items	12
Taste					Sweet-Sour	4		
Dream					About Hypnosis	6		
Age Regression					5th & 2nd Grades	7		
Anosmia					Ammonia	9		
Hallucination					Voice	10		
Visual Hallucination					Boxes	11		

What the HGSHS:A provided for the laboratory investigator was a more time-efficient method of selecting individuals for their degree of responsiveness to challenges following an eye-fixation induction technique. Although the time of administration is about the same as that for the SHSS:A,B, or C, more individuals can be screened in the same amount of time. While perhaps less important to the practitioner, who usually sees patients individually, such a screening device is certainly a saving in laboratory investigations. Like the Stanford Scales, an induction technique is included in the procedure.

The year following the publication of the SHSS:C, a children's scale, was published by London (1963). *The Children's Hypnotic Susceptibility Scale* (CHSS) is an individually administered scale comprised of 22 items (see Table 8.8), the first 12 from the SHSS:A, and the last items from the Stanford Depth Scale (unpublished), on which the SHSS:C is based. The same challenges are used for children from ages 5–16, although the wording of the instructions differs for two age ranges (5–12 and 13–16). Scoring is accomplished by the operator's estimations of the degree of compliance of the subject with each task (Overt Behavior Score) and the degree of subjective involvement the subject showed in attempting each challenge. The Overt Behavior Score can be either a simple pass–fail (0 or 1) or a 0–3 continuum score, depending on the adequacy of the response observed. Subjective involvement is ranked 1–3, with 3 being deeply involved. Total scores achieved in either of the above-scoring categories, or a weighted combination of the two (the sum of the products of multiplying the overt and subjective scores for each item) are used to predict the child's hypnotic behavior following subsequent inductions. The test–retest reliabilities are as follows: .79, for the Overt score; .75, for the Subjective score; and .78, for the weighted combination score, showing a reasonably stable scaling device.

Finally, it is interesting to note that this scale quantifies what the practitioners of both the 19th and 20th centuries have been saying, that children are more receptive to hypnotic induction and suggestions than are adults. Table 8.9 presents the distribution of London's original normative sample for the same categories of responsiveness that appear in Table 8.6. The children's scores are (Table 8.9) more skewed to the highly responsive end

TABLE 8.8. **Items on the Children's Hypnotic Susceptibility Scale**

Part I: Stanford Hypnotic Susceptibility Scale, Form A (except that Item 11, Posthypnotic suggestion, is from Form B)

Part II:		
1.	Posthypnotic Suggestion for Re-induction	6. Smell Hallucination for Perfume
2.	Visual & Auditory Hallucination for Television	7. Visual Hallucination for Rabbit
3.	Cold Hallucination	8. Age Regression
4.	Anesthesia	9. Dream
5.	Taste Hallucination	10. Posthypnotic Suggestion

TABLE 8.9. **Distribution of the Children's Hypnotic Susceptibility Scale Scores ($N = 240$)**

	Distribution of Susceptibility–Depth (in percent)				
	Refractory; Nonsusceptible (Scores 0–5)	Drowsy; Light (Scores 6–23)	Hypotaxy: Moderate (Scores 24–47)	Somnambulism; Deep (Scores 48–71)	Total Susceptibility
Overt behavior	1	12	39	48	99
Subjective involvement	0	8	47	45	100
Total	4	27	36	33	96

of the four-point continuum than are those for the adult nonpatient populations (Table 8.6). They are, in fact, more skewed than the adult *patient population* figures (Table 8.1), with nearly half of the Overt and Subjective scores falling in the Somnambulistic classification. Children's ease of response to hypnosis is also noted in the Total Susceptibility figures of 99%, 100% and 96% for the three types of scoring.

That same year, the Stanford group published another scale, the *Stanford Profile Scales* (SPS) (Hilgard, Lauer & Morgan, 1963; Weitzenhoffer & Hilgard, 1963, 1967). The rationale for this development was that a single score of susceptibility, such as produced by Forms A, B, and C, did not yield enough information about an individual's abilities within hypnosis. Some subjects, for instance, might score high overall, but fail to respond to items that individuals scoring much lower overall passed. It was also felt that a scale offering a profile of several different ability measures would be of particular use to laboratory investigators who wish to study the relationships among other personality traits and the diverse responsivity noted in hypnosis. Consequently, two forms (I & II) were developed, each containing nine suggested effects, each scored 0–3, for a total range of 0–27, inclusive. The challenge tasks for both forms are: Form I: (1) hand analgesia, (2) music hallucination, (3) anosmia to ammonia, (4) recall of meal, (5) hallucinated light, (6) dream (content free), (7) agnosia (house), (8) arithmetic impairment, and (9) posthypnotic task (verbal compulsion); Form II: (1) heat hallucination, (2) selective deafness, (3) hallucinated ammonia, (4) regression to birthday, (5) missing watch hand, (6) dream (about hypnosis), (7) agnosia (scissors), (8) personality alteration, and (9) posthypnotic task (automatic writing).

These subtests have been grouped into six general categories for profiling purposes. Agnosia and cognitive distortion (AG) includes Form I, tests 7 & 8 and Form II, tests 7 & 8; Hallucinations, Positive (HP) includes Form I: 2 & 5 and Form II: 1 & 3; Hallucination, Negative (HN) I: 1 & 3 and II: 2 & 5; Dreams and Regressions (DR), I: 4 & 6 and II: 4 & 6; Amnesia and Posthypnotic Compulsions (AM), I: 9 and II: 9 (Amnesia scored from Stanford, Form A); Loss of Motor Control (MC), motor responses from Stanford, Form A. As indicated by the references to Form A items in AM and MC, SHSS:A is given before the Profile Scales.

Looking at the overall scores of the 112 subjects used in the development of the scale (rather than the profile images, as was intended), 11.5% of the subjects scored 0–3 on Form I (13% for Form II) and 3% scored 24–27 (11% for Form II). These percentages are reasonably comparable to the "refractory" and "somnambulistic" categories for the Stanford Forms A, B, and C in Table 8.6. As indicated above, the reliability of the Profile Scales is near those of the other Stanford forms. Both forms are preceded with an unscored hand-levitation induction procedure following the SHSS:A.

Not satisfied with the SPS special abilities within hypnosis scales, Hilgard and others (Hilgard, Crawford, Bowers, & Kihlstrom, 1979) developed another scale, also intended to aid in the selection of subjects with special abilities in specific areas of hypnotic performance. Stating that the SPS forms were too time-consuming, they investigated the possibility of "tailoring" the SHSS:C by substituting specialized items (e.g., items for positive hallucinations or analgesia or automatic writing or negative hallucinations) into a thus altered form of SHSS:C. The idea was tested on 123 subjects selected for their performance on the HGSHS:A, and it was found that the substitution of one item did not appreciably alter the measurement characteristics of the SHSS:C. The *Tailored SHSS:C* became, then, yet another tool of the laboratory investigator, allowing him or her to select individuals with special hypnotic talents for further study.

No sooner had the Tailored SHSS:C appeared than Hilgard, Crawford, and Wert (1979a,b) published the *Stanford Hypnotic Arm Levitation Induction and Test* (SHALIT). The Stanford group recognized that their scales were intended for the experimental investigator and were rather time-consuming to administer. SHALIT was the recognition that a practitioner's time was valuable and that response to a brief induction procedure could serve as an estimate of further performance during hypnosis, a fact long practiced in the clinical fields. The test is no more nor less than an arm-levitation induction technique during which the operator observes the subject's response to the arm-lightening suggestions. If the arm rises more than 10 centimeters, the individual is a good hypnotic subject (as measured by the longer SHSS:A). An even simpler observation predicts whether the person will perform well in hypnosis: whether the elbow rises off the table on which it rests before the instructions begin. Those individuals whose elbows do rise are good hypnotic subjects.

Whether this arm-levitation induction deserves to be considered a susceptibility scale is a moot point, for it seems only to formalize what most practitioners do as a matter of course, that is, attempt hypnosis with the patient and proceed with treatment without some formal assessment of the patient's a priori responsivity. It is of interest, however, to the experimental investigator to know the relationships among such brief procedures and the more time-consuming SHSS:A and SHSS:C. The SHALIT scores correlated .63 with the SHSS:A, and .52 with the SHSS:C. Self-report scores of hypnotic depth (on a 0–10 scale) and of subject involvement (on a 1–5 scale) correlated somewhat less well with the longer scales, with the exception of the self-report of depth, which correlated .74 with the SHSS:C. The overall test–retest reliability was .88.

The Hilgards had already recognized the need for a scale directed more toward clinical than laboratory use. In 1975 (Hilgard & Hilgard) the *Stanford Hypnotic Clinical Scale for Adults* (SHCS:ADULT) was published, recognizing the perspective that the standard Stanford Scales were too lengthy, possibly too tiring, and probably requiring too much physical effort for some hospitalized patients. The SHCS:ADULT begins, as the other Stanford Scales, with an induction procedure, this time a series of verbal suggestions for relaxation and calm and peace, following a directive for the patient to close his or her eyes. As with the SHSS:C, the induction is not part of the formal scoring. Only the five challenges (moving hands together, dream, age-regression, posthypnotic suggestion to cough, posthypnotic amnesia) are scored. Should the patient be unable to use both hands, a hand-lowering task is substituted for the hand-moving task. Below is the complete scale.

Stanford Hypnotic Clinical Scale for Adults
(SHCS:ADULT)

(Patient may be seated in any kind of chair with arms, or may be in bed, sitting or lying down.)

Introductory Remarks

In a moment I shall suggest to you a number of experiences which you may or may not have and a number of effects which you may or may not produce. Not everyone can have the same experiences or produce the same effects when hypnotized. People vary greatly. We need to know what experiences you can have so we can build on them and know how to make hypnosis best serve you. Please remember always to respond to what you are *feeling,* so we can use hypnosis in ways that are natural for you.

Induction

Please close your eyes and listen carefully to what I say. As we go on, you will find yourself becoming more and more relaxed. . . . Begin to let your whole body relax. . . . Let all the muscles go limp. . . . Now you will be able to feel special muscle groups relaxing even more. If you pay attention to your right foot, you can feel the muscles in it relax . . . feel the muscles in the right lower leg relaxing . . . in the upper right leg relaxing. . . . Now on the left side concentrate on the way that the left foot is relaxing . . . and the left leg, how the lower part and the upper part are both relaxing more. . . . Next, you'll be able to feel the muscles of the right hand relaxing, the right lower arm and right upper arm relaxing. . . . Now direct your attention to your left hand. Let it relax, let the lower arm and the upper arm relax. . . . As you have become relaxed, your body begins to feel rather heavy. Just think of the chair (bed) as being strong, sink into it, and let it hold you. . . . Your shoulders . . . neck . . . and head, more and more relaxed. . . . The muscles of your scalp and forehead, just let them relax even more. . . . All of this time you have been settling deeper and more comfortably into the chair (bed).

Your mind has relaxed, too, along with your body. It is possible to set all worries aside. Your mind is calm and peaceful. You are getting more and more comfortable. . . . You will continue to feel pleasantly relaxed as you continue to listen to my voice. . . . Just keep your thoughts on what I am saying . . . more and more deeply relaxed and perhaps drowsy but at no time will you have any trouble hearing me. You will continue in this state of great relaxation until I suggest that it is time for you to become more alert. . . . Soon I will begin to count from 1 to 20. As I count, you will feel yourself going down further and further into this deeply relaxed hypnotic state. You will be able to do all sorts of things that I suggest, things that will be interesting and acceptable to you. You will be able to do them without breaking the pattern of complete relaxation that is gradually coming over you. . . . 1—you are becoming more deeply relaxed . . . 2—down, down into a deeper, tranquil state of mind . . . 3—4— more and more relaxed . . . 5—6—7—you are sinking deeper and deeper. Nothing will disturb you. You are finding it easy just to listen to things that I say . . . 8—9—10—halfway there . . . always deeply relaxed . . . 11—12— 13—14—15—although deeply relaxed you can hear me clearly. You will always hear me distinctly no matter how hypnotized you are . . . 16—17—18— deeply relaxed.

Nothing will disturb you . . . 19—20—*completely relaxed.*

You can change your position any time you wish. Just be sure you remain comfortable and relaxed.

You are very relaxed and pleasantly hypnotized. While you remain comfortably listening to my words, I am going to help you learn more about how thinking about something affects what you do. Just experience whatever you can. Pay close attention to what I tell you, and think about the things I suggest. Then let happen whatever you find is happening, even if it surprises you a little. *Just let it happen by itself.*

1.   MOVING HANDS TOGETHER (or, if one arm is immobile, go to 1a. Hand lowering)
   All right then . . . please hold both hands straight out in front of you, palms facing inward, hands about a foot apart. Here, I'll help you. (Take hold of hands and position them about a foot apart.) Now I want you to imagine a force attracting your hands toward each other, pulling them together. Do it any way that seems best to you—think of rubber bands stretched from wrist to wrist, pulling your hands together, or imagine magnets held in each hand pulling them together—the closer they get the stronger the pull. . . . As you think of this force pulling your hands together, they will move together, slowly at first, but they will move closer together, closer and closer together as though a force is acting on them . . . moving . . . moving . . . closer, closer. . . .

   (Allow ten seconds without further suggestion, and note extent of motion.)

That's fine. Everything is back to normal now. Just place your hands in their resting position and relax.

   (Score + if hands move slowly toward each other, and are not more than six inches apart at end of ten seconds.)

   1a.   *Hand lowering* (alternative to Moving hands together) If one hand is immobile for any reason, we recommend substituting a hand lowering suggestion, similar to that given as Item 1 in SHSS-C. The arm is held out at shoulder height, with the palm of the hand up. The suggestion is given to imagine something heavy in the hand pressing it down. After a few suggestions of downward movement, if the arm is not completely down, a 10-second wait is introduced. The item is passed if the hand has lowered at least six inches by the end of the 10 seconds.

2. DREAM

Now I am going to ask you to keep on relaxing, and this time you are going to have a dream . . . a real dream . . . much like the kind you have when you sleep at night. When I stop talking to you very shortly, you will begin to dream. Any kind of dream may come. . . . Now it is as though you are falling asleep, deeper and deeper asleep. You can sleep and dream about anything you want to. As soon as I stop talking, you will begin to dream. When I speak to you again in a minute or so you will stop dreaming if you are still dreaming, and you will listen to me just as you have been doing. If you stop dreaming before I speak to you again, you will remain pleasantly and deeply hypnotized. Now just sleep and have a dream.

(Allow 1 minute. Then say:)

The dream is over, but you can remember it very well and clearly, very clearly. . . . I want you now to tell me about your dream while remaining deeply hypnotized. Please tell me about your dream . . . right from the beginning. Tell me all about it (Record verbatim.)

(If subject has no dream:) That's all right. Not everyone dreams.

(If subject hesitates, or reports vaguely: probe for details.)

Inquire: How real would you say your dream was?

Termination: That's all for the dream. Remain as deeply hypnotized as you have been.

(Score + if subject has an experience comparable to a dream . . . not just vague fleeting experiences or just feelings or thoughts. The dream should show imagery, some reality, and not give evidence of being under voluntary control.)

3. AGE REGRESSION

Something very interesting is about to happen. In a little while you are going back to a happy day in elementary school. If you had a choice to return to the third, fourth, or fifth grade, would you prefer one of these to the other?

(If yes:) Which grade?

(If no preference, use fourth grade.)

All right then, I would like you now to think about when you were in the (selected) grade of school, and in a little while, you are going to start to *feel* like you are growing younger and smaller, going back to the time you were in the (selected) grade. . . . 1, you are going back into the past. It is no longer (state present year), nor (state an earlier year), nor (state a still earlier year), but much earlier . . . 2, you are becoming much younger and smaller . . . in a moment you will be back in the (selected) grade, on a very nice day. 3, getting younger and younger, smaller and smaller all the time. Soon you will be back in the (selected) grade, and you will feel an experience exactly as you did once before on a nice day when you were in school. 4, very soon you will be there. . . . Once again a little boy (girl) in the (selected) grade. Soon you will be right back there. 5, You are now a small boy (girl) in school. . . . Where are you? . . . What are you doing? . . . Who is your teacher? . . . How old are you? . . . What are you wearing? . . . Who is with you? . . .

(Ask additional questions as appropriate. Record answers.)

That's fine. . . . Now you can grow up again. You are no longer in the (se-lected) grade but getting older, growing up. You are now your correct age, this is (current day and date), and you are in (locale of testing). You are no longer a little boy (girl), but an adult, sitting in a chair (bed) deeply hypnotized. How old are you? . . . And what is today? . . . Where are you? . . . Fine, Today is (correct date) and you are (correct age) and this is (name place where subject is being tested). Everything is back as it was. Just continue to be comfortably relaxed. . . .

(Postpone scoring until inquiry at end.)

4. POSTHYPNOTIC SUGGESTION (Clearing throat or Cough)

5. AMNESIA
Stay completely relaxed, but listen carefully to what I tell you next. In a little while I shall begin counting backwards from ten to one. You will gradually come out of hypnosis but you will be the way you are now for most of the count. When I reach "five" you will open your eyes, but you will not be fully awake. When I get to "one" you will be entirely roused, as awake as you usually are. You will have been so relaxed, however, that you will have trouble recalling the things I have said to you and the things you did. It will take so much effort to think of these that you will prefer not to try. It will be much easier just to forget everything until I tell you that you can remember. You will forget all that has happened until I say to you: "Now you can remember everything!" You will not remember anything until then. After you wake up you will feel refreshed. I shall now count backwards from ten, and at "five," not sooner, you will open your eyes, but not be fully aroused until I reach "one." At "one" you will be fully awake. A little later I shall tap my pencil on the table like this (demonstrate with two taps). When I do, you will feel a sudden urge to clear your throat or to cough. And then you will clear your throat or cough. You will find yourself doing this but *you will forget that I told you to do so,* just as you will forget the other things, until I tell you, "Now you can remember everything." All right, ready—10—9—8—7—6—5—4—3—2—1—.

(If subject has eyes open:) How do you feel? Do you feel alert?

(If groggy:) The feeling will go away soon. You feel alert now!

(If subject keeps eyes closed:) Please open your eyes. How do you feel?

(If groggy:) You are beginning to feel more alert and refreshed. . . . You feel alert now!

(Hypnotist now taps pencil against table twice. Wait ten seconds.)

(Score + if patient clears throat or coughs after pencil tap.)

Now I want to ask you a few questions about your experience. Please tell me in your own words everything that has happened since I asked you to close your eyes.

(Record subject's responses verbatim. If blocked ask, "Anything else?" and record answers until subject reaches a further impasse.)

Listen carefully to my words. Now you can remember everything. Anything else now?

(Again record subject's responses verbatim. Remind subject of any items not recovered; note these also.)
(Score + if subject recalls no more than two items before memory is restored.)

(If subject is awake and comfortable:) That's all now. You are completely out of hypnosis, feeling alert and refreshed. Any tendency that you may have to clear your throat or to cough is now completely gone.

For Correcting Difficulties When Necessary:

(If there is residual difficulty, e.g., difficulty in restoring alertness or persistence of a cough, proceed as follows with appropriate suggestions:) Please close your eyes and drift back into hypnosis as I count to 5. 1—2—3—4—5. . . . Now I am about to arouse you by counting backwards from 5 to 1. You will feel alert, refreshed, with no tendency to cough. (Wait ten seconds.) 5—4—3—2—1. Fully aroused! (Morgan & Hilgard, 1978/1979a pp. 139–143)

According to Morgan and Hilgard (1978/1979a) the SHCS:ADULT is as reliable as the SHSS:C, against which it was evaluated and has the advantages of a larger scale over single item scales such as Spiegel's Hypnotic Induction Profile (see below) and SHALIT (Hilgard & Hilgard, 1979).

These latter authors (Morgan & Hilgard, 1978/1979b) have also presented the latest in the long list of variations on the original Stanford Scales, the *Stanford Hypnotic Clinical Scales for Children* (SHCS:CHILD). Developed on two normative groups of 98 and 182, ages 5–16 years old, the scale consists of an eye-fixation, relaxation hypnotic induction procedure followed by seven suggested tasks modeled on the older, adult Stanford Scales (hand lowering, arm rigidity, visual hallucination, auditory hallucination, dream, age regression, and posthypnotic suggestion for a quick induction signal for future treatment sessions). As with the SHCS:ADULT and the SHSS:C, the induction procedure is not part of the formal scoring, but is part of the standard procedure. Here are the instructions for the scales, one for general use with children 6–16 years old, and the other, a modified form for children 4–8 years old.

Stanford Hypnotic Clinical Scale for Children (SHCS:CHILD)
Standard Form (Ages 6–16)

Note: Discussion of preconceived ideas that child and/or parent may have about hypnosis should precede administration of the scale. Be sure the meaning of the word "relax" is understood. If necessary, explain it in terms of "letting go" as when the hypnotist holds the child's wrist and lets it drop gently, or "feeling loose like a rag doll."

Introduction

I'm going to help you learn some interesting things about imagination today. Most people say that it's fun (fascinating). I will ask you to think of some different things and we will see how your imagination works. Some people find it easier to imagine some things than other things. We want to find what is most interesting to you. Listen very carefully to me, and let's see what happens. Just be comfortable in the chair (bed), and let's imagine some things. Please close your eyes so you can imagine these things better. . . . Now I'd like you to picture yourself floating in a warm pool of water. . . . What is it like? . . . And can you picture yourself floating on a nice soft cloud in the air? . . . What is that like? . . . That's fine—just open your eyes. . . . Now I'd like to show you how you can feel completely relaxed and comfortable, because that makes it easier to imagine things too . . . I'm going to draw a little face on my thumbnail[1] . . . here it is . . . (Hypnotist draws face on own thumbnail with red felt pen.) Let's put one on your thumb. Do you want to do it or shall I? (Hypnotist or child does so.) That's a good face! Now please hold your hand up in front of you like this (assist child so that hand is in front, thumbnail facing him, with elbow not resting on anything) and look at the little face (thumbnail) as you listen to my voice. Just keep watching the little face (thumbnail), try to think only about the things I talk about, and let your body relax completely. . . . Let your whole body feel loose and limp and relaxed . . . relax completely . . . just let all the muscles in your body relax . . . relax completely. . . . Be as relaxed as you were while you were imagining that you were floating in the pool of water, or floating on a cloud. . . . Feel your body becoming more and more relaxed . . . more and more relaxed. . . . Your eyelids, too, are relaxing. They are starting to feel *heavy*. As you keep watching the face (thumbnail), your eyes feel heavier and heavier. . . . Your eyes are starting to blink a little, and that's a very good sign. That means you're relaxing really well. Just keep watching the face (thumbnail), your eyes feel heavier and heavier. . . . Your eyes are starting to blink a little, and that's a very good sign. That means you're relaxing really well. Just keep watching the face (thumbnail) and listening to my voice. . . . Already your eyelids feel heavy. Very soon they will feel so heavy that they will begin to close by themselves. . . . Let them close whenever they feel like it. And when they close, let them stay closed. . . . Even now, your whole body is feeling so nice, so comfortable, completely relaxed. . . .

IF CHILD SHOWS CONVINCING EVIDENCE AT ANY TIME OF IN-ABILITY TO RELAX, OR UNWILLINGNESS TO LET EYES CLOSE OR REMAIN CLOSED, GO TO MODIFIED FORM.

Now I'm going to count from 1 to 10, and you will find your body becoming even more relaxed. . . . You will continue to relax as you listen to the counting . . . 1 . . . more and more relaxed, such a good feeling . . . 2 . . . 3 . . . more and more relaxed all the time, feeling so good . . . 4 . . . 5 . . . 6 . . . even more relaxed (and your eyes are feeling heavier, heavier . . .) it feels so good just to let go and relax completely . . . 7 . . . 8 . . . 9 . . . very relaxed now . . . 10 . . . .

(If child is still holding hand up:) Just let your hand relax completely too . . . let it relax comfortably on your lap (the bed) . . . that's fine. . . .

---

[1] If drawing a face on thumbnail seems awkward for the older child, eliminate it, and have him simply stare at the thumbnail. Substitute "thumbnail" for "little face" as indicated.

(If eyes have not closed:) Now please let your eyes close, and just relax completely. Just let your eyes close and keep them closed while you listen to me. . . .

(For all children:) And now as we go on, it will be very easy for you to listen to me, because you are so relaxed and comfortable. If you can keep your eyes closed, you can imagine some things better. So why don't you let them stay closed. You'll be able to stay relaxed and talk to me when I ask you to. . . . You are feeling very good. . . . Just keep listening to what I tell you and think about the things I suggest. Then let happen whatever you find is happening. . . . Just *let things happen by themselves*. . . .

   (If eyes open at any time, request child gently to close them because imagination is easier that way.)

1.   HAND LOWERING
Please hold your right (left) arm[2] straight out in front of you, with the palm up. (Assist if necessary.) Imagine that you are holding something heavy in your hand, like a heavy rock. Something very heavy. Shape your fingers around the heavy rock in your hand. What does it feel like? . . . That's good. . . . Now think about your arm and hand feeling heavier and heavier, as if the rock were pushing down . . . more and more down . . . and as it gets heavier and heavier the hand and arm begin to move down . . . down . . . heavier and heavier . . . moving . . . down, down, down . . . moving . . . moving . . . more and more down . . . heavier and heavier . . . (Wait 10 seconds; note extent of movement). . . . That's fine. Now you can stop imagining there is a rock in your hand, and let your hand relax. . . . It is not heavy anymore. . . .

   (Score + if hand lowers at least 6 inches at end of 10 seconds.)

2.   ARM RIGIDITY
Now please hold your left (right) arm straight out, and the fingers straight out, too. . . . That's right, your arm straight out in front of you, fingers straight out, too. . . . Think about making your arm very stiff and straight, very, very stiff. . . . Think about it as if you were a tree and your arm is a strong branch of the tree, very straight and very strong, like the branch of a tree . . . so stiff that you can't bend it. . . . That's right. . . . Now see how stiff your arm is . . . try to bend it . . . try. . . . (Wait 10 seconds) . . . That's fine. . . .

Now your arm is no longer like a branch of a tree. It is not stiff any longer. . . . Just let it relax again. . . .

   (Score + if arm has bent less than 2 inches at end of 10 seconds.)

3,4.   VISUAL AND AUDITORY HALLUCINATION (TV)
It is easier to imagine what I am going to ask you to do if you keep your eyes closed.

---

[2] Either arm may be used for items 1 and 2; if for example, one arm is immobilized, use other arm for both items.

What is your favorite TV program?

(For the occasional child who does not watch TV, substitute favorite movie, and modify the instructions appropriately. Record response.)

You can watch that program right now if you want to, and I'll tell you how. When I count to 3, you will see a TV in front of you, and you can watch (name of program). . . . Ready? 1 . . . 2 . . . 3. . . . Do you see it?

(If yes:) Is the picture clear? . . . Is it black and white or is it in color? What's happening? Can you hear the program? . . . Is it loud enough? What are you hearing? . . . (Finally:) Now the program is ending. . . . The TV is disappearing. . . . It's gone now . . . Very good.

(If no:) That's all right . . . sometimes it takes a little while to catch on to how to do this. . . . Just wait a little while, and I think you'll start to see it pretty soon. (Wait 5 seconds.) There, what do you see now? What are you hearing? (If sees or hears, question as above.)

(If still no:) That's okay. Just forget all about the TV. . . . We'll do something else. . . . Just relax and keep listening to my voice. . . .

(Visual: Score + if child sees a program with sufficient detail to be comparable to actual viewing. Auditory: Score + if child reports hearing words, sound effects, music, etc.)

5. DREAM

Do you dream at night when you are asleep? (If puzzled, explain that a dream is like seeing things going on even when you are asleep.) I'd like you to think about how you feel when you are just ready to go to sleep at night, and imagine that you are about to have a dream. . . . Just let a dream come into your mind, a dream just like the dreams that you have when you are asleep. . . . When I stop talking, in just a moment, you will have a dream, a very pleasant dream, just like the dreams you have when you are asleep at night. . . . Now a dream is coming into your mind. . . .

(Wait 20 seconds)

The dream is over now, and I'd like you to tell me about it.

(Record verbatim, probing as necessary for thoughts or images.)

That's fine. You can forget about the dream now, and just relax. . . . Just relax completely and let your whole body feel good. . . .

(Score + if child has an experience comparable to a dream, with some action.)

6. AGE REGRESSION

Now I'd like you to think back to some very special time when you were younger than you are now. Some time that happened last year, or maybe when you were even younger than that . . . a special trip, perhaps, or a birthday party. Can you think of such a time? What was it? (Record target event.) All right . . . now I'd like you to think about that time . . . . Think about being younger and smaller . . . in a little while, you are going to feel just like you did on that day when (specify target event). I am going to count to five and at the count of 5 you will be right back there again . . . 1 . . . 2 . . . 3 . . . 4 . . . 5 . . . You are now there . . . tell me about it . . . Where are you? What are you doing? How old are you? Look at yourself and tell me what you're wearing.

(Continue as appropriate and record responses.)

That's fine . . . Now you can stop thinking about that day and come right back to today, in this room, with everything just as it is. Tell me how it seemed to be back at (target event). . . . Was it like being there or did you just think about it? How real was it? Did you feel smaller? . . . That's fine. Just relax completely again now . . . .

(Score + if child gives appropriate answers to questions and reports some experience of being there.)

7. POSTHYPNOTIC RESPONSE

That's it . . . very relaxed . . . feeling so good, so comfortable . . . so relaxed. . . . In a moment I will ask you to take a deep breath and open your eyes and feel wide awake, so we can talk a little about the things we have done today . . . . However, while we are talking, I will clap my hands two times, like this (demonstrate). When you hear me clap, you will immediately close your eyes and go right back to feeling just the way you do now . . . completely relaxed . . . You'll be surprised at how easy it is to let your eyes close, and let your whole body relax completely again, when you hear the handclap . . . relaxed and comfortable, just as you are now. . . . All right, then. . . . Now take a deep breath and open your eyes . . . that's fine. . . . Maybe you'd like to stretch just a little so you'll feel alert. . . . You've done very well at imagining these things. . . . Which of the things that I asked you to think about was the most fun?

(After approximately 20 seconds, clap hands. Note response.)
(Score + if child closes eyes and exhibits characteristics of relaxation.)

Do you feel relaxed? Do you feel as relaxed as you did before, before I asked you to open your eyes? . . . That's fine. Now I'm going to count from five to one, and when I get to 1, you will open your eyes and feel wide awake again, and you will know that our imaging things together is over for today. Okay, then . . . 5 . . . 4 . . . 3 . . . 2 . . . 1. Very good. How do you feel now? Let's talk a little about the other things we did today. (Remind child of specific items so that he recalls all suggestions.) Now I'm going to clap my hands again, and this time it will not make you drowsy and relaxed. (Clap hands, record response, and be sure that child is fully alert.)

Termination

You've done very well today. What was the most fun of the things I asked you to do?

Is there anything else you'd like to talk about?—If there isn't, then we're all through.

Stanford Hypnotic Clinical Scale for Children (SHCS:CHILD)
Modified Form (Ages 4–8)

Note: This form may be substituted for the child who cannot relax and does not like to close his eyes. Typically this will be the very young child (under 6 years of age, and occasionally 7 or 8 years) or the extremely anxious child. This form is similar to the standard version except for the active fantasy induction, a few changes in the wording of tests, and the omission of a posthypnotic suggestion.

Induction (If standard form used first, improvise transition)

I'd like to talk with you about how a person can use his imagination to do or feel different kinds of things. Do you know what I mean by imagination?

If necessary, explain: Do you know what it's like to pretend things . . . to "make-believe?" Do you ever pretend things, or make believe that you are someone else? When you can do anything you want to do, what do you do? That is, what are the things you like to do more than anything else in the world?

(Probe for interests, i.e., swimming, hiking, playing on the slide and merry-go-round [playground], having a picnic, etc. Select a favorite activity and engage child in thinking about it. The picnic described here is an illustration.)

Okay, let's do that right now.[3] Let's imagine (pretend) that we are on a picnic, and there's a big picnic basket right in front of us. What does the basket look like to you? How big is it? . . . I'm going to spread this bright yellow tablecloth on the grass here. . . . Why don't you take something out of the basket now? Tell me about it. . . . That's fine. . . . What else is in the basket?

Continue until a convincing fantasy is developed, or child shows total lack of involvement.

You know, you can do lots of interesting things by thinking about it this way. It's like imagining (pretending) something so strongly that it seems almost real. How real did it seem to you? Good. Now let's try imagining some other things, okay?

1. HAND LOWERING
Please hold your right (left) arm[4] straight out in front of you, with the palm up. (Assist if necessary.) Imagine that you are holding something heavy in your hand, like a heavy rock. Something very heavy. Shape your fingers around the heavy rock in your hand. What does it feel like? . . . That's good. . . . Now think about your arm and hand feeling more and more heavy, as if the rock were pushing down . . . more and more down . . . and as it gets heavier and heavier the hand and arm begin to move down . . . down . . . heavier and heavier . . . moving . . . down, down, down . . . moving . . . moving . . . more and more down . . . heavier and heavier. . . . (Wait 10 seconds; note

---

[3] It is not necessary for the child to close his eyes. If closing eyes appears desirable give child choice: Some children find it easier to imagine with their eyes closed. You may close your eyes if you wish to, but keep them open if you'd rather.

[4] Either arm may be used for items 1 and 2; if, for example, one arm is immobilized, use other arm for both items.

extent of movement). . . . That's fine. Now you can stop imagining there is a rock in your hand, and let your hand relax. . . . It is not heavy any more. . . .

(Score + if hand lowers at least 6 inches at end of 10 seconds.)

2. ARM RIGIDITY
Now please hold your left (right) arm straight out, and the fingers straight out, too. . . . That's right, your arm straight out in front of you, fingers straight out, too. . . . Think about making your arm very stiff and straight, very, very stiff. . . . Think about it as if you were a tree and your arm is a strong branch of the tree, very straight and very strong, like the branch of a tree . . . so stiff that you can't bend it. . . . That's right. . . . Now see how stiff your arm is . . . try to bend it . . . try . . . (Wait 10 seconds). . . . That's fine. . . . Now your arm is no longer like a branch of a tree. It is not stiff any longer . . . Just let it relax again.

(Score + if arm has bent less than 2 inches at end of 10 seconds.)

3,4. VISUAL AND AUDITORY HALLUCINATION (TV)
What is your favorite TV program?

(For the occasional child who does not watch TV, substitute favorite movie, and modify the instructions appropriately. Record response.)

You can watch that program right now if you want to, and I'll tell you how. When I count to 3, you will see a TV in front of you, and you can watch (name of program). . . . Ready? 1 . . . 2 . . . 3 . . . Do you see it?

(If yes:) Is the picture clear? . . . Is it black and white or is it in color? What's happening? Can you hear the program? . . . Is it loud enough? What are you hearing? . . . (Finally:) Now the program is ending. . . . The TV is disappearing . . . It's gone now. . . . Very good.

(If no:) That's all right . . . sometimes it takes a little while to catch on to how to do this. . . .

(If eyes are open:) Why don't you close your eyes for a moment and try to see it in your mind. . . . Sometimes it's easier to imagine things like this with your eyes closed. . . . (Continue:) Just wait a little while, and I think you'll start to see it pretty soon. (Wait 5 seconds) There, what do you see now? What are you hearing? (If sees or hears, question as above.)

(If still no:) That's okay. Just forget all about the TV. . . . We'll do something else. . . .

(Visual: Score + if child sees a program with sufficient detail to be comparable to actual viewing. Auditory: Score + if child reports hearing words, sound effects, music, etc.)

5. DREAM
Do you ever dream at night when you are asleep? (If puzzled, explain that a dream is like seeing things going on even when you are asleep.) I'd like you now to think about how you feel when you are just ready to go to sleep at night,

and imagine that you are about to have a dream . . . just let a dream come into your mind . . . a dream just like the dreams that you have when you are asleep.

(If eyes are open:) Maybe you'd like to close your eyes while you do this.

(Continue:) When I stop talking, in just a moment, you will have a dream, a very pleasant dream, just like when you are asleep at night. . . . Now a dream is coming into your mind. . . .

(Wait 20 seconds)

The dream is over now, and I'd like you to tell me about it.

(Record verbatim, probing as necessary for thoughts or images.)

That's fine. You can forget about the dream now. . . . That's all for the dream. . . .

(Score + if child has an experience comparable to a dream, with some action.)

6. AGE REGRESSION
Now I'd like you to think back to some very special time when you were younger than you are now . . . some time that you had a lot of fun . . . a special trip, perhaps, or a birthday party. Can you think of such a time? What was it? (Record target event.) All right. . . . Now I'd like you to think about that time. . . . Think about being back there again . . . in a little while you are going to feel just like you did on that day when (specify target event). I am going to count to 5, and at the count of 5, you will be right back there again . . . 1 . . . 2 . . . 3 . . . 4 . . . 5 . . . You are now there . . . tell me about it. . . . Where are you? . . . What are you doing? . . . How old are you? . . . What are you wearing? . . .

(Continue as appropriate and record responses.)

That's fine. . . . Now you can stop thinking about that day and come right back to this day, in this room, with everything just as it was. Tell me how it seemed to be back at (target event). . . . Was it like being there or did you just think about it? (How real was it?) That's fine. . . .

(Score + if child gives appropriate answers to questions and reports some experience of being there.)

Termination
Well, you've done very well today. What was the most fun of the things I asked you to do? Is there anything else you'd like to talk about? . . . If there isn't, then we're all through. (Morgan & Hilgard, 1978/1979b, pp. 156–160, 164–166)

Summary
As stated earlier, the Stanford Scales are the most elaborately developed and researched susceptibility–depth scales to date. The Hilgards and their army

of colleagues and post-doctoral fellows have literally inundated the field with a continuing stream of scales and with a flood of research pertaining to and using those scales. Normative data for the various scales, particularly the older Forms A, B, and C is extensive. In fact, in many individuals' perception the scales are the standard for the entire enterprise of attempting to measure the capacity for hypnosis. As Bowers, who studied at the Stanford laboratories while on a sabbatical leave, explained, "The Stanford Scales have been a veritable North Star in what would otherwise be a chaotic firmament of hypnosis research" (Bowers, 1981b, p. 79). As new scales develop, both at Stanford and at other research facilities, it has become almost mandatory to compare them to at least one, or several forms of the Stanford Scales. Should a new scale not correlate with the Stanford Scales, in many quarters it is suspected of not really measuring hypnosis. Such, of course, is not the case, but that interpretation needs to be guarded against so that this century does not replicate the last when particular individuals or "schools" dominated thought and direction in the field. There is room for both the Davids and the Goliaths.

There has of late been the beginnings of another battle of Elah. Weitzenhoffer, the principal author of the original Stanford Scales, has recently leveled several criticisms against the scales. (Weitzenhoffer, 1978a,b, 1980a) His two major criticisms are (a) that the scales do not sufficiently consider the subjective experiences of nonvoluntariness, historically a *sine qua non* of traditional hypnotic descriptions, and (b) since, by the inclusion of an induction technique within the scale format, the scales measure hypnotic behavior (assumed depth); they do not tap the other basic of hypnosis—an increase in suggestibility due to whatever takes place through the induction. Thus hypersuggestibility is not tapped by the scales, because to do so would require a pre- and postinduction measure of the behaviors making up the scales. The differences between pre- and postinduction measures are called gain-scores.

Regarding the first criticism, Weitzenhoffer (1974) had discovered that a small percentage of individuals (29 percent) experienced compliance with an ordinary instruction to bring their own hands together in front of them with their arms outstretched as occurring involuntarily. The Stanford Scales do not, he feels, consider "when an 'instruction' is an 'instruction'." Regarding (b) above, "There is a basic ambiguity regarding what scores on scales of the Stanford type indicate" (Weitzenhoffer, 1980a, p. 131). Since the introduction of an induction procedure enhances one's responsiveness to tasks such as appear on the Stanford Scales (Barber & Glass, 1962; Edmonston & Robertson, 1967; Hilgard & Tart, 1966; Ruch, Morgan, & Hilgard, 1973; Weitzenhoffer & Sjoberg, 1961), "It is impossible to distinguish hypnotic from nonhypnotic responses on the basis of the test scores" (Weitzenhoffer, 1980a, p. 132). He even suggested that it would have been more appropriate to have named the scales "The Stanford Scales of Suggestibility," or "The Stanford Scales of Susceptibility to Suggestion," but certainly not "susceptibility" in the sense of susceptibility *to* hypnosis, since the measures are made *in* hypnosis.

However, Weitzenhoffer continues to recognize the Stanford Scales as the best research and researched instruments for measuring whatever they measure. The fault lies not so much in the instrument as in the conceptionalizations of susceptibility, hypnotizability, suggestibility, and depth that underlie the tool. "Whatever deficiencies exist in the assessment of susceptibility are not caused as much by a defective instrument as by a defective conceptualization" (Weitzenhoffer, 1980a, p. 144). He also recognizes the dangers of inundating the field with an instrument, and research about and with that instrument, which, in his view has conceptual superstructure weaknesses. He feels that accepting the scales has "led to the final wide and unfortunate acceptance in scientific circles of a conception of suggestion that essentially eliminated completely the nonvoluntary features of the classical definition as a criterion" (Weitzenhoffer, 1978a, pp. 197–198). An example of this problem is the inclusion of suggested amnesias in the scales, disallowing the possible occurrence of spontaneous amnesias, also thought to be a *sine qua non* of hypnosis at one time.

As the reader might suspect, Weitzenhoffer's remarks were not to go unanswered. Hilgard, although recognizing the need for new revisions of the original Stanford Scales, has responded point for point (Hilgard, 1981a), indicating that he feels that Weitzenhoffer's general arguments rest on a confusion between the concepts of hypnotic depth—which fluctuates with time during hypnosis—and hypnotic talent—the capacity for responding to hypnotic suggestions. Nonvoluntariness does not, he feels, pose any particular or measurement problems and was dismissed on those grounds. The major criticism of the Stanford Scales not tapping changes in suggestibility through pre- and postinduction gain-scores was considered at length. Conceptually, Hilgard feels that it involves a distinction between *becoming* hypnotized and *being* hypnotized, the former being what Weitzenhoffer is advocating we measure (in Hilgard's view). But Hilgard takes more than conceptual umbrage at this point. He provides the interested reader with a detailed accounting of the correlational problems that underlie Weitzenhoffer's advocacy of gain-scores (Hilgard, 1981a). However, his major criticism of the use of gain-scores to assess the capacity for hypnosis is that it would be impractical to implement, and, surprisingly, that "the use of gain-scores results in instances that are counterintuitive to those experienced in hypnosis" (Hilgard, 1981a, p. 33). On this point he also picked a nit by pointing out that the subject's initial response to the induction procedure (eye-closure or arm levitation) was really a response to a waking suggestion (instruction) since hypnosis, at that point, had not yet occurred. It is clear that Hilgard is not pleased with the criticism by his senior author, for even more recently he referred to the discussion as "a little tempest in a teapot" (Hilgard, 1982, p. 398).

Whether a "tempest in a teapot" or not, Weitzenhoffer's remarks have alerted the field to be more cautious in accepting uncritically any measuring device, even the highly regarded Stanford Scales. More importantly, his criticisms led to empirical work investigating the allegation that the Stanford Scales do not measure the "classical suggestion effect," the subjective experience of nonvoluntary response to suggested tasks. By having 24 subjects rate each scale item of the SHSS:A and the SHSS:C for degree of voluntariness on a five-point subjective scale, Bowers (1981a) was able to assess the experience of nonvoluntariness on the scales. He found that Weitzenhoffer was indeed correct with respect to the individual items of the SHSS:A. Subjects experienced passed items as predominantly occurring nonvoluntarily, but not invariably; in fact, 23% of failed items were experienced as nonvoluntary. Unfortunately, the same voluntary–nonvoluntary ratings were not made on items from the SHSS:C. Instead, various nonvoluntary indices were correlated with overall performance on the SHSS:C, using the latter as a criterion. Since the correlations are reasonable, Bowers concluded that the SHSS:C does "reflect a classical suggestion effect" (despite the fact that the nonvoluntary ratings for passed items on the SHSS:A did not correlate significantly), and that while Weitzenhoffer's criticism has "some merit," it "does not have serious empirical repercussions when assessing the hypnotic ability of people over a series of scale items" (Bowers, 1981a, p. 51). He also concluded that all that is needed is a high correlation between the degree of voluntariness experienced and the number of passed scale items. Such a correlation was not obtained in his data ($r = .38$, n.s.), so the reader is left wondering if Weitzenhoffer's criticism does not apply equally to both the SHSS:A and the SHSS:C, rather than just the former. At any rate, it is clear that this controversy is far from over. Hopefully, out of it will come better conceptualizations and improved scales for measuring those concepts.

What does all of this mean for the individual investigator and/or practitioner who wishes to use the original Stanford Scales and their offspring? Use them, but be aware that like their predecessors, they are not perfect; they demand continual updating and revision. Also be aware that, except for the last two scales (SHCS: ADULT and SHCS: CHILD), they are primarily useful in laboratory investigative settings and that their major normative data are derived from nonpatient populations. The clinician may find them too time-consuming for a work-a-day practice, but they are available for the practitioner who wishes to compare his patient's performance in hypnosis with a large body of rigorously developed data.

Hypnotic Induction Profile

In 1970 Spiegel and Bridger published a manual for the Hypnotic Induction Profile (HIP), a six-item test of hypnotizability, which has since gone through two revisions and considerable research evaluation. (Spiegel, 1974—now in its fourth revision; Spiegel & Spiegel, 1978) Developed on 4621 private psychiatric patients, it is touted to be "the only measure of hypnotizability appropriate for clinical settings" (Frischholz et al., 1980, p. 185). Its advantages, in addition to being developed on a patient population, are said to be its brevity of administration (5–10 min.) and its "proven utility in predicting treatment outcome" (Frischholz et al., 1980, p. 185).

The HIP consists of instructions for looking upward and then closing the eyes (Up-gaze, Eye-roll, and Eye-squint), collectively called the Eye-Roll Sign, and five other scorings that depend on the patient's speed of compliance and felt sensations to an arm-levitation induction procedure. The Eye-Roll portion of the HIP has been the most controversial and will be considered separately.

"The HIP assesses a single trance experience as it flows through the phases of entering, experiencing and exiting" (Spiegel & Spiegel, 1978, p. 39). It begins with the Eye-Roll Sign (to be described below). Once the patient's eyes are closed, arm-levitation instructions are begun, which initially include relaxation induction suggestions.

> Keep your eyelids closed and continue to hold your eyes upward. Take a deep breath, hold. . . . Now, exhale, let your eyes relax while keeping the lids closed, and let your body float. Imagine a feeling of floating, floating right down through the chair. . . . There will be something pleasant and welcome about this sensation of floating.
>
> As you concentrate on this floating, I am going to concentrate on your left arm and hand.

At this point the hypnotist touches the patient's wrist, preparatory for the stroking that occurs with the next instruction.

> In a while I am going to stroke the middle finger of your left hand. After I do, you will develop movement sensations in that finger. Then the movements will spread, causing your left hand to feel light and bouyant, and you will let it float upward. Ready?

The hypnotist strokes the patient's left hand and forearm up to the elbow. If the arm does not levitate immediately, the hypnotist lifts the arm for the patient, accompanying such assistance with the following.

> First one finger, then another. As these restless movements develop, your hand becomes light and buoyant, your elbow bends, your forearm floats into an upright position.
>
> Let your hand be a balloon. Just let it go. You have the power to let it float upward. That's right! Help it along! Just put it up there.

Should the arm still not levitate, the hypnotist places it in a position such that the forearm is perpendicular to the arm of the chair, on which rests the upper arm. The elbow is bent at a right angle.

Now I am going to position your arm in this manner, so. . . . And let it remain
in this upright position.

Now the hypnotist issues instructions intended to exit the patient from the
formal trance "ceremony" that has been established through the arm-levitation instructions.

In fact, it will remain in that position even after I give you the signal for your
eyes to open. When your eyes are open, even when I put your hand down, it
will float right back up to where it is now. You will find something amusing
about this sensation. Later, when I touch your left elbow, your usual sensation
and control will return. In the future, each time you give yourself the signal for
self-hypnosis, at the count of one your eyes will roll upward and by the count
of three your eyelids will close and you will feel in a relaxed trance state. Each
time you will find the experience easier and easier. Now I am going to count
backwards. At two, your eyes will again roll upward with your eyelids closed.
At one, let them open very slowly. Ready. . . . Three, two, with your eyelids
closed roll your eyes and one, let them open slowly. All right, stay in this
position and describe what physical sensations you are aware of now in your
left arm and hand.

As the authors see it, it is the formal trance ceremony, not the trance, that is
terminated by the above instructions. The testing now enters what Spiegel
calls the postinduction phase, which includes a question regarding tingling
feelings:

Are you aware of any tingling sensations?

and dissociation of the levitated arm:

Does your left hand feel as if it is not as much a part of your body as your right
hand?

Does your left hand feel as connected to the wrist as your right hand feels
connected to the wrist? Is there a difference?

The patient's forearm, which is still in the upright position, is lowered by
the hypnotist and the latter offers up to four reinforcing statements intended
to encourage the arm to levitate again. During these reinforcements no physical contact occurs between the patient and the hypnotist, as it did during the
induction levitation.

(First reinforcement.) Now turn your head, look at your left hand, and watch
what is going to happen.

(Second reinforcement.) While concentrating on your left-hand, imagine it to
be a huge, buoyant balloon.

(Third reinforcement.) Now, while imagining it to be a balloon, permit it to act out as if it were a balloon. That's right. Be "big" about it.

(Fourth reinforcement.) This is your chance to be a method actor or a ballet dancer. Think of your hand as a balloon or as the arm of a ballet dancer and permit it to act as if it were a balloon. That's right, just put it up there, just the way a ballet dancer would.

If the arm does not levitate after four reinforcements, the patient is instructed to place it back in the upright position. Then instructions are given intended to elicit a response with respect to a perceived difference in the two arms.

While it remains in the upright position, by way of comparison raise your right hand. Now put your right arm down. Are you aware of a difference in sensation in your right arm going up, compared to your left? For example, does one arm feel lighter or heavier than the other? Are you aware of any relative difference in your sense of control in one arm compared to the other as it goes up? (Optional: On a more or less basis, do you feel a difference in control?)

The last question is scored as the Control Differential item. If the patient notes no difference between the two arms, suggestions are again offered for arm levitation and the question of control differentiation is reiterated.

Let it rise like a balloon or ballet dancer's hand. Just let it go up as it did before. This time, do you have more or less control in one arm going up compared to the other?

Now the patient's left forearm is physically moved back to its starting position, flat on the arm of the chair, and the hypnotist strokes it from elbow to hand (the opposite direction from the initial induction, and offers cut-off suggestions).

Make a tight fist, real tight, and now open it. Before there was a difference between the two forearms. Are you aware of any change in sensation now?

If the patient does not feel "back to normal," the hypnotist comments,

Make a fist a few times. That's right. Open your fist and now put your hand down. Now, make fists with both hands at the same time. Lift your forearms up a few times and tell me when you feel that your control is equal.

Now the hypnotist queries the patient to see if a spontaneous amnesia has taken place.

You see that the relative difference in control that was in your arms is gone. Do you have any idea why?

Despite the central role played by amnesia in denoting the presence or absence of a hypnotic condition during the 19th century, this item is not part of the formal scoring of the HIP. However, the response to a final query regarding floating sensation is.

> When your left arm went up before, did you feel a physical sensation that you can describe as a lightness, floating, or "buoyancy" in your left arm or hand? Were you aware of similar sensations in any other part of your body—such as your head, neck, chest, abdomen, thighs, legs, or all over—or just in your left hand or arm? (All instructions, Spiegel & Spiegel, 1978, pp. 46–51)

Thus the items scored as part of the HIP are as follows: Eye-Roll Sign (ER), Signalled Arm Levitation (Lev), Dissociation (Di), Control Differential (CD), Cut-Off (CO), and Float (Fl).

Each of the last five are scored 0–2, except the Lev, which is scored 0–4, depending on the number of verbal reinforcements made in the process of the arm re-levitation. For simplicity sake, this latter score is then halved before combining it with the others to yield a total Induction Score indicating the degree of compliance with the hypnosis. Another score is also derived from the HIP, a Profile Configuration, which consists of the scores of the Eye-Roll, the Control Differential, and the Arm-Levitation subscores. Various weightings of these scores are combined to yield a dichotomy of hypnotizability labeled intact (hypnotizable) and nonintact (nonhypnotizable), although Stern et al. (1978/1979) further divide the dichotomy into intact—regular and special; nonintact—soft, decrement; and zero—regular and special. Recent research into the relationship between the HIP and the SHSS:A and SHSS:C implied that the more detailed breakdown may not have practical value at all. (Orne et al., 1979)

The HIP appears to be a reasonable reliability measure. Spiegel et al. (1976) reported test–retest reliabilities of .76 for the Induction Score, and .66 for the Profile Configuration. Others (Sheehan et al., 1979) have also found similar reliabilities.

In keeping with good psychometric procedures, the HIP has been compared with other measures of hypnosis in a number of studies. Spiegel et al. (1976) reported a correlation of .55 with the SHSS:C in an unpublished study from the Unit for Experimental Psychiatry. That same unit joined forces with the Stanford laboratory and the Spiegels themselves to make a thorough study of the relationship among the HIP, the SHSS:A, and the SHSS:C (Orne et al., 1979) The study was conducted at Stanford and at Pennsylvania on nonpatient volunteers; Herbert Spiegel administered the HIP on the East coast ($N = 87$) and his son, David Spiegel, administered it to the West coast sample ($N = 58$). The HIP Induction Score correlated significantly with both the Stanford Scales in the Pennsylvania sample, but not in the Stanford sample. However, combining the data from both samples an overall significant correlation with both scales was obtained ($r = .34$). Frischholz et al.

(1980) more recently also found a significant relationship between the Induction Score and the SHSS:C ($r = .63$). With respect to the Profile Configurations, Orne et al. (1979) reported that 83% of the Pennsylvania sample and 67% of the Stanford sample were rated "intact" (hypnotizable). These figures are reasonably like those from a patient population of 2000, in which 71% were found hypnotizable (Spiegel et al., 1975). These percentages are comparable to the Total Susceptibility figures in Table 8.6 from nonpatient populations.

Thus, the Hypnotic Induction Profile may be able to fulfill the need of both practitioners and experimental investigators for a measure of susceptibility-depth that requires only a brief time to administer. However, there is one subtest of the scale that has been the center of controversy almost since its introduction in 1970.

The Eye-Roll Sign

At the 1970 Annual Meeting of the Society for Clinical and Experimental Hypnosis Spiegel introduced the Eye-Roll Sign (ER) for hypnotizability, a simple procedure for predicting the capacity of an individual for hypnosis prior to the presentation of an induction technique. (If the ensuing evidence regarding this test had been less controversial, I would have presented it below in the section entitled "Modern Suggestibility Scales," since it does not involve hypnotizing the patient/subject before obtaining a measure.) Actually, the Eye-Roll Sign is similar to Felkin's 1890 observation for determining the presence of an actual hypnotic condition (compared to simulation). As I noted in Chapter 4, Felkin indicated that "the convulsive rotation upwards of the eyes" (Felkin, 1890, p. 31) was a sign of a true hypnotic trance.

The following instructions explain Spiegel's (1972) Eye-Roll Sign:

The patient is asked to:

1. Hold your head looking straight forward;

2. While holding your head in that position, look upward toward your eyebrows—now toward the top of your head (Up-gaze);

3. While continuing to look upward, at the same time close your eyelids slowly (Roll);

4. Now, open your eyes and let your eyes come back into focus.

Instruction four is omitted if the practitioner wishes to proceeed with the rest of the HIP (see above). While the patient performed these eye movements the practitioner observed them and compared their eye positions with the models depicted in Figure 8.1. Figure 8.1*a* shows the scoring criterion for the Up-gaze and the Roll phase as the eyes are closing and Figure 8.1*b* for a Squint, which sometimes occurs during the Up-gaze and/or Roll. Ac-

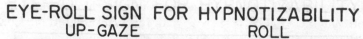

EYE-ROLL SIGN FOR HYPNOTIZABILITY
UP-GAZE   ROLL

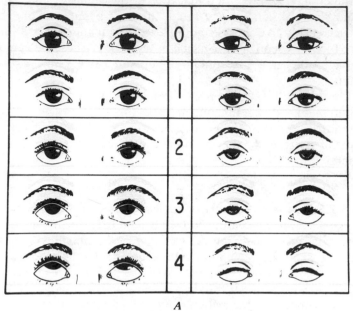

A

EYE-ROLL SIGN (SQUINT)

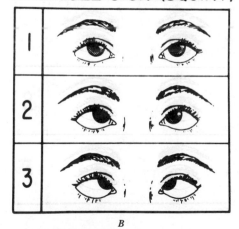

B

Figure 8.1. (*a*) Eye-roll sign for hypnotizability up-gaze, roll. (*b*) Eye-roll sign (squint). (From Spiegel, 1972. Reprinted by permission of the *American Journal of Clinical Hypnosis*.)

cording to Spiegel's original data on 2000 patients, this simple, 5–10 sec observation predicted trance capacity with a 75% accuracy.

Shortly afterward, data started to appear that raised doubts about the validity of the Eye-Roll Sign as a predictor. Switras (1974) showed that the ER was uncorrelated with the SHSS:A $(r = -.07)$ in a student population of 72. Wheeler et al. (1974) reported the same result with the HGSHS:A $(r = -.12$ to $-.27)$ and the SHSS:C $(r = -.17)$ (They did find significant negative correlations for females, however.) Although recognizing the difference of test populations (Spiegel used consecutive appearing psychiatric patients.), these authors questioned the methodology of the ER, particularly the possibility of experimenter bias in the scoring of the task. That same year, Eliseo (1974) reported almost identical data with the HGSHS:A $(r = -.13)$. By 1976 Spiegel (Spiegel et al., 1976) had concluded that "in the overall patient population, ER is at best only slightly predictive of hypnotizability" (Spiegel et al., 1976, p. 309). Sheehan et al. (1979) also reported that the ER was not dependable as a predictor of hypnotizability as measured by the Induction Score of the HIP; however, they did find the test-retest reliabilities of the ER were significant. Whatever it is indicating, it is a consistent intraindividual behavior that can be reliably rated in time by different observers.

However, as late as 1980, Frischholz et al. (1980) reported new and quite different data showing that the ER did, indeed, correlate positively and significantly with the SHSS:C $(r = .44)$. They attributed the nonsignificant findings of the other studies to the failure of those authors to administer the entire HIP and filter out ER "false positives." In fact, when Frischholz et al. (1980) evaluated only those subjects from their 63 Fordham University students who had "intact" HIPs, the strength of the correlation of ER with SHSS:C increased in value if not in significance. In an extensive review of their data, Hilgard (1981b) took exception to their new data and their interpretation of them. He accused the Frischholz et al. report (1980) of offering "as findings misleading interpretations of the value of the ER, based on faulty logic" (Hilgard, 1981b, p. 89). Frischholz et al. (1981) responded, first by pointing out some of Hilgard's own data, which revealed a correlation between ER and acupuncture treatment, and second, and more to the point, by professing justification at evaluating only those subjects who obtained intact scores and dropping out the nonintact group from consideration. Their view is that since psychopathology is a detriment to hypnotizability (a notion in tune with past historical observation, as we have seen), it was reasonable to disregard those data and look only at "healthy patient" data. After splitting the data in this manner, the correlations between the ER and "manifest hypnotic responsivity" were .52 for the "healthy" patients and .15 for the "severely disturbed." Hilgard (1981c) reiterated his concern that many of the claims for the ER are illusionary, a point that he makes more elaborately in a more recent publication (Hilgard, 1982b). Hilgard shows that the ER sign does not have the degree of predictability claimed by its authors, and charges that the Spiegels' interpretation of the ER as 75% successful in predicting hypnotizability is primarily illusionary. This "bowl of marbles" illusion, as Hilgard calls it, is in large part due to not taking into account baseline probabilities of the distribution of high and low hypnotizable subjects on the measures being correlated (the ER sign and the Lev). Thus, according to Hilgard, the predictability of the ER may be as low as 7% above chance, a figure indicating "that the ER does not relate to hypnotizability in an important manner" (Hilgard, 1982b, p. 966).

Depth Scales

While the preceding group of scales for the measurement of the capacity for hypnosis has been labeled "susceptibility–depth" scales because of their historical development from scales formally calling themselves depth scales and the inclusion of an induction technique prior to (or included in) the quantification of the subject's compliance to suggested tasks, the following scales were developed specifically for assessing hypnotic depth, during hypnosis.

The modern scaling of hypnotic depth, or the degree of profoundness of the hypnotic condition following an induction procedure, appeared to have begun with a simple proposal: Ask the patient/subject. Quantification came in the format of providing the subject with a range of numbers to use in response to the question, "How deep are you?" Furthermore, the subject is provided with verbal referents to define the numbers for him or her, either in stages of hypnosis (light, medium, deep, etc.) or in terms of wakefulness–sleep continuum, or the degree to which they feel compelled to comply with the suggestions of the hypnotist ("You are deep enough to experience just about anything I suggest").

The first of these scaling systems was proposed by LeCron (1953) in which subjects were instructed to report their depth on a 0–100 percentage scale, using the following categories: 0–20, light trance; 20–40, medium; 40–60, deep or somnambulistic; 60–80, deeper yet; and 80–100, stuporous state resembling suspended animation. (LeCron did remark that in the latter, plenary trance, it was unlikely that the subject would be able to respond anyway.) What was different about LeCron's technique from what has followed is his instruction to the subjects that they are to allow their "subconscious mind" to respond to the question of depth because it monitors such conditions more accurately than consciousness. LeCron felt that these estimates of hypnotic depth were not only an accurate representation, but were also necessary guides to the investigator–therapist. For example, he suggested that a depth of 40% or more was necessary to obtain age–regression phenomena from a subject.

While LeCron's method was a way of assessing depth *during hypnosis*, Field (1965) developed a questionnaire of 38 true-false items to be administered *following* a hypnotic session. Each of the items (see Table 8.10) corre-

TABLE 8.10.   Field's Inventory of Hypnotic Depth

Item (with response correlated to hypnotizability)

1. Time stood still (T)
2. My arm trembled or shook when I tried to move it (T)
3. I felt dazed (T)
4. I felt aware of my body only where it touched the chair (T)
5. I felt I could have tolerated pain more easily during the experiment (T)
6. I could have awakened any time I wanted to (F)
7. I was delighted with the experience (T)
8. The experimenter's voice seemed to come from very far away (T)
9. I tried to resist but I could not (T)
10. Everything happened automatically (T)
11. Sometimes I did not know where I was (T)
12. It was like the feeling I have just before waking up (T)
13. When I came out I was surprised at how much time had gone by (T)
14. I came out of the trance before I was told to (F)
15. During the experiment I felt I understood things better or more deeply (T)
16. I was able to overcome some or all of the suggestions (F)
17. At times I was deeply hypnotized and at other times I was only lightly hypnotized (T)
18. During the final "countdown" to wake me up I became more deeply hypnotized for a moment (T)

19. At times I felt completely unaware of being in an experiment (T)
20. I did not lose all sense of time (F)
21. It seemed completely different from ordinary experience (T)
22. I was in a medium hypnotic state, but no deeper (T)
23. Things seemed unreal (T)
24. Parts of my body moved without my conscious assistance (T)
25. I felt apart from everything else (T)
26. It seems as if it happened a long time ago (T)
27. I felt uninhibited (T)
28. At times I felt as if I had gone to sleep momentarily (T)
29. I felt quite conscious of my surroundings all the time (F)
30. Everything I did while hypnotized I can also do while I am not hypnotized (F)
31. I could not have stopped doing the things the experimenter suggested even if I tried (T)
32. It was a very strange experience (T)
33. I felt amazed (T)
34. From time to time I opened my eyes (F)
35. I couldn't stop movements after they got started (T)
36. I had trouble keeping my head up all during the experiment (T)
37. My mind seemed empty (T)
38. It seemed mysterious (T)

Source: Adapted from Field, 1965. Copyright 1965 by the Society for Clinical and Experimental Hypnosis. Reprinted by permission.

lated reasonably well with the HGSHS:A total scores and did not indicate that the normative subjects were responding according to a particular response set. Being a retrospective scale, Field's inventory may not have as much value to the practicing clinician, who may want instantaneous, in-state depth measures, as for the researcher. The inventory has the advantage of more rigorous psychometric development than some of the self-rating techniques that have appeared in a number of laboratory studies (e.g., Tart, 1970; Tellegen & Atkinson, 1974).

Tart (1970, 1972, 1978, 1979), on the other hand, has brought more rigorous psychometric techniques to bear on the self-report estimates of depth, and in the process developed a number of different scales. The scales, the North Carolina, the Brief Stanford, and the Long Stanford were designed to use variations on LeCron's original method, and to obtain frequent reports from the subjects during the hypnotic process. The North Carolina scale used a 0–50 range (LeCron used 0–100); the Brief Stanford, 0–4; and the Long Stanford, 0–10. The latter, which Tart feels is the "method of choice for assesing depth"(Tart, 1970, p. 121), was developed by having 35 subjects report their depth following each of the task items on the SHSS:C, presented by tape-recording. In an attempt to evaluate LeCron's notion of the accuracy of the subconcious in making depth estimates, Tart obtained two types of estimates, Instant and Deliberate. Instructions to the subjects for the Instant estimate are as follows:

> Let me explain how you will report your state of hypnosis. When I ask "State?" you are to tell me the first number that pops into your mind, and this will represent your state at that time. We've found that this first impression is more accurate than if you stop to think about just what the number should be. This may seem a little hard at first, but it will get easy as you go along. Just call out the first number that pops into your mind when I ask, "State?" Remember the number zero means your normal waking state, five means quite strongly hypnotized, and ten means you are deep enough to experience just about anything I suggest. Just say the first number from zero to ten that comes into your mind when I ask, "State?" Let's try it now. State? (All subjects called out a zero at this time.) At various times during your experience I'll ask for your state, and you'll call out the first number that pops into your mind. (Tart, 1978/1979, p. 192)

The attempt here was to obtain as rapid a response as possible, and thus tap the subconscious, since, Freudian-like, the ego would not be able to muster its defenses to screen the response before it is uttered. A comparison, however, with the Deliberate report, wherein the subject was not instructed to blurt forth the first number that popped into his or her mind, indicated that the Instant technique was no more nor less related to overall scores of hypnotic behavior (SHSS:C). If the subconscious is more accurate, instantaneous responding does not seem to be the way to demonstrate it.

At any rate, the Long Stanford scale of depth estimate is, Tart feels, the best choice between scales in which the subject is given extensively detailed instructions concerning the meaning of a wide range of numerical values, and the short versions where the categories are broadly defined. The definitions of his scale are: 0, awake and alert; 1, borderline state between sleeping and waking; 2, lightly hypnotized; 5, strongly and deeply hypnotized; 8 or 9, "really very hypnotized"; and 10, very deeply hypnotized and compliant with any suggestion. Kihlstrom (1984) uses a similar subjective report scale in his laboratories at the University of Wisconsin, although he defines the points in a slightly different manner: "1 is wide awake; 2 means you're entering hypnosis, 4 to 5 is a moderate state of hypnosis, the kind that most people can enter easily; and 10 is a deep state of hypnosis; but people can go beyond 10 to a very deep state of hypnosis." He has found it useful in keeping track of the subject's perception of hypnotic depth during experimental sessions and the degree of success achieved by the induction from the subject's point of view.

Assuming that depth of hypnosis is a linear variable, a 0–10 scale seems sufficient for either practitioner or researcher and is being used in a number of studies of the concept (see, for example, Perry & Laurence, 1980).

Modern Suggestibility Scales

The measurement scales included under this heading do not involve a hypnotic induction as part of their standardized procedure. Thus, based on the degree of nonhypnotic suggestibility (defined by the absence of an induction procedure) observed or reported, these scales predict the behavior that will follow any hypnotic induction. A hypnotic induction *may* be given prior to the scale items, but then the scale is being used to assess the changes in responsivity accomplished by the induction, or by any other instructional set (e.g., task motivating instructions). These scales are designed, then, to predict from nonhypnotic behavior to hypnotic behavior, while the scales in the previous section predict from one hypnotic session to another.

Barber Scales

In 1963 Barber and Calverley presented the *Barber Suggestibility Scale* (BSS) to assess "hypnotic-like" suggestibility in both adults and children. It consists of eight challenges (arm lowering, arm levitation, hand lock, thirst "hallucination," verbal inhibition, body immobility, "posthypnotic-like" response, and selective amnesia) requiring about 7 min. for administration. Each of the tasks are scored by the administrator 0 or 1, making a total possible of 8. This score is designated the Objective score to distinguish it from the Subjective score. In the latter, the subject fills out a questionnaire regarding their subjective perceptions of each of the tasks. A 0–3 rating is used for each, making a total possible score of 24. Here are the instructions and scoring criteria.

Barber Suggestibility Scale

As discussed in this paper, the BSS can be administered under a variety of experimental conditions: with and without Hypnotic Induction, with and without Task Motivational Instructions, by means of tape-recording or by oral presentation, etc. With the exception of one study (Barber & Calverly, 1965) the scale has been administered to subjects with their eyes closed.

After one of the experimental treatments has been imposed, as discussed in the monograph, the BSS is administered and scored as follows:

Eight Test-suggestions

1.   *Arm Lowering*. "Hold your right arm straight out in front of you like this." (Guide the subject to extend the right arm directly in front of body at shoulder height and parallel to the floor.) "Concentrate on your arm and listen to me."

(Begin timing) "Imagine that your right arm is feeling heavier and heavier, and that it's moving down and down. It's becoming heavier and heavier and moving down and down. It weighs a ton! It's getting heavier and heavier. It's moving down and down, more and more, coming down and down, more and more; it's heavier and heavier, coming down and down, more and more, more and more." (End 30 seconds)

"You can relax your arm now." (If necessary, ask the subject to lower the right arm.)

Objective score criterion: 1 point for response of 4 inches or more. (Response is measured by placing a ruler near the subject's hand at the beginning of the suggestions and noting degree of displacement at the end of the 30-second suggestion period.)

2.   *Arm Levitation*. "Keep your eyes closed and put your left arm straight out in front of you in the same way. Concentrate on your arm and listen to me."

(Begin timing) "Imagine that the arm is becoming lighter and lighter, that it's moving up and up. It feels as if it doesn't have any weight at all, and it's moving up and up, more and more. It's as light as a feather, it's weightless and rising in the air. It's lighter and lighter, rising and lifting more and more. It's lighter and lighter and moving up and up. It doesn't have any weight at all and it's moving up and up, more and more. It's lighter and lighter, moving up and up, more and more, higher and higher." (End 30 seconds)

"You can relax your arm now." (If necessary, ask the subject to lower the arm.)

Objective score criterion: 1 point for response of 4 inches or more during 30-second suggestion period.

3.   *Hand Lock*. "Keep your eyes closed. Clasp your hands together tightly, and interlace the fingers." (If necessary, the experimenter states, "Press your hands together, with palms touching," and assist the subject to interlock the fingers and to bring the palms together.) "Put them in your lap. Concentrate on your hands and hold them together as tightly as you can."

(Begin timing) "Imagine that your hands are two pieces of steel that are welded together so that it's impossible to get them apart. They're stuck, they're welded, they're clamped. When I ask you to pull your hands apart, they'll be stuck and they won't come apart no matter how hard you try. They're stuck together; they're two pieces of steel welded together. You feel as if your fingers were clamped in a vise. Your hands are hard, solid, rigid! The harder you try to pull them apart the more they will stick together! It's impossible to pull your hands apart! The more you try the more difficult it will become. Try, you can't." (10-second pause) "You can unclasp your hands now."

Objective score criteria: $\frac{1}{2}$ point for incomplete separation of hands after 5-second effort; 1 point for incomplete separation after 15-second effort.

4. *Thirst "Hallucination."* "Keep your eyes closed." (Begin timing) "Imagine that you've just finished a long walk in the hot sun. You've been in the hot sun for hours, and for all that time you haven't had a drink of water. You've never been so thirsty in your life. You feel thirstier and thirstier. Your mouth is parched, your lips are dry, your throat is dry. You have to keep swallowing and swallowing. You need to moisten your lips." (3-second pause) "You feel thirstier and thirstier, drier and drier. Thirstier and thirstier, dry and thirsty. You're very very thirsty! Dry and thirsty! Dry and thirsty!" (End 45 seconds) "Now, imagine drinking a cool, refreshing glass of water." (5-second pause)

Objective score criteria: $\frac{1}{2}$ point if the subject shows swallowing, moistening of lips, or marked mouth movements, additional $\frac{1}{2}$ point if subject indicates during the "postexperimental" questioning that he or she became thirsty during this test (e.g., "I felt dry," "I was parched," "I felt somewhat thirsty"). (See "postexperimental" questions for final scoring criteria on this test.)

5. *Verbal Inhibition.* "Keep your eyes closed." (Begin timing) "Imagine that the muscles in your throat and jaw are solid and rigid, as if they're made of steel. They're so solid and so rigid, that you can't speak. Every muscle in your throat and mouth is so tight and so rigid that you can't say your name. The harder you try to say your name the harder it becomes. You can't talk! Your larynx has tightened up, your throat and jaw feel as if they are in a vise. Your throat is clamped so tightly that you can't talk; you can't say your name. The harder you try the harder it will be. It's useless, the words won't come out; you can't speak your name; it's impossible to talk! The harder you try to say your name the harder it will become. Try, you can't!" (End 45 seconds)

(5-second pause) "Try harder; you can't." (10-second pause) "You can say your name now."

Objective score criteria: $\frac{1}{2}$ point if the subject does not say name after 5-second effort; 1 point if subject does not say name after 15-second effort.

6. *Body Immobility.* "Keep your eyes closed." (Begin timing) "Imagine that for years and years you've been sitting in that chair just as you are now. Imagine that you've been sitting in that chair so long that you're stuck to it! It's as if you're part of the chair. Your whole body is heavy, rigid, solid and you weigh a ton. You're so heavy that you can't budge yourself. It's impossible for you to stand up, you're stuck right there! Your body has become part of the chair. When I ask you to stand up you won't be able to do it! You're stuck tight. The harder you try the tighter you'll be stuck and you won't be able to get up. You're heavy in the chair! Stuck in the chair; you can't stand up. You're heavy and stuck so tight. You can't stand up; you're stuck. Try, you can't." (End 45 seconds)

(5-second pause) "Try harder; you can't." (10-second pause) "You can relax [or sit down] now."

(The subject is considered not standing if he or she rises slightly from the chair without straightening into an erect posture. In this event, the experimenter says "Try to stand fully erect, you can't," instead of "Try harder, you can't.")

Objective score criteria: ½ point if the subject is not standing fully erect after 5-second effort; 1 point if not standing fully erect after 15-second effort.

7.   *"Posthypnotic-like" Response*. (The auditory stimulus consists of tapping once on the metal back of a stop watch with a fountain pen.) (Begin timing) "When this experiment is over in a few minutes and your eyes are open, I'll click like this (experimenter presents auditory stimulus) and you'll cough automatically. At the moment I click (experimenter presents stimulus) you'll cough. It will happen automatically. When I click like this (stimulus is presented) you'll cough immediately. I'll click and you'll cough. When I click you'll cough." (End 30 seconds)

Objective score criterion: 1 point if the subject coughs or clears throat "postexperimentally" when presented with the auditory stimulus.

8.   *Selective Amnesia*. "Your eyes are still closed but I'm going to ask you to open them in a minute. When they're open I'm going to ask you to tell me about these tests." (Begin timing) "You'll remember all the tests and be able to tell me about them, all except for one. There's one that you'll completely forget about as if it never happened! That's the one where I said your arm was becoming lighter and moving up and up. You'll forget all about that and when you try to think about it, it will slip even further away from your mind. You will forget completely that I told you that your arm was becoming lighter. This is the one test that you cannot remember! You will remember that I said your arm was heavy and all the other tests will be perfectly clear but the harder you try to remember that I told you your arm was rising the more difficult it will become. You will not remember until I give you permission by saying, 'Now you can remember,' and then, and only then, you will remember that I said your arm was rising!" (End 45 seconds)

Objective score criterion: 1 point if the subject does not refer to the Arm Levitation item (Test-suggestion 2) but recalls at least four other items and then recalls Test-suggestion 2 in response to the cue words.

"Postexperimental" Objective Scoring of Test-suggestions 4, 7 and 8

"Open your eyes, the experiment is over."

"Scoring of Test-suggestion 7. The "Post-hypnotic-Like" Response item (item 7) is scored at this point. The experimenter presents the auditory stimulus after the subject has opened his or her eyes and before conversation commences.

Scoring of Test-suggestion 8. The experimenter next asks: "How many of the tests can you remember?"

The experimenter prompts the subject by asking, "Were there any others?" "Can you think of any more?" and "Is that all?," until the subject mentions at least four of test-suggestions. If the subject verbalizes the Arm Levitation item during the recital, he or she receives a score of zero on Test-suggestion 8

(Selective Amnesia). If the subject does not include the Arm Levitation item in the enumeration, the experimenter finally states, "Now you can remember," and, if the subject still does not verbalize the Arm Levitation item, "You can remember perfectly well now!"

"The subject receives a score of 1 point on Test-suggestion 8 (Selective Amnesia) if he or she mentions at least four of the test-suggestions, but does not mention the Arm Levitation item before given the cue words and verbalizes the Arm Levitation item when given the cue words, "Now you can remember," or, "You can remember perfectly well now!"

Final Scoring of Test-suggestion 4. The Objective scoring of Test-suggestion 4 is completed when the subject refers to this item during the recital. At this point the experimenter asks: "Did you become thirsty during this test?" If the subject answers, "Yes" to this question he or she receives the additional $\frac{1}{2}$ point of Item 4. If the subject answers, "Yes" but adds a qualifying statement, e.g., "I had been thirsty to begin with," he or she is asked: "Did the imaginary glass of water help quench your thirst?" If the subject now answers, "Yes" he or she receives the additional $\frac{1}{2}$ point.

The maximum Objective score obtainable on the BSS is 8 points.

"Revised" Subjective Scores

After Objective scores have been assigned, the subject is given a mimeo-graphed questionnaire which assesses subjective responses to the BSS and is worded thus:
Please answer the following questions truthfully. Place a check mark above the most accurate answer.

1.   When it was suggested that your right arm was heavy and was moving down, the arm felt: not heavy; heavy; very heavy.

2.   When it was suggested that your left arm was light and was moving up, the arm felt: not light; slightly light; light; very light.

3.   When it was suggested that your hands were stuck together and you couldn't take them apart, the hands felt: not stuck; slightly stuck; stuck; very stuck.

4.   When it was suggested that you felt thirsty, you felt: not thirsty; slightly thirsty; thirsty; very thirsty.

5.   When it was suggested that your throat ws stuck and you couldn't speak, your throat felt: not stuck; slightly stuck; stuck; very stuck.

6.   When it was suggested that you were stuck to the chair, you felt: not stuck; slightly stuck; stuck; very stuck.

7.   When the experiment was over and the experimenter clicked his fingers [presented the posthypnotic cue], you felt: not like coughing; slightly like coughing; like coughing; very much like coughing.

8.   When the experiment was over and you were recalling the tests, you felt that you remembered the test about the arm rising [the test S was told to

forget]: with no difficulty; with slight difficulty; with difficulty; with great difficulty (or did not remember at all).

Each of the above eight items receives a score of 0 to 3; 0 for the first answer ("not"); 1 for the second ("slightly"), and so on. The total Subjective scores on the eight items thus range from 0 to 24." (Barber & Wilson, 1978//79, pp. 98–102)

Both the Objective and the Subjective scores are highly reliable, ranging typically around .88 for test–retest, and .80 for the split-half technique. Originally, the BSS was evaluated on 724 students ranging from 6–22 years old. Later (Barber, 1969), another group of 186 college students was added to the normative data. As shown in Table 8.6, this group distributed itself in a manner comparable to other suceptibility–depth scales when the eight challenge items were preceded by a hypnotic induction. Table 8.11 presents the distribution of Objective and Subjective scores when the BSS is presented in its standard format; that is, without being preceded by a hypnotic induction. Unlike the distributions of the BSS measures following an induction (Table 8.6), which are skewed toward the "deep" end of the categorizations, the distributions of the BSS scores in Table 8.11 are skewed toward the low end. This should not surprise the reader, because as Weitzenhoffer has argued, an increase in suggestibility is to be expected following an induction procedure, and has been found in a number of studies (see above). However, these data do caution the user to be aware that the scores derived from the BSS given in its intended, nonhypnotic format may predict that a particular individual will become less involved in the hypnotic situation than he or she actually does when presented with a hypnotic induction.

Citing the need for a more adaptable scale that could be used either clinically or experimentally and individually or with groups, Wilson (1976) tested a *Creative Imagination Scale* (CIS), which was later further developed in conjunction with Barber (Barber & Wilson, 1977; Wilson & Barber, 1978). The scale consists of 10 challenge items (arm heaviness, hand levitation, finger anesthesia, water "hallucination," olfactory-gustatory "hallucination," music "hallucination," temperature "hallucination," time distortion, age-regression, and mind-body relaxation). Each task is self-scored by the subject on a 0–4 scale, making a total possible score of 40. Here are the instructions for the CIS, along with the self-rating scoring form:

Creative Imagination Scale

1. *Arm Heaviness.* "By letting your thoughts go along with these instructions you can make your hand and arm feel heavy. Please close your eyes and place your left arm straight out in front of you at shoulder height with the palm facing up." [Begin timing.] "Now imagine that a very heavy dictionary is being placed on the palm of your left hand. Let yourself feel the heaviness. Your thoughts make it feel as if there is a heavy dictionary on your hand. You create the feeling of heaviness in your hand by thinking of a large heavy dictionary. Now think of a second large heavy dictionary being placed on top of the first

heavy dictionary. Feel how very heavy your arm begins to feel as you push up on the dictionaries. Push up on the heavy dictionaries as you imagine the weight; notice how your arm feels heavier and heavier as you push up on them. Now tell yourself that a third big heavy dictionary is being piled on top of the other two heavy dictionaries in your hand and your arm is very, very heavy. Let yourself feel as if there are three heavy dictionaries on the palm of your hand and your arm is getting heavier and heavier and heavier. Feel your arm getting heavier and heavier and heavier, very, very, very heavy, getting heavier and heavier and heavier . . . very heavy." [Approximately 1'20" since beginning of timing.]

"Now relax your hand and arm and tell yourself that your hand and arm feel perfectly normal again."

2. *Hand Levitation.* "By directing your thoughts you can make your hand feel as if it is rising easily, without effort. Keep your eyes closed and place your right arm straight out in front of you at shoulder height with the palm facing down." [Begin timing] "Now, picture a garden hose with a strong stream of water pushing against the palm of your right hand, pushing up against the palm of your hand. Think of a strong stream of water pushing your hand up. Let yourself feel the strong stream of water pushing up against the palm of your hand, pushing it up. Feel the force of the water, pushing your hand up. Feel it pushing against the palm of your hand. Tell yourself that the force of the water is very strong and, as you think about it, let your hand begin to rise. Feel your hand rising as you imagine a strong stream of water pushing your hand up, pushing it up, and up, and up higher and higher. Tell yourself that a strong stream of water is pushing your hand up and up, raising your arm and hand higher and higher as the strong stream of water just pushes it up, just rises and pushes and just pushes it up, higher and higher." [End of timing: about 1'10".]

"Now tell yourself it's all in your own mind and just let your hand and arm come back down and relax."

3. *Finger Anesthesia.* By focusing your thinking you can make your fingers feel numb. Please place your left hand in your lap with the palm facing up. Keep your eyes closed so you can focus fully on all the sensations in the fingers of your left hand." [Begin timing.] "Now, try to imagine and feel as if Novocain has just been injected into the side of your left hand next to the little finger so that your little finger will begin to feel like it does when it "falls asleep." Focus on the little finger. Become aware of every sensation and the slight little changes as you think of the Novocain slowly beginning to move into your little finger, just slowly moving in. Notice the slight little changes as the little finger begins to get just a little numb and a little dull. The little finger is becoming numb as you think of the Novocain moving in slowly."

"Now think of the Novocain moving into the second finger next to the little finger. Tell yourself that the second finger is getting duller and duller, more and more numb as you think of how the Novocain is beginning to take effect."

"Tell yourself that these two fingers are beginning to feel kind of rubbery and are losing feelings and sensations. As you think of the Novocain moving in faster, the fingers feel duller and duller . . . more and more numb . . . dull, numb and insensitive. As you think of the Novocain taking effect, the two fingers feel duller and duller . . . more and more numb . . . dull . . . numb . . . insensitive.''

''Keep thinking that the two fingers are dull, numb, and insensitive as you touch the two fingers with your thumb. As you touch the two fingers with your thumb notice how they feel duller and duller, more and more numb, more and more insensitive . . . dull, numb, rubbery and insensitive.'' [End of timing: about 1'50".]

''Now tell yourself it's all in your own mind and you're going to bring the feeling back; bring the feeling back into the two fingers.''

4.)   *Water "Hallucination."* ''Keep your eyes closed. By using your imagination constructively you can experience the feeling of drinking cool, refreshing water.''

[Begin timing.] ''First, imagine you've been out in the hot sun for hours and you're very, very thirsty and your lips are dry and you're so thirsty. Now, picture yourself on a mountain where the snow is melting, forming a stream of cool, clear water. Imagine yourself dipping a cup into this mountain stream so you can have a cool, refreshing drink of water. As you think of sipping the water tell yourself it's absolutely delicious as you feel it going down your throat . . . cold and beautiful and delicious. Feel the coolness and beauty of the water as you take a sip. Now, think of taking another sip of water and feel it going over your lips and tongue, going down your throat, down into your stomach. Feel how cool, refreshing, delicious and beautiful it is as you take another sip . . . so cool . . . cold . . . sweet . . . beautiful . . . delicious and refreshing. Think of taking another sip now and feel the cool water going into your mouth, around your tongue, down your throat and down into your stomach . . . so beautiful and cool and wonderful . . . absolutely delicious . . . absolute pleasure.'' [End of timing: about 1'30".]

5.   *Olfactory-Gustatory "Hallucination."* ''Keep your eyes closed. By using your imagination creatively, you can experience the smell and taste of an orange.'' [Begin timing.] ''Picture yourself picking up an orange and imagine that you're peeling it. As you create the image of the orange, feel yourself peeling it and let yourself see and feel the orange on the outside and the soft white pulp on the inside of the skin. As you continue peeling the orange, notice how beautiful and luscious it is and let yourself smell it and touch it and feel the juiciness of it. Now think of pulling out one or two of the orange sections with your fingers. Pull out part of the orange and bite into it. Experience how juicy, luscious and flavorful it is as you imagine taking a deep, deep bite. Let yourself smell and taste the orange in your mouth and on your tongue. Feel the juice and feel the pulp as you think of taking another bite. Let yourself smell and taste the orange and notice that it's absolutely delicious. Let yourself feel how delicious, beautiful and luscious it is. Just the most beautiful, juicy orange . . . absolutely juicy and wonderful. Let yourself taste and smell the juicy orange clearly now as you think of taking another large bite of the delicious, juicy orange.'' [End of timing: about 1'30".]

6. *Music "Hallucination."* "Keep your eyes closed." [Begin timing.] "Now, think back to a time when you heard some wonderful, vibrant music, it could have been anywhere, and by thinking back you can hear it even more exquisitely in your own mind. You make it yourself and you can experience it as intensively as real music. The music can be absolutely powerful . . . strong . . . exquisite . . . vibrating through every pore of your body . . . going deep into every pore . . . penetrating through every fiber of your being. The most beautiful, complete, exquisite, overwhelming music you ever heard. Listen to it now as you create it in your own mind." [End of timing: about 45″]

[15 second pause] "You may stop thinking of the music now."

7. *Temperature "Hallucination."* "Keep your eyes closed and place your hands in your lap with the palms facing down and resting comfortably on your lap. By focusing your thinking you can make your right hand feel hot."

[Begin timing.] "Picture the sun shining on your right hand and let yourself feel the heat. As you think of the sun shining brightly, let yourself feel the heat increasing. Feel the sun getting hotter and feel the heat penetrating your skin and going deep into your hand. Think of it getting hot now . . . getting very hot. Feel the heat increasing. Think of the sun getting very, very hot as it penetrates into your hand . . . getting very hot. Tell yourself, 'The rays are increasing . . . the heat is increasing . . . getting hotter and hotter.' Feel the heat penetrating through your skin. Feel the heat going deeper into your skin as you think of the rays of the sun increasing and becoming more and more concentrated . . . getting hotter and hotter. Feel your hand getting hot from the heat of the sun. It's a good feeling of heat as it penetrates deep into your hand . . . hot, pleasantly hot, penetrating into your hand now. It's a pleasantly hot feeling, pleasantly hot." [End of timing: about 1′15″.]

"Now tell yourself it's all in your own mind and make your hand feel perfectly normal again."

8. *Time Distortion.* "Keep your eyes closed. By controlling your thinking you can make time seem to slow down."

[The following is to be read progressively more and more slowly, with each word drawn out and with long, i.e., 2–6 second, pauses between statements.]

[Begin timing.] "Tell yourself that there's lots of time, lots of time between each second. Time is stretching out and there's lots of time . . . more and more time between each second. Every second is stretching far, far out . . . stretching out more and more . . . lots of time. There's so much time . . . lots of time. Every second is stretching out. There's lots of time between each second . . . lots of time. You do it yourself, you slow time down." [End of timing: about 1′40″.]

[The following is to be read at a normal rate.] "And now tell yourself that time is speeding back up to its normal rate again as your bring time back to normal."

9. *Age Regression.* "Keep your eyes closed. By directing your thinking you can bring back the feelings that you experienced when you were in elementary school—in first, second, third, fourth, or fifth grade."

[Begin timing.] "Think of time going back, going back to elementary school and feel yourself becoming smaller and smaller. Let yourself feel your hands, small and tiny, and your legs and your body, small and tiny. As you go back in time feel yourself sitting in a big desk. Notice the floor beneath you. Feel the top of the desk. You may feel some marks on the desk top, or maybe it's a smooth, cool surface. There may be a pencil slot and perhaps a large yellow pencil. Feel the under side of the desk and you may feel some chewing gum. Observe the other children around you, and the teacher, the bulletin board, the chalkboard, the cloak room, and the windows. Smell the eraser dust or the paste. You may hear the children and the teacher speaking. Now just observe and see what happens around you." [End of timing: about 1'20".]

10. *Mind-Body Relaxation.* "Keep your eyes closed. By letting your thoughts go along with these instructions you can make your mind and body feel very relaxed."

[The following is to be read slowly.] [Begin timing.] "Picture yourself on a beautiful, warm summer day lying under the sun on a beach of an ocean or lake. Feel yourself lying on the soft, soft sand or on a beach towel that is soft and comfortable. Let yourself feel the sun pleasantly warm and feel the gentle breeze touching your neck and face. Picture the beautiful clear blue sky with fluffy little white clouds drifting lazily by. Let yourself feel the soothing, penetrating warmth of the sun and tell yourself that your mind and body feel completely relaxed and perfectly at ease . . . peaceful, relaxed, comfortable, calm, so at ease, at peace with the universe . . . completely relaxed . . . relaxed, peaceful, lazy, tranquil . . . calm . . . comfortable. Your mind and body are completely relaxed . . . completely relaxed . . . calm, peaceful, tranquil, flowing with the universe." [End of timing: about 1'05".]

"Now as you open your eyes let yourself continue to feel relaxed and yet perfectly alert . . . peaceful, alert and normal again. Open your eyes."

Self-Scoring Form for the Creative Imagination Scale

Please answer each item as honestly as possible. There are no right or wrong answers.

Read the statements below describing the possible responses for each item. Then, circle the number (0, 1, 2, 3, or 4) which corresponds to the statement that most nearly matches your experience.

1. In the first test you were asked to imagine that one, two, and then three dictionaries were being piled on the palm of your hand. Compared to what you would have experienced if three dictionaries were actually on your hand, what you experienced was:

0	1	2	3	4
0%	25%	50%	75%	90+%
Not at all the same	A little the same	Between a little and much the same	Much the same	Almost exactly the same

2. In the second test you were asked to think of a strong stream of water from a garden hose pushing up against the palm of your hand. Compared to what you would have experienced if a strong stream of water were actually pushing up against your palm, what you experienced was:

0	1	2	3	4
0%	25%	50%	75%	90+%
Not at all the same	A little the same	Between a little and much the same	Much the same	Almost exactly the same

3. In the third test you were asked to imagine that Novocain had been injected into your hand and it made two fingers feel numb. Compared to what you would have experienced if Novocain had actually made the two fingers feel numb, what you experienced was:

0	1	2	3	4
0%	25%	50%	75%	90+%
Not at all the same	A little the same	Between a little and much the same	Much the same	Almost exactly the same

4. In the fourth test you were asked to think of drinking a cup of cool mountain water. Compared to what you would have experienced if you were actually drinking cool mountain water, what you experienced was:

0	1	2	3	4
0%	25%	50%	75%	90+%
Not at all the same	A little the same	Between a little and much the same	Much the same	Almost exactly the same

5. In the fifth test you were asked to imagine smelling and tasting an orange. Compared to what you would have experienced if you were actually smelling and tasting an orange, what you experienced was:

0	1	2	3	4
0%	25%	50%	75%	90+%
Not at all the same	A little the same	Between a little and much the same	Much the same	Almost exactly the same

6. In the sixth test you were asked to think back to a time when you heard some wonderful music and to reexperience hearing it. Compared to what you

would have experienced if you were actually hearing the music, what you experienced was:

0	1	2	3	4
0%	25%	50%	75%	90+%
Not at all the same	A little the same	Between a little and much the same	Much the same	Almost exactly the same

7. In the seventh test you were asked to picture the sun shining on your hand making it feel hot. Compared to what you would have experienced if the sun were actually shining on your hand, what you experienced was:

0	1	2	3	4
0%	25%	50%	75%	90+%
Not at all the same	A little the same	Between a little and much the same	Much the same	Almost exactly the same

8. In the eighth test you were asked to imagine time slowing down. Compared to what you would have experienced if time actually slowed down, what you experienced was:

0	1	2	3	4
0%	25%	50%	75%	90+%
Not at all the same	A little the same	Between a little and much the same	Much the same	Almost exactly the same

9. In the ninth test you were asked to think back to a time when you were in elementary school. Compared to the feelings you would have experienced if you were actually in elementary school, the feelings you experienced were:

0	1	2	3	4
0%	25%	50%	75%	90+%
Not at all the same	A little the same	Between a little and much the same	Much the same	Almost exactly the same

10. In the tenth test you were asked to picture yourself lying under the sun on a beach and becoming very relaxed. Compared to what you would have experienced if you were actually relaxing on a beach, what you experienced was:

0	1	2	3	4
0%	25%	50%	75%	90+%
Not at all the same	A little the same	Between a little and much the same	Much the same	Almost exactly the same

(Barber & Wilson, 1978/1979, pp. 102–108)

Test–retest reliability on 22 subjects was .82 and split-half, .89. The distribution of scores for the 217 normative subjects (Table 8.11) is similar to those of the older depth scales of Davis and Husband; Barry, MacKinnon, and Murray; and Friedlander and Sarbin (see Table 8.6), as well as the Stanford Scales. Thus this suggestibility scale, which does not regularly use an induction procedure, distributes subjects in a manner similar to those that do. In fact, Straus (1980) has shown in a clinical setting that a traditional eye-fixation, relaxation induction does not affect scores on the CIS. What Wilson and Barber seem to have created is a suggestibility scale that predicts behavior during hypnosis, without having to measure the subject/patient *in* hypnosis first. In addition, the CIS is well in keeping with the trends of looking at the cognitive processes occurring in hypnosis and measuring such personality traits as involvement (J. Hilgard, 1979) and absorption (Tellegen & Atkinson, 1974), which frequently look like personality traits. The CIS has been shown by other investigators to be a reliable scale (e.g., Sheehan, 1982; Sheehan, McConkey & Law, 1978), which measures at least one cognitive factor (Sheehan, McConkey, & Law, 1978) and most likely a second, ideomotor factor (Hilgard, Sheehan, Monteiro & MacDonald, 1981; Monteiro, MacDonald & Hilgard, 1980). The full scale CIS is highly correlated with both the Stanford Scales—.60—and the Harvard Scale—.55; .28 in Australia (McConkey, Sheehan & White, 1979; Monteiro, MacDonald & Hilgard, 1980).

Tellegen Absorption Scale (TAS)

The search for even more reliable predictive measures of the capacity for hypnosis continues. As indicated above, one of the most promising lines of inquiry into the underlying personality characteristics of individuals who are highly hypnotizable is that outlined by Barber and Glass (1962), J. Hilgard (1970, 1974, 1979), and others, who noted the relationship between an individual's ability to become thoroughly and completely absorbed in an activity and hypnotizability. Tellegen and Atkinson's Absorption Scale (1974) is noteworthy in this regard and has been compared to other scales in a number of studies (e.g., Monteiro, MacDonald & Hilgard, 1980; Sheehan, McConkey & Law, 1978). Quite recently, the TAS has been revised and updated into a 34, MMPI-type item self-response scale (Hilgard, Sheehan, Monteiro & MacDonald, 1981; Tellegen, 1981). The Absorption Items form

TABLE 8.11. Distribution of Barber Suggestibility Scale and Creative Imagination Scale Scores

| Scale | Cases | Distribution of Suggestibility (in percent) | | | | |
		Low (Refractory; Nonsusceptible)	Medium Low (Drowsy; Light)	Medium High (Hypotaxy)	High (Somnambulism)	Total Suggestibility
Barber Suggestibility Scale (BSS) (Objective Scores)	186	37 (Scores 0–1.5)	32 (Scores 2–4)	19 (Scores 4.5–6.5)	12 (Scores 7–8)	63
BSS (Subjective Scores)	186	45 (0–1)	39 (2–4)	13 (5–6)	3 (7–8)	55
BSS (Revised Subjective Scores)	211	34 (0–5)	29 (6–9)	31 (10–15)	6 (16–20)	66
Creative Imagination Scale	217	13 (0–10)	35 (11–20)	34 (21–28)	18 (29–40)	87

one of 11 primary scales in the Differential Personality Questionnaire (DPQ) (Tellegen, 1982) and are imbedded in a total of 300 true–false items on the Questionnaire. The TAS itself measures 9 content categories (see Table 8.12). An individual scoring highly on the TAS is described as follows: "Is emotionally responsive to engaging sights and sounds; is readily captured by entrancing stimuli; thinks in images and has synaesthetic and other 'cross-modal' experiences; can summon and become absorbed in vivid and compelling recollections and imaginings; experiences episodes of expanded (extrasensory, mystical) awareness and other altered states" (Tellegen, 1982, p. 8).

The author prefers the scale to be embedded in "filler" items so that the "powerful demand characteristics influencing subjects' response to the items" are reduced by imbedding the items within the other 266 questions (Tellegen, 1984). To do so will certainly reduce the TAS's attractiveness to those who want a brief scale of hypnotic responsiveness that can be administered in a minimum amount of time. However, to use the 34 items alone, without some sort of masking, filler items will no doubt reduce the high reliability of the scale (test–retest $r = .91$) and the accuracy of its predictibility.

As early as 1980, O'Grady was of the opinion that the TAS was tapping "a relatively new personality dimension." If, however, absorptive behavior *is* the personality underpinning of the capacity of hypnosis, it is as old as the ancients; only our method of quantifying it is new.

But Tellegen is not the only one applying newer methods to the quantification of the capacity for hypnosis. In Sweden, Berger and Arver (1972) have constructed a suggestibility scale (the Multivariate Informational Analysis Suggestibility Scale—MIA-SS) based on a cybernetic model of information theory. Starting with the idea that the basis of hypnotic behavior is suggestibility and that suggestibility is best measured by quantifying the degree to which a subject constructs an elaborate environment from the minimum cues presented by the hypnotist, these authors assessed their subjects' responses to suggestions about the frequency of an auditory stimulus.

Subjects listened to a 660 Hz tone (designated as "10") following suggestions that the frequency of the tone was "10," "15," "20," or "30." They then pressed a recording device with their index finger if the tone seemed to remain the same ("10") after the suggestion, another with their middle finger if the tone sounded like "15," another with their ring finger if it seemed to be a "20," and still another with their small finger for "30." Since the subject knew that the tone was always the same, objectively, the authors claim that they are measuring the degree of information transmission output (response) to a low information stimulus input; in essence, the degree to which the subject compensates for impoverished environmental input by the exaggeration of the importance of unimportant cues. The technique is reliable (test–retest $r = .65$; internal consistency $r = .87$), and relates well to the SHSS:A ($r = .65$). For those interested in information theory and its possible applica-

TABLE 8.12. Content Categories and Representative Test Items of the Absorption Scale of Tellegen's Differential Personality Questionnaire[a]

A. *Is responsive to engaging stimuli.*

 1. I can be greatly moved by eloquent or poetic language.
 2. I like to watch cloud shapes change in the sky.

B. *Is responsive to "inductive" stimuli.*

 1. While watching a movie, a T.V. show, or a play, I may become so involved that I forget about myself and my surroundings and experience the story as if it were real and as if I were taking part in it.
 2. When I listen to music I can get so caught up in it that I don't notice anything else.

C. *Often thinks in images.*

 1. My thoughts often don't occur as words but as visual images.
 2. Sometimes thoughts and images come to me without the slightest effort on my part.

D. *Can summon vivid and suggestive images.*

 1. If I stare at a picture and then look away from it, I can sometimes "see" an image of the picture, almost as if I were still looking at it.
 2. If I wish I can imagine that my body is so heavy that I could not move it if I wanted to.

E. *Has "crossmodal" experiences (e.g., synesthesia).*

 1. Textures—such as wool, sand, wood—sometimes remind me of colors or music.
 2. Different colors have distinctive and special meanings for me.

F. *Can become absorbed in own thoughts and imaginings.*

 1. If I wish I can imagine (or daydream) some things so vividly that they hold my attention as a good movie or story does.
 2. I am able to wander off into my own thoughts while doing a routine task and actually forget that I am doing the task, and then find a few minutes later that I have completed it.

G. *Can vividly reexperience the past.*

 1. Sometimes I feel and experience things as I did when I was a child.
 2. I can sometimes recollect certain past experiences in my life with such clarity and vividness that it is like living them again or almost so.

H. *Has episodes of expanded (e.g., ESP-like) awareness.*

 1. I can often somehow sense the presence of another person before I actually see or hear her/him.
 2. Things that might seem meaningless to others often make sense to me.

I. *Experiences altered states of consciousness.*

 1. Sometimes I feel as if my mind could envelop the whole world.
 2. I think I really know what some people mean when they talk about mystical experiences.

[a] Differential Personality Questionnaire © 1984. The University of Minnesota. (Reproduced by permission of the publisher.)

384

tions to measuring hypnotic capacity, Berger and Arver's monograph (1972) is a good starting point.

SUMMARY

In the last two chapters, I have reviewed the primary methods of measuring the capacity for hypnosis, as well as some indication of the complexity of the conceptual notions that pertain to susceptibility, depth, and suggestibility. Which measurement device the reader chooses will depend on his or her particular needs. For the experimental investigator interested in measuring behavior following the induction of hypnosis and predicting from one hypnotic session to another, the Stanford Scales have the largest data base; for those interested in predicting from the nonhypnotic condition to behavior in hypnosis, the Barber scales, particularly the Creative Imagination Scale (CIS), are available. Any of these scales are also appropriate for the practitioner, although time constraints may dictate using something like the shorter SHCS:ADULT, SHCS:CHILD, SHALIT, or the HIP. The latter is particularly well suited for the practitioner, since its original development and much of the follow-up research was with patient populations. Practitioners seeking quick estimates of the depth of hypnosis achieved by their patients might consider the brief self-report numerical estimates outlined by Tart (1978/1979) and under "depth scales" above. Of all the scales, the CIS and TAS are most clearly related to the modern trend toward investigating the cognitive and imagination components of hypnosis.

Finally, interest in the eyes as indicators both of the presence of hypnosis and the capacity for hypnosis continues. From the earlier chapters of this book, we are familiar with the central focus held by the eyes in the induction of hypnosis. Hull (1933), you will recall, measured the capacity for hypnosis by calculating how long it took the eyelids to close during eye-fixation, eye-closure suggestions. Strosberg and Vics (1962) found reductions of blood supply, the reluctance of the arcades, changes in cornea curvature, and the engorging of the scleral vessels of the eye during hypnosis. The works of Bakan (1969), Gur and Reyher (1973), Gur and Gur (1974), and Dewitt and Averill (1976), have noted a relationship between the direction of lateral eye movements (left) during cognitive activity (questioning) and scores on hypnotizability scales. Smith (1980) on the other hand, has found that highly hypnotizable individuals (as measured by the CIS) have a significantly greater amount of right lateral eye movement when allowed to sit quietly at rest. The main thrust of all of these studies has been to assess cerebral hemispheric activity indirectly through eye movements. Interpretative difficulties of the relationship between eye movement and hemispheric asymmetry aside, what these may eventually lead to is a rapid sign for hypnotizability. Spiegel's Eye-Roll Sign, despite the rather uncertain meaning of the data regarding its usefulness, represents the historical interest in the eyes as indicators of hypnosis. The eyes, the only naturally visible parts of the central nervous system, continue to hold our attention, as they did for the ancients. It may well be that through the eyes will come our understanding of hypnosis and hypnotizability.

NOTE

1. Manuals for the Stanford Hypnotic Susceptibility Scales, Forms A, B, and C; the Harvard Group Scale of Hypnotic Susceptibility, Form A; the Stanford Profile Scales of Hypnotic Susceptibility; and the Children's Hypnotic Susceptibility Scale are all published by Consulting Psychologists Press, Inc., Palo Alto, California. The Tailored Form C manual can be ordered from ASIS-NAPS, c/o Microfiche Publications, New York, NY. (Document No. 03453). The manual for the Stanford Hypnotic Arm Levitation Induction and Test may also be ordered from ASIS-NAPS, Document No. 03452.

References

A Correspondent. (1890, April, 5). Demonstration of hypnotism as an anaesthetic during the performance on dental and surgical operations. *The Lancet*, 771–772.

Aaronson, B. S. (1973). ASCID trance, hypnotic trance, just trance. *American Journal of Clinical Hypnosis, 16*(2), 110–117.

Ackerknecht, E. H. (1948). "Mesmerism" in primitive societies. *CIBA Symposia, 9*, 826–831.

Adler, M. & Secunda, L. (1947). An indirect technique to induce hypnosis. *Journal of Nervous and Mental Disease, 106*, 190–193.

Allen, T. G. (Trans.). (1974). *The book of the dead or going forth by day*. Chicago: University of Chicago Press.

Ambrose, G. (1952). Hypnotherapy for children. In R. H. Rhodes (Ed.), *Therapy through hypnosis* (pp. 105–117). New York: Citadel Press.

Ambrose, G. & Newbold, G. (1958). *A handbook of medical hypnosis*. Baltimore: Williams & Wilkins.

American Society of Clinical Hypnosis—Education and Research Foundation. (1973). *A syllabus on hypnosis and a handbook of therapeutic suggestions* 2250 East Devon, Des Plaines, IL.

Arons, H. (Ed.). (1969). *Prize-winning methods of hypnosis*. South Orange, NJ: Power Publishers.

Ash, E. L. (1906, January 27). Some experiments in hypnosis. *The Lancet*, 216–220.

Ash, E. L. (1906, August 25). The induction of hypnosis. *The Lancet*, 501–504.

Avalon, A. (Ed.). (1969). *Principles of Tantra: The Tantratattva of Śrïyukta Śiva Candra Vidyārnava Bhattacārya Mahodaya* (2 vols.). Madras: Ganesh.

Azam, T. (1887). *Hypnotisme double conscience et alterations de la personnalite*. Paris: J.-B. Balliére et Fils.

Bagnold, M. E. (1848). Mesmerism in India forty years ago. *The Zoist, 6*(23), 250–254.

Bagnold, M. E. (1850). Mesmerism in Africa forty years ago. *The Zoist, 7*(28), 443–445.

Bakan, P. (1969). Hypnotizability, laterality of eye movement and functional brain asymmetry. *Perceptual and Motor Skills, 28*, 927–932.

Bányai, E. I. & Hilgard, E. R. (1976). A comparison of active-alert hypnotic induction with traditional relaxation induction. *Journal of Abnormal Psychology, 85*, 218–224.

Barabasz, A. F. (1976). Treatment of insomnia in depressed patients by hypnosis and cerebral electrotherapy. *American Journal of Clinical Hypnosis, 19*(2), 120–122.

Baraduc, H. (1902). La suggestion phonographique. In E. Berillion & P. Farez (Eds.), *Deuxieme Congres Internationale de L'Hypnotisme Experimental et Therapeutique, Comptes Rendus*. Paris: Vigot Freres.

Barber, J. (1977). Rapid induction analgesia: A clinical report. *American Journal of Clinical Hypnosis, 19*(3), 138–147.

Barber, T. X. (1969). *Hypnosis: A scientific approach*. New York: Van Nostrand Reinhold.

Barber, T. X. & Calverley, D. S. (1963). "Hypnotic-like" suggestibility in children and adults. *Journal of Abnormal and Social Psychology, 66*, 589–597.

Barber, T. X. & Calverley, D. S. (1964a). Effect of *E*'s tone of voice on "hypnotic-like" suggestibility. *Psychological Reports, 15*, 139–144.

Barber, T. X. & Calverley, D. S. (1964b). Comparative effects on "hypnotic-like" suggestibility of recorded and spoken suggestions. *Journal of Consulting Psychology, 28*(4), 384.

Barber, T. X. & Glass, L. B. (1962). Significant factors in hypnotic behavior. *Journal of Abnormal and Social Psychology, 64*, 222–228.

Barber, T. X. & Wilson, S. C. (1977). Hypnosis, suggestions, and altered states of consciousness: Experimental evaluation of the new cognitive-behavioral theory and the traditional trance-state theory of "hypnosis." In W. E. Edmonston, Jr. (Ed.), *Conceptual and investigative approaches to hypnosis and hypnotic phenomena* (pp. 34–47). New York: N.Y. Academy of Sciences.

Barber, T. X. & Wilson, S. C. (1978/1979). The Barber Suggestibility Scale and the Creative Imagination Scale. *American Journal of Clinical Hypnosis, 21*, 84–108.

Barrucand, D. (1967). *Histoire de L'hypnose en France*. Paris: Presses Universitaires de France.

Barry, H., MacKinnon, D. W., & Murray, H. A., Jr. (1931). Studies on personality: Hypnotizability as a personality trait and its typological relations. *Human Biology, 13*, 1–36.

Bartlett, E. S., Faw, T. T., & Liebert, R. M. (1967). The effects of suggestions of alertness in hypnosis on pupillary response: Report on a single subject. *International Journal of Clinical and Experimental Hypnosis, 15*, 189–192.

Baudouin, C. (1920). *Suggestion and autosuggestion*. (E. Paul & C. Paul, Trans.). London: Allen & Unwin.

Baudouin, C. (1922). *Suggestions and autosuggestion: A psychological and pedagogical study based upon the investigations made by the New Nancy School*. (E. Paul & C. Paul, Trans.). New York: Dodd, Mead.

Baykushev, S. V. (1969). Hyperventilation as an accelerated hypnotic induction technique. *International Journal of Clinical and Experimental Hypnosis, 17*(1), 20–24.

Benson, H. (1975). *The relaxation response*. New York: W. Morrow.

Benson, H., Arns, P. A. & Hoffman, J. W. (1981). The relaxation response and hypnosis. *International Journal of Clinical and Experimental Hypnosis, 29*(3), 259–270.

Benson, H., Beary, J. F. & Carol, M. P. (1974). The relaxation response. *Psychiatry, 37*, 37–46.

Berger, G. & Arver, S. (1972). *Multivariate Informational Analysis Suggestibility Scale*. Uppsala, Sweden: Psykologiska Institute, Uppsala University.

Bérillon, E. (1891). *Hypnotisme et suggestion. Theorie et applications pratiques*. Paris: Société d'Editions Scientifiques.

Bernheim, H. M. (1884–1886/1964). *Hypnosis and suggestion in psychotherapy. A treatise on the nature and uses of hypnotism* (C. A. Merter, Trans.). New Hyde Park, NY: University Books.

Bernheim, H. M. (1891/1980). *New studies in hypnotism*. (R. S. Sandor, Trans.). New York: International Universities Press.

Bertrand, A. (1823). *Traité du somnambulisme et des differentes modifications qu'il presente*. Paris: J. G. Dentu.

Bertrand, A. (1826). *Le magnétisme animal en France* Paris: J.-B. Baillière.

Binet, A. & Féré, C. (1888). *Animal magnetism*. New York: D. Appleton.

Birnbaum, K. (1927). *Die psychischen Heilmethoden für Ärztliches Studium und Praxis*. Leipzig: Georg Thieme.

Björnström, F. (1887). *Hypnotism: Its history and present development*. (B. N. Posse, Trans.). New York: Humboldt.

Bloomfield, M. *Hymns of the Atharva-Veda*. In F. M. Muller (Ed.), *The sacred books of the East* (Vol. 42). Oxford: Clarendon Press.

Bonwick, J. (1878). *Egyptian belief and modern thought*. London: C. Keegan Paul.

Bordeaux, J. (1950). Hypnotic experiments with light and color. *British Journal of Medical Hypnotism, 1*(4), 7–17.

Bowers, K. S. (1981a). Do the Stanford scales tap the "classical suggestion effect"? *International Journal of Clinical and Experimental Hypnosis, 29*(1), 42–53.

Bowers, K. S. (1981b). Has the sun set on the Stanford scales? *American Journal of Clinical Hypnosis, 24*(2), 79–88.

Bowers, M. K. (1961). Hypnotic aspects of Haitian voodoo. *International Journal of Clinical and Experimental Hypnosis, 9,* 269–282.

Bowers, M. K. & Glasner, S. (1958). Auto-hypnotic aspects of the Jewish cabbalistic concept of Kavanah. *International Journal of Clinical and Experimental Hypnosis, 6,* 50–70.

Braid, J. (1843/1976). *Neurypnology; or the rational of nervous sleep, considered in relation with animal magnetism*. New York: Arno Press. (Original work published London: J. Churchill, 1843)

Braid, J. (1855/1970). *The physiology of fascination and the critics criticised*. In M. M. Tinterow (Ed.), *Foundations of hypnosis from Mesmer to Freud* (pp. 365–389). Springfield, IL: Charles C Thomas. (Original published Manchester, Eng.: Grant;1855)

Bramwell, J. M. (1896). James Braid: His work and writings. *Society for Psychical Research: Proceedings, 12, Part 30,* 127–166.

Bramwell, J. M. (1903). *Hypnotism, its history, practice and theory*. Philadelphia: J. B. Lippincott.

Brenman, M. & Gill, M. M. (1946). Some recent observations on the use of hypnosis in psychotherapy. *Bulletin of the Menninger Clinic, 10,* 105–109.

Brenman, M. & Gill, M. M. (1947). *Hypnotherapy: A survey of the literature*. New York: International Universities Press.

Brier, B. (1980). *Ancient Egyptian magic*. New York: W. Morrow.

Brotteaux, P. (1936). *Hypnotisme et Scopochloralose*. Paris: Vigot Freres.

Brown, W. (1922). *Suggestion and mental analysis: An outline of the theory and practice of mind cure* (2nd ed.). New York: George H. Doran.

Bruhn, C. (1926). *Gelehrte in Hypnose*. Hamburg: Verlag Parus.

Bunting, E. (1969). *The ancient music of Ireland* (Edition comprising 3 collections, 1796, 1809, 1840). Dublin: Walton's Piano and Musical Instrument Galleries.

Burgess, T. O. (1956). The induction of hypnosis in resistant or refractory patients by means of certain chemicals. *Journal of the American Society of Psychosomatic Dentistry, 3,* 4–8.

Burq, V. (1853). On a preservative and curative treatment of Asiatic cholera with metals: Followed by an account of a particular system of application of metals, intended to popularize the new properties discovered in them by means of magnetism (J. Elliotson, Trans.). *The Zoist, 11*(42), 148–169.

Burrows, G. D. & Dennerstein, L. (Eds.). (1980). *Handbook of hypnosis and psychosomatic medicine*. Amsterdam: Elsevier/North Holland Biomedical Press.

Byers, A. P. (1975). Training and use of technicians in the treatment of alcoholism with hypnosis. *American Journal of Clinical Hypnosis, 18*(2), 90–93.

Cadwell, J. W. (1882). *Full and comprehensive instructions how to mesmerize*. Boston, MA: By the author, printed at W. F. Brown & Co.

Caldwell, C. (1842/1982). *Facts in mesmerism, and thought on its causes and uses*. New York: Da Capo Press. (Original work published Louisville, KY: Prentise & Weissinger, 1842)

Cannon, A. (1936). *The science of hypnotism*. New York: E. P. Dutton.

Cannon, A. (1949). Some hypnotic secrets. *British Journal of Medical Hypnotism, 1*(1), 18–19.

Carlson, E. T. (1960). Charles Poyen brings mesmerism to America. *Journal of the History of Medicine and Allied Sciences, 5,* 121–132.

Carlson, E. T. & Simpson, M. M. (1970). Perkinism vs. mesmerism. *Journal of History of the Behavioral Sciences, 6*(1), 16–24.

Carmichael, A. (1900). *Carmina Gadelica, hymns and incantations* (Vol. 2). Edinburgh: T. & A. Constable.

Chaisson, S. W. (1973). *A syllabus on hypnosis* (p. 14). American Society of Clinical Hypnosis, Education and Research Foundation, 2250 East Devon, Des Plaines, IL.

Charcot, J. M. (1882/1888). Essai d'une distinction nosographique des divers états compris sous le nom d'hypnotisme. In A. Binet & C. Féré (Eds.), *Animal magnetism* (pp. 154–163). New York: D. Appleton. (Original work published Comptes rendus de l'Academic des Sciences, 1882)

Chertok, L. (1967). Theory of hypnosis since 1889. *International Journal of Psychiatry, 3,* 188–211.

Claverie, F. (1889). *Étude sur l'hypnotisme*. Air-Sur-L'Adour: L. Dehez.

Colquhoun, J. C. (1836). *Isis Revelata: An inquiry into the origin, progress and present state of animal magnetism* (2 vols.). Edinburgh: Maclachlan & Steward.

Colquhoun, J. C. (Trans.). (1833/1975). *Report of the experiments on animal magnetism made by a committee of the medical section of the French Royal Academy of Sciences, 1831*. New York: Arno Press. (Original work published Edinburgh: R. Cadell; London: Wittaker, 1833)

Committee on Mesmerism. (1882). First Report. *Society for Physical Research Proceedings, 1*, 217–229.

Conn, J. H. (1949). Hypno-synthesis. *Journal of Nervous and Mental Disease, 109*, 9–24.

Constant, A. L. (Éliphas Lévi). (1913). *The history of magic* (A. E. Waite, Trans.). London: Rider.

Cook, W. W. (1927). *Practical lessons in hypnotism and autosuggestion*. New York: Wiley Book Co.

Cooper, L. M. & London, P. (1978/1979). The children's hypnotic susceptibility scale. *American Journal of Clinical Hypnosis, 21*(2&3), 170–185.

Cooperman, S., & Schafer, D. W. (1983). Hypnotherapy over the phone. *American Journal of Clinical Hypnosis, 25*(4), 277–279.

Coué, E. (1922). *Self mastery through conscious autosuggestion* (A. S. Van Orden, Trans.). New York: Malkan.

Coué, E. (1923). *My method, including American impressions*. Garden City, NY: Doubleday, Page.

Coué, E. (1924). *Ce que j'ai fait. Jugements portés sur mon oeuvre*. Nancy: Chez L'Auteur.

Crasilneck, H. B. (1984). Personal Communication.

Crasilneck, H. B. & Hall, J. A. (1975). *Clinical hypnosis: Principles and applications*. New York: Grune & Stratton.

Crocq, J. (1896). *L'hypnotisme scientifique par Le Docteur Crocq Fils* (Introduction Dr. M. Le Professeur Pitres). Bruxelles: H. Lamertin.

Crone, J. O. (1903). *The magnetic healer's guide, or personal experiences in magnetic and suggestive healing*. Kansas City, MO: Hudson-Kimberly.

Cutten, G. B. (1911). *Three thousand years of mental healing*. New York: Charles Scribner's Sons.

D'Arbois, H. de Jubainville (1892). *Cours de littérature Celtique* (Vol. 5). Paris: Ernest Thorin.

D'Arbois, H. de Jubainville (1906). *Les Druids et les dieux Celtiques a form d'ani maux*. Paris: Librairie Honore Champion.

Darnton, R. (1968). *Mesmerism and the end of the enlightenment in France*. Cambridge, MA: Harvard University Press.

Davis, A. J. (1857). *The magic staff, an autobiography*. New York: Brown.

Davis, L. W. & Husband, R. W. (1931). A study of hypnotic susceptibility in relation to personality traits. *Journal of Abnormal and Social Psychology, 26*, 175–182.

Davis, R. C. & Kantor, J. R. (1935). Skin resistance during hypnotic states. *Journal of General Psychology, 13*, 62–81.

De Courmelles, F. (1819/1970). Hypnotism. In M. M. Tinterow (Ed.), *Foundations of hypnosis: From Mesmer to Freud* (pp. 150–159). Springfield, IL: Charles C Thomas. (Original work published New York: George Routledge & Sons, 1819)

Delboeuf, J. (1889). *Le magnétisme animal à propos d'une visite à l'école de Nancy.* Paris. (See Pattie, 1967.)

Deleuze, J. P. F. (1843/1982). *Practical instruction in animal magnetism* (T. C. Hartshorn, Trans.). New York: Da Capo Press. (Original published translation New York: D. Appleton 1843)

DeM, S. E. (1853). Phenomena observed in mesmerizing water. *The Zoist, 10*(40), 425–427.

Dennys (1904). The folklore of China. In O. Stoll, *Suggestion und Hypnotismus in der Voelkerpsychologie* (pp. 49–50). (2nd Ed.) Leipzig: Veit.

De Puységur, M. (1837). *An essay of instruction on animal magnetism* (J. King, Trans.). New York: J. C. Kelley.

De Rochas, D'Aiglun, A. (1892). *Les États profonds de l'hypnose.* Paris: Chamuel.

Devereux, G. (1966). Cultural factors in hypnosis and suggestion: An examination of some primitive data. *International Journal of Clinical and Experimental Hypnosis, 14,* 273–290.

DeWitt, G. W. & Averill, J. R. (1976). Lateral eye movements, hypnotic susceptibility and field independence-dependence. *Perceptual and Motor Skills, 43,* 1179–1184.

Dictionnaire Universal des Contemporain. (1880). Paris: Librairie Hachette et Cie.

Dittborn, J. M. (1968). A brief nonthreatening procedure for the evaluation of hypnotizability. *International Journal of Clinical and Experimental Hypnosis, 16*(1), 53–60.

Dixon, J. H. (1886). *Gairloch.* Edinburgh: Cooperative Printing Co.

Dods, J. B. (1850). *The philosophy of electrical psychology.* New York: Fowlers & Wells.

Donley, J. E. (1908). The clinical use of hypnoidization in the treatment of some functional psychoses. *Journal of Abnormal Psychology, 3,* 148–160.

Dubois, P. (1904/1909). *The psychic treatment of nervous disorders* (6th ed.). (S. E. Jelliffe & W. A. White, Trans.). New York & London: Funk & Wagnalls. (Original work published 1904).

Dubor, G. (1922). *Les mysteres de l'hypnose.* (G. M. Hort, Trans.). London: W. Rider & Sons.

Duckworth, J. H. (1922). *Auto-suggestion and its personal application.* London: J. A. McCann.

Duffy, J. (1958/1962). *The Rudolph Matas history of medicine in Louisiana* (2 vols.). Baton Rouge: Louisiana State University Press.

DuPotet, Baron. (Jules Denis de Sennevoy). (1852/1927). *Magnetism and Magic* (A. H. Lee, Trans.). London: Allen & Unwin.

Durand, J. P. (1855). *Electro-dynamisme vital ou les relations physiologiques de l'esprit et de la matière.* Paris: J. B. Baillière.

Durand, J. P. (Philips, J. P., Durand de Gros) (1860/1970). A course in the theory and practice of Braidism or neurohypnotism, first conference. In M. M. Tinterow,

(Ed.), *Foundations of hypnosis, from Mesmer to Freud* (pp. 390–401). Springfield, IL: Charles C Thomas. (Original work published 1860)

Durant, C. F. (1837/1982). *Exposition, or a new theory of animal magnetism.* New York: Da Capo Press. (Original work published New York: Wiley & Putnam, 1837).

Durville, H. (1895/1900). *The theory and practice of human magnetism.* Chicago: Psychic Research Co. (Original work published Paris: Chamuel, 1895).

Ebbell, B. (Trans.). (1937). *The Papyrus Ebers: The greatest Egyptian medical document.* Copenhagen: Levin & Munksgaard.

Edmonston, W. E., Jr. (1967). Stimulus-response theory of hypnosis. In J. E. Gordon (Ed.), *Handbook of clinical and experimental hypnosis* (pp. 345–387). New York: MacMillan.

Edmonston, W. E., Jr. (1980, August). Division 30: Directions. *Newsletter of the Division of Psychological Hypnosis of the APA,* pp. 4–5.

Edmonston, W. E., Jr. (1981). *Hypnosis and relaxation: Modern verification of an old equation.* New York: John Wiley & Sons.

Edmonston, W. E., Jr. (1982, April). RSVP. *Newsletter of the Division of Psychological Hypnosis of the APA,* pp. 3–4.

Edmonston, W. E., Jr. & Robertson, T. G. (1967). A comparison of the effects of task motivational and hypnotic induction instructions on responsiveness to hypnotic suggestibility scales. *American Journal of Clinical Hypnosis, 9,* 184–187.

Ekins, Rev. J. (1853). A confirmation of the observations upon mesmerized water. *The Zoist, 11*(41), 84–85.

Ekins, Rev. J. (1854). Further testimony to the peculiar appearance of mesmerized water. *The Zoist, 11*(44), 350–351.

Eliseo, T. S. (1974). The hypnotic induction profile and hypnotic susceptibility. *International Journal of Clinical and Experimental Hypnosis, 22*(4), 320–326.

Ellenberger, H. F. (1965). Charcot and the Salpêtrière School. *American Journal of Psychotherapy, 19,* 253–267.

Ellenberger, H. F. (1970). *The discovery of the unconscious: The history and evolution of dynamic psychiatry.* New York: Basic Books.

Elliotson, J. (1843a). Address. *The Zoist, 1*(3), 227–246.

Elliotson, J. (1843b). Cases of cures by mesmerism. *The Zoist, 1*(2), 161–208.

Elliotson, J. (1843c). Cures of palsy by mesmerism. *The Zoist, 1*(3), 300–349.

Elliotson, J. (1843d). Mesmerism. *The Zoist, 1*(1), 58–94.

Elliotson, J. (1844a). An account of two cases of severe and obstinate diseases perfectly cured with mesmerism; Both of them exhibiting remarkable mesmeric phenomena. *The Zoist, 2*(5), 42–79.

Elliotson, J. (1844b). Case of epilepsy cured with mesmerism. *The Zoist, 2*(6), 194–238.

Elliotson, J. (1846). Case of a contracted foot with severe pain, cured with mesmerism. *The Zoist, 3*(12), 339–379.

Elliotson, J. (1848). Note on M. E. Bagnold's communication. *The Zoist, 6*(23), 254–263.

Elliotson, J. (1851). Note on Thomas Chandler's "A mesmeric scene a thousand years ago." *The Zoist, 9*(35), 226–237.

Elliotson, J. (1852). Two or three practical mesmeric observations by a lady. *The Zoist, 9*(36), 378–379.

Elliotson, J. (1977). Numerous cases of surgical operations without pain in the mesmeric state. In D. N. Robinson (Ed.), *Significant contributions to the history of psychology 1750–1920. Series A, Orientations* (Vol. 10). (pp. 3–56) Washington, DC: University Publications of America (Original work published Philadelphia: Lea & Blanchard 1843).

Elman, D. (1964). *Findings in hypnosis.* Clifton, NJ: By the author.

Erickson, M. H. (1952). Deep hypnosis and its induction. In L. M. LeCron (Ed.), *Experimental hypnosis* (pp. 70–114). New York: MacMillan.

Erickson, M. H. (1958). Naturalistic techniques of hypnosis. *American Journal of Clinical Hypnosis, 1,* 3–8.

Erickson, M. H. (1959). Further techniques of hypnosis—Utilization techniques. *American Journal of Clinical Hypnosis, 2,* 3–21.

Erickson, M. H. (1961). Historical note on the hand levitation and other ideomotor techniques. *American Journal of Clinical Hypnosis, 3,* 196–199.

Erickson, M. H. (1964a). The confusion technique in hypnosis. *American Journal of Clinical Hypnosis, 6,* 183–207.

Erickson, M. H. (1964b). The "surprise" and "my-friend-John" techniques of hypnosis: Minimal cues and natural field experimentation. *American Journal of Clinical Hypnosis, 6,* 293–307.

Erickson, M. H. (1964c). An hypnotic technique for resistant patients: The patient, the technique and its rationale and field experiments. *American Journal of Clinical Hypnosis, 7,* 8–32.

Erickson, M. H. (1964d). Pantomine techniques in hypnosis and the implications. *American Journal of Clinical Hypnosis, 7,* 64–70.

Erickson, M. H. (1967). Further experimental investigations of hypnosis: Hypnotic and nonhypnotic realities. *American Journal of Clinical Hypnosis, 10,* 87–135.

Erickson, M. H. (1980). The dynamics of visualization, levitation and confusion in trance induction. (c. 1940s) In E. L. Rossi (Ed.), *The Collected Papers of Milton H. Erickson on Hypnosis* (*Vol.* 1, pp. 292–296). New York: Irvington.

Erickson, M. H., Haley, J. & Weakland, J. H. (1959). A transcript of a trance induction with commentary. *American Journal of Clinical Hypnosis, 2,* 49–84.

Erickson, M. H., Hershman, S. & Secter, I. I. (1961). *The practical application of medical and dental hypnosis.* New York: Julian Press.

Erickson, M. H. & Rossi, E. L. (1979). *Hypnotherapy: An exploratory case book.* New York: Irvington.

Erickson, M. H., Rossi, E. L. & Rossi, S. I. (1976). *Hypnotic realities: The induction of clinical hypnosis and forms of indirect suggestion.* New York: Irvington.

Erickson, M. H., Aston, E. E., Hershman, S., Kroger, W. S. & Secter, I. I. (undated). *A seminar on hypnosis.* Chicago: Seminars on Hypnosis.

Erskine, A. (1957). *A hypnotist's case book.* Hollywood, CA: Wilshire Book Co. (Original work published London: Rider 1932)

Esdaile, J. (1846/1976). *Mesmerism in India and its practical application in surgery and medicine*. New York: Arno Press. (Original work published London: Longman, Brown, Green & Longmans, 1846)

Esdaile, J. (1852/1975). *Natural and mesmeric clairvoyance with the practical application of mesmerism in surgery and medicine*. New York: Arno Press. (Original work published London: H. Balliere, 1852)

Estabrooks, G. H. (1930). A standardized hypnotic technique dictated to a victrola record. *American Journal of Psychology, 42,* 115–116.

Evans, F. J. (1967). An experimental indirect technique for the induction of hypnosis without awareness. *International Journal of Clinical and Experimental Hypnosis, 15*(2), 72–85.

Eysenck, H. J. & Furneaux, W. D. (1945). Primary and secondary suggestibility: An experimental and statistical study. *Journal of Experimental Psychology, 35,* 485–503.

Faria, L'Abbé de. (1819/1906). *Du sommeil lucide ou étude de la nature de l'homme.* Paris: Henri Jouve, 1906. (Original work published with preface and introduction by D. G. Dalgado, 1819)

Felkin, R. W. (1890). *Hypnotism or psycho-therapeutics.* Edinburgh & London: Young J. Pentland.

Field, P. B. (1965). An inventory scale of hypnotic depth. *International Journal of Clinical and Experimental Hypnosis, 13*(4), 238–249.

Filiatre, J. (1909). *Hypnotisme et magnétisme somnambulisme. Suggestion et télépathie influence personnelle. Cours practique.* Paris: Librairie Fischbacher.

Flint, H. L. (1903). *Practical instruction in hypnotism and suggestion.* Chicago, IL: Flint & Flint.

Fontan, J., & Ségard, C. (1887). *Éléments de Médecine suggestive, hypnotisme et suggestion-faits cliniques.* Paris: Octave Doin.

Forel, A. H. (1906). *Hypnotism or suggestion and psychotherapy (A study of the psychological, psychophysiological, and therapeutic aspects of hypnotism)* (5th ed.). (H. W. Armit, Trans.) London: Rebman.

Frankel, F. H. (1982). Hypnosis and hypnotizability scales: A reply. *International Journal of Clinical and Experimental Hypnosis, 30,* 377–392.

Frankel, F. H. & Zamansky, H. S. (Eds.). (1976). *Hypnosis at its bicentennial, selected papers.* New York: Plenum Press.

Franklin, B., et al. (1784/1970). Rapport des commissaires charges par le roi, De l'examen du magnetisme animal (W. Godwin, Trans.). In M. M. Tinterow, (Ed.), *Foundations of hypnosis: From Mesmer to Freud* (pp. 82–128). Springfield, IL: Charles C Thomas, 1970. (Original work published Paris, 1784)

Freud, S. (1966). Hypnosis (1891). In J. Stachery (Trans.), *Standard edition of the complete psychological works of Sigmund Freud* (pp. 103–114). London: Hogarth Press.

Friedlander, J. W. & Sarbin, T. R. (1938). The depth of hypnosis. *Journal of Abnormal and Social Psychology, 33,* 453–475.

Frischholz, E. J., Spiegel, H., Tryon, W. W. & Fisher, S. (1981). The relationship between the Hypnotic Induction Profile and the Stanford Hypnotic Susceptibility Scale, Form C: Revisited. *American Journal of Clinical Hypnosis, 24*(2), 98–105.

Frischholz, E. J., Tryon, W. W., Vellios, A. T., Fisher, S., Maruffi, B. L. & Spiegel, H. (1980). The relationship between the Hypnotic Induction Profile and the Stanford Hypnotic Susceptibility Scale, Form C: A replication. *American Journal of Clinical Hypnosis, 22*(4), 185–196.

Galdston, I. (1948a). Hypnosis and modern psychiatry. *CIBA Symposia, 9*(11), 845–856.

Galdston, I. (1948b). Mesmer and animal magnetism. *CIBA Symposia, 9*(11), 832–837.

Gardner, G. G. (1974). Parents: Obstacles or allies in child hypnotherapy? *American Journal of Clinical Hypnosis, 17,* 44–49.

Gerrish, F. H. (1909). The therapeutic value of hypnotic suggestion. *Journal of Abnormal Psychology, 4,* 99–119.

Gessmann, G. (1887). *Magnetismus und Hypnotismus. Eine Darstellung dieses Gebietes der Beziehungen zwischen dem mineralischen Magnetismus und dem sogenannten thierischen magnetismus oder Hypnotismus.* Wien: A. Hartleben's.

Gibbons, D. E. (1974). Hyperempiria, a new "altered state of consciousness" induced by suggestion. *Perceptual and Motor Skills, 39,* 47–53.

Gibbons, D. E. (1975). Hypnotic vs. hyperempiric induction procedures: An experimental comparison. *Journal of the American Society of Psychosomatic Dentistry & Medicine, 22,* 35–42.

Gibbons, D. E. (1976). Hypnotic vs. hyperempiric induction procedures: An experimental comparison. *Perceptual and Motor Skills, 42,* 834.

Gibbons, D. E. (1979). *Applied hypnosis and hyperempiria.* New York & London: Plenum Press.

Giles, E. (1962). A cross-validation study of the Pascal technique of hypnotic induction. *International Journal of Clinical and Experimental Hypnosis, 10*(2), 101–108.

Gill, M. M. & Brenman, M. (1959). *Hypnosis and related states: Psychoanalytic studies in regression.* New York: International Universities Press.

Gindes, B. C. (1951). *New concepts of hypnosis.* New York: Julian Press.

Glasner, S. (1955). A note on allusions to hypnosis in the Bible and Talmud. *International Journal of Clinical and Experimental Hypnosis, 3,* 34–39.

Godwin, J. (1979). *Robert Fludd: Hermetic philosopher and survivor of two worlds.* Boulder, CO: Shanbhala Pub.; London: Thames & Hudson.

Goldsmith, M. (1934). *Franz Anton Mesmer.* Garden City, NJ: Doubleday, Doran.

Goldwyn, J. (1929). "Hypnoidalization" its psychotherapeutic value. *Journal of Abnormal Psychology, 24,* 170–185.

Gravitz, M. A. (1983a). An early case of investigative hypnosis: A brief communication. *International Journal of Clinical and Experimental Hypnosis, 31*(4), 224–226.

Gravitz, M. A. (1983b). Early uses of the telephone and recordings in hypnosis. *American Journal of Clinical Hypnosis, 25*(4), 280–282.

Gravitz, M. A. (1983c). Personal Communication.

Greatraks, V. (1666). *A brief account of Mr. Valentine Greatraks, and divers of the strange cures by him lately performed (written by himself in a letter addressed to the Honourable Robert Boyle, Esq.) Where unto are annexed the testimonials of several eminent and worthy persons of the chief matters of fact therein related.* London: J. Starkey.

Gregory, W. (1909/1975). *Animal magnetism or mesmerism and its phenomena* (5th ed.). New York: Arno Press. (Original work published London: Nichols, 1909)

Grill, J. (1889). *100 Lieder des Atharua-Veda.* Stuttgart: Kohlhammer.

Grinker, R. R. & Spiegel, J. P. (1943). *War neuroses in North Africa, The Tunisian campaign (January–May 1943).* New York: Josiah Macy Jr. Foundation.

Gur, R. C. & Gur, R. E. (1974). Handedness, sex, and eyedness as moderating variables in the relationship between hypnotic susceptibility and functional brain asymmetry. *Journal of Abnormal Psychology, 83,* 635–643.

Gur, R. & Reyher, J. (1973). Relationships between style of hypnotic induction and direction of lateral eye movements. *Journal of Abnormal Psychology, 82,* 499–505.

Haley, J. (Ed.) (1967). *Advanced techniques of hypnosis and therapy, Selected papers of Milton H. Erickson.* New York: Grune & Stratton.

Hall, P. (1973). Electrosleep (electrohypnosis?). A resume. *British Journal of Clinical Hypnosis, 4,* 19–22.

Hallaji, J. (1962). Hypnotherapeutic techniques in a central Asian community. *International Journal of Clinical and Experimental Hypnosis, 10,* 271–274.

Ham, M. W. & Edmonston, W. E. Jr. (1971). Hypnosis, relaxation, and motor retardation. *Journal of Abnormal Psychology, 77,* 329–331.

Hamilton, M. (1906). *Incubation or the cure of disease in pagan temples and Christian churches.* London: Simpkin, Marshall, Hamilton, Kent.

Hammer, A. G. & Arkins, W. J. (1964). The role of photic stimulation in the induction of hypnotic trance. *International Journal of Clinical and Experimental Hypnosis, 12*(2), 81–87.

Hariman, J. (1980). A rapid induction technique: My approach. *Australian Journal of Clinical and Experimental Hypnosis, 1*(1), 36–39.

Hart, E. (1896/1982). *Hypnotism, mesmerism and the new witchcraft* (2nd Ed.). New York: DaCapo Press. (Original work published New York: D. Appleton, 1896)

Hart, H. H. (1931). Hypnosis in psychiatric clinics. *Journal of Nervous and Mental Disease, 74,* 598–609.

Hartland, J. (1971). *Medical and dental hypnosis and its clinical applications* (2nd ed.). London: Bailliere.

Hartmann, F. (1891). *The life and the doctrines of Philippus Theophrastus, Bombast of Hohenheim known by the name of Paracelsus.* New York: American Publishers.

Hazard, W. (1849). Mesmeric cures. *The Zoist, 7*(26), 175–184.

Heidenhain, R. (1906). *Hypnotism or animal magnetism, physiological observations* (4th ed.) (L. C. Woolridge, Trans.). London: Kegan, Paul, Trench, Trubner.

Herter, C. A. (1888, October). Hypnotism: What it is and what it is not. *Popular Science Monthly, 33,* 755–771.

Hilgard, E. R. (1965). *Hypnotic susceptibility.* New York: Harcourt Brace & World.

Hilgard, E. R. (1977). *Divided consciousness: Multiple controls in human thought and action*. New York: John Wiley & Sons.

Hilgard, E. R. (1978/1979). The Stanford Hypnotic Susceptibility Scales as related to other measures of hypnotic responsiveness. *American Journal of Clinical Hypnosis, 21*(2 & 3), 68–82.

Hilgard, E. R. (1981a). Hypnotic susceptibility scales under attack: An examination of Weitzenhoffer's criticisms. *International Journal of Clinical and Experimental Hypnosis, 29*(1), 24–41.

Hilgard, E. R. (1981b). The Eye-Roll Sign and other scores of the Hypnotic Induction Profile (HIP) as related to the Stanford Hypnotic Susceptibility Scales, Form C (SHSS:C): A critical discussion of a study by Frischholz and others. *American Journal of Clinical Hypnosis, 24*(2), 89–97.

Hilgard, E. R. (1981c). Further discussion of the HIP and the Stanford Form C: A reply to a reply by Frischholz, Spiegel, Tryon, and Fisher. *American Journal of Clinical Hypnosis, 24*(2), 106–108.

Hilgard, E. R. (1982a). Hypnotic susceptibility and implications for measurement. *International Journal of Clinical and Experimental Hypnosis, 30*(4), 394–403.

Hilgard, E. R. (1982b). The illusion that the Eye-Roll Sign is related to hypnotizability. *Archives of General Psychiatry, 39*(8), 963–966.

Hilgard, E. R. & Hilgard, J. R. (1975). *Hypnosis in the relief of pain*. Los Altos, CA: W. Kaufmann.

Hilgard, E. R., & Tart, C. T. (1966). Responsiveness to suggestions following working and imagination instructions and following induction of hypnosis. *Journal of Abnormal Psychology, 71*, 196–208.

Hilgard, E. R., Crawford, H. J. & Wert, A. (1979a). Protocol for the Stanford Hypnotic Arm Levitation Induction and Test (SHALIT). *Stanford Laboratory of Hypnosis Research mimeo*.

Hilgard, E. R., Crawford, H. J. & Wert, A. (1979b). The Stanford Hypnotic Arm Levitation Induction and Test (SHALIT): A six minute hypnotic induction and measurement scale. *International Journal of Clinical and Experimental Hypnosis, 27*(2), 111–124.

Hilgard, E. R., Lauer, L. W. & Morgan, A. H., (1963). *Manual for Stanford Profile Scales of Hypnotic Susceptibility, Forms I and II*. Palo Alto, CA: Consulting Psychologists Press.

Hilgard, E. R., Weitzenhoffer, A. M. & Gough, P. (1958). Individual differences in susceptibility to hypnosis. *Proceedings of the National Academy of Science, 44*, 1255–1259.

Hilgard, E. R., Crawford, H. J., Bowers, P. & Kihlstrom, J. F. (1979). A tailored SHSS:C permitting user modification for special purposes. *International Journal of Clinical and Experimental Hypnosis, 27*(2), 125–133.

Hilgard, E. R., Sheehan, P. W., Monteiro, K. P. & MacDonald, H. (1981). Factorial structure of the Creative Imagination Scale as a measure of hypnotic responsiveness: An international comparative study. *International Journal of Clinical and Experimental Hypnosis, 29*(1), 66–76.

Hilgard, E. R., Weitzenhoffer, A. M., Landis, J. & Moore, R. K. (1961). The distribution of susceptibility to hypnosis in a student population: A study using the

Stanford Hypnotic Susceptibility Scale. *Psychological Monographs, 75*(8), 1–22.

Hilgard, J. R. (1974). Imaginative involvement: Some characteristics of the highly hypnotizable and the non-hypnotizable. *International Journal of Clinical and Experimental Hypnosis, 22,* 138–156.

Hilgard, J. R. (1979). *Personality and hypnosis: A study of imaginative involvement* (2nd Ed.). Chicago: University of Chicago Press.

Hilgard, J. R. & Hilgard, E. R. (1979). Assessing hypnotic responsiveness in a clinical setting: A multi-item clinical scale and its advantages over single-item scales. *International Journal of Clinical and Experimental Hypnosis, 27*(2), 134–150.

Hilger, W. (1912). *Hypnosis and suggestion, their nature, action, importance and position amongst therapeutic agents* (R. W. Felkin, Trans.). New York: Rebman.

Hockley, M. (1849). On the ancient magic crystal and its connexion with mesmerism. *The Zoist, 7*(27), 251–266.

Hollander, B. (1910). *Hypnotism and suggestion in daily life and medical practice.* New York: Putnam.

Holmes, O. W. (1891). *Medical essays, 1842–1882* (pp. 15–38). New York: Houghton, Mifflin.

Holy Bible. Old and New Testaments. King James Version.

Horsley, J. S. (1943). *Narcoanalysis.* London: Oxford University Press.

Horsley, J. S. (1951). Narcotic hypnosis. *British Journal of Medical Hypnotism, 2*(4), 2–7.

Hoskovec, J., Svorad, D. & Lanc, O. (1963). The comparative effectiveness of spoken and tape-recorded suggestions of body sway. *International Journal of Clinical and Experimental Hypnosis, 11,* 163–164.

Hull, C. L. (1933). *Hypnosis and suggestibility: An experimental approach.* New York: Appleton-Century-Crofts.

Hunt, H. E. (1923). *A book of auto-suggestions.* Philadelphia: D. McKay.

Hunter, R. A. & Macalpine, I. (1956, November). Valentine Greatraks. *St. Bartholomew's Hospital Journal, 60,* 361–368.

Hutchison, A. M. (1919). *Hypnotism and self-education.* London & Edinburgh: T. C. & E. C. Jack Ltd., and Nelson & Sons.

Hyde, D. (1910). *A literary history of Ireland: From earliest times to the present day.* London & Leipzig: T. Fisher Unwin.

Imber, N. H. (1910). *Treasures of two worlds:* Unpublished legends and traditions of the Jewish Nation.

Ince, R. B. (1920). *Franz Anton Mesmer.* London: W. Rider & Sons.

Jackson, K. H. (1964). *The oldest Irish tradition: A window on the iron age.* Cambridge: Cambridge University Press.

Jacobson, E. (1924). The technique of progressive relaxation. *Journal of Nervous and Mental Disease, 60,* 568–578.

Jacobson, E. (1925). Progressive relaxation. *American Journal of Psychology, 36,* 73–87.

Jacobson, E. (1929). *Progressive relaxation.* Chicago: University of Chicago Press.

Jacobson, E. (1977). *You must relax* (5th ed.). London: Souvenir Press.

Janet, P. (1925). *Psychological healing: A historical and clinical study* (2 vols.). (E. Paul & C. Paul, Trans.). New York: Macmillan.

Jeaffreson, C. S. (1892, November 5). Hypnotism during an opthalmic examination. *The Lancet,* 1071.

Jenness, A. F. (1933). Facilitation of response to previous suggestion of a different type. *Journal of Experimental Psychology, 16,* 55–82.

Joyce, P. W. (1920). *Old Celtic romances.* London: Longmans Green & Co.

Kahn, S. (1947). *Suggestion and hypnosis made practical. How to get what you want.* Boston: Meador.

Karambelkar, V. W. (1961). *The Atharva-Veda and the Āyur-Veda.* Nagpur: Ku. Usha Karambelkar & D. G. Lawate.

Katkov, Y. (1941). In K. I. Platonov (Ed.), *The world as a physiological and therapeutic factor* (2nd ed., D. A. Myshre, Trans.). Moscow: Foreign Language Publishing House, 1959.

Kihlstrom, J. F. (1984). Personal Communication.

Kingsbury, G. C. (1891/1967). *The practice of hypnotic suggestion, Being an elementary handbook for the use of the medical profession.* Hollywood, CA: Wilshire Book Co. (Original work published London: Marshall, Hamilton, Kent & Co., 1891)

Kline, M. V. (1953). A visual imagery technique for the induction of hypnosis in certain refractory subjects. *Journal of Psychology, 35,* 227–228.

Knowles, E. E. (1926). *The basic principles of suggestion, hypnotism, telepathy, personal magnetism, character building and the development of the dormant faculties. (Branch one of Elmer E. Knowles system of personal influence and healing).* Brussels: Psychology Foundation.

Krafft-Ebing, R. von (1889). *Eine experimentalle Studie auf dem gebiete des Hypnotismus.* Stuttgart, Enke.

Kraines, S. H. (1941). *The therapy of the neuroses and psychoses.* Philadelphia: Lea & Febiger.

Kratochvíl, S. (1970). Sleep hypnosis and waking hypnosis. *International Journal of Clinical and Experimental Hypnosis, 18,* 25–40.

Kroger, W. S. (1977). *Clinical and experimental hypnosis in medicine* (2nd ed.). Philadelphia: J. B. Lippincott. (Original work published 1963)

Kroger, W. S. & Fezler, W. D. (1976). *Hypnosis and behavior modification: Imagery conditioning.* Philadelphia. J. B. Lippincott.

Kroger, W. S. & Schneider, S. A. (1959). An electronic aid for hypnotic induction: A preliminary report. *International Journal of Clinical and Experimental Hypnosis, 7,* 93–99.

Kronfeld, A. (1925). *Psychotherapie, Charakterlehre, Psychoanalyse, Hypnose, Psychagogik.* Berlin: J. Springer.

Krugsch-Pascha, H. (1893). *Aus dem Morgenlande: Altes und neues* (pp. 43–53). Leipzig: Philipp Reclam Jun.

Kubie, L. S. (1941). Manual of emergency treatment for acute war neuroses. *War Medicine, 4*(6), 582–598.

Kubie, L. S. & Margolin, S. (1944). The process of hypnotism and the nature of the hypnotic state. *American Journal of Psychiatry, 100,* 611–622.

Lafontaine, C. (1860). *L'art de magnétiser ou le magnetisme animal considéré sous le point de vue théorique, pratique, et thérapeutique* (3rd ed.). Paris: G.-B. Baillière.

Lafontaine, C. (1886). *Mémoires d'un magnétiseur* (2 vols.). Paris: G.-B. Baillière.

Laguerre, M. S. (1980). *Voodoo heritage.* Beverly Hills, CA: Sage.

Langen, D. (1965/1966). The method of graduated active hypnosis. *British Journal of Medical Hypnotism, 17*(2), 29–33.

Lapponi, J. (1907). *L'hypnotisme et le spiritisme.* Paris: Librairie Academique/ Perrin et Cie.

Lapponi, J. (1907). *Hypnotism and spiritism, a critical and medical study.* (2nd rev. ed., Mrs. P. Gibbs, Trans.). New York: Longmans, Green.

Leavitt, S. (1910). *Auto-suggestion.* Chicago: Magnum Bonum.

LeCron, L. M. (1953). A method of measuring the depth of hypnosis. *International Journal of Clinical and Experimental Hypnosis, 1*(2), 4–7.

LeCron, L. M. & Bordeaux, J. (1949). *Hypnotism today.* New York: Grune & Stratton.

Leitner, K. (1950). *How to hypnotize: A master key to hypnotism.* New York: Stravon.

Liebert, R. M., Rubin, N. & Hilgard, E. R. (1965). The effects of suggestions of alertness in hypnosis on paired-associate learning. *Journal of Personality, 33,* 605–612.

Lingh, S. & Form, A. (1969, November). Differential effects of valium on hypnotic susceptibility. *Scandinavian Journal for Clinical and Experimental Hypnosis, 8.*

Lloyd, W. W. (1845a). Allusions to mesmerism in the classics. *The Zoist, 3*(10), 156–173.

Lloyd, W. W. (1845b). Allusions to mesmerism in the classics. *The Zoist, 3*(11), 304–316.

Lloyd, W. W. (1847). Magnetism and mesmerism in antiquity. *The Zoist, 5*(19), 273–285.

Loewenfeld, L. (1901). *Der Hypnotismus, Handbuch der Lehre von der Hypnose und der Suggestion.* Wiesbaden: J. F. Bergmann.

London, P. (1963). *Childrens Hypnotic Susceptibility Scale.* Palo Alto, CA: Consulting Psychologists Press.

London, P. (1965). Developmental experiments in hypnosis. *Journal of Projective Techniques and Personality Assessment, 29*(2), 189–199.

Long, M. (1948). *The secret science behind miracles.* Los Angeles, CA: Kosmon Press.

Ludwig, A. M. (1964). An historical survey of the early roots of mesmerism. *International Journal of Clinical and Experimental Hypnosis, 12,* 205–217.

Ludwig, A. M. & Lyle, W. H. Jr. (1964). Tension induction and the hyperalert trance. *Journal of Abnormal and Social Psychology, 69*(1), 70–76.

Luthe, W. (1969). The work of Oskar Vogt and autogenic therapy. In *The Oskar Vogt Institute*. (pp. 31–71). Fukuoka: Kyushu University.

MacCulloch, J. A. (1911). *The religion of the ancient Celts*. Edinburgh: T. & T. Clark.

Marcuse, F. L. (Ed.). (1964). *Hypnosis throughout the world*. Springfield, IL: Charles C Thomas.

Marks, R. W. (1947). *The story of hypnotism*. New York: Prentice-Hall.

Marmer, M. J. (1959). *Hypnosis in anesthesiology*. Springfield, IL: Charles C Thomas.

Mason, R. O. (1901). *Hypnotism and suggestion*. New York: H. Holt.

Matheson, G. & Grehan, J. F., (1979). A rapid induction technique. *American Journal of Clinical Hypnosis, 21*(4), 297–299.

Mayer, L. (1934). *Die Technic der Hypnose*. Munchen: J. F. Lehmanns.

McConkey, K. M. & Sheehan, P. W. (1982). Effort and experience on the Creative Imagination Scale. *International Journal of Clinical and Experimental Hypnosis, 30*(3), 280–288.

McConkey, K. M., Sheehan, P. W. & White, K. D. (1979). Comparison of the Creative Imagination Scale and the Group Scale of Hypnotic Susceptibility, Form A. *International Journal of Clinical and Experimental Hypnosis, 27*(3), 265–277.

McDougall, W. (1908). The state of the brain during hypnosis. *Brain, 82*(31), 242–258.

Meares, A. (1954a). Non-verbal and extra-verbal suggestion in the induction of hypnosis (Pt 1). *British Journal of Medical Hypnotism, 5*(4), 2–6.

Meares, A. (1954b). Non-verbal and extra-verbal suggestion in the induction of hypnosis (Pt 2). *British Journal of Medical Hypnotism, 6*(1), 51–54.

Meares, A. (1958). A dynamic technique for the induction of hypnosis. *British Journal of Medical Hypnotism, 9*(4), 22–28.

Meares, A. (1960). *A system of medical hypnosis*. New York: Julian Press.

Métraux, A. (1972). *Voodoo in Haiti*. (H. Charteris, Trans.). New York: Schocken.

Milechnin, A. (1964a). Hypnotic induction by stimulation of emotional reactions of the stabilizing type (Pt 1). *British Journal of Medical Hypnotism, 16*(1), 2–10.

Milechnin, A. (1964b). Hypnotic induction by stimulation of emotional reactions of the stabilizing type (Pt 2). *British Journal of Medical Hypnotism, 16*(2), 9–17.

Milechnin, A. (1965a). Hypnotic induction by stimulation of emotional reactions of the stabilizing type (Pt 3). *British Journal of Medical Hypnotism, 16*(3), 10–16.

Milechnin, A. (1965b). Hypnotic induction by stimulation of emotional reactions of the stabilizing type (Pt 4). *British Journal of Medical Hypnotism 16*(4), 19–28.

Milechnin, A. (1965c). Hypnotic induction by stimulation of emotional reactions of the stabilizing type (Pt 5). *British Journal of Medical Hypnotism, 17*(1), 11–17.

Miller, H. C. (1912). *Hypnotism and disease: A plea for rational psychotherapy*. London: T. Fisher Unwin.

Moll, A. (1892). *Der Rapport in der Hypnose, Untersuchungen über den thierischen Magnetismus*. Leipzig: Ambr. Abel.

Moll, A. (1889/1897). *Hypnotism* (4th ed.). London: Scott. (Originally *The study of hypnosis*).

Monteiro, K. P., MacDonald, H. & Hilgard, E. R. (1980). Imagery, absorption and hypnosis: A factorial study. *Journal of Mental Imagery, 4*, 63–81.

Morgan, A. H. & Hilgard, J. R. (1978/1979a). The Stanford Hypnotic Clinical Scale for Adults. *American Journal of Clinical Hypnosis, 21*(2&3), 134–147.

Morgan, A. H. & Hilgard, J. R. (1978/1979b). The Stanford Hypnotic Clinical Scale for Children. *American Journal of Clinical Hypnosis, 21*(2&3), 148–169.

Morgan, J. J. B. (1924). *The psychology of the unadjusted school child*. New York: Macmillan.

Morris, F. (1970). Mutual hypnosis: A specialized hypnotic induction techinque. *American Journal of Clinical Hypnosis, 13*(2), 90–94.

Morris, F. (1974). *Self-hypnosis in two days*. Berkeley, CA: Intergalatic Publishing Co.

Moss, A. A. (1955). Rapid hypnotic induction. *British Journal of Medical Hypnotism, 7*(1), 37–39.

Moutin, L. (1887). *Le nouvel hypnotisme*. Paris: Perrin et Cie.

Moutin, L. (1907). *Le magnétisme humain L'hypnotisme et le spiritualisme moderne consideres aux points de vue theorique et pratique*. Paris: Perrin et Cie.

Muthu, D. C. (1930). *A short account of the antiquity of Hindu medicine and civilisation*. London: Ballière, Tindall & Cox.

Nicolas, A. (1852). Du magnétisme animal. *L'Union médicale de la Louisiane, 1*, 19–23.

O'Grady, K. E. (1980). The absorption scale: A factor-analytic assessment. *International Journal of Clinical and Experimental Hypnosis, 28*(3), 281–288.

Orne, M. T., Hilgard, E. R., Spiegel, H., Spiegel, D., Crawford, H. J., Evans, F. J., Orne, E. C. & Frischholz, E. J. (1979). The relationship between the Hypnotic Induction Profile and the Stanford Hypnotic Susceptibility Scales, Forms A and C. *International Journal of Clinical and Experimental Hypnosis, 27*(2), 85–102.

Owens, H. E. (1970). Hypnosis by phone. *American Journal of Clinical Hypnosis, 13*(1), 57–60.

Pagel, W. (1972). Van Helmont's concept of disease—To be or not to be? The influence of Paracelsus. *Bulletin of the History of Medicine, 46*(5), 419–454.

Pascal, G. R. & Salzberg, H. C. (1959). A systematic approach to inducing hypnotic behavior. *International Journal of Clinical and Experimental Hypnosis, 7*, 161–167.

Paton, L. B. (1921). *Spiritism and the cult of the dead in antiquity*. New York: Macmillan.

Pattie, F. A. (1956a). Mesmer's medical dissertation and its debt to Mead's *De Imperio Solis ac Lunae*. *Journal of the History of Medicine and Allied Sciences, 11*, 275–287.

Pattie, F. A. (1956b). Methods of induction, susceptibility of subjects, and criteria of hypnosis. In Roy M. Dorcus (Ed.), *Hypnosis and its therapeutic applications* (pp. 2/1–2/24). New York: McGraw-Hill.

Pattie, F. A. (1967). A brief history of hypnosis. In J. E. Gordon (Ed.), *Handbook of clinical and experimental hypnosis* (pp. 10–43). New York: Macmillan.

Pavlov, I. P. (1927). *Conditioned reflexes, An investigation of the physiological activity of the cerebral cortex.* London: Oxford University Press.

Pavlov, I. P. (1928). *Lectures of conditioned reflexes: Twenty-five years of objective study of the higher nervous system activity (behavior) of animals* (W. Horsley Gantt, Ed. & Trans.). New York: Liveright.

Perry, C. & Laurence, J. (1980). Hypnotic depth and hypnotic susceptibility: A replicated finding. *International Journal of Clinical and Experimental Hypnosis, 28*(3), 272–280

Petersen, H. G. (1897). Medical letters on hypno-suggestion etc. In O. G. Wetterstrand (Ed.), *Hypnotism and its applications to practical medicine* (pp. 119–166). New York: G. P. Putnam's Sons.

Peuckert, W. (1967). *Gabalia*(2nd ed.). Berlin.

Piggott, S. (1968). *The Druids.* New York: F. A. Praeger.

Plapp, J. M. (1976). Experimental hypnosis in a clinical setting: A report of the atypical use of hypnosis in the treatment of a disturbed adolescent. *American Journal of Clinical Hypnosis, 18*(3), 145–152.

Platonov, K. I. (Ed.). (1959). *The word as a physiological and therapeutic factor: Problems of theory and practice of psychotherapy on the basis of the theory of I.P. Pavlov.* (2nd ed., D. A. Myshne, Trans.). Moscow: Foreign Languages Publishing House. (Original work published 1955).

Podmore, F. (1902). *Modern spiritualism: A history and a criticism* (2 vols.). London: Methuen.

Podmore, F. (1909). *Mesmerism and Christian Science: A short history of mental healing.* London: Methuen.

Pokormy, J. (1910). *The origin of Druidism* (pp. 583–597). (Annual Report of the Smithsonian Institution). Washington DC: U.S. Government Printing Office.

Poyen, C. St. Sauveur (1837). *Progress of animal magnetism in New England. (Including "Elements")* Boston: Weeks, Jordan.

Prince, M. (1923). A case of complete loss of all sensory functions excepting hearing but including coenesthesis and visual images of the body. *Journal of Abnormal Psychology, 18,* 238–243.

Quackenbos, J. D. (1900). *Hypnotism in mental and moral culture.* New York & London: Harper & Bros.

Quackenbos: J. D. (1907). *Hypnotic therapeutics in theory and practice.* New York: Harper & Bros.

Rachman, S. (1968). The role of muscular relaxation in desensitization therapy. *Behavior Research and Therapy, 6,* 159–166.

Rader, C. M. (1972a). The relationship of need achievement to hypnotic suggestibility. *American Journal of Clinical Hypnosis, 15,* 38–40.

Rader, C. M. (1972b). Influence of motivational instructions on hypnotic and non-hypnotic reaction time performance. *American Journal of Clinical Hypnosis, 15,* 98–101.

Ravenscroft, K. (1965). Voodoo possession: A natural experiment in hypnosis. *International Journal of Clinical and Experimental Hypnosis, 13,* 157–182.

Reinhardt, C. (1914). *Mental therapeutics or faith, medicine and the mind.* London: London Publicity.

Reiser, M. & Nielson, M. (1980). Investigative hypnosis: A developing specialty. *American Journal of Clinical Hypnosis, 23*(2), 75–84.

Reyher, J. (1973). Can hypnotized subjects simulate waking behavior? *American Journal of Clinical Hypnosis, 16,* 31–36.

Richet, C. (1884). *L'homme et l'intelligence.* Paris: (See Bernheim, 1891).

Riesman, D. (1936). *The story of medicine in the middle ages.* New York: P. B. Hoeber.

Robinson, D. N. (Ed.). (1977). *Significant contributions to the history of psychology 1750–1920. Series A, Orientations (Vol. 10).* Washington, DC: University Publications of America.

Rogers, S. L. (1947). Early psychotherapy. *CIBA Symposia, 9,* 602–632.

Rosen, G. (1948, March–April). From mesmerism to hypnotism. *CIBA Symposia,* 838–844.

Rosen, H. (1953). *Hypnotherapy in clinical psychiatry.* New York: Julian Press.

Rosen, H. (1954). Dehypnosis and its problems. *British Journal of Medical Hypnotism, 5*(3), 18–23.

Rossi, E. L. (Ed.). (1980). *The collected papers of Milton H. Erickson* (Vol. 1). (pp. 133–378). New York: Irvington.

Rothman, I. (1957). Clinical use of drugs in induction and termination of the hypnotic state. *Journal of Clinical and Experimental Hypnosis, 5*(1), 25–31.

Ruch, J. C., Morgan, A. M. & Hilgard, E. R. (1973). Behavioral predictions from hypnotic responsiveness scores when obtained with and without prior induction procedures. *Journal of Abnormal Psychology, 82,* 543–546.

St. Dominique, Countess de (1874). *Animal magnetism (mesmerism) and artificial somnambulism: Being a complete and practical treatise on that science and its application to medical purposes.* London: Tinsley Bros.

Salter, A. (1941). Three techniques of autohypnosis. *Journal of General Psychology, 24,* 423–438.

Sanchez Herrero, A. (1889). *El hipnotismo y la sugestión. Estudios de Fisiopatología y psicoterapia.* J. Pastor, Valladolid.

Sandby, G. (1844). *Mesmerism and its opponents with narrative cases.* London: Longman, Brown, Green & Longmans.

Sanders, H. T. (1921). *Hypnose und Suggestion.* Stuttgart: Franckh'sche Verlagsbuchhandlung.

Sanders, S. (1983, December). Face games: An ideo-kinesthetic approach to mouth biting. *Newsletter of Division 30, APA,* 2–3.

Sargant, W. & Fraser, R. (1938, October 1). Inducing light hypnosis by hyperventilation. *The Lancet,* 778.

Satow, L. (1923). *Hypnotism and suggestion.* (B. Miall, Trans.) New York: Dodd, Mead.

Savage, G. H. (1909). *The Harveian oration on experimental psychology and hypnotism: Delivered before the Royal College of Physicians of London, Oct. 18.* London: Henry Frowde, Oxford University Press.

Schilder, P. (1921/1956). *The nature of hypnosis*. (G. Conin, Trans.). New York: International Universities Press. (Original work published Berlin: J. Springer, 1921)

Schmidkunz, H. (1892). *Psychologie der Suggestion*. Stuttgart: Enke.

Schneck, J. M. (1947). Modified technique for the induction of hypnosis. *Journal of Nervous & Mental Diseases, 106*, 77–79.

Schneck, J. M. (1953). A hypnosis verbal record library. *British Journal of Medical Hypnotism, 4*(4), 20–22.

Scholem, G. G. (1941). *Major trends in jewish mysticism*. Jerusalem: Schocken.

Schultz, J. H. (1953). *Das autogene Training konzentrative Selbstentspannung* (8th ed.). Stuttgart: Georg Thieme.

Schultz, J. H., & Luthe, W. (1969). *Autogenic therapy* (Vol. 1). *Autogenic Methods*. New York: Grune & Stratton.

Scoresby, W. (1849). *Zoistic magnetism*. London: Longman, Brown, Green, & Longmans.

Sears, A. R. & Talcott, M. M. (1958). Hypnotic induction by use of non-meaningful languages. A pilot study. *Journal of Clinical and Experimental Hypnosis, 6*(3), 136–138.

Serlin, F. R. (1970). Techniques for the use of hypnosis in group therapy. *American Journal of Clinical Hypnosis, 12*(3), 177–202.

Sharma, S. (1979). L'Abbé Faria: His life and contribution. In G. D. Burrows & D. R. Collison (Eds.), *Hypnosis, 1979: Proceeding of the International Congress of Hypnosis and Psychosomatic Medicine, Melbourne, Australia, 19–24 August, 1979* (pp. 149–156). Amsterdam: Elsevier North Holland Biomedial Press.

Sheehan, D. V., Latta, W. D., Regina, E. G. & Smith, G. M. (1979). Empirical assessment of Spiegel's Hypnotic Induction Profile and Eye-Roll hypnothesis. *International Journal of Clinical and Experimental Hypnosis, 27*(2), 103–110.

Sheehan, P. W. (1982). Imagery and hypnosis—Forging a link, at least in part. *Research Communications in Psychology, Psychiatry and Behavior, 7*(2), 257–272.

Sheehan, P. W., McConkey, K. M. & Law, H. G. (1978). Imagery facilitation and performance on the Creative Imagination Scale. *Journal of Mental Imagery, 2*, 265–274.

Shor, R. E. (1979). The fundamental problem in hypnosis research as viewed from historical perspectives. In E. Fromm & R. E. Shor (Eds.), *Hypnosis: Developments in research and new perspectives* (2nd Ed. pp. 15–41). New York: Aldine.

Shor, R. E. & Orne, E. C. (1962). *Harvard Group Scale of Hypnotic Susceptibility*. Palo Alto, CA: Consulting Psychologists Press.

Shor, R. E. & Orne, E. C. (1963). Norms on the Harvard Group Scale of Hypnotic Susceptibility, Form A. *International Journal of Clinical and Experimental Hypnosis, 11*(1), 39–47.

Sidis, B. (1898). *The psychology of suggestion*. New York: D. Appleton.

Sidis, B. (1907, March–April). Studies of psychopathology. *Boston Medical and Surgical Journal, 73*.

Sidis, B. (1913). *The psychology of laughter*. New York & London: Appleton.

Silber, S. (1968). Hypno-poetic induction. *Journal of the American Society of Psychosomatic Dentistry and Medicine, 15,* 172.

Silber, S. (1971). Use of poetic hypnogram to reverse obesity, the smoking habit, impotence (Pts 1, 2, 3). *Journal of the American Society of Dentistry and Medicine, 18,* 39–51; *18*(3), 75–82; *18*(4), 117–127.

Silber, S. (1980). Induction of hypnosis by poetic hypnogram. *American Journal of Clinical Hypnosis, 22*(4), 212–216.

Sinnett, A. P. (1897). *The rationale of mesmerism*. Boston, MA: Houghton. In M. M. Tinterow (Ed.), *Foundations of Hypnosis: From Mesmer to Freud* (pp. 5–30). Springfield, IL: Charles C Thomas, 1970.

Skultans, V. (1974). *Intimacy and ritual: A study of spiritualism, mediums and groups*. London: Routledge & Kegan Paul.

Smith, D. E. (1980). Hypnotic susceptibility and eye movement during rest. *American Journal of Clinical Hypnosis, 22*(3), 147–155.

Snyder, E. D. (1930). *Hypnotic poetry*. Philadelphia: University of Pennsylvania Press.

Snyder, E. D. & Shor, R. E. (1983). Trance inductive poetry: A brief communication. *International Journal of Clinical and Experimental Hypnosis, 31* (1), 1–7.

Society for Clinical and Experimental Hypnosis. (1979). Resolution Adopted October, 1978. *International Journal of Clinical and Experimental Hypnosis, 27,* 452.

Solovey, G. & Milechnin, A. (1957). Concerning the induction of the hypnotic state. *Journal of Clinical and Experimental Hypnosis, 5,* 82–98.

Spence, L. (Undated). *The magic arts in Celtic Britain*. London: Rider.

Spiegel, H. (1970, October). *An eye-roll sign for hypnotizability*. Paper presented at the meeting of the Society for Clinical and Experimental Hypnosis, Philadelphia.

Spiegel, H. (1972). An eye-roll test for hypnotizability. *American Journal of Clinical Hypnosis. 15*(1), 25–28.

Spiegel, H. (1974). *Manual for Hypnotic Induction Profile*. New York: Soni Medica.

Spiegel, H. & Bridger, A. A. (1970). *Manual for Hypnotic Induction Profile*. New York: Soni Medica.

Spiegel, H. & Spiegel, D. (1978). *Trance and treatment: Clinical uses of hypnosis*. New York: Basic Books.

Spiegel, H., Aronson, M., Fleiss, J. L. & Maber, J. (1976). Psychometric analysis of the hypnotic induction profile. *International Journal of Clinical and Experimental Hypnosis, 24*(3), 300–315.

Spiegel, H., Fleiss, J. L., Bridger, A. A. & Aronson, M. (1975). Hypnotizability and mental health. In S. Ariet & G. Chizanowski (Eds.), *New dimensions in psychiatry: A world view* (pp. 341–356). New York: John Wiley & Sons.

Stanton, H. E. (1978). Hypnotherapy at a distance through use of a telephone. *American Journal of Clinical Hypnosis, 20*(4), 278–281.

Stern, D. B., Spiegel, H. & Nee, J. C. (1978/1979). The Hypnotic Induction Profile: Normative observations, reliability and validity. *American Journal of Clinical Hypnosis, 21*(2 & 3), 109–133.

Stokes, W. (1902). The death of Muirchertach Mac Erca. *Revue Celtique, 23,* 395–437.

Stokvis, B. (1952). A simple hypnotizing technique with the aid of the color contrast action. *American Journal of Psychiatry, 109,* 380–381.

Stokvis, B. (1960). "Imitation-method" as an aid to hypnosis. *British Journal of Medical Hypnotism, 11*(4), 8–12.

Stoll, O. (1904). *Suggestion and Hypnotismus.* (2nd ed.). Leipzig: Veit.

Straus, R. A. (1980). A naturalistic experiment investigating the effects of hypnotic induction upon creative imagination scale performance in a clinical setting. *International Journal of Clinical and Experimental Hypnosis, 28*(3), 218–224.

Strosberg, I. M. & Vics, I. I. (1962). Physiological changes in the eye during hypnosis. *American Journal of Clinical Hypnosis, 4*(4), 264–267.

Stubbe, H. (1666). *The miraculous conformist: Or an account of several marvailous cures performed by the stroaking of hands of Mr. Valentine Greatarick; with physicall discourse thereupon.* Oxford: H. Hall.

Stungo, E. (1941, April 19). Evipan hypnosis in psychiatric outpatients. *The Lancet.*

Switras, J. E. (1974). A comparison of the eye-roll test for hypnotizability and the Stanford Hypnotic Susceptibility Scale: Form A. *American Journal of Clinical Hypnosis, 17*(1), 54–55.

Tamburini, A. & Seppelli, G. (1882). Contribution de l'etude experimentale de'hypnotisme. *Archives of Italian Biology. 2,* 273–277.

Taplin, A. B. (1912). *Hypnotism.* London: Simpkin, Marshall, Hamilton, Kent.

Taplin, A. B. (1918). *Hypnotic suggestion and psycho-therapeutics.* London: Simpkin, Marshall, Hamilton, Kent; Liverpool: Littlebury Bros.

Tart, C. T. (1967). Psychedelic experiences associated with a novel hypnotic procedure, mutual hypnosis. *American Journal of Clinical Hypnosis, 10*(2), 65–78.

Tart, C. T. (1970). Self-report scales of hypnotic depth. *International Journal of Clinical and Experimental Hypnosis, 18*(2), 105–125.

Tart, C. T. (1972). Measuring the depth of an altered state of consciousness, with particular reference to self-report scales of hypnotic depth. In E. Fromm & R. E. Shor, (Eds.), *Hypnosis, research developments and perspectives* (pp. 445–477). New York: Aldine-Atherton.

Tart, C. T. (1978/1979). Quick and convenient assessment of hypnotic depth: Self-report scales. *American Journal of Clinical Hypnosis, 21*(2 & 3), 186–207.

Teitelbaum, M. (1965). *Hypnosis induction technics.* Springfield, IL: Charles C Thomas.

Tellegen, A. (1981). Practicing the two disciplines for relaxation and enlightenment: Comment on "Role of the feedback signal in electomyograph biofeedback: The relevance of attention" by Qualls and Sheehan. *Journal of Experimental Psychology: General 110*(2), 217–226.

Tellegen, A. (1982). *Brief manual for the Differential Personality Questionnaire.* Mimeo, University of Minnesota.

Tellegen, A. (1984). Personal Communication.

Tellegen, A. & Atkinson, G. (1974). Openness to absorbing and self-altering experiences ("Absorption"), a trait related to hypnotic susceptibility. *Journal of Abnormal Psychology, 83*(3), 268–277.

Teste, A. (1843). *A practical manual of animal magnetism* (D. Spillan, Trans.). London: H. Baillière. (Original work published 1840)

Tinterow, M. M. (1970). *Foundations of hypnosis: From Mesmer to Freud.* Springfield, IL: Charles C Thomas.

Tomlinson, W. K. & Perret, J. J. (1975). Mesmerism in New Orleans: 1845–1861. *American Journal of Clinical Hypnosis, 18*(1), 1–5.

Topham, W. (1847). An instance of great benefit from mesmerism in a case of epilepsy, with the production of clairvoyance and other remarkable phenomena. *The Zoist, 5*(18), 129.

Townshend, Rev. C. H. (1841). *Facts in mesmerism, or animal magnetism with reasons for a dispassionate inquiry into it.* Boston: C. C. Little, & J. Brown.

Trömner, E. (1908). *Hypnotismus und suggestion.* Leipzig: Druck & B. G. Teubner.

Tubbs, W. J. (1844a). Cases of cures of various diseases by mesmerism. *The Zoist, 1*(4), 460–464.

Tubbs, W. J. (1844b). Cases of cures of different diseases. *The Zoist, 2*(5), 124–128.

Tubbs, W. J. (1844c). Cases of cures of different diseases. *The Zoist, 2*(6), 254–268.

Tuckey, C. L. (1892). *The value of hypnotism in chronic alcoholism.* London: J. & A. Churchill.

Tuckey, C. L. (1900). *Treatment by hypnotism and suggestion, or psycho-therapeutics (4th Ed.).* London: Ballière, Tindall & Cox. (Original work published 1889)

Tuke, D. H. (1884). *Illustrations of the influence of the mind upon the body in health and disease, designed to elucidate the action of the imagination* (2nd American ed.). Philadelphia: H. C. Lea's Son & Co.

Ulett, G. A., Akpinar, S. & Itil, T. M. (1971). Investigations of hypnosis utilizing induction by videotape. *Psychosomatics, 12,* 250–255.

Ulett, G. A., Akpinar, S. & Itil, T. M. (1972). Hypnosis by videotape. *International Journal of Clinical and Experimental Hypnosis, 20*(1), 46–51.

Underhill, S. (1902). *Underhill on mesmerism with criticism on its opposers.* Nevada, MO: Weltmer Book. (Original work published 1868)

Venn, J. (1984). The spiral techinque of hypnotic induction: A brief communication. *International Journal of Clinical and Experimental Hypnosis, 32*(3), 287–289.

Vincent, R. H. (1897). *The elements of hypnotism.* London: Kegan, Paul, Trench, Trübner. (Original work published 1893)

Völgyesi, F. A. (1966). *Hypnosis of man and animals.* Baltimore: Williams & Wilkins. (Original work published 1938).

W. C. K. (1891). Hypnotism in the Argentine Republic. *Journal of Nervous and Mental Disease, 18,* 595.

Wagner, F. F. (1951). Hypnotic induction by means of folding hands. *Acta Psychiatrica et Neurologica Scandinavia, 26,* 91–94.

Watkins, J. G. (1949). *Hypnotherapy of war neuroses.* New York: Ronald Press.

Watkins, J. G. (1951). A case of hypnotic trance induced in a resistant subject in spite of active opposition. *British Journal of Medical Hypnotism, 2*(4), 26–31.

Watkins, J. G. (1964). Hypnosis in the United States. In F. L. Marcuse (Ed.), *Hypnosis throughout the world* (pp. 265–299). Springfield, IL: Charles C Thomas.

Weatherhead, L. D. *Psychology, religion and healing*. New York: Abingdon-Cokesbury Press.

Webster, W. C. II (1976). The phreno-magnetic society of Cincinnati–1842. *American Journal of Clinical Hypnosis, 18*(4), 277–281.

Weitzenhoffer, A. M. (1956). Hypnotic susceptibility as related to masculinity-femininity. (Unpublished Ph.D. dissertation, University of Michigan.)

Weitzenhoffer, A. M. (1957). *General techniques of hypnotism*. New York: Grune & Stratton.

Weitzenhoffer, A. M. (1972a). Open-ended distance hypnotherapy. *American Journal of Clinical Hypnosis, 14*(2), 236–248.

Weitzenhoffer, A. M. (1972b). The postural sway test: A historical note. *International Journal of Clinical and Experimental Hypnosis, 20*, 17–24.

Weitzenhoffer, A. M. (1974). When is an "instruction" an "instruction"? *International Journal of Clinical and Experimental Hypnosis, 22*(3), 258–269.

Weitzenhoffer, A. M. (1978a). Hypnotism and altered states of consciousness. In A. Sugarman & R. E. Tarter (Eds.), *Expanding dimensions of consciousness* (pp. 183–225). New York: Springer.

Weitzenhoffer, A. M. (1978b). What did he (Bernheim) say? In F. H. Frankel & H. S. Aamansky (Eds.), *Hypnosis at its bicentennial* (pp. 47–56) New York: Plenum Press.

Weitzenhoffer, A. M. (1980a). Hypnotic susceptibility revisited. *American Journal of Clinical Hypnosis, 22*(3), 130–146.

Weitzenhoffer, A. M. (1980b). What did he (Berheim) say? A postscript and addendum. *International Journal of Clinical and Experimental Hypnosis, 28(3)*, 252–260.

Weitzenhoffer, A. M. & Hilgard, E. R. (1959). *Stanford Hypnotic Susceptiblity Scale, Forms A and B*. Palo Alto, CA: Consulting Psychologists Press.

Weitzenhoffer, A. M. & Hilgard, E. R. (1962). *Stanford Hypnotic Susceptibility Scale, Form C*. Palo Alto, CA: Consulting Psychologists Press.

Weitzenhoffer, A. M. & Hilgard, E. R. (1963). *Stanford Profile Scales of Hypnotic Susceptibility: Forms I and II*. Palo Alto, CA: Consulting Psychologists Press.

Weitzenhoffer, A. M. & Hilgard, E. R. (1967). *Revised Stanford Profile Scales of Hypnotic Susceptibility, Forms I and II*. Palo Alto, CA: Consulting Psychologists Press.

Weitzenhoffer, A. M. & Sjoberg, B. M. Jr. (1961). Suggestibility with and without "induction of hypnosis." *Journal of Nervous and Mental Disease, 132*, 204–220.

Wells, W. R. (1923). Experiments in waking hypnosis for instructional purposes. *Journal of Abnormal Psychology. 18*, 389–404.

Wetterstrand, O. G. (1902). *Hypnotism and its application to practical medicine* (H. G. Peterson, Trans.). New York & London: G. P. Putnam's Sons & Knickerbocker Press. (Original work published 1893)

Wheeler, L., Reis, H. T., Wolff, E. Grupsmith, E. & Mordkoff, A. M. (1974). Eye-roll and hypnotic susceptibility. *International Journal of Clinical and Experimental Hypnosis, 22*(4), 327–334.

White, M. M. (1930). The physical and mental traits of individuals susceptible to hypnosis. *Journal of Abnormal & Social Psychology, 25,* 293–298.

Wicks, G. R. (1982). A rapid induction technique, mechanics and rationale. *Australian Journal of Clinical and Experimental Hypnosis, 10*(2), 117–119.

Wilkie, L. (1975). A blackboard technique used in the treatment of tension. *British Journal of Clinical Hypnosis, 5,* 126–128.

Williams, G. W. (1954). Hypnosis in perspective. In L. M. LeCron. *Experimental Hypnosis* (pp. 4–21). New York: Macmillan.

Wilson, S. C. (1976). An experimental investigation evaluating a Creative Imagination Scale and its relationship to "hypnotic-like" experiences. (Doctoral Dissertation., Heed University. Hollywood, Florida.)

Wilson, S. C. & Barber, T. X. (1978). The creative imagination scale as a measure of hypnotic responsiveness: Applications to experimental and clinical hypnosis. *American Journal of Clinical Hypnosis, 20,* 235–249.

Winbigler, C. F. (1923). *Self healing through auto-suggestion.* New York: American Library Service.

Windische, E. (1880). *Irische Teste mit Wörterbuch.* Leipzig: S. Hirzel.

Wingfield, H. E. (1920). *An introduction to the study of hypnotism, experimental and therapeutic* (2nd ed.). London: Ballière, Tindall & Cox.

Wolberg, L. R. (1948). *Medical hypnosis* (2 vols.). New York: Grune & Stratton.

Wolff, W. (1951). *Changing concepts of the Bible: A psychological analysis of its words, symbols and beliefs.* New York: Hermitage House.

Wood, A. (1851). Contributions towards the study of certain phenomena, which have recently dominated experiments in electro-biology. *Monthly Journal of Mental Science, 12,* 407–435.

Wundt, W. (1892). *Hypnotismus und Suggestion.* Leipzig: W. Engelmann.

Yellowlees, H. (1923). *A manual of psychotherapy for practitioners and students.* London: A. & C. Black.

Zilboorg, G. (1941). *A history of medical psychology.* New York: W. W. Norton.

Zimmer, H. R. (1948). *Hindu medicine.* Baltimore, MD: Johns Hopkins Press.

Zweig, S. (1932). *Mental healers: Franz Anton Mesmer, Mary Baker Eddy, Sigmund Freud.* (Eden & Cedar Paul, Trans.). New York: Viking Press.

Name Index

Numbers in **boldface** refer to pages on which full references appear.

413

Subject Index